PLAGUE WARS

Also by Tom Mangold

The File on the Tsar
Tunnels of Cu Chi

Cold Warrior (with Jeff Goldberg)

PLAGUE WARS

The Terrifying Reality of Biological Warfare

TOM MANGOLD AND JEFF GOLDBERG

St. Martin's Griffin ♨ New York

Library of Congress Cataloging-in-Publication Data

Mangold, Tom
    Plague Wars : The terrifying reality of biological warfare / by Tom Mangold and
Jeff Goldberg.—1st ed.
       p. cm.
   ISBN 0-312-20353-5 (hc)
   ISBN 0-312-26379-1 (pbk)
1.Biological warfare. I. Goldberg, Jeff. II.Title.
UG447.8.M3   1999
358'.38—dc21
                                                     99–17022
                                                     CIP

First published in Great Britain by Macmillan Publishers, Ltd.

First St. Martin's Griffin Edition: April 2001

10 9 8 7 6 5 4 3 2 1

To Kathryn and Jake
To Teddy and George

Contents

Contents

List of illustrations

Chemical and biological warfare expert, Dr Alistair Hay. *Photograph by Martin Keene/PA.*

Israelis during a biological warfare defence exercise. *Photograph by Miki Kratsman/Corbis.*

Anthrax threat in Indianapolis in 1998. *Photograph by Michael Conroy/ Associated Press.*

Anthrax. *Wellcome Trust Photo Library.*

Dying of Ebola in an African hospital ward. *Photograph by Stuart Franklin/Magnum.*

Smallpox. *National Medical Slide Bank, the Wellcome Trust Photo Library.*

George Bush, Mikhail Gorbachev and Ronald Reagan in New York in 1988. *Camera Press.*

Margaret Thatcher and Mikhail Gorbachev. *Photograph by J. Morgan/ Camera Press.*

Alibekov with gun. *Courtesy of Ken Alibek.*

Soviet complex at Stepnogorsk, Kazakhstan. *Paladin Pictures.*

Spy satellite picture of the Biopreparat Institute in St Petersburg. *Paladin Pictures.*

Chris Davis OBE. *Photograph by Tom Mangold.*

The Soviet inspection team during their visit to Pine Bluff, Arkansas in 1991.

Bunker at Pine Bluff. *Paladin Pictures.*

Secretary of State James Baker and Soviet Foreign Minister Eduard Shevardnadze. *Photograph by Peter Turnley/Corbis.*

Dr Wouter Basson in a rare interview with the author. *Courtesy of Tom Mangold.*

The killer screwdrivers. *Photograph by Tom Mangold.*

List of illustrations

Dr Jan Lourens. *Photograph by Tom Mangold.*

The big wink in court. *Photograph by Anna Zieminski/PA.*

Maureen White. *Photograph by Tom Mangold.*

Connie Braam. *Photograph by Pieter Boersma.*

UN weapons experts search for missile parts in Iraq, June 1998. *Photograph by Jassim Mohammed/PA/EPA.*

Frame grab from a 1996 United Nations video. *Associated Press UNTV VIA APTV.*

Richard Butler and Tariq Aziz. *Courtesy of PA/EPA.*

Gabriele Kraatz-Wadsack. *Photograph by Tom Mangold.*

UNSCOM raid on Baghdad University. *Courtesy of Gabriele Kraatz-Wadsack.*

David Kelly. *Photograph by Tom Mangold.*

Nikita Smidovich. *Photograph by Tom Mangold.*

Shoko Asahara. *PA/EPA.*

Aum's lethal attack on a subway in Tokyo in 1995. *PA.*

Foreword

There is a unique ethical repugnance about biological weapons. To employ the very bacteria, viruses and toxins that have threatened life from the beginning is to deal with the enemies of mankind.

Today, no sooner are the terrible Ebola or Marburg viruses discovered in the heart of Africa than men flock to the site to seize and harness them, for eventual use against some adversary. The most virulent anthrax in the world was cultivated in a sewer. Biological weapons conjure up the plagues of the past, give new hope to the vermin banished to the dark, recall the rats of the Black Death whose fleas killed a third of Europe's population – the very scourges with which medicine has wrestled for two thousand years.

Biological weapons are both more immoral and more lethal than their pestilential cohorts in the nuclear and chemical armoury, for in infecting the enemy the aggressor can infect his own side; the pathogens blur the lines between peace and war as they silently spread through the ranks of families and non-combatants.

Biological warfare is cheap, efficient, unselective, and here.

Plague Warriors is not a *tour d'horizon* of the new threat. Rather it concentrates on how three states, Russia, Iraq, and South Africa, have undermined and corrupted honourable men's last dedicated attempts to control the outbreak of biological warfare. (Chemical warfare, so often twinned with its biological partner, is not a subject for this particular investigation.)

At the millennium, the world finds itself facing the spectre of a new weapon of mass destruction just as it did half a century ago after Hiroshima and Nagasaki. The superpowers' nuclear weapons *were* eventually chained, and although their abolition seems unlikely, so does their use. Biological weapons are equal, indeed potentially even more powerful killers, and to contemplate their use is to wink at evil, for pestilence and poison are afflictions as much as weapons.

A note about sources

We have been given exceptional access by primary source contacts from most relevant departments of government, including Western intelligence services. Many interviewees asked for anonymity; some are still in their posts, others cannot by virtue of office be named, some are constrained by civil-service regulations, many found a freedom in anonymity which allowed greater divulgence. Every single confidential interview cited in the book has come from a primary source, e.g. someone who was present at the event or discussion, or who was privy by reason of office to the notes and paperwork ensuing. Wherever possible, information from any confidential interview has been vectored with at least one other independent source. Occasionally, some material did reach us, in verbal or in documentary form, that will have to stand alone. For this decision we respectfully seek the reader's trust and elect to stand by our reputations.

TM/JG, May 1999

CHAPTER ONE

What If . . . ?

In 1998, several Western intelligence services organized a practical war game that was held at a North American airport. The scenario included a biological warfare element. This is what actually happened.

The year is 2001. President George Bush, Jr. is in the White House. Saddam Hussein still rules Iraq. Baghdad has successfully expelled all the UNSCOM inspectors of the United Nations Special Commission from Iraq. So Hussein's biological warfare programme is now no longer subject to any scrutiny.

The Biological Weapons Convention (the treaty banning the use of these weapons of mass destruction, which had been ratified by Iraq) remains toothless. There are no measures written into it to make sure it is being honoured, and no sanctions even if cheating comes to light.

As ten years of UN-imposed sanctions against Iraq are finally lifted (against Washington's and London's advice), Saddam Hussein now seeks revenge against the US for a decade of humiliation.

The Office of the Bureau of the Presidency of Iraq advises Saddam that the biological weapons developed for assassination purposes during the 1980s at the Al-Salman laboratory are readily available to him, having been successfully hidden from the UNSCOM inspectors for ten years.

The Al-Salman facility, which was located on the peninsula south of Salman Pak, some 25 miles south of Baghdad, was bombed and destroyed by Coalition aircraft during the Gulf War. It had been the original research centre of the early Iraqi biological weapons programme. After 1991, the key scientists involved in that offensive programme had been encouraged to remain together as a group, and to maintain and enhance

1

their biological warfare expertise. They had been joined by unofficial Russian experts, who had left their homeland for Baghdad in recent years, attracted by generous salaries and cutting-edge research – a welcome change after serious funding crises had seriously hurt the Russian biological warfare programme.

The Department of Biotechnology at the University of Baghdad has long been involved in isolating virulence and toxic factors associated with bacteria and viruses. Their scientists do this research ostensibly for the development of animal vaccines, but the line between defensive and offensive work is invisible.

The genetically engineered organisms studied are mainly bacteria. However, after starting a successful programme in the late 1980s to investigate smallpox and similar viruses (such as camelpox), the head of the department has developed a genetically engineered smallpox virus which has been integrated with the epsilon-toxin of *Clostridium perfringens* – the third most deadly toxin known to man. Put simply, the Iraqis have developed a chimera or monster virus – a doomsday bug.

The epsilon-toxin had been planted inside the smallpox DNA, so that it helps the processes of infection and death – speeding them up, making the virus more virulent and a ferociously dangerous weapon for a biological attack.

The Office of the Bureau of the Presidency controls Saddam Hussein's Special Security Organization, Amn Al-Kass. This ultra-secret agency trains selected operatives at a special Republican Guard location in northeast Baghdad, and has access to all the resources of Iraq's weapons programmes. Within Amn Al-Kass, a further, and equally elite, cadre of specially trained agents are available. These Iraqis are not thugs or minders, but well-educated, multi-lingual, professional, and ruthless operatives. They travel extensively outside Iraq, as part of trade delegations or diplomatic missions. They use local embassies overseas as their safe houses. They return occasionally to Baghdad for retraining on the use of weapons and emergency decontamination procedures. They are vaccinated against the biological agents they are most likely to use – smallpox, anthrax, Plague, and yellow fever.

These operatives are also skilled in assassination. They have been trained using human subjects, mainly Iraqi political prisoners, as well as Iranian and Kuwaiti prisoners of war. The prisoners used in these so-called tests have been recruited from the notorious Abu Ghraib Prison, west of Baghdad – a place where sudden disappearances and death are no strangers.

The special training for Iraq's elite operatives includes the use of personal weapons to kill or incapacitate individuals or groups of people, in the open or within rooms and buildings.

Iraq is fully capable of producing terrorist quantities of biological agents on demand. Anthrax and botulinum toxin are easily produced at the Al-Kindi Veterinary Vaccine Facility, which makes animal vaccines using simple technology – a 'cottage industry' approach, not previously appreciated by Western intelligence-gatherers. Smallpox is produced at the Serum and Vaccine Institute at Al-Ameriyah, which maintained a long association with Iraq's military programmes. They grow the virus using only a small egg incubator and a few dozen fertile hen's eggs. This readily available technology has been easily established at other facilities throughout Iraq. The tested and evaluated viral strains were never recovered during the days when UNSCOM inspectors attempted to search Iraq. The virulence of these viruses has also been increased by adding strains recently brought to Iraq by Russian advisers.

Saddam, having been reassured that Iraq now has a variety of capable and deadly efficient biological weapons, has tasked his strategists to devise an operational plan to demonstrate to the US that he is capable of undertaking an unconventional attack against the American mainland whenever he likes. Years of enduring the humiliation of Desert Storm, Desert Fox, and the West's numerous sabre-rattling threats and actual missile attacks, have left him obsessed with revenge. He also knows full well that a successful attack on the heartland of 'The Great Satan' will enshrine his status as leader of the fundamentalist Arab world.

Houston, Texas, the fourth largest city in the United States, is chosen as the target. It is a wise choice. The largest city in Texas plays a key role in American heavy industry, and in the oil industry in particular. Disruption of Houston would send tremors through the world's oil market, and enable Iraq to make short-term gains in selling its supply. The attack would not go unnoticed.

From around the Middle East, Iraq now 'wakes' five of its 'sleeper' agents (dedicated, long-term spies under assumed identities waiting for one major assignment). They assemble in Brazil. Four men and a woman are booked on a flight from Rio de Janeiro to San Francisco, with an onward flight connection to Houston. Travelling on forged Kuwaiti passports, they are ostensibly part of the Q8 Company Inc. and are heading to Houston to discuss the acquisition of geophysical scanning equipment from a hardware company.

Before departing from Rio, they are given three aerosol cans carefully disguised as hairsprays, to be carried by the female of the group. They are also issued four containers that resemble water bottles filled with lemon drink. In fact, one of the sprays contains botulinum toxin – the most deadly toxin known to man – and the other two carry anthrax spores. The water containers hold smallpox. So, tucked inside just their hand baggage, they are carrying an arsenal of deadly biological weapons.

All the biological materials have been produced and tested during the preceding four weeks. The containers have been filled in Baghdad four days earlier, and then transported by road to Damascus. Iraqi agents then relayed them by plane from Damascus to Beirut to Madrid to Buenos Aires and so to Rio. These specially prepared biological agents require no refrigeration for the four to five days that they are in transit.

The female is the daughter of a former Iraqi ambassador. She holds Saddam's complete trust. Because of her Cairo and Beirut-based education, she speaks Arabic without the distinctive and heavy Iraqi accent. Her cosmopolitan upbringing allows her to converse fluently in American English, and she can affect a New York accent and imitate a Southern drawl. She is the foil. Her dark features can easily be mistaken for Hispanic.

Although biological terror weapons can readily be used in a confined space, such as an aircraft, the effects are restricted to the aircraft's load – passengers, who can readily be isolated after the flight. The release in an airport terminal is far more serious. It allows extensive dispersal, with the victims (unaware that they *are* victims) subsequently travelling both locally and internationally, spreading the infections wherever they go.

The five Iraqis arrive at San Francisco and, at the American Airlines terminal, collect an extra bag from an incoming flight from San Jose. The bag, containing four pistols, has been transported by a UN-accredited Iraqi diplomat, who had, without difficulty, eluded the slack airport security at San Jose.

Flight AA 252 arrives on time at Houston at 6 p.m. on Friday. Passengers, eager to get home, quickly disembark and enter the large spacious hall, which leads to the baggage-collection point. The hall is well serviced by air-conditioning systems, which partly exhaust outside and partly return the circulation. The ambassador's daughter (having sat in the front row of the first-class compartment) is already at the head of the flow of emerging passengers. She now turns, stands on the baggage carousel, and calmly announces, in her best Southern drawl, that an armed attack is about to take place. She urges the passengers to immediately prostrate themselves in their best interests. As a handful of passengers who have heard her start to laugh, the four male Iraqis produce their weapons – one fires into the ceiling. Slowly, the stunned passengers prostrate themselves as ordered. Two of the Iraqi men secure the doors of the hall. A security guard is disarmed and beaten into submission before being secured with his own handcuffs.

Using an internal telephone in the baggage hall, the female makes her demands in a statement issued in French. There is a predictable threat in the event of non-fulfilment. The airport security officers are ill-prepared for this situation and respond inadequately. The use of French, and much shouting and intimidation, has all been deliberately engin-eered by the terrorists to allow them to use their biological weapons.

The demand is for a senior US politician to come to the scene. But airport security, still reluctant to accept the reality and seriousness of the threat, concentrates on obtaining more local police assistance and finding someone who speaks fluent French.

But all the terrorists really want is an excuse to use their biological weapons. The female deliberately misinterprets the delayed response as an attempt to play for time to mount an armed counter-attack.

Suddenly, and without warning, she orders the use of the spray containing botulinum toxin. The prostrate passengers think they are being gassed. But, as there is no immediate visible reaction to the spray, airport security officers interpret the move as a probable hoax.

The four silent males continue to maintain security with armed force. As the airport authorities slowly react to the stand off, the terrorists now switch demands and suddenly call for safe passage to Damascus. But this demand is refused.

Six hours after the aerosol spray has been used, the first cases of botulinum toxin poisoning become evident. The terrorist's original demand is now repeated, more clearly and in specific detail. Unless a senior US politician is produced to acknowledge the wilful wrongdoings against Iraq by the American government for the past ten years, and, unless he promises that the US will cease to withhold both medical and mechanical technology required by Iraq to re-establish itself, further biological attacks will follow. The Iraq connection is now appreciated. The demand is patently unacceptable – as it is meant to be.

Panic is beginning to sweep the passengers sitting and lying on the floor. But many of them – disorientated, terrified, and denied toilet facilities – are in no mood to offer resistance. A doctor among them is worried by the flu-like symptoms developing in those dosed with the spray.

A new and more high-powered team of US negotiators arrives just as the terrorists threaten to use anthrax. But the American officials refuse to negotiate under threat. Food and water are brought into the hall for the victims, and the emergency services are gathering outside. A SWAT team is waiting well out of sight.

Again without warning, the second and third sprays are produced, and two Iraqi males individually dose several more passengers. Hysteria is beginning to break out and the terrorists know they don't have much longer to remain in control. Realizing that the air-conditioning is still switched on, the female now orders the use of the smallpox.

By now, the Americans recognize the gravity of the situation and the decision is taken to storm the hall. The SWAT team; FBI agents; Bureau of Alcohol, Tobacco and Firearms officers; and local police smash the doors down and quickly fill the hall. There is a short, sharp firefight with the four male Iraqis who are all killed. In the chaos, the 'Hispanic' female takes off her coat, puts on another one from her baggage, assumes her New York accent, and helps a paramedic carry a sick woman out of the hall. She is not seen again.

Houston now faces a major public health problem. It has 120 casualties, or corpses, and the prospect of an emerging epidemic of smallpox. The local television stations issue contradictory and, at times, hysterical statements. Public confidence collapses and panic sets in. Attempts to keep everyone involved at the airport have failed. When impassioned announcements that the emergency services have contained the epidemic are not believed, a huge exodus from Houston begins.

As the panic spreads, isolated gunshots can be heard in the streets, and desperation overwhelms common sense. The airport terminal and its surrounds require immediate disinfection, but both personnel and passengers who might have been exposed to smallpox have in large part fled, and they now need to be traced, vaccinated, and isolated.

Houston becomes a no-go city. The American stockpile of smallpox vaccine is wholly inadequate for nationwide vaccination. As it is, the genetic investigation of the true make-up of the special Iraqi smallpox virus has only just begun. But no one knew about the chimera virus – the doomsday bug.

The Iraqi threat that Houston was to be the first of many such attacks in the next few days means that US security and medical services will become dangerously overstretched. Some cities prepare to declare martial law as the social fabric begins to tear.

Saddam has already warned Washington that the use of nuclear weapons on Baghdad, in response to Houston, would only provoke further indiscriminate terror attacks in the US, as well as at American targets overseas – 'even as Baghdad burns'.

'Iraq Can Take It!' scream the local papers.

Bush's Pentagon advisers warn him that the prevailing winds in the Middle East will carry nuclear fallout and debris south into Kuwait and Saudi Arabia, west as far as Jordan and Israel. The nuclear option, they advise, is not viable in this case.

'God is great – we are the new superpower,' Saddam tells hysterical crowds in Baghdad.

A few days later, a car emitting an unusually white plume of smoke, not unlike lemon juice, is being driven slowly along Whitehall Street in London by a lady with Hispanic features. Shortly afterwards, St Thomas', Hammersmith, Westminster, and Charing Cross hospitals all report cases of patients with the distinctive symptoms of Plague.

Iraq is assumed to be behind the outbreak. As the government's emergency COBRA Committee meets in Downing Street, the Prime Minister is advised by the Chief Medical Officer that the Plague type used appears to be resistant to antibiotics.

It is the second year of the millennium – but London is returning to 1348 and the Black Death.

CHAPTER TWO

1999

'... you asked me what keeps me awake at night, and that bothers
me ... this biological issue ...'

President Bill Clinton, 1999[1]

Now return briefly to the old millennium and to the reality of 1999. The
following is fact.

> Agence France Presse. 19 April 1999. 09.00 GMT
> Dateline: Cairo
> The Egyptian militant group Islamic Jihad has chemical and biological
> weapons it plans to use against US and Israeli targets. Ahmed Salama
> Mabruk, the head of Jihad's military operations, (says) the Jihad had
> drawn up a 'plan for carrying out 100 attacks against US and Israeli
> targets and public figures in different parts of the world'.[2]

Some public figures have taken this threat very seriously indeed.

Whenever President Clinton travels around Washington an anonymous black van tucks itself discreetly inside the tail of the extensive
presidential motorcade. It is the President's personal anti-biological
warfare attack ambulance. This is where he will be carried if contaminated by biological agents in a terrorist, madman, or dedicated biological
assault. On the van's front sits a small biological agent detector, rather
like a weather vane, constantly sniffing the air for the first signs of an
attack.

The van has the acronym 'Hammer' (Hazardous Agent Mitigation
Medical Response) and is fully equipped to decontaminate the President,

wash him down and fill him with the relevant antibiotics.[3] The Secret Service specialists who treat him will wear fully protective anti-contamination suits with special breathing gear. They will look like zombies from hell, but they will be, literally, inside a world of their own, ecologically safe from whatever bacterial or viral ambush has been aimed at their precious charge. Underneath the black van is a special holding tank to contain whatever hazardous material has been brushed or washed or scraped or bled out of the Chief Executive.

This is not 2001. This is here and now.

It's 1999 and in Hollywood they're making the next really big biological warfare thriller – based on Richard Preston's powerful novel in the genre (neatly christened 'Black Biology') called *The Cobra Event*. It is a story about a deranged scientist testing a genetically engineered bioweapon in New York City. People die horrible deaths, their brains liquefy, they gnaw off their own lips, fingers and tongues. But even the fiction of Preston has begun to merge imperceptibly with fact.

President Clinton was given the book to read and became sensitized to the whole security issue surrounding biological warfare. The cynics had a field day. The President reads a page-turner and overnight biological warfare has become a meal ticket for fund-starved Pentagon war-game planners and defence think-tanks turned anorexic for want of work in the post cold-war era. Besides, in 1998 there were some fifty hoax calls about suspected anthrax attacks and there had been sneery newspaper articles and gross over-reaction by federal emergency disaster teams. The FBI, CIA, and every intelligence agency in the West were climbing aboard the biological gravy train.

There were echoes here of Europe's famous 'phoney war' period, the great calm between September 1939 and April 1940 when the British basked through an endless Indian summer of false hope and could not believe it was at war with Nazi Germany. Not until Hitler invaded Norway anyway . . .

The threat of a biological attack today is much more than a war game or think-tank scenario.

In Washington the new national security buzzwords used by Pentagon planners are 'asymmetrical war' and 'catastrophic terrorism'. These tortured military euphemisms are code for the changing nature of war and terrorism. They refer to a small, overmatched enemy (such as a rogue nation or terrorist group) which challenges a vastly superior military power (like the US or Britain) and tries to balance out its own inferiorities by using new forms of weapons of mass destruction – such as biological agents, cyber(computer)-attacks, or chemicals.

The resulting sickness, death, and chaos from such an unprecedented and horrendous act of biological terrorism would be intended to devastate the public's underlying sense of security – like a twenty-first century Dunkirk or Pearl Harbor, or worse.[4]

The United States is not notorious for prolonged bouts of national paranoia or hysterical over-reaction. Her leadership of the West towards total victory in the Cold War remains a lesson in long-term global strategy. So why, in 1999, have the alarms been sounded by those whose fingers are supposed to be on the international pulse? They include the White House, national intelligence chiefs, and numerous senior federal, state, and civic officials. It could be a collective delirium, but chances are it's not.

For instance, the head of the Federal Protective Services, responsible for securing the 8,300 US government buildings, one million federal employees, and several million annual visitors, says that he and other experts no longer considered explosive devices 'the greatest threat' to government buildings. He has warned that they considered 'the chemical and biological threat a far greater danger'.[5]

In a major policy address in November 1998, John Gannon, chairman of the CIA's top analytical division, the National Intelligence Council, warned that the US was unprepared to face the 'ominous' security trends that biological weapons present. Gannon said that biological weapons were 'a clear and present danger for us at home and abroad'. 'The battlefield of the future,' he noted, 'could be Main Street, USA. Warning time may be all but eliminated . . . Our fear is that people will die – a lot of people. The odds of a successful attack are growing, despite our vigilance.'[6]

President Clinton, who, one might safely assume, has read a little more than *The Cobra Event* on the subject, reiterated this warning two months later: 'The enemies of peace realize they cannot defeat us with traditional military means, so they are working on . . . new forms of assault . . . [including] chemical, biological, potentially even nuclear weapons . . . we must be ready.'[7]

The President said it was 'highly likely' that a terrorist group would attempt a biological attack in the US during the next few years.[8] 'I want to raise public awareness of this,' Clinton said, 'without throwing people into an unnecessary panic.'

Even in the United Kingdom, whenever one can penetrate the thickets of semi-secrecy that surround the subject of defence against biological warfare, there are revealing glimpses of the seriousness with which the subject is regarded. The counter-proliferation desks and departments of the Foreign and Commonwealth Office, Ministry of Defence, and intelligence services are tracking every possible symptom of future attack. Scotland Yard's cautious Assistant Commissioner David Veness, head of Specialist Operations, has warned: 'The great nightmare facing anti-terrorist experts is a group with access to significant stocks of chemical, biological or nuclear weapons. That threat . . . is not academic. It is crystal clear that we cannot plan on the assumption that those who gain access to weapons of mass destruction will continue to act with restraint.'[9]

One has only to study the ferocity with which Saddam Hussein has continued to deceive, lie, cheat, and face savage allied bombing raids *only* to protect his covert biological weapons programme to appreciate that this is now a big boy's game.

The threats have been intensifying. Exiled Saudi Arabian terrorist leader Osama bin Laden, the alleged mastermind of the devastating 1998 bombings of the American embassies in Kenya and Tanzania, has threatened (through front groups) to unleash an 'anthrax' attack to kill all American and British citizens in Yemen – unless they leave the country.[10]

President Clinton has recently taken numerous steps to prepare a defence against biological warfare attacks. In May 1998, he signed Presidential Decision Directive 62 that established a special new office to co-ordinate federal counter-terrorism policies and defend the US against 'new twenty-first century threats'. He also selected Richard Clarke, an experienced, forty-eight-year-old member of his National Security Council staff, to direct this new White House Office of Security, Infrastructure Protection, and Counter-terrorism.[11] Clarke has become, in effect, the federal biological terrorism tsar – responsible for developing new programmes, co-ordinating policy between the various agencies, and resolving arguments. With his elevated status, Clarke now sits at the table at all Cabinet-level national security meetings, next to the Secretaries of State and Defense, with voting power equal to the CIA Director and Joint Chiefs of Staff representative.

In a bone-dry mission statement early in 1999, Clarke said: 'We're not doing this just because people in the White House like to read thriller novels and watch movies that have exciting plots. We're doing it because we understand the nature of the potential threat. It's a *real* potential threat. We are not exaggerating it.'[12]

Clarke has since prepared a five-pronged federal response to counter the threat of catastrophic biological terrorism against homeland America, describing the nation's vulnerability to such attacks as its Achilles' heel.[13]

President Clinton has proposed a $1.4 billion annual budget for year 2000 dedicated for local preparedness and defence of chemical and biological terrorism.[14]

For the military, Clinton has approved a plan to give anthrax vaccinations to all two million US soldiers. He is weighing a plan to similarly vaccinate all police officers, fire fighters, and emergency responders in major US cities.[15]

Clinton's White House and cabinet have agreed upon a clear policy of 'deterrence and disruption' of both terrorist groups and rogue state operations which involve biological warfare. This policy includes the ultimate promise that an adversary will 'pay a high price' if they launch a biological attack on the US or an ally. The implicit threat of a nuclear response is intended. As Clarke has explained: 'Attack us and you will unleash a relentless methodical machine against you. We will find you – no matter how long it takes. We will find the terrorist sponsors, whoever they are.'

Clarke added that the US may also take pre-emptive action if it is threatened. 'The US reserves for itself the right of a first strike,' he said, 'for self defence.'

President Clinton has admitted that the terrorist threat that 'keeps me awake at night' is the possibility of a germ warfare attack.[16] 'We are doing everything we can,' he has said, 'in ways I can and ways I cannot discuss, to try to stop people who would misuse chemical and biological capacity from getting that capacity. This is not a cause for panic. It is a cause for serious deliberate disciplined long-term concern.'[17]

Alarmism would indeed be the worst signal to send an uneasy public. But for those in 1999 who still deride the prospect, and therefore the consequences of biological warfare (or BW, as it is known), a short trip back in time may be a salutary reminder that this is something one should never underestimate.

Because, for its victims, biological warfare is truly apocalyptic.

CHAPTER THREE

Unit 731

'The most important thing is to reveal the facts.'
Wang Xuan

On a chilled and dank February morning in 1998, inside Tokyo's District Court, something unusual is taking place.

An attractive forty-five-year-old former English teacher is scratching at the scars of Japan's long-buried memories of an unspeakable crime. She is determined to expose the truth of plague wars to the gaze of a new generation.

Chinese-born Wang Xuan addresses a stony-faced bench. She speaks slowly and carefully as some one hundred Japanese and Chinese look on. 'The Japanese government must acknowledge the facts and officially apologize,' she says quietly.[1] The silence in court seems to absorb her words; but Japan's dirty war secrets are finally being uncovered, like massacre victims from a mass burial site the skeletal arms and bones of a great historical atrocity begin to poke out of the stained ground.

Wang Xuan is speaking on behalf of 108 victims and relatives of the thousands of innocents who were butchered by members of the notorious Unit 731, Japan's first active biological warfare unit.

Well over half a century ago, the Japanese took a conscious decision to research and then practise the new military science of plague war. Their story remains a terrible warning for those who would argue any circumstances for its use.

From 1932–45, Unit 731 of the Japanese Imperial Army was based in Japanese-occupied Manchuria, in northwest China, where it conducted gruesome biological warfare experiments on human prisoners as part of Japan's war with, and occupation of, China.[2]

The unit was commanded by General Shiro Ishii, a strikingly fearsome soldier who was convinced of the necessity for advancing the potential of biological warfare. The fact that BW had been banned in 1925 by the Geneva Protocol only served to confirm for him that its impact could be devastating.[3] Manchuria was the perfect base for Ishii, as there was a limitless supply of Chinese PoWs to be used as guinea pigs during these times of horror.

Today, 108 victims and relatives of those predominantly Chinese victims of the germ warfare project are suing the Japanese government. And in Britain and America, despite denials from the governments, former PoWs are claiming that they, too, were experimented upon. There may yet be a long-delayed reckoning, for there are still important lessons to be learned from that extraordinary story.

Japan's earliest interest in biological warfare began at the end of World War I, but formally matured with the rise of the now notorious Shiro Ishii.[4]

By early 1927, Ishii, a gifted medical graduate, had received his doctorate in microbiology and proceeded to build his reputation as a serious medical scholar, publishing papers in scientific journals. During this period, the young scientist came across a report on biological warfare that would have a profound impact on him. The report was by Second Class (First Lieutenant) Physician Harada, a member of the War Ministry's Bureau.[5] The report centred on the discussions at the 1925 Geneva Disarmament Convention, which outlawed both chemical and biological warfare. The paper had failed to find much response in Japan, but it had a particular resonance for Ishii, who was struck by what he saw as BW's tremendous potential. And so his overwhelming obsession with this science of war was born.

During his time at the Tokyo Army Medical School, Ishii worked enthusiastically on several aspects of BW research, but he was frustrated by his inability to test his laboratory results on human beings. The truth was he needed a concentration camp or two.

Ishii himself put it more delicately. 'There are two types of bacteriological warfare research, A and B,' he once noted. 'A is assault research, and B is defence research. Vaccine research is of the B type, and this can be done in Japan. However, A-type research can only be done abroad.'[6]

The activity of Unit 731 was made possible by the brutal Manchurian Incident of September 1931. In the aftermath of the Russo–Japanese war of 1904–5 and the fall of China's Manchu Dynasty in 1911, Japan had held special privileges in Manchuria – an underpopulated land with rich natural resources. The Chinese Nationalist government complained unsuccessfully to the League of Nations about the Japanese occupation, and left the League. On 1 March 1932, Japan declared the new sovereign state of Manchukuo to be ruled by a puppet emperor. In truth, the commander-in-chief of Japan's Kwantung Army controlled Manchuria.[7]

Ishii, by then an army major and professor of immunology, realized that this remote and underprivileged area would be a superb human test-bed for his BW research.[8] His work could be camouflaged by the poor sanitary conditions of the area; indeed, the *Japan Year Book of 1935* described: '... the insanitary life of extremely primitive conditions ... the risk of the spread of dreadful infectious diseases is rather common. In the past twenty years, Manchuria has often been afflicted by such plagues; for instance, the pneumonic plague of 1910–11, cholera in 1919, pneumonic plague again in 1920–21, and pneumonic plague in 1927.'[9]

So who would ever know the difference between what Nature and what Ishii had intended?

In 1932, in the northern Manchurian city of Harbin, at a village called Beiyinhe, Ishii finally discovered the conditions he had been looking for. The local prison compound harboured people from varied backgrounds. There were members of anti-Japanese guerrilla groups (who persisted with harassment long after the collapse of any organized resistance), communist rebels, or simply innocents who had the misfortune of being rounded-up and branded 'suspicious'. They all ended up at Beiyinhe.[10]

And so the horror began.

The initial experiments tended to be crude versions of what was to follow. An example can be gleaned from the diary of Endo Saburo, a close friend and rival of Ishii who rose to the rank of Lieutenant General.

'Thursday, 16 November [1933]. A bright day. 8.30 a.m. With Colonel Ando and Lieutenant Tachihara, I visited the Transportation Company Experimental Station [a further Ishii-invented pseudonym] and observed experiments ...'

Endo and his fellow visitors took a closer look.

'The Second Squad [which] was responsible for poison gas, liquid poison; [and] the First Squad [which was responsible for] electrical experiments. Two bandits were used [by each squad for the experiments]. 1. Phosphene gas – 5 minute injection of gas into a brick-lined room; the subject was still alive one day after inhalation of gas; critically ill with pneumonia. 2. Potassium cyanide – the subject was injected with 15 mg of it; [subject] lost consciousness approximately 20 minutes later. 3. 20,000 volts – several jolts of that voltage not enough to kill the subject; injection [of poison] required to kill the subject. 4. 5,000 volts – several jolts not enough; after several minutes of continuous currents, [subject] was burned to death. Left at 1.30 p.m.'[11]

One subsequent experiment (conducted in January 1945) involved infecting ten Chinese victims with gas gangrene. These wretched prisoners were tied to posts some 40–50 feet from a shrapnel-type bomb containing gas gangrene bacteria. In order to prevent the victims from instant death from the exploding weapon, their heads and backs were covered with special metal shields and thick cotton blankets while their legs and hips were left bare. After the bomb was electronically detonated, the victims took the force of the bacteria-infected shrapnel in their legs. Each wounded man perished within a week in agonizing pain.[12]

Biological warfare research demanded the most repellent methods.

If Ishii or one of his workers required a human organ, say a human brain, a guard would hold a prisoner down while another smashed his skull with an axe. The brain would be removed, and the dead prisoner's body would be taken to a pathologist and then disposed of at the crematorium.[13]

During the mid-1930s, Ishii and his cohorts – many of whom went on to become prominent scientists, academics, and businessmen after World War II – built several more BW research facilities throughout Manchuria, turning the region into a huge biological warfare laboratory.[14] Large complexes were established in Changchun and Nanking, but by far the biggest of the compounds was at Ping Fan, a group of villages situated 15 miles to the south of Harbin.[15] This 'death factory', as it has been called, became the centre of Ishii's dreadful BW empire. The compound had seventy-six buildings, including laboratories, dormitories for civilian workers, barns for test animals, greenhouses, and a special prison for human test subjects. The scale of evil was enormous. Ping Fan covered an area of six square kilometres and employed an astonishing 3,000 Japanese doctors, technicians, and soldiers. In 1944 alone, the budget for Ping Fan was $2.5 million (in 1944 dollars).

The fundamental contradiction of the Hippocratic oath presented no moral dilemma for Ishii. Harming human beings was simply justified by a small leap of logic – the achievement of a greater good. In his speech formally inaugurating the Ping Fan operation, he addressed the ethical issue of using human subjects.

> Our God-given mission as doctors is to challenge all varieties of disease-causing micro-organisms; to block all roads of intrusion into the human body; to annihilate all foreign matter resident in our bodies; and to devise the most expeditious treatment possible. However, the research work upon which we are now about to embark is the complete opposite of these principles, and may cause us some anguish as doctors. Nevertheless, I beseech you to pursue this research, based on the dual thrill of 1) a scientist to exert efforts in probing for the truth in natural science and research into, and discovery of, the unknown world and 2) as a military person, to successfully build a powerful military weapon against the enemy.[16]

Unit 731 had eight departments working on BW – from those that investigated and cultivated the pathogens, through those responsible for testing animals and humans in the laboratories and in the field, to one that developed special bacterial bombs known as 'Ishii System Bombs', to a dirty tricks department where fountain pens and walking sticks were converted into individual BW attack weapons.[17]

According to undisputed evidence obtained from Unit 731 war criminals at a subsequent Soviet trial in Khabarovsk, Siberia in 1949, Unit 731, at its height, was producing an astonishing 660 lbs of pure Plague bacteria each month. When required, the unit also could make 1400 lbs of anthrax; 2,000 lbs of typhoid, paratyphoid and dysentery bacteria combined; and 2,200 lbs of cholera vibrions. The Plague factory also had 4,500 'nurseries' able to cultivate and harvest 100 lbs of Plague fleas 'in a short time'.[18]

Ishii and his workers studied the full encyclopaedia of diseases and their effect on human specimens. To keep these tests secret, the Japanese told local residents that the guarded compound was a 'lumber mill'; and then, with gallows humour, referred internally to their dehumanized test subjects as *marutas*, or 'logs'. The Ping Fan 'logs' were mainly

Chinese citizens, but also included White Russians; Soviet prisoners; arrested criminals from Mongolia, Korea, and Europe; and hapless mental patients. Ishii's team examined human reactions to Plague, typhoid, paratyphoid A and B, typhus, smallpox, Tularaemia, infectious jaundice, gas gangrene, tetanus, cholera, dysentery, glanders, scarlet fever, undulant fever, tick encephalitis, 'songo' (or epidemic haemorrhagic fever), whooping cough, diphtheria, pneumonia, brysipelas, epidemic cerebrospinal meningitis, venereal diseases, tuberculosis, Salmonella, frostbite, and many others.[19] The 'logs' would be injected with pathogens of various dosages so that the scientists could ascertain what amount would be required to infect enemies. Ishii's researchers would also use many other methods to infect the 'logs' to determine what foods, fabrics, or materials would most effectively transmit diseases. For instance, prisoners would be compelled to eat chocolates stuffed with anthrax, or cakes and biscuits spiked with Plague. Other prisoners would be forced to consume various drinks laced with different germs – including cholera-infected milk.[20]

Further experiments involved injecting air into human subjects to test the speed of the onset of embolisms. Horse urine was injected into human kidneys.

According to evidence not obtained until 1982, Unit 731's biological warfare research included infecting female prisoners with syphillis, having them impregnated by male prisoners, and then dissecting both live babies and mothers. They also drained the blood from prisoners' veins and substituted horse blood.[21]

Few human 'logs' lived longer than a few weeks. They either died as a result of the experiments, or were killed because they were no longer viable test material. Dead prisoners were taken to the pathologist for autopsy where the effect of the pathogens on the bodies' organs would be examined.[22]

But some victims suffered what must be close to the ultimate living nightmare. They were taken for autopsy, *without anaesthetic*, before they were dead.

Almost no contemporary accounts exist of interviews with the perpetrators of these barbarities. The exception is a remarkable conversation in 1995 between a *New York Times* correspondent and an ageing former soldier whose memory has not deserted him.[23]

*

The veteran was an apparently friendly, seventy-two-year-old farmer in Morioka, who even managed to joke as he served the reporter rice cakes made by his wife, before nonchalantly turning the conversation to explain how it felt to stand over a naked, thirty-year-old man who was tied to a bed and about to be dissected *alive*, without anaesthetic. The Japanese farmer was then an army medical assistant attached to Unit 731.

> The fellow knew that it was over for him and so he didn't struggle when they led him into the room and tied him down. But when I picked up the scalpel, that's when he began screaming.
>
> I cut him open from the chest to the stomach and he screamed terribly and his face was all twisted in agony. He made this unimaginable sound, he was screaming so horribly. But then he finally stopped. This was all in a day's work for the surgeons, but it really left an impression on me because it was my first time.

And the reason for the horror? Nothing very special it transpired; the Chinese prisoner was merely part of a research project. After deliberately infecting him with Plague, the Japanese doctors were eager to open him up to see how the disease was affecting his organs.

And why no anaesthetic?

'Vivisection should be done under normal circumstances. If we'd used anaesthesia that might have affected the body organs and blood vessels that we were examining. So we couldn't have used anaesthetic.'[24]

After these live autopsies, the bodies would be taken to one of the compound's crematoria.

The interview continued while there were still rice cakes left. The farmer was generous and polite. Yes, he had helped poison rivers and wells with biological agents, but Unit 731 really was not as cruel as the people now believe.

Experiments on children?

'Of course there were experiments on children' – he crunched a cake – 'but probably their fathers were spies.'

Could it happen again?

'. . . In a war,' the seventy-two-year-old smiled, 'you have to win.'[25]

A Japanese virologist, Yoshio Tamura, recalled how Ishii had a preference for recruiting young boys from his home town to work in Unit 731, because their immature hands could be trained and developed for the sensitive handling of equipment. Also, they could be de-humanized, and were, first by watching animals put to death, slowly, with poison, and then, providing they did not close their eyes or turn away, they were encouraged to watch human beings similarly being put to death.[26]

Ishii also studied the whole problem of BW weaponization.

The city of Anda, situated due north of Harbin, about two hours from Ping Fan, is prosperous by today's standards. During Ishii's reign, Anda was mostly pastureland and a few scattered villages. From June 1941 and until 1944, Ishii conducted a series of crude field tests in the area. Prisoners would be strapped to stakes. Airplanes would then fly over them and release bombs containing deadly germs. Bomb design, types of germs, and the height of the planes would vary as Ishii attempted to discover the most effective way of spreading disease.[27]

The Japanese Army formally authorized Ishii to launch his first wartime BW attack in 1939, when Japan was fighting the Soviet Union in a border war over Manchukuo, Manchuria. At the time, anxious Japanese commanders were facing a possible invasion by Soviet and Mongolian forces from the north. On 12 July, Ishii sent a twenty-four-man sabotage squad into enemy (Soviet) territory up the Halha River. This special operations team took containers with 50 lbs of prepared Salmonella and typhoid bacteria and emptied them into the river. After taking samples from the water, the men hurried back to Ping Fan.[28] The effectiveness of these operations was never determined.

Ishii expanded his testing programme after 1939 to include all of Manchuria as well as occupied and free China. In 1940, he went to Changchun, the Manchukuon capital. When he forecast to the local authorities that a cholera epidemic was about to descend, his warning was believed and he was allowed to 'inoculate' the population. He was actually injecting them with a solution full of cholera germs. An epidemic soon spread through Changchun.[29]

From 1939–45, Nanking housed the so-called Anti-Epidemic Water Unit #1644, which was another important outpost of Ishii's grotesque BW research empire.[30] In a chilling interview given in August 1997, Hiroshi Matsumoto, a medical assistant, described how Chinese prisoners were treated during nauseating biological experiments at Unit 1644. In 1942, Matsumoto's job was to help inject them with live cholera and Plague germs, and allow their bodies to incubate the lethal bacteria so that they spread throughout the blood. Only then did Ishii's technicians harvest this terrible fruit, by draining out their blood while they still lived.

The prisoners were actually housed in animal cages, only 45–50 inches in height, depth, and width. 'They had to have legs crossed always like this,' explained the assistant, as he demonstrated, crouching low with tightly crossed legs.[31] The victims endured this torture for up to six months before they were taken away and chloroformed; then their main artery from the centre of the thigh was cut out using a scalpel. The blood flow was staunched by a clip, while the victim was restrained to the bed by a large belt tied round the chest. Then the bleeding to death began.

Matsumoto continued: 'After the considerable amount of blood flow was gone, when the flow of blood lowered, the whole body was shaking in convulsion. I believe most probably this was the last moment of the person. It was so painful to see the convulsion that rattled the belts that tied his body down. However, I had to climb on the prisoner and step on both sides of the chest in order to squeeze the last drops of blood which came out in the form of small bubbles.'

The Plague-contaminated blood was then used to infect numerous fleas, which would later be dropped against the Chinese to pollute whole villages. Matusmoto's work accounted for the death of at least 40–50 Chinese prisoners – only a tiny fraction of Nanking's many deadly experiments.

In August 1942, a Japanese warplane flew lazily out of the western sky and circled over the small Chinese hamlet of Congshan in Zhejiang Province in eastern China. First, the aircraft dropped down to the rice paddies for observation, then passed over the ornate rooftops that dotted the hamlet. '[It sprayed] a kind of smoke from its back end,' recalled Jin Xianlan in a 1997 interview.[32] She was a child at the time, but today still remembers with clarity the presence of a hostile plane that did no harm. Or so it seemed.

The epidemic began two weeks later when the village rats began to die. Next, fever broke out, carried by the fleas, infecting the villagers like a modern Black Death. The Plague ran rampant through the hamlet for two months, killing 392 out of the population of 1,200. Then Japanese troops arrived and set fire to the plague houses. At its height, this BW attack claimed some twenty lives a day. Some victims just died quietly, some screamed as the terrible infection consumed them; some, delirious, drank stagnant and brackish water from open sewers in a last desperate attempt to put out the burning fire inside their bodies, only to die slow and agonizing deaths.

'You buried the dead knowing that the next day you would be buried,' recalled Wang Peigen, who was ten during the horror and one of the few residents to survive. Another survivor spoke of the slow reversion to medieval terror. 'The thing I remember most is the fear,' said sixty-eight-year-old Wang Da. 'People closed their doors and all you could hear through the night was people dying and people crying for the dead.'[33]

Finally, in one vile act of medical perversion, even the 'helpers' turned out to be masked agents of death. Those villagers who did dare go outside in search of aid might encounter masked Japanese medical assistants in white coats, apparitions from hell who moved silently through the hamlet of death looking for victims who would undergo just one more living nightmare before the sweet release of death. They were needed for live experiments. According to one witness, Tong Jinlan, the Japanese disguised a Buddhist temple in the centre of the hamlet as a Plague treatment post.[34] She recalled how an eighteen-year-old Plague victim, Wu Xiaonai, made the dreadful mistake of falling for the trick. Miss Tong, an old woman in 1997, recounted how she heard Wu pleading for her life as the Japanese doctors tied her down, placed a hood over her head to muffle her screams, and then dissected her – alive – to use her organs for further study.

Wang Rongli was one of Congshan's lucky ones. His withered right arm is a lifetime reminder of where the Japanese doctors had injected bacteria and then left him to die. 'My arm rotted for many years,' he recalled in 1997, 'but I am still alive.'[35]

Today there is no museum nor mark of remembrance to this biological horror unleashed over half a century ago. But the survivors of Congshan would like some help to build one. There is just the small activity centre in a courtyard off the village square, where they still store the large white scrolls that contain the names and ages of the dead and witness signatures to each death.[36] It was these events that brought Wang Xuan to Tokyo, two years ago – for Congshan was her home. 'For us,' she told the Tokyo court, silent but for the traffic hum outside, 'germ warfare is not an event of the past, but still a threat.'[37] She explained that fleas and mice still contain antibodies to the plague used more than fifty years ago. That means the germs are still there, and there could easily be another epidemic. The Japanese lawyers shifted uneasily as Wang Xuan confronted them with their nation's past.

When the Soviet Army swept through Manchuria in August 1945, the activities of Unit 731 were finally terminated. There's little doubt that the speed of the Soviet advance pre-empted further grotesque bacteriological war crimes by the Unit's nearly 3,000 members.

In keeping with the behaviour of all war criminals, orders were given for the evidence to be incinerated. The remaining 150 human 'logs' were peremptorily gassed and their bodies burned. The camp's laboratories and most of its buildings were blown up with dynamite charges. Most of the killers escaped back to Japan, where Ishii instructed them to 'live in the shadows' for their own sakes and for the fatherland.[38]

How close was Japan to using biological warfare against the Western allies? The answer is close enough.

During the years the Japanese spent experimenting on BW, they tried, but failed, to develop a weapon with the potential to unleash mass destruction. But they were never far from it.

Unit 731 had stockpiled some 900 lbs of anthrax for use in a specially designed fragmentation bomb.[39] Known as the HA Bomb, this single-purpose munition was developed in 1941 for dispersal of anthrax spores; it was produced in relatively large numbers ('by the hundreds') indicating plans for a serious aerial biological warfare attack.[40]

There's never been any doubt that the Japanese had plans to attack allied forces with bacterial agents. It was clear to them from the Congshan horror that the use of Plague-fleas had been highly successful. According to Professor Kei-ichi Tsuneishi, an authority on Ishii's germ warfare programme, the Japanese were planning to use BW in 1944 to defend a vital airstrip on Saipan, their Pacific island stronghold. They planned to drop porcelain bombs containing trillions of the Plague fleas on the invading GIs. The plan failed only because a Japanese submarine carrying the BW equipment and specialists was sunk before reaching the island.[41]

During the last frenzied months of war, Ishii was preparing for an even more bizarre attack on the United States. This military operation, code-named 'Cherry Blossoms at Night', called for kamikaze pilots to spread Plague over southern California in September 1945.[42] Toshimi

Mizobuchi, a troop instructor in Unit 731, later explained that the plan was to have a submarine transport a group of Japanese kamikaze pilots and several planes (with folded wings) to the coastal waters near San Diego. They would then fly the planes over the city, dropping Plague-infected fleas.

A pilot under the command of Ishii, Ishio Kobata, recalled the plan in 1998. 'I was told directly by Shiro Ishii of the kamikaze mission "Cherry Blossoms at Night", which was named by Ishii himself. I was a leader of a squad of seventeen. I understood that the mission was to spread contaminated fleas in the enemy's base and contaminate them with Plague.'[43] (Japan surrendered a month before the operation's September 1945 attack date.)

Another ex-pilot of Unit 731, Shoichi Matsumoto, recalled a further equally outlandish plan to infect invading US forces in the Pacific in 1945 with Plague. 'I know there was a plan to release two gliders over the island of Iwo Jima,' he says. 'Each glider, which was German made, had twenty-two seats. My mission was to carry a glider, attached to my plane, from Unit 731's airport over to Iwo Jima, then release it and fly back to Manchuria, where I was to train suicide squad members how to pilot gliders.

'I myself was trained to fly a glider at a Manchurian passenger airline. Only a small glider was available at Ping Fan for my instruction course. A pilot senior to me was supposed to bring the German-made gliders from mainland Japan, but they broke down on the way. They never reached Ping Fan.'[44]

Ishii was desperate to use his new biological weapons on a grand scale. Had the war lasted a few years longer, he may have earned a unique notoriety in military history. As it was, a new weapon, and one that burned with the brightness of a thousand suns, was to bring the war to an end – with the Allies as victors.

After Japan's surrender, Ishii remained devastated and inconsolable. He could not accept that inferior peoples had actually defeated Japan.[45] But his well-honed instinct for survival did not allow him to fall honourably upon his sword. What consumed him first was an older impulse for self-preservation.

First of all, he had destroyed Ping Fan. He also made certain that the principal scientists escaped safely back to Japan. A large amount of documents and equipment from Ping Fan was transported to Pusan, Korea. Many of the most important records ended up buried in Ishii's garden at his Tokyo home.[46]

Back in Tokyo, Ishii decided it was time for a tactical disappearance. A story was planted in a newspaper to the effect that he had been shot.[47] To bear out his untimely death, an elaborate charade of a funeral was held in his home village.

American intelligence officials were not deceived for more than a few months. After an intensive search, he was eventually tracked down by the authorities. The Americans had been pressured into a larger investigation of Ishii and his BW experimental methods after an article appeared in the *Pacific Stars and Stripes* on 6 January 1946.[48] The article alleged that 'members of the Japanese medical corps had inoculated American and Chinese prisoners with bubonic plague virus in experiments in Harbin and Mukden, Manchuria'. The article appeared shortly after the Tokyo headquarters of both US military intelligence and investigators had been inundated with correspondence from Japanese nationals concerning war crimes.

Ishii was tracked down to his home town nearly two weeks later but, curiously, he was not arrested.[49] He was even permitted to stay in his home while the charges against him were being investigated. Under subsequent interrogation, he described his BW research as a small-scale project. Any experiments he had conducted were only with animals. Humans, of course, had never been used. Field tests had certainly not been undertaken.[50]

The work of the American investigators was partly compromised by the needs of the US Army's nascent BW research programme at home. American BW scientists had been frustrated in their work on researching human reactions to biological and toxic agents, because they could use only data received from animal experimentation.[51] They realized they needed to lay hands on the results of biological experiments on human beings.

They also lacked information on BW delivery systems. One scientist claimed that 'we had no first-hand knowledge on how biological warfare agents might be disseminated ... [We had] no background other than conjecture.'[52] Moreover, American BW testing in the field had been extremely limited, yet 'the absolute necessity for adequate field tests of the various means of dissemination was recognized from the beginning'.[53] With the help of Japanese collaboration, it was thought, these problems might be solved.

Ishii soon read the runes. The way in which he had been interrogated by US officials pointed towards a search for BW knowledge, rather than for evidence of bestial behaviour towards civilians. He realized he could trade data for immunity from war crimes prosecution.

When detailed interrogations were carried out by the Americans, Ishii insisted that the meeting always took place at his home, because he claimed he was ill.[54] Then he treated his visitors like an aristocrat suffering the visit of commoners. The interviews were conducted in his bedroom. He sat up in his bed wearing his best kimono. He answered their questions in contradictory fashion, and with varying degrees of honesty. '[I am] wholly responsible for Ping Fan,' he boasted, '. . . I can get all the information for you.

'In the preparation of war with Russia,' he added cunningly, 'I can give you the advantages of my twenty years' research and experience.'[55] This offer, he knew, would touch the spot, and it did.

At times, Ishii would enter into long vainglorious monologues, concluding with a request that he 'would like to be hired by the US as a BW expert'. Moreover, he said he had given a 'great deal of thought to tactical problems in the use of and defence against BW'. He even bragged: 'I can write volumes about BW, including the little thought of strategic and tactical employment.'[56]

By the end of the interviews, Ishii had promised to produce a full account of his two decades of BW experience.[57] Nineteen of Ishii's former underlings also volunteered to the Americans a report on some of their BW experiments, including the 'theoretical and mathematical considerations involved in particle-size determinations', and a summary of a series of lectures 'given to spies and saboteurs by one of the leading BW officials'. They also threw in six hundred pages of articles 'covering the entire field of natural and artificial plague', and a one-hundred-page, printed bulletin concerned with 'some phase of BW or CW warfare'.[58]

Ishii eventually secured his immunity and went on to live well, safe from war crimes prosecutors, until he died from throat cancer in 1959 at the age of sixty-seven.[59]

The irony was that saving the life of one of the world's more repellent war criminals was not necessary. All of that Japanese BW data turned out to be of little use to the United States. A 1982 memorandum from the US Army's archives reveals: 'Scientists in the US programme said the information was not of significant value, but it was the first data in which human subjects were described.'

Closer analysis of the data revealed that the Japanese experiments did not greatly enhance American knowledge of BW. US Army scientists concluded that, 'Within one year of the establishment of its programme (in 1943), the level of US expertise already exceeded that of the team at Unit 731; Japanese weaponry was still crude in 1945.'[60]

There was one final irony.

In 1998, Yoshio Shinozuko, a former member of Unit 731 and a self-confessed war criminal who had publicly admitted his crimes and then publicly recanted, applied to travel to the United States. The purpose was honourable. His intention was to give a series of lectures to young people in America about the truth of Unit 731 and to introduce them to the horrors of biological warfare.

But, because he had sought to assuage some of his guilt and confess to his involvement, Shinozuko was placed on a watch list of war criminals by the US immigration service and was duly forbidden entry.

When appeals were made on his behalf, including some from victims' own relatives in the United States, a senior federal attorney noted, 'I appreciate the irony . . . but the law must be applied in all cases.'[61] The ban was upheld.

The last word regarding Unit 731 belongs to Wang Xuan, to this day still fighting her case in a quiet Tokyo courtroom. 'The most important thing,' she tells the bench, 'is to reveal the facts.

'We are . . . fighting for dignity.'[62]

CHAPTER FOUR

Arms Race

'[BW is] of course "dirty business", but ... I think we must be prepared.'

Henry Stimson, Secretary of War to FDR, 1942[1]

'Biological weapons ... know no boundaries. They are a huge threat to us.'

Secretary of State Madeleine Albright, 1998[2]

Washington's tacit condoning of Japan's research and development of offensive biological warfare during World War II merely reflected the reality that the United States too had begun a similar journey, albeit with a slightly better adjusted moral compass.

The truth is that the potential of biological warfare had whetted military appetites in Britain, Germany, and the Soviet Union at the same time.

Like the Japanese, the Americans needed to suck it and see, find out for themselves. What were the parameters of this unusual form of warfare? Did it have a tactical or strategic role to play? Did it outclass the gun or the bomb? Was it economically viable? There is no evidence that anyone, East or West, Allied or Axis, ever regarded research on biological weapons as morally out of bounds.

In fact, the United States was the last of the great world powers of the 1930s to begin researching biological weapons.[3] In an era before atomic bombs were even a glimmer in the eye of military science, America was slow to appreciate that the large-scale, military use of germs, toxins, and poisons was feasible. However, once American officials discovered during World War II that other nations were developing bio-weapons and the threat was real, the US pursued bio-warfare with typical American ruthlessness, ingenuity, and cash.

By the 1950s, the US Army had created the biological warfare infrastructure that General Ishii and his scientists at Unit 731 had only dreamed of. And by the 1960s, the US had created such a fearsome and sophisticated array of biological weapons that even their own scientists could barely believe what they had accomplished.

At the start of World War II, it was actually the British who were slightly ahead of the game, with scientists from the Chemical Defence Experimental Establishment at Porton Down, deep in the Wiltshire countryside, already preparing to conduct their first testing of a BW agent. A British team led by Dr Paul Fildes and Dr David Henderson (with American officials observing) dropped the West's first anthrax bomb (a 25-pound prototype) amidst several dozen tethered sheep on the rugged, 550-acre Gruinard Island, three miles off the northwest coast of Scotland.[4] This first test in the summer of 1942, conducted under poor safety precautions, created appalling contamination of the island, which was to last half a century. But it proved for the first time that a biological agent – anthrax – could be grown, packed into a weapon, transported hundreds of miles, and effectively exploded over a precise target area.

Most of the sheep died and those that didn't were slaughtered.

Throughout the war, Winston Churchill's coalition government was deeply apprehensive that the Nazis too possessed an offensive biological warfare capability. This fear reached its apogee when Hitler launched the new pilotless V-1 'doodlebugs' over London in 1944. An early assumption was that they might be carrying BW warheads. Allied intelligence further assumed the Germans might use botulinum toxin, so the West stepped up development of antidotes. By 1944, the US Army and Canadian government had made, or commercially acquired, more than one million doses of botulinum toxoid vaccine for shipment to England to protect Allied forces. The vaccines were never required and were destroyed after the war.[5]

But even before the final victory, the Americans had launched a well-funded and serious programme to develop biological weapons. Compared to the Manhattan Project, with a wartime budget of $2 billion to create atomic bombs, the BW programme was still quite small, with an initial budget of only $3.5 million. By the end of the war, however,

BW spending had spiralled to $60 million. Never before had a country thrown together so much money, equipment, and scientific talent with the dedicated purpose of producing biological weapons.[6]

The selection of the actual BW agents by the Americans was critical, with many complex, inter-related factors to consider. The military's shopping list was extensive. They wanted high virulence; low dosage for lethality; consistent effects; reliable growth of the organism during large-scale production; viability during long-term storage; ease of transportation; survivability of the micro-organism in the weapon and on release; and the ability of the agent to 'neutralize' a very large area – up to hundreds of square miles. Most importantly, the weapon user needed to have safe and effective vaccines to counter the agent, while the enemy hopefully possessed no such defensive or therapeutic medical treatments.[7]

Three other more subtle factors later played a big role in the American strategy to develop these weapons: finding agents that might temporarily incapacitate the victims (without killing them); finding agents that were highly infectious to individuals but did not spread from man-to-man; finding agents that did not remain virulent on the battle-field for more than a few days after release. By combining these three properties, an enemy force could be attacked and humanely disabled; and neither the American troops who went in to collect the prisoners, nor the surrounding civilian populations, would have to worry about being infected.

They also had to work out how to deliver the agent in such a way as to infect large numbers of people. No one had ever attempted any mass delivery methods, just small-scale sabotage operations, the use of poisons, and Japan's plans with insects, small bombs, and balloons (which were as yet unknown to the US). Until then, no one had ever thought of using the wind as a carrier of BW agents – to infect people through their respiratory tracts. In 1943, this was a radical new concept; indeed, many of the new scientists assigned to the US programme were sceptical that large-scale inhalation would work at all.[8]

The Holy Grail of biological warfare research was to produce a *dry* bacterial or viral agent. This was to become the most crucial part of the whole programme, but, as of 1943, no one knew how to make dry particles and still maintain the virulence of the living agent. Biological agents were grown only in liquids and produced in a liquid paste form, called slurry, which was the consistency of slightly more viscous than usual whole milk. The scientists eventually realized (long after the war) what they needed to do to make dry, light, small particles, like bath powder, so that the agent could be dispersed in air and inhaled through the lungs.

Size was all important. Through extensive testing, researchers eventually determined that the optimum size of BW particles was between one micron and five microns in diameter (a micron is 1/25,000 of an inch). Tests on animals showed that a one-micron particle was hundreds of times more lethal than a ten-micron particle of the same bacteria. When inhaled, the smaller particles can more easily avoid the body's natural defences – the cilia inside the nose and upper respiratory tract – and reach the lungs.[9] Liquid agents can be made into aerosol particles through intense pressure and released through small nozzles, like a fine spray. But these larger particles drift to earth very slowly in air, degrade very rapidly in heat or sunlight, and are usually too big to be inhaled. Dry agents were far more powerful than liquids – pound for pound they produce many more lethal doses. Dry agents also could be stored much more easily and for longer than liquids.[10]

When the American BW research programme began, it was clear immediately that a new and large site was urgently required.[11] It would need to be near Washington under military control; it had to be relatively nondescript and isolated, for secrecy and safety concerns, yet it had to have room to grow. After considering several sites, Camp Detrick was selected near the foothills of the gently rolling Catoctin Mountains in western Maryland, about 50 miles northwest of Washington. The 1,200-acre rural location was originally the old Detrick Field, a small municipal airport amid a cow pasture that was used by the National Guard as a pilot training facility from 1931–43. (It was named after Major Frederick Detrick, a local physician and World War I hero.)[12]

So in April 1943, Camp Detrick (later renamed Fort Detrick in 1956) became the brain centre of the US programme: the initiation and co-ordination point for all lab research, small-scale production, testing, reports, technical papers, and contact with academia and industry.[13] At its peak in 1945 there were 1,770 officers and enlisted personnel from all the armed services working inside the maximum-security campus, including microbiologists, bio-chemists, medical researchers, engineers,

GIs, WACs, armament specialists, and civilian contractors.[14] It was the world's most advanced biological warfare research unit, inexorably heading down the path General Ishii had first explored, towards the manufacture of weapons that, if used, would return mankind to the future of a new dark age.

They knew the creation of efficient biological delivery systems would not be easy. Taking living bacteria, toxins, or viruses, and placing them inside a military weapon that will successfully deliver them – intact and still virulent – to large numbers of enemy forces, was a technical problem that had only partially been addressed by the earlier British anthrax tests. The Americans had virtually no worthwhile scientific data.[15]

Starting at the drawing board, they split delivery systems into two distinct types. Firstly, bombs, called 'point source'; secondly, liquid (or later dry) sprays, distributed from large tanks mounted on planes, called 'line source'. The benefits of bombs were the comfortable old technology, the efficiency of the small package, and the predictability of hitting the target, even in poor weather conditions. The drawback was that bombs sometimes didn't explode; only 5 per cent of the agent inside discharged on a good drop; and the bombing left a clear 'signature' of what was dropped – so medical countermeasures could be taken.

The benefits of 'line source' were that much larger targets could be attacked with a degree of anonymity in that both the attacker and the agent used might not be revealed for a little while. The downside was estimating with some accuracy wind velocity and direction to maximum effect. The wrong air flow could take the agent away from the target area. Tests showed that optimum wind conditions were between 5 and 30 mph – if below 5 mph the agent did not spread far; if above 30 mph, the wind degraded the agent.[16]

By the time the first US weapons tests were completed, the British were anxiously waiting to lay their hands on finished bombs. In February 1944, Britain's chief science adviser, Lord Cherwell, advised Churchill that the American tests demonstrated that just six of the 500-pound prototype American bombs, loaded with many smaller bomblets and dropped from a plane, would terminate all human life within one square mile.[17] British documents since released suggest that Churchill was so desperate to prevent defeat that he compromised on his humanitarian views to order the use of anthrax against the Nazis if necessary.

In London, military strategists drew up plans to drop hundreds of thousands of the 4-pound anthrax bomblets on six German cities – Berlin, Hamburg, Stuttgart, Frankfurt, Aachen, and Wilhelmshaven. Churchill's staff estimated these attacks would wipe out half the German population in each city and leave the target zones contaminated for many years.

But the British were wholly dependent on the US to supply its anthrax weapons. A deliberate decision had been taken not to set up a large-scale anthrax production site in Britain because it would be vulnerable to Luftwaffe (or V1 and V2) attacks with potentially catastrophic collateral damage to civilians living nearby.[18]

So by June 1944, the US Army actually placed an order for one million of the 4-pound bomblets for their British allies, but the production schedule was delayed and the war ended before any finished bombs were made or shipped to London. As it happened, Churchill never did have to take the final decision to use biological weapons.

Ironically, after the war, Allied intelligence found that the Germans had made no progress on any large-scale offensive BW programme of their own.[19] Captured German intelligence files also showed that after 1942 the Nazis had received no intelligence about the new US BW programme.[20]

After the war ended in 1945, and for the next five years, the initial research at Camp Detrick focused on evaluating the agents that had earlier showed promise during the war, specifically anthrax, botulinum toxin, Brucellosis, Tularaemia, and psittacosis. In 1951, for the first time, the Joint Chiefs of Staff began to set priorities for which BW agents the army should develop.[21]

Throughout the coldest war years of the fifties, other agents were added to the active research list, including: Plague, Venezuelan Equine Encephalitis (VEE), Q fever, cholera, dengue fever, shigellosis (dysentery), and human glanders.[22] The army scientists attempted to make each of these agents more virulent, more stable, more viable, and easier to manufacture. The new techniques included use of additives and mixtures of agents; micro-encapsulation of particles to counter the degrading effects of sunlight; and devising new methods of generating aerosols.[23]

As Camp Detrick was being modernized to meet Research and Development requirements, the US also needed a new, large-scale production centre if the army was finally to make usable weapons. The whole BW programme was given fresh impetus by the Korean War, during which American and British soldiers led a United Nations army against the communist North Koreans who had invaded the South. Both the Congress and the Pentagon feared that North Korea or China might use BW against United Nations forces, and the US would need a retaliatory capability. So, in 1950, Congress authorized funding for the construction of a major production facility at a renovated arsenal near Pine Bluff, Arkansas.

The huge Pine Bluff site, over 14,000 acres in central Arkansas, had originally opened in 1942 as a chemical weapons facility. The new BW plant, code-named X-201, would be added as the army's main centre to manufacture and store BW agents and munitions. Set deep in the forests, and well away from the nearby farming community, Pine Bluff included a ten-storey main building – with three storeys underground, and ten giant fermenters to mass produce biological agents on demand. When the plant finally became operational in early 1954 (at a cost of $90 million), its 858 employees began by manufacturing Brucellosis and Tularaemia. Botulinum toxin and anthrax were added later to the production line. (In 1955, anthrax became safer to make after the first effective vaccine was developed.)

Eventually, in 1963, the plant was modernized again and refitted to handle more infectious viral and rickettsiae agents, including Q fever and VEE. Throughout all of these years, any of the live agents produced at Pine Bluff were stored in bulk, and not inside actual bombs.[24]

Long before the new facilities at Camp Detrick and Pine Bluff were completed, a field-testing programme also began again – but on a far larger scale than during World War II, involving both live agents and simulants.

During the winter of 1948, the US and Britain conducted twenty-two joint tests at sea in the Caribbean. These trials, off the coast of Antigua, included the use of Brucellosis, Tularaemia, and anthrax. From 1952–55 a series of four other secret British tests of Brucellosis, Tularaemia, and Plague were conducted at sea near Scotland and the Bahamas.[25]

As an alternative to aerosols, the Pentagon also actively pursued the concept of insects as a possible virus delivery system during the 1950s. Both Camp Detrick and Pine Bluff (much later) ran entomological facilities, where large-scale breeding of mosquitoes took place. The theory was simple – bites from infected insects would bypass an enemy soldier's protective mask, and, over time, each insect would inhabit an area and infect many people.

In 1953, Camp Detrick started a programme to breed *Aedes aegypti* mosquitoes as a carrier of yellow fever. If necessary, this programme could breed 500,000 mosquitoes per month. From 1956–58, in several tests, the army released *uninfected* female mosquitoes in Savannah, Georgia and Avon Park, Florida – to see how many people were bitten and how far the insects would spread. The Pentagon also developed contingency plans to distribute mosquitoes over enemy territory using aircraft, helicopters, missiles, and bombs. Other insect research included using mosquitoes infected with malaria and dengue fever; fleas carrying Plague; ticks with Tularaemia; and flies with cholera, anthrax, and dysentery.

But this low-tech method of spreading germ warfare eventually fell into disrepute. It might have worked for General Ishii's forces to spread the Plague flea amongst rats in small Chinese villages, but this was not what the mighty superpower of America was looking for. Eventually, by the mid-1960s, army scientists found that the release of insects was much too cumbersome and finicky, and the results were too uncontrollable, unreliable, and inefficient. The insect vector plan was squashed.[26]

Practical war games also became fashionable – to assess US vulnerabilities to potential enemy sabotage attacks. In 1949, the army ran its first 'top-secret' test of a building – inside the Pentagon itself – with sobering results. Scientists inserted a small amount of BW simulant into just one air-conditioning unit and found it was quickly distributed throughout the world's largest office building. The conclusion: if an attacker knew what he was doing, it was relatively easy to incapacitate or kill large numbers of people inside any office building or military facility anywhere.[27] In the land of skyscrapers, this was a lesson that has never been forgotten to this day, when air-conditioning units and ducts remain just as vulnerable.

The Korean War led to hurried testing to assess Allied vulnerabilities to a larger, military-style attack.[28] Open-air experiments with simulants were conducted at sea on US Navy ships in the Atlantic Ocean off Norfolk, Virginia. Clouds of the two leading simulants, *Bacillus globigii* (called 'BG') and *Serratia marcescens* (SM), were released over the ships to assess their vulnerability to attack, and to test prototype detection devices.[29]

In September 1950, the army moved outdoors to San Francisco, California to conduct the first domestic vulnerability tests for large areas of land. The Pentagon wanted to see if an enemy submarine could surface near a major US port city, secretly mount a BW attack, and escape undetected before anyone was aware of what had happened.[30]

From 20–26 September, during six mock attacks, two navy mine-sweepers sprayed millions of particles of *Serratia marcescens* toward the San Francisco coastline.[31] At the time, the army believed SM was harmless, but, three days later, eleven patients with SM infections began appearing at local hospitals – and one man died.[32] Army scientists later concluded that all 800,000 residents of the city, in a 117 square mile area, had been exposed to the clouds of test germs. The test proved that the use of a live agent would have been devastating.

By 1952–53, the US military began to rain BW simulants all over America. As their secret testing programme expanded, planes sprayed clouds of inorganic zinc cadmium sulphide (fluorescent particles) over the populated areas of Winnipeg, Manitoba; St Louis; Minneapolis; Fort Wayne; rural Maryland, and Leesburg, Virginia.[33] Once again, the test results were predictable: a knowledgeable attacker could easily infect many millions of people from a distance as much as 20 miles away from the target area.

In 1957, the army began another series of tests, unsubtly called 'Operation Large Area Coverage', to determine the feasibility of contam-inating huge regions of the country with BW agents dropped from aircraft, tall rooftops, and moving vehicles.[34] The thirty-three urban and rural areas tested covered nearly everywhere within the Canadian and Mexican borders from the Atlantic Ocean to the Rocky Mountains. A variety of simulants (mostly fine fluorescent powders) were tested in various wind conditions to determine the distance and direction they would cover. No illnesses were ever documented from these tests, but the data collected was as grim as ever.[35] The tests with small particles – down to one micron – showed that given favourable winds they could easily cover tens of thousands of square miles at a time.[36]

By 1958, the US had developed its first missile to carry a BW warhead – the 762-mm Honest John rocket. With a 16-mile range, the warhead could deliver 356 4.5-inch spherical bomblets.[37] By the early 1960s, the first long-range US missile, the Sergeant, extended the warhead's reach to 75 miles and the payload up to 720 spherical bomblets.[38]

As the arsenal of 'point source' missiles and bombs was evolving, the army's scientists and war planners knew that dust clouds delivered as a 'line source' from spray tanks on fast-moving planes would have by far the best potential to make BW a truly devastating mass casualty weapon. The problem was that these invisible vapours depended on producing viable dry agents, which were still largely elusive in the early 1960s.

But, after 1963, even that hurdle was finally overcome, and, by the end of the decade, the US knew how to take any potential micro-organism and convert it to a usable dry BW agent, how to stabilize these organisms against the rough handling they would receive before and during weaponization, and how to protect the organisms from decay after spraying.[39] These were huge scientific and military breakthroughs, equivalent to replacing the horse cavalry with the tank.

A crucial technical leap was the ability to freeze-dry large amounts of liquid agents. (For Tularaemia, for instance, droplets of the concentrated liquid agent cultures were frozen with Freon, dried into pellets, and then milled down to a much smaller size. Skimmed milk and sucrose were added to stabilize the resulting agent, which remained viable for three years under proper refrigeration.)[40] Another important technical achievement occurred when the US learned how to fortify agents with unique chemical properties that would keep them stable and virulent during spraying.

Perhaps the gold star went to those researchers who discovered how to produce tiny, dry particles of BW agents without milling them. Milling – the process to make the organisms a smaller, standard size – had always been a serious production drawback because the process tears up the (often fragile) organisms and degrades their potency. The unique new US process concentrated the organisms into the right-sized particles, while maintaining their virulence, without milling them. With this top-secret production technique, the US was able to produce, by weight, the most efficient and lethal agents of any country in the world.

Before 1963, no 'large-scale', 'line-source' tests had occurred using lethal, dry agents as strategic weapons.[41] As the new and improved live agents now became available, the scientists at Fort Detrick and the new

Deseret Test Centre in Utah concluded that even the huge Dugway Proving Ground in Utah, which had served for years as the Americans' testing ground, was no longer big enough to safely contain the tests they now had in mind. The lethality, survivability, and dispersal characteristics of the new agents, and the sophistication and efficiency of the munitions, had all made Dugway virtually obsolete.[42]

The army had to find another test site that could accommodate clouds of lethal pathogens that spread for hundreds of miles. (The actual area covered by the clouds of US test agents remains a highly classified national security secret.)

The only suitable site for large-scale testing, which was owned and controlled by the US military, was Johnson Atoll, four small coral islands in the central Pacific Ocean, 720 nautical miles southwest of Honolulu, Hawaii, from where the US had previously conducted high-altitude atmospheric nuclear tests. The strategically located atoll, which had been a US airstrip and transport centre since World War II, was uninhabited by civilians and isolated from any population areas.

The first ever 'large-scale', open-air American tests with live agents were run at Johnson Atoll from 1963–69. The actual number and type of these tests are still secret. It has been disclosed that one of them, code-named 'Shady Grove', was a series of thirteen trials to determine the effectiveness and decay rate of liquid Q fever and Tularaemia in a warm climate.[43]

Approximately 300 army and navy personnel, technicians and support staff were involved in each of these complicated tests. They used about six tugboats moored in the ocean within the test area as 'samplers'. These boats carried monkeys, guinea pigs, and aerosol sampling devices, which measured the concentration of the agent particles that fell on the boat. By comparing the known breathing rates of the animals with the concentration of the collected samples, the scientists could calculate the quantity of organisms needed to kill a target percentage of the test animals. Achieving a 50 per cent kill rate with the lethal agents was their goal (and remains the acceptable rate to this day).

The invisible BW agents were released from a spray tank mounted on an F-105 Navy jet, which streaked overhead at 600 kph, as it set down the 'line source' for one-to-three minutes. Typically, the tank, which held 90 kg of agent, released three grams per metre over a 30 kilometre release line.[44]

Although the American public was not aware of these secret tests, the Soviets were watching closely. Whenever a test was about to begin, Soviet spy-ships poorly disguised as trawlers would appear on cue in the vicinity of Johnson Atoll. The US Navy sent planes to buzz them and boats to warn them away.

Given the danger of positioning a boat under a shower of deadly germs, the Americans assumed that the Soviet crews had to be militarily and biologically trained and outfitted with protective gear and sophisticated sampling and decontamination equipment.

Their appearance at the right time and place suggested that the Soviets knew full well the US was testing live BW agents.

The Americans ran secret cold-weather tests too in the mid-sixties. There were four large-scale tests in the wilderness of central Alaska, near Fort Greely – to find out how germs and bacteria performed in cold weather. The operational concept behind these trials assumed that the Soviet Union would be America's major opponent in a war and, given the USSR's huge landmass, a US BW attack would inevitably involve operating with bacterial agents and weapons in sub-Arctic temperatures.

Under Arctic conditions, the Americans sprayed agents over densely wooded areas and measured the downwind coverage and decay rates. As expected, the army scientists found reduced bio-decay in the cold, as compared to the warm Pacific islands. This meant the agents would spread better and survive longer.[45]

The army's entire programme placed the United States in pole position to conduct (or defend against) biological warfare in what had by now become a ferocious biological arms race between the superpowers. But, sooner than expected, the time would come when enormous political decisions would have to be taken about this new form of strategic warfare.

Nobody in the West would know for many years, but it would continue for one of them, long after the other had turned its biological swords into ploughshares.

CHAPTER FIVE

The Soviet Programme

'Only at the end of the 1940s, as a retaliatory measure, the Soviet government was forced to . . . fulfil the task of developing military biological weapons . . .'

Russian government statement to UN, 1992[1]

By the late sixties, when the British, the Americans, and the Soviets were locked into a superpower biological arms race, it was the West that decided to call a halt. In a unique gesture of disarmament, the West unilaterally set a moral example (albeit for pragmatic and political reasons only), almost without precedent.

In a move calculated to bring even greater disarmament rewards, Washington and London pulled out of the biological arms race, laid down their deadly weapons, and eventually persuaded a suspicious Soviet Union to sign a treaty too.

But at the very moment when it looked as if the bacteria, viruses, and toxins would be consigned to the autoclaves of history, Moscow decided to cheat. That was in 1972, and, even today, Russia continues to lie and deceive in order to protect a substantial investment in offensive biological warfare. For the last thirty years, Moscow has quietly dealt itself a hand full of aces in the biological warfare game despite every attempt by the other players to cry foul.

American and British work on offensive biological warfare agents and weapons was well advanced when it was voluntarily discarded. The Soviet programme, too, had a long and distinctive background with antecedents traceable back as early as 1928.

Even then, the early Bolsheviks instinctively sensed the future value of this terrible new form of warfare. The Bolshevik government's Revolutionary Military Council signed a secret decree that year ordering the development of typhus as a weapon. In those days, there were no vaccines or antibiotics to treat typhus, and previous major typhus epidemics had shown Soviet Army commanders that the disease could become a very powerful new weapon.[2]

In 1933, the BW programme was put under the control of the OGPU (a forerunner of the KGB), which established a small, experimental research laboratory for bacteria at Pokrovsky Monastery in the quiet town of Suzdal. In 1935, this site was moved to a well-guarded compound on Gorodomyla Island on Lake Seliger – in order to distance the dangerous work and field trials from populated areas. The agents under scrutiny on the island included Plague, leprosy, and Foot and Mouth Disease.[3]

By the start of World War II, the Soviets were able to produce crude weapons using typhus, Tularaemia, and Q fever. They were also experimenting with techniques to manufacture their three best potential agents, Plague, anthrax, and cholera, which they called 'the golden triangle'.[4] But, like those of Japanese General Ishii's team, Soviet delivery systems were still very primitive – with work concentrating on the use of insects as vectors for plague wars.[5]

In the early 1930s, scientists from the Red Army's medical institute also had been ordered to develop lethal germs and bacteria for biological weapons. The army had opened its main BW centre – the Scientific-Research Institute of Microbiology – in the village of Perkhushkovo near Moscow in 1933. Another BW research facility was established in the mid-1930s at the Leningrad Military Academy, where scientists produced both powdered and liquid typhus for primitive aerosol devices.[6] The academy's first test site was the frigid and isolated Solovetsky Island, 160 kilometres north of Leningrad in the White Sea, home of one of Stalin's Gulag prison camps. Prisoners were forced to build a BW laboratory on the island and scientists from Leningrad used it to test typhus, Q fever, and glanders. Some of the researchers (who lacked any antibiotics) fell ill through exposure to the tested pathogens. All the circumstances suggest it is highly likely that prisoners were used as guinea pigs in these early experiments. But there is no firm proof.[7]

When the army was forced to move its secret facilities in 1942, to prevent the advancing German Army from seizing the laboratories, all of the special equipment and samples were relocated to the city of Kirov, 560 miles northeast of Moscow on the Vyatka River, where a huge military hospital already existed.[8]

The army named its new Kirov laboratory the Microbiology Research Institute. But its true purpose remained top secret. There were no signs posted outside, while the barbed-wire fences and concrete walls surrounding the grounds spoke for themselves. During World War II, Kirov also produced the USSR's first batch of penicillin and streptomycin. The Soviets desperately needed these medicines to treat their troops at the front suffering from infectious diseases. Soviet officials later insisted that the facility's post-war work was to make only antibiotics to fight Plague, glanders, and Tularaemia, and the world's best vaccine for anthrax. However, the West still knows very little about what the Soviet military really did at Kirov, since it has never been inspected.[9]

There are some residual suspicions about Kirov because two never explained outbreaks of infectious diseases hit invading German troops in Russia during World War II. In 1942, before the battle of Stalingrad, a severe outbreak of Tularaemia swept through the German Army in southern Russia; the disease eventually spilled over to Soviet troops and local citizens, infecting about 100,000 people in all. In 1943, a similar outbreak of Q fever occurred in the Crimea. Significantly, both epidemics involved biological agents which Soviet scientists were known to be researching at that time and it seems more than a coincidence that no such widespread outbreaks of those two diseases had ever been reported in Russia before these incidents.[10]

After the war, the infamous Lavrenti Beria, Stalin's trusted and all-powerful deputy, was put in overall charge of the BW programme. Beria was chosen because, with Stalin's encouragement, he had helped create and then administer the state's massive secret police apparatus. Inside the army, the Seventh Main Directorate of the Soviet General Staff later ran the programme under the direction of the leading military medical scientist, General Yefim Smirnov, who, during the next four decades, remained a powerful advocate of the strategic military benefits of biological weapons.[11]

In 1946, with Stalin's blessing, the Soviet Ministry of Defence began working intensively to build a more modern BW weapons programme –

now aided by several benefits from the war. The Soviets had acquired German industrial techniques and equipment for large-scale BW production; and they obtained information from Japanese scientists who worked for General Ishii.[12]

The Soviets' need for an offensive BW programme sprang from many factors, including their own perceived vulnerability to invasion and their understanding of the significance of Hiroshima and Nagasaki. There was also the reality that their programme had taken on a life of its own. Anyway, the US, UK, and other nations were also working on biological weapons research, and the Soviet military planners believed they had to have bio-weapons to counter these threats; in other words, there was a BW arms race.[13]

By 1949, the Soviets had clearly learned much from General Ishii's first modern use of biological warfare. The USSR conducted a show trial in Khabarovsk of twelve captured Japanese servicemen who had been preparing to use biological weapons in China and the USSR. The Soviets took extensive testimony of how Unit 731 was preparing for bacteriological warfare (using Plague, anthrax, and cholera), including attacking civilians and poisoning land and water to make cities and regions uninhabitable. The Soviets claimed that it was only their swift military victory over the Japanese Army in Manchuria and the arrest of these suspects that had prevented the Japanese from initiating BW attacks against US and Allied forces.

As part of the worldwide Soviet propaganda campaign from this trial, they indignantly accused (and not without some justification) the US of conducting BW research and protecting Japanese war criminals. This moral outrage against the US was the first of many Soviet efforts over the next four decades to hide and/or justify their own active BW research.[14]

In addition to Kirov, the first post-war Soviet BW site was built at Zagorsk (now Sergiev Posad), 40 miles from Moscow. Called the Institute of Military Microbiology, Zagorsk became the army's centre for researching bio-agents; in the 1950s, these experimental pathogens included anthrax, Tularaemia, Brucellosis, Plague, botulinum toxin, VEE, typhus, and Q fever. A large production site to manufacture these agents was secretly built in 1947 at Sverdlovsk, on the eastern side of the Ural Mountains.[15] (The Soviets relied on captured Japanese blueprints from Unit 731's assembly plants – which were larger and more sophisticated than any existing Soviet facility – to help design the new Sverdlovsk site.)[16]

The Zagorsk centre also supervised the BW programme's field testing site, opened in 1954 on Vozrozhdeniye Island in the huge Aral Sea, between Kazakhstan and Uzbekistan. This isolated site, officially named the Scientific Field Testing Laboratory, was situated south of the fishing port of Aralsk, which is on the northeastern shore of the Aral Sea, then the fourth largest inland body of water in the world.[17] One look at a map of the vast USSR shows the logic for why this particular site was chosen – it was the country's southern-most island (for warm temperatures) on its largest lake that was entirely surrounded by Soviet territory. The location meant privacy, separation from the mainland, and no foreigners.

Ironically, Vozrozhdeniye Island's tongue-twisting name means 'resurrection' in Russian. Because of the biological experiments that took place there, it was soon known by the more apt sobriquet of 'Hell's Island'.

The site's headquarters were located in the coastal town of Aralsk, where the army maintained facilities and housing for up to 1,000 people (including a 400-man battalion of chemical/biological protection troops). From there it took more than an hour and a half by helicopter or small plane to reach the island. The well-guarded base camp included an 80-square-mile test range, shelters for thousands of test animals (including monkeys, horses, donkeys, sheep, rodents, rabbits, and guinea pigs), and facilities and accommodation for as many as 150 scientists, technicians, and soldiers.[18]

The scientists and staff lived in the island's small, decrepit settlement, which included a few residential blocks, a school, and a shop. The 'technical base', where the laboratories, animal houses, and test-grounds were located, was a mile away from the town, encircled with barbed wire. Outside the fence were a few buildings that served as lodging for visiting scientists and servicemen from Moscow, who came to observe tests. This dusty settlement, the labs, and the test site were known as Aralsk-7 to the military and 'Barkhan' (or 'sand dune') to local inhabitants.[19]

There was a continuing problem with some of the more humble servicemen stationed there who were so badly fed that they often stole the higher quality, fresh food rations given to the baboons used for testing. Visiting scientists plagued by the isolation and overwhelming boredom of the posting took to the bottle or sought the pleasures of the flesh with equally bored female workers.[20]

The official purpose of the island was to develop 'defensive' measures against biological warfare; the true function was to test the efficiency of offensive weapons, like bombs, artillery shells, and sprays.[21] Tonnes of anthrax and Plague were dumped, sprayed, and exploded over the island. Brucellosis, glanders, Tularaemia, and some viruses were also tested, even though releases of virus were extremely dangerous because of the possibility of unleashing an uncontrollable infection that escaped the island.

Hamadryas baboons from the horn of Africa were the preferred test animals since they were closest to humans. Since the 1970s, the military had purchased hundreds of these baboons per year, at a steep cost (for Soviets) of $500–$700 each. Each experiment might use up to a hundred baboons chained to posts. After the test agent was released, the specially protected soldiers would collect the dead and dying beasts and take them to a holding unit, where post-mortems were conducted. The island had no crematorium. Instead, a mobile autoclave was driven around the test site to burn the animal corpses, and then the ashes were deposited in mass graves.[22] The island's mass graveyard contained the infected remains of thousands of these test animals.[23]

The Soviets tried to disinfect the island after each test, but it was a losing battle, as the contamination frequently spread into the sea and threatened the mainland.[24] One such occasion occurred in 1972, when a fishing boat with several Kazakhs aboard went missing from a mainland port. When the vessel was eventually found drifting at sea, all of the fishermen were found dead from Plague. They had sailed too close down-wind to an open-air, military test of the potent bacteria. The Soviet government never formally admitted the accident, the exact number of deaths was never disclosed, and the victims' families were never compensated.[25] Some accidents actually occurred on the island; a young woman on the army's first experimental team stationed there died from glanders and was buried in the settlement's cemetery.[26]

Entrance to the site was very strictly controlled. For safety reasons, the tests were usually carried out after dark so that the ambient bacteria would be extinguished at dawn by the rising sun; the homage to Dracula was coincidental. The varying weather conditions on the island –

including different temperatures, winds, and air pressures – were considered ideal for testing the effectiveness of a variety of BW agents.[27]

By the early fifties, as the USSR increased its BW expertise, Soviet generals viewed their programme as a form of warfare in which they now had a significant advantage over the West. This new weapon of mass destruction was now formally integrated into their military planning. BW agents were ominously termed 'weapons of special designation', and could be used not only as strategic weapons, but also to support conventional military operations. For example, the Soviet planners had carefully calculated that BW would be ideal for incapacitating enemy reinforcements or contaminating ports and rail centres.

The Soviets never knew that the United States had no plans to use BW in a strategic manner. However, the early fifties, in the deepest freeze of the Cold War, was no time to consider the equities, or the arithmetic of weapons of mass destruction, in Moscow, or in Washington DC.

CHAPTER SIX

CIA

'Relatively little is known about the nature and magnitude of the Soviet BW programme, particularly its offensive aspects.'

CIA report, 1957

Paradoxically, the view in Washington about the military effectiveness of biological warfare was almost diametrically the opposite of their cold war adversaries. During the early fifties, the fledgling CIA had responsibility for collecting the BW intelligence, analysing and assessing it, and making recommendations to policy makers and the White House.

Senior CIA officials dismissed biological warfare as a hypothetical, futuristic scenario – something from a sci-fi novel. The best guess was that bio-weapons would not have any military significance for another quarter of a century, if then. All the attention was on the looming Soviet nuclear threat. While BW analysis was not ignored, it was placed on the back burner.

This dismissive analysis sprang partly from ignorance as to the extent of the Soviet programme. The early fifties were the days before spy planes or spy satellites and the US was woefully short of HUMINT (human intelligence sources inside the USSR). Even the famous defectors of the next two decades, including GRU Lieutentant General Petr Popov, Colonel Oleg Penkovsky, and Major General Dimitry Polyakov, provided nothing to their British and American debriefers on BW. 'The Soviets compartmentalized their BW programme very efficiently,' recalls a former senior CIA analyst who closely studied all of the Soviet defector reports for more than twenty years.[1]

Some scraps of knowledge did begin to percolate through from other sources. One former Nazi scientist, Dr Walter Hirsch, who had been kidnapped by the Soviet Army during World War II and was later allowed to return to Germany, supplied the West with by far the best BW information. A document prepared by Hirsch guided US and UK analysts for many years afterwards.[2] This voluminous 'Hirsch Report' focused primarily on Soviet chemical warfare preparations (including allegations that the Soviet chemical corps used prisoners and dissidents for human experiments).[3] But Hirsch's report also contained a thin but valuable section on the Soviet BW programme since the 1930s, including some specific technical information. It identified the Soviets' 'golden triangle' of preferred agents – Plague, anthrax, and cholera. His overall analysis showed that the Soviet BW programme after the war was more advanced than either the US or UK programmes.

The CIA also received some confirmatory information about facility locations and sizes from Jewish refugees who had managed to emigrate to Israel. These refugees had been only menial workers (like cleaners or animal handlers) at some Soviet BW facilities, but every little bit helped.

Most years, CIA analysts drew up a major reassessment which described the status of Soviet weapons programmes and future projections of their capabilities. These top-secret National Intelligence Estimates (NIE), which were sent to President Eisenhower and other senior officials, contained a distillation from all sources of the US government's best information about the Soviet BW programme. Despite all of the CIA's efforts, the NIEs as of 1956 contained few reliable clues about actual Soviet bio-weapons capabilities.

For instance, the previously unpublished 1957 NIE begins: 'Relatively little is known about the nature and magnitude of the Soviet BW programme, particularly its offensive aspects.'[4]

A similar CIA report, written months earlier about the threat of Soviet weapons of mass destruction to the US, contained only one paragraph on 'Biological Warfare'. That secret document only noted briefly and blandly that, 'The USSR possesses all the necessary basic knowledge for the production of most BW agents and devices for their effective dissemination.' The most likely bacterial agents the Soviets were researching, the report said, included 'anthrax, Tularaemia, Plague, and Brucellosis' – the same ones the US was studying.[5]

CIA officials also wrote in 1956 that a widespread 'overt' Soviet attack of BW agents against the continental US was not likely in the next five years – since they believed that sufficient delivery systems did not exist and that the storage of large quantities of BW agents was 'infeasible'. The CIA's biggest worry remained that the US's cities and economy (particularly livestock) were vulnerable to possible undetectable Soviet sabotage operations using BW weapons.[6] But the CIA predicted that such clandestine Soviet BW attacks would be unlikely in an all-out nuclear war since the nuclear fallout would make the effects of bio-agents 'redundant'.[7]

The CIA's frustrating reliance on sporadic human sources finally ended on 4 July 1956, when a new era of espionage was launched from an airbase in Wiesbaden, Germany. That date marked the first flight of a high-altitude, U-2 spy plane over the USSR. The U-2, under secret planning for two years, was designed specifically to gather 'strategic intelligence' on the USSR – information about missiles and bombers, and nuclear, chemical, and biological weapons. A prime objective for that first mission was to detect possible Soviet BW plants.[8]

'We started watching everything related to BW and CW,' recalled Dino Brugioni, a founding member of the CIA's photo analysis team. 'To draw up the target sites to film, we used every possible means to gather information.'[9]

By 1957, according to Brugioni, the CIA had a 'good pinpoint' primarily on just two locations: the Soviet research centre at Zagorsk and the open-air testing site in the Aral Sea. The U-2 photos looked for increased movements of troops and equipment to Vozrozhdeniye Island – which indicated important activities were underway. But the CIA could not define the real purpose of these suspected experiments; for all they knew, the Soviets were testing defensive equipment against a wide array of chemicals, simulants or biological agents.

The CIA also searched their photos for specific types of building construction and layouts at other sites across the USSR, which would indicate they might be BW facilities. These so-called signatures included containment features, duct systems, and exhaust stacks.

To supplement the aerial photos, CIA analysts also read Soviet and international publications to obtain clues about which scientists were important, and where they were located. The CIA and Allied intelligence agencies also watched the travel patterns of top Soviet scientists and tried to eavesdrop on their telephone conversations.

In 1958, the Israeli foreign intelligence service, Mossad, supplied an important missing piece to the BW puzzle when a Jewish refugee confirmed that the Soviets had built a major BW production facility near Sverdlovsk, in south central Russia.[10] From then on the CIA made the Sverdlovsk site a priority, placing it on the regular target list for U-2 over-flights. (Coincidentally, when American U-2 pilot Francis Gary Powers was shot down by the indirect hit of a Soviet SA-2 missile on 1 May 1960, he was flying over Sverdlovsk. Part of his mission that day as he left Peshawar, Pakistan and flew on a south-to-north route over the USSR was to film the Soviet biological weapons plant at Sverdlovsk.)[11]

After the Powers debacle, technology saved the CIA. From 1960–72 photographic intelligence was obtained through the untouchable COR-ONA spy satellites, which allowed the US to take pictures every few days over a Soviet target.[12] However, as these satellites focused on suspected Soviet BW production, storage, research, and testing facilities, the Soviets, in turn, began to take better and better countermeasures to disguise their operations from overhead view.[13]

By 1964, the CIA knew – from closely studying Soviet medical and military literature – that Soviet scientists were researching numerous bio-agents, including botulinum toxin, Plague, anthrax, tick-borne encephalitis, Tularaemia, Brucellosis, and Q fever. But the agency just could not confirm that any of these specific agents were being developed for offensive BW usage. The problem was that all these agents were endemic to the USSR and were thus legitimate public health concerns. Furthermore, the US offensive BW programme was developing all of the same agents, so Soviet scientists, who were aware of the American work, had legitimate reasons to do similar research for defensive purposes.[14]

There were several other reasons why the CIA did not see the Soviet offensive programme. First, they still could not prove the Soviets were testing biological weapons.[15]

Secondly, the CIA remained unaware of any Soviet delivery systems for biological weapons.[16]

Thirdly, CIA analysts could find no reference in available classified and unclassified Soviet military documents that an offensive programme existed. All such military writings, the CIA reported, concerned itself 'exclusively with defence'.[17]

So the CIA concluded that the Soviet military command was 'highly unlikely' to use BW agents as a strategic or tactical weapon in a general or limited war because of the 'delayed and unpredictable effects' of such weapons and the 'greater predictability and destructiveness of nuclear weapons'.[18]

So unaware was the agency of the extent and reach of the Soviet BW programme that by 1969, when the CIA's next comprehensive NIE on Soviet BW capabilities was written, the findings remained the same as the 1964 report which had been based on vague and inconclusive evidence. The CIA was adamant that it was 'highly unlikely' that the Soviet military would use biological weapons in a wartime attack.[19]

'Bio-weapons were still considered to be years away,' recalls a former CIA officer. 'The army considered them "desperation" weapons. At CIA we had other more important things to do.'[20]

With its eye off the biological ball, the CIA left Moscow in peace to proceed with its fast-growing programme to wage plague war if necessary. In 1969, the Soviets increased their BW budget to a whopping 3 per cent of the military's total funds. The forward-thinking, offensive plan called for the use of new advances in bio-technology and genetic engineering.[21] One of the most dangerous developments in the cold-war arms race was taking place without the knowledge of Washington. Given the grim political and military philosophy of what became known as 'The Balance of Terror' – by which each side's strength cancelled out the other's – the worst thing that could happen would be for either superpower to be in the tempting position of being able to launch a pre-emptive and technologically superior strike on the other.

Washington's ignorance of this, and its overwhelming reliance and confidence on other weapons of mass destruction, were now to lead to an extraordinary political decision.

CHAPTER SEVEN

The Treaty

'We'll never use the damn germs . . . If someone uses germs on us, we'll nuke 'em.'

Richard Nixon, 1969

On 25 November 1969, President Richard Nixon astonished the rest of the world by announcing the abolition of biological weapons.

So, just as the Soviet Union was placing more and more faith in this weapon of mass destruction, the United States was giving it up.

The US, the President promised, was unilaterally renouncing the use, research, and development of all biological agents, weapons and other methods of biological warfare.[1]

In his speech, Nixon stressed that he was taking these steps for humanitarian reasons: 'Biological weapons have massive, unpredictable and potentially uncontrollable consequences. They may produce global epidemics and impair the health of future generations.'[2]

Nixon also addressed Pentagon concerns by indicating that defensive research on biological agents would continue into the areas of 'immunization and safety measures'.[3]

The British government had made a similar proposal one year earlier at Geneva.[4] But the proposal had stalled. Ironically, President Nixon came into office with no special knowledge of or interest in biological weapons. When the Soviet Ambassador to the US, Anatoly Dobrynin, made his first visit to the Nixon White House on 17 February 1969, their discussion did not touch upon any BW issues. The only arms control issue on their agenda was how to begin talks for a Strategic Arms Control Treaty (SALT).[5]

In January, after becoming Nixon's National Security Council adviser, Henry Kissinger ordered his new staff to produce twenty-two National Security Study Memoranda (NSSM) on key foreign policy issues, including the US–USSR strategic weapons posture. None of these initial NSSMs covered BW issues.[6]

The man who really deserved credit for initiating the US ban on biological weapons was Melvin Laird, Nixon's new Secretary of Defence. His crucial role in this process has never been properly appreciated.

Laird, a politically adept eight-term Republican Congressman from Wisconsin, had given up his increasing power and seniority on Capitol Hill to run the Pentagon for Nixon. He had promised to serve only one term as Secretary of Defense when Nixon chose him in early 1969 – after Nixon's first choice, Senator Henry Jackson (Democrat-Washington), abruptly changed his mind and withdrew.[7]

Upon taking office, Laird asked for a comprehensive review of the BW programme. He was hoping to kill it.

Laird had several reasons for wanting an end to the BW programme. He had served on the defence appropriations committee in Congress since 1953 and was considered an expert in the field of Pentagon budgets. He had been watching, with concern, as the funding for the combined chemical and biological weapons programmes had risen during the Kennedy and Johnson years.

'The Pentagon kept asking Congress for more money in the 1960s,' Laird recalls. 'They told us they needed the increase because of the Soviet Union's increased CBW capabilities.'[8]

Laird also was persuaded that a ban on BW made good sense for political reasons. He felt that the Vietnam anti-war protestors, who were plaguing Nixon, could be deflected if the US ended the use of herbicides and tear gas in Southeast Asia (he had ordered a halt) and if the US moved on BW arms control.[9]

'I saw a red flag,' Laird explains. 'I felt the time had come to take action.'[10]

Surprisingly, in his secret discussions with the Joint Chiefs of Staff, Laird found that they were sympathetic and supportive of his plan from the start.[11] Laird met twice a week with the Joint Chiefs inside the secure conference room called 'the tank'. None of the service chiefs opposed a ban on biological weapons; they fully agreed that these weapons were not militarily effective compared to the US nuclear arsenal. The Joint

Chiefs made several points for why a ban made sense: one, they acknowledged that much of their BW equipment and munitions was ageing or obsolete; two, they understood that a ban on these weapons was a good PR move for the Defense Department; three, they realized a worldwide ban would also benefit US national security, since they were concerned about defending against the Soviet BW programme. The Joint Chiefs also feared that underdeveloped third-world nations, with limited technology, might resort to BW as a 'poor man's atomic bomb' and that eventually these relatively inexpensive weapons would quickly proliferate out of control. The Pentagon would need to set an example, a moral lead (which also made military sense), if the US hoped other countries would follow.[12] It seemed a useful demonstration of *Realpolitik* at work.

The Joint Chiefs insisted on only two pledges from Laird. First, until the Soviet threat was eliminated, the US would have to continue its defensive BW programmes.[13] Second, and most importantly, the Joint Chiefs demanded to keep their chemical weapons capabilities (primarily because they were convinced that the modest US CW stockpile deterred the Soviets from invading Europe in a conventional war).[14]

James Leonard, the Assistant Director of the US Arms Control and Disarmament Agency (ACDA) in 1969, explains: 'I can't stress this enough. The US military did not think there was any military use for biological weapons. This was their main reason for allowing the BW ban to go ahead.'[15]

In late March, Laird invited Henry Kissinger to the Pentagon to discuss these issues at their monthly breakfast meeting. In preparation, Laird sent Kissinger a memo about his plan for BW disarmament. Kissinger's initial reaction was not enthusiastic.[16]

'Kissinger thought there were more important arms control matters on the table,' Laird recalls. 'I told him I thought it was a good thing for the Nixon Administration to do from a political standpoint. After that breakfast, I felt that I had convinced him to go ahead. Once Kissinger came on board, we started moving.'

Kissinger, and Nixon, came to see how Laird's arguments would help them – that a unilateral renunciation of biological weapons, which the Joint Chiefs didn't want anyway, would set the table for nuclear arms control initiatives with the USSR.[17]

Following the meeting with Laird, Kissinger instructed his NSC team to begin a policy review. The initial study concluded it was feasible to eliminate the offensive capability and emphasize defensive capabilities.[18]

In April, Laird made his first direct request to Nixon to take action. He argued that the US should take the leadership on this issue. Laird stressed that the President would be seen as a peacemaker and a great statesman. Nixon, who later wrote that he considered Laird a 'shrewd politician', was receptive.[19] No final decision would be taken until after Kissinger's NSC team completed their study.

That August, the White House directed the army immediately to cease production of all BW agents, in preparation for a major announcement by the President.[20] Three months later, it was a done thing. As part of his announcement, Nixon said all existing BW stockpiles would be destroyed.

Nixon's statement marked the end of the twenty-six-year-old US offensive BW programme. In the final accounting, the Pentagon had spent a total of $726 million since 1943 for everything: facilities, personnel, materials, testing, and storage.[21]

Nixon's November statement was well received around the world. There was only one quibble from other nations, that the administration had inadvertently omitted the word 'toxins' in the ban on biological weapons. 'Toxins' are non-contagious poisons that act like chemicals, but are derived from living substances – like bacteria, fungi, algae, plants, insects, and animals. The most common toxins in the BW field, including mycotoxins, snake venoms, shellfish toxin, ricin, and botulinum, were not covered by the ban. On 14 February 1970, Nixon put it right by extending the ban to fully cover the production and use of toxins.[22]

The total destruction of the US anti-personnel stockpile – incinerating the BW agents at high temperatures and burying the harmless, leftover waste – took a year to accomplish and was completed in May 1972. This disposal plan, which was projected to cost an estimated $12 million, included the full decontamination of the production facilities at the Pine Bluff Arsenal.[23]

Once the US ban was in place, the next step of achieving a worldwide treaty could proceed. This process had actually been percolating since the original British proposals in 1968. A revised UK submission in

Geneva from July 1969 had become the template for the final wording of a treaty, which now had US support.

The next problem, and the toughest, would be how to entice the Soviets to join. Privately, the US felt that it might take another two years or more of hard bargaining. They knew that if the US and Soviet Union – the two superpowers – reached a consensus, then the rest of the world would fall in line.

Soviet representatives had indicated to the US that their position was rock hard and would never change. The US assumed the main reason why the Soviets wanted to keep their biological weapons was that the Soviet military refused to give them up. Period.[24]

Furthermore, whatever might happen in the future, the Allies clearly understood that the Soviets would never, under any circumstances, allow enforceable verification measures – like on-site inspections – to be included in any BW treaty. It was 1970, and that prospect was as real as the tooth fairy.[25]

Indeed, it was in anticipation of future Soviet objections that all of the original language about verification in the 1968 British proposal had been watered down or flushed away. The British draft had proposed merely that a UN-backed team of experts would 'investigate' all accusations of non-compliance. US officials decided it was better to have a treaty with no verification, than no treaty at all. The civil servants even managed to persuade the hard men at the Pentagon to follow this course against all their instincts.[26]

The task of negotiating a worldwide BW treaty for the US, and of overcoming the Soviet objections, had been assigned in mid-1969 to a veteran foreign service officer, Ambassador James Leonard, who was then serving as Assistant Director of ACDA. In February 1970, Ambassador Leonard, a tall, thin, Princeton man, returned to the disarmament talks in Geneva with new instructions approved by the White House. He was told to 'sell' the BW issue hard. To help accomplish this, Washington launched an effort to educate the rest of the world's delegations on the horrors of biological warfare. The idea was to convince the doubters that a BW treaty was worth a try.[27] The wheeling and dealing was further complicated by a strong move within the Soviet-led Warsaw Pact camp to tie chemical weapons into a BW treaty. The Americans (and British) were opposed to this Soviet strategy.

For purely cynical reasons, the Soviets strongly objected to a 1968

British plan to decouple BW from CW. Although publicly the Soviets argued that CW and BW treaties should remain linked, and that a separate BW treaty would only intensify the chemical weapons arms race, privately the Soviets wanted to keep both their biological and chemical weapons. They simply did not want to make it easier for the West to achieve any treaty at all.[28]

In the weeks that followed, the NATO allies and some non-aligned nations gradually moved to join the US and UK. But the Soviet position remained inflexible: that it was absolutely essential to link chemical and biological weapons in one treaty.

As the negotiations dragged on, frustrated senior officials on the US and UK side were ready to give up, partly because the Soviets were winning the international public relations battle. The West was finding it difficult to sustain good reasons for not tying chemical and biological weapons together in one treaty. Senior British Foreign Ministry officials were particularly pessimistic and could find little reason for allowing the Soviets a propaganda win when it was the West that was doing all the work. It looked as if London and Washington might split on this issue.[29]

Suddenly, in August 1970, just when it seemed that the whole arms breakthrough would come to an end and the Cold Warriors would win, when morale in London and Washington was at its lowest, the Soviets unexpectedly flipped their position overnight from no-no to yes-yes. That was the kind of thing that just didn't happen in high-level East/West disarmament talks.

An aide from the Soviet delegation to the Conference on Disarmament in Geneva phoned the US mission and requested an immediate meeting between the two ambassadors.[30] The Americans had no idea what was coming. The chief of the Soviet delegation, Ambassador Aleksei Roshchin, a short, stocky man in his sixties and a protégé of Foreign Minister Andrei Gromyko, motioned to an aide to hand Ambassador Leonard a piece of paper.

There was a minimum of ceremony. 'This is a Soviet draft treaty,' Roshchin explained in a deep baritone voice. 'You will see that it closely resembles your draft treaty. We hope you will be pleased.'[31]

As Leonard and his colleagues slowly read the paper they were unable to contain their undiplomatic smiles. 'Thank you very much,'

Leonard replied. 'We will report to Washington and get back to you after we study your document.'[32]

The reaction in Washington was equally positive. The US called a meeting in Geneva to inform its Western allies that the Soviets had dropped the CW-BW linkage and had agreed in principle to the US/UK language. 'Everyone studied the document for booby traps, and we didn't find any,' Leonard recalls.[33]

Within a week, the US/UK/USSR proposal was on track toward approval.

Why did the Soviets change their position? Leonard's best guess: 'They wanted to do business with the Nixon Administration, this was high politics at a major level and a minor move in a bigger game plan on arms control, involving mainly nuclear issues.'[34]

The Biological and Toxin Weapons Convention (BWC) was considered a model treaty – the first international agreement since World War II that banned the possession and use of an entire class of weapons of mass destruction.[35] It spelled hope for the future.

Article One of the treaty's fifteen stipulations declared a ban on the development, production, storage, and acquisition of all biological agents and toxins in amounts that were not justified for 'peaceful purposes'. All weapons and equipment for delivery of such agents and toxins were also banned. Article Two required that all stockpiles of such materials had to be destroyed within nine months after the treaty took effect.[36]

But the Convention contained the seeds of its own destruction.

To please the Soviets, the provisions for verification were too feeble to work. Article Four stated that each nation must police its own country to ensure compliance. This was like inviting an alcoholic to run a pub on trust. Everyone was placed on their honour. Article Six stated that any nation could complain to the United Nations about another country. Any accused nation was supposed to allow the UN to investigate the allegations but, as there were no formal procedures, reporting requirements or sanctions, it was a meaningless threat. There were no penalties for those who chose to cheat.

Those who framed these inadequate procedures argued that the unique characteristics of biological agents made verification impossible.

Further, Article Ten allowed for the 'peaceful' research of viruses and bacteria – to prevent against a natural outbreak of disease or an unlawful military or terrorist attack. But in order to develop viable protective measures – like vaccines, medicines, and clothing – a country needed to work with real agents. The BWC placed no limits on the quantity of the BW agents that could be produced for this research; no standards were set down either to distinguish between defensive and offensive research – they were so similar that the negotiators could not even agree upon definable criteria.[37]

At the end of the day, those involved in drafting the BWC and approving it decided that the drawing in of the once intractable Soviets was too much of an opportunity to let slip; this was no moment to study the fine print of History.

Ambassador Leonard says it was impossible in the Cold War era of the 1970s even to consider the intrusive inspections or tough enforcement measures that were later considered in the 1990s. 'Nothing the UN has done in Iraq in the 1990s, for instance, was even remotely imaginable with the USSR in the 1970s.'[38]

By August 1971, nearly all of the other nations fell in line. The US, UK, and USSR were then able to report the treaty to the UN General Assembly for consideration and approval.[39] In December, the General Assembly approved the treaty by an overwhelming vote, 110–0.[40] Finally, after more than two years of effort, on 10 April 1972, Secretary of State William Rogers and Ambassador Leonard signed the treaty for the US on behalf of President Nixon, joining seventy-seven other nations.[41]

It took another three years for the national legislatures of each country to ratify the treaty. On 22 January 1975, President Gerald Ford signed the ratified treaty for the US.[42] As he did so, he also finally ratified the fifty-year-old Geneva Protocols for the US. The BWC took effect worldwide two months later, on 26 March.

With fingers crossed, US and British officials prayed that the Soviet government would immediately begin to honour the treaty. They really believed that they had managed to persuade the USSR that plague wars were not a serious military option for either side.[43]

Nixon received the credit he sought (before his early departure from Washington in the Watergate scandal) as a closet peacemaker (as Laird had promised he would), and the Pentagon had no reason to complain.

The truth is Nixon had never cared about the morality or consequences of biological warfare one way or the other.[44] When his speech-writer, William Safire, questioned him in private about the wisdom of eliminating the entire BW stockpile without retaining a few bio-weapons in case future retaliation was required, Nixon replied: 'We'll never use the damn germs, so what good is biological warfare as a deterrent? If somebody uses germs on us, we'll nuke 'em.'[45]

CHAPTER EIGHT

Cheating

'Mel, the Soviets are not doing a damn thing to stop. They are saying one thing, but they're doing another.'

Richard Helms, 1972

The cheating began before the ink was dry.

Shortly after the BWC was signed in 1972, Secretary of Defense Melvin Laird began receiving alarming reports from the Pentagon's Defense Intelligence Agency (DIA) and the CIA that the Soviets were not sticking to their solemn treaty commitments.

The evidence came from US satellite intelligence, the so-called spies in the sky, that were taking pictures from space of Soviet BW facilities. They were the only means of verification. Richard Helms, then the hard-line CIA Director, warned Laird: 'Mel, the Soviets are not doing a damn thing to stop. They are saying one thing, but they're doing another.'[1]

Laird slowly realized that the Soviet leaders had all along wanted the US to disarm unilaterally, so they could continue their BW programme without competition. Hence the sudden change of heart at Geneva. It was as simple as that.

Why didn't the US complain to the Soviets and trumpet their knowledge to the outside world?

'I raised hell,' Laird recalls. 'I told our diplomatic team to put on a full court press. "They're violating the treaty!" I said. But officials at ACDA turned their cheek. They wanted to go on to other things – like SALT-1 and SALT-2 – which they felt were more important. They didn't want to accuse the USSR of treaty violations because they feared they would lose their other programmes by making such accusations.'[2]

This single dilemma – applying the stick on BW treaty violations or offering the carrot on major nuclear disarmament – was to become a recurring theme of East/West political negotiations from that day to this. The 'maximalists' wanted action now; if the Soviets couldn't be trusted to sign solemn arms control undertakings, then there was little point in negotiating for them in the first place. The 'minimalists' argued that restraint was all for the greater good; that even the USSR was not a monolithic entity that spoke with one voice, that it had its own hawks and doves. The minimalists argued for the softly-softly approach.

Intelligence analysts (usually maximalists) would acquire evidence that showed the Soviets appeared to be cheating on the BWC, and minimalist officials at ACDA, the State Department, and the White House, along with members of Congress, would choose to ignore the evidence or argue it was not proof positive, or simply that it came at the wrong time.

Until the BWC was formally ratified in 1975, the Nixon and then Ford Administrations had no incentive to accuse the Soviets of violations – since paradoxically the allegations would tarnish the treaty and focus attention on the lack of verification.

But the cameras in the US satellites kept turning out photos that continued to show suspicious activities at the Soviet military's BW facilities. In August 1975, four months after the BWC became law, frustrated CIA officials, tired of the minimalist approach, leaked some material to the press for the first time. The CIA charged that questionable activities appeared to be continuing at the old sites – Kirov, Zagorsk, and Sverdlovsk – and expanding to several new ones – Omutninsk, Berdsk, and Pokrov. The overhead photos ominously showed new-building construction at several suspected sites, including incinerator stacks and large cold-storage bunkers used to stockpile BW agents.[3]

But the press leaks provoked no official US response against the USSR. The sceptics argued the CIA had no hard proof. Anyway, it was always possible the cameras were filming legal and legitimate activities – such as permitted defensive measures or the making of herbicides. The silent satellite photos had no way of telling or determining intent. Only a good human source could ever do that.

*

The first break came in 1975.

At last a Soviet defector emerged who knew something about the USSR's real BW intentions. He was Arkady Shevchenko, a senior Soviet official at the United Nations in New York, who became the highest-ranking Soviet diplomat ever to spy for the West. While serving in New York as the UN's Under-Secretary General, he was recruited by the FBI. As an agent-in-place he was to share a wide range of valuable, Soviet foreign policy secrets with them (and the CIA). Then, in April 1978, fearing he was under suspicion by his government, he suddenly defected for good into American hands.

First, Shevchenko confirmed to his US debriefers that the Soviet government was deliberately violating the BWC. He said that the Soviet military decided to pursue a biological weapons programme, in spite of the treaty, because the treaty was unverifiable. Hence the USSR could get away with violations.[4] Shevchenko further confirmed that the Soviet Ministry of Defence had adamantly rejected any kind of international inspections or 'oversight' during the treaty negotiations because it would 'reveal the extent of the development of these weapons and would show Soviet readiness for their eventual use'.[5]

It got even worse. Shevchenko said that his boss and mentor, Foreign Minister Andrei Gromyko, had agreed to the BWC for 'propaganda purposes'.

'The Soviet Union,' Shevchenko later wrote, 'had consistently depicted itself as a leader in the effort to destroy these ghastly weapons. In fact, the USSR has always continued to increase and expand its sophisticated chemical and biological weapons production programmes.'[6]

Both the Politburo and the Soviet military had approved this strategy of deception, Shevchenko revealed. Defence Minister Andrei Grechko, a long-time friend and ally of Premier Leonid Brezhnev, had advised Gromyko to sign the treaty, because the military wanted to retain the programme. Without effective international inspections and controls, Grechko argued, no one in the West would know what they were doing. The military not only insisted on keeping their existing weapons, but under the shield of the BWC they were actually initiating a top-secret programme to develop more of them.[7]

If Shevchenko was speaking the truth (and there was no reason to disbelieve him), this was the worst possible news, for minimalists and maximalists.[8] It meant the Soviet Union was utterly cynical and ruthless and prepared to deceive its treaty partners in a way that could destroy all trust and make a mockery of future, unverifiable arms control treaties.

However, even an official as senior as Shevchenko could not tell the CIA the full extent of the new Soviet BW programme – because it was kept so secret and compartmentalized by the military.

What is now clear is that with the approval of Premier Brezhnev, the Politburo, the Communist Party Central Committee, and USSR's Council of Ministers, the Soviet military embarked on a massive new project in 1972 to hide their BW research from the West under the cover of a bona fide civilian research organization.

The first military director of this new programme was General Vesvolod Ivanovich Ogarkov, who had previously headed the military's BW production facility in Sverdlovsk. The Soviets had deliberately changed the name of his new programme several times in the first year, but everyone informally called it the Ogarkov System or (as in a John Grisham novel) just 'The System'.[9] Funded and controlled by the Ministry of Defence, The System eventually expanded into eighteen scientific/research institutes, more than 30,000 scientists and workers, and five production and storage plants.

It is impossible to maintain a large conspiracy within a democracy, a little easier within a political dictatorship. One must nevertheless pay tribute to The System that it stayed as secret as it did, for as long as it did. This is partly because The System was marked by the strictest need-to-know compartmentalization and patrolled by Soviet intelligence officers. Even The System's own scientists were kept isolated from their colleagues – it was need to know, or ignorance. And the sole purpose of this secret empire was to develop and produce a formidable and efficient offensive biological warfare programme, capable of inflicting the most horrendous damage to the people the USSR considered its enemies. Within that programme, work continued in order to produce new and more deadly biological agents, weapons, and delivery systems, and it was all done in deliberate circumvention of the BWC.

Nixon may have signed the document with utmost cynicism – but the West did stick to its obligations and commitments.

Shevchenko shone the first light into the darker corners of the Ogarkov System and Soviet betrayal, but it was to take many more years to reveal the full truth.

CHAPTER NINE

Incident at Sverdlovsk

'. . . the official Soviet version is riddled with inconsistencies, half-truths and plain falsehoods.'

Peter Gumbel, *Wall Street Journal* reporter, 1991

Shortly after sunrise on Monday, 2 April 1979, the worst accident in the history of biological weapons production occurred at a top-secret Soviet military facility in the southern-most district of Sverdlovsk (now reverted to its old White Russian name of Ekaterinburg).

Sverdlovsk, then a city of 1.2 million people, was the industrial centre of the Ural mountains region, 900 miles east of Moscow. Scores died, hundreds were injured, and the Soviets were forced into the greatest cover-up of any biological warfare tragedy. Coincidentally, Ekaterinburg was no stranger to lies, cover-ups, and deceptions. On 16 July 1918, the Bolsheviks murdered the last Russian imperial family in the woods outside the town and kept the details secret for half a century.

Military Compound 19, officially known as the Microbiology and Virology Institute, had been built in 1947 as the Soviet Union's main centre for producing special bacteria and toxins suitable for bio-weapons. In the USSR a compound like No. 19 was actually a small self-contained military garrison, typically housing about 2,000 troops and their families. Originally, this compound was built outside the city, but during the next thirty years, as Sverdlovsk's urban development spread, the military base became engulfed in a residential and industrial neighbourhood. In 1979, despite the danger to the many nearby civilians, military technicians wearing gas masks and rubber protective suits still worked inside the compound. Their main product – large quantities of dried, powdered anthrax spores – was the perfect biological weapon.[1]

The facility included an outer residential zone (with shops, schools, and apartment houses for 5,000 people) and a heavily guarded inner zone, surrounded by ten-foot high, double barbed-wire fences. This inner area included the top-secret production buildings and research labs. The CIA, which had been closely watching this site for many years with spyplanes and later satellites, knew it was a BW facility because the photographs revealed special vents, smokestacks, animal pens, refrigeration units, concrete storage bunkers, special rail lines, and extremely tight military security in the inner area.[2]

On the south side of Compound 19 was an adjacent army base known as Compound 32. Further south was a residential neighbourhood – the Chkalovskiy district – which was mostly comprised of small private houses and a few apartment buildings, factories, shops, and schools.

On the morning of 2 April, sometime between 6 a.m. and 8 a.m., a workman inside Compound 19 launched the programme to commence the anthrax production cycle. However, after work had stopped on the prior Friday, there had been a routine maintenance check-up at the production facility. During the inspection two workers removed a key filter to the exhaust system attached to the drying and milling equipment. These round filters, about 24 inches in diameter, were made of a special synthetic fibre surrounded by a metal rim. They were regularly changed about once a week, but on this occasion the crew carelessly forgot to replace the filter with a new one.[3] So when the plant went back into production on Monday, the next team of workers had no idea that the exhaust was unfiltered.

Because of this error, several pounds of deadly powder was inadvertently released through an air duct.[4] A narrow plume of microscopic anthrax spores belched into the sky and was blown unseen by the wind in a southerly direction from Compound 19, settling mostly over Compound 32, the nearby residential area, and a ceramic pipe plant less than a mile away.

As the plume widened and dispersed, a less concentrated cloud of anthrax spores drifted down invisibly to a half-dozen small villages further south.

Such is the silent nature of biological warfare that accidents like this are a harbinger of the real thing. No one even knew the accident had occurred, so no warning could be sounded. Nobody in the surrounding population had ever inhaled anthrax spores, let alone weapons-grade anthrax spores, so there was no knowledge of what would happen, how it would happen, or when.

There are three variations of anthrax infection – cutaneous (from contact with the skin or through open sores), gastrointestinal (from eating tainted meat), and pulmonary (from inhalation). The skin and gastric forms rarely cause death in humans. Breathing anthrax spores is almost invariably fatal, but this form of contact is extremely rare in nature. Pulmonary anthrax is essentially a man-made and very efficient biological weapon.

The first clear symptoms of anthrax inhalation take one or two days to emerge. The first signs are a headache, coughing, mild fever, chills, and grogginess. As the dormant spores of bacteria become activated inside the body, they quickly multiply, secreting deadly toxins that eventually overwhelm the immune system. It is a most unpleasant way to die.

What happened at Sverdlovsk was a perfect example of how ruthless and indiscriminate a real BW attack would be. Most of the first casualties were located within a few hundred yards downwind of the anthrax plant. They included people who just happened to be near open windows, standing outside, or walking in the streets. The worst affected were military personnel from the production site, troops stationed at the adjacent Compound 32, various men on their way to work, and about twenty people already working at the nearby ceramics factory. That rundown building, which faced Compound 19, had some large holes in the walls and broken windows which allowed the deadly cloud of spores to seep in.[5]

At first, the weakened victims believed they only had a cold or the flu. But, by the end of the first evening, the local emergency rooms at Hospitals No. 20 and No. 24 were flooded with calls. Two days after the accident, dozens of victims started appearing at the hospitals with more severe symptoms, including breathing difficulties, high fevers, vomiting, and, ominously, lips turning blue. The doctors, who had received no warnings from military officials, did not know what was causing the illness. At first, they diagnosed what seemed to be pneumonia but, as more and more patients appeared, panic developed among the shocked medical staff who now feared they were facing an unknown infectious disease. As dozens more victims arrived in various states of distress, doctors too began to panic and simply gave the patients every medication available – including penicillin, antibiotics, and steroids. By the fourth night, before further tests could be completed, many patients began to die with fluid-filled lungs, blood in their throats, and odd dark blotches and lesions on the bodies. The medical teams were now helpless to stop the mortality rate climbing; there were 42 corpses at Hospital 20 alone. Some people didn't get to hospitals in the first place and either died at home or were found unconscious in the streets.[6]

The civilian doctors, who had never seen inhalation anthrax symptoms and were unaware there was a secret military production site in town, simply had no idea what they were facing for several more days. It was only after the first autopsies had been completed that one experienced female pathologist was puzzled to see infection in the lymph nodes and lungs, and, significantly, haemorrhaging in the small blood vessels of the brain membrane – producing a so-called 'cardinal's cap'. It was she who realized that these bloodied brains were probably caused by anthrax.[7] But if that was the case, where on earth had the anthrax come from?[8]

After a confused and frightening week, the doctors from all hospitals were ordered to move all remaining patients and new ones to the 500-bed infectious disease wing at Hospital 40, for special screening, intensive care, and autopsies. By then, a quarantine had been imposed around the infected area. Vaccines were administered to tens of thousands of people. Suddenly, Moscow was in the loop and senior health and military officials started turning up. Rather prudently they flew over the site by helicopter, refusing to enter the danger zone.[9]

In the absence of any authoritative or credible public announcement from government officials or the state-controlled media, wild and alarming rumours about the cause of the tragedy began to take hold. Most people heard that cattle in a nearby village had been contaminated with anthrax. A local newspaper, *Vercherny Sverdlovsk*, carried a warning about 'Siberian ulcer', a Russian term for anthrax infection. Terrified families started getting rid of their meat.[10]

Some people suspected the answer had to lie inside the secret military facility.[11] The work at Compound 19 was so classified, however, that even the local KGB chief did not know what was going on there. Using his initiative during the burgeoning crisis, he ordered his men to tap the phones of the secret laboratory and soon learned the truth – about the technicians, the missing safety filter, and the inadvertent release of anthrax through a vent.[12]

But this information was immediately zipped tight by KGB head-quarters in Moscow as the huge cover-up now began. Local residents, Russians, and the rest of the world were to be kept in the dark, for this was something that could never be admitted – for obvious security, political, and diplomatic reasons. So the KGB seized all hospital records, autopsy reports, and epidemiological surveys with the give-away 022 code, which denoted anthrax in Soviet medical documents. They simply falsified other reports to delete all references to inhaled anthrax.

The cover-up now needed an alternative theory, an explanation for the deaths. First, it was necessary to deflect attention from the military base, so health officials distributed 50,000 leaflets warning local residents not to eat contaminated meat or touch stray animals.[13] The big lie was taking shape.

It took several months to complete the extensive and dangerous decontamination of the area. Soldiers wearing distinctive grey-green protective suits and gas masks took soil samples and sprayed the streets, sidewalks, and trees with disinfectant. Bulldozers ripped off the topsoil in contaminated areas and several contaminated dirt roads were surfaced with asphalt. Firemen scrubbed the roofs, walls, and sidings of all homes and buildings with caustic solutions.

To justify the big lie of the cover story, and as a prudent precaution to prevent further spread of anthrax, wild animals and stray dogs were hunted down and shot; uninspected meat was confiscated and burned.[14] It was all very convincing.

This perilous decontamination process led to even more deaths as people inadvertently inhaled invisible dust which still retained the tough, virulent anthrax spores. The deaths continued for up to six weeks after the initial accident.[15]

The final death toll remains unknown, the truth buried under the dirt of the lies. Estimates range from 64 to over 600 people.[16] The final official Soviet tally of civilian victims – issued years later – showed that 96 people were stricken, of whom 64 had died. But doctors in Sverdlovsk say these numbers were much too low.[17] Up to 200–300 military personnel also were rumoured to have died, but this suspicion was virtually unverifiable as the military closed ranks, took over their own hospital and confiscated all records. These were scarcely the actions of those who had nothing to fear or hide.[18]

Many of the anthrax victims were buried in Section 15 of the city's Eastern (Vostochny) Cemetery, which was promptly declared a no-go area. The grave sites were covered in chlorinated lime and then cordoned off, so that no one would ever dig near them again. Near the civilian tombstones were dozens of other graves, each marked only with a metal spike topped by a red star. These other burial sites were rumoured to contain the remains of some of the military personnel killed in the accident.[19]

By the summer of 1979, the massive cover-up operation had succeeded. The truth was known to only a handful of local military officials, the KGB, and senior officials in Moscow. The Kremlin and Ministry of Defence determined both the outbreak and the subsequent medical decontamination process were to be treated as state secrets. For the next twelve years, the Soviet government attempted to maintain the big lie and deceive its own people and the rest of the world.

Soviet officials could hardly admit they had deliberately been violating the BWC, especially as they continued to violate it. The price of supporting the big lie meant deceiving the United Nations and the Carter, Reagan, and Bush Administrations. Astonishingly, the Soviets very nearly got away with it, proving again that a well-ordered conspiracy engineered inside an undemocratic state remains eternally feasible and stands a very high chance of success.

The story of how this conspiracy was eventually exposed is one of the defining scientific, political, and propaganda struggles of the Cold War.

Western intelligence first heard rumours about Sverdlovsk shortly after the accident occurred.[20] Britain's MI6 received uncorroborated, low-level reports from ethnic Germans travelling from the USSR to East Germany about deaths possibly caused by a release from a biological weapons plant. British defence intelligence analysts produced a written assessment that this information was plausible. But some policy makers in the Foreign Office were preoccupied with demonstrating that the BWC was effective, and strongly opposed giving the accusation any credibility.

Without proof these civil servants and diplomats were unwilling to believe the Soviets were cheating on the treaty. It was this group that managed to persuade Britain's Joint Intelligence Committee (which directly advises the Prime Minister) to take a soft line in their ultimate assessment. The more suspicious defence analysts were seen as nagging Cold War alarmists, and their views failed, at first, to hold sway.

Once again, the maximalist/minimalist tensions emerged. These were not simple hawk/dove divisions, but they were differences in approach. Maximalists were for the stick, then the carrot; minimalists were for the carrot first, and maybe no stick. Both groups sought to avoid dangerous confrontation, but some thought it was more expedient to be tough and nasty to achieve policy ends, while others wanted to try the nice approach.

Eventually, six months after the accident, the Western press and public heard the first murmurs. The first published article about a mysterious bacteriological accident in the USSR appeared in early October 1979 in *Possev*, a small Russian-language paper based in Frankfurt, Germany, which regularly reported rumours and gossip from the Soviet émigré community about events in the USSR. *Possev* ('sowing' in Russian) was the partial newspaper of the anti-Soviet Peoples–Workers Alliance. Details were very sketchy in this first, unsigned report – the date was wrong, the city was wrong, anthrax was not mentioned, and the death toll was estimated at several thousand people. Because the source was such an obscure and partisan newspaper the story was ignored.[21]

Three weeks later, on 26 October, the first English-language press account appeared in the now-defunct London news magazine *NOW*. The article, headlined 'Russia's Secret Germ Warfare Disaster', was based on the *Possev* story and the account of a 'traveller' who had visited the USSR in April. The article claimed that the Soviet government was trying to 'hush up' an accident at a germ warfare factory in Siberia that had left 'hundreds' of people dead, thousands 'seriously injured', and the city closed where it occurred. The 'traveller' said the corpses were 'covered in brown patches' and were buried in sealed coffins to prevent the spread of death. However, the *NOW* report, like *Possev*, got the date wrong by two months (it said 'June') and the city wrong by 1,000 miles (it cited the 'southern outskirts of Novosibirsk').[22] But the first threads in the unravelling process had been tugged.

In January 1980, *Possev* reported more precise details, now citing a source using a pseudonym 'NN' (Russian for 'XX'). This second article said the accident, now called an 'explosion', had occurred at a military base near Sverdlovsk on 4 April. The explosion had released a cloud of anthrax over a nearby village. An estimated 1,000 people had died; no cases of animal disease were reported; the military had taken charge to calm the population; civilians had been vaccinated; and top soil had been covered over in nearby areas.[23] This was getting warm.

The second *Possev* report sparked additional articles in mid-February in larger European publications, including the respectable *Bild Zeitung*, a widely circulated Hamburg tabloid magazine, and the authoritative *Daily Telegraph* of London.[24] *Bild Zeitung* repeated the basic *Possev* story – that a cloud of 'deadly bacteria' had been released near Sverdlovsk, at a secret military installation. *Bild* said that 'more than 1,000 people died in great pain' after a strong wind carried the cloud away from the heart of the city. It described choking deaths, cremated corpses, and decontamination efforts involving bulldozed topsoil and dirt roads covered with asphalt. *Bild* reported that a 'Soviet government' cover-up had lasted ten months.

The detail included in the *Bild* article finally caught the attention of the mass of the Western press and eventually provoked the first response from the Soviet government. On 19 February, the state-controlled Tass news service called the Western news reports about an anthrax epidemic 'malicious inventions'.[25]

The US government stayed silent, biding its time, waiting for something hard from the CIA. The agency routinely retained all satellite photo evidence on file, but analysts had not appreciated the true value of the April 1979 Sverdlovsk 'take'. It was not until the first press reports the following year that the analysts realized what might be on the films.[26]

It turned out that the CIA's store of information was very good.[27] Remarkably, they had photos of Compound 19, both before and after the event for comparison. They immediately spotted signs of the decontamination vehicles and checkpoints on roads around the vicinity – indicating a quarantine. Why, the analysts asked, would a tainted meat incident have caused the Soviets to close off their important military facility?[28]

The US intelligence analysis included an estimate of the wind conditions by the CIA's Office of Scientific Intelligence to determine which way the plume would have drifted. Best of all, the ultra-secret

National Security Agency (NSA), America's electronic eavesdropper, delivered valuable communications intelligence from the USSR – having recorded the Soviet military reaction to the accident. The CIA learned, for the first time, that Soviet Defence Minister Dmitri Ustinov had gone to Sverdlovsk after the accident. This unscheduled trip raised suspicion – why would the defence chief go to the facility if the incident was just an outbreak of tainted meat?[29] Two days after Ustinov's trip, the Soviet health minister and chief epidemiologist from Moscow also arrived *deus ex machina* unannounced, with a team of assistants – raising additional suspicion.

By February, the CIA began receiving good, corroborative evidence from reliable human sources in the Soviet émigré community, who were secretly speaking and writing to contacts in the USSR.[30] One important informant was Mark Popovsky, a Russian scientific writer who emigrated to the US in 1977 but maintained contacts in Moscow. He obtained information about Sverdlovsk via letters smuggled out through underground channels.[31] Soviet Jews who emigrated to Israel also provided valuable information which confirmed an anthrax accident had occurred at Compound 19.[32] Most importantly, an unnamed credible source added new details obtained from a doctor in Sverdlovsk who treated patients.[33] The victims, the CIA was told, had high fevers and trouble breathing and, according to second-hand accounts of autopsy results, the victims' lungs were filled with fluid – which tended to support the inhalation anthrax theory. The CIA also learned that possibly 200–300 civilians had died, despite heroic efforts by Soviet doctors to save them. Other guesses ranged up to 1,000 total civilian and military deaths.[34]

By early March, Washington, despite the usual maximalist/minimalist disputes, was ready to act. President Carter himself agreed that there was enough intelligence on hand to ask the Soviets for an official explanation.[35]

On 17 March 1980, the Carter Administration delivered a diplomatic inquiry to the Soviet Union demanding an explanation of the 'outbreak of disease' in Sverdlovsk. In Moscow, US Ambassador Thomas Watson specifically asked a senior Foreign Ministry official if the deaths were caused by an accident during a biological warfare test.[36]

Washington was in a bullish mood with Moscow. The Soviets had invaded Afghanistan four months earlier.[37] It was no time for diplomatic niceties. So the next day, without waiting for the Soviet response, a State

Department spokesman in Washington publicly confirmed for the first time that the US had received 'disturbing indications' that a 'lethal biological agent' may have been released in Sverdlovsk. The resulting epidemic, the spokesman said, 'raised questions' about whether a violation of the BWC had occurred.[38]

The first responses from the Soviet Foreign Ministry denounced the US accusation as 'blatant slander', a 'fabrication of American propaganda', and an 'epidemic of anti-Soviet hysteria'. The Soviet Union, a spokesman solemnly pledged, had always 'strictly observed' all provisions of the BWC. Another official said the USSR 'firmly rejected any attempt to cast doubt' upon its 'conscientious' adherence to its obligations.[39]

The Soviets next feigned anger with the American tactics and sought to turn the tables in the fast developing propaganda war.[40] They accused the US of violating the BWC by going public with accusations before giving them a fair chance to respond. The 1975 treaty allowed the parties to 'consult' one another and 'cooperate' when an accusation of non-compliance was made. The Soviets refused to cooperate now because they claimed the US had violated the spirit of the agreement by making the accusations public.[41]

On 20 March, the Soviet Foreign Ministry now retaliated with 'facts' and offered its first public explanation of what happened in Sverdlovsk. Their official position was an unctuous and reassuring version – there had been a minor, routine, public health problem in Sverdlovsk. Due to poor food controls, they said, some anthrax-tainted meat was sold on the black market and caused an outbreak of illness. This version of the story meant the victims had died from intestinal anthrax after eating contaminated food. The Soviets claimed that both anthrax disease in livestock and the sale of black market meat were common in that region of their country. If this were all true, it meant that the people of Sverdlovsk had suffered, in this instance, the worst human outbreak of anthrax – from natural causes – in the twentieth century.

This lie was a good one. It solved, at a stroke, any problem with violation of the BWC, and kept hidden the illegal anthrax BW production facility in Sverdlovsk.[42]

The cover-up was not well received in Washington. A State Department spokesman responded that the US had 'ruled out natural causes as being a likely explanation' for such a disaster.[43] In other words, the Soviets had to be lying.

The Soviets now went to extraordinary lengths to buttress their lies and make them supportable and credible worldwide. What had begun as a local cover-up in Sverdlovsk, now became an international fairy tale, a fiction of breathtaking audacity.

In May, the Soviets published their first scientific explanation of the accident, in a prestigious medical journal in Moscow. Two senior Soviet physicians/epidemiologists produced a government-approved report which stated that they had traced the cause of the anthrax disaster to two families who purchased tainted meat from private sellers at 'make-shift markets'. Another family, the report said, had eaten 'diseased sheep'. To authenticate their argument that such anthrax outbreaks in animals were relatively common, the paper stated that the disease had occurred 159 times in the Sverdlovsk region between 1936–68, each time from contaminated soil.[44] One did not argue with authoritative reports like these.

Nevertheless, that same month, members of Congress, led by Senator William Proxmire (Democrat-Wisconsin), passed a resolution that called on the Carter Administration to take stronger measures against the Soviets to establish the real truth about Sverdlovsk. But there had been a subtle change of heart in Washington, and the minimalists had now caught Carter's ear. In responding to Proxmire, Deputy Secretary of State Warren Christopher wrote that the administration had raised the issue twice and was clearly 'dissatisfied' with the Soviet responses. But because of the 'gravity' of the issue, explained Christopher, the US was making 'special efforts' not to treat it as 'a political ploy with which to embarrass the Soviets'. Although these views seemed to contain some paradoxes and non sequiturs, that softer line was to remain the official American political position for a while.[45]

The maximalists had their own view. In June, the House Intelligence Oversight Subcommittee held classified hearings on Sverdlovsk with witnesses from the CIA, State Department, and ACDA testifying. The subcommittee's report found that the 'incomplete' Soviet explanations about the cause could not be true. The inquiry's conclusions were spot on, the epidemic had been caused by inhalation anthrax from a military biological weapons facility.[46] The subcommittee, chaired by Representative Les Aspin (Democrat-Wisconsin), found that the Soviets had probably 'cheated' on the BWC by researching and developing bio-weapons.[47]

Aspin understood the broader implications of the Soviets' deception when he noted that 'the future of arms control hangs in the balance' until the Soviets provided a 'full, accurate account' of how the people died in Sverdlovsk.[48]

In the months that followed, the Soviets maintained the big lie as best they could and with it the air of injured innocence. They had suffered a terrible public health tragedy, that was bad enough without the United States' slanders. This was only happening, argued Moscow mournfully, in retaliation for the Soviet invasion of Afghanistan and (curiously) to promote the boycott of the Olympic Games in Moscow. The state-controlled Soviet media faithfully accused the US of conducting 'psychological warfare'.[49]

Ultimately, there were other, equally important, international issues to deal with, and the Sverdlovsk affair looked like it would end in a stand-off, relegated to the historical sidelines. Then the USSR suddenly had a lucky break.

Throughout the rest of the 1980s, Matthew Meselson, a respected Harvard professor of microbiology and longtime arms control activist, unwittingly helped the Soviet caravan of deception and disinformation gain acceptance in the West.

Meselson emerged as the leading scientific expert to oppose his own government's interpretation of Sverdlovsk in favour of the Soviets' old tainted-meat cover-up. He defended the Soviets' case publicly and doubtless from the most honest of beliefs. President Reagan was now in the White House and, no matter how forcefully his administration complained about Sverdlovsk, Meselson remained utterly convinced that there had been an accident with bad meat and it had nothing to do with any secret biological weapons plant.[50]

Since the mid-1960s, Meselson had become deeply involved in advising and lobbying US officials on policies to control biological weapons worldwide. For him, the successful signing of the BWC was the fruit of his endeavours and he seemed loath to accept the possibility that any one of the signatories might deliberately violate it.

With his well-deserved and impressive academic/scientific creden-tials, his views were usually sought and carefully listened to. He also became an important figure for the US media to consult. His opinions about Sverdlovsk were widely quoted in the serious press, books, and prestigious scientific journals. The record shows that after 1980 his publicly stated views on Sverdlovsk broadly agreed with the explanations issued by the Soviets themselves.

In August 1986, Meselson finally gained approval from the Soviet Foreign Ministry to make a four-day visit to Moscow to confer privately with several senior Soviet health officials about the Sverdlovsk evidence.[51]

These officials now told him yet another, more detailed story about the outbreak; they claimed it had been caused by contaminated cattle feed. In a story uncannily reminiscent of the Mad Cow Disease tragedy, BSE, they explained that contaminated bone meal from dead cattle and sheep, which was used to supplement the cattle fodder, had not been properly sterilized before being fed to privately owned cattle.[52]

The scientist who had dreamed up this explanation was Dr Pyotr Burgasov, the USSR's deputy Minister of Health and Meselson's host for the visit. Trouble was Burgasov had a slightly partial background. He had been a Major General in the Soviet Army and had previously served at Compound 19 from 1958–63 as a senior officer in the BW programme.[53] Worse still, when the Sverdlovsk tragedy happened in 1979, it was actually Burgasov who had hurriedly been dispatched from Moscow to Sverdlovsk, right after the accident, to help direct the cover-up. Now, in 1986, he was still leading the disinformation campaign for a Soviet military which must have seen the presumably unaware Meselson as their *deus ex machina* sent to save their face.

Meselson had asked to visit Sverdlovsk during his trip, but this facility was denied him. He was allowed only to hold conversations with four officials in Moscow. When the Harvard professor returned home, he did not immediately publicize his conclusions. Instead, he invited Burgasov and the other Soviet officials to come to the US at some future date to present their new medical evidence themselves in a lecture tour.

A year and a half later, in April 1988, Dr Burgasov, and two other senior Soviet health officials, finally accepted Meselson's invitation. It was shrewd public relations and an unprecedented effort by the Soviets to calm the still lingering American concerns about the incident. It was also the kind of East/West event that American scientists were eager to host.

One of several presentations was made at the prestigious National Academy of Sciences in Washington; two others were conducted at Johns

Hopkins School of Public Health, and the American Academy of Arts and Sciences. These were not exactly village halls. The audiences were supplemented by scores of interested and concerned scientists, medical experts, government arms control officials, and journalists.

Burgasov faithfully reiterated what he had told Meselson in Moscow: there was no doubt that Sverdlovsk was a case of food poisoning from infected meat. He assured anxious listeners that a military accident was 'impossible'. He repeated the explanation about contaminated cattle feed. He emphasized, with sadness, that he simply could not understand the continuing doubts from Americans.[54]

Unsurprisingly, Meselson now added his considerable prestige, by explaining that he found the Soviet presentation completely 'plausible and consistent with what is known' from medical literature and recorded human experiences with anthrax.[55]

The Soviet doctors and their presentation seemed so well informed and sincere that US officials were forced on to the back foot and found they could not properly rebut men who were, after all, primary sources.

Additional political problems were hurting the US rebuttal. The conservative Reagan Administration had passed through its 'Evil Empire' phase with the USSR. It was a time when substantial sections of the American press and the American scientific community were still highly sceptical of the US government's attitudes towards Warsaw Pact nations. Furthermore, the CIA and DIA still refused to release enough of their classified evidence to mount a credible public relations counter-attack to the Soviet scientists' triumphant lecture tour. Those maximalists, who were convinced the Soviets were lying, went through a long period of great frustration.[56]

Meselson himself continued to ignore any doubts or inconsistencies in the Soviet story, while implying that all prior US government analysis had been biased.[57] In 1988, he wrote in a scientific journal, 'Contrary to the US government version, there is no evidence of inhalatory anthrax ... It is clear that the US version of the Sverdlovsk anthrax outbreak is in need of careful and objective review.'[58]

And that's where it looked as if one of the great Cold War deceptions would end up – written into the history books. Truth badly wounded by good and bad intentions, and given the *coup de grâce* by naïveté.

*

It was not until Soviet communism's collapse that the truth was revived and the full horror of Sverdlovsk revealed.

By 1990, Mikhail Gorbachev was the new leader of the Soviet Union, and his policy of openness, glasnost, allowed some courageous Soviet journalists to begin to uncover the facts about Sverdlovsk. Physicians and medical personnel who had treated the patients and performed the telltale autopsies began to speak openly of death by inhalatory anthrax. Slowly, a clear and truthful picture of what had happened on that bad day in Sverdlovsk began to emerge in the Soviet press.[59] The revelations continued although a distracted Western press at first failed to follow through.

The breakthrough occurred in October 1991, when the *Wall Street Journal* sent its Moscow Bureau chief, Peter Gumbel, to Sverdlovsk to re-examine the facts from the Soviet news reports and to find victims of the outbreak. Gumbel made three visits to Sverdlovsk, where he interviewed numerous families, hospital workers, and doctors, and uncovered previously hidden medical records. He found 'the official Soviet version' of events 'riddled with inconsistencies, half-truths and plain falsehoods'.[60]

Gumbel made one particularly startling discovery that seriously damaged Meselson's arguments.[61] Based on information supplied by the Burgasov group, Meselson had written in 1988 that the bad bone-meal supplement had originated from a meat-processing plant near Sverdlovsk, where sterilization procedures had been lax. But Gumbel found that no such slaughterhouse existed.[62] Gumbel's subsequent articles showed that some of Meselson's previous statements were not only incorrect, but had been based, in part, on fabricated Soviet information.[63]

Now, the sluice gates opened. One month after Gumbel's report, retired General Andrei Mironyuk, the acting head of counterintelligence for the Urals Military District in 1979, confirmed to *Izvestiya* that the Sverdlovsk accident was indeed caused by a laboratory employee who failed to turn on 'the safety filters' inside the Compound 19 anthrax facility.[64]

Next, *Izvestiya* was told by General Yu Kornilov, the former KGB chief in Sverdlovsk, that he was ordered by no less than the KGB boss in Moscow, Yuri Andropov, personally to supervise the extensive clean-up of Compound 19 – which took five years to complete. In decontaminating the labs, he said, they had even 'changed the floors and removed the plastering'.[65] Rarely has such a complex conspiracy been so neatly exposed.

But the guilty involvement reached even higher. Next, it emerged that Boris Yeltsin himself also must have known about the cover-up. In May 1992, Yeltsin's new Russian government formally acknowledged what was now well known, but still had no official imprimatur. The man who had been the powerful communist party chief of the Sverdlovsk region in 1979 was none other than – President Boris Yeltsin. He now admitted that the outbreak had been caused by an accident at the biological weapons facility, and not by natural causes.[66] This presumably correct version became the official position of the Russian government, and remains so to this day.[67]

Meselson, however, remained unfazed. In the face of Yeltsin's admission and the Russian and US press disclosures, the professor assembled a team of expert American scientists and went with them to Sverdlovsk in June 1992 to see for himself. They interviewed two outstanding Sverdlovsk doctors – Faina Abramova and Lev Grinberg – who participated in the 1979 autopsies at Hospital 40. For thirteen years, these brave pathologists had secretly hidden incontrovertible medical evidence from the KGB – including preserved tissue samples, slides, and autopsy reports – which proved that the victims had died from breathing in the anthrax.[68]

Meselson later claimed that he and his team had made the discovery of the new truth from these important witnesses, but again, the facts were against him. The two Russian doctors had previously spoken to Soviet reporters and the *Wall Street Journal*, so Meselson was simply following old, published leads. He nevertheless persisted in taking credit for being the final arbiter who had authenticated the evidence.[69]

After making a second trip to Sverdlovsk, Meselson finally published his results in 1994 in the journal *Science*; the article accepted that the tainted-meat story was bogus. But, perversely, he still would not admit that the US government had been right for fifteen years, or that he had been wrong. Rather, he trumpeted the fact that *he* and his team had finally uncovered the 'definitive proof' that the true cause of the outbreak was pulmonary anthrax.[70]

'This should end the argument about where the outbreak came from,' Meselson somewhat pompously told the *New York Times*. 'Right up until now, people have still been debating the matter.'[71]

Yet, to the bitter end, Meselson still clung to a benign interpretation of Soviet motives. He noted that the cause of the accident was still not determined, which implied that it may have involved only a Soviet *research* centre, one for finding an antidote to an anthrax attack, and not a military production centre for biological weapons. By clinging to this position, he could still argue that the Soviets were not violating the BWC, but were conducting permissible research under the treaty.[72]

For the Soviet Union, by then dissolved into Russia, the Sverdlovsk revelations should have been a lesson and a warning. Meselson's cartwheels to one side, Moscow might have finally absorbed the reality that the persistent Soviet breaches of the BWC were now known to the West. It might have been the right historical moment to call a halt to the violations, for the sake of international credibility and honour, and because the times were fast changing.

But it was not to be.

CHAPTER TEN

The Juniper Channel

'A policy decision was made to deal with this topic quietly . . .'
Former US State Department official, 1998

In late November 1987, US intelligence analysts were poring over routine radar printouts and satellite pictures of Soviet missiles launched from their Kamchatka test range in eastern Siberia. This was the basic intelligence 'take' that typically accompanied every Soviet ICBM test launch. It was gathered from a mixture of electronic eavesdropping by US naval vessels in the Pacific, spy satellites, and other euphemistically named 'national technical means' by which the superpowers kept an eye on each other.

The desk analysts quickly spotted something odd about the trajectories of a series of test firings. There were clear flight anomalies which needed urgent explanation. The slightest variance from normal was a matter of immediate concern to the Western allies, and the printouts were quickly distributed throughout the relevant US intelligence agencies.[1]

A top-secret report about the Kamchatka mystery was issued by the CIA's technical staff of missile experts, under the signature of DCI William Webster. The very tightly held document did not speculate about the reasons for the flight anomalies or even hint at the possibility that new non-nuclear warheads might be involved. Nor did the report contain any conclusions; it just described the odd profile of the test flights. The experts were asking, in effect, does anyone in the US government know anything about what might be causing this to happen?[2]

There were no immediate answers – yet there had to be explanations.

America's top technical experts on missiles worked on this problem for the rest of the Reagan Administration. They investigated a wide range of possibilities: including different weight distributions and various payloads. All of this painstaking analysis took time. About six months were needed, for instance, just to decode the encrypted telemetry of the missile firings. When the analysts finally confirmed these were Mod 4 (fourth modification) of the Soviet SS-11 ('Sego') multiple-warhead missile, the US intelligence community initiated high-priority surveillance of all known sites in the USSR where those strategic missiles were assembled and deployed.

It took nearly a year, but the effort was to prove worthwhile. Finally, in October 1988, the small, dedicated intelligence team made the breakthrough. It began when US satellite photos showed that the Soviets had attached large units with tubes and hoses that were connected to the missile warheads in storage silos and at the launch sites. These strange units had never been seen before in this configuration with warheads. No one knew what they were. Many hypotheses were floated. Were these a new type of multiple warhead? Could the units involve some sort of new electronics? Just what on earth *were* the Soviets playing around with?

It took another two months to confirm – through sophisticated thermal analysis by which highly sensitive spy satellites can 'read' the body temperature of objects thousands of miles away – that the unidentified units were . . . refrigerators!

Refrigerators.

American reconnaissance experts had never before seen refrigerators attached to Soviet missiles on launch sites.[3] Since it was unlikely that the Soviets were going to launch an intercontinental ballistic missile attack on the West using iced-beer warheads, a serious and gloomy atmosphere settled over the analysts. Finally, using age-old logic and the process of elimination, a group of CIA experts cracked it. It was only a hypothesis, but it was the one that worked best; it was also the one that augured the most depressing conclusion.

The refrigerating units were keeping something cool, therefore alive, for the journey through space. And, if it was living, and offensive, it had to be bacteria or viruses.[4] There was a brief pause as the message sank home. Relief at the discovery was soon tempered by the dawning of the dreadful truth that they had uncovered. The Soviets had developed a new weapon of mass destruction for strategic warfare by mounting biological weapons on long-range missiles that could reach North America. A fearsome new milestone in war had been reached.

The chief arms control analyst at CIA, Douglas MacEachin, immediately delivered the information to the National Security Council's senior advisory group. Incredulity and disbelief were the first reactions. This was followed by an understandable reluctance at first to accept the information.

'You must understand, there was still a dearth of intelligence on the Soviet BW programme,' concedes a former senior CIA official, who was later briefed on MacEachin's presentation. 'Even some senior CIA analysts still did not believe that the Soviets had a BW programme. So some people in authority did not believe they had this rocket capability. The believers didn't know for sure. They had never seen the Soviets test offensive BW missiles before. The CIA had seen Soviet activities at Vozrozhdeniye Island, but we were never certain what it was.'[5]

The 'believers', however, were in the ascendancy and their conclusions could not be ignored.

The news about BW missiles was brought to the White House during the post-election, transition period from Presidents Ronald Reagan to George Bush, just a few weeks before Bush was to be inaugurated. But because the outgoing president was a powerless 'lame duck', the problem was forwarded to the new president and his incoming team. President-elect Bush and his senior advisers were promptly informed.

At this stage, the US did not tell any of its allies (not even the British government) about what they had discovered, despite the global implications and special intelligence-sharing relationships. This was such a serious development that US policy makers were determined not to go off half cocked. They felt it was still too early, since the CIA had arrived at only a preliminary conclusion. The assessment had to be fortified with more hard evidence and analysis before any action could be taken.

This caution was also rooted in the frustrations of the Reagan years, when information about the Soviet BW programme had been hard to come by. It was a time when the USSR had continued to cheat and lie by consistently claiming that it had no offensive weapons and that it was in full compliance with the treaty. Even after Mikhail Gorbachev took power in 1985 (long before the final Sverdlovsk revelations) and instituted new policies centred on the concepts of perestroika (restructuring) and glasnost (openness), every US/UK allegation about the Soviet BW programme was simply denied.

The Reagan Administration officially complained six times to the Soviet government about its offensive BW programme. These démarches were presented in two batches: the first batch – in October 1984, February 1985, and December 1985 – concerned suspicious activities at BW facilities, including Zagorsk. The later batch – in August 1986, July 1988, and December 1988 – demanded explanations for the accident at Sverdlovsk. None of these formal diplomatic protests produced any worthwhile responses, just more shameless denials.[6]

During the second Reagan term (1985–88), the CIA's awareness of the Soviet BW programme was contained in several National Intelligence Estimates (NIE) prepared for the White House. These secret NIEs concluded that the Soviets had a very aggressive biological research programme.[7] With hindsight, the NIEs were even more accurate than their authors realized. The secret CIA analyses found that the Soviets might be manufacturing biological weapons at nine possible facilities run by the Ministry of Defence. But only two of them were confirmed – Sverdlovsk (due to the 1979 accident) and Zagorsk (based on its high security and visible bunkers). The rest were categorized as 'suspect' – Omutninsk, Aksu, Pokrov, Berdsk, Penza, Kurgan, and a storage site at Malta (in Siberia). The intelligence reports also noted that the Soviets were thought to be producing the following BW agents: anthrax, botulinum toxin, Tularaemia, Plague, cholera, and several toxins – basically the same list of threats the US had suspected since the 1950s.[8]

Since 1984, the CIA had also been tracking suspicious construction at several new molecular biological institutes in the USSR – including one at Obolensk, 40 miles south of Moscow near Serpukhov, and another in Kol'tsovo, near Novosibirsk, Siberia. The CIA believed the Soviets might be using these 'civilian' locations for secret, military research on genetic engineering. American and British analysts estimated in 1986 that the Soviets might produce weapons with newly created pathogens in three to five years. But little else was known in the West about the true purposes of these facilities.[9]

After George Bush had taken the oath of office, he told his senior National Security Council staff (led by NSC Adviser, General Brent

Scowcroft, and his deputy, Robert Gates) that he wanted them to find a new way to handle arms control, including chemical and biological weapons. Bush wanted the US to press the Soviets to force them to modify their activities. He instructed his new administration to conduct a full strategic review. Orders went out to accumulate BW intelligence from all possible sources; the aim was to consolidate what was suspected and then to establish beyond all reasonable doubt what it was the Soviets actually were working on.[10]

To meet this urgent requirement, the CIA set up a special new top-secret intelligence reporting system which was assigned the random code-word 'Juniper'. This 'Juniper Channel', as it was known, was designated to hold all information related to the Soviet BW programme and future US–Soviet diplomatic exchanges on these issues. The tightest possible compartmentalization was imposed on Juniper information – equivalent to the shrouds of secrecy that had been draped over such previous sensitive material as the Cuban Missile Crisis.

Initially, only twenty-six officials in the Bush Administration (in addition to about ten CIA technical experts) were cleared to read Juniper reports. These documents were among the two or three most sensitive topics inside the US arms control establishment in 1989. The designation meant that only the highest-level officials in the government had access – including the President, Vice President, NSC Adviser, Secretary of Defence, Secretary of State, Director of ACDA, CIA Director, Joint Chiefs of Staff, DIA Director and their relevant senior deputies.[11]

It was to take nine months for the administration to establish its new policy on how to handle the Soviet BW issue. During that time, the Bush team did not take any public or diplomatic action against the USSR. Then, in September 1989, President Bush announced his intention to undertake an intensified arms control initiative with President Gorbachev. The White House noted that this initiative would include biological weapons (on which subject the files were now bulging), but no new details were revealed about US information, complaints, or future negotiations. The policy of no publicity was still in effect.[12]

'A policy decision was made to deal with this topic quietly – with no media,' recalls a former State Department official. 'That's what made this issue so sensitive. They decided not to seek a Soviet-bashing solution.'[13]

The reasons were obvious. The world was passing through a period of intense and exciting change; Soviet communism was teetering and this was no time to encourage hardliners in Moscow. The cautious, minimalist approach by Western diplomats was to cause serious divisions between intelligence analysts and policy makers in both Washington and London, but, for the time being anyway, Washington spoke softly and kept its big stick out of sight.

Robert Gates explains that President Bush did not so much initiate a new policy, as resolve to push the Soviets harder to find the truth. 'We just became more determined to make the Soviets come clean,' Gates says. 'It was a matter of pushing them to rectify an unacceptable situation. We still were trying to get more information on what they were doing.'[14]

And there were other considerations. The political situation in the Soviet Union and the status of other arms control negotiations were equally important factors in how the Bush Administration proceeded. Mikhail Gorbachev had been in power for more than four years. Both he and his country had travelled far since he took over the USSR's leadership in March 1985, following the three unexciting years when two successive ailing General Secretaries, Yuri Andropov and Konstantin Chernenko, had briefly been in charge. At home, Gorbachev's programmes of perestroika and glasnost were taking hold and capturing the imagination of the world. Internationally, Gorbachev won praise for initiating an unprecedented series of arms control agreements with President Reagan. After decades of cold stagnation, the diplomatic rivers were beginning to flow and sparkle.

In 1986, at their summit in Iceland, Gorbachev had proposed a sharp reduction in the Soviet stockpile of ballistic missiles. In December 1987 in Washington, Gorbachev and Reagan signed the treaty on Intermediate Nuclear Forces (INF), which eliminated a whole category of superpower nuclear armaments. This success was considered a major breakthrough in arms control.[15]

The following August, that enduring fixture of negative, foot-dragging, Soviet foreign policy, Andrei Gromyko, retired and was replaced with the Soviet Union's first new foreign minister in thirty years, Eduard Shevardnadze, a Gorbachev ally from the Republic of Georgia. The switch was to mark a major change in the way Soviet foreign policy was handled – from the age-old Soviet 'don't give an inch' hard line of Gromyko to the progressive new initiatives of Shevardnadze.

On 8 February 1989, Gorbachev announced in a nationwide TV

address a complete Soviet troop withdrawal from Afghanistan. The pullout was completed on 15 March, ahead of schedule, when Soviet forces marched across the Termez Bridge back to the USSR – ending a costly and bloody war that had severely damaged US–Soviet relations for ten years.[16]

Dramatic signs of thaw continued throughout 1989, as an historic rush of major political changes swept through Eastern Europe. With breathtaking suddenness, the Cold War was melting, as every communist government in the region (except Albania) was removed from power. The Bush team understood full well that Gorbachev and Shevardnadze had allowed these reforms with no Soviet military interference.[17]

In December 1989, one month after the Berlin Wall came down, Gorbachev met President Bush at a summit in Malta, where they agreed that the arms race, mutual mistrust, and ideological struggles 'should all be things of the past'. The two leaders discussed START, reduction of Conventional Forces in Europe (CFE), on-site inspections of nuclear missiles, and even the pending re-unification of Germany.[18] There was something new in the air, this was no time to ask embarrassing questions about treaty compliance. The BW issue stayed in the pending tray.

One key to all of this progress was Secretary of State James Baker's increasingly warm relationship with Foreign Minister Eduard Shevardnadze.

Baker had first met Shevardnadze in Vienna, March 1989, just months after he became Bush's Secretary of State. To relax and get better acquainted, Baker later invited Shevardnadze and his top advisers to join him in Jackson Hole, Wyoming, where Baker owned a nearby 1,500-acre ranch amid the scenic splendour and abundant wildlife of the Grand Tetons, some 50 miles south of Yellowstone National Park.[19]

Baker, a wealthy, sixty-year-old corporate attorney from Houston's legal and social aristocracy, had been a longtime friend, confidant, and political adviser of George Bush, as well as the powerful White House Chief of Staff and later Treasury Secretary during the Reagan years. As Bush's Secretary of State, he was both trusted and given real authority.

The four-day session in Wyoming with Shevardnadze, in late September 1989, had established a strong bond and solid working relationship between the world's two senior diplomats. Baker and

Shevardnadze also signed a major agreement on chemical weapons, designated the 'Wyoming Memorandum of Understanding', which called for US–USSR reciprocal verification and data exchange on CW stockpiles and production facilities, leading to an eventual global ban.[20]

'The Wyoming ministerial radically altered Jim Baker's view of how to deal with Shevardnadze and the USSR,' recalled one of Baker's senior advisers who was present.[21]

'These actions reinforced the notion that Gorbachev and Shevardnadze were trying to do the right thing on arms control,' recalled a participant. 'We began to think to ourselves: maybe, Mrs Thatcher's famous statement was true, that, "We could do business with this man, Gorbachev".'[22]

For Washington's and London's BW minimalists, who might reasonably have expected a rise in superpower tension after the BW warhead discoveries, it all sounded too good to be true. And it was.

Just one month after Wyoming, a middle-aged man from Leningrad slipped unnoticed into London. What he brought with him was to transform, at a stroke, the euphoria that had settled over East/West arms control discussions into the all too familiar dark cloud of mistrust.

At last, a top scientist from right inside the heart of the Soviet BW programme had defected to the West.

CHAPTER ELEVEN

The Defector

'This new source was giving us very frightening confirmation of what we suspected.'

Former UNGROUP member, 1998

In October 1989, Dr Vladimir Pasechnik, a leading Soviet bio-chemist, defected to Britain after attending a meeting in France. Pasechnik had been Director of the Institute for Ultra Pure-Biological Preparations in Leningrad (now St Petersburg) since 1980. This large facility with the ungainly name hid a top-secret centre for Soviet BW research of which the West knew nothing.

Pasechnik looked unlike a typical scientist – he was short and stocky, with a round, craggy face, a muscular build, and unusually beefy, artisan's hands. He was also the first primary source from deep inside the Soviet BW programme who was in a position to see what the spy-satellites could never see – what was actually going on inside the plants and what the Soviets were really thinking.[1]

And now, he belonged to the West.

Pasechnik was first taken into care by Britain's Secret Intelligence Service, MI6, which assigned him the code name 'Truncate'. His information was so voluminous that the British assembled a special task group of intelligence officers, technical analysts, and scientists to evaluate it. Officers from MI6 did the initial debriefings, assisted later by Dr David Kelly, then senior principal scientific officer at the Chemical Defence Establishment at Porton Down, and Surgeon-Commander Christopher Davis, Royal Navy, of the Defence Intelligence Staff.[2] Kelly, an experienced microbiologist, was called in because his technical expertise was needed to fully understand and evaluate the science of what Pasechnik was saying. Davis carefully pulled from Pasechnik additional details on other Soviet institutes, personnel, and future research programmes.[3]

Pasechnik brought with him a cornucopia of priceless biological warfare information, which he proceeded to spill out in front of his wide-eyed debriefers. First, he disclosed the existence of a massive infrastructure of Soviet bio-research laboratories and production plants under a supposedly non-military conglomerate called Biopreparat. This was a classic Russian *Matryoshka*, the doll within a doll within a doll; in this case, an ostensible civilian biological research programme was deep cover for a huge military programme. Biopreparat – the renamed, updated version of the Ogarkov System – was neat, cynical, and a gross violation of the Biological Weapons Convention.

Biopreparat simply hid sites built after the BWC was signed in 1972. The heavily guarded locations were spread across the wide country, from big cities like Leningrad and Moscow to small, obscure towns like Obolensk, Kol'tsovo, Chekhov, and some fifteen other locations. All were operating under secret direction and funding from the Ministry of Defence.

Both British and American intelligence agencies had known for some time that some of these sites existed, and they had also known, in general terms, that an organization called Biopreparat existed as a sub-section of the Soviet Ministry of Medical and Biological Industry.[4] But they were astonished to discover they had never been aware of what was going on inside Biopreparat's huge organization – even though, as Pasechnik explained, it had so many locations, more than 30,000 workers, and a yearly budget of several hundred million dollars for research, production, testing, and equipment design. (Co-ordinated military activities raised these totals to 60,000 employees and nearly $1 billion in annual spending.)[5]

MI6 quickly realized that Pasechnik was a man of huge importance to the West. He helped the task force confirm, clarify, and develop much of their old fragmented BW information from the USSR. Slowly the disparate puzzle pieces were linked into a single picture. Now, for the first time, the West had solid evidence, first-hand from a primary source of unimpeachable character, that could not be discredited.[6]

Pasechnik's voluminous knowledge about the entire Soviet biological weapons system sprung from his position on the Science and Technical Committee of Biopreparat and his visits to many of the sites. Overall, his startling disclosures confirmed two important British/American fears: the Soviet Union had violated the BWC from 1972 to the Gorbachev years, *and was continuing to do so*; and, worse still, the USSR was extensively involved in engineering germs and bacteria to develop new kinds of biological weapons against which the West would be defenceless. In other words, the Soviets weren't just ahead, they had 'done a Sputnik' in BW terms against the West. Their code word for the whole offensive programme was the Russian word 'Ferment', which means enzyme.[7]

The detail of Pasechnik's account was horrific. Since 1984, he revealed to his British debriefers, a top priority of the four hundred scientists at his former institute in Leningrad was the development of bacteria, including Plague and Tularaemia, that were more lethal than ever before and resistant to heat, cold, and antibiotics. He said they were able to make this bacteria resistant to all known Western medicines by growing it in flasks filled with specially engineered plasmids, and repeating the process many times. The Soviet scientists made sure the resulting super-Plague could be counteracted with secret antidotes, which only the Soviet military possessed. In that way, they could vaccinate their own military forces while leaving enemy troops defenceless. This Plague was the Soviet weapon of choice because it was so lethal and transmissible from person-to-person.[8]

This was heady stuff. The defector was telling the West that the Soviets had created a strategic biological weapons arsenal to which there was no defence, which worked, and which would return the industrialized world to the Middle Ages – to a horse and cart economy, and there certainly wouldn't be enough of them to bury the dead.

Pasechnik also described how that the Soviets were packing a dried, powdery form of this super-Plague into munitions, like rocket warheads, bombs, and artillery shells. Just a small amount of these powders, he warned, could kill half the population of a small city in a week. Mankind would be reacquainted with the horrors of the fourteenth-century's Black Death, when Plague spread by fleas killed a third of the population of Europe.[9]

Pasechnik confirmed that the USSR was perfecting other new strains of bacteria and viruses in weaponized aerosol form.[10] For research and testing purposes, he said, the Soviets had stockpiled a much greater amount of BW agents than the West suspected. Senior military officials had told him that the USSR kept on hand a twenty-ton stockpile of Plague for weaponization at any given time. This huge, standby amount was replenished on a regular basis.[11] Full-scale production could be started at any time the military gave the signal.

He also verified what the West had long suspected, but couldn't prove, concerning the Soviets' germ warfare test site in the Aral Sea. He confirmed they had conducted offensive trials that killed hundreds of tethered test animals; he knew about these trials on Vozrozhdeniye Island because he had been called upon to assess the results.[12]

Perhaps most ominously, Pasechnik revealed tantalizing clues that the use of biological weapons had been integrated into the Kremlin's special war plans, and that the Soviet military had developed a diabolical range of tactical and strategic weapons to carry out the mission.[13]

So, crudely, they had the weapons, the delivery systems, and the bacteria and viruses specially treated and engineered, and they had taken the political decision to use them in the event of all-out war. As the task force listened in silence, the small cassette tapes that recorded Pasechnik's revelations rolled silently on.

Pasechnik disclosed areas where biological weapons development was underway – although, as a civilian, he had no direct personal access to the military's weapons or delivery systems. From his initial leads, and later information obtained from other sources, Western intelligence analysts were eventually able to fill in the picture.

Since the late 1960s, the Soviets had maintained a small fleet of about twenty specially equipped planes, based in the Volga region, that could be used to carry bio-weapons for tactical attacks. These Ilyushin-28 (IL-28) medium-range bombers carried spray-tank delivery systems which could distribute deadly clouds of weaponized anthrax, Plague, Tularaemia, glanders, and Brucellosis over enemy forces.

For long-range attacks in Europe and America with biological weapons, the Soviet Union's primary strategic warplane was the TV-95, which carried cluster bombs filled with weaponized bio-agents. These cluster bombs, each holding more than a hundred special bomblets inside, had been tested successfully many times on baboons tethered to stakes on Vozrozhdeniye Island. Several military facilities (including Kirov and Zagorsk) kept pre-deployed containers of BW agents to fill these bomblets and spray tanks.

And, yes, the Americans had got it right with their surveillance satellites – the USSR's ultimate biological weapons were ICBMs capable of delivering warheads to any target in the world. According to Soviet military doctrine, these missiles would be used only if 'total war' was declared with the West. 'Total war' was defined as an all-out battle of 'mutual destruction' with direct fighting between the US/UK and USSR, including the use of nuclear weapons.[14] (The Vietnam War, by comparison, was considered a 'regional conflict'.) In 'total war' the Kremlin would have no moral reservations against using BW warheads. The Soviets, with malice aforethought, would kill entire Western populations rather than risk losing the war. This ruthlessness was motivated, in part, by memories of the unspeakable Nazi atrocities committed on the Soviet civilian population during World War II. The policy represented not so much payback time for those horrors, but a grim determination never ever to allow a potential invader to secure a foothold on Mother Russia's soil. Hence, whatever it took, including biological weapons, would be used to break the enemy's spirit long before tanks began to roll east over Europe's central plains. Whatever pragmatic, historic or emotional justification the USSR had for deterring attack, it was nonetheless a policy that made their solemn treaty commitments to the BWC look like nonsense.

The basic objective of these ICBMs was to cause catastrophic epidemics that would completely disrupt an enemy country's civilian activities. The key destinations – called 'deep targets' – included London, New York, Washington, Chicago, Seattle, and Los Angeles.[15] The Soviet ICBMs could carry anthrax or Plague (and other highly contagious viruses were in development). In peacetime, biological warheads were not stockpiled in a ready, weaponized state like nuclear warheads (it would have been impossible to keep the bacteria and viruses alive and fresh anyway). Instead, these BW warheads were to be hurriedly assembled and loaded at Biopreparat's production plants only during a 'special period' of preparedness and mobilization that the Kremlin would declare during heightened world tensions just before an imminent war.[16]

The biological agents for these non-activated warheads were kept in special hermetically sealed containers inside assembly rooms at four of Biopreparat's facilities – Berdsk, Omutninsk, Sverdlovsk (before 1979), and Stepnogorsk (after 1981). Two workers needed about one hour to arm a single warhead.

The first of the Soviet BW rockets – developed during the 1960s and

1970s – was called 'monoblock', which meant the high-altitude missile held just one warhead. In the 1980s, the newer, much larger Soviet rockets – SS-18s – carried multiple warheads (up to ten warheads per missile). Several SS-18s, with a range of 10,000 kms, were dedicated to the BW programme. Just one of these huge anthrax-loaded SS-18s would have been able to wipe out an entire big city population.[17] Interestingly, nothing like multiple-warhead ICBMs loaded with biological weapons had ever been contemplated in the West before BW was renounced in 1969.

But even more significantly, the Soviets were also working on a tactical cruise missile system that could deliver biological warheads at more than one pre-determined 'drop off' point – in a dreadful kind of lethal bus run.[18] These deadly accurate, air-breathing, 'doomsday doodle-bugs' were the last word in non-strategic warfare. Each cruise missile was supposed to carry a payload of multiple wet or dry biological cannisters which would be released at pre-ordained targets. The missile could be launched from the ground, from stand-off strategic bombers, or from submarines or warships. In any one flight, only a single cruise missile would need to penetrate the air defences to cause untold havoc in the target country.

The Soviet military handed Pasechnik's laboratory the assignment to design these cruise missiles. So serious were the implications of this form of biological warfare that the West has kept this knowledge top secret until 1999.

Western experts were also stunned by how the Soviets had managed to solve the problems of delivering fragile pathogens thousand of miles in ICBMs, while surviving the enormous atmospheric pressures in-flight; the intense heat involved with launch, and re-entry; and the destructive forces of final explosive dissemination.[19] Starting in the late 1960s, top Soviet rocket scientists, supervised by the USSR's Special Rocket Forces, had addressed all of these problems. The warhead's re-entry from space to the target was handled just like an astronaut's return to earth. The BW rockets were fitted with the same special cooling and protective systems that kept the astronauts from being 'cooked' when they splashed down. Simple. The Soviets fully anticipated that some of the pathogens inside the warhead would be destroyed in the explosion. However, a significant amount would survive and remain lethal. Ample redundancy was the name of the game. The 'bugs' themselves were cheap after all.

The Soviets knew their biological warfare programme would work because they had thoroughly and secretly tested their rockets and warheads, using bio-simulants. These tests had taken place over the Atlantic and Pacific Oceans during a period of many years – and the Western intelligence services had missed their significance. Using anthrax, the tests showed that nearly 100 per cent of the payload would survive. With most of the other pathogens, some 10–30 per cent would survive. But who would be counting as the wind blew incurable epidemics through the cities and across the countryside, finally leaving the dead and dying rotting where they lay?

Asked many times in different ways why he brought this precious information to London, Pasechnik always gave the same answer: he couldn't stop the Soviet programme by working from within, so he defected to warn the West.[20]

Vladimir Artemovich Pasechnik had never intended that his scientific career would take such a dramatic turn.

Born in Stalingrad in 1937, he studied molecular biology at a prestigious school in Leningrad and was spotted as one of the country's brighter young scientists. He wanted to apply his research talents toward peaceful purposes, particularly cancer research. In 1974, however, General Ogarkov and the Ministry of Defence made the then thirty-seven-year-old microbiologist an attractive offer. They recruited him to establish a new, high-tech laboratory in Leningrad for Biopreparat. He would be given whatever funds were needed to buy new Western equipment and to hire the USSR's top scientists to work for him. General Ogarkov had a clear rationale for establishing the new laboratory – he wanted Pasechnik's team to conduct serious science to eliminate certain non-biological problems that always cropped up during the production, storage, and use of bio-weapons. Pasechnik's laboratory would carry out advanced bio-chemical studies for Biopreparat to improve the stability, viability, and dissemination characteristics of micro-organisms used in biological weapons.[21]

Pasechnik was told initially that his work would have only civilian applications, like vaccines and crop control, or that it might be used for military defences. He accepted, he said, because in those days in the Soviet Union only the Defence Ministry had the vast funds necessary to support the most advanced scientific research.[22]

After years of planning, the new institute finally opened in 1980. It did not take long for Pasechnik to realize he had been conned and that his laboratory's work-product was actually intended to support the development of offensive biological weapons for the Ministry of Defence. The military installed an explosive chamber and aerosol test rooms at his laboratory, even though it was located in a densely populated city. He said he developed a 'disgust' for his work, but, in the Soviet system, he was trapped with no alternatives.

By 1989, Pasechnik, then fifty-one, had privately confided to a Biopreparat colleague that he was frustrated and somewhat depressed about his career path. He was worried about his upcoming retirement and how he would survive on a meagre pension of only 120 rubles per month. Although his co-workers missed the warning signals – such frustrations were prevalent in the Soviet system – in his own mind Pasechnik was ready to leave.[23]

In early October, his chance came when his superiors at Biopreparat authorized his first-ever trip to the West. On a Thursday, Pasechnik went to Toulouse, France, with a subordinate – his laboratory chief – for an officially sanctioned meeting with a French equipment manufacturer. They were due to return home that weekend. Instead, acting on his own, a nervous Pasechnik initiated contact with the West.

His first choice was to defect to Canada and he duly knocked on the door of the Canadian Embassy in Paris. But the Canadians wanted nothing to do with the balding Russian scientist with the nice smile and, to his surprise, he was shooed away. He had no interest in defecting to the United States, because he was unsure if the American offensive BW programme was still underway, and if it were, he feared he might be made to work inside it. (Incredibly, Pasechnik claimed he had never been told about the existence of the BWC and learned of it first from his British debriefers!)

So, he turned to Britain.[24]

Pasechnik phoned the British Embassy in Paris and informed a surprised official that he wanted to defect to London. This time the response was swift and positive. The MI6 station chief was informed.

Pasechnik was quickly and quietly collected and flown straight to London under a false identity. Then he was taken to an MI6 safe house outside London, and, after a short, respectable break for re-orientation, the intensive debriefings began.[25]

Pasechnik's former colleagues never saw him again. His military bosses in Moscow realized by Monday, when the laboratory chief returned alone, that Pasechnik had probably defected and would never return. It was the very first time that Biopreparat had been hit by a defection and it was to shake the Soviet institution to its roots.[26]

Pasechnik's boss was Major General Yuriy Tikhonovich Kalinin, an old unreconstructed Stalinist.[27] A tall, thin man with high cheekbones and neatly combed jet-black hair on an aristocratic face, Kalinin was known for being an intensely clever manipulator who had danced from one rolling political log to another during the turbulent years since the death of Brezhnev. His background included engineering degrees and a long spell with the army's vaunted Chemical Corps.

He started his BW career as the first director of the All-Union Scientific Research Institute of Biological Instrumentation (part of the Biopreparat empire). His rise to power began when he left his first wife, the daughter of a laboratory director, to marry the daughter of a senior general in the Soviet Defence Ministry. Later, after he arrived at Biopreparat headquarters, he had an affair with his secretary, Tatyana, a relationship of mutual benefit which resulted in her being paid more than the deputy directors.[28]

In 1979, General Yefim Smirnov, then head of the offensive BW programme in the Ministry of Defence, appointed the under-qualified, but malleable, Kalinin, then age forty-one, as director of Biopreparat. Kalinin soon became an empire builder, increasing the size, scope, and political importance of Biopreparat, eventually making it five times larger than the organization he had inherited from Ogarkov.[29]

Kalinin's headquarters was a grim-looking, nineteenth-century, yellow brick mansion with a green roof, set behind a concrete wall on the small and narrow Samokatnaya Street in Moscow's old 'German Quarter'. From his large, high-ceilinged office on the second floor, where he ran the building's 150 administrators and staffers, Kalinin remained a ferocious proponent of the USSR's offensive BW programme.[30]

In 1989, Kalinin took immediate and deft steps to survive the Pasechnik debacle. First he managed to incriminate his deputy director for science with responsibility for the disaster, and, then arranged for the unfortunate man to be fired as a sacrifice to the Kremlin.[31] Next, Kalinin and other military officials steered a security report to the Kremlin which sought to minimize what the loss of Pasechnik meant to the USSR.

To decrease further the possible damage, officials from Biopreparat and the Ministry of Medical Industry, working under Kalinin's careful guidance, prepared plausible cover stories to counter the information that Pasechnik would give the British government. All of the classified papers and records at Pasechnik's institute were systematically destroyed. A Soviet security team shredded and burned several rooms full of papers. This step was taken so that Biopreparat officials later could deny everything that Pasechnik said he had done there. In the unlikely event an official inspection of the Leningrad facility was conducted by the UN, or even the British or American governments, nothing would be found. Plausible deniability would take over.

Should Pasechnik try to phone or write to his former colleagues in Leningrad, the security officials also wanted to be sure that no future backsliders had any paperwork to send him.[32]

As the airbrushing of history began, officials in Moscow also devised and implemented a completely transformed scientific programme for Pasechnik's institute, involving only defensive and civilian research. Now, there never had been an offensive programme. 'Ferment' was a figment of Pasechnik's imagination. All work related to the offensive BW programme was immediately halted at Leningrad to allow for denials. By the time Kalinin had finished, the plan was to have changed the backdrop, rewound the clock, got rid of the actors, and rewritten the entire script. Thus, Pasechnik's allegations would be shown to be the ravings of a lunatic, the paranoid fantasies of a disgruntled scientist. There would be the usual behind-the-hand murmurings about his mental health – the KGB had good experience with all of that.

As usual in such defections, the Soviets also mounted an effort to woo him back. The Russian Ambassador in London complained that the British were holding Pasechnik against his will and asked to speak to him. In a telephone conversation, which MI6 permitted with Pasechnik's agreement, the Ambassador urged Pasechnik to return home. He promised him there would be no problems and all his concerns would be fully addressed. Pasechnik was unconvinced. Instead, he wrote a long letter to the Soviet government resigning from the Communist Party and setting out his reasons for defecting. He even enclosed a detailed financial statement of his trip to France and returned the expense money he had not spent.[33]

MI6 officials did not tell the CIA of Pasechnik's defection until several months after he arrived.[34] There had been a delay, the British explained, as they finished the initial debriefing and satisfied themselves that Pasechnik's credentials and story were sound. During the winter of 1990, MI6 shared all the debriefing reports with CIA analysts. The British first sent highly classified digests of this information to Washington and then sent a two-man team, including Chris Davis, to brief the CIA.

A group of CIA officers, in turn, was given full access to Pasechnik in London. After a full debriefing they left certain that he was the real thing.[35]

In February 1990, once Pasechnik's initial debriefings had been fully analysed and verified, CIA analyst Douglas MacEachin went to a White House meeting to inform the rest of the government about the defector's information. Pasechnik's news was still so closely held that the CIA's Directorate of Operations had not even distributed it within the agency. Pasechnik's name and job description were also tightly classified. To anyone without a need-to-know, he was referred to only as 'a highly reliable human source'.[36]

The White House meeting was a regularly scheduled session of the 'UNGROUP', a secret team of senior advisers on arms control policy established by the Bush Administration. The mordant humour of the group's title was deliberately Kafkaesque because, as no one was supposed to know about them, the unofficial UNGROUP didn't exist. The members came from the Under Secretary or Assistant Secretary level of their respective agencies: NSC, CIA, State, ACDA, Defense, Joint Chiefs, and Energy.[37]

After the usual business was concluded, MacEachin asked for the room to be cleared of all staff and assistants. Only the eight principal UNGROUP members remained.[38] 'We have some reliable new evidence from a HUMINT source,' MacEachin began. He then spoke for about ten minutes, explaining Pasechnik's essential information.

The Americans soon split once more into minimalist and maximalist groups. The minimalists were not quite sure about this new intelligence 'take'. They wanted more proof, corroboration. It all sounded a little far out, and this was no time to interrupt the delicacies of dealing with the prospect of real breakthroughs in discussions with a fast-changing Soviet Union under the progressive Gorbachev. Besides, argued some of the minimalists, they were wary of maximalist ambushes. Indeed, some minimalists used to disparagingly call them the 'Armageddon types'.

But some of the maximalists comprised the most experienced and dedicated arms control analysts in the US government. These weren't Evil Empire men, but seasoned intelligence officers from the CIA, Defense Department, and State Department, who were fully supported by their British counterparts, including David Kelly, Chris Davis, and senior MI6 analysts.

Some doubters listening to MacEachin's presentation, for instance, wondered how it was that the CIA previously had missed Pasechnik's crucial new information about the civilian Biopreparat apparatus. The CIA had never uncovered anything about this huge BW programme for the first fifteen years of its existence! British intelligence didn't know about it either. How could such a huge intelligence failure happen?

The answer was depressingly simple. Western intelligence had wrongly assumed that the whole Soviet BW programme was a very small operation hidden *deep inside the military set up, not the civilian Biopreparat*. Using templates from their own pre-1969 US offensive programme for comparison, they mistakenly believed the Soviets would need only a few military facilities (like Fort Detrick, Pine Bluff, and Dugway). When the US confirmed the Sverdlovsk disaster in 1979, they assumed, incorrectly, that they had spotted the main Soviet production facility. By continuing to watch the Sverdlovsk compound more closely, they felt they had the heart of the Soviet programme under surveillance. At its simplest, no one ever imagined that such huge biological warfare complexes run by such a vast organization would be required. Ironically, the so-called 'Armageddon types' who were often scolded for exaggerating the size and scope of the Soviet programme, had actually greatly underestimated it. The maximalists had been right all along to be suspicious, and Pasechnik's information began to slowly turn the tide in their favour.

The minimalists, however, wanted to ensure that there be no room for doubt about this astonishing information. Their representatives on the UNGROUP called for several corroborative sources for the Pasechnik take. Reasonably enough they could see the politics of this issue under-mining the great détente that had settled on East/West affairs. As veterans from the Reagan Administration, several UNGROUP members remem-bered the agonies of accusing the Soviets of treaty violations, like Sverdlovsk, that could not (at that time) be fully supported in public with presentable sources.[39]

'We were worried about not being able to convince people because our evidence was secret,' recalls one UNGROUP member.[40] 'There was a fear of criticism in the back of everyone's minds.'

Agreement between maximalists and minimalists developed in small stages. Firstly, there was complete accord that whatever happened next would have to be done in complete secrecy. There could be no Reagan-era bashing of Soviets. The Evil Empire was disintegrating too quickly for that.

The UNGROUP had another important reason to be cautious, to go slow, to keep things quiet and reach consensus. MacEachin was bringing them not just hot new intelligence, but, more significantly, a major foreign policy problem – which he somewhat indelicately called 'the turd in the punchbowl'.

The eight men in the room were very concerned about their obligation to inform Congress that the Soviets appeared not only to be in grave breach of the BWC, but also to be several generations down the path of offensive biological warfare. And there was nothing the US could do about it. But would Congress leak to the press? The last thing the UNGROUP wanted was public ventilation of an issue so emotional and sensitive that rational discussion might be impossible and the White House might be forced into rash action.

MacEachin stressed at the end of his briefing that this new infor-mation could not be withheld from Congress. The CIA and UNGROUP were legally required to report forthrightly to the relevant oversight committees. (It was also a major requirement for ACDA to annually inform Congress of arms control violations and compliance.)

'If the information is misused by Congress,' shrugged MacEachin, 'then they will be responsible.'[41] That settled that.

But the biggest problem by far was the very nature of future superpower relationships and the trustworthiness of Moscow's signature on arms control agreements. This was basic stuff. Could the Soviet Union ever be trusted again? Once powerful conservatives like Senator

Jesse Helms (Republican-North Carolina), chairman of the Senate Foreign Relations Committee, got hold of the Pasechnik debriefings, he would surely speak against any further arms control treaties with the deceitful nation whose word and signature were not its bond. But a world without superpower treaties was almost unthinkable.

'We knew we could not take the START (Strategic Nuclear Arms Reduction Treaty) to Senator Helms for confirmation if we had not dealt with Pasechnik,' an UNGROUP member explained. 'Senator Helms would eat us alive. He would say: "Your treaty is dead!" And all future treaties after that would be held hostage by Senator Helms.'[42]

In the end, the UNGROUP members agreed they had no choice but to tell Congress everything promptly and risk a leak. It would be catastrophic if the Congress heard about the story first from the press.[43] The advisers agreed to inform the sixteen senior Congressional members with jurisdiction. This group, the so-called 'Big Eight' from each body, included the House Speaker and Minority Leader; the Senate Majority and Minority Leaders; and the chairman and ranking minority member of the House and Senate Foreign Relations, Armed Services, and Intelligence Committees.

The Bush team, which took pride in keeping secrets, now braced itself. But the story never did leak; their fears had been unjustified.

Next, the US also had to convince the British government to acquiesce with this quiet approach. But many officials in Prime Minister Margaret Thatcher's government were urging that everything should be made public. The Prime Minister, who had read chemistry at Oxford in her student days, had been kept fully informed of Pasechnik's debriefing and was fascinated by the details he was revealing, as a scientist, a politician, and a world-ranking leader. She was also following guidance given by Sir Percy Cradock, then chairman of the Joint Intelligence Committee, who reported directly to her as foreign policy adviser. Cradock had devoted considerable time talking to Pasechnik, and came away a dedicated maximalist, convinced that strong action had to be taken to stop the Soviet programme.[44]

Inevitably, a reasonable compromise about how to proceed was reached between the US and UK leadership teams. Not everyone was happy, but it was a start.

'Thatcher actually dragged a reluctant American president into a more forceful policy,' explains a senior British official. 'If it had not been for Thatcher the chances are that, even with Pasechnik's information, there would have been no political will to see it through.'[45]

'The British were hot to get going,' recalls former State Department intelligence analyst Gary Crocker, a dedicated maximalist. 'They wanted to accuse the Soviets of violations and to shut down the Soviet programme. They were more aggressive than the US.'[46]

The compromise, given the extraordinary times, was that neither London nor Washington would publicize the Pasechnik revelations – a concession to the minimalists. However, the 'Ferment' problem would be tackled head-on (point to the maximalists) using quiet diplomacy at the top and back channel negotiations at a lower level.

Much of this strategy would have to be built on the warm, developing relationship between Baker and Shevardnadze, a relationship founded on good personal chemistry and mutual trust.

If that bond were to pull apart, or the Soviet deceptions at the highest levels continued over the BW issue, the maximalists would be proven right.

CHAPTER TWELVE

Protests

'I will consider this matter very seriously.'
Eduard Shevardnadze, 1990

By the spring of 1990, the key question in Washington and London concerning the illegal Soviet biological warfare programme was not just how to put an end to it, but, more importantly, what did Gorbachev himself and his foreign minister, Shevardnadze, know about it, and should this matter become a litmus test for the new relationship between Moscow, Washington, and London?

On 30 April 1990, the US and British Ambassadors to Moscow – Jack Matlock and Sir Curtis Keeble – took the unusual step of secretly issuing a joint démarche to the Gorbachev government, demanding an end to the Soviets' offensive BW programme.[1] The official protest from the two governments was presented to Anatoly Chernyaev, Gorbachev's senior foreign policy adviser. Secretary Baker had wanted the protest lodged before he arrived in Moscow in May for his next round of arms control discussions with Shevardnadze.

As expected, Chernyaev conceded nothing as he calmly accepted the document. He promised only that Gorbachev would look into the accusations.[2]

On 2 May, Baker's team arrived in Moscow for their four-day ministerial meeting, which included preparations for the upcoming Bush–Gorbachev summit in June. Essentially the same groups from Jackson Hole, Wyoming, had gathered again.[3] During a break in the talks, Shevardnadze decided to entertain Baker with a side trip of about forty miles to a famous fourteenth-century Russian Orthodox monastery at Zagorsk. Thousands of Soviets made pilgrimages each year to this Trinity St Sergius monastery to drink from the sacred waters. Shevardnadze planned to introduce Baker to the archbishop, and light candles in the chapel.[4] The mood was cordial, and the good chemistry showed no signs of spoiling.

Before the drive, the CIA's Douglas MacEachin, who was on Baker's team, was asked to write a short paper for Shevardnadze which laid out, in blunt, assertive language, some of the new evidence that was alluded to, but not spelled out, in the more diplomatic April démarche. MacEachin produced a carefully worded, two-page memo, based on previously approved, inter-agency guidance, which succinctly made the case that the Soviets had an active civilian and military BW programme that was producing illegal pathogens. As evidence, the document cited brief examples, with dates, of where alleged Soviet violations had occurred.[5] Behind this paper lay the knowledge of Vladimir Pasechnik. As part of the forthcoming conversation, Baker's aides also urged him to point out, forcefully, to Shevardnadze, how damaging these BW violations would be to US-Soviet relations and to Congressional approval of all future treaties.

During the drive, while they were alone together in the back of a black ZIL limousine, Baker confronted Shevardnadze with the very sensitive paper.[6] After reading the document, Shevardnadze appeared genuinely shocked. He finally replied, in the present tense, that he 'didn't think they could be doing this'. Baker presumed this reply was carefully crafted language. Shevardnadze did not say: 'We did not do this.' The conversation ended with Shevardnadze promising to elucidate more information and give it to the Secretary of State as soon as possible.[7]

Baker left Moscow with the significant impression that Shevardnadze had appeared 'distracted' during their meetings. Baker later wrote that they were 'going nowhere slowly' on arms control and that Shevardnadze 'seemed unwilling to make decisions or show initiative, as he had done in the past'.[8] Baker also noted, with considerable prescience: 'The military now seemed in charge of arms control.'[9]

In fact, it's now known that after the 30 April joint British/American démarche was received, General Yuriy Kalinin, the director of Biopreparat, was asked to prepare a confidential response for the Kremlin. After several working sessions with his staff to anticipate how much the West already knew, Kalinin decided to continue the bluffing. The reply would fully reject all accusations.

His one-page memorandum to Gorbachev's office stated, in essence, that the USSR was not in breach of the BWC, and that the nation possessed only a defensive biological programme, which involved *inter alia* working on vaccines and testing defensive equipment.[10] It was the Big Lie, now told with a straight face by the Soviet military to its own new political masters.

Kalinin's position was fully supported by other, even more powerful hard-line generals who controlled the BW programme in the Ministry of Defence, including General Vladimir Lebedinskiy and General Valentin Yevstigneev.[11] They, in turn, were backed at the very top by the Minister of Defence, Marshal Dmitry Yazov.[12] *Pace* Pasechnik, this lie was to become the template for all future responses from the Soviet military to any inquiries about their offensive BW programme, whether it came from the West or from their own civilian leadership in the Kremlin.

Neither Washington nor London needed an analytical genius to establish the position of the Soviet military establishment. What remained puzzling, however, was the original question of just what the Kremlin political establishment was being told by its generals. Just what did Gorbachev and his wily Georgian Foreign Minister really know about these serious BWC breaches?

'Frankly, the US did not know what Gorbachev and Shevardnadze were hearing behind the scenes in their own government,' recalls a former State Department official. 'Initially, in 1990, it seemed that Gorbachev and Shevardnadze were lying to us. We believed they knew about the BW programme. But we were guessing.'[13]

Sir Percy Cradock, then chairman of Britain's Joint Intelligence Committee, had no doubt that Gorbachev knew about 'Ferment'. 'He may not have known the detail,' Cradock explains, 'but he would certainly have known the broad extent of the programme. And, yes, he knew the Soviets were cheating, and he lied to the West about it.'[14]

Sir Percy, through whose hands went the most secret intelligence analyses of Moscow's activities at that time, is adamant that 'the scale of the Soviet biological programme was such that it could not possibly have been seen as defensive by Gorbachev'. 'Remember,' he stresses, 'Gorbachev was a patriotic Russian – he knew he was the West's blue-eyed boy and he reckoned he could get away with it.'

And Shevardnadze? 'He may not have known everything,' concedes

Sir Percy. 'He may have been more on the fringes and did not sit on the right committees.'[15]

Some US officials hold a contrary view that is more sympathetic to Gorbachev. They have revised their personal opinions of what was happening in Moscow in 1990 based on new evidence obtained long after the USSR collapsed – from defectors and high-level government sources in Russia. They now believe that Gorbachev, in part, and, more so, Shevardnadze were actually strong opponents of the Russian military, and they were genuinely taken aback by the extent of the BW programme when they tried to look into it.[16]

The Soviet military tried to sell the BW programme to Gorbachev, according to the revised view, by arguing, in part, that it was needed to defend their homeland against 'the Chinese threat'. The Soviet generals claimed that this 'defensive' BW programme was the Soviet 'equalizer' which would prevent millions of Chinese soldiers from invading across the USSR's southern border. For many years, the Soviet military had stressed this same argument to the Kremlin – that the threat to their national security was not just the US and NATO to the west and east, but China to the south.[17]

Certainly, as of 1998, Ambassador Jack Matlock, the former US envoy to Moscow, was still not sure what Gorbachev actually knew in 1990. 'From their behaviour,' Matlock recalls, 'I think the people at the top probably did not know everything. There is plenty of evidence that shows these people were not able to get the information they wanted, because the system was so secret and the political authorities had so little control over the military and KGB. And they had no reliable way to check up on the information they did get.'[18]

The US government has also learned that Gorbachev *did* try to take some actions to curb the BW programme – but these steps went undetected or unappreciated in the West, and later were secretly undermined by the Soviet military. For instance, on 5 May 1990, immediately after the US/UK démarche and Baker's paper to Shevardnadze, Gorbachev issued an unpublicized decree that closed down and forbade further testing of BW agents. Work at some test chambers was halted as a result.[19] But military hardliners, led as ever by General Kalinin and his more senior backers, cleverly revised the document by adding a crucial caveat to an addendum, which allowed Biopreparat to continue its work under 'special circumstances'. This brief addition, apparently unnoticed by Gorbachev, meant that Biopreparat would maintain its 'mobilization preparedness' functions under a new organization outside its previous chain of command. The bottom line was that most of the BW work continued as before. Now, it was just better hidden from the civilian leadership.[20]

The next meetings between Soviet, American, and British heads of state took place in early June 1990. First, President Bush and Gorbachev met in Washington. Then, Prime Minister Thatcher and Gorbachev met in Moscow a week later. The US and UK had assumed a 'good cop/bad cop' strategy in dealing with Gorbachev. Bush and Secretary Baker would play the low-key role, trying to coax cooperation; Thatcher and her senior aides would be tougher and more forthright.[21]

Starting on 1 June, the mood was as warm as the weather when Bush and Gorbachev met for three days in Washington (only Gorbachev's second-ever summit there). The two leaders declared a new era of superpower cooperation. Bush publicly praised Gorbachev as an agent of change; Gorbachev stressed perestroika as the 'pivotal point of world politics'.[22]

In private, however, Bush raised the issue of Soviet non-compliance with the BWC. Gorbachev responded that the USSR was ready to answer the US/UK questions – and put to rest all concerns – but first he needed time to collect more information and personally question the responsible Soviet officials.[23] Speaking about all strategic weapons, Gorbachev told Bush: 'We won't use our weapons against the United States.' He asked Bush to 'trust' him.[24] Bush did not press Gorbachev on the BW issue because of all the other important world concerns on their agenda.[25]

The summit ended memorably at Camp David when Gorbachev scored a direct hit with a horseshoe on his first try and was photographed driving a golf cart with Bush. The images were a distinct change from the frozen face, aching gait, and dead hand of Brezhnev. Gorbachev then flew on to inspect American businesses in Minneapolis-St Paul and San Francisco.

But, at home, his political situation was weakening. Four days earlier, on 29 May, as Gorbachev was leaving for the summit, his emerging political rival, Boris Yeltsin, was elected chairman of the Russian parliament.[26]

*

On 8 June, Prime Minister Thatcher, in her tough-cop role, bluntly asked Gorbachev if the Soviets were or were not making new biological weapons as Pasechnik alleged.[27] 'Are you hiding secret research to develop weapons of mass destruction?' she further demanded.[28] The Prime Minister quietly threatened to put Pasechnik on international television if Gorbachev didn't cooperate and stop the programme. The General Secretary replied that the Soviets had no programmes to develop BW or toxins. He repeated his pledge to question the military officials in charge.[29]

Gorbachev's denial was his first substantive comment on biological warfare since the April démarche. In London and Washington, his response was taken as might be expected – with predictable fears that he was lying, by the maximalists, and with continued urging for caution, by the minimalists. The truth is no one was sure. Nor was there a good answer for the West, since either Gorbachev could not be trusted, or a superpower's leader did not have control of his own military.[30]

While the CIA pushed harder to establish how much Gorbachev actually knew, the case against Foreign Minister Shevardnadze appeared to be more damning. One piece of evidence looked grim. British officials learned from Pasechnik that, in Gorbachev's absence, Shevardnadze had chaired a high-level Kremlin meeting in 1988 during which Biopreparat's future programmes and budgets were approved. Pasechnik learned about this meeting, he said, from General Kalinin, who had also attended.[31]

As if this was not enough in itself, Pasechnik's information appeared to be supported by a new human source in Moscow whom the US had recently recruited and developed. This new informant confirmed that Shevardnadze had personally approved the allocation of funds for Biopreparat for 1991. If true, it meant that the decision had been made in 1990 – that very year![32] It now looked bleak for Shevardnadze's trustworthiness, for he had stood by silently in Moscow when Gorbachev had issued his denial of offensive biological warfare activities right to Mrs Thatcher's face.

The raw intelligence reports from the new American source were handed to Secretary Baker on special 'blue border' paper, which designates secret HUMINT. After Baker read these reports, the normally composed and affable Texas lawyer flashed his rarely seen but formidable temper. Baker was inconsolably furious at what he saw as a betrayal by his new-found Soviet counterpart whose friendship and trust were playing such an important part in the new superpower dialogue. If Pasechnik and the new HUMINT source were speaking the truth, then Shevardnadze had deliberately lied to Western leaders about the Soviet BW programme. The implications were grave, and, for a while, even hardliners tried to see another side.

'We tried to rationalize that report about Shevardnadze,' Robert Gates recalls. 'We thought it might be something he had not paid any attention to, and that he did not know the details about it.'[33]

But that view simply led Washington and London down a new and equally dangerous path. If Shevardnadze said the Soviet programme didn't exist, or he didn't know about it, or he couldn't get the information, then it meant he was probably powerless to turn it off.

Ultimately, the evidence in hand forced the US and the British to conclude that Shevardnadze, at the very least, had full knowledge that the BW programme existed.

But even if Shevardnadze had been caught with his hand in the till, it would not be easy publicly to accuse and punish him. Baker understood full well that the penalty for embarrassing the Soviet minister could be a new chill or even freeze just at the moment when Shevardnadze's role in helping bring the Cold War to a peaceful conclusion had become so critical.

'Baker was angry because he felt he had been lied to,' Gates confirms. 'But he also felt all other arms control issues could still be jeopardized.'[34]

The US strategy of 'quiet diplomacy' now hung in the balance as Baker assessed the three key pieces of evidence he was holding: 1) Pasechnik's accusation that Shevardnadze – and presumably Gorbachev – had approved the ongoing funding for the BW programme; 2) Gorbachev's denial to Thatcher; and 3) a new source alleging Shevardnadze's approval of the 1991 budget.

In fact, in recent years as the full truth has slowly emerged, with hindsight and fresh knowledge and brand-new sources, it seems that Baker and his staff were not, at that stage, seeing the full picture, and, what they did see, they may have inadvertently misread.

New evidence, obtained by the US and UK governments from sources in Russia during the years since Gorbachev and Shevardnadze left office, strongly suggests that Shevardnadze had indeed attended meetings where senior military officials, including General Kalinin, made presentations about the BW programme. These meetings – which the

CIA and Secretary Baker had viewed as so damning to Shevardnadze – were actually attempts by the Foreign Minister to find out what was going on in his own government. He was trying to determine where the money was being spent. It had been Ministry of Defence policy to keep from Shevardnadze and his Foreign Ministry any real details of how the offensive biological warfare programme was being handled. He was *not* approving the programme, but nor did he have any means to influence it.[35]

'The Soviet leadership – Shevardnadze and Gorbachev – did not know in detail what the Soviet military was really doing about the BW programme,' explains a former State Department officer. 'Former officials in the Soviet Foreign Ministry – who served under Shevardnadze and were themselves opposed to the BW programme – have since told us: "You people didn't understand what Gorbachev and Shevardnadze were trying to do." '[36]

In 1990, however, the Bush Administration, still steeped in Cold War doubts, could only guess at Shevardnadze's motives. After a full review of what looked like damning evidence, Baker concluded that he would need to confront Shevardnadze face-to-face during their next scheduled meeting.[37]

The showdown between the superpower foreign ministers took place on 1 August 1990, when Baker and Shevardnadze met at Irkutsk, an industrial centre of about 600,000 people in southern Siberia. Between their work sessions to prepare for the next Bush–Gorbachev summit, Shevardnadze sought to repay the hospitality that Baker showed him ten months earlier at Jackson Hole, Wyoming; so both men took a hydrofoil up the Angara River to nearby Lake Baikal, the largest (by volume) and deepest body of fresh water in the world. They then enjoyed a relaxed dinner at a rustic fishing lodge.[38]

Finally, when it came to the prickly subject of the Soviet Union's alleged BWC violations, Shevardnadze began by responding to a jointly prepared US/UK memorandum that Baker had given him in Paris in mid-July. That note – a written follow-up to the Bush and Thatcher summits with Gorbachev – had described the West's concerns about the illegal Soviet programme in greater detail than the previous démarches. The US/UK memorandum had included sharply focused questions on four specific Biopreparat research centres built after the 1972 BWC had been signed: 1) Lyubchany, a site run by the Ministry of Health, south of Moscow; 2) Obolensk, a large complex southeast of Moscow; 3) Kol'tsovo, a huge institute in Siberia known as Vektor; and 4) Leningrad, which was Pasechnik's former laboratory.[39]

Shevardnadze produced a document which he said was the formal response to all the Western allegations about Soviet BWC breaches, including the Paris Memorandum, summit meeting conversations, and the démarche. The Soviet document, he explained, had been prepared and approved by the senior Soviet political leadership, after a full review of the issues. As Baker and his aides studied the Soviet paper, they could see that on the face of it, the reply merely reiterated the military's previous hard-line denials. But at the end of the document, there was something excitingly new.

For the first time, the Soviets were offering a conciliatory, and very unmilitary-like, glimmer of hope. The document proposed that there should be steps taken to build confidence that the USSR really was abiding by the BWC. Then, surprisingly, Shevardnadze offered the United States and United Kingdom the chance to have their own inspectors visit the four Biopreparat sites in question. Even more remarkable, the Soviet Foreign Minister expressed his willingness to allow American scientists to work at those four facilities, effectively to serve as observers in place.

The energetic Georgian had not yet given it a name, but he had launched what was to become known as 'The Trilateral Process', a revolutionary system involving the USSR, the US, and the UK in a procedure for arms control verification that had the potential to change the face of history. The prospect of the Soviet Union actually inviting Western experts into its most secret scientific institutions was mouth-watering.[40]

Baker's initial response was deliberately low key. He recognized the significance of the inspection offer, but he was still concerned at the substantive denials that Moscow was running a covert offensive biological warfare programme in defiance of the treaty. Privately, he was also much exercised about Shevardnadze's own possible complicity.

Having read Shevardnadze's document and retained a non-committal view about it, Baker decided he still needed to confront his opposite number privately about the nagging BW concerns. He waited until the two of them were again alone inside the black ZIL limousine.[41] His aides had prepared a one-page paper laying out the essence of the case against

Shevardnadze. Both the note, indeed the whole scenario, had been carefully orchestrated, with President Bush's approval.

When Baker handed Shevardnadze the paper, he watched the Soviet Minister's face intently to gauge his reaction. Shevardnadze went pale. He did not launch into an immediate refutation. Baker made some personal comments about his disappointment with Shevardnadze for having denied these matters to Mrs Thatcher.[42]

'I will consider this matter very seriously,' Shevardnadze said, as he folded up Baker's paper and put it in his pocket.

Baker let it go at that. He had made his point. Not only had the Soviet Minister now offered a potentially breakthrough inspection procedure, but, even as they rode in the heavy Soviet limousine, new and pressing world events were overtaking the BW issue. Coincidentally, during that same car ride, Baker informed Shevardnadze that he had just received word from Washington that Saddam Hussein's army had invaded Kuwait. Although details were sketchy and Shevardnadze initially did not believe that Saddam had behaved so recklessly, the shrewd American already realized that the Western allies would need the support of the Soviet government in their effort to reverse Iraq's actions.

On 11 September, one month after Irkutsk at a meeting in Paris, Secretary Baker gave Shevardnadze an encouraging written response to the Soviet proposal for inspections and placement of scientists. Suddenly, the new buzzword was 'transparency'.

The US said that the Soviet plan, depending on the details, could offer a constructive approach to the whole BW problem. The Americans now produced a series of proposed guidelines for the Soviets, which would increase openness and build confidence in the new trilateral procedure. These basic principles of conduct included: a full description in advance of the organizational structure, research programmes, and personnel at each facility; access to the entire facility, including the insides of all buildings, laboratories, and bunkers; interviews with any staff scientists or technicians; access to financial records; and sampling and photography permitted where necessary and mutually agreed.[43] This plan was intended to be the template for the future, a system that would try to forge a compromise between two opposing cultures – one secretive, paranoid, suspicious, and hurt; the other open, naïve, over-trusting, and over-exuberant.

Assuming these ground rules would be adopted and adhered to, the Americans were ready to start visits to the USSR by November. They would want to devote a minimum of three days to each site. Washington also placed the Soviets on notice with requests for inspections to seven additional Soviet BW facilities (beyond the original four). The new ones included three production plants – at Stepnogorsk, Berdsk, and Omutninsk; two military sites – at Zagorsk and Kirov; the outdoor test site at Vozrozhdeniye Island; and a biological equipment design plant in Moscow.[44]

Three days later, London too was on board following bilateral talks in Moscow between British Foreign Secretary Douglas Hurd and Shevardnadze.[45]

Inevitably, perhaps, the Soviet Ministry of Defence now uncoiled in all its wrath. The Soviet military had never accepted the Shevardnadze plan for the inspections and quietly urged the Foreign Ministry to slow down. In fact, they were anxious to kill the whole idea of visits. Failing that, the Ministry of Defence wanted to stall the visits as long as possible and impede the effectiveness of the inspectors.[46] They began an extensive foot-dragging operation, allowing Biopreparat more time to deal appropriately with any incriminating evidence at the sites. Openness was not to be interpreted too literally.

As a quid pro quo, the Generals also demanded equal inspection rights at the US military's biological facilities. They demanded access to Fort Detrick, Dugway, and Pine Bluff – in early 1991, after the first round of visits to the USSR were completed. At first, the Americans cavilled at this suggestion, pointing out that they were not, nor had they ever been, accused of BWC treaty violations.

By 8 November, however, a basic compromise agreement had been ironed out which called for a two-step process. First, a US/UK team would visit several pre-designated 'suspect' Soviet sites starting on 28 November. Then, later, as a face-saving gesture, a comparable Soviet team would visit several US facilities. But since these American sites were all legal, defensive facilities – fully abiding by the BWC guidelines – the stated purpose would be to show the Soviets how offensive programmes could be dismantled and/or converted to commercial and/or non-harmful uses. In diplomatic language, the Soviet visit to the US would not be based on a 'correspondence of concerns'.[47]

In the rush to move forward, the US/UK diplomats chose to finesse any other problems that might develop given this unique procedure. It was assumed that the Soviets would play by the Marquis of Queensberry rules and abide by the principles of conduct that Baker had proposed – which allowed full disclosure, unimpeded access, and flexibility. Ominously, as of early November, however, the Soviets were still raising nagging new questions about those conditions, which remained unresolved.[48]

In the enervating spirit of the times, the West dispensed with the dotting of the i's and the crossing of the t's in order to launch a radical new approach to arms control, at the end of which the almost uncontrollable genie of biological weapons would be corked forever in its safe and transparent bottle.

CHAPTER THIRTEEN

Inspection

'I had never seen anything like this before.'
Dr Frank Malinoski, 1998

On 8 January 1991, very early on a dark, freezing and gloomy Moscow morning, an ancient bus containing British and American inspectors and their Soviet minders was heading out of the city when suddenly there was a loud boom and the driver screeched on his brakes as the front windshield shattered. The driver, covered in glass fragments, managed to bring the hurtling vehicle to a stop. Before a replacement bus could be summoned at a police roadside box further on, the entire windshield had to be knocked out. The little heat from the bus escaped and a bitterly cold, sub-zero wind now whipped into the vehicle. The driver was forced to bundle himself inside three coats just to survive. As the coach picked up speed, the shivering passengers, one by one, retired to the rear to avoid the icy blast. Within a few miles, Americans, British, and Soviets swapped decorum and political differences for one huge, snug, Cold War embrace to share each other's body heat.

It was an eerie, symbolic gesture for the first hours, of the first day, of the first ever inspection of the USSR's biological warfare plants.

Much had happened in the previous months after Baker and Shevardnadze had agreed to the opening of the trilateral process. Only three weeks before the first trip, Foreign Minister Eduard Shevardnadze stunned the world by resigning his post as 'a protest against the onset of dictatorship'.[1] Ominously, he warned the Soviet Union that it was returning to its terrible past, with reactionaries gaining power and reformers scattered. He was to explain later that he had been under severe pressure from the military and had received no support from Gorbachev.

The General Secretary was indeed under pressure and preparing to use force to put down uprisings in the Baltics. Needing the army's support, Gorbachev swung towards the conservative forces in his government, including Defence Minister Dmitry Yazov and KGB chief Vladimir Krychkov, the very men who were secretly plotting to oust him.[2]

Shevardnadze's sudden exit and Gorbachev's reaction was to be a setback for all US–Soviet relations, including the BW negotiations.

On the biological warfare issue, there had been negative movement since the Irkutsk meeting. General Valentin Yevstigneev, head of the Soviet military's offensive BW programme, and General Yuriy Kalinin, head of Biopreparat, had plotted endlessly to frustrate the inspections. Senior scientists involved in the project supported Kalinin since they knew they'd be out of work once the true nature of their tasks was uncovered by the Western inspectors.[3] Kalinin was unable to countermand the Kremlin's decision to allow the inspections and realized his best option was to sanitize the facilities and disguise the true BW programme. His greatest fear was that he might be forced to show the West his huge BW production facilities at Berdsk, Pokrov, Omutninsk, and Stepnogorsk. He was only too aware that once these sites were inspected the game would be up. If the inspectors were restricted to laboratory tours then he would be safe, since his team would be able to argue endlessly about the true nature of the work inside. Kalinin was lucky that Shevardnadze had been powerless to override military objections and open up these give-away sites. It was Gorbachev who took the final decisions and he relied on the advice of Generals Yevstigneev and Kalinin.[4]

Washington and London, unaware of the machinations in Moscow, prepared the joint team for the historic visit. A senior ACDA official, Edward Lacey, was placed in charge of the field investigation.[5] Lacey, a broad-shouldered six-footer with thinning hair and sharp, blue-grey eyes carried the confidence of the West's arms control community. He was a former CIA analyst specializing in Soviet nuclear weapons, and a year earlier had been named by President Bush to be Deputy Assistant Director for Verification and Intelligence at ACDA.

The thirteen-member US/UK delegation included specialists from the State Department, CIA, MI6, DIA, (British) Defence Intelligence

Staff, Fort Detrick, and two translators. Co-leader of the delegation was Peter Davies, head of the Arms Control Department of the Foreign and Commonwealth Office, and he was supported by two senior British specialists (who had helped MI6 debrief Pasechnik), Dr David Kelly, the ubiquitous Biological Warfare Adviser to Porton Down, and Dr Chris Davis, a Royal Navy Surgeon-Commander in charge of the Biological Warfare Desk of the Defence Intelligence Staff. The mission was so heavily classified that one specialist, Dr Frank Malinoski, the team's physician and representative from the US Army Medical Research Institute of Infectious Diseases (USAMRIID) at Fort Detrick, was told he could not even tell his family where he was going.

There were prolonged delays throughout November and December caused by wrangling in London with their Soviet hosts, led by Nikita Smidovich, a veteran arms control negotiator. The good news was that the delays gave the team time to review all of the new ground rules and their objectives for the trip. The experts would be looking for certain tell-tale 'offensive' signs: excessive production capacity for bio-agents; aerosol and explosive test chambers; BL-4 laboratories (the maximum safety and security level biological and viral containment facilities); research with large primates; unusual security precautions; and military connections to civilian sites.[6] The visitors were especially determined to find out who commissioned and paid for all of the work.[7]

At its simplest, they wanted to see and record anything and every-thing, and they wanted to go in and out of every room in every building. Even though they had the Pasechnik 'take', they knew that trained experts can tell much more by eyeballing. There would also be sharp and pointed questions to officials and workers at the sites. It had been agreed they could not take any photos inside the facilities unless a Soviet official used the camera for them.

Finally, on 6 January, the team flew to Moscow – and two mornings later began with the first awful bus ride.

The first site on their tour was the smallest and least significant of the four destinations. The Institute of Immunology in Lyubchany (near the town of Chekov) was (to have been) a relatively short drive outside of Moscow. When they finally arrived at the institute, they found one of Biopreparat's key centres for producing defensive medications to treat BW agents, including vaccines for Plague, anthrax, and Tularaemia.

It was here that they met the Deputy Director of Biopreparat, Dr

Kanatjan Alibekov, who would be the most senior technical official to accompany them on the tour. General Kalinin, Alibekov's boss, was nowhere to be seen.[8] (Kalinin was the invisible man of the Soviet BW programme; never attending meetings with the West, inaccessible on the phone, a man whose presence was spiritually overwhelming, but physically remote.)

The forty-year-old Alibekov, a military-trained medical microbiologist, had a soft-spoken, engaging but unassuming manner for the enormous power and prestige he wielded within the vast Biopreparat organization. Originally from Kazakhstan, he was a short, well-built man with thick black hair, a dark complexion, and Asian features. As Biopreparat's Science and Technical Director, he was in charge of all of the system's equipment and facilities. It was a fact of life in the USSR at that time that a non-Russian had to possess extraordinary qualifications to be promoted that far to the top of a covert national security programme.

Alibekov wore the same drab brown, pullover sweater every day, in contrast to other senior Soviet officials who always dressed more formally in proper coats and ties. But despite his distinctive sartorial style, the visitors marked Alibekov as clearly the most knowledgeable and impressive of all the Soviets they met on the entire trip.

'Alibekov seemed to know everything about all of their facilities and programmes,' Malinoski recalls. 'He had intellect, access to everything, and seemed to know more about production of biological agents than even experts in the West. There was never a question he couldn't answer.'[9]

What the inspectors did not know was that beyond his strong scientific background, Alibekov was also Kalinin's 'fixer' on the trip, whose job it was to implement Kalinin's complex cover-up strategy for the whole tour.[10] Firstly, Alibekov orchestrated a pattern of constant delay (although the bus incident had not been a part of it).

Constant tension developed because the visiting team always wanted to start early (i.e. before 8 a.m.), push on faster, ignore set meals, and work longer hours to see as much as possible. The Soviets, however, repeatedly (and deliberately) complained about the gruelling pace. They wanted to start each day later, take leisurely meals, and knock off earlier. As the suspicious Westerners encountered each new endless and pointless lecture, logistical problem, or travel delay, it soon became obvious what the Kalinin plan was.[11]

In fact, we now know that General Kalinin had given top-secret instructions to Alibekov and the rest of the Biopreparat team to employ shortened workdays and continual delays throughout the tour. This deliberate strategy included forcing the visitors to endure as many long speeches and boring briefings as possible on mundane topics like science and safety – any device was to be employed to limit access time at the laboratory buildings. The plan was that the hell of boredom would be assuaged by the heaven of post-briefing cognac and vodkas – large ones, and frequently, to help keep the visitors' minds off the matters at hand.[12]

The delays made a very tense atmosphere even more stressful.[13] As the first Westerners ever to visit these facilities, the team members were suddenly confronting Soviet officials who had worked for decades on a secret offensive programme. These Soviets knew they were about to be challenged by foreigners walking all over *their* turf and demanding plausible explanations for illegal activities.[14] This was not how the old Soviet Union had been run.

In fact, the first two days at the heavily sanitized, nearly deserted institute in Lyubchany were relatively uneventful and unforthcoming – as the Soviet cover-up strategy worked well. The visitors' only findings, from persistent interviews, were that the Ministry of Defence financed 40 per cent of the institute's work, which supported research at Obolensk.[15]

The team next began their visit to Obolensk on 10 January. The All-Union Scientific Research Institute for Applied Microbiology, built under a Communist Party Central Committee decree in 1974, was located about 40 miles southeast of Moscow. During the Cold War, Obolensk had been a closed city – no Westerners allowed. The visitors would soon find out why.

Obolensk had originally been chosen to visit because Pasechnik said it was an important Biopreparat facility, with sophisticated equipment, where the Soviets were researching deadly organisms for offensive purposes, especially Plague and anthrax, but also Tularaemia, Brucellosis, and glanders. All the analysts in Washington could tell from satellite photos was that Obolensk was indeed a huge complex.[16]

They came across it half-hidden among pine forests groaning under the weight of snow. The thirty-building site was enormous, and from the ground it seemed even bigger to the visitors than the overhead photos had indicated. They estimated it was about ten times the size of

USAMRIID headquarters in Maryland; what's more, Fort Detrick did not have razor-wire fences around the perimeter. Oddly, the whole place seemed deserted, even though a 4,000-person staff normally worked there, including about 800 scientists.[17]

Dr Nikolai Nikolaevich Urakov, the facility director since 1986, was a natural leader, an army general who had been deputy director of the military's secret BW facility at Kirov. A tall, gaunt, grey-haired man, Urakov gave an opening presentation, welcoming the first Westerners ever to visit the facility and setting down the ground rules. He explained that his laboratories were only developing defensive methods (particularly vaccines) to fight anthrax and Tularaemia.

Urakov's long and time-consuming speech was followed by a get-acquainted bus tour of the facility – which allowed for only a preliminary assessment of the site. That was the first day, largely wasted. Afterwards, everyone returned to the administration building to plan the second day. There was too much to see in the remaining time so the visitors broke into three sub-teams when they returned – and even then they had to omit many rooms. Everyone concentrated on their own responsibilities based on the planned requirements.

The British sub-team's priority was to penetrate Obolensk's explosive test chamber, where, Pasechnik warned, the Soviets had simulated detonations of BW munitions carrying Plague and Tularaemia. Off to one side of the chamber, he advised, was a long tube-like chamber where they could place animals to expose them to the aerosols.[18]

The importance of finding an explosive test chamber was that its existence would be highly indicative of the existence of an illegal offensive BW programme. The ability to detonate bacteria-filled bomblets so that the pathogens are not themselves immolated in the explosion is one of the great challenges of BW bomb-making. It would be nigh impossible to have an explosive test chamber without tell-tale pitting on the walls.[19]

As soon as the British group asked to be taken to the chamber, the Soviets nervously resorted to a series of evasions.[20] At first, they claimed they were unaware of the building (in the hope that the British didn't know either). But that excuse collapsed when a British inspector pulled a map from his pocket and helpfully showed the Soviets where the chamber was located deep inside a maze of buildings. Then there was some theatre about a lost key and more Monty Pythonesque farce until it slowly dawned on the hosts that the British had very detailed information – it could only have come via Pasechnik – and, given the rules of the game, they wouldn't be deterred.[21]

The tension couldn't have been greater on both sides as they finally stepped inside.

Dr Chris Davis of the Royal Navy, who led the way for the British group, is a gimlet-eyed defence analyst, with a steel trap for a brain; he tolerates fools poorly and is an old-fashioned patriot. His forthright, slightly confrontational style did not always go down well with the Soviets, or, on occasions, the minimalist tendency on his own side, but character is fate with men like Davis. For any diplomatic *faux pas*, the young intelligence officer made up with a ruthless determination to stand his ground and play by, and to the very limits of, the agreed rules.

What happened next between Davis and his Soviet minder – the first major confrontation of the trip – was intensified by Cold War mistrust, real cultural differences, and, embarrassingly, some unfamiliarity by the Soviets with Western technology.[22]

When Davis and his group finally stepped inside the window-less, eight-sided, steel chamber, they were brimming with anticipation at having finally reached their target. Then, suddenly, the lights dimmed and the chamber was plunged into darkness. In the confusion, Davis was showered with Soviet excuses for the untimely 'accident' – a bulb had blown, a switch had failed, there was a power cut-off . . . shoulders were shrugged . . . these things happen.

Smartly, a colleague handed Davis a small, steel Maglite flashlight. Davis switched it on.[23] His Soviet minder, a senior scientist at Obolensk, was startled. The man had never left the USSR and had never seen such a device before. He immediately suspected it was some kind of exotic spying equipment, perhaps a digitized, miniature, and very sophisticated electronic sampler. According to the previously agreed trip guidelines, the visitors could not use any kind of 'electronic' equipment without prior Soviet consent. The minder promptly grabbed Davis's left wrist in a vice-like grip.[24]

'That is prohibited,' the Soviet protested. 'Switch that off or give it to me.'

'Please take your hand off me,' Davis replied.

'No electronic devices!' the burly Soviet minder shouted as he grappled for the light.

'Will you please ask this gentleman to remove his arm from mine,' Davis asked the translator. 'We are on an official diplomatic mission sanctioned by your president. This is not the way to behave.'[25]

A tense and ugly face-off ensued. Davis stood his ground, held on to the flashlight and was prepared to wait indefinitely, knowing the Soviet minder had made a big mistake in laying hands on him. The Soviet scientist was finally persuaded that the flashlight was only a flashlight and not something from Q's laboratory for 007. But the minder would not immediately back down for fear of how his superiors would regard this gaffe.

Finally, light, sanity, and *amour propre* were restored in equal parts. Davis and his colleagues were at last able to examine the tell-tale marks of explosions on the submarine-like door to the test chamber. The double thickness door, with lighter-weight steel on the inside, was, as the Brits had guessed, very heavily dented.[26]

'What are these dents all over the door?' Davis asked his escorts. 'How did that happen?' It was Monty Python time again.

'Er ... a workman using a hammer damaged the door while installing it,' came the unblinking response.[27]

When David Kelly asked why he could see 'evidence of shrapnel within the chamber', the Soviets insisted it was just 'natural wear and tear' and 'metal fatigue'.[28]

It was all lies.[29]

'It would have been laughable, had not the whole thing been so serious,' Davis recalls.[30]

Now, for the first time, fully qualified and authorized Western inspectors had seen with their own eyes what had been suspected for so long. Here was the first-hand evidence of a covert programme. It was, in a small way, an historic moment for arms control.

From the sublime to the slightly ridiculous, Lacey and the British were upset that Davis had been physically restrained. But before Lacey could complain, the Soviet team leader, the crafty Nikita Smidovich, got his blow in first with a formal objection about Chris Davis.[31] He complained that Davis had broken the rules by using an 'unauthorized electronic device' – since the flashlight was battery-powered. It was a neat twist, technically correct, and diplomatically a face-saver by the Soviets.

'We found it difficult not to laugh at the sheer absurdity of it all,' Davis recalls.[32]

As it turned out, no Soviet ever again attempted to restrain an inspector.[33] What really mattered now was that the dogs had seen the rabbit. And the tour was still young.

'The explosive test-chamber incident convinced us,' Malinoski recalls, 'that we were getting close to areas the Soviets didn't want us to see. It just made us more suspicious.'[34]

The visitors next went to their final stop at Obolensk, the main research centre – named Corpus One (or 'Building One' in Russian). This huge, eight-storey building was one of the world's largest bio-laboratories, with one and a half million square feet of floor space. Corpus One covered five acres by itself, surrounded by security that included triple razor-wire fences, ground vibration sensors, infrared detectors, and armed guards.[35]

Inside the building there were the Soviets' highest containment laboratories, built like boxes within boxes for extra protection. The Soviet scientists were very proud of this sophisticated layout and their special safety equipment. Different bacterial agents – including Plague, Tularaemia, anthrax, glanders, and melioidosis – were studied on each of the first five floors. Between each floor of working laboratories was a separating 'infrastructure' floor that hid all the tubes, piping, wiring, and other special equipment. The visiting team wanted to walk through each laboratory, but the Soviets arbitrarily restricted them to just one area on one floor of the building, which severely limited what could be seen.

Only David Kelly, who donned a Soviet AP5 special protective suit, was allowed inside one part of the BL-4 section.[36] Unexpectedly, Malinoski, who was designated to accompany Kelly, was denied entrance to the 'hot zone' at the last minute. A female Soviet physician politely insisted that he was ill with a 'red throat'. No one carrying an infection, she said, was allowed into the laboratory. Malinoski, a doctor, felt fine and knew he was not ill. He and the team leaders complained vigorously, but their hosts were inflexible.[37]

'These are our procedures,' Urakov declared.

The expert American virologist was livid. Malinoski had come 5,000 miles and now was being excluded from the one place he really wanted to inspect. But his skills were too well known to the Soviets, and, using a pretext which they believed they might just get away with, they left him to peer through the windows and portals of the outer wall of the laboratory.[38]

'I was completely healthy,' Malinoski recalls. 'The Soviets were exerting control and limiting our access. It meant one less set of eyes and ears in their laboratory.'

Corpus One also had extensive testing facilities for small animals, like rodents, rabbits, and guinea pigs. Up to ten cages could be hooked up to one central aerosol generator via a series of stainless-steel tubes and connecting pipes. The multi-port generator could pump test germs through ceiling vents into enclosed cages, where the experimental animals were tethered to the floor.

The focus of Corpus One's research was allegedly defensive work on Plague. But Pasechnik had strongly warned the team in London that in fact the Soviets were *designing* Plague that could be used in strategic biological warfare weapons. He added they were also trying to genetically engineer highly contagious strains of Plague that were resistant to all known antibiotics, ultra-violet light, and nuclear radiation – so the bacteria could even survive a nuclear explosion.[39]

Significantly, inside several laboratories the visitors did indeed find that the Obolensk scientists were developing plasmids, on a 'pilot' scale, to manipulate the genes of Plague and anthrax.[40] As further evidence of offensive BW work the inspectors were astonished to see numerous giant fermenters inside Corpus One – four of them were twenty feet tall with a 10,000-litre-plus capacity. Since these commercial-size vessels were mounted *inside* the BL-4 containment, they were clearly used to grow deadly bacteria in very substantial quantities. The Soviets admitted that each floor of Corpus One could make 900 litres of a given biological agent per week.[41] Why on earth, wondered the visitors, would the Soviets need such enormous production capacity for legitimate defensive work?

When challenged, Dr Urakov claimed he only developing defences against Plague for peaceful purposes, because outbreaks of the bacteria were a major, recurring problem in the USSR. They needed active research and surveillance of these diseases, he said, because they faced strains that the US and Europe had not encountered.[42] The excuse was seen as nonsense. The entire USSR had suffered some ten Plague cases per annum. Furthermore, endemic and localized outbreaks of Plague can be controlled with antibiotics like tetracycline and streptomycin – both readily available in the Soviet Union. The real defence against the natural spread of Plague was not to embark on a programme like Urakov's – but to employ more rat catchers throughout the Soviet Union.

Suspicions merely hardened when Urakov adamantly refused to allow Kelly, or any of the others, to visit the two floors of Corpus One where the most sensitive Plague research and testing was underway. Urakov's excuse this time (and one that ostensibly stayed within the rules of the game) was that a quarantine of nine days to three weeks was mandatory after anyone visited those laboratories, even though this restriction did not apply to his own workers. He recited a long story about a local man who had once gone into the laboratory, and then had gone home and infected his village. This excuse made no sense to the visitors, who felt that at least Kelly, a fully inoculated, expert microbiologist from Porton Down, should have been allowed inside.[43] Their arguments failed.

As the inspectors drove back to Moscow that evening and compared notes, the significance of what they had seen at Obolensk became obvious.

The massive scale of the complex, the ability to ferment large quantities of BW agents, and the confrontation in the explosive test chamber were, according to Malinoski, 'eye opening and troubling, and really hit home'. As a relative newcomer to Soviet BW issues, he admits, he had been a little sceptical before the trip about some aspects of Pasechnik's information. After Obolensk, he had changed his mind, as had any other doubters on the team.[44]

Now there were still two more stops to go.

After a rest day in Moscow on Saturday, 12 January, the next stop was a two-day visit to the Vektor laboratory complex near Novosibirsk, Siberia, south-central Russia's major industrial centre and a transport hub on the Ob River and the Trans-Siberian railway. It has become something of a rustbelt, with potholes in the roads big enough to accommodate entire families. The locals, however, are still proud to call their country's fourth largest city, the 'Russian Chicago'.

The team travelled all day and night on Sunday (their flight was re-routed and delayed by a snowstorm), and they arrived very early and very tired on Monday morning, and then waited patiently in a huge unheated aircraft hangar that passed as a baggage waiting lounge. Outside the temperature was forty degrees below zero (Fahrenheit) and heavy snow covered the ground. For the first time, they encountered real Russian hospitality and were taken to a large dacha in the wooded countryside that was used to entertain important visiting dignitaries. The Soviets referred to it as the 'Presidential Palace' because Gorbachev stayed there whenever he visited. Lacey found himself in a huge, ornately decorated suite which included a large bed, massive bathroom with gold fixtures, and enormous living room furnished with a grand piano, numerous antique sofas, and a generous supply of class vodka. He remarked that they could play a game of soccer in the fifty-yard-long room.[45] Chris Davis too was delighted with his ample and luxuriously furnished suite. Out of habit and curiosity, and using age-old tradecraft, he set a trap ('just a little something, old boy') to establish whether his luggage would be searched while he was away. It was.

After a two-hour rest, the visiting team was driven to the main site of the several scattered locations and institutes that make up the large State Research Centre of Virology and Biotechnology, known as Vektor laboratories. Vektor's 'Centre' – called the Research Institute of Molecular Biology – is an ugly hundred-building complex that stands in a large, silver birch clearing in the anonymous hilltop town of Kol'tsovo, near Novosibirsk.

As with Obolensk, the team had prepared for the visit by studying maps and overhead photos. Even so, they were again impressed by the sheer enormity of the complex. The breadth and scope of the Soviet programme was remarkable.[46]

The purpose of Vektor, they were to confirm, was simple and terrible. It was the largest, most sophisticated facility ever built in the world to research and produce viral agents for biological weapons.

The first building went up in 1975; by 1991, the site had expanded into four laboratory buildings, two animal houses, and numerous other 'experimental' buildings. A newer, adjacent site, constructed since 1985, housed vaccine and pharmaceutical production facilities. The staff of about 4,500 workers included about 160 important Ph.D.-level scientists. The entire complex was surrounded by a low security wall and was bordered by a sort of exclusion zone of fields sparsely planted with exhausted silver pines. The stench of oil persistently rode the wind.[47]

The day began with another interminably long and pointless Kalinin-inspired lecture by Vektor's founder and director, Dr Lev Sandakhchiev, a small, gentle-looking intellectual from Armenia, with a nut-brown face and Asian features, black hair flecked with grey, and teeth, like many Soviets, with ostentatious gold inlays. His manner exuded friendliness and sincerity. A discreet silver and bronze badge on his lapel proudly showed that he was a member of the highly prestigious Soviet Academy of Sciences. Inside Biopreparat he was recognized as one of the most knowledgeable and experienced viral and genetic engineering experts.[48]

When his seemingly endless lecture came to a close, the visitors divided into teams and spread out to tour the facility, which was much larger than Obolensk.

'The pace was fast,' Malinoski recalls. 'Everyone was looking in different directions to see as much as possible.'[49]

As had happened at the other sites, large areas of the complex had been sanitized of all workers, research projects, and animals, giving the laboratories an almost holiday-like atmosphere. Kalinin had ordered that as few workers as possible be placed in a position to meet the visitors.[50] Every room and laboratory they entered had been thoroughly disinfected recently with bleach and formaldehyde so there were no surfaces to swab for samples.

'They made damn sure nothing was there of an incriminating nature,' Davis recalls. 'Everything was clean and sparkling.'[51]

As the inspectors toured the office space and outer laboratories of Building One, the leading British experts, Kelly and Davis, came across a handwritten note, in English, left on the end of a workbench in a laboratory. It read: 'The eagle cannot catch a fly.' That odd message, with its symbolic implication, was left unexplained. The two visitors thought a sympathetic Vektor scientist might have deliberately left it as an Agatha Christie-like clue; it was probably just one of those useless English aphorisms Russians like to note down.[52] Nevertheless, the perplexing message heightened suspicions for the visiting team as the tour moved on.

The visitors were next taken to a large animal laboratory – four floors filled with monkeys of all varieties – from small rhesus to chimpanzees and baboons. The presence of these higher primates was significant for they make the best models to compare the effects of viruses on humans. The Soviets even grew crops on the site to feed the numerous animals.[53]

In one special building the Soviets showed the visitors a sophisticated computer modelling system that plotted how aerosols spread through various landscapes and terrain under given wind conditions.[54]

'I had never seen anything like this before,' Malinoski recalls.[55]

The Soviets justified using the computer programme to track the movements of specially designed viruses and bacteria used to fight ecological and environmental problems, like crop pests. They claimed they could compute the coverage that was needed from the modelling. The visiting party was privately incredulous at this explanation. The computer model was precisely what one would develop to estimate offensive biological warfare distribution using the aerosol vector. The 'defensive' explanation was viewed as absurd. Who would devote the staff, time, and money to a problem which had already been solved by legitimate agricultural industries around the world?

The truth is, the visiting inspectors didn't know how right they were.

The software, fifteen years in the making, actually mathematically modelled how various biological payloads would spread under many circumstances, including type of agent, meteorological conditions (time of day, temperature, and wind), and geographic location (including urban or rural environments).[56] By analysing computer data from numerous field tests, Biopreparat's goal was to predict the consequences of various attacks and to learn the optimal conditions for using any agent in its arsenal. The research even covered terrorist applications, such as how agents and aerosols would contaminate different buildings and underground railway systems.[57]

Ten of the senior officials and scientists who worked on this computer project, led by Dr Sandakhchiev and General Kalinin, were all supposed to receive the Lenin Prize in 1991. The paperwork approving the prestigious honour had been completed. But the ceremony and the awards themselves were cancelled when the Soviet Union collapsed.[58]

What also was not known to the US/UK investigators, and what was to emerge only later, was the full extent of the sophisticated viral research programme that the personable Dr Sandakhchiev was running for Biopreparat. Pasechnik had alerted them about Vektor's importance, but he was not a virologist, so his knowledge of Sandakhchiev's actual programmes was limited.

Sandakhchiev, the West would later learn, maintained a bank of 10,000 of the most dangerous and exotic viruses known to man, one of the biggest collections in the world, including smallpox, Ebola, Marburg, Lassa fever, Machupo, VEE, Crimean-Congo haemorrhagic fever, and Eastern equine encephalitis. The actual list was then a top Soviet secret, but it included 140 strains of smallpox and three kinds of Ebola.[59]

Contrary to persistent Soviet denials, Sandakhchiev's work also focused on genetically altered viruses for offensive biological weapons. He was manipulating smallpox, Ebola, Marburg, and VEE – and experimenting with combinations of each of them.[60] In fact, the Soviets' virus of choice was smallpox. It had been chosen as the preferred 'mass casualty weapon' because it was so contagious, had a high mortality rate (about 30 per cent), and would cause panic and chaos in the targeted city.[61]

Only a year before the inspectors arrived at Vektor, Sandakhchiev had developed a new industrial technique to manufacture huge amounts of the virus on demand for biological weapons.[62] The Vektor team kept hundreds of litres of the highly concentrated virus on hand for this purpose. The laboratory's careful analysis of smallpox was meant to map the virus so that it could be more readily combined with other viruses, through genetic engineering, to make it even more infectious and deadly. Monkeypox, mousepox, and smallpox vaccine were used as substitutes in these experiments.[63]

But none of these crucial details about Sandakhchiev's intent, or the scope of his work, was known to the American and British inspectors as they slowly walked through the huge complex. The most important site by far that they saw at Kol'tsovo was Building 6A, a sophisticated centre for aerosol testing and animal research. Pasechnik had alerted the visitors about 6A, but they did not fully appreciate its significance until they entered.

Buildings 6–6A were actually two large, rectangular, four-storey, brick buildings side by side, ringed with small outside windows. Inside Building 6A was another huge box-within-a-box, BL-4 high-containment structure.[64] Among its notable features, Building 6A housed a large aerosol test-chamber complex, like the one at Obolensk – only this one was even newer and more innovative. This Vektor testing system included a computerized control panel area for each floor, which could send germ-laden air to the test animals (rodents, sheep, and primates) kept in different rooms. These electronic remote controls included special dials to adjust the pressure flows. Nothing comparable to this system ever existed in the US or Britain.[65]

Predictably, the visitors were forbidden to enter the control rooms and could view them only through thick glass windows. As the visitors peered through the glass and started firing questions, the Soviets became increasingly uneasy and the atmosphere grew very tense. The visitors sensed that the Soviets had been recently conducting very sensitive tests here, but everything had since been cleaned up.[66]

'After seeing the way the elaborate equipment was configured in 6A,' recalls a team member, 'we knew this facility was "dirty". This equipment was designed exclusively for offensive research, any microbiologist would know this.'[67]

Once again, predictably, the Soviets announced that they would not let the visitors into the innermost containment laboratories in Building 6A where Sandakhchiev's staff worked on the most dangerous viruses.[68] Just as Malinoski had been barred on a flimsy excuse at Obolensk, this time everyone was advised that entry was forbidden for reasons of 'quarantine'.[69] Rather than waste valuable time making arguments they knew they would lose, the visitors resigned themselves to viewing the laboratory only through the outside windows.

Even then, the skilled interviewers on the team managed to elucidate some surprising admissions from their hosts. First, the Vektor scientists boasted that they had studied Marburg virus extensively. They were doing full nucleotide sequencing on Marburg (as well as Ebola and Lassa).[70] They showed off their equipment, which could spray Marburg in aerosol form into animal test chambers. It was all being researched, of course, to develop a vaccine for Marburg. The vaccine was needed, they claimed, after a laboratory worker had become infected with the virus.[71] The visitors were puzzled – why should the Soviets have been working with Marburg in the first place? It is a virus which, like Ebola, poses no serious threat outside the deepest heart of Africa, its indigenous home.

The more the pure science was discussed, the more relaxed the atmosphere was. David Kelly, for whom there is no such thing as scientific small talk, was asking the right questions and listening sympathetically to all the answers. Suddenly, a mid-level researcher let slip to Kelly that this laboratory also was studying smallpox virus, which the Soviets always referred to by its proper scientific name, 'Variola major', or the Russian word, 'Ospr'. Kelly and his colleagues went very quiet. Speaking gently through an interpreter, Kelly made the man repeat his statement about 'Variola major' three times to ensure there was no ambiguity, that no one could plead a translator's error when the full import of what the man had said was recognized. The fact that the Soviets were working on smallpox at Vektor was headline news.[72]

'The guy talking to Kelly probably didn't realize how much he was supposed to be hiding,' Malinoski recalls.[73]

The very presence of smallpox in Siberia was a huge and alarming surprise. Under a 1983 World Health Organization programme for the eventual elimination and destruction of smallpox, the only remaining samples of the virus in the world were supposed to be stored in just two places – at the Centres for Disease Control in Atlanta and a Ministry of Health laboratory in Moscow. After centuries of smallpox epidemics, the dreadful virus had been trapped and eradicated throughout the planet save for the two remaining samples.

The Soviets had never before disclosed that the Vektor laboratory now had the virus. Its presence there in Kol'tsovo meant the visitors had uncovered an apparent violation of both strict WHO regulations and the BWC.[74] (The real reason that the Soviet smallpox stores were moved originally from Moscow to Vektor was Sandakhchiev's desire to have the samples in his laboratory for advanced offensive research.)[75]

As an experienced virologist, Malinoski immediately recognized the danger. 'Smallpox can cause a devastating plague,' he explains. 'A whole generation in the US and the entire world – under age twenty-five – are not immunized and are susceptible. Vektor did not have any written WHO approval to have the virus. If they did, they would have given us a good explanation. Kelly, Davis, and I were absolutely shocked. Everyone understood this was very serious.'[76]

It was David Kelly who first began to cotton on to what was really going on at Vektor. He appreciated that the Russians knew that smallpox was the strongest candidate of viral agents for use in biological warfare. 'It's a robust virus,' he explains, 'it is lethal, it is readily transmitted, it can be disseminated very effectively by aerosol, and it will survive a blast dissemination.'[77]

Kelly, and many other experts, believe that smallpox is the most terrifying virus that confronts the world as a biological weapon. 'If smallpox were reintroduced,' he says, 'it would be potentially a catastrophe.'

To make matters even more serious, from what the US/UK team

had seen already during their tour (and heard earlier from Pasechnik) they were confident that Vektor's laboratories had the ability to genetically engineer smallpox into an even more virulent pathogen.

In the light of the smallpox revelation, Kelly also now reassessed what they had seen at the specially controlled aerosol test chambers in 6A, where both static and explosive disseminations were being worked on. The Soviets had told Kelly they were studying the spread of 'monkey pox' (a less virulent cousin of smallpox) in the explosive chambers for defensive purposes, but, wondered Kelly, could that have been a cover for offensive smallpox testing? The implications in terms of offensive biological warfare, accidental release of the virus, or accidental infection were grim.[78]

Kelly and Davis now began asking more pointed questions, which immediately led to suspicion amongst the Soviet scientists and the minders. A 'situation' developed in which the two Britons were asked to stay in an office for an hour, while frantic telephone calls were made to locate senior Vektor officials (occupied with other sub-groups), to obtain help in handling the answers.[79]

Finally, everyone was reassembled and returned to the conference room at the administration building for a discussion. This had now become a serious matter for both sides. The visiting team, led by David Kelly, sat across the table from the Soviets for an hour in a tense and detailed question-and-answer session about the smallpox research. Dr Sandakhchiev fielded the majority of the enquiries. Tape recorders were out and copious notes were taken. The visitors had to wait interminably after each question and reply for the translations of the difficult, scientific points. Sometimes answers were repeated back-and-forth a second time, to make sure the visitors understood precisely what Sandakhchiev was saying.

It became evident almost immediately that the Soviets would stonewall as long as they could.

'They had slipped up in the laboratory,' Malinoski recalls, 'but then they quickly caught themselves.'[80]

The more Kelly pressed, the more the Soviets fudged. Kelly has needle-sharp concentration backed up by world-recognized expertise in every aspect of biological warfare. Opponents have learned to their cost that it is pointless to obfuscate or dissimulate with him.

As the hosts answers became increasingly evasive, the translations became more and more muddled. First, Sandakhchiev categorically denied they had *live* smallpox organisms.[81] Next, he claimed they were working only with 'the DNA of the smallpox virus'.[82]

Kelly saw through that one too. The Soviets were attempting to draw a fine line between working with the infectious virus, which was illegal, and working on just the DNA, which they said was used for 'cloning' purposes. Sandakhchiev insisted they were merely mapping the sequence of nucleotides – to define the genes necessary for Variola major.

But why would they need to clone the smallpox in the first place?

The answers were vague and occasionally exotic. They claimed that they needed to research the virus because there was a real danger that global warming might lead to the slow melting of the permafrost in Siberia, which, in turn, might uncover old graves of people who had died in pre-World War II smallpox epidemics. Since the virus could still be active there was a danger of a new outbreak and, in that event, the Soviets would need to be prepared.[83]

The visitors listened with growing astonishment to this *X-Files* scenario. Some shook their heads in disbelief.[84] While it was remotely possible that melting grave sites could happen, and even more remotely possible that a new infection or two might occur, a localized outbreak could be contained without the extensive Vektor research.

The visitors knew that such cloning work could also be adapted to making entirely new and more deadly forms of smallpox. There was also the possibility of combining smallpox with other viruses in genetic engineering experiments. (They suspected, for instance, that Vektor's monkey pox was a candidate for such a smallpox combination.)

So had they created new strains of smallpox? The Soviets declined to answer.

Had they mixed smallpox with other viruses or made a version that was resistant to vaccines? Again, no answer was forthcoming.

Finally, the Soviets offered a highly significant reason for their work – they were researching the virus because they believed the US had continued a secret BW programme after 1972 to develop a smallpox weapon. It was a stunning admission, and after it had been made, a flustered Sandakhchiev said he would not respond to further questions about the virus or the cloning.[85]

'We were shocked,' Malinoski recalls. 'We had caught them in a significant breach of international law.'[86]

But Vektor had managed to hide the very worst.

After leaving Vektor, the team flew on 16 January to Leningrad to spend two days at Pasechnik's former facility, the All-Union Scientific Research Institute for Ultra-Pure Biological Preparations.

The visitors knew that the Leningrad site, and its 600-person staff, filled several important functions for Biopreparat – all involving advanced research for optimizing the manufacture, concentration, storage and release of biological agents.[87] The institute's scientists used highly sophisticated equipment and advanced techniques to test aerosol dissemination of micro-organisms; to determine the best additives which protect bio-agents once they are released; to find the various agent properties which best survive an explosion; and to increase quality control to grow the most lethal pathogens.

During Biopreparat's planning for the visit, Kalinin and Alibekov had realized that the British experts, armed with Pasechnik's information, would know much more about where to go and what to see at the comparatively small institute. So the Soviets went to even greater lengths in Leningrad to devise cover stories and hide incriminating evidence.[88]

It was evident from the outset that Pasechnik had become an unperson to the Soviets. His replacement, who gave the opening lecture, described the facility and its history without ever referring to its founder and long-time director. During the subsequent tour, the staff avoided mentioning Pasechnik's name or asking the British visitors what had happened to him. The sanitizers did make one little error. Chris Davis found proof of Pasechnik's former existence on a wall just outside the first-floor main office. Hanging on a noticeboard was an old, long-forgotten announcement with the defector's name and signature at the bottom.[89]

The three-building institute, situated downtown on ordinary city streets, included a newer main building and two converted structures at separate locations. The main building housed a two-storey explosive test chamber. The visitors were surprised to see such a dangerous enclosure in a heavily populated city. (No such explosive chambers still existed in the West.) The Soviets repeated their mantra that they only used simulants in this chamber – and that all of the research was defensive.

Inside a second seven-storey building in another part of the city, the institute operated a huge static/dynamic aerosol test chamber on the top floor. This chamber, which was attached to a generator and ductwork a yard wide, allowed for flow testing of simulants. The Soviets could start a flow of air at one end and measure the distribution of particles throughout the long ducts – more than fifteen yards on one floor.

The Soviets did not want to show this chamber to the visitors. But the US/UK team insisted. When they asked for an explanation of what the chamber was used for, the Soviets replied that it was needed to test bio-pesticides. By now, the inspectors were becoming acclimatized to the environment and just smiled at this well-rehearsed response.[90] They knew it was untrue just by examining all the other incriminating BW equipment they saw scattered about the three buildings.

In the main building, for instance, there were special dryers and large-capacity, 'jet stream' milling machines (which used strong blasts of air, instead of heavy ball bearings, as a less aggressive method to generate small particles for weapons). None of this custom-made Soviet equipment – which Pasechnik had personally developed – was needed for defensive work or 'bio-pesticides'.

When the visitors asked for an explanation about the milling equipment, the disingenuous reply came back that these machines were used under a commercial contract to make aerosols of 'salt' for medicinal purposes. While such salts *are* used to treat asthma and other respiratory diseases, both the Soviets and the visitors knew it was a preposterous explanation. No advanced biological-research laboratory would be milling salt; but it was the best cover story available.[91]

The full inspection team – both Americans and British – returned to Washington on 20 January for a final debriefing and the writing of a joint report for their respective government leaders. This classified document, more than 200 pages long, was supported by photos, audio tapes, and video. The report concluded:

1. The US/UK team had found disturbing evidence which confirmed that the Soviets had a massive, offensive biological warfare programme run by Biopreparat and the military. It was the largest such programme that the world had ever known. Key indicators of offensive intent were the type and configuration of the equipment and the huge BW production capacity – which went well beyond the requirements of legitimate bio-research.[92]

2. Biopreparat officials and scientists admitted extensive connections to the Soviet military. At every facility, the visitors heard about or

observed military personnel on the staff; a large amount of work that was classified; and a substantial percentage that was funded by military contracts.[93]

3. Specific evidence of disturbing treaty violations emerged – including smallpox research, genetic engineering of dangerous pathogens, and explosive aerosol testing.

4. Soviet officials had done everything possible to limit the scope of the visits – through evasion, obfuscation, and prolonged negotiations. Due to the swift pace, the Obolensk and Kol'tsovo tours were considered incomplete and unsatisfactory. The visitors had been too rushed to see everything or to verify important information they were given. Many laboratories had clearly been sanitized, so it had been impossible to define with accuracy the kind of research going on inside. Many scientists were absent and could not be questioned. The Soviets had refused all requests for samples of disease-causing agents or genetically altered organisms.[94]

5. During the entire tour, no Soviet official had been open, frank, or truthful about any aspects of the offensive programme. Whenever the Soviets were cornered and could not properly explain suspicious activities, they had resorted to excuses about doing purely 'defensive' research against potential threats from the rest of the world. The visitors were certain that these answers were not truthful.[95]

When the British team returned to London, Kelly, Davis and the others quickly reported to their senior leaders and wrote a JIC (Joint Intelligence Committee) paper. The committee is the highest level at which all British intelligence is drawn together (the equivalent of the CIA's NIE) and the distribution list includes the Queen, followed by the Prime Minister and the Secretaries of State for Defence and Foreign Affairs.[96]

In Washington, Ed Lacey briefed ACDA Director Ronald Lehman, who, in turn, informed the UNGROUP, Secretary Baker, and President Bush.[97]

The team returned in triumph from the historical voyage to a Washington and London that was deeply pre-occupied with weightier matters. The audience had moved to another theatre where Iraq was now the lead feature. Desert Storm had begun and with it the bombing campaign. Margaret Thatcher was out of office and John Major had taken over. The Middle East was about to go up in flames and the West urgently needed Moscow's compliance with its plans. Gorbachev's own political position was becoming shakier. Shevardnadze had gone. Once again events had moved against the BW maximalists, now proven broadly right in their fears about the Soviets' serious breaches of the BWC, but once again, this was not the right time to confront Moscow. Anyway, the West had its hands full.

Surprisingly, the reaction in Moscow after the US/UK team departed was upbeat. The invisible General Kalinin was satisfied that the visit had been a success.[98]

Within a week, he was asked to file a report for President Gorbachev describing the results. His succinct, one-page reply informed the Kremlin that the four facilities had been scrutinized by the American and British experts without incident. The note ended with Biopreparat's firm assurance that the visitors had not found any proof that an offensive BW programme existed in the Soviet Union. Once that report was submitted, no further Soviet analysis was requested about the trip. Gorbachev's office did not respond to Kalinin's memo.[99]

CHAPTER FOURTEEN

Gorbachev

'The Soviets had still not come clean . . .'
US Ambassador John Hawes, 1998

It was not until March 1991, after the Gulf War, that Washington and London once again began to address the problems the inspectors had spilled across their desks following the winter visit to the USSR.

Even when the BW arms control negotiations started once more, the West had difficulties in steering the talks out of the shallows. From March through to July, President Bush, Prime Minister Major and their senior diplomats – in their dealings with either Gorbachev or his top deputies – tried more than ten times to elicit a response that squarely addressed the inspectors' continuing fears about the ongoing Soviet offensive programme.[1] Gorbachev and his new Foreign Minister, Alexander Bessmertnykh, responded by obstinately sticking to a point-by-point rebuttal of every Western allegation and denying that they had ever violated the BWC.[2]

So with the process becalmed, the Bush Administration for its part continued to delay persistent Soviet requests for a return visit to US facilities. Finally, on 29 July in Moscow, Secretary Baker dangled a carrot in front of Foreign Minister Bessmertnykh. If a planned meeting of trilateral experts in late August could successfully address the US/UK concerns from the winter inspection, then a return Soviet visit to the US could be tentatively scheduled for mid-October.[3] The Soviets took the bait.

But on 19 August, came the surprise coup attempt by hardliners against Gorbachev. Five days later (after the plot failed), Gorbachev resigned as head of the disbanded Communist Party. As power began to slip from him, the Soviet Foreign Ministry notified the State Department that the scheduled trilateral meeting and the October visit to US facilities would have to be indefinitely delayed.[4]

A week later, on 1 September in Moscow, a now politically weakened Gorbachev met John Major, who again raised the BW issue – only this time even more forcibly than before.[5] Now changing his tune, Gorbachev blamed the coup plotters, Minister of Defence Dmitry Yazov and others, for previously misleading him about the BW programme. Gorbachev promised to get at the real truth and work to create mutual trust. (Afterwards, both London and Washington privately recognized that the badly wounded Gorbachev probably would be unable to confront the military or ever dismantle the BW programme.)

By mid-October, Russia had set up its own Foreign Ministry, separate from the Soviet Foreign Ministry, which meant that President Bush now had a formal diplomatic channel to the emerging power in Moscow, Boris Yeltsin. The Bush Administration then decided to take a huge calculated gamble – effectively to place a bet on Russia by secretly telling Yeltsin everything that the West knew about the *Soviet* BW programme. This was very high-stakes diplomacy, full of risk. The US had to assume that Yeltsin didn't know of, nor approve of, the illegal Soviet BW programme. So the UNGROUP prepared a paper, about fifteen pages long, which laid out in unprecedented detail what the US knew about the Soviet programme. The document, drafted by the CIA with inter-agency approval, contained the essence of the Juniper channel intelligence.[6] The sensitive message was secretly conveyed to Yeltsin through diplomatic channels – both orally and in writing. The prompt response came directly from Yeltsin's senior aides. In sum, it said that Yeltsin did not challenge the Western allegations, rather, he tended to believe them. Furthermore, the situation might even be worse than the West knew. This was an urgent problem, they acknowledged, that would be dealt with as promptly as possible.[7]

While the West waited anxiously for evidence of Yeltsin's deeds, the political prognosis on Gorbachev grew even more glum. When the long-delayed trilateral meeting was finally held in Moscow in mid-October (to discuss the troubling findings from the January visit), no progress was made to address Western concerns. The meeting demonstrated only that the Soviet military, even after the disastrous coup attempt, still retained a dominance over all BW issues.[8]

On 18 November, with Gorbachev now in terminal political decline, the Soviet leader belatedly responded to the promise he had made John Major in September. The British Ambassador in Moscow was informed that Gorbachev had issued orders to end the Soviet BW programme. In the light of the failed trilateral meeting a month earlier, both London and Washington responded with coolness.[9]

In a further gesture calculated to boost Yeltsin, and as a clear quid pro quo, President Bush's next move, taken in November, was to authorize the long-delayed Soviet visit to the Pentagon's former BW installations in the United States.[10] The plan was to set a shining example of Western openness and honesty.

Washington would prove once and for all there were no rabbits in the hat or cards in its back pocket.

Now, at last, for better or worse, the Soviets/Russians were coming.

CHAPTER FIFTEEN

The Soviet Visit

'Some of us assumed that they would go back and tell the Ministry of Defense what they wanted to hear.'

Colonel Jim Bushong, 1998

The Pentagon had been both planning and dreading the Soviet visit.

Just as the prospect of Western arms inspectors on Soviet soil had appalled their Moscow equivalents, so now the American brass hats viewed the return visit with a distinct absence of enthusiasm.

However, their spin-doctors and public relations consultants saw it otherwise. Here was a golden opportunity to set a wonderful capitalist example of openness and honesty. As the Americans had nothing to hide, they had nothing to lose. Naïve, but very American in their evangelical fervour, the planners determined the Soviet visit would be the antithesis of everything unpleasant that had happened to the British and American inspectors the previous winter. They would show the Soviets the benign face of their society. There would be no freezing buses with broken windshields or nightmare travel delays, and there would certainly be no hard-faced, glaring minders to intimidate.

So they selected Lisa Bronson, a very bright and capable thirty-one-year-old attorney in the Pentagon's office of arms control negotiations, to handle the very delicate assignment of hosting the visit.[1]

A petite woman with short hair and a friendly manner, Bronson was the daughter of a schoolteacher from Massachusetts. She graduated as an attorney from the ROTC programme at Cornell University, becoming the first female colonel in the corps. In 1987, while serving in the army's Judge Advocate General's office, she was dispatched to Geneva to assist the American team negotiating the chemical weapons treaty. While serving there, she became enamoured with arms control issues. In April 1989, after leaving the army, she was assigned as a civilian to the Pentagon's small 'Negotiations' office, which handled all arms control issues for the military (then primarily involving nuclear and chemical weapons).

Colleagues remember her as a meticulous workaholic who was totally dedicated to guiding and protecting Defense Department interests.[2] Her selection was a neat move. The irony of Bronson's assignment was evident from the outset – an attractive, young, female lawyer, with no prior BW experience, would be America's main host to an all-male group of Soviet scientists, military officers, minders, and spies.

Bronson was excited at being invited, but later conceded that she had no idea what she was getting into.[3] Her superiors had given her total responsibility to prepare the American sites and to look out for the Pentagon's interests during the process. She was told to prepare four locations that the Soviets had specifically requested: Fort Detrick, Maryland (home of USAMRIID and the former US offensive BW research programme); Dugway Proving Ground in Utah (the main US test facility); Pine Bluff Arsenal in Arkansas (the former US BW production facility); and the Salk Institute in Swiftwater, Pennsylvania (the army's primary contractor for manufacturing vaccines).

The Defense Department's instructions were clear and simple: the army was to set a glowing example for the Soviet military by demonstrating a degree of openness and friendliness on the American side that was expected in return from the Soviet side on future visits. The Pentagon's mission was to be as accommodating and hospitable as possible, and present a model of transparency; then reap the harvest for its own boys when they went East again.[4]

Bronson's team was briefed on the difficulties that had occurred during the US/UK visit to the USSR. They knew that the Western experts had felt mistreated by the Soviets. The tense, physical confrontation at the Obolensk chamber was an example of 'atrocious behaviour' that the US welcoming team swore to avoid. No recriminations would be voiced either about Soviet violations, such as the work on smallpox, or super-Plague, or explosive tests. Nothing would be done to provoke the Soviets in any shape or form.

Bronson organized several dry runs of each of the four sites. From these practice sessions, both Bronson's team and the site personnel learned a great deal. Even though the US had nothing to hide, the army had to be ready in case the Soviets heard incorrect information, or misinterpreted innocent evidence, or were determined to provoke a confrontation by making outright false accusations. Of all these concerns, the Pentagon was worried most about 'ambiguity'; for example, that the Soviets would see something innocuous and misinterpret its purpose as part of a covert offensive BW programme.[5]

It was determined that all Soviet questions would be funnelled through Bronson, so that a co-ordinated reply could be prepared. She would respond to the entire Soviet group, so that everyone heard one answer and the Americans did not contradict themselves.[6]

The ground rules for the visit – by mutual agreement on both sides – called for no publicity whatsoever. The Pentagon officially classified the trip as 'secret' and took every precaution to ensure the press did not get wind of this historic visit.[7]

'Our primary concern was what happens if this goes public,' recalls Ambassador John Hawes, the State Department's senior representative to the trilateral process. 'We didn't want the press to ask us: "What do you mean you have a bunch of Soviet officials crawling around old US Army BW facilities in the midst of total chaos in Moscow?" We were really worried about how we would explain that.'[8]

The thirteen-man Soviet team flew from Moscow to Washington on Saturday, 7 December 1991 – the very day the Commonwealth of Independent States was officially formed.[9] They were met at Dulles Airport and were driven to the Soviet Embassy to spend the night. The team leader was Grigoriy Berdennikov, forty, a smooth and cultured career diplomat who spoke fluent English and had extensive arms control experience. He was not known as a cold warrior or hardliner. Earlier, he had been allied with Shevardnadze against the Ministry of Defence and he had secretly encouraged US diplomats to push the military harder on the BW issue. Berdennikov had been elevated to Deputy Foreign Minister after Shevardnadze resigned and had become a pragmatic Yeltsin supporter.[10]

From Biopreparat, the most important delegates were three familiar faces. Dr Kanatjan Alibekov was the senior technical officer. Dr Lev Sandakhchiev of Vektor and Dr Nikolai Urakov from Obolensk were the two senior scientists.[11]

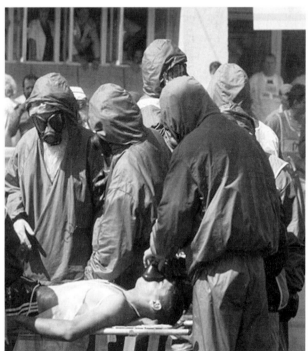

Above: Chemical and biological warfare expert, Dr Alistair Hay, dressed in a gas mask and protective suit similar to those worn by British forces in the Gulf.

Right: Israelis during a biological warfare defence exercise. Each home in Israel has a specially equipped 'safe room' where the owners can seal off the door space and windows from biological agents if they are attacked. The nation is on the front-line for BW attacks by Iraq, Libya, Syria or Iran.

Down Your Way. This is how it will look if there is a BW terrorist incident in your street. Grotesque, white-suited, 'Michelin Men' figures, protected against airborne bacteria or viruses, will man the front-line. Here firemen hose down after dealing with an anthrax threat at a school in Indianapolis in 1998. It was a false alarm.

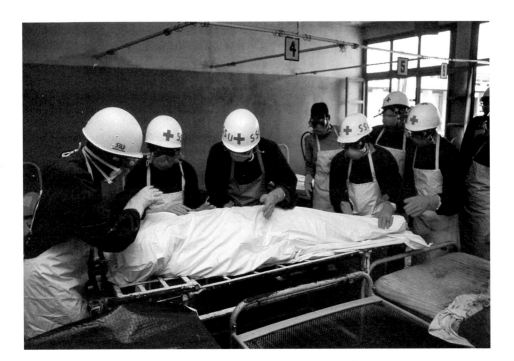

Above: Dying of Ebola – one of the more recently discovered haemorrhagic diseases – in an African hospital ward. South Africa's biological warfare programme – Project Coast – investigated Ebola as a candidate weapon for assassination. Ebola reduces the body's organs to bloody pulp before death.

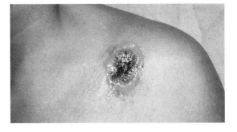

Right: Anthrax, the biological weapon of choice, now refined to travel on ICBM warheads and treated to become antibiotic resistant. Indigenous in Africa, it was deliberately used during the Rhodesian struggle for independence in the late 1970s.

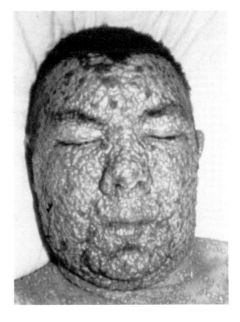

Bottom right: Smallpox – one of mankind's greatest scourges – was produced by the tonne by the Soviets to attack the West in a strategic war. Although successfully brought under control by the WHO and due for final destruction in June 1999, both Washington and Moscow have decided to keep their stocks ('for defensive research purposes only').

The view from the West. George Bush, Ronald Reagan and Mikhail Gorbachev in New York in 1988. The superpower thaw had begun but Gorbachev did not tell the truth about the Soviet Union's huge arsenal of biological weapons.

Margaret Thatcher and 'the man we can do business with' in London during the Soviet leader's three-day visit. But, behind the scenes, Thatcher's intelligence chiefs were grimly aware of the substantial breaches by the USSR of the Biological Weapons Convention. Tension over these violations was minimized by the need to end the Cold War and support the Soviet leader.

Alibekov (with gun) years before his defection to the West. He became one of the Soviet Union's top Plague Warriors, and saw for himself the horrendous build-up of the deadliest biological arsenal ever created.

'Hells Kitchen' – the huge Soviet complex at Stepnogorsk, Kazakhstan – the largest BW production facility ever built in the world. This is where, in the 1980s, then-Major Kanatjan Alibekov manufactured the world's most virulent anthrax and later tested bombs loaded with Marburg virus.

A spy satellite picture of the Biopreparat research institute in the main part of Leningrad (now St Petersburg), where Vladimir Pasechnik directed a scientific team that engineered antibiotic resistant super-Plague for long-range Soviet missiles.

Surgeon-Commander Chris Davis OBE – the arms inspector with a steel-trap brain. He helped prove the Soviets were still cheating on their biological warfare preparations. When they staged a light-failure in a sensitive chamber, Davis produced a small hand-torch which a minder attempted to seize. 'Please take your hand off me – now,' said Davis very cooly.

Secretary of State James Baker and Soviet Foreign Minister Eduard Shevardnadze. The men were friends but it took a quiet ride in a Black Russian Zil before the truth of the Soviet's biological warfare programme was confronted.

Now inhabited only by mosquitoes, this bunker at the Pine Bluff Arsenal in Arkansas became the focus for the unreasonable suspicions of the Soviet inspection team during their contentious 1991 visit. The Soviets were to make the wholly false claim that these bunkers were still on standby to store US offensive biological weapons.

The Soviet inspection team during their top-secret inspection visit to the old US BW site at Pine Bluff, Arkansas in December 1991. The Russian team found nothing so they faked evidence of American non-compliance with the Biological Weapons Convention. Alibekov was so disgusted he eventually defected. *Back row: far left,* Chris Davis. *Front row: 3rd from left,* Lev Sandakhchiev; *4th from right,* Lisa Bronson; *3rd from right,* Kanatjan Alibekov.

The Ministry of Defence was also well represented with five officers. The senior military man and deputy head of the delegation, Colonel Nikifor Trofimovich Vasileyev, forty-three, was a rising power in the Soviet biological warfare hierarchy. A vintage hardliner, built like a Russian bear, Vasileyev was an expert on BW defensive issues and a recognized authority on anthrax.[12]

The military's number-two officer was Colonel V.I. Zyukov, forty-four, a shorter version of Vasileyev, more aggressive, though not quite as tough looking. Zyukov had extensive experience in the Soviet chemical corps. Another Colonel appeared to be a senior officer from the Soviet GRU (military intelligence), although even some of the Biopreparat members on the team were not sure who he was; they were told only that he was an interpreter.[13]

On Sunday morning, the Soviets were treated to a ride on Air Force Two, the Vice President's plane, to Salt Lake City, where they were put up at the Airport Hilton (the Pentagon and State Department paid the tour's hotel bills).

That afternoon, the first official greeting and briefing session was held in a hotel conference room. On the American team, Ambassador John Hawes served as the senior diplomat – Berdennikov's opposite. But, at the sites, it was Lisa Bronson's show. She was the Defense Department's senior representative, supported by three colonels from the Pentagon, including veteran army officer, Jim Bushong, a senior analyst from the Negotiations office who had been assigned to assist her from the start. Colonel Bushong, fifty, was a take-charge Arkansan who had been a 'Tunnel Rat' commander in the Vietnam War and then served in the army's Chemical Corps.[14]

Also present throughout the tour, as official observers, were those indomitable Brits, Drs David Kelly and Chris Davis, the invaluable veterans of the USSR trip.

As expected, the all-male Soviet team was surprised and puzzled at first by Bronson's presence.[15] She presented something of a challenge to Soviet military thinking, which respected age, status, gender, and rank. The Soviets didn't quite know how to deal with an attractive, energetic, and very bright young lady as the leader of the US team. They weren't sure exactly who she was; and they didn't understand why everyone on the American side, including colonels, took orders from her. At first, they challenged her in little ways to test the limits of her authority, but once they saw that she could clearly deliver on whatever they asked for – access, information, and transportation – they began to accept her.

On Monday, the Soviet team left the hotel at 6 a.m. and was driven by bus 80 miles southwest through the near barren, high mountain desert – past Skull Valley and an Indian reservation – to the huge Dugway Proving Ground facility in western Utah.

The Dugway command's opening presentation explained that the vast facility – 1,300 square miles of salt flats, sand dunes, rolling hills, and low mountains covered with juniper – was where the Pentagon now developed, tested, and evaluated defensive equipment (like masks, clothing, detectors, filters, and decontamination materials) to protect US forces from chemical and biological attacks. Before the 1969 ban, it had been the United States' major testing ground for offensive biological weapons.

As the Soviets, led by Colonel Vasileyev, examined the thousands of acres of test grounds, they were allowed to collect as many soil and grass samples as they wanted. The Americans watched passively as a few Soviets poked around the scrub, trying to pick up debris from the ground. All of these samples, placed in small bags, were later packaged for them in airtight metal cans for carriage back to Moscow.[16]

'We had no concern at all about them taking away any evidence or old debris from Dugway, since we had nothing to hide,' Colonel Bushong explains. 'I have to say whenever we demonstrated that we were willing to give them whatever they wanted, they quickly lost interest.'[17]

Early on the second morning, they again drove to Dugway. The Soviets were very interested to see tests performed on tanks and other vehicles mounted with special collecting particle filters. They also took 'swipe samples' of dust after they learned that the army used BW simulants (like BG and *Serratia marcescens*) during some experiments.[18]

The visit was finished by noon, when everyone broke for a buffet lunch, followed by a few farewell remarks by the Dugway commander, Colonel Frank Cox. As a very American gesture, each visitor was presented with a souvenir of their visit – a geode (the locally renowned, spherically shaped, crystalline rock) mounted on a base which displayed a Dugway Proving Ground crest.[19]

The group flew back to Washington that evening and the following day were picked up at 6 a.m. for the one-hour bus ride to USAMRIID headquarters at Fort Detrick. The Soviets then toured the BL-4 facility. Unlike the contentious and secretive Vektor visit, no one who asked to go inside was barred from these high-containment labs.[20]

Colonel Vasileyev led a group of Soviets on a tour of the second floor Pathology Division, where the inspectors showed their first flash of suspicion. The facility had kept its three, large, expensive electron microscopes in a three-room suite in this area. To keep out all electric pulses, these rooms were specially shielded with a tin covering and could be entered only through large freezer-style doors.[21]

Coincidentally, when the Soviets entered the suite, the three rooms were empty and the electron microscopes were gone. Several weeks earlier, as part of a long-standing reorganization plan, USAMRIID had moved the entire pathology centre to another building in the nearby city of Frederick. Only holes were left in the floor where the microscope apparatus and worktables had once been bolted down. But that was enough to get the Soviet team going. As soon as the Soviets saw the configuration of these rooms with its vacant spaces, they became very agitated and began talking in an excited way among themselves in Russian. The Soviets apparently thought they had found some special chambers that the US Army was using for testing biological agents on humans and that it had been sanitized for the visit.

Colonel David Franz, USAMRIID's deputy commander, sat down and slowly and patiently explained to them about the microscopes, the shielding, and the recent move of the division. The Soviets refused to believe him. They spent forty-five minutes examining the suite inch by inch – while rejecting his repeated attempts to explain. They argued that such heavy and suspicious shielding was not justified for the minimal equipment left behind in the rooms.

Finally, in desperation, Franz got down on his hands and knees and measured the distances between the holes on the floor, then drew a scale diagram of all of these measurements. Next, he commanded an extra vehicle and personally drove the three-man Soviet sub-delegation to the town of Frederick to see the new pathology centre for themselves. With the diagram for precise reference, they were able to measure the electron microscopes and compare them to the holes in the floor at Fort Detrick. Point made. Embarrassed grins.

It was becoming clear that the visitors had their maximalists and minimalists too.

'While a few colonels were taking detailed tape measurements of our labs,' recalls Ambassador Hawes, 'others, like Berdennikov, were rolling their eyes and discreetly shaking their heads at all the nonsense.'[22]

The Soviets returned to Fort Detrick early Friday morning for a full tour of the entire facility.[23] To maintain the open hands US approach, Lisa Bronson told them they were allowed to choose – without prior announcement – any five sites that they particularly wanted to see. They were told to mark off their choices on a map.

Like the US/UK team in January, the Soviets had studied their own satellite photos of Fort Detrick before arriving and they selected five sites which looked suspicious to them. After indicating their selections, four members of their team, led by Colonel Zyukov, boarded a bus and headed out to inspect those locations. Dr Charles Bailey, the former USAMRIID commander, was their army guide.[24]

The first stop was an unfamiliar place to Bailey since the tiny, unidentified building was on the National Institute of Health side of the sprawling complex. As Bailey directed the driver to the appropriate street, they finally pulled into the driveway of the Fort's cone-shaped, salt-and-sand storage facility. The large bay door was open, revealing the pile of greyish matter inside that was used to cover icy winter roads. Salt.

'The four visitors started talking in Russian faster than you can imagine,' recalls Bailey. 'Their translator then asked: "What is that?" I told them: "Road salt – for ice." '[25]

To their credit, the Soviets started to laugh, but just to be sure, one of them stepped from the bus, took a pinch of the substance, and tasted it. He nodded, and everyone laughed again.

Bailey learned years later that Colonel Vasileyev had spotted the strange looking, round-shaped building from satellite photos and suspected it might be a new aerosol test chamber. The Soviets had been hoping to find something there to offset the damning Obolensk chamber incident.[26]

Later that day, the full Soviet delegation was shown the two remaining symbols at Fort Detrick of the old US offensive programme: the pilot production plant and the 'Eight-Ball' – the famed one million-litre, spherical test chamber. As they stepped from the bus outside the chamber, the last stop of the day, the army guide carefully explained what they were seeing.

During the army's earlier dry runs, Lisa Bronson had worried about how she would explain the status of the 'Eight-Ball' to the Soviets. Why would the Department of the Interior put a brass plate at the entrance designating this inactive building – which had once been tasked to investigate the most horrible ways of killing – as a national historical monument that can never be destroyed? Why would the US do that, the Soviets might ask, unless the government intended to use the building again?[27] Would the visitors ever understand the cultural divide between West and East, and American's fierce pride in its military technology, no matter how obscene its ultimate use?

The army guide carefully recounted all of this history to the visitors – including how the structure around the 'Eight-Ball' had burned down and why what remained had been declared a national monument. The guide stressed that the 'Eight-Ball' had not been used since before 1969.[28] The Soviet delegation listened intently, without raising objections, and the Americans breathed sighs of relief.

At Fort Detrick's farewell ceremony, the new USAMRIID Commander, Colonel Ron Williams, gave each Soviet representative a baseball cap and coffee mug with the 'Fort Detrick' insignia on them. The Soviets again seemed pleased to receive these tokens of their visit.[29] So far so good. It wasn't a holiday tour, but it wasn't hell on wheels either.

'The goodbyes were cordial, almost emotional,' Colonel Franz recalls. 'Given the situation in Moscow, they didn't know what they were going home to. We actually felt a bit sorry for them.'[30]

The Soviets were given most of the weekend to themselves in Washington, prior to their departure for the Pine Bluff Arsenal. On Sunday afternoon, everyone flew to Little Rock, and early on Monday morning, the visitors were driven some 40 miles south, following the Arkansas River, to the massive arsenal, located just north of the city of Pine Bluff. After introductory briefings for most of the morning, the Soviets broke up into small groups and spent most of the afternoon walking through the old US production facility, which had been converted since 1972 into a modern, non-military laboratory for animal and plant research.

The new establishment was called the National Centre for Toxicological Research (NCTR). The old filling equipment – for pre-1969 US BW munitions – was still there, covered by the dust of the ages.[31] The Americans had made no attempt to hide what had been the framework of a full BW production facility. They could easily have levelled the Pine

Bluff plant to the ground in the early 1970s; and, in doing so, destroyed all of the pre-1969 evidence. That move, with one stroke, would have eliminated any future Soviet arguments that the US was capable of quickly reactivating their offensive production capacity. But, to save money, the Nixon Administration had chosen to convert the buildings, effectively leaving much of the old and rotting infrastructure in place. But these old financial decisions were to prove a hostage to fortune twenty years later, as Soviet military inspectors trod the ground of America's long discarded biological warfare arsenal.[32]

As the tour began, one sub-group of Soviets, led by Colonel Vasileyev, asked to see the huge 'mosquito room', where the old US programme had kept large water tanks used for breeding vast numbers of insects as possible wartime delivery systems of BW agents. Coincidentally, this room, in Section 5B of the NCTR, was one of the key areas at Pine Bluff that had concerned Lisa Bronson's team during their pre-planning sessions. They were always worried that the Soviets might misconstrue what they found there. And they were right.

The room contained a mammoth, stainless steel vat on legs; the dimensions around the edges were about 60 feet long, by 60 feet wide, by 2 feet high. This vat, which once held several plagues of mosquito larvae, was now being used by the Pine Bluff staff to raise young catfish fingerlings – for civilian bio-research projects. To this end, the NCTR had recently refitted the room's plumbing with new equipment – pumps, valves, filters, tubes, and connectors. These improvements meant that this room was the only place in the entire former US offensive BW programme where, instead of rusting, rotting, decaying pipework, one could see modern valves and tanks.

As soon as Vasileyev and his colleagues entered Section 5B and spotted the new equipment, they became agitated. Ignoring their American guides, as they tried patiently to explain the minutiae of catfish breeding, the Soviets assumed they finally had found an active part of the US offensive programme. Until that point, the tall GRU officer accompanying Vasileyev had occasionally recorded places of interest with a small, Japanese-model, video camera he had strapped to his hand. Now a very excited Vasileyev tore the camera away from his colleague and started taking close-ups of the new equipment spread throughout the room.[33] This seemed to be his crowning moment.[34]

Perhaps the most absurd incident of the entire visit occurred when

Colonel Zyukov decided to show off both his thoroughness and climbing skills. While touring the facility on the bus, he asked the driver to stop as they approached a tall water tower.[35] Zyukov alighted alone and started climbing the ladder. The other Soviets began giggling and took pictures as they watched his ascent to the top. When he finally returned to the bus a colleague asked what he had found.

'Water,' snapped Zyukov.

Everyone returned to the hotel that night. As some of the visitors gathered for cocktails in the hotel restaurant, Dr Alibekov separated himself from the pack and approached Lisa Bronson while she was standing at the bar with one of the translators. Alibekov had been the quiet and thoughtful one on the tour. He did not appear to be aligned with any one group. He seemed to have taken everything in, had asked intelligent and penetrating questions, and shown he understood the answers. Nothing had passed him by. To the amused relief of Kelly and Davis, who had met him in the USSR, he had replaced his favourite brown cardigan with a sports coat and jeans.

Taking Bronson's hand, Alibekov said to her, through the translator: 'You are a nice lady. You have been good to us. Thank you.'

Somewhat unusually, he then asked for her business card. She handed him one, with her Pentagon address and phone number on it. He thanked her again before rejoining his colleagues. Bronson was pleased by the gesture. She took it to mean that the reasonable guests – like Berdennikov and now Alibekov – were impressed by the level of openness they had seen. As a scientist, Alibekov seemed to understand that the US had nothing to hide, whereas there was now a pervasive feeling amongst the hosts that the hard-line military officials might never be convinced.[36]

On Tuesday morning, everyone arrived back at Pine Bluff at 8 a.m. As they began to plan the day's agenda, the Soviets made it clear from the outset that they primarily wanted to see the earth-covered bunkers at the Arsenal. This was a perfectly reasonable request, but it contained a difficult bureaucratic problem for Lisa Bronson and the Pentagon.

Most of these bunkers, when in use, now stored chemical munitions – bombs, shells, rockets, and mines. They were located on another side of the Arsenal – the chemical side, which was clearly separated by a fence from the NCTR labs and the old BW production facilities. The Americans had made a firm decision in planning the visit that the Soviets would not be allowed to go beyond the fence which marked the limits of the old biological warfare facilities.

The twenty or so bunkers in question had originally been built to store biological munitions – before the 1969 ban. Adjoining each of them was a small concrete pad on which had stood refrigeration units to cool the bunkers when perishable agents were inside. Each pad was now bare and it was clear that the refrigerators had been removed some time ago.

Denying access to what was now a designated part of the United States' chemical weapons store and *not* part of the trilateral agreement was a matter of principle for the US side. There was nothing of any biological warfare relevance inside these bunkers. Most of them were empty; some were used to store old paint cans, ladders, and cleaning cloths. But the army didn't want the Soviets to enter any part of the chemical side of the Arsenal, since it was not covered by the visit agreement and would have set bad precedent.

Another consideration was the ongoing US–USSR negotiations to strengthen the chemical weapons treaty. As part of those continuing inspections, the Soviets were asking to see the production facilities and storage areas for US binary weapons at Pine Bluff. The US did not want to give away a 'free' look at that site at this stage – especially since some members of the Soviet BW team (like Vasileyev and Zyukov) also had been chemical inspectors.

At the morning meeting, Bronson did not reveal any of the underlying US motives to the Soviets; she explained only that the bunkers were strictly off limits and were not part of Pine Bluff (Biological). She offered to show anything the Soviets requested on the NCTR side that was covered by the agreement.[37]

The Soviets were not placated, and it must be admitted, did have an argument. They pulled out their own map of the site, based on their satellite photos, which showed the line of bunkers, and, specifically, the refrigeration pads. They had correctly pinpointed these pads as the 'signature' for biological weapons storage. Why couldn't they see them now?

As a compromise, Bronson proposed to take the Soviets to see four similar and empty BW storage bunkers on the NCTR (i.e. the *correct* side) of the fence. She asked them to pick any two at random for inspection.[38] At first, the Soviets refused the offer, but then finally agreed.

When they arrived at the old BW bunkers around 10 a.m. the Soviets quickly searched through two of them and found nothing. To alleviate any further suspicion or possible complaint, Bronson then offered the two remaining old BW bunkers for inspection.

But this sincere, voluntary gesture only elicited greater suspicion. Vasileyev was overheard asking Berdennikov: 'Why can we now see the other ones? Is it a trick?' The Soviet colonel just wouldn't let it go, and he and several other Soviets stood on top of an old BW bunker, looked over the fence, and pointed at the other bunkers on the Arsenal side.

'We want to see those bunkers,' he demanded.

Everyone then was escorted back inside the NCTR building by a grim-faced Lisa Bronson. The good will that had prevailed evaporated like puddles in a heat wave. The tension had been building and now a full-blown argument ensued for the next half-hour – with each side atavistically reverting to hard-line, cold-war postures. Only Alibekov stayed out of it. It became the most heated confrontation of the entire tour – a rough equivalent of the argument after the embarrassing Obolensk chamber incident.

Bronson tried to remain calm.

'What you are asking for exceeds the limits of our agreement,' she repeated to them. 'You can look over the fence and even take photos, but you can't cross the fence line.'

Even the relaxed Berdennikov, now prodded by Vasileyev and the other military officers, started turning up the rhetoric and accusations.

'You are denying us access to something that is critical,' he complained. 'You obviously have something to hide.'

Bronson stood her ground. After several heated and escalating exchanges, she finally recommended that both sides separate for a few minutes, and reconvene after they had had a chance to cool off.

All thirteen Soviets stormed outside for a smoke. From inside, the Americans could see them engaged in intense and animated conversation. The angry Soviet military officers, led by Vasileyev, were clearly pushing their diplomatic leader, Berdennikov, to get tougher.[39] On their return, both sides squared off again minutes later, but Bronson remained firm. 'You can't go,' she told them, time and again.

'It will be noted in our report that you refused,' Berdennikov replied.

Ironically, neither Bronson nor Berdennikov was really angry with each other. Both understood that there were roles to play. Bronson was personally delighted when the Russian diplomat privately apologized to her afterwards. But the confrontation chilled any warmth that had been established over the previous week between the military officials on the two sides and was to leave the entire inspection tour with a sour taste.[40]

The Soviets left Pine Bluff at noon on Tuesday. Fortunately, no souvenirs had been planned at this stop, which was just as well, for, after the confrontation, none of the Americans would have wanted to hand out any gifts that day anyway.

And now the visitors had even more to worry about. The news from Moscow that day, 17 December, was equally grim. Gorbachev announced that the USSR would cease to exist as of 31 December.[41] The team had left as Soviets and would be returning as Russians (and one Kazakh).

After a final, uneventful visit (in rural Pennsylvania), the Soviet team boarded an Aeroflot flight at Dulles Airport on Saturday. The partings from their American hosts were not sweet sorrow. The American plan to set a new example for future BW arms control inspections had essentially failed.

But that was not the initial view in Washington, where the Defense Department concluded that the tour had gone about as well as could be expected. With cool hindsight, Bronson and her team decided that the war of wills at Pine Bluff had been predictable, and probably not deliberately planned as a provocation. They recalled that similar tense situations had occurred during prior chemical and nuclear inspections.[42] And they were pleased nothing had leaked to the press.

As for the Soviet/Russian government's reaction, Pentagon officials had low expectations from the outset and were now even less hopeful based on the hard-line performance of Colonel Vasileyev and his men.

'Some of us assumed,' Colonel Bushong recalls, 'that they would go back and tell the Ministry of Defense what they wanted to hear.'[43]

It was a remarkably prescient assumption.

Hardly had the Moscow-bound flight taken off before the Russian team began comparing notes on the most damning evidence they had found in America.

What the Americans did not know, but might have guessed, was that the tour had been a set-up. Prior to the Soviet team's departure, officials from the Ministry of Defence and Biopreparat held numerous meetings to plan what they wanted to see at the American facilities, whether they were operational or not. Their mission was made crystal clear before they left. General Valentin Yevstigneev, head of the military BW programme, had despatched his officers with an unmistakable threat, namely to find physical evidence of an American offensive biological warfare programme. If they did not find it, heads would roll. It was as brutal as that.[44]

Some of the military men began scribbling draft reports on the flight. Even the famous Eight-Ball chamber explanation, so painstakingly given by the Americans, was corrupted for the benefit of Generals Yevstigneev and Kalinin. The final report was to state unequivocally that the chamber could easily be put back into operation.[45]

As the plane headed north for Canada and the Atlantic crossing, one of the colonels suddenly revealed that he had managed to find something tangible that would satisfy General Yevstigneev. He showed the others a tiny metal fragment he had picked up from the ground at Dugway without the Americans apparently noticing.[46]

With some drama he opened his fist, displayed the fragment and announced it was part of a biological warfare bomblet.[47] It was a green-coloured fragment, one inch by half an inch, with black and yellow stripes on it. He explained that this was how the Americans had marked their BW weapons. A colleague expressed scepticism that this very old remnant constituted any kind of proof of a US violation.

'It doesn't matter,' replied the Colonel.[48]

A few seats away, Dr Alibekov held his counsel and remained even more deeply lost in thought.

CHAPTER SIXTEEN

Yeltsin

'No more lies – ever.'
Boris Yeltsin, 1992

By the New Year of 1992, Soviet Communism and the USSR had collapsed, Gorbachev was history, and Boris Yeltsin, the bluff, exciting new leader of Russia and the Commonwealth of Independent States – the USSR's old empire – was in charge. Now, finally, the biological warfare treaty violations and the whole edifice of the old Soviet BW programme could be eliminated at a stroke. That was the hope in Washington and London.

As early as 10 January 1992, Yeltsin quietly sent President Bush a letter that conveyed the kind of message the West had been longing to hear. Essentially, it was over; no one would now stand in the way of removing the old BW programme that Russia had inherited from the USSR. Yes, there had been treaty violations. That would stop.[1]

Ten days later in Moscow, during preparations for the first Yeltsin–Major summit, British Foreign Secretary Douglas Hurd held the West's first face-to-face discussion with Yeltsin about those assurances to put a stop to all illegal BW activities.[2] Yeltsin began the long talk with an important revelatory admission. When Gorbachev and his former Defence Minister handed over the reins of government, Yeltsin explained, they had promised him that the Soviet BW programme had been terminated. Yeltsin admitted point blank that this claim was not true. The programme, he had since discovered, was continuing in secret.

In brutally frank language, Yeltsin called the men in charge of the covert BW programme 'fanatics' and 'misguided geniuses'.[3] He promised to do his best to close down the offensive facilities, fire the officials in charge, and get rid of the entire Biopreparat system. He said the leader of the programme (whom he did not name) would have to 'retire immediately' and other scientists 'would have to be demoted'. He pledged that an international commission would be invited to Russia to verify for themselves that the programme had ended. The Foreign Secretary could not have asked for more.[4]

On 29 January, Yeltsin repeated these assurances to Secretary Baker at a planning session in Moscow for the first Yeltsin–Bush summit three days later.[5] Yeltsin promised Baker that the Soviet BW programme would be 'dismantled within a month'.

Later that same day, Yeltsin delivered a major televised address to the Russian people, setting out the country's entirely new disarmament programme. This transformed policy, he said, included a renunciation of the use of biological weapons and 'rigorous implementation' of the 1975 BWC. He even renounced the right of retaliation in kind against a foreign BW attack, an argument that the Soviet military had used to justify their need for having an offensive programme. Yeltsin said Russia now favoured verification, openness, and confidence building measures.[6] London and Washington could scarcely believe their eyes as they read the official despatches.

The following day, en route to Washington, Yeltsin stopped in London to consult Prime Minister Major. Yeltsin repeated everything he had told Hurd and Baker, including his promise to close down the BW facilities – though he extended the deadline slightly to forty-five days.[7]

On 1 February, at a working summit with President Bush in the rustic setting of Camp David, Yeltsin reiterated his firm commitment to ending the Soviet programme.[8] But, ominously, he also warned Bush that his aides were having difficulty finding out from the military what really was happening on the inside.[9] There were very few officials in the government, he cautioned, who were knowledgeable and forthcoming about this subject. Biopreparat was highly compartmentalized, he said, and, most ominously, the military was moving and hiding facilities. 'I am trying to find out everything I can,' he told Bush.[10]

As evidence of how hard it was to get answers, Yeltsin volunteered some intriguing comments about the accident at Sverdlovsk. Something troubling had happened there, he conceded, but he claimed he could never elicit the truth when he was the Communist Party leader of the region.[11] Yeltsin did not explain why he had never before spoken out publicly to correct the cover story of 'infected meat'. Instead, he offered a rambling excuse and complained that the KGB and military had lied to him in 1979 that the BW production facilities had been dismantled after the anthrax outbreak. Yeltsin took these assurances to mean that the USSR had 'completely scrapped' its entire BW programme. He claimed he didn't know that the Sverdlovsk facilities 'were simply moved . . . and the development of the weapons continued'.

Bush and his advisers chose to accept Yeltsin's version that he was untainted by Sverdlovsk, especially since they detected no signs that he intended any continuing cover-up. Their reaction was to encourage his search for the truth. He had, after all, achieved more in one week than his predecessor had in six prevaricating years.[12]

At the joint press conference after their private talk, neither Bush nor Yeltsin mentioned biological weapons. Rather, they chose to accentuate the positive, emphasize the historic end of the Cold War, and stress that their 'new relationship' was 'based on trust'.[13]

After the two leaders departed, Yeltsin's senior military adviser disclosed publicly for the first time the specific pledges that Yeltsin had made privately to Bush and Major. The spokesman said Yeltsin had already closed a number of BW centres, had halted all BW research and military funding to such programmes, and intended to convert the Russian BW sites into medical and pharmaceutical facilities.[14]

The Cold War was melting in front of everyone's eyes.

But these were the high points of those halcyon days. The honeymoon was already about to end, as the old Soviet military began to reassess their position and quietly reassert command of the one programme involving weapons of mass destruction which were impossible to verify. For reasons that remain unclear to this day, the old Soviet offensive biological warfare programme was worth lying, cheating, and deceiving for, even as a new Russia emerged blinking into the sunlight.

The first warning signs were innocuous enough.

On 16 February, at follow-up talks between Secretary Baker and Yeltsin (and his top aides), the Russians were still at their most encouraging, but once again they extended the deadline; another one-to-two months were needed, they said, to deal with the BW problem.[15]

On 28 February, Yeltsin announced the establishment of a new national panel: the Committee on the Convention Problems of Chemical and Biological Weapons. The committee's assignment was to study the situation surrounding Russia's CW and BW and implement steps to prevent further development, production, or stockpiling of such weapons.[16] But, at about this time, British officials were warned for the first time, by a reliable source inside the Russian Foreign Ministry, that the military was fiercely fighting the progressive, pro-Yeltsin diplomats to gain full control of this new reform committee. It was the first real indication given to London and Washington about the struggles to come.[17]

Another secret British source in Moscow warned that the Generals were still controlling all decisions on BW policies and were certainly lying to Yeltsin's team, just as they had deceived Gorbachev. For instance, the Soviet group that had recently visited the US was warning that their tour had proved conclusively that the American BW facilities were only 'mothballed' and could be readily reactivated at any time. This 'evidence' alone was reason enough, the Russian Generals argued with Yeltsin, why Russia should retain its BW programme.[18]

Nevertheless, in March, Yeltsin's government announced that they planned to make a full disclosure to the United Nations of past Soviet BW activities – a 'transparent' declaration of the entire programme and history.[19] This UN declaration, called Form F, was a new requirement of the amended BWC. It was the first official BW report the new Russian government would file; and the US and Britain viewed it as a vital test of the promises of reform and openness that Yeltsin had made to Bush and Major. Full disclosure was also considered an absolute prerequisite for a trusting future relationship. US and British officials were quietly sanguine about the UN report, which was due to be filed in April, although they knew from a British source inside the Foreign Ministry in Moscow that the Russian document might be delayed because the military was resisting its release.[20]

On 4 April, British Ambassador Rodric Braithwaite and US Ambassador Robert Strauss went together to see Yeltsin in Moscow.[21] It was now two months since Yeltsin's promises to Bush and Major. What progress had been made? Yeltsin reaffirmed his commitment to end the illegal programme, but he urged patience and once again extended the deadline. Now he said the task would take another three months.

On the plus side, Yeltsin enumerated his progress so far: he had appointed the special committee; he had ordered the closing of BW facilities and test sites; he had ordered the redeployment and retraining of 200 scientists; and he had promised to open two important military sites – Kirov and Sverdlovsk – for inspection.[22] In the course of this conversation, he conceded that he was having an intense battle with the military about all of these plans. At this point, the two ambassadors decided not to press him about the West's serious concerns that the new clean-up committee would, in fact, be controlled by the military.

One week later, on 11 April, in his most positive and definitive move yet, Yeltsin issued a formal decree (Edict 390 of the Russian Federation) ordering that Russia would stop all BW production. But, on the very same day, he also announced who would head the important new committee. Yeltsin appointed General Anatoliy Kuntsevich to serve as his personal adviser on chemical and biological disarmament; the deputy chairman would be General Valentin Yevstigneev.

It was like asking Burke and Hare (the notorious Victorian grave robbers) to take over the administration of Highgate Cemetery.

This was the first clear indication that something was fundamentally wrong within the new Russian Administration, that the old military lobby was mounting a successful counterattack. These were both old-guard Soviet generals – Kuntsevich was from the chemical side, Yevstigneev had the strong biological warfare background. Neither had any association with the reform movement.

Previously, Kuntsevich, while serving as the long-time deputy chief of the Soviet Chemical Warfare Troops, had played a major part in developing the Soviet Union's vast chemical arsenal. In 1991, Gorbachev awarded him the Lenin Prize for supervising the secret development of a new Soviet binary nerve gas, which was intended to bypass the limitations of the Chemical Weapons Convention.[23] The file on Valentin Ivanovich Yevstigneev was even more troubling. He had spent most of his military career in the BW field before becoming head of 15th Chief Directorate of the Soviet/Russian Ministry of Defence, which directed the entire illegal BW programme. Like General Kalinin (a rival for power whom he personally disliked intensely), Yevstigneev had long been an invisible force behind the BW programme, acting as the great 'no' man for requests for inspections of military BW facilities and ordering the collection of incriminating 'evidence' against the US.

To stunned US/UK arms control experts, these appointments were scarcely propitious.

Both Washington and London formally complained about Kuntsevich several times to the Yeltsin government in the weeks that followed – but to no avail. Some senior Western policy makers made allowances and tried to see the best in these appointments – arguing that Yeltsin should be given the benefit of the doubt. This benign view held that the presence of Kuntsevich and Yevstigneev did not necessarily mean that Yeltsin himself was trying to deceive the US. Rather, the two generals were more a symbol of the military bureaucracy's last ditch attempt to protect one of its key weapons programmes. Ministry of Defence officials recognized they were losing strategic nuclear weapons superiority (due to the Gorbachev/Shevardnadze/Yeltsin arms control agreements), that their reduced nation was in serious economic trouble, and that Russia might have difficulty maintaining its superpower status. Biological weapons, it could be argued, were one (unverifiable) capability which would retain that status for the new Russia. This essentially minimalist Western interpretation held that the problem might just be transitional, a housekeeping chore with which Yeltsin would eventually catch up.[24]

Once more, the prevailing view in Washington and London was not to confront Yeltsin at this stage.[25]

That spring another bad omen surfaced quite unexpectedly in London. MI6 collected another important defector from Biopreparat. Coincidentally, this new catch was a junior-level bench scientist who had worked on Plague research in Pasechnik's laboratory in St Petersburg. British authorities have never publicly identified or acknowledged the existence of this man whom they code-named 'Temple Fortune'. Although Temple Fortune was not as highly placed as Pasechnik, he helped the West in two major areas. First, he fully corroborated Pasechnik's previous revelations. Secondly, and much more significantly, he brought valuable, updated information about what was actually happening at the St Petersburg laboratories in 1992 – even *after* Yeltsin had ordered the programme terminated. The defector revealed that his laboratory was secretly continuing its research to develop new forms of Plague for offensive use in biological warfare.

Biopreparat, he disclosed, was building a new, larger facility just outside St Petersburg, in a place called Lakhta, about three miles from the institute. The planned Lakhta site, he warned, would be a huge complex of buildings covering the equivalent of a large square block in London. Biopreparat's cover story was that the so-called 'Biotechnology Facility at Lakhta' would conduct research on vaccines and interleukin II. The truth was, however, that the location would work, in conditions of great secrecy, to develop a new and improved super-Plague for the Russian offensive programme. This new Plague, he explained, would not only be even more resistant to multiple antibiotics, heat, and cold, it would be made with special new processes that gave it a truly fiendish dimension. In its initial form, the Plague would not be virulent – so it would be safe to handle and store, and, more importantly, it would not appear to be produced for offensive purposes. However, Russian scientists had found a way to convert this non-toxic Plague back into a deadly, antibiotic-resistant form as soon as it was needed for weaponization.[26]

This information came as a blow to even the most hardened and cynical British BW experts; it was the most alarming news from Russia since Drs David Kelly and Chris Davis had discovered the covert smallpox programme at Vektor. British analysts were now well aware that the Soviet/Russian military BW programme considered smallpox (from Vektor) and Plague (from St Petersburg) to be the strategic weapons of choice – the two most efficient and effective biological agents that could be carried on missile warheads for launch on US and UK cities. The potential danger and threat to the West from such missiles was as great as large megaton nuclear weapons. The permutations for further BWC treaty breaches using the new convertible super-Plague – stored in its non-lethal state – would give the Russian military even further deniability. This was a threat, the intelligence analysts warned the policy makers, that had to be taken very seriously.

After a careful debriefing, British officials shared Temple Fortune's 'take' with the Americans and then began to urge Washington to join in another joint démarche – as had been done after Pasechnik's arrival two years earlier. The Bush Administration urged patience, to give Yeltsin's team a chance.[27]

But more uneasiness grew in April when Russia's UN declaration, the famous Form F, was yet again delayed, for unexplained reasons.[28] The US and UK had submitted their own similar draft declarations to the Russians, as an example of full disclosure, but the Russians did not reciprocate as expected with their Form F document. London learned privately, from contacts with senior Russian diplomats, that the Russian Ministry of Defence vigorously opposed any release which confirmed even the existence of an offensive programme.[29] However, eventually, ten days late, on 22 April, the Russian Form F declaration, which had been personally approved by Yeltsin and his advisers, was handed over to expectant US and UK representatives.

Grigoriy Berdennikov, who had led the Russian visit to the United States in December and had since been promoted to Russia's deputy Foreign Minister, made the formal presentation of the document. He was still battling the military behind the scenes. In handing over the Form F, Berdennikov placed the best possible interpretation on it – he pointed out the declaration admitted that the USSR had violated the BWC and pledged that all illegal activities had ended. But then Berdennikov conceded the bad news. The document had been difficult to produce, he said, because the old-line BW experts were reluctant to end their work and Yeltsin's team was facing difficulties acquiring accurate information.[30] Despite these problems, Berdennikov insisted that the disclosure was the Russian government's 'best effort'. It was important now, he urged, to draw a line – to separate the past from the future. Yeltsin was hoping to put the BW issue behind and move on.

Compared to the similar American and British disclosures to the UN, the Russian paper was sketchy at best – comparable to a confession without any details of the crimes. On the one hand, the West was pleased that the document admitted the Soviet government had violated the BWC until 1992. At least that statement was formally on the record. But the admissions were not specific and failed to describe what the violations were. They avoided each of the key, lingering issues – like Sverdlovsk, Pasechnik's charges, evidence from the January 1991 visit, military facilities, and Russia's continuing BW capabilities.[31] The Russian document, for instance, cited only four BW production and testing centres dating back to the early 1950s – Sverdlovsk, Kirov, Zagorsk, and Vozrozhdeniye Island – and not the other twenty military and Biopreparat sites known to the US and Britain in the 1990s. No word was included of such bigger, newer facilities as Stepnogorsk, Berdsk, Pokrov, and Omutninsk. Vektor, Obolensk, and Leningrad/St Petersburg were dismissed in passing as research centres where 'insufficient' scientific methods and 'poor instruments' produced no 'significant military results'.[32]

Equally disingenuous, the UN declaration failed to explain how, when, or where the Soviets actually produced their BW agents. They admitted to having four BW plants – but they didn't seem to make anything there. The paper tersely noted the standard BW agents the Soviets had developed – 'anthrax, Tularaemia, Brucellosis, Plague, botulism, VEE, typhus and Q fever.' But there was no word whatsoever about their research on smallpox, or other deadly viruses like Marburg, Ebola, and Lassa fever.[33] The paper was also silent about the Sverdlovsk accident. Even though Yeltsin had admitted that it was a military release of anthrax, the UN declaration ignored the subject altogether.[34]

To expert US/UK analysts, the declaration's lack of content, and frankness, confirmed that the Russian Foreign Ministry had lost the battle with the Kuntsevich/Yevstigneev Committee and the Ministry of Defence.[35]

Finally, on 5 May, the disappointed US and British governments formally issued a démarche on the subject of the Russian Form F.[36] The complaint cited specific omissions. But Washington and London still decided the best approach was the confidential trilateral one, which would not undermine support for Yeltsin's still precarious political position.

One further overture was also pursued. On 4 June, Ambassador Reed Hamner, Deputy Director of ACDA, held a long private meeting with General Kuntsevich to go over the Form F declaration.[37] The General was impassive. He stressed that the UN document met all legal requirements and provided exhaustive details. When Hamner pressed him for answers to several of the most important US/UK concerns, the well-rehearsed responses were totally evasive.[38] For good measure, Kuntsevich added that all information the US/UK side had received from Soviet defectors was 'rubbish'. He dismissed these sources as 'impostors'.[39]

In some parts of Moscow, the Cold War still chilled the air.

Eleven days later, on 15 June, the Russians formally responded to the démarche by giving the US and UK a second Form F declaration. But this supposedly revised document was essentially the same as the first one, with only a few insignificant edits. Tellingly, it was Kuntsevich, and not a Foreign Ministry representative like Berdennikov, who made the presentation this time. The General insisted this was now the 'full story'. There would be no further additions. That was it.[40]

The next day, Yeltsin travelled to Washington to attend his second summit with President Bush since the collapse of the USSR. On 17 June, the Russian leader addressed a joint session of Congress to rousing applause. As he denounced communism, Yeltsin promised that Russia had 'done away with the practice of double standards in foreign policy'.

'We are firmly resolved not to lie any more . . . to our negotiating partners . . . or any other people,' he said. '. . . There will be no more lies – ever. The same applies to biological weapon experiments . . . We are inviting the cooperation of the US and other nations to investigate these dark passages of a former Empire.' As Yeltsin uttered these memorable words, and especially the neatly honed sound bite – 'no more lies, ever' about US–Russian relations, the packed chamber gave him one of the dozen standing ovations he received, amid chants of 'Boris, Boris'.[41]

Later, back at the White House East Room, Bush and Yeltsin signed seven major agreements, including an unprecedented pledge to cut US and Russian nuclear weapons by one-third within eleven years.[42] In this respect, the new relationship was paying handsome dividends. Amid all of this euphoria, excitement, and progress, Yeltsin promised Bush, during their private discussions, that Russia would produce another more complete UN declaration.[43] Once again, there could not have been a more inopportune moment to raise the growing displeasure about the Kuntsevich/Yevstigneev axis.

On 4 July, because of an absence of progress, a frustrated maximalist leaked the story to the press for the first time. A report in the *Washington Times* now revealed the existence of an unnamed Soviet defector (Pasechnik) who had told the British government two years earlier, in great detail, about the illegal Soviet BW programme.[44] The article cited the inadequacy of the Russian UN declaration and raised questions about whether the Russian military was still withholding information from Yeltsin about the continuing BW programme.[45]

Three days later in Moscow, British Ambassador Rodric Braithwaite and US deputy Ambassador James Collins responded to the second Form F declaration with yet another joint démarche, delivered in private to the sympathetic Russian Foreign Minister, Andrei Kozyrev. The protest demanded disclosure of more information. Sir Rodric reminded the Russians that Yeltsin had promised President Bush 'no more lies, ever'.[46]

Kozyrev replied that he had spoken to Yeltsin about this matter and they were doing their best to 'rid this house of its old ghosts'. He complained that the recent US press leak had not been helpful in this effort.[47]

Three weeks later, the US and UK learned that the Russian government had submitted, without further consultation, their final version of the Form F to the UN – and that this document was unchanged from the second one and remained hopelessly incomplete. Sources in Moscow privately conveyed to British officials that Kozyrev and the Russian Foreign Ministry had been excluded from the process of revising the declaration. General Kuntsevich and his backers were in complete control of the policy.[48] The Russian military had won another important victory over the reformers.

The West was now running short of new ideas.

In August, the US and UK presented a third démarche – this one based on Temple Fortune's Plague revelations.[49] The British had been urging just such a step for months.

On 24–25 August in London, Foreign Minister Douglas Hurd and the new Acting Secretary of State, Lawrence Eagleburger (who had replaced James Baker), jointly delivered the démarche to Foreign Minister Kozyrev and Deputy Foreign Minister Berdennikov.[50] The two Western diplomats complained that the Yeltsin government had made no progress with the UN declaration since April.[51] They cited specific concerns that the Russians were still developing an antibiotic-resistant strain of Plague. They again asked for proof that Russia had ended its offensive BW programme.[52]

In his response, Kozyrev tried to be helpful, but he was clearly hampered by the military domination of the issue. Nevertheless, the Russian Foreign Ministry was still supportive. He stressed that he could not properly address the Plague allegations because the new Yeltsin government still did not know everything about the military's BW programme.[53] The Russian official suggested that some sort of trilateral group meeting should be held, with senior Russian Ministry of Defence officials present, to address any specific Western concerns. Kozyrev also suggested that new inspections could be held to investigate suspected violations at specific Russian sites.[54] Two days later, at a follow-up meeting, Kozyrev revealed to Eagleburger that Yeltsin had decided to replace Kuntsevich and set up a new commission. But these actions would require more time and more patience from the West.[55]

By now the maximalists were gaining the upper hand in Washington and London, and their frustration with the lack of real progress was overwhelming. Within a week of Eagleburger's return home, the Bush Administration, with Prime Minister Major's assent, approved a leak to the press (as the British had been urging all along). On 31 August, a page-one article in the *Washington Post*, based on unnamed high-level sources, revealed the US and British unhappiness with the repeated delays, the incomplete UN declaration, and the démarches.[56]

Responding to the *Post* report in *Izvestiya*, a Russian Ministry of Defence spokesman repeated that the West's allegations were false, since all offensive Soviet BW work had stopped in 1975 and the Russian military did not possess any more biological weapons! General Kuntsevich added that the UN declaration was comprehensive and demonstrated evidence of Russia's good faith.[57] This 'full' disclosure, a spokesman said, would not be rewritten again.[58]

And it never was.[59]

CHAPTER SEVENTEEN

Trilateral Agreement

'You are as guilty as we are.'
General Valentin Yevstigneev, 1992

In early September, senior American and British diplomats decided to accept Kozyrev's offer to hold a trilateral meeting in Moscow, with senior Ministry of Defence officials present.[1] The US/UK side sought to use these non-technical talks to push for several political objectives, including yet another effort to persuade the Russians to rewrite the now notorious Form F UN declaration and to encourage them to restate publicly the basic principle that biological weapons were immoral.[2]

There were growing political pressures on the Bush Administration to hold this meeting. Now that the complaint about the Russian UN document was public, members of the Congress were expected to ask questions, such as: could the country that had violated the BWC ever be trusted to implement the even more important START? Key Senators had warned the White House that major US–Russian arms reduction treaties would not receive congressional approval unless the Russians made a full disclosure of the BW programme.[3] The objective in Moscow, therefore, was to bring back a new US–UK–Russia Memorandum of Understanding on biological weapons that could be shown to a sceptical Congress.[4] President Bush was also pushing for the hastily convened Moscow meeting because he was concerned about the imminent November presidential election, only two months away.[5] If doubts about Russian trustworthiness on BW issues spilled over to contaminate all the other pending nuclear and chemical arms control negotiations, then the adverse publicity and the attacks in Congress might damage Bush's chances for re-election.

The Americans were well aware that the Russian military's quid pro quo for any compromises would be 'reciprocity' – equal inspections in the US. The planners in Washington agreed beforehand that they would not grant any concessions that would somehow implicate the US as being an equal violator of the BWC.

So a high-powered team of US/UK senior policy makers was hurriedly assembled to go to Moscow. The US contingent, which included four UNGROUP representatives, was led by Under-Secretary of State for Security Affairs Frank Wisner, a newcomer to BW issues.[6] The five-person team of British arms control diplomats was led by Paul Lever, Assistant Under-Secretary from the Foreign and Commonwealth Office.[7]

It was mutually agreed that no technical or intelligence experts from either the US or UK would be invited on the trip. No spooks. The experienced maximalists were deliberately excluded from these policy discussions to avoid undue tensions or delays in securing a deal.[8] The entire visit was scheduled to last only a little more than twenty-four hours. Washington and London wanted results.

The Americans arrived in Moscow at noon on 10 September. After a quick strategy session with their British allies, the first meeting with the Russians began at 4.05 p.m. at the Foreign Ministry. More than forty Russian officials filled the room. The atmosphere was confrontational. Foreign Minister Kozyrev opened the ceremonial speeches, and then departed, leaving his deputy, Grigoriy Berdennikov, in charge. At his side, inevitably, was the ubiquitous General Valentin Yevstigneev, who ran the military's so-called defensive biological programme and was deputy director of the Yeltsin clean-up committee. The senior Biopreparat representative was its deputy director, Dr Vladimir Davydov, a close ally of General Kalinin. The visitors were told that Kalinin, the invisible man, was 'on vacation'. Also noticeably absent was General Kuntsevich, the head of the committee, who had left town, the US/UK team was pleased to learn, 'to visit' a BW site. (No one mentioned that the US had advised the Russians beforehand that it would be 'helpful' if Kuntsevich were otherwise engaged.)[9]

The preliminary discussions dragged on hour after hour, with time needed for translations, as the visiting side waded through their objectives, point by point, and Berdennikov tried to offer encouragement that his side sincerely wanted to resolve the outstanding issues.[10] But when the talks focused on the UN declaration and the prior démarches, the mood abruptly changed, as the military now showed its hand.

General Yevstigneev, speaking in Russian, took the predictably hardline stand that the Form F was 'complete'.[11] No corrections were needed, he insisted, because the UN had not criticized the Russian report. If there were no complaints, he said, then no Russian response was required. All Russian BW activities had been 'terminated', he added, so no current programmes had to be reported either. The visitors had a frustrating sense of *déjà vu*.

The General then switched to the offensive. He said the Russians had questions about the US and British declarations. 'You are as guilty as we are,' he declared.[12] He threw out this accusation – alleging American and British violations – several more times throughout the evening, without offering any details or evidence. Each time the visitors remained silent and did not respond.

Next to speak was Dr Davydov, a fluent, but tough, hardline colonel from Biopreparat, who launched into a prolonged rebuttal of the August démarche – starting with a contemptuous attack on Pasechnik's credibility.[13] Davydov insisted that the defector could not be believed because he was 'obviously looking for information with his finger tips' (a Russian euphemism for inventing allegations for money).[14]

Davydov claimed that Pasechnik's accusation that Biopreparat had weaponized Plague was preposterous, as Plague research would never be undertaken in a populated area like St Petersburg.[15] Western intelligence agencies must be confused, he added, because Pasechnik's old laboratory had not worked for the military in five years; instead, it was actually conducting research for the Veterinary Institute to develop a vaccine to protect chickens from a pseudo-plague of birds, called 'hen cholera' or 'chicken Plague'. He described in detail a natural outbreak of 'hen cholera' that had recently killed many poultry in Lakhta. He assured the visitors that there was no reason for the West to worry about anything the Russians were doing in Lakhta or St Petersburg.[16]

At 10 p.m., when the day's session eventually concluded, the two sides were still negotiating basic items for the proposed understanding.

The full groups reassembled late the next morning for a session that was supposed to produce the final written agreement before the visitors' scheduled 4 p.m. departure.[17] The Russians must have sensed the visitors' haste to leave, for instead of addressing the agreement, General Yevstig-neev felt it was necessary first to respond to the previous American questions about why the accident at Sverdlovsk had been entirely omitted from the UN declaration.[18]

He brazenly described three 'plausible' explanations for the outbreak – none of which squared with President Yeltsin's previous admissions that the accident was caused by a release of anthrax during military production. The visitors were forced to sit patiently as the General turned the clock back to these previously discredited Soviet theories, including contaminated meat, an accident during defensive research, or deliberate sabotage to discredit the facility.[19] He said the military was being incorrectly and unfortunately blamed for the outbreak only because its *defensive* work on anthrax was secret. Then came his pièce de résistance. Since Russian experts could not agree on the exact cause of the Sverdlovsk outbreak, the government decided it could not mention anything about it in the UN report. 'We didn't know enough about the cause,' he said, in a final piece of impenetrable logic.

After the General eventually fell silent, Davydov launched into a long defence of Biopreparat's funding, structure, and programmes, which, he insisted, had never involved any offensive military component, past or present.[20] He said that Biopreparat only made vaccine preparations for the Ministry of Defence.

When Wisner and Lever expressed some scepticism about this explanation, General Yevstigneev jumped in to defend Davydov. All BW activities of a *military* nature, he replied stiffly, were performed only by the Ministry of Defence.[21]

After the General and Davydov had finished, both Wisner and Ber-dennikov tried to draw the meeting to a close on a note of optimism.[22] The two sides had at least agreed on a memorandum of understanding – which they now formally christened the Trilateral Agreement.

For the West, the document's most significant new commitment was that a US/UK team would be allowed to visit any non-military Russian sites requested. This team would be allowed to go anywhere at these Biopreparat sites to view equipment, interview personnel, recover sam-ples, and record on video. Later, the team would also be permitted to inspect Russian military sites – a key concession the West had sought. But the Russians refused to define the precise timing and locations of these military visits. Instead, as a concession to the Russian military, it was agreed that 'working groups' of experts from each country would refine the details later.[23] In other words, it went on the back burner.

The visitors did secure one of their primary political objectives – the Russians agreed to democratize the Duma's oversight of the BW programme. This meant that their parliament would recommend new legislation requiring the Yeltsin government to enforce the country's obligations under the BWC (thereby hopefully marginalizing the military).[24]

Then, at the very last minute, with an agreement apparently in hand and the American and British officials now under time pressure to catch their flights home, the masters of chess executed a superb move that was to have a profound impact on the future course of the entire three-nation process. The Russians demanded that the agreement had to include a clause permitting their experts to inspect equivalent non-military sites in the US and Britain – in other words, *private* biological research and drug companies. Once the next US/UK visit to Biopreparat sites was completed, the Russians would demand their reciprocal round of inspections to unspecified American and British commercial pharmaceutical labs. These visits, the Russians claimed heavily, would 'remove ambiguities'.[25]

When the visitors protested, the Russians laid it out as simply as they could. No return visits – no agreement – no deal.

It was a brilliant stroke. With one move, the Russians had equated Biopreparat with American and British pharmaceutical houses – even though nothing could have been further from the truth. Next, there was the tacit implication that the US and UK had something to hide in terms of their own violations of the Biological Weapons Convention – that too was wholly without foundation. For a nation deeply involved in a massive deception with its own secret offensive biological warfare programme, twice caught out by defectors, it was a stunning return to the diplomatic front foot.

As the Russians had guessed, this eleventh-hour ultimatum caught the US/UK team off guard and threatened to undo everything the trip had accomplished. It was also contradictory to the US pre-trip pledge of not acquiescing to Russian equivalency demands for reciprocal inspections.

As the Americans and British huddled among themselves to agree on a course of action, small minimalist/maximalist tensions developed. The concession opponents made several points. Firstly, reciprocity to commercial sites was uncalled for – since it did not correspond to anything under question in Russia. Secondly, neither the US nor UK governments had the power to force any private companies to submit to foreign inspection. The delegation did not have the authority to sign an international agreement promising that private firms would agree to such terms. Finally, there were those who argued the whole thing was a huge Russian bluff, as they were as anxious as the visitors for the agreement, because of the availability of substantial amounts of congressional funding for Russian disarmament if these BW talks were successful. The Russians had their minimalists too, it was argued.

The senior team leaders, led by Wisner, finally overruled the objections based on their determination to go home with a deal. The reciprocal clause was quickly drafted into the agreement. The single key sentence read: 'After initial visits to Russian facilities there will be comparable visits to such US and UK facilities on the same basis.' These few innocuous sounding words would later hang like a dead-weight around the necks of the Americans.

The homecoming was celebrated by press releases, briefings, and diplomatic fanfares. The Russians too held an on-the-record press conference in Moscow to praise the document.[26] In Moscow, Berdennikov, with General Yevstigneev forever by his side, announced that the three-government joint statement reaffirmed Russia's 'commitment to full compliance' of the BWC and acknowledged that 'biological weapons have no place in their armed forces'. He further announced that Russia had cut the staff of its military biological programmes by 50 per cent and reduced the related military research budget by 30 per cent. In sum, he said Russia would stop offensive research, dismantle the related research and testing facilities, and eliminate the division within the Ministry of Defence responsible for the past offensive BW programme. None of the previous BW violations committed by the Soviets, he reiterated, was continuing.[27]

General Yevstigneev added, somewhat elliptically: 'We have some questions to put to the British and US side.'[28]

In Washington, Under-Secretary Wisner, speaking on background, forcefully played up his team's achievements in Moscow. All doubts from the previous démarches, and the repeated Russian failures to respond, were swept aside. With congressional hearings on nuclear arms control, and an election pending, he accentuated only a very positive message – that the agreement was a major breakthrough.[29] The Bush Administration, he said, was pleased that 'all of the relevant ministries' in Russia – defence, health, industry, and security – had supported the agreement.[30] For good measure, he added that he believed the Russian military was now 'responsive to civilian direction in this matter'.[31] He stressed that he was now convinced that the Russian military would abide by the demands of the Yeltsin team, which now had 'the authority and discipline [and] . . . consensus' to end the BW programme. He said the results in Russia in less than a year, created by the change from Gorbachev to Yeltsin, had been 'dramatic'.

The maximalists in London, including some officials who had not been invited to Moscow, saw the deal with greater cynicism. They felt the Wisner team's visit had accomplished nothing, since the Russian military had made no real concessions, had provided no new information about their current or past programme, had not changed their dishonest UN declaration, and had besmirched the credibility of two defectors. Yet the Russians had gained reciprocity in writing. One British official derisively called the result: 'Munich in Moscow.'[32] Another, Dr Chris Davis, recalls: 'Once that deal was made, we knew the real biological warfare inspection process was over. The Russians had got away with it.'[33]

CHAPTER EIGHTEEN

Alibekov

'I did a lot of very bad things. God will forgive me.'
Dr Kanatjan Alibekov, 1998

A few days after the Wisner team had returned from Moscow in mid-September 1992, and even as the backslapping and self-congratulatory memoranda were still flying around Washington, Lisa Bronson received a propitious phone call at her Pentagon office.[1]

The nervous caller, an unidentified female with a Russian accent, insisted on meeting Bronson privately to discuss a matter of great importance. She was calling from New York, she said, on behalf of their 'mutual friend'.[2] The same woman had briefly phoned Bronson several months earlier, mentioning, somewhat mysteriously, this 'friend's' desire to live in the US. Intrigued, Bronson now agreed to see the woman the next day.

When they met, the woman handed over the very same business card Bronson had given Dr Kanatjan Alibekov during the Soviet inspector's visit to the United States a year earlier. The woman then delivered the most sensational news.

Dr Alibekov – one of the world's leading Plague Warriors, who had been second only in rank at Biopreparat to General Kalinin – was ready to defect to the United States.

There were only two conditions. He wanted the US government to grant him permanent residence and to accept his wife and three children with him.

Bronson was very excited. A Pentagon lawyer, with no intelligence experience, she was about to pull off what the CIA's best case officers had not managed to achieve in twenty years – bring in not just a defector from inside the heart of Biopreparat, but the number-two man in the whole set-up.

The business card was Alibekov's sign that Bronson could be assured this was the real thing. Bronson whistled quietly to herself and reasoned that the scientist must have known a year ago that he might defect. The secret operation to retrieve him and his family was then handed over to the CIA. Some four weeks later, in mid-October, Bronson received confirmation that everyone had arrived safely in Washington.

For whatever reason, no one at the CIA ever thanked or commended Bronson for helping lure Alibekov to the US. She had to celebrate this success on her own and in silence. She was not even allowed to meet him for another six months. When they finally did reunite inside her Pentagon office, he gave her a huge hug and then thanked her profusely for helping him and his family. The memory of that intimate moment would be Bronson's enduring reward.

Alibekov remained out of sight for the next six years, as his presence in CIA hands was kept a priority national security secret. (MI6 debriefers were the only outsiders given access to him.) At last, as he spoke in private, the full, terrible story of Soviet biological warfare began to tumble out.

Before Pasechnik arrived, the West's information about the Soviet BW programme was comparable to a series of black-and-white snap pictures from space, supported by educated guesses. After Pasechnik, these photos became an out-of-focus black-and-white film with expert narration. The visit to the four Soviet sites added focus to the film, and context and confidence to the narration. But Alibekov changed the production into feature-length, full colour – with surround sound.

Alibekov had seen everything from Moscow head office point of view and he possessed a wonderful memory. He had been General Kalinin's point man on the US inspections and he'd helped run the Soviet deceptions at the sites visited by the British and the Americans. He knew not only where the bodies were buried, but who had killed them, and how and why. He knew about high-level meetings with the Kremlin from 1987–91. He had studied secret files – dating back to the 1930s, and had interviewed old-time officials about their experiences. He had worked at or visited every single major facility in the Biopreparat complex. He personally knew most of the employees. He knew every detail of how the USSR developed and tested their biological agents and weapons since he ran that programme. He even knew about the programme's future plans.[3]

Unlike Pasechnik, who was a civilian scientist, Alibekov was an army Colonel who had dealt with senior military officials and KGB officers. He had served as Kalinin's deputy for four years. He had directed Biopreparat's teams during the USSR and US visits so he knew the behind-the-scenes strategy. In the intelligence business, it was hard to imagine a better source. Put simply, he was bringing the West the crown jewels of Soviet BW.

Again, unlike Pasechnik, he readily conceded that his driving motive during the Soviet years was to defend the motherland, by helping the USSR win what he understood to be a BW arms race with the US.

His Pauline conversion came about because of the traumatic inspection of the old American BW sites a year earlier. In that sense, the Pentagon's attempt to let the democratic process shine a light on the Soviet team had been an evangelical triumph as far as Alibekov was concerned. Day after day, in Utah, Arkansas, and the other locations, he slowly realized that there was no covert American BW programme. The United States really *had* abandoned all offensive biological weapons many years earlier. *The enemy spoke the truth.* At that point, he began to lose faith in the Soviet system.

Like Pasechnik, he was coming to the West, with all the fervour of a convert, to undo the damage he had caused by helping in the programmes that produced such horrific weapons.

As he began talking, it became very clear there was no good news.

Since World War II, he told the CIA, the Soviets' crude biological warfare arsenal had been expanded to include: anthrax, Plague, cholera, VEE, glanders, Brucellosis, smallpox, and Marburg. Under research and development were: Ebola, several haemorrhagic fevers (Machupo and Junin), Lassa fever, yellow fever, and Japanese and Russian encephalitis.[4] In all, Alibekov said the Soviets possessed an incredible *fifty-two* different biological agents that could be used as weapons.[5] The highest-rated ones, appropriately called 'battle strain', were the most infectious and the easiest to manufacture and transport.[6]

The Soviets made the acquisition of biological warfare agents a full-time, and suprisingly efficient, cottage industry. To ensure they acquired only the newest and most exotic types of bacteria, viruses, and toxins, the organizers of the programme relied on the ubiquitous KGB to act as procuring agents. KGB officers throughout the world were placed on special alert to seek and acquire. Biopreparat code-named the KGB, somewhat childishly, 'Capturing Agency One'. The 'Agency', in turn, regularly, and rather alarmingly, sent samples of these emerging pathogens back to Moscow simply packed in diplomatic pouches. The unwitting airlines were, of course, never forewarned that they were transporting miniature plagues around the globe. It is fortunate there were no recorded mishaps.

Using these extraordinary methods, Biopreparat even obtained strains of AIDS virus and Legionnaire's disease from the US, although, after further study, neither candidate was found to have any military usefulness (due to their instability).[7]

Of the 'battle strain' bacteria, the preferred agents by the 1980s were a special type of anthrax (up to 90 per cent mortality rate), Pasechnik's super-Plague (up to 100 per cent death rate if untreated early), and Tularaemia (a special Soviet version about which little had been known in the West).[8] Alibekov revealed that the Soviets first obtained their most potent strain of Tularaemia – a hot lethal strain called 'Schu-4' that was not found naturally in the USSR, Europe or Asia – from a routine medical exchange with the US in the 1950s. In the officially sanctioned exchange, the US received a new Soviet vaccine for Tularaemia; in return, the US supplied the Soviets with a Schu-4 sample, supposedly for future medical research. The Schu-4 was severely infectious, with a 10 per cent lethality rate compared to 3 per cent for other strains.[9]

The USSR, Alibekov disclosed, had prepared and stored literally hundreds of tonnes of weapons-grade anthrax and dozens of tonnes of Plague and Tularaemia – all ready to load into bombs and ICBM warheads at short notice.[10] As Pasechnik had warned, Alibekov now confirmed that the Soviets were attempting to make all three of these bacteria resistant to antibiotics. By 1991, Alibekov added, Soviet R&D experts had 'improved' anthrax, super-Plague, and Tularaemia so that they also could overcome all immune systems and current medical treatments.[11]

Alibekov said the Soviets produced enough anthrax and super-Plague to have killed the Earth's entire population several times over.

He also confirmed that the Soviet Army, since 1947, had specifically focused attention on smallpox as the most effective viral weapon.[12]

In 1959, KGB officers in India obtained samples of a highly virulent, rapidly infectious strain of smallpox, which, after several years of careful development and testing, became the main Soviet 'battle strain' of the virus. By the 1970s, this smallpox strain, code-named 'India-1' by Biopreparat, became the Soviet military's virus of choice. The Soviets produced some *twenty tons* of it each year (the virus had a one-year shelf life) and stored the supply at a secret lab in the army's Virological Centre at Zagorsk.[13]

But still not content with this cornucopia of death, General Kalinin ordered his research team in 1987 to develop a yet more virulent smallpox weapon. Biopreparat then built a large smallpox reactor inside Vektor's new Building 15 in Kol'tsovo – the first of its kind in the world. Alibekov and Dr Lev Sandakhchiev jointly managed this expanded, industrial-scale smallpox programme. This team, Alibekov revealed, had successfully tested their first improved smallpox weapon inside Vektor's explosive chamber in December 1990 – just one month before the US/UK inspectors visited the site when they were blandly assured that no such work was ever contemplated.[14]

Alibekov also confirmed that the Soviets were attempting at Vektor to genetically engineer entirely new life forms – super-viruses – which, if successful, were intended to cause unimaginable consequences to the world's population.[15] These 'doomsday' viruses were combinations of the most deadly germs available – smallpox, Marburg, Ebola, VEE, and Machupo. The grotesque 'marriage' would be between speed of infection and high-kill factor. The aim was to insert genes from one virus, like Ebola, into another, like smallpox, to create an even more lethal 'chimera' virus.

By 1990, Alibekov alleged, the Soviets had successfully created the first 'chimera' – by inserting genes from VEE (a brain virus, that causes a severe coma) into smallpox.[16] Biopreparat spent several million dollars on this programme. Subsequent combinations under development included the insertion of Ebola and Marburg genes into smallpox.

(Alibekov's claims about this 'chimera' research were later vociferously denied by Sandakhchiev. Western intelligence analysts believe such a programme is still in its infancy; however, to dismiss it as a potential threat, they say, would run contrary to everything the Russians have achieved in their biological weapons development programmes so far.)[17]

Alibekov described the entire range of special technologies and engineering used by the Soviets to manufacture agents and weapons: cultivation; preparations; formulas; instruments; and milling, drying and freeze-drying techniques. He recounted a wide array of testing methods in chambers and the open air. He recited precise testing results – including gruesome infection ratios and kill rates. For every piece of equipment or process, he also carefully explained how each technique applied to every primary BW agent in the Soviet arsenal. He gave personal profiles of all the key Soviet officials and scientists in Biopreparat, including their research work, tendencies and vulnerabilities. He described the layouts of every facility in depth and concluded his technical presentation with an insight into Soviet defensive innovations, equipment and vaccines – that is, how they planned to fight off an enemy attack.

Alibekov also confirmed that the Soviets had conducted large-scale aerosol tests inside the USSR's borders, near civilian populations, using BW simulants (including *Bacillus thuringiensis* and *Serratia marcescens*). These experiments, held from 1979 through 1989, had occurred near Novosibirsk, at a military site near Nukus, in the Caucasus, and several times inside the Moscow subway system.[18]

In terms of strategic planning, he confirmed Pasechnik's insight that the Soviet BW programme had operated under the highest security classification possible in the USSR's political/military system – even higher than the nuclear programme. This classification, 'Special Importance', which was higher than 'Top Secret', indicated, by itself, that the Soviets equated their strategic BW missiles with their nuclear weapons.[19]

Alibekov explained Soviet delivery systems of BW agents, describing with precise detail the tactical aircraft with spray tanks; long-range strategic bombers carrying cluster bombs; strategic missiles with multiple warheads; and cruise missiles under development. In the event of all-out war, he added, the biological agents used to strike strategic targets – like American and British cities – would not just comprise super-Plague and anthrax, but also viruses that cause serious epidemics, including smallpox and Marburg.[20] Each city would be attacked with a cocktail of bacteria and viruses – at least three to five agents per attack – so that enemy activities would be fully disrupted within a couple of days; the civilian infrastructure would collapse and there would be few survivors. The will to continue war fighting would die with the people.[21]

Soviet BW production information was considered so sensitive, Alibekov said, that nothing was shared with any foreign government, not even Warsaw Pact nations. Inside the Kremlin, all Soviet leaders since Brezhnev, including President Gorbachev, had understood the extent of the BW programme. But only a few other high-ranking members on the Politburo (like the Defence and Health Ministers), who were directly responsible in the chain of command, and took care of the funding, were kept fully informed; other officials only had a generalized overview.[22]

This Mafia-like secrecy, a kind of military/political *omerta*, ensured that only a tiny handful of very senior officers and their immediate aides and juniors, men like Yevstigneev and Kalinin, had the knowledge and were able to administer the whole programme.[23] That alone helped explain Gorbachev and Yeltsin's confusions, hesitancies, and contradictions when talking to the West about BW treaty violations.

At the very end of months and months of long and careful debriefing, Alibekov was invited to write a study paper for the CIA of all the information in his possession on the entire Soviet BW programme. This long paper was considered so potentially dangerous should it ever fall into the wrong hands that it was given the highest US security classification that exists, and even Alibekov was not permitted to keep a copy or ever see it again.[24]

Kanatjan Alibekov was born in September 1950 in the small settlement of Kauchuk, in a farming region of south central Kazakhstan, then a Soviet republic south of Russia.[25] His father, Bayzak, a Kazakh, was a Soviet army veteran of World War II who became a career militia officer (local police). His mother, Rosa, also a native Kazakh but with Slav features, was a descendant from a prominent, aristocratic family in the pre-1917 era, though she inherited no wealth. Her second son, young Kanatjan, favoured his father's Asian appearance – with thick, straight, black hair and a wide, roundish face with a light brown complexion.

In 1951, when Alibekov was a baby, the family moved 800 kilometres east to Alma-Ata, the capital of Kazakhstan near the Chinese border, where his father was promoted and eventually became Regional Commander for all militia forces. His mother, meanwhile, became a department chief administering the local directorate for surveyors. With such good posts, both parents remained loyal Communist Party members and strong believers in the Soviet system.

Young Alibekov was not a particularly good student, indeed, for three years as a teenager he attended school at night and worked full-time by day in a small factory that made washing machines. This tiresome and dreary experience changed his life and forced him to face the reality that without a good education he would be a cipher.

At age seventeen, after receiving a high-school equivalency degree, he decided to become a physician and enrolled in the medical institute in Alma-Ata, a six-year, tuition-free course for civilian doctors. After four years, he decided to become a military physician. Once in the army, he eventually chose epidemiology and infectious diseases as his medical speciality.

He graduated from the medical military college at Tomsk, Siberia in June 1975 at the age of twenty-four. Just before the ceremony, he had an inkling that something special was brewing when unidentified security officers, probably from the KGB, interviewed him on campus several times, because, they said, he was being considered for 'important and interesting scientific work' that was 'classified'.

On graduation day, he learned he was being assigned to a top-secret new directorate of research that the Kremlin had established two years earlier. The official name was the Special Military Directorate of the Council of Ministers of the USSR. The open name was 'Biopreparat'.

No one told him why he was selected for this job or what it would entail. He had no idea yet what Biopreparat was established to do. In August 1975, he reported to his first assignment in Omutninsk, a small city of 20,000 people about 400 miles northeast of Moscow. At the Omutninsk BW facility, a complex of some thirty buildings and more than 3,000 workers, the normal activity did not involve pathogenic agents. Rather, the facility, like several others in the Biopreparat system, was an 'on-call' site where the Soviets could launch a full BW programme of production and weaponization if a war was imminent.

The Soviets actually devised complexes like Omutninsk to bypass the 1972 BWC, which prohibited the signatories from preparing any BW agents for weapons. The special Soviet 'standby' concept allowed them to begin full production of weapons with only a few days' notice by always remaining totally prepared and fully staffed. Special Mobilization

Departments kept everything ready; but since no agents were produced for weapons, the Soviets could argue that these sites were not technically violating the treaty.

The Soviet policy specified that wartime production would only begin during a 'special period' of high tension – just before a declared war. Once mobilization was ordered, these supposed 'civilian' facilities, like Omutninsk, would immediately convert to military facilities. An encrypted message from Moscow to the facility director would specify what kinds of biological weapons to start producing. At Omutninsk, the assigned agents were Plague and Brucellosis.

Alibekov spent seven months in Omutninsk as a junior scientist learning the basics of technical microbiology and BW research. In March 1976, he was transferred to Berdsk, about 50 miles south of Novosibirsk, Siberia. His new facility, the Berdsk Biotechnology Plant, did essentially the same work as Omutninsk – planning to produce weapons with Plague, Brucellosis, plus Tularaemia. As a trained junior scientist, Alibekov was now empowered to start his own independent scientific research.

Alibekov, now married, remained in Berdsk for four years, rising to senior scientist and then laboratory chief in charge of seventeen people. Soon after he arrived, he first caught the attention of senior Biopreparat officials in Moscow by showing unusual initiative – he organized a special research laboratory for developing processes for cultivating and concentrating a wide spectrum of micro-organisms. This laboratory was considered a significant accomplishment. A self-starting scientist who demonstrated initiative attracted notice in the still relatively new Biopreparat system. Although Alibekov did not know it, his future career path was already being plotted by General Yuriy Kalinin, who toured Berdsk in late 1977 and was very pleased to see the new laboratory.

Kalinin quietly adopted the young Kazakh and made sure Alibekov was promoted rapidly (ten times in the next ten years), a meteoric rise that would eventually take him all the way to Kalinin's side in Moscow. In 1980, the General offered him the first of these new jobs: to go back to Omutninsk as chief of the technical department supervising 150 people. He would be in charge of all cultivation, generation, and final formulation of BW agents.

Much of his work now took place in high-containment laboratories, where he developed incapacitating organisms, like Brucellosis. Kalinin promoted Alibekov a year later to be Deputy Director, and then soon Acting Director of Omutninsk's entire military section, supervising all 400 military personnel. Alibekov's major accomplishment during the next year was to produce and successfully test Biopreparat's first vaccine-resistant Tularaemia bomblet.[26]

In August 1983, Alibekov was named military director for the BW facility at Stepnogorsk, Kazakhstan, where he now supervised 1,000 people at a much larger, more prestigious site than Omutninsk. A year earlier, the Soviet government had signed a highly classified decree ordering Biopreparat to develop a new variant of anthrax. To do this, the army needed a new manufacturing facility to replace the closed anthrax plant at Sverdlovsk. The existing Stepnogorsk site, which previously did not handle lethal agents, was renovated for this sensitive new work. General Kalinin selected Alibekov to develop this important weapon and prepare the expanded facility for production.

The complex he now ran was vast; the largest BW production facility ever built in the world, so secret it was never shown on any map. 'The Progress Scientific and Production Association', as the military eerily called it, was the Hell's Kitchen of Biopreparat, the mother of all biological warfare breeding, loading, and weaponization plants.

Inside the heavily guarded site, the huge production buildings were all numbered rather than named.[27] Building 221 alone, the main production hall, had ten twenty-ton fermenters on the ground floor, for producing anthrax and Plague. Just one twenty-ton fermenter can produce *fourteen tons* of bacteria at a time. Just one millilitre contains two billion organisms.[28]

The deadly end products from Building 221 – concentrated, weapons-grade biological warfare agents – were then safely stored in refrigeration units. From the building's basement, a tunnel led to nearby Buildings 241–244, where all the 'filling' of weapons took place in huge, semi-underground bunkers. The bacteria were loaded into what the Soviets called cassettes, and then trundled off to Buildings 251 and 252 for handling and assembly on the ground floor, where there was space to park large vehicles. Here the cassettes were loaded into sophisticated, melon-sized bombs and warheads, and driven off for storage.

It was a well-organized and efficient production plant that produced disease by the ton. It was all nicely self-contained and bomb-proofed.

Only seven days were needed to crank the whole plant into full-scale production activity.

Building 600, the second largest structure at the site, housed the research laboratories and two large test chambers, where Alibekov's staff tested anthrax, Plague, Tularaemia, and glanders. Building 261, the quarantine building, held a 45-bed isolation unit. Security was much tighter throughout the entire compound than at Sverdlovsk to ensure there were no more disasters like the anthrax emission and to prevent potential international scrutiny or espionage.[29] In order to frustrate any attempts at electronic eavesdropping by Western spy satellites, the complex deliberately had only a special, land-line telephone system (using buried, high-frequency cables encased in metal pipes) and no radio communications. In the event of conflict, Moscow would have had to tone-dial up the end of the world.

Alibekov delivered three important accomplishments for his boss at Stepnogorsk. First, he developed a new, more efficient industrial process for making anthrax – both liquid and dried. This 'Alibekov anthrax' was three times as lethal, by weight, as the powder used in previous Soviet weapons.

The actual anthrax type that the Soviets had prepared for use against the West had all the pedigree and class one might associate with a top-quality French truffle. It was prosaically called 'Strain 836', but happened to be the most virulent and vicious strain of anthrax known to man. It was created by pure chance in 1953 following an accident at Kirov, the Soviet military's first anthrax development site, when large amounts of live anthrax spores were inadvertently spilled into the city's sewage system.[30]

Three years after this unfortunate little mishap, Kirov's senior scientist, Vladimir Sizov, suggested that a team might usefully enter the sewers and find out if the anthrax carried by the rats of Kirov had mutated and become stronger (since rodents do not die from anthrax infection). The designated ratcatchers were duly despatched, and infected rat offspring were trapped, brought to the surface, killed, and dissected.

To their joy, the scientists under Sizov discovered that the rats had indeed incubated a new, and naturally selected form of anthrax. It had survived years in the darkness and filth of the sewers and proved to be an unusually tough, virulent spore. It was christened Strain 836. (In 1979, it was this strain of anthrax that leaked at Sverdlovsk.)

In 1984, under Alibekov's direction at Stepnogorsk, Biopreparat decided to test Strain 836 to assay its virulence against all comers – to see if it was still the most potent after nearly thirty years. There would be a sort of clinical trial against the toughest competition. The KGB was instructed to collect the most lethal anthrax strains in the world. Soviet officers scoured the world, literally, and eventually brought back fourteen different strains from places as diverse as the US, France, Spain, and Southwest Asia.

Mice, hamsters, and guinea pigs were used to conduct the trials. Strain 836 emerged as the clear winner of this grotesque beauty contest, a full 10 per cent more virulent than its nearest rival.

But *still* the Soviets weren't satisfied. By 1986, Alibekov's team at Stepnogorsk had *tripled* the potency of the original strain 836 (as confirmed by animal testing at Vozrozhdeniye Island). The Stepnogorsk plant could manufacture two tons of this finished anthrax every day, Alibekov later explained, 'in a process as reliable and efficient as producing tanks, trucks, cars or Coca-Cola'.[31]

As of 1992, the Alibekov-enhanced 836 still remained the preferred Russian military strain of anthrax. The other benefits of this rodent-produced anthrax were its good resistance to both heat and cold and inclement environmental factors; and, crucially, its easy adaptability to aerosol spraying.

Alibekov's second achievement at Stepnogorsk was the development of glanders as a biological weapon. In only one year, he established the usefulness of this previously under-used bacteria and devised new production procedures to manufacture it. Found in horses, mules, and sheep, glanders is highly infective and transmittable to humans; it inflames the skin, causes deep ulcers, attacks the internal organs, and is often fatal if untreated. After Alibekov's work, the Soviets concluded the agent was stable in aerosol delivery systems and was indeed lethal in low doses. Glanders was added to the Soviet arsenal as a tactical, battlefield weapon.[32]

Alibekov's third and crowning achievement at Stepnogorsk was supervising the first-ever Soviet tests to assess the Marburg virus as a biological weapon. In this breakthrough development, he worked closely with Dr Sandakhchiev's Marburg research team at Vektor laboratories in Novosibirsk. By 1983, the Vektor group already had spent several years working with this terrible virus, but their laboratories did not yet have the right equipment to test its behaviour in explosive dissemination.

So Alibekov staged the first Marburg tests inside Stepnogorsk's Building 600, a five-storey, brick and concrete structure built like a box within a box. Inside its core was a large (400-cubic-yard) explosive chamber linked to a nearby static chamber. Attached to this static chamber by sealed pipes was a series of smaller capsules that housed test monkeys. From these capsules, the animals would breathe in the contaminated air sent by explosive dissemination via the connecting pipes and chambers.

In all, Alibekov ran about twenty different Marburg experiments to measure a variety of agent efficiency factors, using at least four monkeys per test.[33] No one else in the world had ever considered weaponizing Marburg this way, much less testing it to prove it could work. The desire to use the Marburg virus as an offensive biological weapon is to flirt with evil. In the table of biological and viral horrors, Marburg is at the top.

But, inevitably, the Soviets discovered a military/scientific justification for developing this virus. Marburg was preferred, because testing at Stepnogorsk showed the equally appalling Ebola virus was not quite as stable in storage or sturdy against environmental factors, such as sunlight. On the plus side, both viruses required a very low infectious dose and did not respond to any known treatment. Only a tiny amount, just a few particles, was required to infect a human; so a millilitre of a virus like Marburg actually contained billions of contagious particles; billions of doses. Very efficient.[34]

By 1990, following Alibekov's experiments with Marburg at Stepnogorsk, the Soviets had completed all preparations for manufacturing the virus as a weapon. Even Soviet scientists spoke with awe about the virus's deadly power. If it were ever deployed, they knew, the consequences would be unimaginable.

How did they know? Alibekov had brought with him one of the great true horror stories of biological warfare research.

On 13 April 1988, Nikolai Ustinov was working with a young assistant, Sergei Krotov, on the deadly Marburg virus inside the high-containment laboratory at the Vektor viral research centre in Kol'tsovo.[35]

Ustinov, a ruggedly attractive and talented forty-four-year-old scientist, held a struggling guinea pig in his gloved hand, while Krotov prepared to inject it with the virus. The guinea pig was squirming, and, at the precise moment of injection, Krotov stuck the needle into and through the animal's body, missing the intended spot. Instead, the tip pierced Ustinov's rubber glove and delivered some of the virus into his thumb. Because Marburg has an extremely low infectious dose, Ustinov knew instantly that he had been sentenced to death.[36]

Ustinov remained outwardly calm. He left the laboratory through an air lock and used an emergency phone to report the accident. He was immediately placed into a special bed inside a high-containment isolation unit equipped for such emergencies. Inside, the air is sterilized and all staff and visitors must first go through a chemical shower. Nurses wear biologically secure space suits. Even the patient's faeces are 'cooked' before exiting the hospital through a separate sewage unit.

Inside the sterile suite, Ustinov knew exactly what was coming. As did his handsome wife, Yevgenia, who also worked at Vektor in paediatrics and was the mother of his two young sons, Sergei and Nicolai.

'When I heard the news my heart shrank and never grew again,' recalls his wife. 'He told me: "Don't worry, everything will be fine," but I knew and he knew, and he knew that I knew . . .'

As his temperature began to rise, he asked for a diary so he could record his own death in full clinical detail. By the fourth day, his eyes had turned red, as small haemorrhages developed in them. On the eighth day, Yevgenia began to prepare herself for the worst. The Marburg virus slowly destroys and then liquefies the body's internal organs; as they disintegrate, the body eviscerates them. Blood begins to seep from the skin, the mouth, the gums, the nose, the eyes, the anus, and the nipples. It is no longer able to clot.

Ustinov scribbled furiously through the last days. When his wife came to see him, she was permitted only to look through the protective glass and communicate by phone. Physical contact had long since ceased. In order to protect her during the visits from the reality of his mouldering body, they had carefully wrapped him in sheets to his chin. When she left, he continued writing. She was with him as he wept just before he died. He had begun to sweat blood.

The autopsy was on the seventeenth day. They took the body into a sterile isolation room, built as a box within a box. They knew exactly what they had to do. They had his permission.

They wore Soviet-made hooded containment suits made of light-weight rubber the colour of fresh grass. Over their trousers, they wore black, knee-high lab boots, and, on their hands and arms, two pairs of flesh-coloured gloves.

They removed Ustinov's liver and spleen, and sucked large quantities of his damaged blood from a leg vein, using a special nine-inch glass syringe. Then they froze it. They needed to keep the Marburg strain alive and replicating. This was, by grotesque coincidence, just what the laboratory had been praying for – a fast-acting and deadly strain of Marburg, ideal for weaponization.

They called it Variant U (for Ustinov), and soon replicated the virus in flasks. Once it had been dried and processed into particles small enough to be inhaled, it was ready to be passed over to the weaponization boys at Stepnogorsk, where it would be factory-fed into the necessary armaments, shells, cluster bombs, even ICBM warheads ready for target-ing against London, New York, Washington, and Los Angeles.[37]

Oddly, they didn't cremate the remains. Instead, what was left of the corpse was placed inside a triple-lined, rot-proof, zinc coffin and was buried in a local cemetery. His widow, who never remarried, visits his grave often. In traditional Russian orthodox fashion, she first kisses his photographic image on the headstone, then 'shares' a drink with him to celebrate a birthday or a holy day.

According to Alibekov, by 1991, the illegal Soviet/Russian biological warfare programme had produced sufficient Marburg virus to wipe out the world.

In August 1987, General Kalinin rewarded Alibekov for his performance at Stepnogorsk with his first post in Moscow – Biopreparat's Deputy Director for Special Biosafety. His new job was only a temporary stop. Kalinin actually intended to familiarize Alibekov with all of the key positions at headquarters. During the next ten months, he promoted Alibekov four times, each time with increased authority, until, finally, in May 1988, he became Kalinin's first Deputy for Science and Technology, a powerful number two post he held for the next three years. Since

Kalinin was primarily a military administrator – with little scientific background – Alibekov had essentially become the chief scientific planner for all of Biopreparat.

Such were Alibekov's skills, and the highly classified nature of his work, that, since Stepnogorsk, he was being paid more than twice as much as a typical Soviet minister serving in Moscow. Along with this large salary and his prestigious positions came the perks, including a personal limousine and driver, access to special food, exceptional medical coverage, and a spacious three-bedroom apartment.

It was at Biopreparat headquarters that Alibekov first discovered the full extent of the Soviet BW programme. Until 1987, he had been aware of only certain aspects of the overall programme. Even as his level of understanding now grew, he remained proud that his country possessed such a serious offensive capability, because he firmly believed that the US had a similar programme. The Soviet programme, he believed, was an appropriate response to the deadly American weapons.

The defection of Pasechnik in 1989 shook all of Biopreparat. Alibekov had known Pasechnik for more than a decade; most recently, as director of all Biopreparat research, he had been Pasechnik's immediate supervisor. From that insider's position, he was able to describe to the CIA and MI6 the Biopreparat reaction after Pasechnik fled.

First, there was an immediate KGB investigation. Both Kalinin and Alibekov were fully cleared of any responsibility. Next, Alibekov was put in charge of the cover-up. He was instructed to prepare misleading stories to counter the damaging information that Pasechnik would give the British government. He also went to Leningrad to supervise the destruction of all classified papers and records at Pasechnik's institute. A large security team removed, shredded, and burned every document relating to Pasechnik and his military work. Alibekov also devised and implemented a new scientific programme for the institute which appeared to involve only defensive and civilian research. All obviously identifiable offensive work for the military was halted in Leningrad.

Alibekov then began to have his first nagging doubts about the programme.

After the April 1990 Washington/London démarche, Biopreparat received instructions from Gorbachev's office to prepare Soviet facilities for possible future US/UK visits. Alibekov sensed a wind of change blowing through the old Soviet BW system. By December 1990, now increasingly uncomfortable in doing offensive BW research, Alibekov decided to de-emphasize his military work. Rather than abruptly leave his post as Kalinin's deputy, however, he first tried to ease his way into more acceptable work by asking for additional responsibilities in legitimate civilian medical research. When Kalinin agreed, Alibekov also became director of science and technology for Biokhimashproeket (Biological Machinery), the civilian branch of Biopreparat, which designed laboratory and production equipment. Alibekov hoped it was his first step out of the military programme.[38]

That same month, coincidentally, the Kremlin ordered Kalinin to open up the four Biopreparat facilities for the US/UK visit. Kalinin placed Alibekov in charge of sanitizing those facilities and co-hosting the visit. Alibekov was now making noises at Biopreparat meetings suggesting that there should be meaningful BW disarmament talks between the USSR and the US/UK, with Soviet admissions of past violations, but Kalinin firmly overruled him. Instead, Kalinin sent Alibekov out with top-secret instructions to employ evasions and constant delays throughout the visit.[39]

Alibekov confirmed to his CIA debriefers how much the Soviets had lied throughout the 1991 inspections. They had hidden every piece of sensitive equipment from all the laboratories and buildings, especially the drying, milling, and filling devices, as well as all traces of the weapons themselves, like bomblets and spray tanks. If there was no plausible 'defensive' explanation for an item, they had removed it and put something else in its place. Everything the visitors had spotted which might be incriminating was incriminating. Alibekov confirmed that the British experts – Kelly and Davis – had been dead right when they identified the pitted marks inside the Obolensk test chamber. Because this was irrefutable proof of an offensive BW programme, the Soviets had prayed this evidence would not be uncovered.[40]

When Kalinin named Alibekov to lead Biopreparat's contingent on the US tour in December 1991, it meant Alibekov would be taking his first trip to the West. At preliminary meetings, he soon learned that Colonel Vasileyev, who would head the military side, had declared the US guilty of maintaining a covert offensive BW programme even before they left Moscow.[41]

After touring the Dugway site in Utah for two days, Alibekov, to his dread, knew all he needed to know. As the world's foremost BW production and testing expert, he knew exactly what to look for, and he saw nothing that remotely could be considered operational for offensive purposes. It was obvious to him that anything related to Dugway's offensive BW programme had been shut down long ago. He also noted that none of the rooms, laboratories, or chambers had been specially sanitized for the visit in the way he had sanitized his locations. He was impressed that the Americans allowed the Soviet team to use video cameras wherever they went (which he had not permitted in the USSR). This freedom, he concluded, indicated that the US had nothing to hide.[42]

On the plane back to Washington, he realized that Dugway was his breaking point. If the US was not using Dugway as an active testing facility for biological weapons, then there was no offensive programme. It was that simple. The US could not have such weapons if they did not test them. Thoroughly deflated, Alibekov knew in his heart there would be nothing serious left to find on the rest of the trip. The Soviet myth of a BW arms race, which he had embraced for so long, made him utterly disillusioned, for it meant only one side was violating the BWC.[43] The visits to Fort Detrick and then Pine Bluff only confirmed this conclusion. That's why he had asked Lisa Bronson for her card.

He was so profoundly moved by what he had seen, and not seen, in the US that he decided, within a week of his return, that he would resign from both the army and Biopreparat.[44] When Alibekov informed Kalinin of his intentions, the General was stunned.

'It's impossible for such a young man, in charge of so many people and such important work, to leave,' Kalinin told him. 'You are stupid to do this.'[45]

When Alibekov insisted that his mind was made up, Kalinin angrily called him a 'betrayer'.[46]

On 13 January 1992, Alibekov formally resigned his commission as an army colonel. Three weeks later, he stopped working at Biopreparat and gave up all of his administrative responsibilities in both the military and civilian programmes.[47]

He now had no work, no salary, nor a pension. Worse still, the KGB had started following him almost every day. A special militia booth was installed on the block near his apartment and he suspected his phones were tapped.[48]

A hoped-for government job in Kazakhstan's Health Ministry failed to materialize. Instead, in June 1992, Alibekov attended a meeting at the

Kazakh Ministry of Defence, where the First Deputy Minister offered him a newly created position – to be director of Kazakhstan's new 'offensive' BW programme. They promised to make him a General in Kazakhstan's army if he said 'yes' immediately.[49] They explained that Kazakhstan wanted him to reopen the giant Stepnogorsk facility. Ironically, it was Alibekov who had given the orders from Moscow in late 1990, as deputy director of Biopreparat, to dismantle the dreadful place. Now, the government of his homeland, never before involved with biological weapons, was asking him to reactivate the facility he once ran. Unhesitatingly, he refused the offer. Once he had turned down the Kazakhs, he felt he would have no further opportunities for important work in either Kazakhstan or Russia. Alibekov decided he had no choice but to leave with his family for the West.

With CIA help, Alibekov, his wife, and three children managed to obtain travel papers and leave Moscow by commercial airliner, for an undisclosed third country, before flying on to New York in October 1992.[50] When he finally arrived at JFK Airport, he felt an enormous sense of relief, combined with fear of the unknown. He didn't know what to expect; he didn't speak any English – not one word.

It took time but, like so many immigrants, he became acclimatized. The CIA gave him an English tutor for the first two months, he started buying stylish clothes, and he anglicized his name to Ken Alibek.[51]

Today, sitting at his favourite bar in his favourite hotel in Roslyn, Virginia, the once anguished defector is unrecognizable. He is not wholly anonymous, with his distinctive and rather handsome Kazakh features; but he is conventionally and nattily dressed, like so many of Washington's Beltway consultants who drink their martinis in the friendly and noisy location after work, and he is clearly at ease with himself.

As he buys his round at the glass and aluminium bar, then threads his way back to the table, nobody would guess they are rubbing shoulders with one of the most fearsome Plague Warriors of our age.

Asked whether he could square his conscience with what he had done in the past, he thoughtfully struggles to interpret the correct meaning of his answer. 'Yes,' he says quietly, 'I did a lot of very bad things. God will forgive me.'[52]

CHAPTER NINETEEN

A Walk Through Pokrov

'The status of the [Soviet BW] programme . . . remains unclear.'
ACDA Report, 1993

In the New Year of 1993, as Alibek's debriefings continued in earnest, the Bush Administration's time came to an end, having tried hard, but having failed, to end the Soviet/Russian BW programme.[1] Russian BWC violations were now President Bill Clinton's problem.

The arrival of the Clinton Administration brought with it an entire new cast of policy makers, and, accordingly, a complete re-evaluation of the BW policy. In this transition, the Democrats, who had been out of power for twelve long years during the Reagan–Bush era, installed a new generation of senior policy makers who had to be educated about the issues and review sheaves of classified intelligence – which meant delays in action. Further complicating matters, this new Clinton team was more moderate than their predecessors and was viscerally opposed to reigniting a cold war or attacking Boris Yeltsin and his new Russia in any way.[2]

But central issues remained unresolved: how much did Yeltsin know? Was the illegal programme continuing, even if only trickle funded? And, crucially, how and why did the military retain control of the offensive BW programme?

The most ominous sign of Yeltsin's complicity was the continuing presence at the helm of the programme of hard-line military officials, like Generals Kuntsevich, Yevstigneev, and Kalinin. None of Yeltsin's 'madmen' and 'fanatics' had been removed from Biopreparat laboratories either, as he had promised a year earlier.[3]

In London, Britain's Joint Intelligence Committee came to a slightly different assessment. They concluded that the Russian military lied to Yeltsin when it claimed that their BW work was not actually breaking the treaty. The Generals were ignoring his 1992 decree by secretly classifying all ongoing scientific research in the offensive BW field as 'defensive' work. By using this semantic sleight of hand, most of the old research was continuing, only now it was wrapped differently. This 'defensive' programme was necessary, the Generals argued, as an insurance policy in case Russia was ever attacked by any powerful enemy – to the south (China) as much as to the west. According to the JIC, Yeltsin probably accepted this argument and now left well enough alone.[4]

In October 1993, after a year of policy debates and transition delays since the Trilateral Agreement had been signed in Moscow, a US/UK team finally took their first tour to Russia under the controversial new 'reciprocal' guidelines negotiated by the Wisner team in Moscow. Four Russian sites were to be examined in two trips of two sites each. This trip would be the West's first access to Russian production and weapons-filling capabilities. The first two facilities, at Pokrov and Berdsk, were both considered Biopreparat institutes under military control (but not pure military facilities like Zagorsk or Sverdlovsk). The second visit, three months later, would include another Biopreparat site, Omutninsk, and a return to Obolensk (in order to document changes since 1991).

The joint Anglo/American inspection team arrived on 2 October.[5] At Pokrov, the visitors verified that there was still BW production capacity in working order. Under the military's secret mobilization plan before an all-out war, Pokrov's industrial-scale production line could quickly be converted to make many tonnes of viral agents.[6] The Russians claimed that they were researching only Foot and Mouth Disease prevention, yet the visitors found two large production lines with fermenters that could hold more than ten tons of live virus! David Kelly, who was again the team's co-leader, was stunned by that capacity. The inspectors were also shown huge, hardened bunkers which held hundreds of thousands of hen's eggs. The Russians said they were for growing influenza and cattle disease virus, for vaccine research. But Kelly didn't believe it. The bunker was set up, Kelly concluded, to grow 'massive quantities' of smallpox.[7] The only reason for having such a large amount of that virus, he adds, would be to 'sustain a strategic weapons system'.[8]

Dr Kelly, the West's leading biological warfare inspector, walked away feeling that Pokrov was 'the most sinister facility' he had yet seen in Russia.[9] Furthermore, his team had seen proof that the full array of Soviet offensive capabilities, even in the new Yeltsin era, was still potentially operational.

At the Berdsk facility near Novosibirsk (which Alibek previously ran), the visitors saw an extensive fermentation capacity that was up and running inside the main production building. Four huge 64,000-litre fermenters, the largest-sized, Soviet-made fermenters, were in use. The Russians said they were making a bio-insecticide, BT (*Bacillus thuringiensis*), in these enormous vessels.[10]

Under questioning, the Berdsk director said he changed products in these units 'twice a month'.[11] His answer meant that the Russians could completely sterilize the production line and start making a second bacteria every two weeks. This meant the Russians still had the capacity – 256,000 litres worth – to make any bacteria the military requested, and make it fast.

The visitors saw an even more astonishing sight at another huge, but incomplete, building. Construction on this concrete and steel structure (about 300 yards long and fifty yards wide) had stopped in 1990, apparently after Gorbachev issued orders to cut back on Biopreparat's expansion programme. Inside this unfinished building, the long, tall, central room had been prepared to hold four rows of 64,000-litre fermenters – with ten units in each row. Although none of these forty vessels was ever installed and hooked up, the planned total capacity would have been an astounding 2,560,000 litres!

By contrast, the visitors knew that previous UN inspections to Iraq had found that Saddam Hussein's total BW production capability before 1991 was 77,000 litres – for the whole country. So at Berdsk, just one single Russian fermenter was nearly equal to the entire Iraqi programme.[12]

On 10 January 1994, a second US/UK team, again co-led by David Kelly, began an inspection of Omutninsk, where they saw more ready-to-use equipment and encountered more Russian evasions.[13]

The final stop was Obolensk. The team went there a second time to document the changes the Russians had promised to make in 1991. Here the visitors indeed saw some positive signs; for instance, the famous explosive test chamber – the site of so much controversy in 1991 – had now been removed.[14]

The visitors also closely re-examined the giant Corpus One research centre. Much of the building was vacant and most of the incriminating equipment had been stripped out, though the building itself remained intact. The building's aerosol chamber was gone (thus limiting the animal testing capability), but the huge and sophisticated air handling system remained (so the chamber could be easily reinstalled).

Other positive signs were that new construction at Obolensk had been halted and the staff size and work activity had been greatly reduced. The Russians attributed all of the changes to a severe cutback of funding for the programme.

Perhaps the most encouraging sign that Obolensk had fallen on hard times was the team's discovery of a vodka distillery right inside a BL-3 lab. The enterprising Russians had knocked out holes in the tiled containment walls and had run new hoses and pipes into fermenters previously used to grow BW agents. When the chief scientist showed off the still, he explained that his laboratory was so strapped for money that his staff had resorted to making vodka as a cash crop. In a very capitalist enterprise, they were turning out sixteen gallons a day and selling the bottles in town as their last attempt to keep the laboratory afloat.[15] Business was brisk at this unique swords into ploughshares location. There was some gallows humour in the sight. Death by vodka seemed infinitely preferable to death by Plague.

But the same people were still in charge of running Obolensk.

'In essence,' remarked Kelly, 'the place had gone dormant rather than been converted by converts.'[16]

That, in sum, was the consensual conclusion of the inspection. The old Soviet programme had not been shut down per se. It had, at worst, gone into sleep mode; at best, it might decay, starved of finance and clear political support.

Nobody knew it, but the much vaunted trilateral process was winding down. There was just one more inspection left.

This time, for the second time, the Russians would come to America.

CHAPTER TWENTY

The Pfizer Fiasco

'. . . we're not just in business, we're in business for life.'
Pfizer advertisement, 1999

It should, and could, have been different if the new spirit of honesty and cooperation between the trilateral signatories – America, Britain, and Russia – had been rooted in good faith. The second visit by Russians to the US could have been the best chance to make informal bilateral arms control visits the template for future arms control agreements. It could have been the best opportunity to nail the violations of the BWC and ensure that this weapon of mass destruction would be kept firmly corked in its bottle.

But history and habit turned out to be fate.

The thirteen-member Russian team arrived in Washington on Friday, 11 February 1994, three weeks after the US/UK team returned from their last Russian inspection. The Russians were led by Oleg Ignatiev, a senior member of General Kuntsevich's committee on biological problems and a former head of Russia's industrial programme to produce biological weapons. Ignatiev, a short man with a high forehead and booming baritone voice, was a forceful defender of hard-line Ministry of Defence interests. The ubiquitous and emollient Dr Lev Sandakhchiev of Vektor led the Biopreparat contingent.[1]

The US side did not know which three sites the Russians would ask to see, since, under the trilateral rules, the choices did not have to be revealed until just before each visit. The Russians' first request turned out to be only a mild surprise to the American officials. The visitors wanted to go to the Terre Haute, Indiana, to inspect the army's old Vigo production plant – which had not been used since World War II. The Vigo Ordnance Works was an old weapons facility which the army had selected in 1944 to be their very first anthrax plant – a forerunner for Pine Bluff. The plan was to make thousands of anthrax bomblets at Vigo for Britain to use against Nazi Germany. But the plant never actually produced any BW agents or bombs before the war ended; it made only simulants before it was decommissioned in 1945. The site was sold after the war to Pfizer, the huge pharmaceutical company. Pfizer left most of the army buildings standing and built a modern drug-manufacturing facility adjacent to them. The Russians wanted to see that new Pfizer complex too, as part of the same visit. Given the well-known World War II production connection, the Russians had adequate justification, under the agreement, for asking to visit the Vigo/Pfizer site. The Americans were not worried about the now vacant Vigo site. It was old, run-down, and decrepit.

White House staffer Elisa Harris, the CBW issue specialist on the National Security Council, phoned Pfizer officials with the unpleasant news of their selection. Pfizer was not overjoyed, but the company reluctantly went along with the government's request after assurances were given that the formal rules governing the process would be enforced and that their concerns would be addressed.[2]

The trilateral process had established 'visits', not 'inspections'. To arms control experts, there was a big difference. As defined by other formal arms control agreements, 'inspections' were very formal, legalistic events with strict requirements. 'Visits', by contrast, were considered much more flexible occasions, where the visitors had fewer rights and any problems that arose could be negotiated on the spot.

Before these 'visits' to non-military facilities could begin, the US, Britain, and Russia had to negotiate additional procedures to protect the proprietary information of private companies. This document, called the Proprietary Agreement, was finally signed by the three parties in Moscow on 12 May 1993, without any publicity.[3]

The Proprietary Agreement set down special new 'protocols' for the non-military visits, which further restricted access, interviews of personnel, sampling, and audio/video taping.[4]

Exactly how a dispute would be decided on the spot remained a problem. While the so-called 'Rules of the Road' were meant to be comprehensive, they were actually the product of typically diplomatic compromise. Key words and phrases – like 'inappropriate', 'justifiable reason', 'unrelated to concerns', and 'reasonable necessary steps' – remained undefined because the treaty drafters could not reach agreement on precise semantics. These imprecisions were an invitation to intractable disputes. For instance, how would the hosts be able to protect classified or proprietary information, while also permitting the visitors to access all areas within a facility? These contrary provisions were not clearly defined.[5]

For industry representatives, the problems were even more profound. An unofficial census discovered that there were about 3,000 'dual-use' commercial facilities and 500 BL-3 labs in the US that the Russians could ask to inspect under the agreement – including businesses totally unrelated to biotechnology. Anyone with a large fermenter was a candidate: like producers of bio-medical goods (antibiotics and vaccines), chemicals (ethanol and citric acid), foods (yoghurt and yeast), beverages (beer, wine, and liquor), and a wide range of industrial and university research labs.[6] One of the great curses of biological warfare research and production is its ability to hide inside the respectable cloak of bona fide civilian, commercial work.

For American and other Western pharmaceutical and biotech firms, the fear of losing valuable trade secrets to Russian experts was predominant. Industry officials argued that the loss of just one secret process or innovation for developing a new micro-organism – like the genetic engineering technique for mass producing human insulin – could cost more than $1 billion to a US company. To the industry, 'proprietary' secrets also included: new products under development; production capacities; cost of manufacturing; equipment design; manufacturing recipes; computer programmes; and manufacturing strategies.[7] Pfizer was even then researching Viagra, a product destined to make huge profits.

But there was much more than that. The image, reputation, and good name of these companies were also at stake. Who would wish to buy a sleeping pill from a pharmaceutical company allegedly making Plague, anthrax, and smallpox on the sly? How long before the demonstrators were gathered outside company HQ, and how long before television picked up the scent and product embargoes followed? The scenarios were infinite and all ended in tears. A Russian inspection could do for Pfizer's sales what Lockerbie had done for PanAm.

Ultimately, Pfizer gave way. In a closely regulated industry like pharmaceuticals, company officials were reluctant to refuse a very strong government request. There was also a sense of national responsibility and even national security involved. Privately, however, the industry believed that the demands of the government should not outweigh their constitutional rights – so reservations abounded.

On Monday, the entire group of Russians and Americans, with British observers, flew from Washington to Indianapolis aboard Air Force Two. They drove 75 miles west to Terre Haute and spent the next three days, 15–17 February, touring the Vigo plant and the Pfizer facility.

Amongst other inconsequential sights, they saw the old production plant, a huge empty building that was padlocked shut. Pfizer officials explained that the large, obsolete fermenters inside were utilized during the years immediately after the war to make penicillin, but had not been used in decades.

The Russians became very agitated and argumentative when Pfizer officials explained that it was less expensive to let the building and the fermenters sit undisturbed, than to destroy the site. The Russians adamantly refused to accept this explanation. They insisted that the old, idle fermenters proved that Vigo could still be converted to produce BW agents. Their attack, the hosts soon realized, was a direct response to the US/UK accusations about the huge fermenters at Pokrov and Berdsk.

To the Russians, this still-standing Vigo/Pfizer building was evidence of suspicious US activity after the BWC was signed in 1975 – neatly mirroring the same accusation the US and UK were making about the Russian sites.[8]

The Russians insisted that the old facility would not have been kept there unless the US government intended to use it again or was indeed still using it secretly. Why hadn't the US or Pfizer torn it down, they demanded to know?[9]

The Pfizer officials patiently repeated their explanation. They insisted they had no reason to lie. But their attempts to satisfy the Russian questions were fruitless. In the end, the Pfizer officials, who had no experience in convoluted arms control politics or dealing with suspicious Russians, just shook their heads silently and gave up.

The next day, the tour of the more modern Pfizer facility also went sour. Again, the biggest issue the Russians raised was the 'production capacity' of the giant fermenters that Pfizer used to manufacture commercial pharmaceuticals. The Russians counted the reactor vessels. From their size, they could calculate the facility's overall production potential. Using the same argument that the Americans had raised in Pokrov and Berdsk, the Russians claimed this capacity could be converted quickly to produce vast quantities of BW agents. Pfizer officials, who worked for a commercial company in a nation that had definitively abandoned offensive biological warfare, were unamused.

On 18 February, Pfizer breathed a huge sigh of relief as the Russians boarded Air Force Two to leave. But, with the plane still on the ground, the Russian team leader, Dr Ignatiev, approached his State Department hosts for a private chat. Speaking through a translator, Ignatiev informed them of the next site the Russians demanded to see. To the US officials' dismay, Pfizer copped it a second time. And this time the Russians weren't kidding around – they demanded to visit Pfizer's main research complex in Groton, Connecticut. It was, the Russians claimed, another 'dual-use' site that could be converted to BW production.

The Pfizer Central Research Center in Groton, a seaside town in southeastern Connecticut, was the company's largest single location – a 75-building complex on 137 acres. Since 1959, it had been Pfizer's international research headquarters, a high-technology centre where 3,700 employees developed new drug therapies and animal-health products. Some 100 projects were under way at any one time, investigating more than twenty disease areas.

The American officials went into a huddle to decide who would now have the unpleasant chore of inviting Pfizer to open up its precious storehouse of pharmaceutical research and laboratory secrets.

The short straw was drawn in Washington by the NSC's Elisa Harris. She telephoned Pfizer again, now with even worse news than her call five days earlier. To pre-empt the inevitable, she now used the big gun – the White House would be very grateful: if necessary, Vice President Al Gore himself was ready to get on the phone with the Pfizer CEO to make the case and explain why the visit was so important to US national security.[10] Arms were now gently being twisted.

Despite the blandishments, Pfizer officials were livid, complaining, with some justification, that the US government was imposing a totally unfair burden on their private company. They returned again and again to their biggest concern – that the Russians would demand to see very sensitive proprietary research and take samples. They stressed there were many things they could not and would not show them.[11]

Indeed, Pfizer, the maker of numerous wonder drugs, was well known as an innovative, research-intensive company. At the Groton centre, the company invested more than $2 billion annually in R&D, one of the largest amounts spent by any healthcare business in the world.[12] A new medicine approved by the FDA could cost as much as $500 million to develop – and there were lots of disappointments along the way. Pfizer could not afford to have the Russians stealing any of this information.

Pfizer was further concerned that the unwanted visitors might inadvertently contaminate their precious 'clean room' facilities, where expensive clinical trials were conducted with test animals. These special germ-free rooms, with positive air pressure, keep the test animals totally sanitized during experiments. Pfizer did not want to risk having a team of officials wandering through these sterile areas; they were adamant that the Russians would not be permitted inside these clean rooms – even if they complained about a violation of their trilateral rights.

It was finally agreed – in a compromise between Pfizer and US officials – that the Russians could tour only the offices and corridors of the clinical trials building, but they would not actually enter the sterile areas where the animals were kept. With that plan, and reassurances that US national security required such a visit, Pfizer, with corporate heart in mouth trepidation, reluctantly said, 'OK.'[13]

The visit to Groton covered three days, from 23–25 February.[14]

As expected, when the Russians were denied access to the sterile areas in the clinical building, tension began to rise. The Russians were permitted to view as much as possible inside the testing areas through windows and TV monitors, but, as expected, they complained that this limited access wasn't good enough.[15]

On the final day, Pfizer's senior managers attempted to answer, yet again, all of the Russian questions about why they had not been allowed into the sterile areas. Pfizer took the capitalist approach, explaining patiently how many years and millions of dollars were required to complete the research and trials, and how company profits and livelihoods depended on this work.

The Russians took copious notes, but no formal protest was mentioned.

US officials assumed they would hear the complaints through diplomatic channels after the Russians returned home. There were no fond farewells as the Russians flew back to Washington to prepare for their third and last destination. Their choice turned out to be the Department of Agriculture's facility at Plum Island, off the northeastern coast of Long Island, New York.

The isolated island belonged to the government and was used for non-military, defensive research against highly infectious animal plagues that might spread to US horses, cattle, and hogs.[16] The main viruses under study included Foot and Mouth Disease and African swine fever. Outbreaks of such feared diseases could cost billions to the US meat and dairy industries. In 1994, the centre had a staff of about 100 people and an annual budget of about $14 million. The Russian visit was uncontroversial.

As the Russians departed on the last day, Dr Ignatiev was non-committal about what his team had seen.[17]

The Russians flew back to Moscow on 3 March. Once again, their American hosts felt the tour had gone quite well. Pfizer had been open, the sites fully inspected, there had been nothing to hide. These were different times now and Washington and Moscow were furthering a new and closer relationship. The Americans weren't taking bets, but, had they done so, the stakes would have been against the return of a Cold War on the biological warfare front.

Washington only had to wait four short weeks for the Russian reaction. It came in a 5 April news report from *Izvestiya*. Any optimism, the Moscow report confirmed, had been wildly misplaced and any progress on biological weapons control had been consigned to the deep freeze of the bad old days, and, once again, truth had become the first casualty.

An unidentified Russian official – apparently representing the Yeltsin government – was now publicly accusing the US of violating the BWC.[18] *Izvestiya* charged that the March inspection of Pfizer showed conclusively that the US had advanced production facilities for biological weapons. Specifically, the report charged that Pfizer's Indiana site maintained 'redesigned and modernized' BW production equipment 'in good working order'. Similarly, the Groton laboratory had special equipment and 'manufacturing areas' for 'micro-organisms' which the Russians found suspicious. The 'possibility' existed, the Russians claimed, that Pfizer's suspect buildings could produce 'pathogens of dangerous infectious diseases'.[19]

To rub salt in, the Russian official claimed that his country had given American experts total, 'unhindered' access to all requested facilities in Russia since 1992. By contrast, he charged that Russian experts had faced serious obstacles and were denied access during their recent visit in America. For instance, he said the Russians were not allowed into a number of laboratories and one Pfizer building that were suspected of producing biological weapons. The Russian official further complained that 'certain restrictions' were placed on them, including the refusal to let them take 'biological tests'.[20] He claimed that the Groton facility was opened only after a 'delay', and then only when the Russian Embassy intervened. All of these restrictions, the Russian official complained, violated the rules that were stipulated in the Trilateral Agreement. And, as a final knee in the groin, the unnamed Russian official explained why the Russian government was making these charges public. He claimed the US was resisting *Russian* attempts to tighten compliance of the BWC.[21]

No official from the Yeltsin government disavowed the *Izvestiya* report.

US officials were furious, and now nobody wanted the Russian experts to ever come back again.

The perversion of truth was not lost on the US pharmaceutical industry either.[22] Pfizer retained a dignified silence, but the message was clear. Being nice to Washington to help international arms control on the spread of biological warfare was not going to bring any reward. The episode poisoned the relationship between the industry and the White House – which was blamed for coercing Pfizer to participate. Worse still, the Clinton Administration later backed away from accepting any responsibility for the fiasco and carefully wiped its prints off the evidence. At private meetings later with industry representatives, White House officials would not accept any blame for convincing Pfizer to participate. They said that the visit had been 'voluntary' on Pfizer's behalf.[23]

In 1994, after Pfizer, the Russians visited one site in Britain, Evans Medical Laboratories, a vaccine plant in Speke, near Liverpool. During the Gulf War, the facility had packaged anthrax vaccine for British soldiers. After the uneventful visit, the Russians made exactly the same complaints about the British company as they had about Pfizer.[24]

The whole Pfizer affair, which should have been a shot in the arm for the trilateral process, became a shot in the head instead. A leading pharmaceutical company lobbying association in Washington, PhRMA, even decided to take an active role in preventing future new additions to the BWC that would force their members to accept similar terms.[25]

The worst fears of those who had criticized Wisner's 1992 agreement in Moscow had been confirmed. After two years of negotiations and inspections, the Pfizer debacle had crippled the trilateral process.

Ultimately, the Pfizer fiasco also highlighted the depth of East/West cultural differences and political suspicions, as well as, inevitably, the continuing military control in Russia of their illegal BW programme. The chance to come clean had been declined. The Generals continued to risk the new détente by fighting tooth and nail to protect their illegal offensive biological warfare programme.

The question remains. What is it about biological warfare that remains so close to the heart of the Russian military and makes it worth jeopardizing the new superpower relationship with lies, deceptions, and dissimulations?

CHAPTER TWENTY-ONE

Postscript: Russia

'We remain concerned about a continuing Russian capacity for
biological warfare.'

Sir Percy Cradock, 1998

On 7 April 1994, two days after the *Izvestiya* article attacked Pfizer,
President Yeltsin fired General Kuntsevich as head of the Russian
committee investigating biological problems.[1]

The reasons for Kuntsevich's hasty departure did not reflect well
on the honesty and incorruptibility of Russia's BW oversight programme: it was disclosed that he had been caught trying to sell five
tonnes of VX nerve gas components to middlemen from the Syrian
government. All of the chemical precursors in the deal had been filched
from Russian military facilities. The final destination of the illegal
shipment was suspected to be Iraq. For pocket money, Kuntsevich
also had allegedly sold another 1,760 pounds of chemicals to unnamed
Middle Eastern buyers – while he was still heading Yeltsin's clean-up
committee.[2]

But even before they launched the corks off the champagne bottles
in London and Washington to celebrate Kuntsevich's departure, the
second shoe dropped. The new man, it turned out, would be none other
than the committee's deputy director, General Valentin Yevstigneev, the
hardliner and nemesis of Western arms control negotiators who had
headed the BW 'defence' programme since 1985. This was the man who
still dissembled about Sverdlovsk and every other important BW issue.
Yeltsin had replaced Bonnie with Clyde. It was another clear signal that
the military were very much in charge.

During the rest of 1994, the Trilateral Working Group met four times in secret in an attempt to plan future inspections of the never-seen Russian military BW facilities – which the US and UK were most anxious to visit.[3] Each of these long, frustrating negotiating sessions – in London, Vienna, Washington, and Moscow – ended in failure.[4]

Then, in May 1995, at a Clinton–Yeltsin summit, President Clinton pressed the Russian leader for inspections of the military sites. Yeltsin agreed and the visits were tentatively scheduled for August. But once again, the inevitable procrastination and delays surfaced and the visits never took place.[5]

It was the last gasp of the trilateral process.

From that day to this, all Anglo/American inspection teams have been barred from the Russian military sites where work on biological warfare programmes is taking place.[6]

Since Alibek's defection, neither the UK nor the US has had any major defectors or intelligence breakthroughs about the Russian programme.[7] There is an ironic reason for this. Western intelligence officers are deeply concerned that some of Russia's top microbiologists and BW scientists from cash-strapped labs like Vektor and Obolensk, might leave Russia for 'rogue' states like Iraq or North Korea or Libya. As of 1998, there were about 10,000 scientists inside the Biopreparat system, of whom some 1,500 are considered top researchers with experience with lethal viruses and bacteria.[8] There is also a growing fear that samples of deadly viruses and bacteria from Russian laboratories with less security might be vulnerable to theft by terrorist groups or rogue governments.[9]

So the US and UK intelligence services have asked Russian officials to keep a closer eye on their top BW officials, to make sure they are not lured away. The Russians have responded enthusiastically by increasing their own internal security – to make sure there won't be another Pasechnik or Alibek. But, by encouraging the Russians to do this, the West has effectively choked off its own new sources of information.[10]

Consequently, the West still has little insight into what the Russian military are doing with their biological warfare programme, or why they are doing it. Sir Percy Cradock, former head of Britain's JIC, is deeply pessimistic.

'The trilateral process is stalled,' he says. 'There is now little enthusiasm for meetings with Russian officials who consistently lie, and who demand that the UK and US undergo a programme of visits to any

Western facility chosen by the Russians – none of which has anything to do with biological warfare – in exchange for limited access to Russian BW facilities.

'Until we receive a credible account from the Russian government of the Soviet BW programme which they inherited ... we will remain concerned about a continuing Russian capacity for biological warfare. We just don't know why they are so determined not to allow access to the BW facilities run by the military.'[11]

Meanwhile, alarming information continues to surface that offensive research rolls on. For instance, in 1998, there were persistent news reports from Russia that the scientists at Obolensk have successfully produced genetically engineered strains of anthrax that are resistant to all known antibiotics and vaccines.[12]

In September 1998, the American Defense Intelligence Agency and the CIA separately reported their concerns in writing to Congress. The DIA stated that 'key components' of the former Soviet BW programme remained 'largely intact and may support a possible future mobilization capability'. The DIA added that, 'Work outside the scope of legitimate biological defence activity may be occurring now at selected facilities within Russia.'[13]

In concurring, the CIA noted that some Russian BW facilities 'may retain the ability to produce BW agents'. 'We cannot establish,' the CIA said, 'that Russia has given up this capability and remain concerned that some of the individuals involved in the old Soviet programme may be trying to protect elements of it.'[14]

As of 1998, the British Joint Intelligence Committee has maintained a similar assessment of the Russian programme for the prior five years. The JIC has concluded that Russia's BW research capability and production facilities remain intact and could be reactivated with ease.[15] Since the arrival of Tony Blair, there has been so little new to report that the JIC has supplied only one new paper on the subject to Downing Street.

In Washington, the Clinton Administration is spending millions of dollars on more than a dozen programmes intended to block the brain drain from Russian research institutes to rogue nations; the ultimate goal is to disarm the biological warfare establishments by firing hard currency at them for productive, non-military work.[16]

In one such programme, the National Academy of Sciences (acting with Pentagon approval and funding), began the 'Pathogens Initiative' in

1995 to expand cooperation between scientists in the Russian BW programme and American microbiologists, by spending $38.5 million over five years to fund Russian research projects. The programme – which focuses attention on Vektor and Obolensk – is intended to instil cooperation, which would hopefully allow the West to learn more about the ongoing Russian BW research.[17]

The Pentagon also plans to spend up to $6 million to upgrade security at Vektor's laboratories, to prevent the theft or diversion of dangerous pathogens, like smallpox and Ebola, from its lethal virus collection.[18]

Since 1997, another Pentagon programme has been underway to arrange projects with both Vektor and Obolensk covering a variety of topics: vaccine production, bio-medical research, pharmaceutical production, counter-terrorism, emergency response, detection, and new technologies. US and Russian officials hold regular bilateral meetings nearly every month.[19] The end game for the West is always to divert activity away from offensive biological warfare research and development and into peaceful commercial projects.

The US, UK, Japan, and several European countries are also financing the International Science and Technology Centre in Moscow, which tries to find peaceful work for former weapons scientists.

But there are substantial problems in attempting to attract private capital into private business ventures with Russian laboratories, since they are still government owned and their personnel have a limited grasp of Western business practices or private capital investment procedures. In 1997, Dr Sandakhchiev told a White House meeting of scientific advisers that it was important for Vektor to 'adapt to the new world'.[20]

Sandakhchiev has told the US that he needs two main things for Vektor to survive: a 'strategic partner' to help him develop new products for sale; and expert consultations on a complicated range of privatization issues. But American pharmaceutical companies remain wary of Russian facilities and business practices. Safety standards in some cases are regarded as simply unacceptable. There is also some apprehension about dealing with crafty scientific entrepreneurs like Sandakhchiev who still takes orders from his real boss, General Kalinin.[21]

And here is the nub of the problem. The cast list running the Russian BW programme remains immovable. The very same Ministry of Defence and Biopreparat officials who directed the programme during the Cold War are still in charge seven years after Yeltsin took over. Yevstigneev, Ignatiev, Vasileyev, Kalinin, Sandakhchiev are still in place. These are the abominable no-men of Soviet and now Russian offensive biological warfare programmes. These are the very same men who have decided it is morally acceptable, in strategic warfare, to bombard the enemy with smallpox, Plague, and anthrax, and drive them back to cave life. And to achieve an unbeatable lead, they agreed and signed a treaty which they have seen only as an opportunity to cover up their work. They are serial cheats.

Even now the Russian military can maintain the BW programme without the infusion of any major funding from the Yeltsin government as most of the major capital expenditures were laid out prior to 1992. The programme is now essentially in a maintenance status which can be either slush-funded or funded from normal defence allocations.

Western intelligence has also spotted some new, better hidden BW sites, but these have not been named publicly because the CIA and MI6 need to keep secret which ones have actually been spotted.[22]

Ultimately, the maximalists are surely right, that Russia, even under these relatively new and hopeful times, still cannot be fully trusted. The minimalists have been right too in encouraging a softly-softly approach at a time when Yeltsin and his democratic government seems terribly vulnerable once more.

No better example of the intolerable dilemma exists than when Presidents Clinton and Yeltsin met in Moscow in September 1998. Clinton was besieged by the Lewinsky scandal and Yeltsin seemed ill, and even inchoate, at the final press conference. The intractable biological warfare problem had been on their agenda, but their public statement following the summit made no mention of any problems surrounding the BW issue. Instead, it recited only an anodyne reaffirmation of a US and Russian commitment to 'enhance the effective implementation' of the BWC.[23]

CHAPTER TWENTY-TWO

Rhodesia, 1978

'Why keep to the Queensberry rules . . . ?'
Eugene de Kock

They crawled out of the night and they made dark history . . . the first soldiers to unleash modern biological warfare. They were specially trained, but could hardly have understood the enormity of what they were doing.

The soldiers and their civilian advisers stealthily distributed the deadly anthrax spore among the hungry cattle of the Rhodesian tribal trust lands, and seeded cholera into the rivers. The big, rich white farms were left in peace. The logic was brutally simple. Kill the black man's cattle, and food for the Rhodesian guerrillas dies with them; kill the cattle and blame the guerrillas and win a psychological victory at the same time. Spread cholera epidemics among the villages and destabilize the guerrillas and their infrastructure.

The consequences of these strategies were to endure long after the whites lost their war and Rhodesia became Zimbabwe. Anthrax remains in the soil; it has become indigenous to Zimbabwe, an evergreen bouquet of poison left by the departing losers. Long, long after the dirty war for Rhodesian independence had been settled, the white administration overthrown and the blacks had taken control of their own destiny, the effects of that biological attack still trickle through the lifeblood of the nation. Biological warfare is like no other conflict – once released, it is already beyond control, distinguishing between neither aggressor or defender, good or bad. It is incapable of honouring a truce, let alone a peace.

And long after the political issues have melted into history, the bacterial spores will sleep and wake, hibernate and then re-infect, still fighting a long gone war like some mad mechanical infantryman too wound-up and besotted with conflict to call a halt.

By the late 1970s, Southern Africa was turning into a crucible of revolutionary and/ counter-revolutionary independence struggles. South Africa's National Party, under its new, hard-line premier, P.W. Botha, had defined the wars against its authority as one of 'total onslaught'. In other words, a mandate to fight what was essentially a racial war with uncompromising ruthlessness. Faced with what it saw as local communist insurgencies supported by Moscow's gold, South Africa unleashed a series of internal and external military and paramilitary operations which involved murder, torture, smuggling, forgery, propaganda, and subversion as 'legitimate' weapons. In this febrile atmosphere, the use of offensive biological warfare was but one malignant idea away.

A UN report has estimated that the South Africa-backed 'dirty wars' were to claim over one-and-a-half-million deaths and some $60 billion in losses in the neighbouring black countries of Zimbabwe, Mozambique, Angola, and Namibia.[1] They were prosecuted by a combination of South African and Rhodesian security and special forces, intelligence agencies, and mercenaries. They were helped by the porous border between Rhodesia and South Africa, the combat skills of white soldiers (some of whom had once fought with honour), and the sense that this was the racial war that would determine the continent's future for the next millennium.

In South Africa, the banned African National Congress (ANC) had moved its military wing, MK (Umkhonto we Sizwe), to safe bases in Tanzania.[2] They envisaged a strategy known as 'hacking the way home', which would involve opening up a Ho Chi Minh trail to South Africa. There were also alliances with ZIPRA, the armed wing of the Zimbabwe African People's Union (ZAPU), then Rhodesia's leading nationalist movement. After a joint MK/ZIPRA force had infiltrated Rhodesia in August 1967, South African police units were sent to work alongside the white Rhodesian security forces. By 1975, more than 2,000 South African policemen were stationed in Rhodesia. By 1979, the South Africans were extremely active inside Rhodesia; combat tracker units of the South African police were deployed alongside regular units of the Rhodesian Army and operated in the Matibi Tribal Trust Land. The presence of these forces inside Rhodesia was vigorously denied by both sides.[3] They, in turn, worked with regular South African soldiers, South African special forces, and the now notorious Selous Scouts, who specialized in 'pseudo operations' – a technique learned from the British forces in Malaya and Kenya. The scouts, in turn, used large numbers of black troopers (called askaris) disguised as nationalist guerrillas who would operate in enemy territory capturing and interrogating real guerrillas and using the intelligence gathered to launch immediate surprise attacks. Battle-hardened, psychologically and socially divorced from their own communities, and compromised by their treachery, askaris were well suited to some of the grisliest acts of war. The White fighting philosophy was best summed up by apartheid's leading assassin, Eugene de Kock (currently serving 212 years in prison for seven individual murders and numerous lesser charges), who stated: 'Why keep to the Queensberry rules and fight one boxer, when you can kick them in the balls and kill all three?'[4]

In the late 1970s, the orders were given to use biological warfare against the enemy. Because of its insidious and unusual nature, no one would even know that the weapon had been used.

Today, the journey from Harare to the district of Kweke is uneventful. A lean, grey mist hangs over the gentle plains. 'WORMS FOR SALE' announces one sign hammered to a tree, 'LION PARK' and 'SNAKE WORLD' announce others. But Disney won't catch on here. Zimbabwe is poor. There were bread riots in the streets of the capital when we left.

We drive through Selous (named after the explorer and hunter F.C. Selous), which gave its name to the infamous Selous Scouts. By 8 a.m., the mist has risen and the early dawn lights the brilliant wild Jacaranda. Noisy street vendors are hawking bananas from wheelbarrows, the acacia trees rustle with life. Suddenly it's light in Africa.

As we approach Ngwenya village, the earth loses its richness and becomes harder, sending dusty red clouds into the car. The luxurious greenery gives way to thorny scrub. We see the first kraal fences and wattle huts that stand on this overworked land that has given of its best, but now harbours the worst. We are in the anthrax zone.

This is where bad men planted the spores twenty years ago. Now, the anthrax which endures has become virulent once more. Forty-seven human cases and countless cattle have died in this district alone, all in the last six months. The cattle are all these proud and dignified people have. No televisions, few radios, bank accounts or cars. Just wattle huts, cattle, and ubiquitous bicycles. When the health workers (all five of them) go out and find the anthrax-infected meat in a butcher's stall, they order the carcasses to be burned. But it's a poor land here, and that meat is someone's livelihood. Money may change hands and the infections continue.

The spores are everywhere, activated when the chemistry of the earth works its voodoo – mixing the right cocktail of alkaline pH, nitrogen, calcium, and organic matter. Then the brew needs cooking with the correct, extreme weather conditions for the spores to compete successfully with the other micro-organisms in the soil. A drought followed by heavy rains is most helpful and often precedes an outbreak.

Atalia Ngwenya is sixty-two-years-old, broom-stick thin, with a fine, handsome face, and eyes that hold ours with unblinking curiosity. She has come with her family to pour beer on the common-ground grave of her husband, whose name was Tommy, and who died aged forty-eight, when the soldiers brought the anthrax to the district. Atalia is a Ndebele, and this small, spirit ceremony marks another anniversary of her life as a widow. The family kneel, and chant and talk, and, because it is bad manners to exclude the departed host, they pour a measure of the warm beer onto his grave; then they drink a little themselves, and then just one more for him.

Afterwards, standing awkwardly under the bone-dry Mzambani tree, Atalia speaks softly and quickly, with the strange cadences and rhythms of her click tongue. 'He became sick and we did not know what was wrong with him. We took him to Mpilo hospital and they did an operation, but it wasn't OK. He died in our hut, he was in pain. I dabbed him with water because he said he was feeling so hot. He began to swell all over and coughed and coughed. He knew he was going to die. He said to me, you will remain alone, who is going to look after the children? This disease was brought by war, now it has come back, but we are no longer at war ... when will it leave the earth? Will our children die too?'[5]

By now, the relatives of other dead victims are waiting to talk to us. Elijah Dube lost his brother Mbuyazwe, who was only twenty-eight. His anthrax began as a sore on the finger and ended when God released him from the agony in hospital. Elijah, a Seventh Day Adventist from the village of Tete, leaves to join the choir in the modest hut they call a church. 'In the inevitability of death, God shines like a star,' he sings.

But those anthrax deaths were all man-made. Here, in the hard bush life, some things are not the will of the Almighty.

It was years before anyone found out.

The first to suspect a modern war crime was an American doctor, Meryl Nass, MD, then with the Department of Internal Medicine at the University of Massachusetts Medical School. From 1989–92, she researched the epidemiology of the largest outbreak of anthrax in history in Rhodesia/Zimbabwe in the late 1970s. While ploughing through the statistics, she realized that an inexplicable spike in the casualty figures had occurred during the years 1979/80. Anthrax is endemic in parts of Southern Africa, but Rhodesia, with its fine veterinary services and human health care, had reported only an average of thirteen human cases a year before 1978. However, in the two years 1979/80, a staggering 10,738 human cases were recorded and 182 humans died of the illness. Thousands of cattle were infected and had to be slaughtered. The disease spread over time from area to area, into six of the eight provinces.[6] Significantly, virtually no commercial, white-owned farms were affected.

Even more puzzling was the way in which the anthrax spores were transported over very large distances – across areas *where no bovine cases were known to have occurred.*[7] If the cattle had not spread the spores, then who or what had? Dr Nass suspected the worst.

The epidemiology and circumstantial evidence pointed in one direction, but confirmation had to wait for years. The earliest corroboration was probably in a secret report sent by a US Defense Intelligence Agency officer to the Pentagon. 'According to [source deleted], a member of the Rhodesian Selous Scouts admitted in 1978 that "they" had tried both chemical and biological warfare techniques to kill terrorists.'[8] The DIA report also spoke of Rhodesian ground forces poisoning water systems with dead bodies and ground forces 'attempting to infest the water system with *Vibrio cholerae*'.[9]

To this day, there is no proof of how the anthrax was delivered. The most logical source of the first modern use of BW was an old-fashioned, but highly reliable, vector – the cattle cake (a livestock food).

Today the Zimbabwe Ministry of Health is certain that the strain of anthrax came from the United Kingdom. That, in itself, is not necessarily sinister. Both Britain and the United States exported BW pathogens for 'legitimate' research in those days. They were relatively easy to acquire, and a buyer only had to produce the appropriate documents. Forgery was dead simple in the catalogue of tricks used during the dirty wars in Southern Africa.

In 1943, the British War Cabinet prepared a requirement to retaliate against the Nazis had they used biological warfare against British live-stock. The ultimate plan had been to use anthrax spores released by 500-lb cluster bombs, each containing over 100 small 4-lb bomblets containing the spores. During simulant trials at Porton Down, such cluster bombs had been shown to produce an effective aerosol concentration of spores that covered nearly 100 acres from the impact area. However, there were problems in developing the right quantities of bombs in the time, so the quick-fix solution was a weapon requiring no special munitions or hardware. In the end, the British simply charged ordinary cattle cakes with anthrax spores. It was neat and simple, and would have been wholly effective, because of the precision of deliverance, literally down the throat and into the stomach of the targeted cattle.

The British manufactured a stockpile of five million of these cakes. This stockpile was destroyed after the war, apart from one or two boxes which were retained as memorabilia until 1972.[10] The technology was simple enough for anyone to copy once they had access to the anthrax spores.

Dr Tim Stamps was born in Cardiff, Wales, but has eagerly joined the White Tribe of Africa. Today, he is Zimbabwe's Minister of Health. He is also a member of the Executive Board of the World Health Organization. He has personally ordered an official investigation by his ministry 'for substantial information indicating the use of biological agents as tools of war in Zimbabwe (Rhodesia)'.[11]

The 112-acre farm he owns outside Harare is everything that binds men like Stamps with such passion to this part of Africa. It is cool, fertile, spacious – a picture-book farm with plump, contented Guernseys. Large white egrets poke around the damp grass. As we talk, his wife serves coffee and cakes on the patio. We could be in the verdant English county of Sussex.

Stamps is tall, handsome, grey-haired, and mostly gentle. His real passion ignites when he talks about biological weapons and the anthrax and cholera – and maybe worse – that were used against his country.

'No doubt about the anthrax,' he mutters grimly. 'You only have to look at the figures. No doubt about the cholera either. Cholera was new to this country. Odd, isn't it, that it spread so quickly, particularly during a period of hostility when human movements were very, very severely restricted in the Eastern districts of Zimbabwe, where the cholera broke out. Now, if these outbreaks had been endemic, we would have expected them to continue and reoccur, especially with our health services in disarray.

'We had another outbreak in 1993, which I think was another BW attack. Odd, isn't it, that we managed to control that outbreak within three months and eliminated it within seven.[12]

'We had a localized outbreak of bubonic plague during the dirty wars, and it reoccurred twice more in that area. But why so local? It was a place where there was intense fighting between the forces of liberation and the regime.

'I have my suspicions about Ebola too. It developed along the line of the Zambezi River, and I suspect that this may have been an experiment to see if a new virus could be established to infect people. We looked at the serological evidence on strange cases, including a fifteen-year-old child which occurred in 1980. Nothing really made epidemiological sense.

'Do I have evidence? Only circumstantial. In fact, the Rhodesian security forces were more expert than the Nazis at covering up evidence.'

Dr Stamps is speaking weeks before the remarkable evidence was presented by South African soldiers and scientists at the 1998 Truth and Reconciliation Commission's hearings on South Africa's covert biological warfare programme. The Health Minister doesn't know just how close to the truth he is.

Stamps begins to talk gloomily about the revived epidemic of anthrax which now stalks his land. 'Even the wild animals have been infected – antelopes, elephants . . .' The voice trails off, then picks up again. 'We've asked the American Centers for Disease Control to come and help us, but they work only on a cost plus basis and my budget is very small.'

We talk about the anthrax. 'If you can destroy a person's cattle, you can destroy his livelihood,' he says. 'If you can kill a few people in the process, then you can subjugate a large number of people. And the stuff lasts forever. That is the evil of biological warfare.'

Who brought it in?

Stamps picks up a cake knife and points to the south. 'Where do you think? South Africa, of course.

'This was the highest form of inhuman murder ever known to man. They targeted *my* Africans, and they did it without regard to the future. Anthrax will stay in our soil for at least fifty years and we do not have the resources to remove it. The people who did this should be brought to justice before the international community. We are talking war crimes here.'

It is hot now. The armed police guard, standing in the shade at the farm gate, cradles his rifle and yawns. Stamps – angry – and restless, heads for his beloved Guernseys. The interview is over.

A few miles away, much closer to Harare and later that evening, a lean, square-jawed man with a razor haircut waits by the electronic gates to his substantial home as they groan open and let us enter. In each hand he holds the lead of a snarling Doberman. An alien from outer space would recognize the man as an ex-soldier. Colonel Lionel Dyck smiles and shrugs apologetically. 'I'm sorry, but there have been several murder attempts on me. Home's a bit of a fortress.'[13]

It certainly is. Peace has not brought peace to this fifty-four-year-old former Commanding Officer of the Rhodesian African Rifles, who, after independence, stayed loyal to the new flag and joined the Zimbabwe Parachute Brigade and Special Air Service. There are some unforgiving people in South Africa who do not believe Dyck should have worked with the new rulers. They have already come for him with guns at his home.

It turns out he doesn't just have two Dobermans. There's a Rott-weiler inside the house too.

There were honourable white men sucked into the dirty war, fighting for Queen and country, kith and kin. Dyck was one of them. As a soldier, he served the new flag, and still does. Today, he runs a company that clears mines from Africa and Bosnia. He is absurdly fit and active. And he knows one small, but important, part of Rhodesia's BW mystery.

'The regular Rhodesian soldiers were not involved,' he insists. 'It's true, commanding officers at the time would give us briefings about certain places and we would be warned that the drinking water or, you know, the wells, might have been poisoned – but our soldiers didn't do it. There were places where we were categorically told that the waters had been salted [sic] with cholera and we would have to be careful. Truth is, Rhodesia was being used as a laboratory. There were civilian operators, strange types from South Africa . . . they did it.'

To be more precise?

'To be more precise, it was South African military intelligence.[14]

'The anthrax they put down,' he continues, with some passion, 'it's hit this amazing herd of elephants. They had previously mutated – if that's the right word – to become desert elephants, and they move around the outskirts of the desert, from water hole to water hole. They're unique because they don't destroy their own habitat, so there's always food for them. Now they've started dying of anthrax.'

The full story remains elusive. A former Rhodesian intelligence officer, now active for the new Zimbabwe Administration, has written a kind of *mea culpa* which contains the ring of truth.[15] The letter, in part, reads: 'It is true that anthrax spoor was used in an experimental role in the Gutu, Chilimanzi, Masvingo and Mberengwa areas, and the anthrax idea came from army Psyops [Psychological operations]. The use of anthrax spoor to kill off the cattle of tribesmen . . . was carried out in conjunction with [the] psychological suggestion to the tribes people that their cattle were sick and dying because of disease introduced into Zimbabwe from Mozambique by the infiltrating guerrillas.

'The use of cholera was . . . restricted to external use only as it was believed at the time that an outbreak of the disease within Zimbabwe would seriously affect the security forces operating in the bush.

'Rhodesian Security Forces were given the job of polluting watering points close to guerrilla camps in Mozambique, i.e. stagnant pools or slow moving streams, but this tactic was said to be of very limited use due to the quick dispersion of the bacteria.'[16]

Jeremy Brickhill, a white Zimbabwean activist who joined the guerrilla forces during the war of liberation, was himself a victim of a South African military hit squad in 1987, when he was severely injured in a car bomb attack. He recalls the role of the Rhodesian Central Intelligence Organization in Rhodesia's offensive biological warfare attacks.

'In the mid-seventies, in the most closely guarded secret operation of the entire war, the CIO embarked on a programme of chemical and biological warfare. Doctors and chemists from the University of Rhodesia were recruited by the CIO and asked to identify and test a range of chemical and biological agents which could be used in the war against the nationalist guerrillas.'[17]

Brickhill alleges that by 1975 clinical trials were performed on human guinea pigs at a remote Selous Scout camp at Mount Darwin in north-eastern Rhodesia. The CIO provided victims from their detention centres, choosing little-known detainees who had been arrested on various security charges. 'In the secrecy of the camp,' he writes, 'the doctors administered various chemical and biological agents to the prisoners, experimenting with delivery systems and dose levels. The local CIO Special Branch disposed of the bodies in local mine shafts.

'By 1976, the CIO Special Branch and the Selous Scouts [carried out] the actual deployment of the successfully tested chemical and biological weapons in target areas. They were assisted by . . . South African military and security personnel who not only acted as advisers and monitors, but likely played some part in the development of the chemical and biological agents.'

Henrik Ellert, formerly with the British South Africa Police in Rhodesia and former head of a section in its Special Branch, recalls how thallium (a lethal, heavy-metal toxin similar to rat poison) was injected into tins of corned beef and fed to guerrilla fighters. Predictably, one of the tins fell into the hands of innocent villagers living in the Arcturus District, who ate it. Many died. A detailed investigation, both by the innocent manufacturers of the corned beef and the government Ministry of Health, established the facts.[18]

Ellert further described the use of an unspecified poison, which was responsible for the death of some 200 non-combatants after the Selous Scouts poured it into the single reservoir that fed the Cochemane Administrative Centre in the Tete Province.[19] Ellert also reported the use of 'measured quantities of bacteriological cultures', possibly cholera, in the Ruya River wild-life area near the Mozambique border. People living along the river banks died soon after the water was poisoned. The deaths were attributed to cholera.[20]

Because the use of anthrax, cholera, and thallium in Rhodesia was no biological Hiroshima, the events were never clearly marked for the historical record. Far worse things happened in the dirty wars. It was, perhaps, a moment that was missed for its real significance in terms of the use of a new weapon of mass destruction.

So, when it was all over, biological warfare was recorked and some of the men who had used this dark science slipped back south across the border, returned to South Africa, and studied the lessons of Rhodesia.

There was another racial conflict looming in their own homeland. There would be much work to do.

CHAPTER TWENTY-THREE

Nothing Personal

'They've done terrible things to me.'
Connie Braam, 1998

He's a big chap. Large ruddy face, huge frame sagging in the middle under the weight of years and a beer belly. The blue blazer and regimental tie date him, sartorially, somewhere in the mid-seventies. He'd look at home in a bourgeois English café or propping up the bar in a suburban saloon, inseparable from the blazer that carries an (unofficial) carefully woven, gold-threaded flash stitched into the distinctive and proud-winged dagger of Britain's Special Air Service. No ex-SAS man would be seen dead in that rig, but 'Taffy' (an acquired *nom de guerre*) is not in a quiet English town. He's in Pretoria, sitting in a bar at the Holiday Inn, a white supremacist stranded by the tides of history. Now, still clinging to the insignia and uniforms of yesteryear, Taffy has his memories and his thin, grey flannel trousers and mirror-polished shoes, while Africa moves on and ignores him.

Yet he has a story. It was men like Taffy of Rhodesia, a mere twenty years ago, who first used biological warfare and toxins to kill or attempt to assassinate the perceived enemies of the state.

And Taffy's great claim to fame, the reason there's always a drink at the bar from the good old boys, is that he's the man who very nearly murdered President Robert Mugabe.

The use of biological or toxic agents as a method of personal assassination was to reach its triumphal peak in Southern Africa during the 1970s and 1980s. This was something the 1972 BWC, or to give it its full title, 'Convention on the Prohibition of the Development, Production, and Stockpiling of Bacteriological and Toxin Weapons and on Their Destruction', could never have foreseen. The treaty, ratified three years later, was meant to be employed as a tool with which to fight the new weapons of mass destruction. But for some who wore cloaks and broke the rules, exotic bugs and toxins were preferable to daggers.

Rhodesia was never a signatory to the BWC.

Taffy prefers to remain anonymous. Smart move for someone like him currently living under a black ANC government in South Africa.

'It was nothing personal, you understand,' he says meaningfully, 'it was war.'

He was a former British soldier who graduated through the Parachute Regiment to the elite, but even more murderous, Special Air Service Regiment. The SAS is to covert action what the flame is to gunpowder.

In the late 1960s, when a Socialist Prime Minister sat in Downing Street, some men of the far right found this prospect so offensive that they moved to Southern Africa to find a life more in keeping with their view of the world. Taffy, having left the army, went first to Zambia (the job failed), then to Salisbury (now Harare), the capital of Rhodesia, in 1970. In 1973, Prime Minister Ian Smith closed the border with Zambia, and Zambia, in turn, allowed Rhodesian guerrilla groups to establish base camps near the Rhodesian border. The gloves were already being removed as Rhodesia tooled up for civil war.

Taffy's old skills were now much in demand. And he soon became an undercover agent for the Rhodesian Central Intelligence Office. The CIO was less an information-gathering and analytic intelligence service, so much as a pro-active and ruthless white strike force that organized dirty tricks and ran small, illegal operations that included the use of biological warfare against blacks in Rhodesia.

In 1979, Taffy was called into his director's office to be told that the CIO was planning to murder Robert Mugabe, the long-time black nationalist leader in Rhodesia, during the all-important Lancaster House Talks in London. It was at this meeting that the conclusion to the vicious Rhodesian civil war was to be negotiated with Mugabe's powerful guerrilla force, Zimbabwe African National Union (ZANU).[1]

Taffy, when invited to become Mugabe's assassin, found no moral impediment at the prospect.

Because the murder would have to take place in high-profile circumstances in London, Taffy was keen to select a method that would not
necessarily involve shooting and explosives.

He was introduced to a Professor Robert Symington, who then
headed the Anatomy Department at the University of Rhodesia. Symington, who later left Rhodesia for South Africa after independence, has
been credited with being the father of Rhodesia's biological warfare
expertise.[2] Taffy says he knew him socially and that 'he informed me
that he had been producing and testing and using toxins to supplement
[*sic*] the war effort for the Rhodesian forces. The toxins had been used
for killing terrorists.'[3]

We have moved to a hot and darkened hotel room up from the bar.
Taffy begins to relax and warm to the subject. 'The toxins we used came
under three headings. One of them was ricin, which comes from the
castor bean and has to enter the body intravenously. The second one
was a heavy metal called thallium, which has to enter the body orally
and kills, like ricin, within a matter of three days. There was a third one,
researched and used by Symington, which was called Parathion, that was
something I had never heard of before. It enters the body through the
hair follicles.' (Parathion is an organo-phosphate, a highly dangerous
and potentially deadly toxin used by farmers on the land. It was to
become a favourite murder agent of the South Africans, too.)

Taffy made ricin his toxin of choice.

He concluded that the best way to kill Mugabe would be to fire the
ricin into his body with a rifle. In order to ensure that the ricin pellet
stayed in the body long enough, the enterprising Welshman took an
ordinary rifle bullet, ground off the head (which is made of cupro-
nickel), drilled a hole into the centre of the lead inside, and filled it with
ricin. This dum-dum bullet not only held the ricin, but also had the
advantage of spreading inside the flesh and not exiting the body, thus
ensuring the poison stayed where it would do its work.

Unhampered by any overpowering sentimentality towards canines,
Taffy picked up a couple of large dogs from the local Society for the
Protection of Cruelty to Animals to test his theory. He shot the dum
dums into the dogs. It worked. The dogs took three days to die.

For his flight to London and entry through customs, the resourceful
Taffy put the ricin (and some back-up thallium) into separate glass vials,
carefully undid the wrong end of a toothpaste tube, squeezed out much

of the paste, inserted the vials, and then rolled the tube up as if it were already half used. The scheme worked and he entered the United Kingdom without difficulty.

Then, in a sensible *Day of the Jackal* gesture, he moved into a small, back-street hotel in Victoria.

'Robert Mugabe was staying in the Royal Lancaster Hotel, as was Joshua Nkomo [then leader of ZAPU, the Zimbabwe African Peoples Union]. The CIO had said that if one of them became amenable to the talks, and one of them was difficult, it was the difficult one I was to get rid of.'

The go-signal was to come from his CIO bosses in Salisbury in a telephone message which would say somewhat cryptically: 'See you in November.'

As it turned out, the message never came and the assassination plot was called off. Taffy, who had previously bumped off one or two awkward people for the CIO in Zambia, was phlegmatic. He disposed of the toxins and returned to base like a good soldier.

Despite its anti-climactic conclusion, the Mugabe plot was a chilling foretaste of the extent to which biological warfare could, and would, be used extensively by whites fighting a desperate rearguard action throughout Southern Africa.

Mugabe had been a potentially high-profile target. But there were other lesser-known people involved in the African struggles who were not so lucky.

Connie Braam, small, an immaculately trim figure, a pretty and intelligent face – a Dutch Jane Fonda in her day, but her day is still not over.

She ran weapons for the military wing of the ANC during the 1960s and 1970s and took real physical risks for which she was nearly murdered.

Connie Braam, sitting in an Amsterdam apartment within a cigarette-flick of the busy Central railway station, still wearing her combat trousers incongruously matched with an attractive red blouse. And looking tired, because she's got cancer, but still looking good and twenty years younger than her age.

Connie Braam, unwilling victim of a terrible practical experiment.

First in Rhodesia, and, after he fled, in South Africa, Professor Bob Symington's experiments with the organo-phosphate, Parathion, were successful. The toxin, an insecticide that was first synthesized in the 1940s, was an anticholinesterase – a substance which retards natural and important enzyme activity in the brain and thus interferes with nerve conditions, which can lead to serious poisoning and death. In humans, organo-phosphates will invariably cause nausea, headaches, excessive salivation, vomiting and diarrhoea, visual problems, disorientation, and mental confusion leading to respiratory arrest. Some organo-phosphates are carcinogens; depending on the amount of exposure, it is believed that they can eventually cause growths and tumours.

The appeal of organo-phosphates as weapons of assassination is that it is extremely difficult for anyone other than an expert to detect traces of these rare substances in the human body. This means that correct diagnosis and treatment may be delayed long enough to allow death.

The method of application for offensive use against humans is bizarre. The poison needs to enter the body's largest hair follicles, underarm or around the crotch. Hence, smearing some (it is odourless and colourless) on underwear is the most efficient method.

In September 1987, Connie Braam, always heartily despised by the hard right-wing white Rhodesians and South Africans as a pro-black activist, attended a Children's Conference in Harare. She was then chairperson of the influential Dutch anti-apartheid movement. She stayed at the Bronte Hotel, as she had many times before.

'In my room, I opened the closet and there were two jackets hanging in there. Now, let me say straight away, I can take care of myself. I've been a target long enough. They've tried everything. But over the years, I had changed my clothes a bit, less the combat jeans and something more fashionable.

'I guess they figured I'd fall for the clothes thing. Anyway, these two jackets were really beautiful and very much beyond me money-wise. One was real wool, black, and the other one was cotton, but with a print and a design. Oh God, I mean it must have cost a fortune, and, what was most amazing, they were absolutely my size.

'It had been very hot during the day, and, in the evening, it got very cool, and I was terribly tired. I had been wearing only a small dress at the conference and I had a lot of skin exposed. So, anyway, I put the black woollen jacket on, and I sat at my hotel table and wrote my conference report. I worked on it about an hour. After that, I took it off and went to bed, without even taking a shower.

'I think I woke up about three or four in the morning because of my own screaming and the knocks on the door. The pain was incredible, beyond belief. I've had a child, and it was a difficult birth, and this was much worse than that, much worse. The pain would start to build up and build up and then would reach an unbearable pitch.'[4]

The knocks on the door came from the guest in the next bedroom, a friendly Dutch cameraman, Jan de Graaf. Braam crawled along the floor and managed to let him in. Then she returned to bed and began to lose consciousness from the pain. De Graaf thought it might be food poisoning and tried to help Connie vomit, but it made no difference. Eventually, a doctor arrived.

'Now there's this mysterious man hanging over me. I was worried, because he was a stranger, and a man with a heavy South African accent to boot. He kept pressing me here [she points to her stomach] and said I had an ulcer. He immediately produced a little brown bottle and said I should take the pills. But I knew I didn't have an ulcer, and how could he diagnose it so quickly even if I had? The whole thing was very odd. There was a new receptionist on the desk who was unknown to me. He had called the doctor, who miraculously arrived within minutes – at that time of night. I ask you!'[5]

The 'doctor' then made some remark about Connie Braam being the right age for ulcers and left, after again strongly advising her to take the pills. But, coincidentally, de Graaf actually had an ulcer. He examined the pills and declared he had never taken 'rubbish' like that, and threw them down the toilet. De Graaf and a colleague took turns to baby-sit Connie for the rest of the night. She returned to Holland and immediately saw her own doctor, who checked her thoroughly for ulcers – and found nothing.

About three months later, in March 1988, Connie Braam woke up and discovered a huge swelling the size of a ping-pong ball had suddenly developed on the bridge between her vagina and anus. She was rushed to a hospital. The diagnosis produced nothing and she underwent an immediate operation for its removal. But then, to her horror:

> The wound they left wouldn't close, it just wouldn't heal. I lived with
> a plastic bowl and surgery soap and, three times a day, I had to sit on
> it to clean that wound. There was no pus and no blood, it just stayed
> open. Apparently, my blood wasn't good enough to heal the wound. It

stayed like that for a year. The hospital was completely baffled. After a year, they said: 'This is ridiculous, we're going in a second time.' And then they started to cut my vagina to pieces, and they started to dig in, but they just didn't know what they were looking for. And you know, they found nothing, nothing, nothing.

Finally, after another five or six months, it began to heal. But it's a bad and vulnerable scar. It still splits open very easily, it gets red and itches. There's poison in my body, that's why, it was that jacket. I know. I feel it.

Now I have to be careful with my personal hygiene, and it has badly affected my sex life.

Then, last year, I got cancer.

Finally, very feminine and after a long silence, she cries a little. 'I think it was the jacket. They've done terrible things to me.'[6]

While it is unlikely that one single exposure to Parathion would cause cancer, it is possible that Connie may have been exposed at other times in other ways. Ominously, the insults to her body defy conventional medical explanation. Biological warfare, when it fails to kill, can scar for life. It does not have the brutal finality of the bullet or the bomb. For Connie Braam, it remains an obscenity.

The Reverend Frank Chikane is one of those cheerful vicars of Christ, like Archbishop Desmond Tutu, who bless their enemies at the drop of a bible and seem incapable of harbouring anger, revenge or hatred. Yet Frank Chikane, internationally respected as General Secretary of the South African Council of Churches, and a former ANC activist, also found himself targeted by the killers who engineered toxins for the assassination of their enemies. Like Connie Braam, he is lucky to be alive; unlike her, there seems no lasting damage.

He was a key member of South Africa's first democratic government, serving as Director-General of the Office of Deputy President Thabo Mbeki (now Nelson Mandela's successor). His status gives him a substantial office in Government House, where black civil servants and black ministers scurry round corridors in a reassuring demonstration of the smoothness of the political transition.

Chikane is small and unfailingly cheerful. Like Tutu, he is always on the verge of a giggle, unpompous and workmanlike, with a steady handshake and penetrating eye contact.

In April 1989, he drove north to Namibia from South Africa to meet various contacts. He had previously been barred from entry, but once the UN moved in on 1 April he felt free to take the risk.

> Suddenly, I felt I needed to vomit. I became very sweaty, and seemed to lose all my energy. I got the car to stop and threw up. It was now clear something was wrong, and I was rushed to hospital. By the time I got there, I couldn't move and I was carried in on a stretcher, and, I must tell you, I was in agony.
>
> Do you know, I was now in a remote hospital in northern Namibia; there were only two doctors on duty and the hospital stopped for five hours to save my life.[7]

Chikane returned to South Africa as an emergency medical case; and, after six days of treatment, he recovered. In the absence of any other recognizable cause, the rather limp verdict was that he had been suffering from fatigue.

The following month, on 10 May, he left for the United States as part of a four-person team of church leaders to meet top Senators, Congressmen, and, finally, President Bush. But, within a few hours of arrival, he had another severe attack. He was in Madison, Wisconsin and was again rushed to a hospital. The same symptoms emerged: nausea, sweating, salivating, and vomiting.

> My body began shaking and twitching, my eyes became watery and vision blurred. I could hardly walk or turn my body in a sleeping position. Then came the hyperventilation. I lost consciousness and had to be placed on an artificial respirator.
>
> I'll tell you, my wife left my bedside that evening thinking I was dead. That terrible night, they called Desmond [Tutu] and said, 'He's dying.' And so they sent me an Anglican bishop, and, when I opened my eyes in the morning, I found this bishop with me and he was there for the last rites, and he said the prayers and then left.[8]

Chikane is silent for a moment, then smiles to himself, as if savouring some clerical inside-joke.

Oddly, he travelled from near death to rude health within a couple of days. It didn't make medical sense. Yet, each time he returned to his hotel he began to get sick again. On three separate occasions, he bounced in and out of the intensive care unit – to the growing perplexity of the American doctors. They asked him delicately if he had a drinking problem, since there seemed to be a touch of pancreatitis. More and more doctors crowded around his bed to examine him. This wasn't the Namibian outback; and the Americans wanted answers.

Finally, on his third return to the hospital, one doctor, frustrated by the lack of logic to these turns, took himself off to the library and burned some midnight oil over a pile of medical reference books. Eventually, he discovered that the symptoms related to organo-phosphate poisoning.

Samples were flown to California laboratories and the call came back: 'They're positive.' They'd cracked it. Chikane missed his date with President Bush, but at least he was alive.

It's now 1998. Has he forgiven the perpetrators? 'Oh yes, I've forgiven them. Why should I not? If I don't, then I carry the pain in my system. People who do awful things carry the scar. It was a struggle, and I'm prepared to forgive, especially those people who were used in the process because they were instruments.'[9]

A few weeks later, less than a mile from Government House and Chikane's office, a medium-sized man with salt and pepper hair, rimless glasses, a checked shirt, and a shaking hand, testified before South Africa's Truth and Reconciliation Commission. He had actually worked with the men who tried to kill Chikane with Parathion.

'Ja,' intoned the witness, without emotion, 'I was told there were mistakes with Frank Chikane. The intelligence was bad, we were counting on very little forensic capability in Namibia. Then, when he went to the US, the stuff was smeared over his underwear, but too little was used to kill him outright. They got it all wrong.'[10]

Chikane watched that testimony of the stranger who had wanted to kill him – and promptly forgave him too.

The Braam and Chikane bungled murder attempts (there were others that succeeded) are new evidence of the value of biological and toxic devices as weapons of assassination. What is only now becoming apparent is the true role of South Africa in this new form of warfare.

During the 1980s, this was a nation state that prided itself on its civilized and civilizing ways, reflecting the highest values of the white man. South Africa was even an original signatory to the BWC in 1972.[11] But only ten years later, and faced with enemies inside and all around the white laager, South Africa removed any restraints on the use of biological warfare. Rhodesia had been an interesting experiment. Now, the lessons would be put into practice.

CHAPTER TWENTY-FOUR

Wouter Basson

'Medicine's my profession, but war's my hobby.'
Dr Wouter Basson

Dr Wouter Basson.

If he hadn't been real, the Republic would have had to invent him. Single-handedly he developed South Africa's biological warfare programme, drove an ox and cart through the Republic's solemn international BW arms control commitments, and then turned the official BW programme into a vehicle for biological murder and mayhem.

Single-handedly, too, he showed the world how one dedicated man, well financed, could create an offensive biological warfare programme in secret, rendering valueless the checks and balances in current BW arms control legislation. All that, and he's still, on the face of it, a nice guy, with a firm handshake, a handsome, friendly face, a finely honed sense of humour, and enough charisma to overwhelm even his fiercest enemies.

In the Keg and Hound bar and restaurant shop near his lawyer's office in Pretoria, sits the man now regarded as the Mengele of South Africa. If the Republic's Attorney General is to be believed, he is a man who has both instigated and conspired to commit murder, caused grievous bodily harm, is a serious drug dealer, has conspired to pervert the course of justice, and committed fraud involving sixteen million pounds.[1] Basson lazily sips his espresso. The piercing blue eyes twinkle as he talks. But the conversation needs to sparkle, for he is easily bored and the good humour in his eyes can morph in an instant to defensive aggression. He denies every allegation, as one might expect him to. He was merely 'a soldier', he says, who fought an honourable war. His lawyer is present.

But this is only a very brief get-to-know-you meeting. On parting, he gives a wildly exaggerated Masonic handshake, then roars with laughter and walks away. 'The spooks will have taken pictures of us,' he says gaily, as he leaves. They had too.

Once South Africa had successfully used neighbouring Rhodesia as a human laboratory for its primitive biological warfare attacks, it began its search for the man who would convert the amateur to the professional, the tactical to the strategic, the man who would wage the first modern offensive biological warfare programme since the 1940s. Basson, a scientist and a warrior, was the perfect candidate. The Rhodesian civil war ended in 1980 with the birth of Zimbabwe. For the units of South African police and South African military intelligence who had fought with the whites, the war had been a vital learning curve in preparation for the new smouldering border wars with Angola, Namibia and Mozambique. The Rhodesian Selous Scouts, the so-called pseudo-operations group, gave inspiration to South Africa's Special Forces units (and several other specialized counter-insurgency units) who were mobilized for these border wars.[2]

P.W. Botha's elevation to the premiership of South Africa in 1978 not only brought with it the ruthless military policy of 'total onslaught', but the implementation of another dangerous euphemism, 'segmentary destabilization', which actually meant using economic sanctions, sabotage, sponsorship of anti-government groups, and even the use of criminal bands, in order to create chaos in the target country. Botha's cardiologist was a young and promising military doctor called Wouter Basson.

Basson operated within a system where, officially, sabotage operations in neighbouring countries, the use of death squads to assassinate opponents of the government at home and abroad, and the use of torture simply didn't exist. All the relevant military equipment used for these incursions was purchased overseas (usually in Britain) by a special South African procurement unit. The protagonists of all this deception included specialist units of the South African police, the South African

Defence Force, Military Intelligence and Special Forces. Particularly Special Forces.

And it was in the crucible of paranoia, guilt, hatred, and the partial breakdown of civilized conduct that 'Project Coast' (*Jota* in Afrikaans) was born. It was the code name for South Africa's official, but secret, programme to develop offensive and defensive chemical and biological warfare weapons. The annual budget was in the region of £4–5 million, a staff of some two hundred were involved.

There *was* some small military justification for the creation of a defensive *chemical* programme. Cuban troops allegedly armed with chemical weapons had arrived in Angola in the late 1970s and early 1980s; and there was evidence of the use of basic chemical weapons in Mozambique. It made military sense to take defensive precautions. But there was no possible justification for South Africa to embark on a covert biological warfare programme; not a shred of evidence existed to suggest that her enemies were using BW.[3] Nevertheless, Project Coast went ahead.

Nominally, the responsibility for the project was passed to South Africa's new Surgeon-General, Niels Knobel, a former Professor of Anatomy at the University of Pretoria Medical School and a member of the Citizen Force (Territorial Army) from 1971 onwards. Knobel appointed as Coast's project manager a young physician with a Masters in chemistry, now a talented Lieutenant Colonel, Wouter Basson.

There was during these febrile years a political/military paradox in the way South Africa organized its defences against her border enemies. Although under Botha the state was being rigidly centralized, there was an increasing tendency for covert units to act within a decentralized system of command – in order to promote operational effectiveness, while minimizing the risk of embarrassment to senior officials. The 'need-to-know' principle generally used in covert operations precluded knowledge of the trade from circulating through normal managerial channels. This system also enormously increased the possibilities of corruption and mismanagement and encouraged the tendency for these secret programmes to fracture into vertically integrated patronage struc- tures. This, in turn, allowed covert operators in the field to carry out illegal operations on the authority of just one senior central official, thus by-passing various committees designed to co-ordinate and monitor government actions.[4] When it came to biological warfare, there was also the little matter of South Africa's signature on the BWC – dated 3 November 1975.

This curious covert system allowed Basson to accrue the power and the budgets that enabled him to create and develop, almost single-handedly, a national offensive biological warfare programme. His enthusiasm for the task was boundless, and he answered to no one.

Knobel may have been his nominal boss, but Basson did not feel himself constrained by the Surgeon-General's rank or personality. Knobel signed the cheques, but asked merely to be kept informed. Basson would have understood only too well the need for plausible deniability. So Knobel slipped Basson's leash and allowed him to travel the world, often in a private jet, to acquire whatever South Africa needed. At Basson's disposal were placed South Africa's embassies, safe houses, and High Commissions, along with their spies and dirty tricks people. Basson's programme was to become one of the Republic's greatest illegal and sanctions-busting operations.

Basson controlled the programme, seeing himself more organ grinder than monkey, regarding both Knobel and his superiors with occasional disdain, calling them 'chicken heads' and similar unflattering sobriquets.[5]

Even today, most of the who, what, where, and why of Project Coast remain wrapped in enigma. The official documents have been largely shredded, fingerprints carefully wiped, responsibility sloughed onto very junior shoulders, or, better still, onto those who have since died. Those who should have known were not told, those who were told have poor memories. So, little is known about how Project Coast was planned, developed, or executed.

To Knobel's slight irritation (for he was, after all, Basson's *nominal* boss), Basson was actually 'tasked' by the most dangerous and powerful men in the land, a deadly 'kitchen cabinet' including the Minister of Defence, the Head of the Defence Force, the Commanding Officer Special Forces, the Commissioner of the South African Police, and the Director General of the National Intelligence Service. With friends like that, Basson scarcely needed Knobel's patronage. Whenever Basson carried out an operation for his masters, Knobel was usually advised *post hoc*, a humiliation he simply had to learn to live with.[6]

That was the *official* Project Coast, on the face of it, the programme to defend against the use of biological weapons by the nation's enemies.

But under Basson's energetic leadership, and with the knowledge and approval of the men above him, an unofficial Project Coast soon emerged, linked to but hidden deep inside the official version. And *this* Project Coast involved the use of offensive biological warfare in a pseudo-military series of operations against South Africa's perceived enemies on the border. But there was still more. Project Coast also involved the targeting of individuals, both inside South Africa and outside the Republic's borders, as far away as Europe and the United States. Basson was given licenses to make money and kill.

The first impression of General Niels Knobel is of a courteous, honourable, slightly plodding and pedantic man; decent, rather bureaucratic, a functionary, precise, and slow, but always reliable and loyal. A man who, despite his rank, might have been better at receiving and executing orders than giving them.

He is a frequent visitor at the home of Magnus Malan, the former defence minister. Malan's home sits high in the hills of Arcadia, a white and well-off suburb outside Pretoria with a passing resemblance to some of the vulgarities and exotica of Beverly Hills. The jacaranda seems in permanent blossom, and each large mansion is heavily fenced and sprouting enough barbed wire to repel a bad day at Ypres. Fences and walls still carry the large-lettered, day-glow security warnings that have become the trademark of so many prosperous homes of the ever nervous whites in South Africa.

Malan's generous spread has electronic gates with a speakerphone, and the man himself, with unfailing courtesy, waits by the main house entrance to greet guests, his faithful Rhodesian Ridgeback bitch at his heels. The black mini-cab driver is steered with utmost courtesy towards the shade and offered a cold drink.

Inside, it is cool, civilized, spotlessly clean. The English tea comes from English china, the cakes are small and delicate and fresh. This is the Africa that Malan and his tribe always dreamed of. Outside the double-glazed French doors, the heat doesn't dare invade. Later, as cool evening settles, the chilled white wine is served from a vintage cut-glass decanter.

Knobel is over six feet tall, wears slightly sinister blue-tinted glasses, predictable grey flannel trousers, laced black shoes, and is fractionally overweight. He has a curious, almost obsequious relationship with his former defence minister, whom he persists in calling 'Minister' to this day. When discretion calls, both men break into Afrikaans.

Knobel, the midwife of Project Coast, is sixty-one-years-old, an anatomist who earned his Ph.D. in Edinburgh. He gleams with pride at still serving his nation (having stayed in the post during the transition to Mandela, leaving government only in 1997). Indeed, somewhat paradoxically, he is today a member of South Africa's Council for the Non-Proliferation of Weapons of Mass Destruction, a poacher now playing gamekeeper's rules.

By giving Project Coast to Basson, Knobel effectively handed it to South Africa's Seventh Medical Battalion, a unit specifically tasked to provide medical support to the SADF Special Forces during the wars. Basson had joined the SADF in January 1979 as a medical officer with the rank of lieutenant. He spent two years at military hospital specializing in internal medicine. From March 1981, he served as a specialist adviser at headquarters and worked within Special Projects for the Surgeon-General.

When promotion to field rank was in the offing for Basson, he both worked and played hard to achieve the honour. While on a senior management course at the Voortrekkerhoogte military headquarters in Pretoria, Basson did well with his homework, but forgot there was a physical side to the test which involved a day of tough, marathon examinations. The candidate felt he would need some extra chemical stimulus to pass. Whatever it was he took certainly achieved the desired result, as he sped through the day. However, the after-effects of whatever he had taken were punishing and potentially dangerous.

So he placed himself on a life-saving drip, and, that evening, drove to an important social event with the drip still in place. He survived the evening with the apparatus somewhat anachronistically, but carefully, lodged on his shoulders.

He got his promotion.[7]

By 1985, Basson had reached the rank of Colonel and, three years later, Brigadier. But it was as a lieutenant colonel that Basson finally took command of the Seventh Medical Battalion. The soldiers of 'Seventh Med' (as everyone calls it) were not like the American paramedics in Vietnam, who often choppered in to deal with the dead and wounded and then exited with all speed. Seventh Med was expected to fight as well as heal, and they earned a ferocious and deserved reputation as a special forces unit in their own right, having been trained in parachuting, rappelling, unarmed combat, and rope work.[8]

To this day, Knobel believes that Basson should have been given a medal and not a criminal charge sheet. 'My knowledge of this man stretches over twenty years. I've never had any reason to doubt his integrity. I've seen him in action under fire, and he is cool, calm, and collected, and a gentleman.'

Today, Knobel justifies South Africa's work on BW because he always believed that diseases that were endemic to Southern Africa might have been used as offensive biological weapons against the Republic. Besides, there was the underlying mistrust of what the Soviets and their surrogates were up to.

Project Coast, he insists, was always a defensive project.

Untrue. A top-secret letter from South African Military Intelligence, dated 25 March 1992, states unambiguously:

'Project Coast is a project organized by the Surgeon-General with Brigadier Dr Wouter Basson as project officer. The aim of the project is to provide the South African military with *offensive* and defensive methods of chemical and biological warfare [our italics].'[9]

This means Knobel must have known all along.

Knobel first sent Basson around the world on a feasibility study. The keen young officer returned and submitted a long report on trends, doctrines, and the main modus operandi of the superpowers, including the USSR. The clubbable Basson soon found himself comfortable in the small and tightly knit world of toxicologists and microbiologists. He adopted their language, did his homework diligently, and used charm and an endless supply of cash to smooth his way through these important networks. Project Coast was now already 'black' funded, which meant financial control and knowledge were in very few hands. In fact, Basson could have been buying beer and cigarettes with the cash, no one would ever have known.

After the feasibility study – the commission. In 1982, Project Coast was launched. Nearly everything about it was criminal or illegal. Knobel smiles as he reveals some of the secrets.

'Listen, we had to do some penetrations. So we penetrated the American biological programme, we penetrated the Russian programme, we penetrated the United Kingdom. And we had wonderful information from them, and some of the scientists who were later on sent to look at *our* programme were the very scientists who had given us information in the first place.'[10]

How did Basson do it?

'Look,' Knobel replies, 'this was a covert operation. Basson goes into a pub with this guy or he meets him at a scientific conference, they begin to talk. Scientists like to exchange information.

'He went to Porton Down, he got the tour in Porton Down. And he went to Fort Detrick. I'm telling you, he infiltrated them all.[11]

'Let me give you an example. The Soviets had that flesh-eating bug, necrotizing fasciitis, right. Now, we obtained that and its antidote from the Soviets and gave it to the Americans, and they were astounded. We really obtained our capability from the superpowers.

'Basson managed to get manuals. Whether we stole them, or whether they were given to us, I do not want to elaborate, but they were top-secret manuals from the Americans, the British, the French, and the Germans.'

As Basson blithely bought, bribed or stole his way into what were supposed to be tightly secured and sophisticated defensive biological warfare programmes, London, Washington, and Moscow seemed unaware about this haemorrhage of information. In Britain, the main responsibility for preventing the proliferation of knowledge on any weapon of mass destruction (including biological) rests, in the first instance, with the Proliferation Desks of the home and foreign intelligence services. (Today, MI5, the counter-intelligence agency, is still trying to find out if, and how, Basson managed to enter the top-secret Porton Down BW defensive plant in Wiltshire and if there were breaches of national security.)

In Malan's drawing room, Knobel warms to the praise of his protégé, turning every now and then to Malan for approval, or confirmation, or clearance to reveal what he is revealing. Malan is mostly silent, an occasional nod, a small grimace, nothing one could ever attribute directly to him. Knobel always defers.

Knobel is praising Basson again: 'This man has the capability of going anywhere and talking to anybody ... he went all over the place, he went to the cartels in Colombia, he went to Iraq and Iran, he went to the Philippines, to Northern Korea, to Croatia, all over the world – and he made friends and contacts and he obtained information. There was a lot of sympathy for South Africa at the time.'

A visit by Basson to the United Kingdom in 1985 (partly to talent-spot microbiologists working at Porton Down) illustrates how easily he moved between the formal and informal world of BW acquisition. In April of that year, a London company, Special Training Services (STS), with close connections to British intelligence, had a stand at a military medical exhibition in Bloomsbury, London. One of the company directors was Jim Shortt, a former special forces soldier who now runs an international bodyguard firm in Croydon. Shortt recalls Basson asking STS for information about nuclear, biological, and chemical matters; and also for help in establishing an 'R2I' (Resistance to Interrogation) course.

STS reported the contact to MI6, Britain's foreign intelligence service, which opened a file on Basson. Then the story becomes a little opaque. Shortt says, and can prove, that in order to make a credible presentation to Basson, he was sent by 'the authorities' on a one day's nuclear, biological, and chemical defence skills course at Winterbourne Gunner, the government's training establishment near Porton Down in Wiltshire. A subsequent 'block prospectus' detailing what STS might be able to sell the South Africans was then prepared.[12] Basson did not go ahead with the deal.

Shortt met Basson again at the Second World Congress of the International Association of Forensic Toxicologists in Ghent, Belgium during the following August (1986). The list of participants included a who's who of the biological warfare world – Arabs mixed with Jews mixed with Americans and Eastern Europeans. Basson modestly described himself as coming from: 'Forensic Science Laboratories. Private Bag X620. Pretoria.' It was at these gatherings that the personable and very well-heeled South African engineered the networks that delivered the bacteria, viruses, and knowledge into the secret files of Project Coast.

By now, Project Coast had grown into the world's second largest offensive biological warfare programme. Knobel had authorized the use of several front companies, ostensibly civilian, but wholly financed by the Ministry of Defence and run by the Special Forces.

One of these companies was the Roodeplaat Research Laboratories, located ten miles north of Pretoria, which was the locus of Project Coast's secret BW work. Outside were large steel gates and a double-row

Dr Wouter Basson ('charming, charismatic and very, very dangerous') in a rare interview with author Tom Mangold during a break in the TRC hearings in Cape Town.

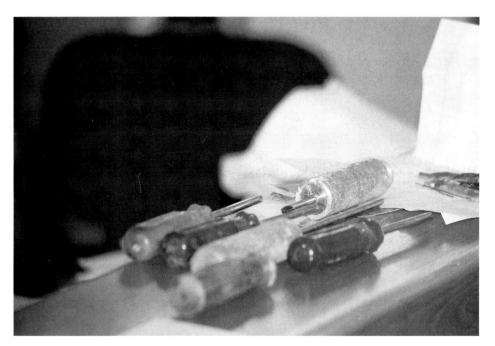

This collection of harmless-looking household screwdrivers had been specially adapted and engineered to become lethal injectors of toxic substances to be used for individual assassinations in London by killers allegedly hired by Wouter Basson.

The big wink in court. Wouter Basson acknowledges a friend at the TRC hearings. Unfailingly cocky and arrogant but always personable, Basson's smile may have deserted him when he subsequently found himself charged with sixteen counts of murder and thirteen counts of conspiracy to murder many victims using biological weapons.

Above: Dr Jan Lourens – a former South African Special Forces officer who blew the whistle on Wouter Basson at the TRC hearings in Cape Town. His evidence was breathtaking.

Top right: Maureen White in a Kent garden. Her South African soldier husband died mysteriously while working with Special Forces. Dr Basson supplied the death certificate. South African intelligence officers believe he was murdered with snake venom.

Right: Connie Braam. 'The pain was incredible, beyond belief . . . they have done terrible things to me.' The Dutch anti-apartheid heroine nearly murdered by organo-phosphate poisoning.

UN weapons experts wearing protective clothing use high-tech sensors during a search for missile parts in June 1998 in the dunes at Al-Nibai, 45 kilometres north of Baghdad, in a bid to verify Iraq's claims that it has buried all its biological and chemical missile warheads.

'The Iraqis play monstrous games, you should hear some of the lies they have told me about their biological weapons.' UNSCOM's tough Australian weapons chief, Richard Butler, a man with a deep loathing of biological warfare, shown here meeting Tariq Aziz, the Iraqi foreign minister.

A frame grab from a 1996 United Nations video which shows the UN blowing up an Iraqi biological weapons plant at the Al Hakam base 60 kilometres southwest of Baghdad. The UN said the weapons plant was used to manufacture botulism, anthrax and other deadly germ warfare agents. It believes 600,000 litres of biological agent was made at this plant, making it probably the biggest biological plant in Iraq.

Left: Lt-Col Gabriele Kraatz-Wadsack, the German Army Plague Warrior and scourge of the Iraqis. As an UNSCOM Chief Inspector she unearthed BW growth medium and investigated allegations of experiments with biological weapons on human beings. Iraqi thugs tried to intimidate her – 'They'll have to try harder, I just love this job.'

Below: Colonel Kraatz-Wadsack (foreground) on an UNSCOM raid moments after BW documents were found hidden in an administrative office at the University of Baghdad. 'I'm sure the Iraqis have managed to hide most of the incriminating paperwork.'

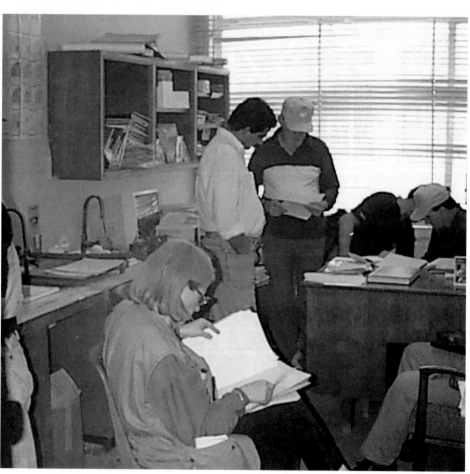

The Inspector's Inspector. David Kelly *bête noir* of the Russians and the Iraqis, respected and feared by both. One of Britain's finest Plague Warriors and a world expert dedicated to forcing compliance of the Biological Weapons Convention.

A rare picture of Nikita Smidovich – Soviet poacher turned UN gamekeeper. Once he was dedicated to fooling Western BW arms inspectors in the USSR, then he joined the United Nations Special Commission on Iraq as an inspector himself. Quietly patient, astute and capable of facing down the worst of Iraqi threats and blusters.

Half blind, quite mad, but the first modern plague warrior Shoko Asahara, leader of the secretive Japanese Aum Supreme Truth cult. He supervized Botulinum toxin attacks against the Japanese parliament and US troops stationed near Tokyo.

Aum's lethal attack on a subway in Tokyo in 1995. Twelve people died. Five thousand were injured. It was the West's 'wake-up call' to the dangers of modern apocalyptic terrorism.

of electrified fencing. Guards with dogs patrolled the wire. When asked why such extraordinary security was necessary for an ordinary civilian plant, a spokesman answered laconically that it was needed to protect the laboratories from 'industrial espionage and irrational animal rights groups'.[13] Inside was a 40-metre-square BL-3 (Biosafety Level three) containment laboratory, where work on all but the most lethal bacteria and viruses could be conducted. (When Basson wanted the safety level raised to the highest number, BL-4, two British scientists, one on an unauthorized visit from Porton Down, came to help and advise.)[14] All the programme's microbiological laboratory work, testing, and inhalation experiments were performed at Roodeplaat, or RRL, as it was known.

A large part of the building was hidden underground, where there were operating theatres and two-way mirrors through which visitors could be observed. There was, inevitably, a decontamination room with showers in case of accidental exposure to bacterial agents or toxins.

Down below were the cages which held primates and beagles for biological testing, and an incinerator for disposal of the animal cadavers.[15]

Baboons, trapped up-country in Kruger Park, were shipped by the crateload to RRL for biological tests. Some of the incapacitant tests were done on the baboons *en plein air* in the park. The researchers used poison darts, which took several hours to incapacitate or sometimes kill the primates. This led to complaints from tourists and the swift termination of that visible aspect of the programme.[16] Nevertheless, so strictly compartmentalized was the work at RRL that some of the civilian employees were ignorant of the deception and sincerely believed they were working for a legitimate private commercial establishment. (Today, the laboratories are used as the headquarters of the Plant Protection Institute.)

By the mid-1980s, Basson's energy and diligence had produced a sophisticated and deadly arsenal of biological weapons. RRL was working on anthrax, Plague, cholera, Tularaemia, E. coli, staphylococcus enterotoxins, necrotizing fasciitis, ricin, botulinum toxin, gas gangrene, and the so-called anti-matter bacteria, a state of the art pathogen which destroys materials, including plastic.[17]

When Basson acquired the bacteria, according to Knobel, he invariably transported them himself, and only in a private or chartered plane, so there would be no risk to ordinary commercial passengers should there have been an accident or breakage.

More ominously, RRL also worked with the new killers, the African haemorrhagic fevers: Ebola, Marburg, and Rift Valley. Original viral samples had obligingly been sent to Pretoria in eight separate shipments by the Centres for Disease Control in Atlanta in 1984, ostensibly for the South Africans to devise vaccines or countermeasures.[18] This cooperation was a perfect example of the weakness of the BWC in failing to make a clear and legal distinction between legitimate defensive/medical research and illegal offensive development.

RRL had two ten-gallon fermenters for growth medium and a few smaller ones, which allowed for small-scale production. No serious attempt was made to weaponize BW agents on a grand scale, as it was clear that biological warfare would be waged in a series of low intensity, regional skirmishes, and, of course, individual assassinations.

Some of the grey areas of Project Coast are still being investigated. Only a fraction has been exposed. Daan Goosen was managing director of Roodeplaat between 1983–86 and knows where some of the bodies are buried. Any suggestion that Project Coast might be a defensive BW programme was never communicated to him. Indeed, the reverse was true – he was categorically informed the programme was offensive. 'It was spelled out to me as such,' he recalls.

For example, Project Coast worked on fertility drugs. Goosen was well acquainted with this research. 'There was a project to develop an oral contraceptive which would have been applied clandestinely to blacks. Knobel knew all about it. We were told that the black population, because of its high birth rate, would outgrow the resources of this country . . . and that the fertility project was the most important research we could work on. We developed a vaccine for males and females, but we had to develop something that could be given without the knowledge of the recipient. It had to be given either orally or as an injection. The blacks would have been made sterile without their awareness.'[19]

General Knobel's recollection of this extraordinary project, potentially a war crime, is different. 'Er . . . yes, there was an investigation into fertility. I'm hesitant to tell you what the basis was, but it was in fact that the Chinese [were the clients]. It was carried out for them in exchange for some of the equipment that they made available to us.'

The General denies abuse of the programme, but found no great political paradox in Pretoria working with Peking to confront the spread of communism in Southern Africa.

The fertility programme was just a small part of Project Coast. One of its dedicated aims was to repeat the Rhodesian experience, by using biological warfare offensively in the scrub, bush, and jungles of the border areas of Angola, Mozambique, and Namibia, where South Africa found herself hard pressed by increasingly organized guerrilla groups, and even regular fighting forces. Furthermore, there was the ANC's military wing (Umkhonto we Sizwe) to cope with – a constant threat, even if it delivered less than it promised. Botha's government, feeling itself under siege, now opened up 'total onslaught' using the germs and the germ-knowledge acquired by Basson.

Biological warfare broke out, quietly, and secretly, and the plan was the world would never find out.

CHAPTER TWENTY-FIVE

'Gert'

'Yeah, [we used] thallium, botulinum toxin in food and water, Hepatitis A. Look, it was a dirty war.'

'Gert'

Not surprisingly, when South Africa's Truth and Reconciliation Commission (TRC) invited amnesty applications from those plague warriors who had actually used biological warfare in the bush, they received not one response. Who would be sufficiently unwise to incur the wrath and hatred of the community and expose himself as a war criminal in return for state mercy? Besides, there is now a revived and toughened War Crimes Court in The Hague, and Pretoria could not guarantee immunity from that tribunal.

And, equally problematic, if the lowly executioners of BW, the ones who were 'only obeying orders' came forward, then how long before the Godfathers of BW, the men who gave the orders, were exposed too?

In his investigation into the men he called 'Apartheid's Assassins', journalist Jacques Pauw explained how the structure of state-run assassination worked.[1]

'The men had their own rules, their own language, their own culture. Informal rules required that only two people should ever be present when orders were given, turning the only witnesses into co-conspirators. The conspiracy needed its own language, one that didn't leave any suggestion of blood, pain, loss or suffering. Never but never, did they use words like "kill" or "murder" or "assassinate". (Rather) "*Maak 'n plan met*" (make a plan with), "*vat hom uit*" (take him out), "*raak ontslae van hom"* (get rid of him), *"los die probleem op"* (solve the problem), and the favourite *"elimineer"* (eliminate).'

So, using the side-of-the-mouth euphemisms much beloved by organized crime, these men invented a language which allowed the killers to pray, attend church, marry, raise God-fearing children, and weep when their pets passed away.

They dehumanized the opposition, branding children in the townships armed with sticks and stones as 'armed terrorists', civic leaders who led disobedience campaigns as trained revolutionaries, and all others were *ipso facto* Marxists and Communists. The political mind-set was best encompassed in the ominous expression 'total onslaught'. A speech by Minister of Defence Magnus Malan in parliament in September 1981 symbolized the state of fear that gripped the ruling Nationalist Party: 'At point of departure we have to accept that the onslaught here in southern Africa is Communist-inspired, Communist-planned and Communist-supported . . . They want to establish a dictatorial state for elite black Marxists in the Republic of South Africa . . . The security of the Republic of South Africa must be maintained *by every means at our disposal* [emphasis added].'[2]

The institution that set the parameters for murder was highly secret and varied, a quasi-masonic structure for like-minded men who did not need to meet to conspire, rather they knew instinctively what was required of them. Impenetrable, safe, and plausibly deniable. At its head was the State Security Council (SSC), which had been established by law in 1972, but with a secret membership and secret proceedings. Its task was to co-ordinate the security of the state in general, which included oversight of the police but which also included almost all other branches of state policy. At the SSC's base were numerous autonomous and camouflaged units and committees sanctioned by SSC guidelines, including the Counter Revolutionary Information Target Centre, better known by its Afrikaans acronym of Trewits. This apparatus was founded in 1985 to identify human targets for removal. Each month representatives of the security police, Military Intelligence, Special Forces, and National Intelligence Service would hold meetings at which intelligence information would be swapped and targets identified and if necessary hit-lists 'for removal' created.[3]

Then there was the Directorate of Covert Collection, a secret dirty-tricks unit within Military Intelligence.

But the ultimate killing machine – and one that certainly involved the use of biological warfare – was first formed in 1986. It became active towards the end of 1988, when a small group of South Africa's best-trained and most feared soldiers joined together to create a master plan for a very special South African Defence Force unit. This group studied the structures of the CIA, KGB, and Mossad, and concluded they needed a component that could function and survive completely independent of the SADF.[4]

It had to generate its own funds, obtain its own weapons, and gather its own intelligence. It had to be sufficiently secret to survive investigation and ensure it was never exposed. No member should know the identity of any other; even the men at the top would not know all the members who worked for them, and – vintage tradecraft this – there would have to be members who did not know for whom they were working. There would be one golden rule for members involved in operational work – 'their tracks should never be traced back to the SADF'.

Thus, an extraordinary organization with a civilian façade was formed. It was eventually called, with a fine sense of ghoulish humour, the Civil Cooperation Bureau (CCB). Although it formed part of the SADF's Special Forces (as, in essence, did Basson's Seventh Med), there was no overt indication of this. At Special Forces, it functioned under the code name 'Triplane'.

In fact, the CCB had begun life under another banner, 'D40', in the early 1980s, and it included former members of the Rhodesian Security Forces who had emigrated south after Zimbabwe's independence.

In his submission to the TRC in May 1997, General Malan admitted he had approved the formation of CCB 'for the infiltration and penetration ... and disruption of the enemy'. Asked what he meant by 'disruption' the former Minister, never short of a few bons mots to demonstrate an endearing sense of humour, answered: '... You can throw sugar in [the enemies'] petrol.'[5]

But with Malan's sly wink and nod, the CCB became a monster with tentacles that stretched not only over South Africa and the border states, but all the way to Europe. At its most venomous, the CCB spent a fortune in establishing a network of agents who spied on anti-apartheid activists, acquired weapons on the black market, and hired professional assassins and criminals to execute the nominated enemies of the state.

The use of biological weapons, although exotic, was also pragmatic in a part of the world where killer epidemics and local disease outbreaks were commonplace. Anyway, it had been tried in Rhodesia and it had worked. There were other advantages as well, now well rehearsed by the professionals. BW could be used often without detection, endemic sources could be blamed, and its use gave time for the killers to escape. If used correctly against black targets, the natural proliferation of disease would be a bonus in the dirty war. The undetectable incapacitants, which had been researched on wild baboons in the Kruger Park, could be used on humans; allowing CCB killers to hurl them out of windows in apparent accidents or suicides.[6]

The CCB was so well protected that when the South African Police Forensic laboratories were called in to investigate a particular crime, they would first check with the CCB to establish whether they had been involved. In that case, the investigation quickly dried up.[7]

Only one CCB operator, Pieter Botes, has spoken openly about his unit's use of biological warfare, and even he made only a glancing reference to it.[8]

For two years, Botes was one of CCB's elite; he was a captain in the Special Forces 'recces' – best described as South Africa's own SAS. Botes admitted in a personal conversation with Jacques Pauw that the CCB had devised a plan to put cholera and the yellow fever virus (provided by an army doctor) into the drinking water of Swapo refugee camps in northern Namibia. This operation had been successfully executed at the refugee camp at Dobra, but the bacteria did not survive because, Botes explained, the chlorine content of the water had been too high. Botes' boss had discussed with him plans 'to distribute disease in the camps'. Botes admitted to another cholera attack on the Mozambique border (using germs obtained from South African military intelligence). Since these admissions, Botes has prudently vanished. South African investigators finally believed they had unearthed him in an African country early in 1999, but it was in a location too dangerous for an ordinary detective to travel.[9]

It was against this background of omertà that we met 'Gert'.

The introduction was arranged by Nico Palm, then a senior director with the notorious 'Executive Outcomes', in its day, one of South Africa's leading companies that supply mercenaries. Until 1998, the firm's offices were located on a large and beautifully manicured ranch just outside

Pretoria.[10] Curiously, once inside the high-walled location, on an appointment, a sense of a deep mystery took hold. There were BMWs in the parking lot; each one sparkling clean, but the drivers were missing. Inside, the offices were spotless – but still no people. There were classrooms, lecture halls, and the whole feel and atmosphere of a well-endowed English public school – but the place was hauntingly empty. Only one immaculately coiffured receptionist and the equally immaculate Nico were in attendance.

Nico, thin, incongruously city-groomed – in dark suit and blue crease-less shirt with matching blue tie and not a hair on his head out of place – looks like what he is not, a slightly effete, mid-thirties, ad-man. In fact, he's a military hard-man, having served with distinction in the South African Defence Force as an engineer. The bad old days have left him nervous and troubled; he has an album with ghastly photographs of bomb victims (blacks and whites), and he produces it frequently. Peace has handed him a mental in-tray of unfinished business, but the contents remain ill-sorted. He is an earnest and serious young man, unfailingly polite and, like others who know him, we like and trust him instantly.

Yes, he'd heard about the use of biological warfare during the border wars. Yes, he knew all about Seventh Med. 'They check each other out when people like you approach them,' he explained. 'They warn each other. It's very tight. These guys didn't always wear uniforms, the doctors were civilians.'[11]

Palm spoke enigmatically of 'Die Organisasie', a pulp fiction *nom de guerre* (which he calls, even more melodramatically, the 'Spider Network'). It is a group of white South Africans who wait patiently for the demise of the ANC government and a return to the old days. They are not the mad pseudo-Nazis of the far right, but something far more organized, well financed, and patient. Other people know them as 'The Third Force'. We are to hear of them time and again from ex-soldiers like Nico Palm all the way up to South Africa's deputy defence minister, Ronnie Kasrils. Significantly, files have also been opened by MI5 in London, where Die Organisasie is recognized as a small, potent, and potentially significant union of like-minded South African right-wingers. All of them are ex-pats now living in the United Kingdom, who may support the destabilization of any black South African government.

Palm says he has a primary source who used biological warfare against the enemies of South Africa during the covert border struggles of the 1980s. This contact may be prepared to talk on guaranteed non-attributable terms.

Three days later, we drive in Nico's pristine BMW to an office near Centurion Park, a few miles from Pretoria. Gert, as he wishes to be called, is waiting. He's about fifty years old, with brown hair showing no sign of grey, slim, with very slightly puffy eyes. He wears a short-sleeve, chequered shirt. Nothing very distinctive. His English is good, and he is used to giving orders and being obeyed. He says he wants the truth told. Like Nico Palm, he is angry at the many crusaders who benefited financially from the dirty wars in the bush and left their underlings to face the music. He wants no money, nor favours, and has no objection to being audio-taped for accuracy.

The noise of the air-conditioning in the office overwhelms the tape-recorder and has to be switched off. The heat is stifling. It is well over 95°F outside. A secretary brings in endless coffee and orange juice.[12]

Gert teases with some hints about his personal background, but not enough to make an identification. 'I was recruited by Basson,' he says casually. 'I had the same rank and status, I was a colonel.'

Gert belonged to a Task Force attached to Seventh Med. Slowly, his story emerges like a jigsaw, with pieces that ought to fit, but never quite inter-lock. That's how he wants it.

What was used in the bush?

'Thallium, botulinum toxin in food and water, Hep. A [Hepatitis A] . . . Look, it was a dirty war.'

Against whom?

'Anyone we were acting against . . . the enemy.'

How do you know this?

'I was there when it was put in.'

The bacteria and viruses, he says, were delivered in containers and used in northern Namibia. Bacteria were placed into a water source 'wherever you identify one, or wherever you identify one destined for human consumption'.

'When Hep. A was used, we had to make sure that the operators had a gamma globulin injection first. Cholera was pretty widely used also. I used it. I personally was involved in the Eastern Transvaal against FRELIMO in Mozambique. We placed the cholera upstream . . . we looked for areas, and you don't have to be a rocket scientist to work this out, where they didn't filter the water or don't clean it – places where there was no chlorination, so you drop it in and prod it.'

Who did this? Soldiers?

'No, no, no, no. Never, ever did it happen by ordinary soldiers. You can't blame any of the normal forces for that. Although sometimes some of our own soldiers did get infected by the cholera that we put in the water.

'This is what I'm saying, usually the guy who did it, who placed it, was dispensable – he would have been very well selected, he's someone you can compromise, he's either on drugs, or he drinks too much, or he's got his hand in the cookie jar. That was all done here in Pretoria.'

Who did the selection? Basson himself?

'He selected the guy with the criminal background ... It was a criminal operation. The guy would wear civilian clothes.'

How did you feel, you are obviously a doctor? How did you feel when you saw cholera, hepatitis, and botulinum toxin being used in action?

'Look, it's too bad, I didn't like it at first, I still don't like it ... Of course I am responsible. I have to accept responsibility for it, but, at the level at which I operated, it was something which I had to protect myself, otherwise I'll die ... I was part of an indoctrination process which started off in this country since I was a child – and I grew up with it and I honestly believed at that time it was right.'

Gert senses he is saying too much – the unspoken feeling transmits around the room. He remains coy about his background, coy about the chain of command, coy about the use of biological agents.

Did people die from the BW attacks?

'Yes.'

How do you know this happened?

'Because I saw the bodies.'

Oh, really?

'Because I was in the target area, I had to report on what happened to the target.'

After an hour, Gert is beginning to relax. He has said more than he intended, and is ready to go just a little further. The coffee helps concentration and the skin is beginning to acclimatize to the steady run of sweat in this hot, stale, and exciting room.

'Look, I know what one of the very, very, very secret specialized units had. We had to test it. And that was viral capsules that were specifically related to Congo fever and the haemorrhagic fevers.'

Ebola?

'Yes.'

So Gert is beginning to corroborate Dr Stamp's suspicions in Harare that Ebola and Marburg, although indigenous, were also artificially seeded into Southern Africa. Basson, says Gert, was involved in all this. (When the last terrible Ebola outbreak occurred in Kikwit, Zaire, as late as 1995, Gert claims that Basson was there, unofficially. Twenty years earlier, when the village of Yambuku in northern Zaire witnessed one of the first major Ebola outbreaks, two South African scientists were there, allegedly working hand in glove with US military personnel from Fort Detrick.)[13]

Slowly, patiently, Gert confesses that these terrible viruses were 'researched' for offensive use by South Africa. Next, he talks elliptically about 'taking out' certain enemy units, even though these actions had no military value. It was done in order to find the one soldier who, according to military intelligence, had contracted an haemorrhagic fever. These sick people would then be evacuated from the border areas to South Africa, 'to see what the effect was, obviously'.

You wanted to see the effect because you had sown the disease?

'For sure . . . I can tell you that I know of this thing because I did it myself. I did the evacuations. It was up in Eastern Angola, we're talking mid-eighties.'

Gert lifts another veil. 'There was some HIV tampering,' he says.

Meaning?

'I mean all you have to do is get one covert guy, he's HIV positive, he's of the area. You get him to infiltrate the whole town and screw the whole lot . . . get him out and shoot him.'

Was that really done?

'If I tell you, it was obviously done.

'Look, I was a wild guy. At one stage, I worked with the police, I worked with national intelligence, I worked with military intelligence, I worked with Seventh Med, I worked with everybody. I was never identified, because only a very few people knew where I was positioned.'

Was Basson your boss?

'No, it was higher up, both military and political.'

We return to the subject of biological assassinations, but with serious cautions from Gert to be most discreet. On occasions he wants the tape switched off. He acknowledges some ten assassinations carried out using bacterial agents. Often the victims were ill and vulnerable, already in a sick bed. There was a politician, he claims, who 'was given thallium with his penicillin injections ... another, a journalist, who was murdered using BW'.

And Basson's role? Did he know about the biological assassinations? 'For sure.'

Did he talk about assassinations to you?

'Yes, to me personally.'

Using bacteria?

'Yes.'

Gert denies he ever used BW himself.

'I never dirtied my hands ... I never gave the orders, but I saw the effects. You must remember, I was behind the scene. I had to report what happened.'

In his reporting role, he says, he was flown by private plane on two occasions to meet a small group of South Africa's top military officials and politicians – he knew them all by sight. They wore civilian clothes and waited inside the air-conditioned HS125 jet they had flown in to meet him. There could be no witnesses. Inside the plane, they talked BW – was it working, what were the effects, was it efficient?

It is within this context that Gert now raises the question of Die Organisasie. He is clearly apprehensive of its power, and it is the only moment he appears truly concerned. 'These are people who take no prisoners,' mutters Nico. Gert grimly nods his head.

A few weeks later, another meeting with Gert – on this occasion, for dinner. It is a more relaxed and friendly session. But this time, another side of him is on display – a little arrogance, more self-confidence, more soldierly. He has some rather nasty stories about the use of certain interrogation methods – perhaps he used them himself. It is the last meeting.

CHAPTER TWENTY-SIX

Truth and Reconciliation

'I've got one daughter, and one day the blacks will take over, and if my daughter asks me what did you do to prevent this, my conscience will be clear.'

Dr Wouter Basson[1]

Basson's unofficial Project Coast included the development of a bizarre range of biological agents and delivery systems for individual murders that would have been the envy of the Borgias. There were cholera organisms by the millions and anthrax planted in the gum of envelopes, into the filters of cigarettes, and inside chocolates. There was thallium and ricin and organo-phosphates; there was snake venom, paratyphoid, Plague, Hepatitis A, HIV, and the terrible Ebola and Marburg viruses. There was botulinum toxin secreted inside beer bottles and Salmonella germs hidden in sugar. Most of the 'bugs' were freeze-dried, where possible, for more effective use. Rarely can death have been prepared in such eclectic and obscene forms.

An investigating South African intelligence officer was stunned by the evidence he saw. 'The whole thing scares the shit out of me. There are nights when I can't sleep. We are looking at perhaps some three hundred individual murders. It's like something from Heinz Konsalik [the German science-fiction writer].'[2]

Who were the victims? The world will never know. Who can determine years later that a death from cholera, or Plague, or a supposed heart attack, or a stroke, or something terrible in the stomach, or an illness that defied diagnosis was the result of a biological murder? In places where physicians and coroners have not been trained to identify the signatures of biological warfare, and where bodies are quickly disposed of in the heat, who was to stop the burial, voice suspicions, or ask the right questions?

The hearing rooms of South Africa's Truth and Reconciliation Commission, on the twelfth floor of a deeply ugly skyscraper in Cape Town, is an unlikely setting for the unravelling of some of the truth about Project Coast. In fact, 106 Adderley Street did once have a more salubrious background. It was originally part of the Dutch East India Company's gardens before becoming Colonial Mutual's headquarters. In 1958, the city demolished the old building and replaced it with the present architectural carbuncle.

One of the quiet arrangements made between President F.W. de Klerk's outgoing administration and Nelson Mandela's incoming government was that there would be a minimum of angry recrimination, showtrials, or hounding of the architects and enforcers of apartheid. If that was the price of peaceful transition, most South Africans must have paid it gratefully – for the alternative was unconscionable.

The Truth and Reconciliation Commission (TRC) was a sincere and Christian attempt by the new South Africa to come to terms with the horrors of apartheid, without the concomitant revenge. The commission was more an approach than an event – an attempt to understand, then come to terms with evil, an attempt at a moral and spiritual catharsis under the watchful eye of trained counsellors. The priority was to restore the dignity and self-respect of the victims, often by bringing them face-to-face with those who had given or carried out the orders. The commission was not a tribunal or a properly constituted court of law, nor was there any attempt at show trial histrionics. The TRC had its own peculiar rules and rhythms and was the better for it.

Given the seriousness of what was paraded in public, the TRC was an extraordinarily relaxed and informal process. This was no Nuremberg – the guilty men sat in no dock, scowling; rather, they sat next to their lawyers, grinning or chatting. The rules of evidence were slack, and the men and women who sat as TRC commissioners eschewed the garments of formality and authority – no wigs, no gowns, just an unfailing gentleness and helpfulness.

With Archbishop Desmond Tutu as the TRC's chairman, it could never have been anything less. Most days, he set the informal tone, this familiar and diminutive chairman touring the chamber before the hearings, blessing the congregation (even the press!), beaming, gossiping, and giggling.

One of Basson's willing helpers was a mild-mannered veterinarian, with yellowing, grey hair and ordinary glasses, who ran the animal laboratories at RRL, the front company created by Knobel to work on biological warfare research. Dr Schalk van Rensburg was recruited by Basson in 1984 to become director of RRL's laboratory services. His testimony was revealing.

'The most frequent instruction [from Dr Basson],' he disclosed, 'was for the development of a compound which would kill, but [would] appear to make the cause of death look natural. That was the chief aim of the Roodeplaat Research Laboratory.'[3]

And biological killings *were* ordered.

Van Rensburg addressed one key document, found in Basson's possession, which detailed a list of biological and toxic 'weapons' which were drawn from the RRL stores in one brief, seven-month period in 1989.[4]

This biological murder arsenal included: anthrax on envelope gum; botulinum toxin and thallium hidden in beer bottles; Paraoxon (an organo-phosphate of the type used against Frank Chikane); Salmonella hidden in paraquat bleach, whisky, and sugar (and used against ANC activists at a meeting with unknown consequences); twenty-two bottles of cholera; Camel cigarettes with anthrax-spiked filters; snake venom (including some from the Mamba); para-typhoid hidden in deodorant; a baboon foetus; fourteen doses of coffee- or peppermint-flavoured chocolate spiked with anthrax or botulinum toxin; plus much more. And all of it was formally issued and signed for by men with no names, only initials, in just one *seven-month* period!

A closer study of the list suggests these bio-weapons must have been targeted at people on the move, vulnerable and exposed in hotels, like Connie Braam or Frank Chikane.

Van Rensburg admitted that Daan Goosen, then managing director of RRL, once told him: 'If you let us down, you are dead.' The vet also revealed that both Prime Minister P.W. Botha and General Knobel knew about this exotic biological and toxic murder factory. 'Of course they knew,' he said angrily, when pressed, 'that's what it was all about.'

More detail tumbled from his monotonous testimony. Russian military advisers had been murdered by anthrax in Lusaka. Basson had talked about thallium poisoning causing a death that might look like meningitis. 'We gave thallium to Steve Biko before he was beaten to death by the police,' said van Rensburg. (A belt and suspenders indeed.)

Basson had discussed 'sorting out' the Eastern Cape with cholera. Van Rensburg added that 95 per cent of the biological and toxic work at RRL was offensive; nearly everything was shredded after the place was closed down.

And what was in it for those involved in the whole business? Van Rensburg put on his bleakest face: 'Good pensions, a nice car, perks, housing subsidy . . .'

Mike Odendaal, a humble microbiologist who worked at RRL for eight and a half years, did what was asked and did it without question. Perhaps that is why he was such a company asset.

On the witness stand, bible in hand, Odendaal is undistinguished and indistinguishable, hewn from the blandest of clays. Everything about him is average – his height, his weight, his horn-rimmed glasses, his nylon shirt and dull tie, his featureless face, his persona. Yet Odendaal was one of those very necessary craftsmen employed in RRL's little biological murder shop.

He prepared some 260 ml of cholera germ, enough, he admitted, to cause 'a very serious epidemic'. Yes, his conscience stayed clear, for biological warfare, as he understood it, was to be used 'in a war situation' and not within South Africa's borders. When it was pointed out to him that cholera was a particularly despicable biological weapon (as it tended to target the very young and the very old), Odendaal thought about this for a while, one felt for the first time, then answered, 'Yes, this is true.'

It was this mild-mannered and inoffensive young scientist who mixed the anthrax and other biological agents with chocolates, alcoholic drinks, and cigarettes. And, no, he had no idea how they were eventually used. He had been told by one of his bosses that they had subsequently been given to 'operatives'.[5]

Odendaal spoke of the offensive use of a resin that would attack aircraft fuel, of methods of causing sceptic shock, of E. coli research (in which baboons were injected), of experiments on hundreds of Alsatian dogs, of causing pneumonia in cattle, and of work on anthrax to produce an antibiotic-resistant strain – the ultimate in BW research.

The SADF had ordered freeze-dried BW pathogens, including Salmonella, anthrax, cholera, and Plague. RRL had performed scores of effectiveness tests to determine the LD50 (the lethal dose required to kill 50 per cent of the targeted victims) for more than *forty-five* strains of anthrax alone. Odendaal admitted running tests on botulinum toxin to establish which household drink would be the most efficient vector – beer, whisky, milk, or water. 'We were seeking anything that could aid the ingestion of botulinum,' he added, somewhat redundantly.

He worked with the bacteria *Brucella melitensis*, which causes a terrible infection, Brucellosis, first of wild or domesticated animals and then of humans, who come down with it either by drinking milk or eating dairy products, or through direct contact with infected animals. This disease can also be sprayed from a household aerosol container.[6]

In animals, the Brucella organism causes abortion, foetal death, and genital infection. When humans are infected, they can develop even more numerous symptoms, including: fever, arthritis, muscle pain, malaise, depression, headache, irritability, insidious chronic infections (including the genito-urinary tract, bladder, and kidneys), cough, pleuritic chest pain, dyspepsia, weight loss, and many others. This medical dictionary of illnesses can last up to a year, and often reoccurs after ten years.[7]

'It's not lethal,' Odendaal brightly told the commissioners.

'Would you like to have it?' he was asked, meaningfully.

'Er . . . no, I would not like to have it,' was the reply.

Odendaal, who said Basson was involved in every aspect of these dreadful events, made a bland apology for his misdeeds, but few on the twelfth floor felt themselves in the presence of a profound man or one whose moral compass had been finely tuned. These were the little men who worked in the basement of South Africa's biological warfare programme. Their evidence mere confirmation of the banality of evil.

Daan Goosen sits in a chrome and red-painted fast-food joint in Pretoria, not eating his French fries, too frightened to raise his voice, which is already overwhelmed by Chuck Berry's guitar from the big fifties-style jukebox speakers. The former managing director of RRL – squarely built, early middle-age, pugnacious – has decided to talk, but he believes there is now a contract on him, and his personal and family's security is at risk. The meetings with him are melodramatic – made by mobile phone appointments, usually changed at the last moment – always at noisy fast-food restaurants or crowded bars. All good B-movie stuff. What he says is equally melodramatic.

> I was asked by Basson to provide biological agents and poisons to eliminate enemies of the state, no doubt about that. He was looking for stuff that would not be very detectable or traceable. There would be ... [Goosen searches for the right euphemism] clandestine applications.[8]
>
> The fertility business was Basson's plan to curtail the black birth rate. He said 45 million blacks [in South Africa] was too many. Should I have helped? I don't know. I think I made a mistake. I'm not a racist. We just weren't thinking rationally. It would have been like America's Star Wars project, and would have given the government a powerful negotiating tool that could have resulted in white people staying in power.
>
> Knobel knew everything. He called it 'the most important project for the country'.
>
> You know there was an amazing thing happened in Europe in 1983/84. Someone handed our military attaché in the London High Commission a scientific document which purported to show that there was a class of bacteria that would kill only pigmented people. Basson heard about this paper and asked me to investigate the scientific feasibility of such a bug. Well, we organized a search of the literature and concluded it was theoretically possible.
>
> The anonymous provider of the original document in London had told our people they should place an ad in a certain newspaper if they wanted to take this further. Well, we discussed this with Knobel and it was decided it would be a good thing if the government acquired such a weapon. It was decided I would go to London to set things up.
>
> However, that week, some of our people walked into an ANC trap in Paris, and, because of that incident, we cancelled at the last moment.

Goosen speaks about Basson's thoughts on how to murder an enemy using snake poison; simply by injecting the victim using a very small-bore syringe and then leaving a dead snake next to the body. Goosen and Basson had equally bizarre discussions about the possibility of 'infecting' Nelson Mandela with cancer, although nothing further came of it.

Did Knobel know about the biological murder weapons?

'Yes, we discussed targeting individuals with him. We were worried about the legitimacy of the targets.'

Goosen was eventually downgraded at RRL and finally replaced by an even more compliant managing director.

The most interesting of Basson's plague warriors turns out to be a mild-mannered, rather handsome, bespectacled young scientist, Dr Jan Lourens, a former South African Air Force officer, subsequently recruited by the Special Operations Unit headed by Basson. Lourens was to become a star witness in the TRC hearings.[9]

During his time with Basson, Lourens recalled, there was the infamous fertility programme (which Knobel claimed had been created for Peking) run by the unfortunately named Dr Riana Borman. The plan had indeed been to produce a blacks-only non-fertility pill. There was no doubt that the ultimate aim of Dr Borman's work with baboons in this area (which thoughtfully and delicately included the use of an electronic masturbator to produce their semen) was to 'manipulate the fertility of people in South Africa on an ethnic basis'.

As Lourens began to give his evidence to a hushed hearing, one of the Afrikaaner lawyers sitting a few feet from the witness issued a loud stage-whisper to his junior counsel, hissing that Lourens had become 'a self-torturing little arsehole'. (An embarrassed court official later translated the offending Afrikaans phrase as 'martyr'.) Lourens, who was meant to hear this gross insult, stopped half-way through an evidential sentence and complained bitterly to the commissioners. Given the impertinence of the act, and its symbolic meaning, the offending lawyer (General Knobel's representative) was lucky not to be thrown out. He was reprimanded and subsequently apologized, but the point had been made. It's not over yet in South Africa.

Stung, but not intimidated, Lourens now began the slow exposé of an even darker side of Project Coast, with revelations about some of the main vectors designed and manufactured to deliver the biological and toxic weapons as a lethal dose. These devices included an eccentric array of rings with secret compartments; walking sticks and umbrellas with secret sprung syringes that could inject an untraceable polycarbonate ball containing ricin straight into the body (as was used in the notorious assassination of Bulgarian dissident Georgi Markov in London in 1978); and, finally, a tool box of screwdrivers all adapted by hand to become biological murder weapons.

These killing tools were all theatrically produced at the TRC hearings by the man from South Africa's National Intelligence Service and arrayed on a bench with a grim warning to the commissioners not to handle them.

During the early 1990s, Basson maintained a regional headquarters-cum-safe house, in a small, rented cottage near Ascot in Berkshire, England. Curiously, the property – Number 1 Faircloth Farm Cottage, Watersplash Lane – is still owned by WPW Instruments Inc. (the acronymn stands for the christian names Wouter [Basson], Phillip [Mijburg], and Wynard [Swanepoel], all of whom have been named by the TRC as being involved in the South African biological warfare programme).

The land registry of the cottage (BK 275140) shows WPW's address to be a solicitor's firm in Fleet, Hants, England. In fact, the company is registered in the Cayman Islands. There was a plan to purchase the adjoining cottage, Number 2, and then knock down the wall to make a single property large enough to house visitors on special missions from South Africa. That plan was shelved, but it is significant that the property remains listed under Basson's name, and that there are still mobile telephones registered out to the address. A small Basson flourish exists in the bathroom, which is decorated with specially created WPW insignia bath tiles.[10]

This cottage was the location, Lourens told a hushed commission, to which he had been ordered in 1992 to take one of the murderous screwdrivers, together with two glass vials containing toxin. His assignment was to deliver it to another South African whom he knew only as Trevor. (The man's full name is in fact Trevor Floyd, a short, stout South African estate agent, now in his late forties, who was then an operative of the notorious CCB [Region 5], which comprised Europe – including the UK.) When the handover took place in the cottage, Lourens accidentally got some of the toxin on his thumb and into his mouth. He promptly fainted, then revived, drank some Dettol (an antiseptic), and threw up in the lavatory. This moment was black farce, but the intent behind the whole screwdriver operation was clear.

'Did you realize the weapon was going to be used on someone in Europe?' Lourens was asked.

'This was my first interface [sic] with someone who would kill someone else,' he replied.

Lourens bought the British newspapers after the meeting to see whether anyone had actually been murdered. They hadn't.

In fact, the court indictment against Basson now alleges that Trevor Floyd's job had been to study the movements of prominent ANC members living in London, and he had recommended that two of them, Ronnie Kasrils (then a senior intelligence officer with MK, the ANC's military wing, and now South Africa's deputy defence minister) and Dr Palio Jordan (now South Africa's Minister of Environmental Affairs and Tourism) should be assassinated. (The method of killing was to be a straight imitation of the notorious 'Markov umbrella' used by the Bulgarian Secret Service years earlier.)

Dr Lourens, the charge against Basson alleges, brought the South African umbrella and a special toxin, called Aryl-Silatrane, to London, and handed both to Floyd during a clandestine meeting on a train. Basson's cottage was then used to show Floyd how to handle the murderous device.

Floyd next gave the umbrella and toxin to a two-man South African hit-team in London, both of whom were Portuguese-speaking Angolans who had worked with the SADF in their home country.

For reasons still unexplained, this assassination attempt also failed. (Floyd is expected to be a future prosecution witness against Basson.)

These revelations have now led to a prolonged murder investigation by Britain's MI5 (together with South Africa's intelligence service), who believe that up to half a dozen enemies of apartheid could have been murdered in the UK, or other European countries, from the mid-1980s through the early 1990s. One leading anti-apartheid activist in Amsterdam, Klaas de Jonge (a friend of Connie Braam), was certainly attacked by organo-phosphate in his clothes. He subsequently lost an eyeball because of the toxin.[11]

One possible murder victim was a South African soldier, Garth Bailey, who died under mysterious circumstances in Pretoria's Number 1 Military Hospital in January 1984. At twenty-two, he had been a member of South Africa's elite and somewhat notorious '5 Recce' (Fifth Reconnaissance), a unit that worked in the bush and was frequently involved in targeted political assassinations.

Bailey was a fit, young, second Dan black-belt karate expert, who played squash three times a week and had undergone punishing survival courses.

His widow, Daphne White, now lives in Maidstone, Kent, England, and is certain her husband was murdered. She is convinced that not only did he know too much about the recce unit's murders, he had also expressed his reservations about what both he and his team had been tasked to do, and had decided he wanted to get out.[12]

He was suddenly taken ill while serving up-country near Katima Mulilo. Eventually, while at a hospital in Pretoria, he came under the care of Dr Wouter Basson.

The paperwork on Bailey's death shows a remarkable inconsistency of medical evidence. The cause of death was variously attributed to botulism, rabies, natural causes, cardio-respiratory arrest (with diarrhoea as a contributory factor), or bacterial intoxication.

Mrs White was refused access to his medical records, so she stole them. Despite her objections, the SADF insisted on cremation, and her late husband's ashes were subsequently forwarded to her in a white shoebox. Dr Basson wrote 'heart failure' as cause of death on the coroner's certificate.

All of the papers in the Bailey case are now with South Africa's National Intelligence Service and the Attorney General's Special Investigation Unit in Pretoria. A formal inquiry has begun into Bailey's death on suspicion that it was caused by human-delivered snake venom.[13] The Attorney General's dogged special investigator, Torie Pretorius, came to Britain in late October 1998 specifically to interview Mrs White.[14]

As the TRC hearings progressed, it slowly became clear that the biological and toxin murder campaign, far from being a 'justifiable' act of war, had continued *long after* the enemy had won the battle. In fact, the campaign had developed a momentum of its own.

Counsel for the Commissioners seized on this point when they asked: 'In 1992 [the date Lourens took the screwdriver weapon to London], who *exactly* was the enemy?' Soviet communism had collapsed, and, with it, the communist expansion threat in Southern Africa. So who was there who needed murdering?[15]

Lourens spoke quickly in reply: 'We did not expect Mandela to be so kind-hearted. We did not think [the handover] would work so well.'

But the point had been graphically made. Project Coast had rolled on long after even the most pessimistic members of South Africa's doomed Nationalist Party realized the game was up.

Before he sat down, Lourens could not resist a final swipe. Knobel, he revealed, was known as 'The Mug' by insiders for the way they could manipulate him. But Basson was feared and had once warned Lourens: 'You cheat us, we kill you.'[16]

Finally, the TRC was reminded that the main office for most of these biological killers was always RRL – the Roodeplaat Research Laboratories. Here there was a safe in the director's office with a refrigerator inside, and inside this fridge was where they kept Basson's arsenal of active and inactive bacteria and toxins, as well as a frozen, dried-blood sample containing the HIV virus (provided indirectly by Basson), a range of organo-phosphates, and a clutch of nerve gases (including Sarin, Tabun, and VX).

When RRL was finally dissolved in 1993, before privatization, the directors allowed Dr Basson personally to remove all of the vital research documents. They were packed into two blue trunks supplied by, and then taken away by, Basson. South Africa had finally agreed to end its BW programme, but all that biological warfare knowledge could not be allowed to be lost.

So Basson calmly decamped with it. The bacteria and viruses were burned.

Remarkably, it looked, at first, as if South Africa's dirty little secrets might stay secret for ever.

CHAPTER TWENTY-SEVEN

Revelations

'I was totally unaware of any unofficial biological warfare programme...'

Former Surgeon-General Niels Knobel, 1998

By 1992, South Africa, under President F.W. de Klerk, was slowly moving towards its great historical *Tsunami* – the peaceful transition from the brutality of years of apartheid governments to majority rule under Nelson Mandela's African National Congress.

The move had begun in earnest, and with visibility, in 1989, when President P.W. Botha was taken ill and the leadership of the National Party, and later of the government itself, passed to F.W. de Klerk, a politician on the conservative wing of the party. He is a skilled and intelligent man, infinitely more subtle and less cruel than the crafty and ruthless P.W. Botha.

As the nation moved awkwardly towards democracy, De Klerk inevitably found himself facing the growing hostility and resistance of the hard right-wing Afrikaner groups. As the National Party opened talks with Mandela's ANC, it became obvious that there were significant elements within the party, and not far outside it, who would do what they could to frustrate De Klerk and return to white supremacy. The most determined of these whites came to be known as 'The Third Force'. They comprised not the mad neo-Nazi right, but revanchist politicians and hard men in the military, and the military intelligence and civilian intelligence agencies, and the myriad covert action groups involved in fighting clean or dirty, internally or externally, to maintain white supremacy.

On 18 November 1992, De Klerk appointed the SADF Chief of Staff, Lieutenant-General Pierre Steyn, to investigate in secret the loyalty of the armed forces – with particular emphasis on the numerous military intelligence groups. In a devastatingly honest report, Steyn warned that Basson's Seventh Med was involved in a biological warfare programme, which included toxin murders and the handling of drugs for operational use. The violent activities, he informed De Klerk, ranged from targeted assassinations to acts of random violence. An 'elimination group' under Dr Brigadier Wouter Basson, Steyn reported, was said to be in charge of all SADF removal actions.[1]

Steyn identified Project Coast as the secret code name of Basson's CBW programme. No one was formally accused in Steyn's report, but the implication was clear – here was a group of men who were dangerously opposed to the new administration.[2]

What mattered most, however, was that South Africa's covert biological warfare programme had at last been exposed internally; the full implications and the details would take another five years to emerge publicly, but the countdown had begun.

On 31 March 1993, just twelve weeks after De Klerk received Steyn's first report, Brigadier Wouter Basson was quietly retired from the South African Military Medical Service. De Klerk simultaneously ordered the closing down of Project Coast's extensive biological warfare research and operations.

F.W. de Klerk had been conversant with some aspects of Project Coast upon taking office, having been briefed about it by Surgeon-General Knobel. But the new President knew only what he was told. 'The briefing essentially said that the programme was aimed at developing our defensive capability,' he recalls. '. . . It was never the policy that it should be used.'[3]

But Steyn's subsequent investigation began to open De Klerk's eyes. 'I was deeply shocked when I heard that we might have been involved in assassinations and the like. I have never been part of any policy decision which said it would be OK to commit these heinous crimes and these gross violations of human rights.'[4]

By then, Basson's name was beginning to circulate beyond the claustrophobic offices of Pretoria. The South African Office of Serious Economic Offences was taking an interest in the financing of Project Coast and had opened a file on Basson. More seriously still, word was beginning to reach London and Washington that the South Africans might be in very serious breach of their solemn BWC commitments. Breaches of treaties that may involve proliferation of nuclear, chemical, or biological warfare materials are the responsibility of dedicated desks in London, of MI6, and in Washington, at the CIA.

So, by 1993, information regarding the truth about Project Coast and its biological warfare programme was being passed from agents of MI6 and the CIA in South Africa to London and Washington.

By the late autumn, it was becoming clear that both the United States and the United Kingdom were increasingly anxious about what they were hearing concerning South Africa's covert BW programme. A démarche was now imminent.

To add to the growing international unease, the unemployed but far from unemployable Dr Basson took a decision to work as a consultant for a South African industrial conglomerate, called Transnet, and he promptly travelled to, of all places, Libya to drum up business for their transportation and hospital equipment interests.

So an extraordinary situation was now developing. South Africa's chief Plague Warrior, the man who single-handedly had created a national biological warfare programme from scratch, who had travelled the world in a chartered jet and procured an arsenal of biological agents, the brilliant scientist and BW weapons engineer who retained unique BW contacts throughout the world, was now trying to do business with one of the world's acknowledged rogue states, with a long and unpleasant history of involvement with international terrorism.[5]

Colonel Mu'ammar Gadhafi's pursuit of a chemical weapons capability is legendary. At the time of Basson's visits, Libya already possessed two large chemical weapons production complexes at Rabta and Tarhunah. Spot a chemical complex, goes the saying, and a biological warfare plant will be carefully hidden somewhere inside. In addition to the Tarhunah plant, the Libyans were building an extensive underground network of pipes running more than 2,000 miles through the nearby mountains – its purpose then was unclear.[6] What *was* clear, however, was that Libya's undeveloped biological warfare programme was quietly seeking ideas and technology from anywhere in the world.[7] This was no place for Basson to be seen wheeling and dealing.[8] And there was another major political complication – which was left unspoken, but very seriously worried both London and Washington.

Nelson Mandela's ANC had received valuable assistance from Libya (as well as Scandinavia and some Eastern European countries) during the dark years of struggle. The ANC's military wing, MK, had been afforded training facilities in Libya. Nelson Mandela remembered his friends. Although all the evidence showed that Tripoli wanted to concentrate on developing chemical warfare capabilities, MI6 and the CIA asked themselves if it were possible that the next leader of South Africa would repay his debts by allowing Libya to become BW proficient as well? The very prospect was deemed wholly unacceptable.

At the end of 1993, President de Klerk received a formal, joint démarche from London and Washington which stated in uncompromising terms that both nations were alarmed with South Africa's existing and future biological warfare programme; and that they were concerned with Basson's presence in Libya and the potential proliferation issues he created.[9]

De Klerk now recalls this very secret event somewhat ruefully. 'A specific name did come to the fore,' he says, 'a certain Wouter Basson.'[10]

Speaking five years later from his well-furnished skyscraper office overlooking Cape Town, De Klerk recalls: 'A special meeting was set up through the secret services. My initial reaction, after having listened to the British and the Americans, was to firstly restate the sovereignty of the South Africa Republic. They were initially quite aggressive, and they had a long list of demands. I said that because I could give them certain assurances, we could not simply accede to all sorts of demands.'

But the West was in no mood to deal with problems of national posturing. 'They wanted five things,' recalls a senior South African official who was present at every meeting. 'They said: "Destroy all your BW records, destroy all your capability, make a public declaration in this regard, and inform Mr Mandela. We also want access to all your records, we must be able to look through them all." I told them to go jump in a lake.'[11]

Supported by President de Klerk, this official counter-attacked. 'What about your biological warfare stockpiles?' he asked the UK and US visitors. 'We are not going to do what you say.'

'There was a major confrontation,' the official recalls, 'and we refused to see them again. Later, they had to come back and eat humble pie and we made friends again.'

However, the truth of the meetings was less flattering to South African *amour propre*.

Both MI6 and CIA had collected considerable covert intelligence about Project Coast. The CIA even had a crucial primary source, a very senior South African, who was well placed (and, more importantly, still in place), and who was giving them some information, not for cash, but because even *he* was frightened about the future of South Africa's biological warfare programme. It was Washington who first learned about Basson's trips to Libya from this source, who had grown deeply concerned about those visits and the implication that Gadhafi might buy a South African biological warfare programme off the shelf.[12]

The Western allies learned that Basson had been working on three main biological agents: cholera, botulinum toxin, and Hepatitis A. The only good news the CIA source provided was that Basson had not devised any serious weaponization plans for these agents; nor had he undertaken any aerosol testing either. The main vectors were 'natural' – comprising water, food, alcohol, and similar items of daily chemistry.

Both Britain's MI6 and MI5, and the CIA, next launched a major investigation into Basson's frequent overseas journeys, his many bank accounts, his interests in brass-plate corporations, and his American connections – a long and tortuous enquiry that continues to this day.

A former senior CIA officer recalls: 'We knew about Basson quite early, and we started watching the South Africans to see how closely they were watching Basson and what meaningful steps they would take to close the programme down.'[13]

At the same time, a CIA agent in Libya was tasked to explore Basson's alleged commercial approaches to Tripoli. 'It all had a bad smell to it,' recalls the senior CIA officer. 'Gadhafi had been trying to get a BW programme for years – without success. He had incompetent people in place – that was the only reason he failed to get a BW programme up and running. Now, suddenly, we saw him with a man who our source was telling us was South Africa's top BW expert. You can imagine how we felt.'

By now, MI6 (which, with its very good sources, had been first on the case), MI5, Britain's Defence Intelligence Service, the Pentagon, and the CIA were all sharing their joint intelligence 'take'. The British were satisfied from an early stage that Basson's programme was essentially devoted to the assassination of internal enemies. They concluded that the unofficial part of the BW programme did not technically breach the BWC. This judgement was based partly on a tour they were given of the Roodeplaat Laboratories. They were satisfied that what they saw did not amount to an offensive biological warfare programme within the meaning of the Biological Weapons Convention.

But even as these assessments were being recorded, a new and invisible problem emerged. De Klerk's order to Knobel to destroy the entire biological warfare programme had been passed to Basson for action. Basson promised he would carry out this directive. The biological 'hardware', the bacteria and viruses, the cultures, and all the experimental stuff were indeed destroyed. That left 'the knowledge' of the entire BW programme, the formulae, the contacts, and the experiments that had worked and those that had not – a priceless library of biological warfare information and research that had cost millions of dollars to acquire. Naïvely, Knobel assumed that Basson would destroy this vital information too.

Incredibly, it is now apparent that despite the overwhelming evidence, even at that time, of very serious abuses in Project Coast, Knobel did not personally oversee Basson's claimed destruction of the BW intellectual property. It was decided instead that the paperwork would be transferred on to a set of CD roms before being shredded. The CD roms, in turn, would be held under a double lock and key in a safe inside the bleak headquarters building of the Seventh Medical Battalion on the outskirts of Pretoria. One of the two keys required to open the safe would always be in the possession of the President of the Republic or his personal nominee.

Theoretically, given the awesome value of 'the knowledge', this solution was regarded as the best compromise between containing the programme and not destroying what had been learned. The trouble was, the whole thing rested on the honesty of Wouter Basson.

Not for the first time, Knobel's poor judgement would turn out to be disastrous.

The UK/US démarche – despite some bad-tempered exchanges and huffy protestations of national sovereignty – did produce agreement for all three nations (South Africa, the UK, and the US) to work together towards a common goal of disarmament, not only of the Republic's biological and chemical weapons, but also of its small nuclear arsenal. De Klerk had been reluctant to turn over the state's nuclear bombs to Mandela. The solution was simple. One evening, three giant US Air Force C-5 transport planes quietly removed the bombs and the military nuclear infrastructure.[14]

Ironically, De Klerk wanted the US to remove all of their biological warfare equipment at the same time, including the indestructible hardware, such as fermenters, *and* any incriminating records. But Washington declined the offer, mainly because the US did not wish to take responsibility for closing the South African programme. The US had two sensible reasons for this reluctant stance. Firstly, Washington would never really know whether everything had really been handed over; and, secondly, it would be easy enough for the Republic to restart the programme some day in the future. Either scenario could leave the US looking deeply embarrassed if it had previously confirmed the end of the South African BW programme. The South Africans also wanted the Americans to take possession of 'the knowledge' – the set of CD roms that contained all the essential details of Basson's programme, including how it worked (the manufacturing processes and parameters) and how it was set up (the biological agents, test results, virulence studies, and so forth). But the US could never be certain that there was only one set of CD roms – so it didn't want them either. It turned out to be a most prescient decision.

Somewhat predictably, with the transfer of power to a new government of National Unity, with Mandela as the new president and De Klerk as deputy president in 1994, the BW issue remained unresolved. The three-nation contacts had continued after the first démarche, with MI6 now taking the lead role in the exchanges of intelligence information. But, by 1995, Basson continued to visit Libya – he made at least five visits to Tripoli – and London and Washington's apprehensions persisted. British and American intelligence officers still considered Basson to be fundamentally dangerous.[15]

In the end it was British representatives who decided to approach President Mandela, with a minimum of fanfare, to advise him that he was inheriting an ugly biological assassination programme from the previous administrations. Mandela's first reaction was: 'Oh my God!' He was initially terrified that the South African 'Third Force' elements, including such organizations as Eugene Terre'Blanche's ultra right-wing and fanatical AWB, might lay their hands on it. He specifically asked British officials for their assistance and advice.[16]

The British advised a gentle approach to entice Basson to cooperate in ending the BW programme and proving he had done so. This would require some formal interviewing. Mandela agreed.

A US/UK team subsequently met Basson in a conference room adjoining Knobel's office in the headquarters of the SADF in Pretoria. Knobel was present. The session began at 10.00 a.m., and except for a forty-five minute lunch break in the officer's cafeteria, Basson was interrogated until 4.30 p.m. According to one of the Americans present, Basson was initially 'testy and arrogant', but, faced with the detailed precision of the questions, he began to lose the front. He was quizzed very closely by an MI6 officer about the type of bacteria and viruses, production techniques, delivery systems, testing, efficacy, weaponization, drying, milling, detailed specifications, everything. His polite but firm interrogators were most anxious to know if there had been any open-air tests of bacterial agents. Basson confirmed that no such trials were held; explaining that neither the climate nor the targets were suitable for aerosol dissemination. He added that secreting toxins, bacteria, and poisons in the food and water systems had been far more effective. He nodded agreement when asked whether botulinum toxin had been his BW weapon of choice. When asked about anthrax, Plague, and the 'standard' viruses, Basson said that none of these agents had been weaponized – although, ominously, the South Africans had been trying to find suitable vectors for them in the food chain! Curiously, Basson consistently denied working with cholera.

Did the South African programme retain any BW stocks? Basson tried a variety of responses on the British and Americans. First, he denied making any BW agents. 'That response didn't even pass the laugh test,' explains one of his questioners.[17] Then, the doctor alleged that no stocks had been made beyond the testing stage. Finally, he admitted that if any stocks ever *had* existed, they had all been destroyed when Project Coast had been dismantled. 'How?' he was asked. 'The way anyone would do it,' he answered. 'Heat and bleach.'

At the end of the session, the allied team met Knobel on his own and told him bluntly that they thought Basson was a pathological liar.

But, on balance, they accepted Knobel's assurances that Coast was now dead, that the stocks were destroyed, and that 'the knowledge' was secure on the CD roms inside a safe inside military headquarters.

That left just one outstanding problem – Basson's continuing Libyan connections; benign, malign, authorized, or not, these contacts were still felt to be both unwise and unhealthy. The decision was reached to focus Basson's mind on the risks. A covert operation was conceived, brilliant in its economy, clarity, and brutality.

On his next (and last) trip to Libya, Basson went on to Tunisia before returning home. In Tunis, one of the South African Transnet representatives was approached by a man he believed was from the Mossad, the Israeli foreign intelligence agency. 'Tell your colleague, Dr Basson, that the next time he is seen in Tripoli, he will be dealt with,' was the bleak message, delivered forcefully and without ceremony. This warning was speedily conveyed to Basson.[18]

'Scared? Jesus, I was shit scared,' recalled Basson later.[19]

He never returned. The Basson/Libya problem was solved.

There is one final irony. Despite the fears, and persistent allegations in South Africa that Basson *was* trying to sell BW to Colonel Gadhafi, the truth is that Basson was not dealing. A British MI6 operation, mounted, quite coincidentally against the very Libyans with whom Basson was in contact, revealed he had been innocent all along. The contacts had indeed been commercial and legitimate.[20]

One last issue remained. What was to be done with Basson now? Should this dangerous, talented, and knowledgeable scientist be left unemployed, rolling like a loose cannon around a nation which was still in uncharted waters on its journey to political rebirth?

Basson was now to biological warfare what Gatling had been to the Colt 45; he had travelled around the world, made extensive contacts, knew where the bodies were buried. He was a man of inestimable value to those rogue states which were intent on achieving their own BW programmes. So what was to be done with him?

The answer was a celebration of Lyndon Johnson's famous aphorism on J. Edgar Hoover's malign presence in Washington: 'It's better to have him inside the tent pissing out, than outside the tent pissing in.' Following some delicate back-channel communications with London, the government in Pretoria was advised that there would be no international outcry if Basson were to be re-instated in government service, even placed in a high-profile civil service job, where, to put it bluntly, he could be seen travelling to and from work every day.[21]

Eventually, President Mandela accepted London's arguments and took the decision to bring Basson back 'in the national interest, in order to regain some control over his movements and activities and to minimize the possibility of proliferation ... of ... technology with regard to biological warfare'.[22]

In 1995, Basson was appointed as consultant physician and head of the Department of Cardiology at 1 Military Hospital, Voortrekkerhoogte, Pretoria. There was a huge outcry in the press, but the appointment had the personal approval of President Mandela, Deputy Presidents Mbeki and De Klerk, the Minister of Defence and his deputy, and the Minister of Justice and Intelligence.

The move simply proved that knowledge is power. Like the vile General Ishii of Japan's Unit 731 notoriety, it looked as if Basson was not going to be prosecuted for what were clearly crimes of war and crimes against humanity. It was hoped that his silence could be purchased through the judicious use of state bribery. All Basson now had to do was to leave well enough alone, and get on with his nice new job.

But character is fate, and instead of just keeping his head down, and clocking in and out of the nice new sinecure, he began the actions that were to lead directly to his downfall.

CHAPTER TWENTY-EIGHT

Arrest

'You know, it would be very foolish of me to talk more about this.'
Juergen Jacomet, 1998

On 29 January 1997, Dr Wouter Basson was arrested in possession of 1,000 Ecstasy tablets.

The South African drugs squad police had earlier arrested another dealer and 'turned' him to betray his supplier. The informer agreed to entrap Basson in what would appear to be a deal for the Ecstasy tablets. The exchange was to take place at the Magnolia Dell Park, almost opposite Basson's house in a prosperous and comfortably white suburb of Pretoria.

The informant was wired for sound, and a detective hid in the boot of his white Nissan car. Other detectives hid in the bushes around the venue. When Basson arrived, also in a white Nissan, he got out and the two men greeted each other like old friends, which indeed they were. A police radio communications officer heard the deal taking place, and, as the money changed hands, the hidden detectives pounced.

Basson sprinted away and was chased by narcotics Superintendent Giel Ehlers, who shouted at him to stop. Basson was running for his life, convinced that foreign intelligence agents had caught up with him to implement 'The Tunis Warning'. The chase turned to low farce as Basson dived into what he thought was a river, but was a mere shallow stream. This heroic escape attempt ended when he stood up, a good suit covered in mud, his bald pate glistening with water, and his hands behind his head in total surrender. When Ehlers identified himself and showed the drenched Basson his warrant card the Plague

Warrior almost sobbed with relief to discover he was not about to be assassinated.

How and why Basson allegedly became a drug dealer is for the courts to determine. But it seems an incongruous development in his exotic career. Now back on the defence payroll, working as a well-paid and respected cardiologist, Wouter Basson was not short of money or respect. His home, at Queen Wilhelmina Drive in Pretoria, was a large, comfortable, detached house where he lived with his wife and young daughter.

So what was Basson up to that night? He says simply that he was framed.[1] Another version has it that he did it purely for personal gain; there is a third explanation, that it was a mixture of personal gain *and* helping to raise funds for the Third Force, of which Basson is considered to be a member.

Basson's possible connections with the Third Force were elliptically referred to by Juergen Jacomet, the former Swiss military intelligence agent who worked with Basson on money-laundering aspects of Project Coast in Europe. When we met Jacomet he was suffering from a serious facial and neck cancer; he had elected to go beyond conventional treatment and was in the hands of a private healer in the Philippines. Despite this serious illness, he remained a cheerful man, philosophical and optimistic, a good friend of Basson and of the old regime in South Africa.

While in London on business in 1998, Jacomet was formally interviewed by officers of MI6 in room 114 of (appropriately) the Sherlock Holmes Hotel on London's Baker Street. They too wanted information about Basson, the biological warfare programme, and Jacomet's role in the whole affair. According to Jacomet, he told them virtually nothing.

In fact, back in the mid-1980s, the Swiss agent had first worked with General Lothar Neethling, South Africa's Police Forensic Chief, delivering arms to South Africa, in an extensive sanctions-busting arrangement. Neethling introduced Jacomet to Basson, and the two men became friends. Basson often visited Jacomet at his Berne home. Eventually, Jacomet travelled to South Africa on several occasions to help Basson and Neethling in the dirty wars of the 1980s.

Now, sitting in a quiet West London garden on an early spring day in 1998, Jacomet relaxes with coffee and cigarettes and discusses the arrest of Basson and the Ecstasy allegations. He scoffs at the prospect of his friend being a profiteering drug dealer. 'It makes absolutely no sense if you know him. It makes no sense that he would mix with street dealers. If it happened at all, there must be a higher interest.'[2]

Such as?

'It might be to procure money to support a certain group which represents the interests of South Africa and wants the return of a white-dominated government.'

Jacomet, now nervous, is pressed to expand a little.

'There is a group of people here in London,' he says. 'One could call them the friends of South Africa. They have it in mind to see a strong white South Africa again. There are American connections too. They need funds, and it is possible that the drug business has helped them. You know, it would really be very foolish of me to talk more about this. They are serious people.'

Jacomet searches for the popular expression, and, remarkably, finds the same aphorism used by Gert about the same people. 'They don't take prisoners,' he says finally.

And who are 'they'? Jacomet mentions some well-known South African names – men previously associated with Third Force activities. He also refers to an American name known to Britain's MI5 for his alleged involvement with Basson in money laundering, sanctions busting, and biological agents procurement.[3]

Once again, Die Organisasie is mentioned in respectful tones, and, once again, the details remain scant and elusive. Jacomet remains silent. (He died months later of the cancer).

It transpires that MI5 officials also take Die Organisasie very seriously. They hold details of a small group of once powerful South African and/or ex-Rhodesians who have residential rights in the United Kingdom, but who share a community of interest in the future of South Africa. The men comprise a closely knit group, which would welcome, and might be prepared to help, the return of a traditional white government to the Republic. These men are not political fanatics, nor is their political motivation sufficiently visible to make them liable to closer supervision. Nevertheless, they remain a troubling point of political focus for Pretoria, where both the National Intelligence Agency and the Ministry of Defence also take them very seriously indeed. The relationship between Die Organisasie and Basson is indistinct, but troubling.

Events after his arrest quickly confirmed that Basson was not merely an alleged drug dealer. There was much more to it than that.

Shortly after the Magnolia Dell chase, narcotics squad detectives took Basson back to his luxurious home just opposite the park to search for further drugs. They found none – but what they did find was far more volatile.

When the detectives arrived at the house, the first person they met was the tall, bearded figure of Mike Kennedy, the counter-espionage chief of South Africa's National Intelligence Agency, and one of the men who had relentlessly targeted Basson. The men from the two government agencies stared at each other, and then the explanations began. It transpired that the NIA had had Basson under observation for some considerable time and had been baffled by the turn of events in the park. Finally, ruffled feathers were smoothed and the spooks and cops worked together to search the house. Inside was Basson's wife and young daughter. Later, his lawyer arrived.

First they searched the doctor's study and seized some papers found in five boxes inside filing cabinets and other documents found inside a safe.[4] At this stage, according to Detective Superintendent Giel Ehlers, the arresting officer, both Basson and his lawyer were still fairly relaxed. It was only when the search moved to his garage that polite smiles began to freeze.

Inside the garage, the NIA officers discovered two steel trunks, both padlocked. In a subsequent search the next day, further documents were retrieved and a third trunk was found at the home of a friend of Basson's, Sam Bosch.

Inside the trunks, they discovered the crown jewels of Project Coast.

After General Knobel had instructed Basson to dispose of everything to do with Project Coast, the resourceful Plague Warrior had indeed collected the paperwork from the Roodeplaat Research Laboratories. But he had not merely transferred the knowledge of South Africa's biological warfare programme to CD roms and then destroyed the documents. Instead, he had kept the documents and taken them home. The reasons for doing this were complex.

Basson needed documentary evidence that what he had done, he had done for the State on the orders of the State. He also needed the documents in order to put pressure on people should the necessity arise. Finally, there was also the pride in his own scientific ownership of so much biological warfare research. It is not inconceivable that he also reasoned that this BW treasure trove might one day be cashed in – so it was worth keeping as insurance for all kinds of reasons.

Kennedy and his men took the top-secret documents back to intelligence headquarters in Pretoria. As they pored over the paperwork, they could not believe what they were seeing. Here was the proof, the confirmation, the corroboration, and much more, that had been missing ever since Steyn had aired his suspicions five years earlier. Here was the evidence that South Africa under Botha's imperial presidency had deliberately cheated on its solemn treaty obligations and had developed a large, potent, and offensive biological warfare programme. Here was evidence too that these weapons were used against innocent civilians in South Africa and the border states, and in individual murders of enemies of the Republic. (It was these crucial papers which allowed the Truth and Reconciliation Commission to mount such informative hearings one year later.)

One recently retired South African intelligence officer, who read the documents, realized that Basson must have had instructions from a very superior quarter – both on the direction of the programme's development, its use for murder, and the selection of targets.[5] These instructions did not, on the evidence from the papers, come from General Knobel. The evidence also showed that time and again, Knobel's authority over Basson was trumped by the then-Chief of the Defence Staff (General Liebenberg), who ran Basson from a wholly different agenda.

The documents also contained evidence that a private British company had been involved in the intended creation of a BL-3 containment laboratory at Roodeplaat, which would have been used for offensive BW work on the haemorrhagic fever viruses – Ebola and Marburg. This British role, however, was not officially sanctioned; it involved one former Porton Down employee who had joined Porton International, a private commercial firm formed by 'old boys' from Porton Down.

As it turned out, that lab-building plan had only failed because De Klerk ordered the termination of Project Coast. Despite denials from London, there was evidence of some British assistance to Basson's programme. 'This was a dirty game, a dirty game,' says an NIA officer.

'The British helped on the margins, but it was still help. The papers showed that both the British and Americans have behaved hypocritically over this, but so did the Germans, the Israelis, the Swiss, and a large number of greedy academics.'[6]

How?

He would not amplify.

We meet Basson for the last time by the Greenpoint Lighthouse, a short drive outside Cape Town at Mouille Point, a beauty spot that defines the raw splendour of the city's location. At a place where the mountains slash the horizon, and the South Atlantic crashes angrily against the land, we meet the man who spent years throwing civilization into reverse, a doctor who did not heal, but instead called disease back from the darkest caves of expulsion.

His charm is undiminished ('I'd love to talk to you, but I've been told to wait for the trial'), although his style is cramped by the brown-leather jacketed NIA bodyguard, who is never more than a few feet away from him.

Basson cheerfully denies any wrongdoing and sees himself as a victim of major political conspiracies. He poses against the spectacular backdrop of the nation he loves, all the while insisting that his per-secutors simply do not have the full picture. His trial, he insists, will reveal all. He will surely plead that his work was in the national interest and that he was only obeying orders. It will be a familiar-sounding defence.

He is unfailingly cocky; where does that confidence come from?

We recall there was, in the documents found at his home, a fax from Britain. It stated that should Basson ever find himself in trouble – real trouble – there was a safe house ready for him not half-an-hour from London. All he had to do was to make his own way to Heathrow. The signature on the fax had been whited out. In fact, the message had been sent by a former Rhodesian/South African citizen who now lives and works in West London, was once very close to Basson, and worked with him on the biological warfare programme. He is ex-Special Forces, and linked to Die Organisasie. Now he is a businessman, married with family, whose permanent residence is in London.

When South African special investigator Torie Pretorious flew from Johannesburg to London in October 1998 to ask this man for help in providing evidence against Basson, he was given the polite brush off.

We ask Basson about this.

He smiles, looks at his watch, summons his bodyguard, and returns wordlessly to his car.

Post-script

On 29 October 1998, the Truth and Reconciliation Commission's report on South Africa's biological weapons programme was published.

The commissioners concluded that the military command under the former government was grossly negligent for approving a biological and chemical warfare programme it did not understand.

Retired Surgeon-General Niels Knobel was accused of gross negligence. He knew of the production of murder weapons, but refused to address the concerns that were raised with him. Knobel made no attempt to understand the medical, chemical, and technical details of the programme. The overall understanding and co-ordination of the programme, as well as its direction, was vested in the hands of one person – Wouter Basson.

The biological warfare programme opened the way, the TRC said, for a 'cynical subversion' of its ostensible aims, through the production of murder weapons for use against individuals.[7]

The trial of Wouter Basson was scheduled to begin in October 1999 and is expected to last for two years.[8] The criminal investigation of him, according to the 300-page charge sheet, is pursuing twenty-nine counts of instigation to murder and conspiracy to murder more than 200 victims (using poisons created at state laboratories). Other serious charges include: defeating the ends of justice, improper possession of classified material, illegal manufacture and possession of Mandrax and Ecstasy, twenty-four counts of fraud, and theft of 57 million rand in government funds.[9]

CHAPTER TWENTY-NINE

Iraq

'All I maintain is that on this earth there are pestilences and there are victims, and it is up to us as far as possible not to join forces with the pestilences.'

Albert Camus

The failure to disarm Russia of its biological weapons or to terminate its continuing research is seen as a serious blow to the prospects of a continuing, verifiable, and fully honoured Biological Weapons Convention.

Equally, the failure to disarm smaller regional powers of their existing biological warfare material or simply to exert pressure on their biological warfare aspirations will add significantly to the apparent reach impotence of civilized nations to abolish BW as a weapon of mass destruction.

Policy makers, military academicians, and concerned scientists have a consenual view that now is the time to set the standards – for this is the moment when the genie is half out of the bottle.

The best Western military strategists believe the first biological war of the millennium will not be a cataclysmic superpower exchange, but a low-intensity regional conflict between a 'rogue' state (beyond the control of a global consensual morality) and its neighbour.

Iraq qualifies.[1]

This nation, under the control of a man perceived to be beyond control himself, has already taken the Middle East to the very edge of biological conflict. If Russia is tomorrow's BW threat, Iraq is the immediate danger, indeed it has been for a decade.

In December 1990, one month before Desert Storm (the Coalition's operation to drive Saddam Hussein's forces out of Kuwait), General Charles Horner, the US Air Force Commander at CENTCOM in Riyadh, and his deputy, General Buster Glosson, faced the West's first-ever modern, military biological warfare dilemma.[2]

Military intelligence had pinpointed eighteen suspected Iraqi BW sites, production facilities, and heavily fortified storage bunkers. Horner had to draw up a bombing target priority list; both he and General Norman Schwarzkopf, the officer commanding Desert Storm, wanted all the sites to be blasted.

But others, including General Colin Powell, chairman of the US Joint Chiefs of Staff, and the British and Soviet governments, were justifiably wary of spreading clouds of lethal germs throughout the Middle East as the munitions blasted biological debris into the skies. President Gorbachev went so far as to order Soviet intelligence to monitor the USSR's southern border for possible bacterial fallout.

Horner sought professional advice from Fort Detrick, and concluded the risks were worth taking. He even argued that a minor outbreak from collateral damage might be a useful lesson to discourage other third-world nations. For redundancy, Horner added nearby electrical stations to his targets list, to ensure that power would be cut off from all BW-related refrigeration units. The plan called for an attack just before sunrise, so that any BW agents which *did* escape would rapidly deteriorate in the full sunlight.

Although Horner cleared the operation with his superiors, the truth was that the Americans were straying into the twilight zone of biological warfare. Nobody really knew what the secondary effects of the bombing would be: whether displaced anthrax spores might float up and head for Iran, Saudi Arabia (and the US bases there), or even Bahrain; or whether there were genetically engineered viruses that would be freed by the bombing, with potentially devastating effects on all mankind.[3]

So the military called in the veteran, sixty-four-year-old William (Bill) Patrick, one of the world's foremost experts on military BW programmes.[4] Patrick had worked on the previously abandoned US offensive BW programme and was (and remains) the repository of most relevant knowledge in the West about BW production and delivery systems. Based on experiments carried out by the US in the 1960s, Patrick estimated that less than .0001 per cent of the anthrax fall-out in

Iraq would prove viable; the rest would either be killed by the blast and the ultra-violet rays of the sun, or would disperse particles too large to hurt humans. He also calculated that the Coalition's own troops, and the Kuwaitis, would be safe from fall-out. But even his expert estimates were based entirely on the supposition of what it was that Saddam's plague warriors had been brewing.

It turned out that Patrick's calculations proved to be right. The bombing raids went ahead and no collateral damage was reported. The world's first modern plague war spasm ended with victory for the good guys.

But the air strikes were the least of the biological warfare problems facing the planners of Desert Storm. The nightmare scenario was of an Iraqi BW attack, using anthrax or botulinum toxin (agents the Iraqis were known to possess), against Allied troops that might infect and kill thousands. How could the diseased corpses be returned to the US? Fort Detrick came up with the grim answer: saturate the bodies with Clorox and seal the remains in body bags. The Pentagon promptly ordered 100,000 new bags in preparation.[5]

Substantive problems also arose with the vaccines needed to cope with such an Iraqi attack. Firstly, there weren't enough; secondly, what *was* available was not guaranteed safe or effective; and, finally, no one could say who would receive them and who would not. The situation with anthrax was bad enough, but with botulinum toxin it was potentially catastrophic. So, throughout the autumn of 1990, a series of urgent meetings were held at the Pentagon. In order to make the serum needed for the production of the vaccine in the laboratories, the army needed first to find a horse with botulinum toxin (BTX) antibodies. A Defense Department search revealed that there was only one single horse in the entire military command which had been immunized against BTX. First Flight was a twenty-six-year-old former funeral caisson hauler, which had been retired to Minnesota to produce anti-toxins.

But the production of BTX vaccine in a horse is slower than a cortege on a winter's morning. It takes several months for nature to get the manufacturing and processing plant up-and-running inside the equine. Nor could the faithful First Flight, even under optimum conditions, produce enough vaccine to inoculate the American troops, let alone all of the allied forces. (By then, General Peter de la Billière, the British Commander in the Gulf, was demanding his men be vaccinated as well.)[6]

So, orders went out from the Pentagon to Colonel Charles Bailey, the acting commander of USAMRIID at Fort Detrick, to do what it took to solve the problem.[7] He found a horse broker at the nearby Charlestown racetrack and negotiated for thirty healthy thoroughbreds (all had disappointing track records) for $800 each. It was their good fortune as they were destined for the slaughterhouse anyway. The horses were divided into five groups, one for each known sera type of BTX. All five had to be developed, as the Americans did not know which type of toxin the Iraqis were working on. (Scientists from Porton Down prepared similar BTX vaccines using forty-five goats, which goat milk producers were persuaded to release – in the national interest.)[8]

Ironically, very little of the American BTX vaccine was ever used. Only some 8,000 shots were dispensed, mostly to Special Forces units. The bulk of the vaccine was placed into storage at Fort Detrick.

By contrast, some 150,000 American soldiers received anthrax shots.[9] Substantial quantities of Ciprofloxacin, a broad spectrum antibiotic, were also made available in the event of anthrax infection. Iraq had, in fact, produced at least 1,850 gallons of wet anthrax for offensive use. None of it was activated against Coalition targets during Desert Storm. This was very fortunate, as Coalition forces were woefully unprepared to fight a biological war. The field troops had few vaccines, no efficient bio-detectors, and only a handful of high-speed armoured carriers (Fox vehicles) specifically designed to find and mark nuclear, biological, and chemical contamination anywhere on the battlefield. (Even today, the US Army still has no efficient system for the instant detection of most of the likely biological agents to be used in a conflict. Even the very best system has a built-in forty-five-minute delay between the detection of a biological agent and its correct analysis. By that time, of course, most of the soldiers in the area will have been afflicted. Worse still, the military equipment can only detect a limited number of bacterial agents, and no viruses.)[10]

The Gulf War was to prove the turning point (the 'wake-up call', as the Americans put it) for the West to take seriously the prospect of a strategic or tactical conflict involving the use of biological weapons. Until then, the subject held scant interest for the planners in the Pentagon or the Ministry of Defense. Saddam Hussein was to change all that.

Iraq signed the Biological Weapons Convention in 1972. Although Saddam's regime (which came to power in 1979) never ratified it, international precedence usually determines that it should have been morally binding on the nation. Iraq, however, adopted a secret policy only two years later to acquire biological weapons. A covert research centre at Salman Pak, about 25 miles south of Baghdad on a bend in the Tigris River, was up and running by then. Work continued intermittently at Salman Pak during the 1980s under a government organization called the Technical Research Centre, which housed special Biosafety Level 3 buildings, together with a forensic research laboratory. Saddam eventually gathered the top Iraqi bio-chemists to work on his secret BW programme, including the formidable Dr Rihab Taha (known to Western intelligence as 'Dr Germ' or 'Toxic Taha'), who had earned her doctorate in micro-biology (plant toxins) from East Anglia University's John Innes Institute in Norwich, England between 1981 and 1984.

The programme involved research on a broad spectrum of offensive biological warfare agents including anthrax, botulinum toxin, cholera, Plague, Salmonella, ricin, Staphylococcal enterotoxin, camel pox (as a model for smallpox), aflatoxins, and haemorrhagic conjunctivitis virus.[11] In assessing these efforts, the Pentagon later stated: 'Iraq developed the largest and most advanced biological warfare programme in the Middle East.'[12] Originally, it is believed, the Iraqis planned the military applications of this programme for possible use against Iran, with whom Iraq had been engaged in a bitter war, and almost certainly Israel, a permanent enemy.

In 1985, as part of a concentrated five-year plan to produce germ weapons, Iraq developed a small biological weapons research facility at Al-Muthanna, Iraq's giant chemical weapons plant. Later, this project was moved to Salman Pak. The plan included targeted research on anthrax, botulinum toxin, and *Clostridium perfringens* (gas gangrene).

By 1988, Iraq's scientists were conducting inhalation and blast experiments using biological agents of various kinds on large animals, beagle dogs (supplied by Germany), sheep, donkeys, Rhesus monkeys (obtained in 1978 from the UK), and chimpanzees. (Iraq tried unsuccessfully to buy some chimpanzees from Britain's Chipperfield's Circus.) Special animal test centres were established at Salman Pak and at an extensive new BW production centre (posing as a chicken feed factory) at Al-Hakam, deep in the desert. Germ-laden aerosols were sprayed near the animals, which were watched in their death throes to assess which strains were most effective and lethal.[13] Crude field trials on test animals – of aerial bombs and 122-mm rockets – also began that year. Production of anthrax and botulinum toxin for offensive use began in the spring of 1989.[14] By 1990, Al-Hakam was making 1,300 gallons of concentrated botulinum toxin and 1,800 gallons of anthrax culture.[15] The facility actually was designed to make up to 11,000 gallons of anthrax, botulinum toxin, and other BW agents a year.[16]

Western intelligence sources are also satisfied that Iraq embarked on, and still maintains, a programme to develop Plague as an offensive weapon. The British SIS (MI6) obtained two good sources for this information; one of them confirmed it a year before the Gulf War. This first source revealed that the Iraqis were making Plague in 20-gallon fermenters, then freeze-drying the bacteria, and storing them in glass vials. It was a small-scale operation, but enough to fill a couple of bombs.[17] The work was done at the chemical warfare complex at Al-Muthanna. According to subsequent information from the same inform-ant, this Plague project remained undetected even after the war, because the evidence was hidden in the nearby workers' housing compound, and these dwellings were never searched by inspectors from UNSCOM – the UN Special Commission on Iraq tasked with finding and destroying Iraq's weapons of mass destruction.

A second British source revealed that the Iraqi leadership had been as exercised as the Americans during the Gulf War as to what would happen if their Plague stocks were hit by Coalition bombs. The Iraqis were known to have bought about 1,000 doses of Plague vaccine before the war. Western intelligence analysts believe this supply was probably used for their Plague production line workers – a small team, working in shifts. No sensible explanation for the purchase was ever offered by the Iraqis.

Such was the credibility of the SIS intelligence that it led directly to the United Kingdom's decision to vaccinate its military forces against Plague before the Gulf War.

In 1991, after the Plague alert was first sounded, SIS also spotted in Baghdad a scientist from Vektor laboratories in Kol'tsovo, Siberia. (An inordinate amount of time and energy is spent by MI6 and the CIA in monitoring the movements of all the world's key microbiologists.)

Vektor was then (and remains) Russia's main viral research institute, and it was where the US and UK had just learned that Biopreparat was developing smallpox as an offensive biological weapon. What worried Western analysts is that the Iraqis later admitted working with camel pox, a safer cousin of smallpox. Iraq's official explanation for this camel pox research was revealing (but not necessarily complete). The people of Iraq, Jordan, and Sudan worked with camels, so they were immune to camel pox. Therefore the Iraqis admitted that camel pox could be used, as an ethnic weapon against the more vulnerable Westerners and Israelis![18]

A more logical explanation would be that camel pox, like monkey pox, is a safe and useful working model for research into smallpox as an offensive weapon. The same cell cultivation and growth techniques can be used for both viruses, but camel pox is more readily available and certainly far less dangerous to work with. After a prolonged analysis of this information, the best intelligence guess by Britain's SIS was that Iraq had begun a dedicated smallpox programme.[19]

Despite numerous American and British intelligence reports during the 1980s on the development of Iraq's formidable and unique regional biological warfare capability, the political reaction in London and Washington (essentially the self-styled guardians of the BWC) before the Gulf War remained one of general unconcern. Biological warfare was still widely regarded as an unlikely weapon of mass destruction. More importantly, Iraq and Iran were then at war, and the US and UK found it opportune to take a broadly pro-Iraqi stance.

Most of Iraq's original strains of biological agents were purchased, without difficulty, during the 1980s from the American Type Culture Collection (ATCC), a non-profit supply house for academic and government researchers then in Rockville, Maryland. In those days, ATCC supplied the most virulent organisms to microbiologists throughout the world without ever checking on who, why, or where the germs would end up. Iraq purchased thirty-six strains of ten different pathogens from ATCC. All were sent first to the University of Baghdad, ostensibly for vaccine research. But Iraq's military actually paid the bills, and the glass vials soon ended up in Salman Pak and Al-Hakam.[20] Hardware for BW production came from the continent of Europe. The growth medium to produce bacteria by the ton came from the United Kingdom. (Growth medium, a culture which looks rather like dried milk powder, is commonly used by civilian institutions, such as hospitals, to grow bacterial samples. Bacteria feed on it. The growth medium is also used for offensive biological warfare programmes to produce substantial quantities of bacteria.)

Production was placed in the care of two British-trained scientists, General Amer Al-Sa'adi, who obtained his masters in chemistry at

Oxford, and Dr Taha. (She later married General Amer Al-Rashid, who supervised the secret missile programme during the 1980s and became Iraq's Oil Minister in the 1990s. Rashid, too, had a British connection, with a London University education and a year's training in the Royal Air Force.)[21]

In early August 1990, after Iraq's invasion of Kuwait, Saddam ordered a crash programme for his biological warfare team to begin loading warheads in bombs and rockets. Within four months (according to Iraq's own unsubstantiated admissions), the Iraqis had filled 157 bombs with botulinum toxin, fifty with anthrax, and seven with aflatoxins (a mould, called Aspergillus, that grows on plants and can cause jaundice, internal bleeding, and liver cancer in humans). They also filled sixteen missile warheads with botulinum toxin, five with anthrax, and four with aflatoxin, and field-tested artillery shells and battlefield rockets with anthrax simulant. They also modified aerial pesticide sprayers to disperse bacterial agents, and worked at creating remotely piloted aircraft ('death-drones' as they were to be called later by British Defence Secretary George Robertson) that carried special tanks filled with bacterial agents which would be sprayed down on the enemy.[22]

During 'Desert Fox' (the December 1998 joint US/UK air attack on Iraqi BW installations), these 'death drones' became a primary target for the British Tornadoes. Defence Secretary Robertson revealed that the planes had bombed two bases where the Iraqi-modified Aero L-29 Delfin basic flight trainers had been stored. 'This aircraft had been fitted with two underwing stores [tanks] carrying 300 litres of anthrax . . .' Robertson reported. 'If this were to be sprayed over a built-up area, such as Kuwait City, it could kill millions of people.'[23]

In early January 1991, just before the Gulf War began, the Iraqi BW bombs and warheads were given to Iraqi Air Force commanders at four bases near Saudi Arabia and in Western Iraq near Israel. The field commanders were given full authority to use them in the event that an American or Israeli nuclear attack on Baghdad disrupted all communications.[24] Rolf Ekeus, the first Executive Chairman of UNSCOM, reported on 11 October 1995 to the United Nations that the authority to use these weapons also had been pre-delegated to Iraqi field commanders as a second strike capability against Coalition forces in the event that Baghdad was overrun.

On 9 January 1991, a classic example of the old Cold War military philosophy of MAD (Mutual Assured Destruction) in action took place in Geneva. (This principle of deterrence argues that no nation possessing the means of mass destruction can win a war as long as its opponent is able to survive the first strike and can respond with equal, or even more, ferocity with the second strike. Hence no nation will initiate such a war.) Secretary of State James Baker met his Iraqi counterpart, Tariq Aziz, in Geneva for the final talks before the launch of Desert Storm. Baker carried a written warning from President Bush. If Iraq used chemical or biological weapons, the US would retaliate in 'the strongest possible way', and Iraq 'would pay a terrible price'. Although the word 'nuclear' was never used openly, neither side had any difficulty understanding the sub-text of the message.[25]

It is now accepted that Iraq's biological sword – poised for use in the modern world's first official, state-sponsored act of international biological warfare – remained sheathed only because of the promise of a nuclear Armageddon.

The latest, but still unverified inventory on Iraq's Plague War armoury was as follows:

- 157 bombs (100 filled with botulinum toxin, 50 with anthrax, 7 with aflatoxin).[26]
- 25 Scud/Al Hussein missile warheads (16 filled with botulinum toxin, 5 with anthrax, 4 with aflatoxin).
- Several 122-mm rockets filled with anthrax, botulinum toxin and aflatoxin. (Iraq says these rockets were for trials only, and not deployment.)
- Spray tanks and drop tanks ready for fitting to fighters or remotely piloted vehicles (drones) capable of spraying 2,000 litres of anthrax over a target.
- Four 155-mm artillery shells used in trials for ricin dissemination.[27]
- An unknown and unspecified quantity of primitive delivery systems for the dissemination of freeze-dried Plague bacteria; and possibly smallpox.

In March 1991, after the Gulf War, Iraq agreed to a ceasefire and to halt further work on weapons of mass destruction (nuclear, chemical and biological), and to allow UN inspectors to locate and destroy whatever documentation, hardware, and software that Saddam possessed. UN

Resolution 687 decreed that Iraq must unconditionally accept the destruction, removal, or rendering harmless of its weapons of mass destruction and ballistic missiles with a range of more than 90 miles. As a condition of surrender, Saddam was supposed to declare all his nuclear, chemical, and biological weapons within fifteen days and to reveal the location and details of all related research, development, production, and support activities.

A new UN body was created, UNSCOM (United Nations Special Commission on Iraq) to verify compliance. The Swedish diplomat, Rolf Ekeus, was its first chief (1991–97); the Australian diplomat, Richard Butler, its second head (1997–99). Iraq began its dealings with UNSCOM as if it intended to continue as before – by denying it had an offensive biological weapons programme or any biological arms.

Ekeus assembled a large team of inspectors from thirty UN member nations. They were staffed 'as you would cast an opera', with each person bringing to the Inspectorate special disciplines and different skills which complemented the others. Their base and HQ were established in the main UNSCOM offices on the thirtieth and thirty-first floors of the UN building in New York, overlooking the East River.

What both parties – the UN and Iraq – may have naïvely predicted as a relatively short post-war inspection process, was to drag on for seven years – seven years of Iraqi lies, deceptions, cheating, false promises, spying, and counter-spying in order to protect their covert offensive biological warfare programme. Through 1998, UNSCOM inspectors made seventy-two separate, dedicated biological inspections, with, at best, meagre results. The inspectors were faced with the daunting task of exploring between 80 and 100 sites in Iraq which might be hiding BW equipment, including pharmaceutical plants, vaccine facilities, university research laboratories, medical supply companies and stores, food-testing laboratories, agricultural research laboratories, breweries, and dairies. On the inspectors' target list were documents relating to BW matters (including old purchase orders for dual-use equipment such as fermenters and filters), associated hardware, and munitions that had been adapted – anything that might point the UN in the direction of the programme.

The inspectors were guided principally by Western intelligence reports, their own forensic science instincts, and an evolutionary knack for patient and shrewd interviewing. The inspections were to become one of the great international hide-and-seek games of arms control, but they were played for real. At stake, possibly, the security of the entire Middle East as a region.

After a long and dispiriting start, the UNSCOM inspectorate finally benefited from a few breaks in the fourth year of its difficult and frustrating search. In November 1994, Saddam's former director of military intelligence during the Gulf War, General Wafiq al-Samarra'i, defected and gave MI6 and CIA officers much useful information during debriefings in Turkey.[28]

The biggest and most sensational break came on 8 August 1995 with the defection to Jordan of Lieutenant General Hussein Kamel, who was Minister of Industry and Minerals and the former Director of Iraq's Military Industrialization Corporation, with responsibility for all of Iraq's weapons programmes.[29] Kamel possessed full knowledge of the secret biological warfare programme. He was one of Saddam's son-in-laws and had fled Iraq after a private quarrel during a family dinner, which left six bodyguards dead. Kamel's defection would have a profound effect on the floundering UNSCOM mission, even though he revealed very little after he arrived in Amman.

Ironically, although Kamel chose not to talk freely, the Iraqis feared that he *was* talking. Saddam's intelligence officers assumed the worst, namely, that Kamel would eventually give away the whole store – biological, chemical, and nuclear.

Consequently, Iraq took an extraordinary preemptive step in order to account for the years of denial about the biological warfare programme. First, they pretended that Kamel had actually deceived *them* about the existence of the BW programme. Next, to forestall Kamels' revelations, Saddam authorized the release of over two million of Kamels' research records – pages and pages of documents which laid out valuable details about the size and scope of the state's programme to make weapons of mass destruction. The haul of biological warfare documents was small. It came in a single wooden box, about two feet by two feet by two feet, which contained some 200 documents. Half of them were previously published biological warfare papers from universities and military think tanks around the world. The remaining 100 or so documents dealt with bacterial agents, but they mentioned nothing at all about aflatoxins, viruses, or weaponization. Britain's David Kelly, serving on loan as one of UNSCOM's top weapons inspectors, was not fooled by this 'take'. 'The

Iraqis pretended these documents were the crown jewels,' Kelly explains, 'but they most certainly were not. So where is the real archive?'[30]

The 'Chicken Farm Documents', as Kamel's papers became known (because they were shown to UNSCOM inspectors at Kamel's chicken farm near the Baghdad airport), did not turn out to be a Pandora's box. Nevertheless, other items at the farm did finally prove what had been suspected all along, that Iraq had a mature, offensive biological warfare programme.

Inside one of the chicken sheds, Ekeus' team found a bright-red photo album containing neatly mounted pictures of petri dishes, fermenters, freeze dryers, BW munitions, and dead test animals (including donkeys, monkeys and dogs covered in lesions).[31] Eventually, UNSCOM seized 147 boxes and metal trunks, including microfiches, computer discs, and videotapes. The tapes, which remain locked in UNSCOM's vaults in New York, show hideous injuries to experimental beagle dogs and monkeys.

However, none of the records revealed any details about how to develop, build, and use biological weapons. All of the 'know-how' documents, explained an UNSCOM official, had been weeded out – by design. Nevertheless, the inspectors now had a trail to follow. The official papers *did* confirm that there had been five BW production facilities in Iraq: Salman Pak, Al-Hakam, Taji, the Water and Agricultural Resources Centre at Fudaliya (where aflatoxin was produced) and Daura Foot and Mouth Institute.[32] There was evidence that Iraq had produced 4,000 gallons of botulinum toxin, 1,800 gallons of anthrax, 530 gallons of aflatoxin, ricin, and 90 gallons of *Clostridium perfringens* (a highly toxic bacteria which causes gas gangrene, a potentially fatal series of painful lesions). The papers also mentioned that Iraq was developing a dangerous viral programme.

In February 1996, six months after Kamel's defection, Saddam enticed him back to Iraq on a promise of safe conduct, full forgiveness, and reinstatement. Kamel accepted his leader's word of honour. Shortly after his return, his home was attacked. As he walked outside to find out what was going on, he was cut to pieces by machine-gun fire. His remains were unceremoniously thrown on to a rubbish pit.[33] (What has now been revealed is that Kamel defected along with sixteen other top Iraqi officials. Once Kamel had been butchered, they decided, wisely, to stay in place in the West. Many of them are now working with allied intelligence agencies running agent networks against Iraq.)

After Kamel's death, UNSCOM redoubled its efforts to implement Resolution # 687. The team of inspectors had access to aerial photographs of Iraq taken by an American U-2 spy plane; information recorded by five American intelligence satellites; helicopters, supplied by Chile, to move inspectors quickly around the countryside; and a large base in Baghdad, which served as a Verification and Monitoring Centre. This centre maintained dozens of special tamper-resistant monitoring cameras and air samplers at key locations throughout Iraq.[34]

But, by then, Saddam had begun withdrawing cooperation from UNSCOM.

Although, ultimately, Baghdad was forced to admit it had produced enough biological agents to kill the world's population four times over, UNSCOM inspectors found precious little prima facie evidence and no biological weaponry intact. That lack of success was scarcely a great surprise. Hiding or disposing of bacterial accoutrements was hardly beyond the wit of a regime to whom lying, cheating, and deceiving was second nature.

In December 1998, the US and UK launched the Desert Fox air attack on Iraq following yet another series of Iraqi broken promises to cooperate fully with the now weary UNSCOM inspection teams. Many missile sites were attacked in Iraq, together with other military facilities. Officially, the allies confirmed that the short operation had successfully 'degraded' Saddam's offensive warfare capabilities. The truth is, the Desert Fox raids had little impact on Iraq's biological warfare programme.[35] Generally, public opinion did not support the strikes, which were regarded as politically motivated and militarily ineffectual. President Clinton was facing impeachment proceedings at the time, and it was alleged that the raids were intended to be a distraction from his extensive political dilemmas.

Inevitably, sharp international criticism of UNSCOM's work followed. Why, critics asked, had it taken seven years to uncover so little? Could this not mean there was nothing there left to uncover?

In August 1998, Scott Ritter, a ferociously aggressive American inspector, had resigned in disgust, alleging that UNSCOM had become a 'cover' for allied espionage operations against Iraq. This was just the news that Baghdad had been waiting for. By late December 1998 and early in 1999, allegations of UNSCOM's abuse of intelligence input began to flourish – much encouraged by Ritter's growing revelations. The evidence from New York and London suggested serious misconduct and breaches of good faith by well-intentioned but jejeune UNSCOM decisions. In the UN Security Council, UNSCOM's 'bosses' – France, Russia, and China – had begun to work for the dismissal of UNSCOM Chairman Richard Butler. In February 1999, under severe pressure, he announced he would not stay beyond the end of his contract in June. UNSCOM was now fatally holed beneath the water line. It had clearly trespassed beyond its mandate; there was even evidence that intelligence information collected by its inspectors had been handed to the US/UK military targeters for Desert Fox. The mission was running out of steam. Worse still, there was little to show for its work.

The truth is that much of UNSCOM's progress in the biological warfare field has been, by necessity, slow, tortuous, and incremental, and has depended ultimately on the skill, courage, and sheer rat-like cunning of its inspectors. As of early 1999, it looked as if this extraordinary team would be disbanded and a new, anodyne version of arms control introduced. Yet the inspectors' individual stories have never been told in detail, and their achievements deserve to be placed on the record.

CHAPTER THIRTY

The Inspectors

'I know what these bastards are like . . . we've got to win.'
Ambassador Richard Butler, UNSCOM, 1998

Gabriele Kraatz-Wadsack – Germany

She is an unlikely biological warfare defender.[1] Petite, blonde, blue-eyed, with a wide, generous smile. Forty-four-years-old, a lieutenant colonel (non-combatant) in the German Army Medical Service, she is on permanent loan to UNSCOM as an inspector. In July 1998, she seemed hopelessly out of place when she confronted the thugs and bully boys of Saddam Hussein's Air Force deep inside the command post of their six-storey headquarters; and all this in a temperature of 130°F, with the mercury and tempers rising as the Iraqis crowded round the diminutive but determined inspector. She had managed, through sheer force of character, to persuade them to open a safe filled with documents. She was looking for evidence of past manufacture, possession, and use of biological agents or weapons.

The Iraqis had lied and lied – saying the documents in the safe were irrelevant to her enquiries and were only current 1998 operational papers. In that case, challenged the German, you can show me the papers.

What the Iraqis did not know was that she had learned enough Arabic to read numbers and a few key words. One of the first documents taken out of the safe was dated 1997 and contained the all too familiar word 'Khas' – 'special', the euphemism used by the Iraqi military for biological and chemical warfare matters. As she took the document (as she was fully entitled to do), her UN interpreter confirmed that it appeared to contain written evidence of munitions used by the Iraqi Air Force. Those weapons included LD-250 bombs, which Iraq had used to test biological warfare agents, such as anthrax and botulinum toxin. This was very clearly a key document. The Iraqi Air Force officers and the attendant state security officers maintained the document was not relevant and could not be abstracted by the diminutive Colonel. She held her position, and a compromise was reached that the document could be photocopied. The original would stay in Iraqi hands, the copy would go to UNSCOM in New York. As Colonel Wadsack tried unsuccessfully to make copies from a machine that appeared to have been sabotaged, the Iraqis made urgent phone calls to Baghdad. They came back and informed her that she could not make copies after all, but she could take notes.

As she began doing that, there were more phone calls to Baghdad and, this time, a security officer bore down on her and instructed her not to take any more notes. He then asked to see something on the document on a pretext, and, as she showed it him, he snatched it from her, thus crossing an important line between verbal harassment and physical coercion. (There have been endless debates amongst her peers as to whether she should have allowed that document to float around long enough for it to be snatched away eventually. The golden rule seems to be, get a document you need and secure it *at once*. Colonel Wadsack herself remains uneasy about what happened.)

Wadsack next dashed out to her United Nations Unimog vehicle. And, using her satellite phone, called her chief executive officer, Richard Butler, on his mobile in New York. Butler first instructed her not to leave the site without an authentic copy of the document. But later, after discussions with the Iraqi Oil Minister, it was agreed that the disputed document would be placed in a tamper-proof plastic envelope with four UN seals at each end. The Iraqis would keep the document, but it would eventually be revealed.

Wadsack had been on site for over twelve hours and had taken the heat, literally and figuratively. She left with pleasure and returned to her hotel in Baghdad.

A complaint was made to the UN Security Council, and it was agreed that Butler would formally open and examine the document on a visit to Baghdad the following month. But when the chairman arrived in

August, Tariq Aziz, the voluble Iraqi Foreign Minister, determined that the document was none of UNSCOM's business – because it only concerned the Iraq/Iran War. Butler, UNSCOM, and the authority of the Security Council were once more flouted. The document remains unexamined.[2]

The 'mildly aristocratic' Gabriele Kraatz-Wadsack agrees that she was not destined in youth to become the gentle hammer of the Iraqis. In the staff canteen of the United Nations she fiddles with her coffee cup as she recalls the events that took her from research into microbiology at the University of Munich – where she did her Ph.D. – through a captain's commission in the German Army, to a long loan as a lieutenant colonel and chief arms inspector at UNSCOM. En route, she acquired a husband and four children. Her ambitions have been limited to excellence in science, not intimidating fracas with hostile thugs. Her youngest son, Merlin, is eight years old. Whenever she goes to Iraq, and she went very often before Saddam's clampdown in August 1998, she tells Merlin she's going 'to cure camels'.

In New York, she wears natty gold-rimmed glasses and neat pants suits. She's photogenic and has the kind of intelligent and attractive face that Hollywood needs when casting female leads in science films.

It was Wadsack, the real-life plague wars defender, who, in January 1998, was handed the most volatile brief of all by Richard Butler. UNSCOM had received hard intelligence that the Iraqis had used prisoners for live human experiments with biological agents in 1994 and 1995 (even as UNSCOM inspectors were roaming Iraq). Both she and Butler regarded this information as sufficiently well sourced and authoritative to merit further investigation.

So UNSCOM inspection #215 took her to the notorious Abu Ghraib Prison, some 20 miles from Baghdad on the main airport road. The Iraqis had prepared for her visit by allowing selected prisoners to leave their cells to scream anti-West political slogans at her. The Colonel told her escorts to lock the men back up before she toured the site. They agreed. It was still a tricky inspection. She did not anticipate finding any forensic evidence, but the Iraqis are paper-crazy when it comes to bureaucracy so she marched straight to the prison's administrative offices to demand the prison records for 1994–95.

They were missing.

'They've been returned to the appropriate ministries,' leered an official, giving the excuse the Iraqis always offer when challenged for missing evidence.

'But I see you have papers for the years *prior*, namely 1992 and 1993, how can that be?' demanded Wadsack. The Iraqi official shrugged and turned away.

Before she left, they invited her to inspect the Amputees Room, where limbs were removed for punishment. She declined.

The Executive Chairman, Richard Butler, picks up the story: 'That inspection was fully justified on the basis of the intelligence handed to me. I personally believe those human experiments happened, and I'll tell you something. When it's all over, come the day and the revelations, I shall be astonished if someone does not provide the evidence.'[3]

'Look, I love this job,' Wadsack says, making it sound like a confession. 'My father was a lawyer in Munich, he told me, whatever you do, make sure you are happy at work. He's right. I am. I wouldn't want to do anything else. Do I worry about the children?' A heavy sigh. 'Yes, it can get nasty. The more intrusive we become, the more unpleasant it gets.

'I fear we are getting nowhere on the control of biological warfare in Iraq. If we fail there, it will have a bad effect on the BWC. I have a sense the world is watching us. This sounds pompous, but I think we are trying to make arms control history here.

'Funny thing is, I really like the Iraqi people. They have been so nice and respectful to me. But that government of theirs . . . ugh.'[4]

Terry Taylor – United Kingdom

'The assignment came in April 1997. There's no security inside the UNSCOM office in New York, and the Iraqis have their agents everywhere, so the only way you can talk about things in safety is in someone's apartment or in a restaurant. So we all piled off to this Thai restaurant on Third Ave – me, Gabriele, and two American inspectors.'

Terry Taylor, late-fifties, tall, grey-haired, angular, with a passing resemblance to James Stewart. A former colonel of the Royal Anglian Regiment, working-class background, self-made, joined the British army as one of the last National Servicemen – as a private, and was commissioned from the ranks. Then some curious military attachments took him to Ghana and Zaire, and later South Arabia, the Far East, Malaysia, and Northern Ireland. There are few soldiers with that kind of tour behind them nowadays. He then finished up in Geneva, as the military adviser to the UK delegation on the Conference on Disarmament, specializing in nuclear, chemical, and biological matters. Divorced, restless, young at heart, roguish smile, very fast brain. He had been selected by the Ministry of Defence as a biological weapons investigator on the Soviet/Russian inspections and was an old hand when UNSCOM called him in on a consultancy basis. The Iraqis soon got to hate him. He rather likes that.

We were after one particular scientist who had worked on biological warfare agents in the past, and who might still be at it. Gabriele had this theory that scientists never ever dispose of their papers. We needed to find him and his papers. We didn't even know what he looked like. It was a classic long shot.

We war-gamed the whole assignment over Thai noodles and chicken ginger soup in the restaurant. It was all very dramatic really, diagrams on paper napkins . . . that kind of thing.

We flew to Bahrain to prepare in more detail. There's an intelligence feed there and UNSCOM has a small administrative HQ. We pick up briefings, cameras, tape recorders, local currency, and so on. Then we have to dump all our Western credit cards, personal notes, address books, and personal items which could give information away about us. Once we get to Baghdad and stay in the UN allotted hotel, we know our rooms will be searched and then bugged by the Iraqis. It's a good idea to give them nothing that they might eventually use against you.

We also have access to a special building in Bahrain where we dry run our inspection, work out which teams are going where, and how to handle the situation if an Iraqi leaps out of the window clutching documents. We make sure we have people outside in case files are hurled out of windows . . . They have been in the past, you know.

Then we agree on the use of key code words so we can say things of operational importance in front of our Iraqi minders. There's no question of physical force – that's forbidden in the rules of this game. If we were to be attacked, my instructions as chief inspector would be to withdraw the team.

When we reached Baghdad on this assignment – the destination was actually the University of Baghdad, where we knew this scientist was doing research work – we obviously gave the Iraqi escorts and minders no hint as to where we would be heading. They would beg us for any clue on the pretext that the traffic would have to be organized or whatever. We told them nothing, just to wait and see which direction our convoy took in the morning. There's no point giving them a hint of the ultimate destination as they can and will sanitize the place within hours.

I forbade all operational discussions on internal phones in the Baghdad hotel, or even in public places or rooms. Important communications had to be scribbled down and shown to the person concerned. All very le Carré, but all very necessary, believe me.

Even when we set off in the morning, we have to make sure that if we are using maps in our UN vehicles, their security men don't look through the car windows. So you have to keep your hand over the relevant bits. On this trip, we used a very small, prepared, route map and a portable GPS (Global Positioning System), so we could use the co-ordinates on the screen and the Iraqis couldn't see and work out where we were going.

We had mainly Toyota Land Cruisers or Nissan Patrols, all painted white with clear UN markings. We took off with our escorts and headed very quickly for the College of Pharmacology at Baghdad University. We had a good plan of the place, and we knew the building in which our man might be working, but that was all.

So we arrived, leaped from our vehicles, and walked briskly into the building.

The man Taylor was looking for was Professor Shahir Al-Quedi, a bona fide microbiologist who had worked with the deadly toxin ricin, a favoured toxin for individual assassination. The Iraqis had persistently lied about their work with ricin; they claimed that only a very limited amount of research had been done in connection with anti-tumour therapy. The ricin, they said, with straight faces, had been used only on mice.[5] UNSCOM's analysts had their doubts. Al-Quedi had a strong academic and scientific background, having been trained and earned his Ph.D. in Britain. He had also worked briefly in the West before returning to Iraq. Under Saddam's rule, this kind of scientist might well have been induced to work on the nation's biological warfare programme.

We arrived at about 9.30 a.m., and I think we took them by surprise. But it was tricky, there were scores of students milling around, all carrying papers. I had people on the gates checking what they could, but it was real needle in haystack time. By the middle of the day we still had not found our man. We'd checked the smaller buildings and were in the main college building, which is large and has four floors. One of my teams was checking names on registers in the Dean's office, but still no joy.

Anyway, I now positioned myself near the big central staircase on the second floor. I just wanted to see who was going where and what kind of state they were in, and, especially, if they were carrying loads of documents.

So it's now past 3.00 p.m. and I think I've missed it. Then, suddenly, while I was talking to a colleague, I noticed out of the corner of my eye an Iraqi Brigadier General going up the stairs rather quickly, which alerted me. After all, we were on a campus which is non-military, so what was this high-ranking officer doing? I moved even closer to the stairwell. Five minutes later, a very distinguished looking man in a double-breasted grey suit, moustache, grey hair, quite well built, came down the stairs. I didn't have a photograph of the man I was looking for, but I just sensed this might be my man.

So I did a very British thing. In my experience, if you step forward, proffer your hand and give your name, the man you want to meet will respond instinctively. So I did that, shot my hand out and said, 'Hello, I'm Terry Taylor,' and he immediately identified himself correctly. I saw he was carrying a plastic transparent folder with some papers in it, some twenty to thirty pages. After some pleasantries, I asked him if I could see his papers. He became a little embarrassed and said they were only personal papers. I insisted, as was my right, and he somewhat reluctantly handed them over.

The first document was a photocopy of an application for his wife's driving licence, nothing wrong with that. But the last document in the set was the same photocopy. When I rifled through the rest of the papers, my interpreter realized we'd struck pay dirt. These were the papers on the ricin research we'd been looking for. They described the research, the tests on animals, its efficacy as a weapons agent, and details of the production processes – answering the question of whether Iraq could manufacture in bulk. And there was more, the paper also proved something we had suspected, which was that the Biological Section of the Iraqi Scientific Research Centre – a civilian programme – was also involved in support of the military's biological weapons programme.

Wadsack, who was on this inspection too, picks up the story:

> I'd staked my reputation on scientists hanging on to old studies of theirs. After Terry stopped Al-Quedi, I led a team into his office, which turned out to be on the third floor, and we took the place apart, everything, under the carpet, behind the pictures, real B-movie stuff. I found this old binder next to a pile of very old scientific magazines. Inside was one of his documents on ricin research. I don't think he even knew it was there.

Taylor again:

> The next thing was to get these papers back to the vehicle as quickly as possible. That Unimog is a piece of UN territory; it's a four-wheeled, light-armoured vehicle, no weapons, but hardened against small-arms fire. Inside is a small photocopier and a satellite burst transmitter, so we can flash the stuff to New York within seconds if we feel threatened. Otherwise, we make several copies and place them in sealed containers.
>
> That operation against Professor Al-Quedi was one of the key assignments which proved the extent to which the Iraqis were lying about the size of their offensive biological warfare programme.

Sadly, it was also destined to be one of the last major successful UNSCOM operations to uncover biological warfare knowledge and equipment.

Nikita Smidovich – Russia

The quintessential poacher turned gamekeeper; the bad Soviet who metamorphosed into the good Russian; the gangster who took his secrets over to the Feds and became an investigator.

The big, brooding Russian sits in his tiny, trophy-laden office on the thirtieth floor of the United Nations building, scowling at the world in general. He is to publicity what the Pope is to bungee jumping. A shapeless, green polo shirt tries unsuccessfully to cover a menacing paunch; the trousers have not seen a press this year. He is tall, smells of tobacco, but beneath the defensively hostile glare hides an intelligent and compassionate face.

Eight years ago, when Nikita Smidovich was a hired gun working for the other side, he was tasked by the managers of the Soviet Union's BW programme to fool British and American inspectors on the first, hesitant trilateral inspections. It was he who helped General Kalinin and General Yevstigneev orchestrate the theatrical moments, the delays, the language incomprehensions, the lies and deceptions when the David Kellys of this world first came to see what the Soviets were doing with their offensive programmes. Smidovich's battle honours during the Soviet plague wars included tactical successes over Western adversaries at Obolensk, Kol'tsovo, and St Petersburg.

He joined the Soviet Foreign Ministry as a junior diplomat in 1975, and, by 1980, he was with the Soviet UN Mission in New York. Later, back in Moscow, he handled chemical and biological warfare issues, before being sent (like Terry Taylor) to Geneva for the disarmament talks. There he was talent-spotted both by Rolf Ekeus, the senior Swedish delegate, and by Richard Butler, the Australian representative who sat opposite him between 1983 and 1987. Both Western officials developed considerable respect for the big Russian's intellect and negotiating skills, and when they asked around the lower ranks, they heard nothing but tight-lipped and grudging admiration for him.

Smidovich adapted comfortably to the rapid decline of Soviet communism and was able to join UNSCOM's permanent staff as an inspector in June 1991. He has travelled to Iraq sixty times since then, while living with his wife and son in a modest apartment in Riverdale, Bronx.

He is a symbol of what the United Nations could still become, a gene pool of the best talents in the world, irrespective of previous political or national affiliations. But it's a symbolism that may yet cost Smidovich dearly. The word in the UN corridors is that he won't get back to Moscow that easily when his contract ends. His enemies see him as a legal defector to the West, doing his job too enthusiastically. They say the Russians won't forget this in a hurry and Smidovich should start applying for American citizenship if he wants to continue working.

Ironically, as a weapons expert, Smidovich is still looking for the missing Iraqi Scuds which were sold to Baghdad by the Soviets.

The burly Russian has become one of UNSCOM's legendary negotiators with the Iraqis. 'I worked for [Andrei] Gromyko for ten years,' he says. 'I know how stonewallers think.'[6] Consequently, he has all the cunning of the Russians, the patience of the Arabs, and none of the impatience for instant gratification that can mark some of his Western colleagues. 'It's true,' he says, 'I will go on for hours and hours, and I like the detail, and I immerse myself in it.'

Smidovich led the UNSCOM team to one particularly confrontational meeting with the Iraqi Minister for Oil, General Amer Al-Rashid, who is rude, has a vile temper and an intimidating stare, shouts a great deal, and is probably deaf. During this key session, Rashid suddenly lost his cool and started yelling personal obscenities at the UNSCOM officials. There was enough diplomatic fire in his outbursts to ignite World War III. Smidovich heard the man out, then stayed eerily silent for three nerve-wracking minutes before saying very quietly: 'Shall we now resume?'[7] Later, when Rashid had another outburst, Smidovich adjourned the meeting until the minister was able to regain his composure.

Fuelled by a stream of black coffee and nicotine, Smidovich is the Duracell Man of UNSCOM's talks with the Iraqis. He thinks ahead, understands their mentality, and is unbluffable. In July 1996, he calmly faced down a crazed Arab who was pointing a loaded Kalashnikov at him. His knowledge of weapons systems is awesome; he can poke around a munitions scrapyard and detect a whole story from just a mangled piece of aluminum (several of which surround him in his office).

'I've never worried too much about Scud warheads as a method for the delivery of biological weapons,' he says, talking almost to himself. 'They have no good proximity fuse for detonation, so the Israelis don't need to worry too much about an Iraqi BW missile strike.

'I happen to think biological warfare is inevitable though. I don't think it will be strategic, but a low-intensity regional outbreak. The aggressors will use drop-tanks, probably mounted on RPVs [remote piloted vehicles]. Now that would be nasty.

'I am pessimistic about the control of biological agents and the whole issue of proliferation. I'm not a moralist or an idealist, this is a professional challenge. What we have done here is to put an arms control system into place which may just control the spread of biological warfare. It's a beginning. However gloomy we may feel, it's better than nothing. Before us, there were only lies and no attempt to stop the spread of BW.'

He smiles enigmatically when asked whether he will return to Moscow at the end of his contract. 'Why not? I don't think the Russians hate me. We are like tax collectors.'

David Kelly – United Kingdom

If David Kelly were a tax inspector, he would recoup Britain's entire national debt. With his soft voice and his semantic precision, he is an inspector's inspector. He's led teams in the Soviet Union, then Russia, and is the oldest hand on the UNSCOM inspectorate; he is also the most respected – and, in Iraq, the most feared. He wears Clarks shoes, saggy comfortable pullovers, and silver-rimmed glasses. He is a Welshman from the Rhondda Valley, where you either drift into a life of local unemployment or rise to great heights elsewhere. He is married with three daughters, has been to Iraq thirty-five times, and knows where most of the biological bodies ought to be buried. Despite real strains on his marriage, he has made this assignment his life-work in the autumn of a long and honourable career.

He is currently the senior adviser on biological defence to the Ministry of Defence, which makes him one of the world's leading plague wars defenders. You take on Kelly, you take on a truly hard man. The Iraqis know this and treat him with considerable respect. He is quiet, persistent, well informed, scientifically indomitable, and, in terms of biological warfare knowledge, cannot be overtrumped.

UNSCOM's first real breakthrough occurred in January 1995, when Kelly went to the apartment of a Canadian inspector, David Ezekiel, on First Avenue and Thirty-eighth Street in mid-town Manhattan, very close to UN headquarters. A French female UN inspector, Annick Paul-Henriot, had arranged a meeting with an Israeli military intelligence officer. Over lemon tea and biscuits, the visitor passed over documents showing that British and German companies had exported some 32 tons of growth medium for bacteria to the Iraqis. The 32 tons was substantially more than could ever have been required for normal civilian use; it was an indefensible figure, and for Kelly it was the 'Gotcha' moment.[8]

He immediately reported to the then-Executive Chairman of UNSCOM, Rolf Ekeus, who was astonished at what he heard. 'From then on,' says Kelly, 'we knew we had to trace the material.'[9]

Australian inspector Rod Barton led the hunt. The Iraqis lied and lied about that growth medium. They claimed to have lost it, they said it had been stolen in food riots after the Gulf War, they said some had 'fallen off a lorry' – unaware of the English connotation of that remark. Then they said they had destroyed it after its five-year sell-by date expired, but Barton knew perfectly well that the date was actually a manufacturer's 'best-by' date and that as long as the heavy duty, double-wrapped powder never got wet, it had at least a ten-year shelf life.

Colonel Wadsack got pulled into this search too. 'Rod Barton and I found it,' she recalls. 'The Iraqis claimed it had gone to hospitals in small containers for civilian use, but the point always was that it was the wrong growth medium for civilian use anyway. Furthermore, hospitals take the stuff in 500-gram or 1-kg or 5-kg containers. When we found much of it at Al Adile, a warehouse in Baghdad, only after a huge paper trail hunt, it was in 25-kg, 50-kg and even 100-kg containers. So, again, the Iraqis had lied to us.'

Kelly, Barton, and Wadsack established that some eighteen tonnes of growth medium had been used by the Iraqis for growing substantial amounts of anthrax and botulinum toxin. When the final count was completed, Barton realized that two tonnes still remained unaccounted for to this day. 'They say it's been stolen, but we actually have evidence that this is not true. We can't find it now, but it's there and it's good to grow bacterial agents for years to come. My guess is they'll use it for anthrax.'[10]

Kelly is gloomy about much of what he has seen, and equally gloomy about what he has not seen in Iraq.[11]

The Iraqis have been working on three viral programmes – camel pox, rotaviruses, and haemorrhagic conjunctivitis. Why the last? It's inspired. This is a robust, indestructible little virus, which you can spray on clothes and skin. The moment you rub your eyes, it will infect them, causing acute pain and profuse bleeding. The effects last for one week and there is no antidote. It's a wonderful incapacitant. Why have they developed this? It's a mystery to me, but it's a very effective weapon.

Iraq denies working on Plague, but I find its absence conspicuous. There's some intelligence evidence showing that they imported the correct growth medium to grow the Plague bacteria. We came across some of the medium at their Al-Hakam facility, and, as usual, the Iraqis couldn't account for it. At first, they said they had imported it [together with Plague vaccine, in the late 1980s] as a contingency in case the Iranians used bacteria on them. But if that had been true, the growth medium should have been stored at their Food Examination and Analysis Laboratory in Baghdad, and not at their biological weapons plant in the desert. I remain deeply suspicious.

I also remain deeply suspicious about the sudden and unaccountable disappearance of Iraq's expert on the development of aflatoxins as weapons.

(Aflatoxins would be an unusual BW agent – as they do not kill or incapacitate quickly. One theory is that Saddam wanted to use them as a form of long-term ethnic cleansing against the Kurds, since aflatoxins cause serious illness, including cancer, after a period of years. Saddam may have calculated that the use of an aflatoxin weapon would ensure that no moral opprobrium would fall on his regime, as such an attack would leave no smoking gun.)

Kelly continues:

The missing scientist was Dr Emad Diyab. He was recruited by the Iraqis in 1988 and became responsible for producing the aflatoxins that were experimentally loaded into their 122-mm rockets. We found him in September 1995, and he gave us some pretty useful accounts of those weapons' trials. Suddenly, while we were still acquiring information from him, he vanished. 'Ah,' said the Iraqis, at their most ludicrous, 'he's probably emigrated to Britain or the United States.' But we know he hasn't gone to either country, so where is he?

Current Iraqi biological warfare capability? They could send a couple of Scuds with anthrax warheads against Israel or Kuwait today. The Israelis would certainly shoot them out of the sky. The Kuwaitis – not sure. There are still about eight missiles missing, and the bio-warheads can be made in any foundry. They can easily produce the 30 gallons of anthrax per warhead; we know they've hidden the growth medium. In a crude operation, they could use this stuff internally by spraying it from a helicopter. I believe they now have a dormant biological weapons programme. Remember it was a programme always destined to mature in the late 1990s and it would have done so, but for the Gulf War. Even after our inspections began, they continued their research and development right up to 1995, when, I think, the defection of Hussein Kamel and the discovery of the chicken farm documents *did* put an end to the active programme. But it won't take much to re-ignite the whole thing.

My investigative technique has always been to go in hard, but to be courteous. I remind my interviewees of the seriousness of the UN mission, I explain my role, I treat people with respect and dignity, a little bit of humour, and no threat. I've done six-hour interviews, with *very* short coffee breaks, where I thought people were holding back; [I do] nothing nasty, but they tell me I *am* rather persistent.

I love Iraq; in my spare time there I go to a special bookseller in Baghdad and read about the British occupation. It's a fantastic country, the people are lovely. On a day off, I try to get down to Al Hatra, south of Mosul, to the world heritage site – all two-thousand-year-old temples and tombs. There are no other tourists there, and the isolation is wonderful.

This could be such a wonderful land.

Hamish Killip – United Kingdom

Sitting in the dark bar of New York's Crowne Plaza hotel on Forty-second and Second, Hamish Killip looks like a rubicund British farmer in his checked shirt and tweed jacket, out for the day to sell a couple of cows or sheep. He has a jolly red face topped by thinning, fair hair; he smiles a lot, and the farming background is there – in his family on the Isle of Man – but Killip is a soldier. Like so many other recently retired UNSCOM ex-Colonels, he brings a special discipline from the Royal Engineers. He is a weapons expert and a chemical engineer, and one of the great specialists in reading complex drawings and blueprints. He also served a spell in British military intelligence, but it is his two years with UNSCOM that have earned him his prestigious Member of the British Empire. A bachelor, he now spends two-thirds of his time in New York or Iraq. Over a glass of indifferent Californian Chardonnay, Killip recalls the January 1996 inspection in which he found a part of Iraq's well-hidden biological bombs arsenal.

> It really was a long shot. We were at Al Azzizziyah looking at fragments of bombs which had been destroyed. We dug away and bingo, struck pure gold – three bombs with black stripes on the warheads. The Iraqis had always denied these bombs even existed. I didn't want to drill through the casings there and then, in case the warheads were pressurized and anthrax blew all over my face and the cloud then floated off somewhere else. The bombs required special equipment to open them up. After I obtained that gear, we returned and did the job.

We drilled into the heads and discovered de-activated botulinum toxin. There was a burst charge in the centre of the bombs for explosive dissemination of the bacterial agents. The bombs were R-400s – about eight feet long and some two feet in diameter. I think they were intended for use against Israel. But I don't think we'll ever unravel the whole story.

I agree with my pal Nikita. It's the Iraqi drop-tanks that will really send biological warfare over the horizon. They've invested a great deal into converting them for BW use. They took these tanks, capacity about 450 gallons, look rather like wing-fuel tanks, and they added a special drain and a couple of British-invented, Venturi electric valves, which simply force the bacterial agent out in a nice, controllable spray.[12] They really thought the whole thing through. Then, they married the tanks to a Mirage F1 fighter/bomber, and, in test flights, worked out the ideal attack height – which is about 160–320 feet.

They would have used anthrax. The whole project had an operational title, *Thul Fiqar*, which means something like 'The Double-Edged Sword of the Cousin of the Project'. Now that's ominous, because the Iraqis don't give names like that to a project that's not going to war.

The prevailing winds in that part of the world are from the northwest to the southeast, so I guess that puts Kuwait and Saudi Arabia on the target list. Well, they kept this delivery system in a very special shelter at Abou Obeydi base near Al Kut, some 70 miles from Baghdad. We went there the moment we received intelligence about it, but they told us that the system had been destroyed during an air raid in the Gulf War. I demanded to see any remains, but they produced absolutely nothing. Not a nut or a bolt.

Worse still, the Iraqis had an unmanned drone which they tested with a piloted MiG-23 flying alongside. They deny the two projects, the Mirage F1 and the remote vehicle, were ever linked, but that's just another lie, as we now know they were co-ordinated by the same person. I'll tell you, that RPV carrying biological warfare drop-tanks filled with anthrax, now that's an effective weapon; incredibly simple and incredibly awful. Once you have that drone up and running, it would be the most ghastly weapon, like the Nazis' V1 buzz bombs.

Killip and his colleagues have discovered that Iraq has also been working on an equally dangerous BW delivery system – simple aerosol sprayers attached to helicopters and slow-moving fixed-wing planes.[13] The so-called 'Zubaidy Device', named after its expert developer, Dr Tariq Saleh Mohammed Zubaidy, is basically a converted crop sprayer, normally used for dry chemical pesticides sprayed from a helicopter. Zubaidy managed to adapt this sprayer, link it to a small volume tank to take small-particle aerosols, and successfully tested an anthrax simulant as far back as August 1988. Any commercial helicopter or plane fitted with a standard hook device to its belly could take between six and ten Zubaidy sprayers, which would be ample to lay down a huge amount of 'line source' biological agent, dry or wet, to cover a very large area. The consequences, given the right conditions, would be horrendous.

Two Iraqi engineers who worked with Zubaidy took his ideas and modified his BW spraying device to fit a smaller drone aircraft. Because these short-range planes are much lighter and more unstable than piloted aircraft, the spraying device attached to the bottom of the fuselage had to be very sleek and compact, vibration free, and capable of withstanding buffeting in high winds. Iraqi representatives had to hunt around Europe to find just the right device; and, in 1988, they eventually located what they wanted at a small Danish company. During the negotiations a price of $10,000 was fixed, in cash, for each device – a substantially inflated amount, suggesting both sides were prepared to enter a questionable and untraceable deal. UNSCOM cannot prove the devices were ever delivered to Iraq. Once again, it looks as if compliant sanctions busters got clean away with it.[14]

Scott Ritter – United States

He is the ultimate plague wars defender – Action Man in a blue beret, the Rambo of the UNSCOM inspectors, a loose cannon who eventually rolled right off the deck.

Some of Ritter's story, carefully promoted by himself, is well known – the gung-ho, go-getting, forward-thrusting, ex-Marine who joined UNSCOM's inspectorate and eventually allowed his mouth and his actions to facilitate a premature departure from the UN. There was a series of rancorous quarrels, lethal publicity for UNSCOM itself, and trenchant position-taking. This was not the way UNSCOM wanted to do business, and it's not the way it should have done it.

Where David Kelly was Poirot, Ritter was John Wayne; where

Smidovich was a Russian Colombo (an ostensible shambles, but deadly cunning), Ritter was in your face – with hog's breath. Where UNSCOM needed Inspector Morse, it got Clint Eastwood. Ritter's philosophy on the subtleties of inspection protocol are best summed up in his view of how his inspection team should hit an assignment: 'I am the alpha dog. I'm going in tail high . . . gonna spray urine all over their walls . . .'[15]

Ritter, may have lacked the rank and eloquence of a MacArthur or a Patton, but not their determination. He displayed qualities that the more wimpish side of UN diplomacy despised, but might, if properly handled, have been of value. Ritter could as easily have won a purple heart as the odium that has followed his departure.

He's even larger in the flesh than the videotapes of him from Iraq suggest. If you were from the moon, you'd spot him as an American Marine Major at 3,000 yards. Very self confident, very physical, dangerous to cross, a good friend in a tight corner, honour, tactlessness, bravery and poor diplomatic skills; ultimately a more complex man than his own promotion suggests. Americans like him win wars the hard way, they don't talk their way out of them.

He quickly understood that the UNSCOM inspectorate, unlike previous arms controllers, possessed powers that were almost warlike in their fight against Iraqi deception. They could mount surprise challenge inspections; they could go where they liked, when they liked; and they had substantive powers of seizure. In terms of an international arms control and inspection procedures, none of this had ever been tried before.

Ritter was a junior Cold Warrior, an army brat who firmly believed that one day he really would be killing 'commies'. After a dedicated career in the military – including service as a junior intelligence officer in the Marines – Ritter spent time monitoring Russia's compliance with the 1987 Intermediate-range Nuclear Forces Treaty.

When Saddam invaded Kuwait, Ritter, who regards war 'as a good thing', was assigned to Central Command Headquarters in Riyadh, Saudi Arabia, where he assessed the bomb damage the Coalition forces were inflicting on Iraq. Somewhat inadvisably, he was to cross swords with, of all people, General Norman Schwarzkopf. They disagreed over the correct interpretation of how many Scuds and their launchers had been destroyed by allied forces. The General was probably playing high politics when he publicly released his numbers (while Ritter's analysis was probably right), but it was still a poor career move for the then young Captain. After the war, he and the Marine Corps parted company.

Eventually, through an old arms control pal from Russia, Ritter ended up in New York as an early UNSCOM inspector.

Probably his greatest contribution in the course of a hectic but stimulating shift with UNSCOM was to help fashion a strong link with Aman (Israeli military intelligence) from contacts in New York and Tel Aviv. This was a personal matter, and he ran the Israeli operation from his hip pocket.[16] Sometimes he met the agents in New York, sometimes (together with colleagues) he flew to Tel Aviv to collect and trade information.

The fact was, UNSCOM inspectors, despite some valuable if limited successes, had never really found the prima facie evidence needed to present to a sceptical UN Security Council. Even though Iraq was supposed to demonstrate compliance to the UN, the political reality was that UNSCOM needed to *prove* that Iraq was still involved in an active BW programme or at least maintaining a dormant offensive one. Ritter's Israeli material was very helpful to the team.

After much patient analysis of information from their own agents, the Israelis told Ritter that they reached the conclusion that Saddam had issued a Presidential Directive in April 1991 ordering Iraq to deceive UNSCOM and to hold on to its weapons of mass destruction by any means.[17] A month later, the biological materials and know-how were turned over to Iraq's Special Security Organization (SSO) and Special Republican Guard (SRG) – the President's own security forces, his personal SS.

The SSO is one of the most secretive organizations in Iraq, numbering some 5,000 people. It was this organization that was tasked with running a vast three-card monte trick against UNSCOM's inspectors. So, even as the inspectors bore down on the right locations, the SSO would be just ahead, removing the incriminating materials, and keeping them away from the men and women in blue berets.

In 1997, the SSO removed temperature-sensitive biological materials in two dedicated fleets of vehicles: one comprised red-and-white refrigerated trucks painted up as the Tip-Top ice-cream company, the other were unmarked green Mercedes tractor-trailers from the fleet of Segada Transportation Company (named after Saddam's wife).[18] The plan for this extensive 'find-the-lady' trick was that the vehicles would shuttle from ever-changing storage sites to a network of temporary hide sites whenever UN inspectors drew close. The SSO ran the strategy, the SRG did the guard duties and the rough stuff.

The mastermind behind this plan, said the Israelis, was Abed Hamid Mahmoud, the Presidential Secretary and probably second most powerful man in Iraq.

As these revelations reached Ritter, he realized that to take on the SSO and the SRG, he would need access to very sensitive sites that had not yet been challenged, and many more surprise inspections. He would also need the full backing of a tough UN and the US/UK governments, prepared to threaten and carry out strikes as a sanction for Iraqi non-compliance.

As the Iraqis got to know Ritter and his tactics better, serious tensions developed between Baghdad, Washington, and UNSCOM itself.[19] Richard Butler, UNSCOM's new Executive Chairman as of July 1997, supported Ritter's efforts to confront Iraq's special security organs. But there was nervousness about his 'Alpha Cat' behaviour on the ground, and, by now, there were two serious intelligence problems dogging him. Firstly, there were the security clearances of a Russian lady he had married; secondly, Washington and the UN were becoming increasingly nervous about Ritter's tight Israeli connections, which had not gone unnoticed in Baghdad.[20]

By February 1998, the Iraqis were declaring that specified 'Presidential sites' (including several of Saddam's palaces) were off limits to UNSCOM inspectors. Given the deadly game of biological hide-and-seek, Iraq was now moving the goalposts out of sight. A few days later, in order to avoid what appeared to be an almost inevitable conflict between allied forces and Iraq as a consequence of Iraqi non-compliance, UN Secretary-General Kofi Annan travelled to Baghdad and made a peace, which further undercut Ritter and the inspectors. Sensitive sites, it was agreed, would now be accorded a different, special inspection protocol. War had been avoided, but few observers believed the Secretary-General had not been taken for an Iraqi ride. Indeed, by August 1998, even that accord had broken down when Saddam halted cooperation with the visiting inspectors, making it impossible for them to work in Iraq.

By the end of the month, Ritter had resigned, noisily, charging that Annan and the US had failed to stand up to Baghdad and were now party to 'an illusion of arms control'. There was some truth in that charge. But he was to allege far more. The CIA, he claimed, had used UNSCOM inspectors as a Trojan horse to penetrate Iraq for its own purposes. In the trade, they call the intelligence acquired by spies on target, and in place, as 'Ground Truth'. It is the ultimate prize of intelligence collection.

UNSCOM's inspectors are a tightly knit bunch. Their village is on the thirtieth floor of the UN building, with its cramped offices and its drab civil-servant paintwork, relieved only by stunning East River views.

Here, the consensus amongst the inspectors is that Ritter was a formidable inspector, that he has always spoken the truth, but that his political judgement, in the indelicate Americanism, 'sucks'. His biggest sin, they allege, is that he gave Baghdad the Israeli intelligence card, a mistake when so many neutral, third-world countries are watching the poker game. His subsequent writings and revelations, after he quit the Commission, about UNSCOM's alleged spying role did little to help him or UNSCOM's reputation amongst the powerful friends of Iraq within the Security Council. With so much of Iraq's biological warfare concepts, software, hardware, and God knows what else, still unaccounted for, Ritter must be held accountable for retarding, albeit inadvertently, the process of biological disarmament of one of the most dangerous rogue states in the world today.

Critically, he also damaged the perception of UNSCOM's political impartiality and integrity, by revealing that Western intelligence services had both legitimately used, but also abused, the Commission's unique powers on the ground in Iraq.

To add to UNSCOM's difficulties, Washington and London finally mounted Desert Fox, the short, sharp, and furious air attack on scores of Iraqi targets in December 1998. Those who sensed the strategy seemed more in keeping with destabilizing Saddam Hussein than seeking and destroying his outstanding biological weapons infrastructure may have been right. Ritter argues cogently that intelligence acquired by the CIA, through its penetration of UNSCOM, was given to the Pentagon for targeting use before Desert Fox.[21] If that proves to be the truth, and Ritter has never been found to be lying, then UNSCOM may well be doomed.

Meanwhile, what is left of Iraq's biological warfare materiel is now hidden even deeper within the fabric of Iraq's voluminous and confusing folds, and Saddam dances on and plots the next move.

Ambassador Richard Butler – Australia

He's an Australian. What can one expect? Diplomacy? Tact? Tortured euphemisms?

The Executive Chairman and Commanding Officer of the United Nations' tiny platoon of plague wars defenders is very tall, slightly overweight, and exudes authority. He wears a lot of dark blue, plays rugby at No. 8 position, and carries the burden of one who has spent too long dealing with too many international sociopaths. He has had a distinguished career as one of Australia's foremost diplomats specializing in nasty arms control negotiations. He was deeply involved in the negotiation of the Cambodian peace agreements. His curriculum vitae shows he's no time-serving parvenu, nor would he be at home in a sun-hat with corks hanging from it. If he lacks the suave, oleaginous, and duplicitous manner of the seasoned diplomat, it is because he's just not like that, and, anyway, he's good with the press. Most Australians are.

It's Day One of the latest Iraq/UNSCOM crisis and he flees from the waiting New York camera crews camping by his office and seeks refuge in a tiny airless room full of stationery.

Butler is jacketless and in suspenders and there is real passion in his voice. 'I cannot understand why Saddam is prepared to keep sanctions on his people for the sake of his biological weapons programme. It doesn't make sense. Of all his weapons programmes of mass destruction, it's the biological warfare one that he's really hanging on to. I just cannot see why.

'You know, you should hear some of the lies they have told us about their BW for the last eight years . . . they play monstrous games . . . listen to this.' (Butler's now getting angry, and he begins to pound his fist on a desk.) 'They explain everything away by blaming errant girlfriends, mad generals, clerical foul ups . . . food riots, for Christ's sake. What do they think we are?'

Ritter?

'The Ritter thing hasn't helped,' he says grimly. 'I like the man, we're still friends, but it didn't help.'

Butler hates being lied to, and he feels disgust at other men's inability to find their moral bearings. He knows exactly where he stands and has a deep visceral loathing of BW as a weapon of mass destruction.

'Listen, I went to one of my first meetings in Baghdad with General Sa'adi, one of their top guns, right. He then explains to me in an appealing and cajoling way.' (Butler does both the drama and the accents.) '"Mr Chairman, you must understand, our biological warfare programme was flawed and shabby, we do not have any Ph.D.s working on it. I don't mind admitting had we been better, we would have gotten more done."

Butler stares unblinkingly at us. 'Can you imagine it, not only does he admit that they had a biological warfare programme' (now really angry) 'but they apologize it wasn't better.'

We get the drift. It's like Hitler apologizing for some of the inefficiencies of the Auschwitz gas chambers.

'Well, later that evening, I'm with Tariq Aziz, and in front of Sa'adi I tell Aziz that I wish to record my shock and concern that a colleague of his has entered a most lamentable explanation in justification of a biological warfare programme. Well, that moral view fell on stony ground. Aziz simply said: "Yes ... so what." He clearly didn't understand my point. I couldn't believe my ears. These people are actually dedicated to biological warfare. This homicidal regime is in time warp. It's very, very serious. I'm telling you.'[22]

What is the one thing he'd like his inspectors to find?

'It would be the biological warfare agent manufacturing network, the dual-use equipment they've failed to declare, the hidden fermenters, the key personnel who have disappeared without a trace or explanation. We've had intelligence reports of BW mobile facilities and munitions still filled with bacterial agents. We know they're still trying to get BW material from supplier countries. All this points to an ongoing BW programme which is still being concealed from us.

'I'll bet you my balls that there's a safe with the central directive for the use of offensive biological warfare locked inside it, under the direct control of Saddam's private secretary. There's a central directive, and there has to be a central committee in charge of concealment.'

Friends of Butler say he believes that Tariq Aziz runs such a committee.

Butler is said to believe that Kofi Annan made a mistake in negotiating the Memorandum of Understanding with Saddam during the February 1998 crisis. He believes Annan should not have given ground on the sensitive sites issue and that he should have realized too he was dealing with a dangerous and disturbed man. It's said that Butler has not discouraged the use of the word 'Chamberlain' in connection with that February negotiation.[23] He is said to like and respect Annan personally and to believe that the whole experience has left the Secretary-General a sadder and wiser man.[24]

It is no secret that Butler finds the Iraqi regime deeply repugnant, run by a bunch of moral lepers who happen to hold keys to the biological warfare box. He is an eloquent man when he so chooses, but uses street language to illustrate his revulsion at the absence of moral behaviour by those Iraqis who should know better.

'There was this really revolting moment. I'm with Tariq Aziz and some heavies. Suddenly, it's like a B-movie, I'm not kidding, the nasties lead in this humble peasant, right. It's real master and slave stuff as this poor, humble guy is led into the exalted presence, and then ordered to roll his sleeves up to show me a scar on his arm.'

(One provocative photograph found amongst the chicken farm documents showed a scarred human arm, which suggested that the Iraqis had conducted at least one biological experiment on humans. Aziz tried to dispel this theory to Butler by producing, he claimed, the very same arm.)

'So the heavies all say to this poor bugger: "Tell us how you got the scar." This is now Monty Python for real, I promise you. So this poor fucker is shitting himself in the presence of all these thugs and UN people, and he blurts out what they've previously told him to say.

'I mean, Christ, what a way to treat another human being. It tells you all you want to know about them. You just want to go away and have a hot shower.

'Listen, I had to deal with the charmers of the Khmer Rouge. I know what these bastards are like.'

Why does BW matter so much to the Iraqis?

'I just don't know,' he sighs. 'Once Aziz told me that their use of chemical weapons against the Iranians in the marsh wars had saved Iraq. Maybe it's that.'

So is UNSCOM winning, losing or holding? A glimpse of the diplomat emerges as he puts the best face on their work. 'Look, we've done a lot.' He strides to an erasable white board hanging on the door.

One senses he's drawn this simple diagram before. 'This is the BW we've dealt with, say 80 per cent, I suspect there's another 20 per cent concealed. We're getting there.'

But what if the concealed figure is much higher than the declared figure of 80 per cent?

Butler scowls and doesn't answer.

Earlier, over a long working breakfast with Terry Taylor, the lanky British UNSCOM arms inspector theorizes that the best form of arms negotiations are informal, state-organized, bilateral deals – involving gentlemen's agreements, some useful offers of aid, minimum publicity, no great loss of face, and the slow and consensual move towards the destruction of weapons. Taylor believes there is no evidence that a world body like the United Nations, which is so high profile and so wracked with its own politics, could achieve biological disarmament.

We try that on Butler, who half agrees.

So how is a world authority ever going to implement a biological warfare arms control agreement? Butler is mildly pessimistic. 'You need a moral consensus against biological weapons in the target country, then you need that country's political commitment to disarmament, and finally you need commonly agreed verification procedures. If any part of that formula is inadequate, then you have a problem. We simply cannot prevent clandestine activity if we cannot detect it.'

That's a gloomy conclusion.

'Look,' he says almost despairingly, 'it's better to have something rather than nothing.

'I know when it comes to biological warfare that Iraq is the paradigm case, a pioneer case. UNSCOM is making a matrix for the future here, and we simply must not lose. If we do, the decent world will never be able to control biological warfare. I'm telling you.'

He is still talking as the elevator hits the ground floor and he rushes off to a Security Council meeting.

A few weeks later, in December 1998, Butler's damning report to the UN Security General on Iraq's tricks of deception on his inspectors finally led to Desert Fox, an operation that was successful neither in destroying the BW facilities nor in unseating Saddam Hussein.[25]

A few days later, there was open speculation that the 'sometimes abrasive' Richard Butler might end up as the first Western casualty of Desert Fox.[26] There were calls among Security Council diplomats for a fundamental overhaul of UNSCOM, which was code for, amongst other things, the removal of Butler. Kofi Annan, the UN Secretary-General, was asked about Butler's future and replied in a way that suggested he had already heard the carpenters hammering the gallows together outside. Would Butler be moved on?

'That is a question I would prefer not to answer today,' Annan replied, hardly overwhelming his UNSCOM chief with unconditional support. 'You have heard all the discussions going on, several governments saying we need a new structure, we need a new inspection mechanism.

'I don't know what that means, and I do not know what kind of structure.'[27]

And on that decisive note he strode off.

It got worse.

Scott Ritter's damning revelations about UNSCOM's complicity in spying operations left Butler spluttering about exaggerations and dissimulations, but the Ritter stuff sounded too true for comfort.[28] Now Iraq's Security Council friends climbed on board, and suddenly the already beleaguered Australian found himself facing a Russian who seemed pathologically obsessed with getting rid of him, and a French and Chinese couple whose cloaks barely concealed their daggers.

To crown the indignity of it all, both US State Department officials in Washington and UN officials on the thirty-eighth floor (the Secretary-General's floor) began briefing journalists in order to discourage Butler's continued stewardship of the fast-sinking UNSCOM vessel.

By February, Butler could feel the icy water flowing through the holes below the water line. At the time, his contract was due to end in June 1999. He indicated he would not seek its renewal. Privately, it became clear that as long as this tough, proud, and committed diplomat were not further humiliated, he would not resign.

Either way, Saddam and the biological warfare team around him were undisputed winners in a battle to which decent people throughout the world might have contributed more. In the words of Edmund Burke: 'The only thing necessary for the triumph of evil is for good men to do nothing.'

Richard Butler – a great plague wars defender; down but not out.

CHAPTER THIRTY-ONE

Rogue State

'I can hardly overstate my concern about North Korea...'
CIA Director George Tenet, 1999[1]

In 1952, at the height of the Cold War, the Americans were caught red-handed using biological warfare against their enemies. Or so it seemed.

On 22 February, a senior North Korean minister formally complained to the United Nations that American aircraft involved in the UN war against North Korea had dropped disease-bearing insects in seven raids over the communist state. Two weeks later, Chinese Premier (and Foreign Minister) Zhou Enlai, the North's ally, charged the US with despatching 448 aircraft on 68 missions to spread Plague, anthrax, cholera, encephalitis, and meningitis amongst the North Koreans.

On the face of it, the accusation meant that the Americans had been the first nation to use biological warfare since the Japanese had employed it against the Chinese in the late thirties. And now the US had been caught.

This was a deadly serious charge, made by real heads of state, and there was supporting evidence. Two North Koreans had died mysteriously of Plague; twenty-five American POWs had signed confessions admitting they had used biological weapons.

A communist-backed 'International Scientific Commission for the Investigation of the Facts Concerning Bacterial Warfare in Korea and China', led by Joseph Needham, a British bio-chemist and avowed Marxist, carried out a detailed enquiry *in situ*.[2] Slides of Plague tissue from the alleged North Korean victims were examined. The Commission produced a 669-page report that affirmed the charges. The allegations stuck, despite explicit denials from Secretary of State Dean Acheson; they hung as an awkward black mark on American foreign policy even as late as the war in Vietnam fifteen years later.

But it was all an elaborate set-up, demonstrating, if nothing else, that biological warfare can be faked with surprisingly successful results. The whole episode had begun as a carefully staged piece of disinformation, prepared by North Korea, China, and the USSR.

First, Plague samples were obtained by North Korea's health minister from the Manchurian city of Mukden, which had, notoriously, been bombed with bacterial agents by the Japanese in the thirties. Next, two convicted North Korean criminals, facing death sentences, were deliberately infected with the Plague bacillus. The men were allowed to die and their diseased tissues were harvested.

The relatively unknown process of brain-washing, so effectively used by the North Koreans, extracted the false confessions from the American prisoners of war.

The whole thing had been a conspiracy at the very highest level.

Chairman Mao Zedong personally sent a secret message to Joseph Stalin asking him to join the propaganda campaign against the US. Stalin and Lavrenti Beria, his infamous head of Soviet security-intelligence, along with Mao and Zhou Enlai, then all enthusiastically joined in and backed the conspiracy to denounce the innocent Americans in the international court of public opinion.

Only in 1998 did a Japanese newspaper find the tell-tale documents (in the still-secret Presidential Archive in Moscow) which revealed the truth.[3]

In fact, the Soviets had extricated themselves from the conspiracy in the new political atmosphere following Stalin's death in 1953, although they never admitted their part publicly. When the Soviet ambassador to China privately informed Mao of this revised policy, the Chairman too thought it prudent and began to wipe his fingerprints from the failed conspiracy. He now claimed the BW accusations had merely been based on uncorroborated reports from Chinese battlefield advisers to the North Koreans. At this private meeting, the Soviet ambassador later reported, Mao displayed 'some nervousness, smoked a lot, crushed cigarettes, and drank a lot of tea'.[4]

Nearly half a century later, North Korea retains one of the world's last communist regimes.[5] Like Iraq, it remains diplomatically isolated, a secretive, unaccountable international pariah. The West calls these nations 'rogue states' because of their unpredictability in domestic and foreign behaviour and their separation from generally accepted norms of decent conduct.

Like Iraq again, North Korea is certainly researching, and probably already possesses, a real offensive biological warfare capability.

Although North Korea's interest in BW probably dates back to the period when the Japanese attacked the Chinese in the late thirties, their active research programme did not accelerate until the early 1960s, when work seems to have focused on ten to thirteen different strains of bacteria.[6]

Western intelligence, which devotes considerable resources in attempting to penetrate the fogs of secrecy that swirl around North Korea, currently believes that their military scientists are working with anthrax, botulinum toxin, cholera, haemorrhagic fever, Plague, smallpox, typhoid, and yellow fever.[7]

The Pentagon officially reported in 1996 that North Korea's military-run BW programme had facilities at universities, medical institutes, and special research centres.[8] North Korea also maintains several BW production sites and tests its BW agents at a remote island territory – which the US scrutinizes by satellite. One news report claims that North Korean scientists conduct advanced genetic engineering research at Kim Il Sung University.[9]

A major motivation for North Korea's offensive programme is believed to be the so-called equalizing factor that biological warfare endows the user. Over the years, in its seemingly endless confrontation with the American-backed South Koreans, the North has been increasingly unable to match the quantity and quality of the forces that oppose it. In terms of hi-tech military equipment such as 'smart' weapons, North Korea is not even in the ballpark. As the American military presence in the region has become more powerful, and political determination to hold the 38th parallel strengthened rather than weakened, North Korea has been forced to confront the uncomfortable reality that it will never be able to achieve its objective of reuniting the Korean peninsula with a purely conventional weapons attack.

So Pyongyang has been forced to consider alternative strategies, including biological weapons, which are cheap, relatively easy to manufacture, efficient, and terrifying.

Because of this threat, the Pentagon staged a substantial war game four years ago, in order to test all its gloomiest assumptions about a possible conflict on the peninsular. Based on intelligence analysis, the planners included a new dimension – a major biological warfare attack would be used by the aggressor.

The exercise was called Global 95, and its results were so catastrophic that much of what happened during the war game still remains highly classified.[10] The details which have leaked confirm that military planners were obliged to confront the reality of a surprise attack in which US ports and airfields in South Korea were hit with biological (and chemical) weapons that North Korea was known to possess.

The actual plot of Global 95 was based, in part, on top-secret information received by the CIA from a defector serving in place in North Korea. This secret informant was one of the very few primary sources with knowledge about the North's BW programme that the West has managed to acquire.

From 9–15 July 1995, senior US military and intelligence officials gathered at the Naval War College in Newport, Rhode Island. The plot of Global 95 simulated forty days of world-shaking events. The scenarios spread wider than Korea, encompassing also a secondary major regional conflict in Saudi Arabia.[11]

The exercise began with a North Korean spray attack of a BW agent on US forces encamped south of the Parallel. The assault, which started at night, was mounted in the two ways American planners fear most: from stealth speedboats positioned just offshore and from North Korean special forces teams which infiltrated through tunnels along the DMZ (demilitarized zone between North and South Korea on the 38th Parallel).[12] The consequences were devastating.

A former senior Pentagon official, who closely studied the war game's classified findings, explains: 'To tell you the truth, Global 95 fell apart very fast. It was so bad [for the US forces] that in order to save the exercise at all, the referees decided to grant the players a "miracle" for each game day. The referees said: "We will allow you one chance to wipe away a bad move or an indefensible mistake." '[13]

But even self-awarded miracles couldn't save the world's superpower from a humiliating defeat at the hands of a tiny, low-tech assault force armed only with bacteria, chemicals, and high-powered patrol boats mounted with aerosol sprayers. 'Frankly,' the former Pentagon official adds, 'the exercise was basically over after the opening action by the North Koreans. It fell apart for the good guys as soon as the bad guys breached the DMZ and seized all the BIDS units [then the army's only detector vehicles for BW agents] away from the US forces.'[14]

Without the precious detectors, the participants soon discovered that the allied forces were basically helpless in the face of a sneak aerosol BW attack at night. To make matters worse, there simply were not enough BW detectors to go around, nor did the defending Americans know where to put the few that they had. Without the BIDS, the US commanding general had no way to confirm either a BW attack nor the type of agent used; so, if he suspected one had occurred, his only option was to get the hell out – and fast.

In the game, the officer in charge ordered a full retreat – but then he discovered there were not enough vehicles to handle the get-away. An added complication was that the commander was unable to organize enough firepower to cover his retreat.

It would have required a millennium of miracles to save the defenders. Pinned down by an invisible bacteriological enemy, BIDS vehicles taken out, and unable to mount an orderly retreat, it soon became obvious that US forces would not be able to reach safety in Seoul, the South Korean capital. Nor, disastrously, were there enough protective suits for the US troops. To their horror, the US commanders discovered that most of the CBW suits that could have saved lives were stored in a warehouse in Indiana and would take two weeks to ship to Korea, by which time it might safely be assumed that a substantial number of soldiers would have become infected with anthrax, Plague, smallpox or whatever was in those North Korean aerosols. And that's exactly what happened.

By the end of Global 95, 50,000 US troops had been infected with, as it turned out, anthrax.

The gloomy post-game analysis showed even more glaring weaknesses in the US defence. Air bases and ports in host countries (like Korea and Saudi Arabia) are particularly vulnerable to biological attack because the vital workers there are civilians, contractors, and third-country nationals who are unprotected and untrained in biowarfare defence. Once this crucial support staff is contaminated, incapacitated, or killed in an attack, it will drastically erode the ability to supply and reinforce the friendly 'guest' troops. Furthermore, if these workers were to see the American soldiers donning protective gear during a biological strike, they would fear for their lives and wonder why they were not similarly protected. Understandably, many would flee in panic to their families. Without the workers to unload ships or maintain the planes, the ports and airports would close down, reducing movements to logistical paralysis.

'As a result,' says another senior Pentagon official, heavily, 'the entire US reinforcement plan was thrown into disarray.'[15]

The frustration of the US commanders was compounded by the realization that an effective overland counter-invasion of North Korea would be impossible once the North had demonstrated a willingness to use biological and chemical weapons.[16] There is just a thin line of passage from the DMZ through the mountains that the US forces would have to travel through to reach the North Korean capital. It soon became apparent that the North Koreans could have booby-trapped this passage with trip wires or timer devices that would set off more BW (or CW) sprayers.

Given the indefensible nature of a surprise scenario, like Global 95, the only viable option would have been for the US to attempt to deter a BW attack, in advance, with threats of nuclear retaliation. Indeed, the nuclear response might be the only military option once biological agents have contaminated large, populated areas of the South.

In fact, the White House has been forced to confront this very possibility. Under a new set of Presidential Decision Directives signed by Bill Clinton in 1998, a US president now has authority to order a retaliatory strike using nuclear devices in the event of a BW attack.

The former senior Pentagon official who closely studied the Global 95 outcome explains: 'We know the North Koreans have already weaponized their missiles with BW agents, but these devices are not considered such a big threat. There are only a few of these weapons, and they don't work that well. But that misses the point.

'One of our main worries remains the thought of one man, from North Korea's well-trained special operations force, carrying a portable BW sprayer on his back and silently launching a devastating anthrax attack on a US base at night. No one would get sick for one-to-three days, and, by then, it's too late. If detectors are not deployed on the site, or they don't work, or they don't work quickly, no one would know of the attack until it's too late.'[17]

To add to the nightmare, the Global 95 scenario was designed as a two front war. Days after the devastating North Korean BW attack was reported around the world, and the US had responded as best it could, a Middle Eastern dictator (modelled after Saddam Hussein) decided that the US was so distracted and weakened, that it would be the ideal time to take advantage. So the dictator's army launched its own BW attack on a small, neighbouring oil country, comparable to Kuwait. As part of this plan, the attacking nation used BW weapons on US bases in Saudi Arabia, principally as an act of terror to kill some American soldiers, to erode the capabilities of other US forces, and to panic the civilian population.[18]

The vulnerability of US forces was again highlighted. The war game participants found there were no biological sensors in Saudi Arabia to detect the attack, nor enough protective suits for US troops. As a consequence, the defenders were powerless to respond to this second assault. All available defensive BW materials, including protective suits, were already on their way to North Korea.

In this second front scenario, an anthrax attack on Dhahran killed more than one million civilians, most of whom lived or worked near US bases. The multi-faceted Iraqi attack also used specially rigged crop-dusting aircraft to spray US carriers in the Gulf.

The only response left to Washington was to order nuclear weapons to be dropped on the aggressor nation – an event which sharply focused minds and brought the conflict to a swift conclusion – but at a horrendous price.[19]

Global 95 underscored a fundamental problem in dealing with North Korea: the difficulty in securing accurate and reliable information about the capabilities and intentions of Pyongyang's BW programme. A former senior Pentagon official stresses that the intelligence received about this offensive programme comes from limited human sources. 'We have very little information about North Korea,' he says. 'And what we have cannot be corroborated.'[20]

The problem is that 'normal' intelligence collection is almost impossible. Says another former Pentagon official: 'We simply can't get close enough to their facilities to do what we need to do – such as taking soil, air, and water samples near suspect sites. We don't have good communications intercepts either.'[21]

What little information has reached US intelligence agencies in recent years has been increasingly alarming. 'North Korea's BW programme is more advanced than Iraq's,' explains a former senior CIA official. 'They have a wider range of agents they are looking at – more agents and more types of agents.'[22]

The increased US concern over the North Korean BW programme is based to a large degree on precious information acquired from the CIA's lone source-in-place in North Korea. This source was so valuable that even the South Koreans were not given his 'take'.

'We had concerns about North Korea before 1995,' says the former CIA official. 'This source pinpointed and confirmed matters for us. The source enabled us to piece together lots of little things we had before and added some details. We had some technical information before. The new source gave us precise details to focus on – including BW facilities, agents, and names of people who are involved in the programme. We still don't know all of the biological agents they are making. We know they are working with the main ones we have long suspected – anthrax, botulinum toxin, and Plague. These are the most common ones used by all nations who have a programme.[23]

'But that is not all the North Koreans are doing,' the CIA officer adds. 'They are making curious things, like special, weird agents and other unusual toxins. But we don't know much about this. We do know they also have the ability to produce weapons.'[24]

Western military analysts have long been suspicious that the North Koreans modelled their BW programme after the Soviet military's programme. Some US officials even suspected (but had no proof) that the Soviets helped the North Korean BW programme during the Cold War – prior to 1991 – because everything the North Koreans seemed to be doing was a poor copy of the Soviet system, facilities, and agents.[25]

Further suspicions about Soviet–North Korean cooperation centres around the special make-up of North Korean anthrax, which has a distinctive Soviet fingerprint on it. This sensitive information about the identifiable anthrax came from the CIA defector-in-place in North Korea.[26] He claims that Pyongyang's microbiologists have done two markedly revealing things to their anthrax. First, they have produced particles in the 4–5 micron range, which is the ideal size for human inhalation, and is thus far more lethal in aerosol form than other anthrax spores. Few nations, besides the USSR and US (before 1969), were ever technically proficient enough to make this optimum-sized anthrax. This achievement alone reveals that the North Koreans possess an advanced and sophisticated level of production.

Secondly, North Korean scientists have managed to coat their anthrax with special organic compounds, which shield the spores from the harmful UV rays of sunlight that decay and weaken normal anthrax. This coating process – called microencapsulation – is also considered evidence of possible Soviet assistance, since only the Soviets and Americans (before 1969) managed to coat anthrax in this way. Even the Iraqis have not attained this level of biological weapons engineering yet.

Some other rare nuggets of information about the progress of North Korea's BW programme have emerged from a tiny handful of civilian defectors who have fled the North. Although some of their stories must be treated with circumspection, especially after the South Korean government has spun them for propaganda reasons, several of the people who escaped have been taken seriously by Western intelligence analysts.

The essence of these stories – promoted by the South Koreans – is that the North has conducted BW experiments on unwitting humans, including political prisoners and dissidents.[27]

Lee Sun Ok, who escaped from the North in 1997, is one such informant.

Today, she sits in one of the many coffee shops in Seoul which are frequented by student couples holding hands and office ladies who finish their chocolate cakes before preparing to go back to work. Lee Sun Ok, age fifty-one, does not stand out amongst them.[28] She is neatly dressed, and looks much like any other South Korean 'ajuma' or auntie – the name given to a respectable married woman. Only the lilting North Korean accent and vocabulary peculiar to that country (one which actively protects its language from foreign influences) distinguishes her. Deep wrinkles, only partially obscured by fashionably large glasses and sad eyes, hint at the terrible hardships this woman has endured.

Her personal story is an Odyssey in its own right. But, if true, it reveals something important about a regime that may now possess its own instruments of mass destruction in the form of weaponized bacterial and viral agents.

Lee Sun Ok spent more than eight years incarcerated under draco-nian North Korean laws. The 'crime' that led to her imprisonment? Her honesty in what she saw as a corrupt society. When a security director asked her to supply him illegally with some suits from the supplies of the Commerce Administration, where she worked as a supply chief, she refused. He had her arrested by the police, after falsely accusing her of misappropriating government property. She was to finish up as one of 200,000 North Koreans then imprisoned in the state's pseudo-concen-tration camps, where, it is alleged, some 400,000 inmates had previously died.[29]

After her arrest (and separation from her husband and son), Lee Sun Ok was held in a police detention camp for fourteen months as an unconvicted prisoner. There, she was subjected to relentless torture in an attempt to force her to admit to charges that she embezzled state property and failed to abide by the Party's commercial policies – crimes she did not commit.

She has told her American and South Korean debriefers that her naked body was hung on a wooden frame as she was thrashed. She also would be tied to iron bars with her hands and feet in fetters and beaten with rubber whips. Oak sticks, she says, were placed between her fingers and twisted until the agony was unbearable. Sometimes, she would not be permitted to sleep for three or four days, during which time she was given no food. The guards would then take pleasure in escorting her to a dining room to watch police officers eating their meal.

On other occasions, she says, she was placed in a burning hot kiln immediately after baked bricks had been removed from it. She would be thrown into the kiln, which was still filled with hot dust, and would faint within seconds. Then, she would be taken out of the kiln, cold water would be poured onto her, and she would be placed back in the kiln. The process would be repeated three times.[30]

Here there is a pause in her story, and she falls silent and looks away. Even her interpreter is embarrassed. It is impossible in the quiet and friendly warmth of the coffee shop for her listeners, with no comparable experience, to give shape and meaning to what she alleges. It would be an impertinence at this moment to seek out physical scars to authenticate her account.

She says it took fourteen months before they broke her and she agreed to admit to the fabricated charges. She was then taken to court, where the presiding judge asked her to confess her guilt. But, once in court, she could not bring herself to do it. Two policemen, who were standing beside her, became infuriated by her change of heart and began to beat her in front of the judge. She fell to the floor, bleeding from her nose and mouth. The judge did not even reprimand the two officers. Instead, he dismissed the preliminary court and scheduled a full trial for that same afternoon.

At that moment, Lee Sun Ok says, all resolve ended. She then made a false statement admitting the charges and the judge immediately sentenced her to thirteen years of imprisonment in the Indoctrination Camp No. 1, located in Kaechon City.

After seven years of incarceration, she was granted amnesty for working hard and allowing herself to become 'reborn ideologically'. After her release, she lived in such fear of being returned to a camp, that she took the momentous decision to flee North Korea. She eventually managed to take her son with her to China, and four months later, they reached South Korea.[31]

In Seoul, she was debriefed at length, and what attracted the attention of Western intelligence analysts were those segments of her narrative which suggested that biological agents may have been used by her jailers to subjugate or even kill inmates in the camps. The evidence is sketchy, but has value.

'It was around May of 1988,' she recalls. 'About fifty people were fed with Chinese cabbage soaked in salt water. And all of them died right away. We were never usually given side dishes like Chinese cabbage to supplement our diet of rice in the camp. But the fifty were especially selected to eat the prepared Chinese cabbage. The people who were selected were those who were unable to work productively at the camp. There were hunchbacks and people with deformed legs. The majority of them were physically disabled.[32]

'It was the job of some prisoners to remove the corpses,' she continues. 'When the fifty disabled prisoners died, some prisoners, who were not given masks, were sent to gather the dead bodies.[33] The people who cleared the bodies were later infected with unknown contagious diseases. They suddenly started having nosebleeds and coughing up blood.'

Lee Sun Ok believes that biological agents were involved in those tests. She spoke to prisoners who had practised medicine before being incarcerated and were subsequently ordered to serve as medics in the camp. They told her that 'this was a test of pharmaceutical liquids'.

She also recalls overhearing some prison guards saying that the 'elements for the weapons' that were being tested 'seemed to be working very well'.[34]

After the incident, she says, prison officials in sealed suits entered the room and performed extensive disinfection. For three or four years afterwards a number of inmates had severe fever; others had sores, blisters, and nosebleeds, and coughed blood. The contagious illness appeared to spread to other parts of the camp in sporadic outbreaks during the next four years and many died.

Which bacterial agent was used? The best guess by Western micro-biologists who have read her testimony is that it was anthrax, which would explain the sores and the pulmonary afflictions leading to the coughing of blood. However, the use of food as a vector for anthrax would make no sense. The real question is whether Mrs Ok has made a mistake in associating the cabbage with the bacterial outbreak. The North Koreans may have secretly used another method of dissemination of which she was never aware. Or, it could have been something else entirely. Without forensic evidence, the world will never know.

General John Shalikashvili, the Chairman of the Joint Chiefs of Staff in 1997, warned that North Korea posed the greatest threat to Asia, because floods and famine have driven the economy to ruin and made the government increasingly unpredictable. He said 'the security situation on the Korean Peninsula [was] worse than it was twenty-five years ago', when he served there as a military planner.[35]

The decision in North Korea to employ biological weapons currently rests with Supreme Commander Kim Jong Il, who has four means of delivery at his disposal: artillery, aircraft, ballistic missiles, and unconventional systems.[36]

Following the military 'catastrophes' of Global 95, the Pentagon currently regards a small-scale, third-world, special forces or terrorist attack, using portable or boat-mounted aerosol sprayers, as the greatest danger faced by its troops stationed overseas. North Korea remains the most likely flashpoint.

Sensible critics of these scary views will argue, cogently enough, that the Pentagon and all Western ministries of defence, and the whole battalion of military academicians, are playing internal politics when they exaggerate the threat of a possible biological attack by a rogue state or even by terrorists.

The critics' arguments might carry greater validity but for a series of extraordinary events in next-door Japan that happened, by coincidence, a few months before the hypothetical Global 95 was played out.

Except that in Japan what happened was no war game. It was the real thing.

And real people died.

CHAPTER THIRTY-TWO

Apocalypse Delayed

'... with terrorist groups today ... we're in a new era ... where the unthinkable could be done with unthinkable destructive power by groups that are willing to do the unthinkable.'

Senator Sam Nunn, 1996[1]

It's one thing when the state, like North Korea or Iraq, formally authorizes the use of biological warfare. But what happens when terrorists beyond all control decide to use it?

The only consolation when it comes to state-sanctioned use of any weapon of mass destruction remains, traditionally, the vulnerability of the aggressor state to massive retaliation. There is an army to fight, a state capital to bomb, a leader to be displaced – a balance of terror.

But none of that applies to unaligned terrorists should they decide to use a weapon of mass destruction such as biological agents. Until 1995, the concept had been given no considered thought. Then, suddenly the world received its wake-up call.

On 20 March 1995, just before the height of the Tokyo rush hour, invisible clouds of lethal sarin nerve gas began to drift through five high-speed trains inside Tokyo's teeming subway system.[2]

Twelve people were killed and more than 5,000 were injured.[3] Pictures of victims fighting for breath, lying on the Tokyo streets in agony while the emergency services struggled to cope with the magnitude of what had happened, were transmitted to stunned audiences around the world. This was the worst act of terrorism ever to have taken place on Japanese soil.

Aum Shinrikyo – the apocalyptic cult responsible – has usually been identified with that one nerve gas attack, but what is not fully appreciated is that the sect ran a parallel biological warfare programme with the intention of causing massive deaths throughout the world. Aum did come very close to achieving great devastation.

In fact, the cult carried out at least nine biological attacks. These attempts failed not from a lack of effort, but only because Aum did not use bacteria of sufficient virulence and because the execution of the attacks was persistently amateurish.

Aum Shinrikyo is now the world's most notorious so-called 'apocalyptic sect'. These are quasi-religious and highly eccentric groups of like-minded fanatics who place themselves outside the norms of accepted social behaviour. Their powerful beliefs and obsessions tend to focus on a time when the planet will be destroyed by universal forces beyond the control of man.

Apocalyptic sects have begun to overtake 'conventional' terrorist groups as points of international concern, for they have no political agenda, no desire to save themselves or their loved ones, and do not accept that this is a world worth living in. Some pose no threat to the real world, others do. On balance they have tended to remain a tolerated and somewhat patronized backdrop in the fabric of most societies.

But 20 March 1995 changed all that. Awareness that biological warfare capability had slipped down the national structure and into the hands of a bunch of apparent crazies would alter the West's perception of the potential of BW for ever.

Aum Shinrikyo had been in existence since 1987. For seven years, the group had been involved in secretly developing chemical and biological weapons. They carried out numerous unsuccessful attacks, often using biological agents with far greater destructive potential than sarin. At its height, the group's financial base may have been as much as $2 billion in assets.[4] Yet the activities of the doomsday cult were virtually unnoticed by Japanese, American, and British intelligence organizations. After the Tokyo gas attack, US officials were astonished to discover that neither the CIA nor the FBI had a single file on the sect. It is only by good fortune that the cult failed in its many attempts to commit mass murder.

John Sopko, who thoroughly investigated Aum in 1995 for the US Senate, has summed it up: 'Although the findings may initially sound far-fetched and almost science fictional, the actions of Aum ... create a terrifying picture of a deadly mixture of religious zealotry ... anti-government agenda ... and the technical know-how of a Dr Strangelove.

'... the Aum incident is a remarkable yet frightening case study of the threat modern terrorism poses to all industrial nations.'[5]

Aum Shinrikyo – the name is formed with a conjunction of the Hindu mantra (pronounced 'Ohm') and 'Shinrikyo', which means 'the Supreme Truth' of the universe – was created by Shoko Asahara, the half-blind charismatic 'guru', easily recognizable today with his long beard, the trademark colourful robes, and his icy stare.

Asahara was born on Japan's southern island of Kyushu in 1955, the fourth son of a weaver of *tatami*, the straw floor mats often seen in Japanese homes. Even as a child, Asahara discovered the strange hold he could wield over his peers. Chizuo Matsumoto, as Asahara was then known, was born with infantile glaucoma, which left him blind in one eye and with only limited vision in the other. His parents sent him away to a boarding school for the blind – where the one-eyed child was king. He bullied his classmates and used his partial sight to earn money from them through various schemes. Through high school he showed flashes of his cunning, volatility, and violent temper, and always dreamed of a grand future full of wealth and personal power.[6]

After failing his university entrance exam, in 1978 Asahara opened a one-room Chinese herbal medicine and acupuncture clinic in Funabashi, southeast of Tokyo. His business – selling expensive, fake potions to the frail and elderly – thrived, but he was later caught selling orange peel soaked in alcohol as a cure, and he was fined and briefly jailed.[7]

By the early 1980s, Asahara had moved to Tokyo and acquired an interest in the spiritual life. In later years, he claimed to have had an out-of-body experience at the age of three, but this assertion, as with many of Asahara's statements, can be treated with a degree of scepticism. He began to study Chinese medicine, fortune-telling, astrology, and the writings of Shinji Takahashi, founder of the new religion GLA (God Light Association), who claimed to be Buddha incarnate – though he incorporated Christian theology into his teachings.[8]

In 1984, Asahara created a new company, which he named Aum Inc. At first the company amounted to little – just a one-room yoga school where Asahara was still peddling his snake-oil to the gullible.[9] But, like so many schizophrenics, he was about to receive important messages that would override social norms. On a beach on Japan's Pacific coast in 1986, the future guru received a 'message from God'. The voice told him: 'I have chosen you to lead God's Army.' Later that same year, he says, he met a radical historian at a spiritual retreat in the mountains. The man informed him: 'Armageddon will come at the end of the century. Only a merciful, godly race will survive. The leader of this race will emerge in Japan.' The close conjunction of these two formative events led Asahara to the ineluctable conclusion – he had been chosen to save the world.[10]

He now began to attract students to Aum, publishing advertisements that promised followers the ability to see the future, read other people's minds, make wishes come true, attain x-ray vision and levitation, and take trips to the fourth dimension. He also wrote his first book, *Secrets of Developing Your Supernatural Powers*.[11] The cult was beginning to take shape and there was no shortage of the lonely, the vulnerable, and the disturbed to share such a glorious vision.

Asahara's first speech on the approaching apocalypse was made at a seminar in May 1987. 'Japan will rearm herself in 1992,' he predicted. 'Between 1999 and 2003, a nuclear war is sure to break out. I, Asahara, have mentioned the outbreak of nuclear war for the first time. We have only fifteen years before it.'[12]

From the ashes of this global fire, a new race of superhumans would arise phoenix-like. World War III would not be a problem, at least not 'for one who has attained enlightenment', the guru explained.[13] The exact timing of the coming apocalypse, however, was subtly altered on a regular basis. The gods that spoke to Asahara were occasionally inconsistent.

Gradually it became clear that the apocalypse might need a little help on its way – and Aum would be in the vanguard of those prepared to offer their assistance. Asahara and his followers would ensure that worldwide destruction would arise from (yet another) vast conflict between the United States and Japan. It was all good top-of-the-mountain-end-of-the-world stuff, but for one thing. By now, these crazies had quietly begun to accumulate a small, but potent, biological and chemical armoury.

A handful of Japan's gifted youth was seduced by Aum's dramatic claims to supernatural power, its warnings of an apocalyptic future, and its esoteric spiritualism. By 1989, Asahara had gathered about him a potent mixture of talented young disciples – including doctors, biologists, and computer programmers – who recognized the vast destructive potential of biological weapons. He set about assigning positions to these followers so that the power structure of Aum reflected the organization of the Japanese government (which he planned to take over).[14] Seiichi Endo became the cult's biological warfare chief, or 'Minister of Health and Welfare'. Before joining the cult, Endo, twenty-eight, had been working in genetic engineering at Kyoto University's Viral Research Centre.[15] The new recruit, with his shaven head and beady eyes, took on a new job at Aum to discover which lethal germs could be converted into the most efficient weapons.

To fund his weapons programmes and cult operations, Asahara promoted a variety of schemes. For instance, new cult members were told to wear a bizarre electrode-laden shock cap known as the PSI, or Perfect Salvation Initiation. The cap was designed to transmit the guru's brain waves to cult members. The strange head-dress soon became standard issue and a huge money-maker for the cult, since followers were required to pay $7,000 per month to use them.[16]

What made Aum less laughable and more ominous was the co-existence between the bizarre, the insane, and the realities of biological and military science. Fascinating insights into the sophisticated types of research, testing, and production conducted by Aum's scientists have been discovered inside the main laboratory at the cult's largest centre at Mount Fuji. This laboratory, which was first set up in 1988, was later sealed and left to decay after the infamous sarin attack.[17] Aum also had laboratories at Mount Aso in central Kyushu and had ordered equipment for these places from around the world, through various front companies the cult controlled.[18]

A forty-minute video of the interior of Aum's Mount Fuji laboratory, taped after the Tokyo attack by a freelance Japanese reporter, has provided rare visual evidence and confirmation of the cult's biological terrorism infrastructure. The video revealed a maze of new laboratory equipment (equivalent to components found in major pharmaceutical companies), glassware, animal cages for guinea pigs and rabbits, and photos of the guru on the walls.[19] The equipment included freeze dryers, high-pressure bacteria concentrators, huge high-tech incubators, electron microscopes, containers to preserve cells in liquid nitrogen, and water distillers. The laboratory also had a library of 300 biochemical books and recipes for making BW agents.

A former senior Pentagon official, who saw the video, says the bio-equipment was very advanced.[20] Aum also kept highly professional documentation of their animal-testing programme, including the doses they used in the experiments and logs of how the animals died. Although the video only shows that Aum was working with anthrax, the truth is they were experimenting with a far greater range of BW agents.[21]

The Pentagon official explains: 'Our analysts were astonished at the high quality of the research lab. It was top flight. It was not as good as CDC [the Centres for Disease Control in Atlanta, Georgia] or Fort Detrick, but very good by world standards.'[22]

A CIA officer, who studied the tape, recalls that Aum cleverly made up for any deficiencies in sophisticated devices they lacked. 'To an expert,' he explained, 'the video tells a lot. It showed that Aum had some crude, improvised production equipment that was nevertheless effective. Their bio-fermenters, for instance, were simply modified 55-gallon drums. To analysts, this modification shows that a terrorist group does not need to purchase top-of-the-line fermenters from a large company in Europe or the US. You can use common drums to make agents.'[23]

To help midwife the coming Armageddon, Asahara wanted the most powerful weapons of mass destruction possible. His microbiologists studied the available literature and concluded that they would work with *Clostridium botulinum*, the most toxic bacteria known to man, which causes botulism. Botulinum toxin struck Aum's dedicated young scientists as the ideal killer, since it was cheap to produce and seemed to be within their capabilities to develop as a biological weapon.[24]

The cult obtained its first sample of botulism-causing germs in March 1990 during a special trip made by Endo to the northern Japanese island of Hokkaido, at a wilderness area near the Tokachi River, where he had previously lived.[25]

Aum's scientists also tried to develop an antitoxin to counter botulism, using horse serum.[26] Experiments were conducted at the Mount Aso complex. Asahara ordered the building of a stable and purchased horses, for a continuing live blood supply. The *Clostridium botulinum* was then tested on laboratory rats by dropping it in powder form onto their feed. The scientists waited patiently, but no rats died.

Endo then tried sprinkling the powder directly over the rats. When that too failed, he then injected a supposedly toxic solution directly into the rats, but still they did not die.

In fact, that failure was a useful step on Aum's learning curve of how to apply biological agents. They had been murderously careless with the powder, for, as they grated it, some speckles flew into the air and could easily have been inhaled.

Eventually, Endo identified the problem. *Clostridium botulinum* is an anaerobic organism, which means it dies in the presence of oxygen. But if it is cultured in a special liquid growth medium and then concentrated into a powder, it becomes botulinum toxin, which does survive exposure to the air. Aum's laboratories required more sophisticated equipment; and since money was never a problem, everything necessary was immediately purchased for the cult's head of biological warfare. By April 1990, Endo was convinced that he could maintain the toxicity of botulinum toxin.[27]

Aum then went for the big one. With some hubris, the cult concluded it was now ready to take on the United States, and it duly prepared for the first-ever biological warfare assault by terrorists on American armed forces.

That month, Aum despatched a three-truck convoy, each vehicle carrying spraying devices and a reservoir of botulinum toxin, into the streets of Tokyo. The guru's personal chauffeur, Shigeo Sugimoto, was one of the drivers that day. Sugimoto subsequently testified in court that the convoy drove through most of the Tokyo Bay area to attack two American bases. In a daringly insane biological assault, the vehicles went first to the US Navy installation at Yokohama and then on to the base at Yokosuka, headquarters of the Navy's Seventh Fleet.[28] The convoy then moved on to Narita, Japan's largest airport, which is situated about 40 miles northeast of Tokyo. At each of the sites, Sugimoto said, the trucks sprayed clouds of invisible botulinum toxin mist.[29]

But once again, the attacks failed. Asahara and the cult waited in vain for news of casualties. Nothing on the television, nothing on the radio, and nothing in the newspapers. Once again the apocalypse was postponed.

BW specialists in the United States remain unsure whether the botulinum strain was weak or the toxin was fickle, or the wind direction unhelpful, or all three. Since the potencies of the hundreds of strains of botulinum toxin vary widely, effective dissemination is very difficult, even for experts.[30]

Aum returned to the drawing board.

While Endo's team took time to re-examine its methods and agents, Aum was having remarkable success in setting up overseas bases of operation, especially in Russia.[31] The decision to develop the sect in Russia was taken shortly after Aum began to develop a weapons capability in 1991. Aum began a vigorous recruitment programme in what seemed to be virgin territory, perhaps because the former Soviet Union had been so intolerant of religious worship that it had left something of a spiritual vacuum among the people.

The cult even signed a three-year contract for airtime on state-run Mayak Radio, broadcasting an hour-long daily programme together with transmissions from Russia's '2X2' television station. Aum's hocus pocus seemed to draw a serious audience, particularly among disaffected students. In 1995, a Russian government investigation into the sect's activities discovered that membership in the country had reached an astonishing 35,000, with another 55,000 lay followers who attended Aum seminars on an occasional basis. These Russian figures dwarfed the cult's 10,000 Japanese followers.[32]

Aum's main interest in Russia was in using cash and new converts, including scientists, former military officers, and KGB veterans, to acquire weapons technology.[33] Numerous delegations were sent to Moscow. One went to discuss laser weapons with a Russian expert; another smuggled back submachine-gun manufacturing blueprints and other weapons data to Japan; and there were even efforts to obtain nuclear intelligence. Aum's shopping list later also included Russian Army helicopters, MiG-29 fighters, Proton rocket launchers, and chemical weapons. From a senior Russian official, Aum actually obtained a blueprint from a Russian sarin production plant and information on how to manufacture the deadly chemical.[34] Significantly, the sect also tried to penetrate Russia's illegal BW programme, when Endo made an exploratory trip to Russia to see if he could acquire expertise or purchase any biological agents. There is no evidence, however, that he succeeded. Russia's secret BW programme was neither for inspection nor sale at that time.[35]

As worldwide recruitment soared, the development of biological weapons was continuing in Japan. In 1992, Aum attempted to acquire strains of the deadly Ebola virus in Zaire. A US Senate report on Aum confirmed that the sect craftily sent a purported medical mission to Zaire to assist in the treatment of Ebola victims at several hospitals. This forty-person 'humanitarian' team, cutely named the 'African Salvation Tour', was led by Asahara himself. 'We were trying to save African lives from sickness and hunger,' cooed an article in *Enjoy Happiness*, a cult magazine. Not so. In fact, the cult was trying to harness the notorious new and highly lethal virus as a weapon of mass destruction. To this day, no one knows if they succeeded in acquiring a virus sample; however, it is notable that Endo later discussed the potential of using Ebola as a BW agent during a 1994 radio address.[36]

Aum was also peering into the future of biological terrorism and began ambitiously pursuing genetic engineering strategies. The cult attempted to buy genetic engineering equipment as early as May 1993, and despatched Endo that month to a major Japanese research institute to study new techniques in cell multiplication technology (which are used to grow viruses). In a subsequent book published by Aum, Endo predicted that 'new microbes and biological weapons produced through gene technology will be used in the next world war'.[37]

Aum also attempted to purchase sophisticated molecular design software from two American companies – these computer programmes, normally used to develop new therapeutic drugs, could be adapted to create new BW agents.[38] And there were enquiries to a New Hampshire company about buying advanced air filtration media for use in bio-laboratory 'clean rooms'.[39]

In June 1993, Asahara's fevered mind settled for a moment on the impending imperial wedding of the crown prince, Naruhito, and his bride, Masako Owada. This high-profile event, he reasoned, would lend itself to a spectacular attack. At first, Asahara demanded that a laser weapon should be used to vaporize all of the corrupt Japanese leaders gathered at the Imperial Palace.[40] When he was advised the laser gun would take more time to perfect, he turned to good old reliable Endo, who assured him that this time he'd really cracked the bacterial problems and had two efficient and highly lethal biological weapons ready for use.

Asahara's team began preparing Plan B. While the eyes of Japan were firmly focused on the royal wedding, Aum would seize control of the military and capture the Imperial Palace, the Diet, and the Prime Minister's residence. Nothing less. His plans were soon so developed that

Aum followers actually considered renting convenient office space near the palace and government buildings.[41]

The reality, however, was more prosaic. At the last moment, Asahara was gently advised that Aum was not quite ready for a biologically fostered *coup d'état*. So, instead, a slightly less ambitious Plan C was developed, by which Aum would again spray botulinum toxin, this time through central Tokyo. Once the city was overcome by death and fear, Asahara would hold a press conference to blame the US military for the attack and for killing so many people.

A vehicle was set up with a special spraying device. The technology was simple, the agent available, the moment was right.

This time, the guru himself, beaming with pleasure, joined the terrorists inside the vehicle as the deadly attack began. But midway through their tour of Tokyo, Asahara was suddenly overwhelmed by paranoia and became convinced that the killing mist was leaking back into the vehicle. He screamed at the driver to stop and leapt out and ran. His obedient sprayers finished their assignment.

Endo, however, had failed his master again. The new batch of botulinum toxin killed nobody. No one even knew the attack had taken place.[42] Endo, more Groucho than Karl as a revolutionary Marx, now found himself drinking in the last chance saloon.

He promised an angry Asahara that the next attack would succeed, because he was changing the delivery method and the agent. When the time came, three weeks later, Endo took the guru on a tour of the cult's latest bio-laboratory, located on top of an eight-storey building in eastern Tokyo.[43] On the roof of the building, Endo showed him a contraption that appeared to be a large cooling tower. In fact, it was an industrial sprayer hooked up to a huge fan.

Endo explained to his fellow cultists that he had now given up on botulinum toxin and had embraced anthrax. The lethal bacterial spores would be pumped from the top of the building and waft across the city, spreading the deadly disease on a vast scale.

This plan, with its truly apocalyptic potential, received the guru's assent. In late June 1993, cult workers in protective clothing poured a liquid solution of anthrax spores into the dispersal device.[44] For four days, a strange kind of toxic steam poured onto the city below. The first signs were promising. Neighbours complained of a foul odour, and some people lost their appetite. Small birds and pets grew ill. Plants died. One local resident told the press: 'When we smelled the horrible odour, some people who had survived World War II said it was the smell of burning flesh.'[45]

The local authorities were called in to the Aum building, but cult members turned them away. The matter was not pursued and was soon forgotten. Asahara later explained to residents that the odd smell had come from burning soybean oil and perfume to purify the building.

But once again the biological assault failed. There were no casualties, no deaths. What the hapless Endo did not understand was that possession of a biological agent and a dispersal device is not enough in itself. The strain's potency, spore size, rate of human inhalation, effect of sunlight on the spore, wind shifts ... all these factors have to be just right for an attack to succeed – especially since he was not using a dry agent. In this instance, the strain of anthrax Endo had obtained was relatively weak; the sprayers became clogged; and the mist was too 'heavy' for the anthrax spores to be inhaled directly into human lungs.[46]

Weeks later, in July, Endo tried again, twice. This time, he used a truck to spray his anthrax solution around central Tokyo – first, near the Diet, and then with the Imperial Palace as his main target. But the results were the same each time, no one got sick, no one died, no one knew.[47]

The year 1993 was a busy time for the cult. Several months earlier, in April, two senior members turned up in Perth, Australia, where they were met by an Australian real estate agent of Japanese origin. Over the next few days, Asahara's two followers were shown around various sheep-grazing properties before they decided to purchase, for $400,000, the remote Banjawarn Station, about 400 miles northwest of Perth.[48] The huge sheep ranch (about 500,000 acres), located in the midst of a mineral rich region of western Australia, was acquired for three main purposes: to mine for uranium to fuel Aum's planned nuclear arms; to serve as their test site for weapons of mass destruction; and to become a cult hideaway during the planned apocalypse.[49]

On 9 September 1993, Asahara and twenty-four cult members arrived in Perth from Tokyo. At the airport, the weird-looking band of cultists was stopped by customs officers and thoroughly searched. Their luggage was strange. They were carrying a wide variety of chemicals, including hydrochloric and perchloric acids (in large bottles marked 'hand soap'), picks, shovels, generators, a mechanical ditch digger, respirators, and gas masks. The mining equipment was confiscated and two cult members – 'Minister of Health and Welfare', the unlucky Seiichi Endo, and Tomomasa Nakagawa, the guru's personal physician and a top cult official – were briefly detained and fined for transporting dangerous substances aboard an aircraft.[50]

Asahara and his followers spent a week at the ranch (collecting uranium samples) and then returned to Japan. In October, when the guru and four others applied for visas to return to Australia, their applications were rejected. But even though Asahara himself was not allowed back into the country, cult activity at the Banjawarn Station continued until the property was sold in August 1994.[51]

Australian authorities later discovered that Aum had set up a laboratory in the outback that rivalled its facilities back in Japan. The laboratory boasted numerous computers, digital equipment, glass tubing, glass evaporators, beakers, Bunsen burners, ceramic grinding bowls, and a new supply of the chemicals that had been successfully smuggled in.[52]

The cult also purchased a large number of sheep and used them for experimentation with chemical agents. After Aum vacated the site, the new owner discovered the carcasses of twenty-nine sheep (killed by sarin), as well as chemicals on the property.[53]

A former senior CIA official says that a careful review of Aum's actions by US analysts has concluded that the ranch was also used to research biological agents and acquire materials that could support a BW programme. The CIA is reluctant to disclose details of this evidence. With deliberate vagueness, the former official explains: 'The Aum group was thinking of other things to do in Australia. They were acquiring BW-related materials in Australia to ship back to Japan.'[54] A major motivation for buying the ranch, some US intelligence officials suspected, was to obtain sheep, cattle, and rabbits so that more potent strains of Tularaemia and anthrax could be obtained.[55]

US officials also theorize that Aum may have been researching Q fever, a highly infectious, incapacitating agent that was a mainstay of both the US and Soviet offensive BW arsenals. This rickettsia-like organism (discovered in Australia) can be harvested from cattle and sheep and grown in fertilized chicken eggs. Such eggs were found at an Aum laboratory in Japan.[56]

There was one additional clue about Aum's interest in Q fever. In a television interview recorded days after the Tokyo subway sarin attack, Asahara, looking ill and weak said: 'My body is considerably damaged now.' He alleged that unidentified airplanes had sprayed his Australian compound with Q fever. Western analysts suspect that Aum members accidentally infected themselves.[57]

After the Australian venture, Asahara, now back in Japan, began exploring other bizarre plans, while Endo continued refining his BW agents in the laboratory. CIA analysts later concluded that Asahara's team was apparently hoping to launch airborne CW and BW attacks over Tokyo and other cities using unmanned aircraft and a helicopter which were retrofitted with spray tanks. Japanese police later found two radio-controlled drones (from US Navy surplus) that the cult hoped to use to distribute biological agents. The sect also managed to smuggle a Russian military MIL-17 transport helicopter into Japan. A former Russian military officer trained four Aum members on how to fly it.[58] In more sophisticated and experienced hands, this arsenal of BW-orientated equipment could have had potentially devastating consequences.

Fortunately it was Asahara's delusions that kept turning possible tragedy into farce. He told his scientific team that he wanted to launch worldwide germ warfare attacks by releasing large balloons filled with botulinum toxin. This scheme was part of his plan to 'rule the world'.[59] In apparent preparation for such attacks, an Aum front company in Tokyo ordered 400 Israeli-made gas masks from a firm in New York (but the shipment was later seized by US customs before delivery was made).[60] However, Japanese police later found about 200 large metal drums of peptone, enough growth media to culture a huge quantity of bacteria.[61]

In early 1995, Asahara ordered yet another biological attack on Tokyo. They reverted to botulinum toxin, still the cult's biological agent of choice.

This time, the attack was to be on the Tokyo subway system, in the station at Kasumigaseki on 15 March 1995. Here, it was hoped, an enclosed space would help to concentrate the deadly mist.[62] Kasumigaseki Station is a major transit hub used daily by tens of thousands of commuters, including many officials who work at the nearby Tokyo police headquarters and central government ministries. Underground stations and their connected tunnel networks, everywhere in the world, are properly regarded as the most profitable targets for biological terrorists. The reasons are straightforward: the bacteria and viruses will not be exposed to degrading sunlight; the artificial air-flows through tunnels are ideal dispersants for biological agents; and, obviously, the networks teem with people. As a bonus, the well-dispersed bacteria usually vent through giant air ducts and filtration systems into the street, where they can continue their destructive work.

The cult's weaponeers, having learned from previous mistakes, were now beginning to refine their devices for disseminating the bacteria.[63] The plan this time was to insert a solution of the pathogen in vinyl tubes, mounted on a ceramic diaphragm. This apparatus, in turn, was placed in a dispenser that fitted neatly into a briefcase. The battery-driven dispenser was designed to turn the solution into a mist, which would be blown from the briefcase by a small fan. Three such briefcases were prepared (hundreds more were being planned).[64] They could be activated by the vibration of a passing train or by an unwitting passer-by who might lift one up and carry it to the lost-and-found office. It may have been hi-tech nonsense, but the potential for disaster was immense.

A cultist slipped into Kasumigaseki Station, and, in the rush-hour crush, simply left the three briefcases on platforms as instructed. The cases were soon picked up, as expected, by stationmasters. Two of the cases failed to activate, but the third case did click into action and began to emit a fine mist.

Unbelievably, this successfully activated spraying device also proved to be a dud. The unidentified cult member who deposited the briefcases had suffered a last-minute crisis of conscience and had decided not to arm any of the three devices with the toxic solution.[65]

The infamous sarin gas attack took place five days later.

Afterwards, the police raided Aum's Mount Fuji base under the pretence that they were investigating the disappearance of Kiyoshi Kariya, a notary who had been abducted and murdered by Aum. On 22 March 1995, a thousand police dressed in riot gear and protective suits approached the complex at Mount Fuji. They brought a variety of gadgetry with them – electric saws, blowtorches, guns – and even caged canaries, the oldest early warning system for poison-gas emissions. A convoy of armoured trucks, water cannons, and ambulances followed just behind. For the next few days, an astounded nation looked on as police discovered an immense array of strange equipment, germs, and chemicals – the raw materials for the biological/chemical instruments that would help bring about the apocalypse.[66]

Two months later, on 16 May, Asahara was arrested at Mount Fuji.[67] The guru just couldn't stay away from his seat of empire. He was discovered by police investigators amid scenes that might better have suited Howard Hughes. They removed the door to Bloc Satian #6 with the aid of blowtorches and began searching the building. In a tiny chamber between the third and fourth floors of the building, they came upon the crestfallen and tired-looking guru. Beside him were a cassette-player, medicine, $100,000 in cash, and an AK-47 assault rifle. Asahara made no attempt to escape or to defend himself. 'Don't touch me, I don't even let my disciples touch me,' he said.[68]

As the full truth about Aum was slowly revealed, the US Senate ordered hearings on the who, what, and why of Aum, with particular reference to the lessons to be learned by the West. Biological terrorism was an entirely new phenomenon, and, rather like the Soviet Union's successful first leap into space with Sputnik, the Americans found it hard to accept that there was a new form of terrorism which had been launched even before they had knowledge of its existence.

During the hearings, the much respected, senior Democrat, Senator Sam Nunn of Georgia, wondered aloud how this could have happened. 'Another troubling aspect of this case,' Nunn said, 'is that despite the Aum's overt and far-flung activities, no US law enforcement or intelligence agency perceived them as dangerous, much less a threat to national security, prior to the March 20 subway attack this year [1995]. How does a fanatic, intent on triggering an Armageddon between the United States and Japan, with virtually unlimited funds and a worldwide network of operatives, escape the notice of Western intelligence and law enforcement? What happened to the co-ordination between the United States and Japan?'[69]

There were, a senior FBI executive explained patiently, serious civil rights and constitutional constraints (in both the US and Japan) that restrict investigations of any chartered religious organizations.[70]

Perhaps then the CIA should have known more? Gordon Oehler, a senior CIA official, replied to Nunn: '... Aum was a registered religious group in Japan ... Being a registered group in Japan, it had a lot of protection from even the Japanese investigative services.'

Oehler went on to agree with the FBI view. '... I really do not see any inclination here or abroad,' he said, 'to have the CIA running around peering into religious groups around the world to see who is naughty and nice.'[71]

John Sopko, the deputy chief counsel who led Senator Nunn's inquiry into the Aum sect, believes that intelligence agencies have to change the way they deal with religious groups like Aum, but he is less optimistic that mankind will be saved much longer by the screw-up factor – the probable failure of such groups to achieve their aims because of their innate propensity to get things wrong. He points out that only a fairly rudimentary scientific knowledge is required to conduct research on biological agents; he warns that 'either Aum members still at large or other terrorist groups may be more successful in the future'.[72] Sopko was closer to the truth than even he imagined.

Incredibly, the story of Aum is still far from over.

Japan's fervent determination to be a good democracy has inadvertently led to a *revival* of the Aum sect, even before its old leaders face their criminal trials. Only eight weeks after their arrest, in May 1995, other lesser members of the cult showed a renewed interest in the end of the world by mounting another gas attack on the busy Shinjuku train station. Catastrophe was only averted as police acted swiftly to put out a fire under two plastic bags, one of which contained sulphuric acid, the other hydrogen cyanide: Had the noxious fumes combined into hydrogen cyanide, there could have been massive casualties.[73]

To compound the irony, late in January 1997, Japan's Public Security Commission, an independent body, announced that it had decided not to outlaw Aum. The Commission rejected a request, filed in July 1996 by the Public Security Investigation Agency (a branch of Japan's Ministry of Justice), to apply the 1952 Antisubversive Activities Law to outlaw Aum. Their reasons? 'The cult can no longer pose a threat to Japanese society.'[74]

The official word from Aum is that they are not engaged in violent activities. 'Our believers are sharing a quiet decent life,' says Hiroshi Araki, the cult's chief spokesman.

But Aum today is in a state of renewal. The Public Security Investigation Agency has repeatedly warned that the cult is attempting a rapid resurgence, and a Japanese police report states that Aum 'remains very active and this calls for due vigilance' (a complete *volte-face* from the views of the Japanese Public Security Commission).[75]

And, just to retain the sense of *déjà vu*, Asahara's followers are once again plotting Armageddon. 'They are talking about arming themselves again,' says a Japanese police report. 'Members are hearing sermons telling them Armageddon is coming ... and to prepare themselves for the return of the guru in 2008.'[76]

Most ominously to the Japanese authorities, the cult is again buying land and buildings; it owns 33 facilities and 100 dormitories throughout Japan. At these communal locations, members are immune from Japanese law. They obey only Asahara's laws.[77]

As of early 1999, the group still boasted some 2,000 faithful members in Japan, and the numbers are rising, as the cult focuses recruitment on its key target group of university students – especially those with a good microbiology or chemical science background.[78] Recruiters are often spotted at university campuses, offering yoga lessons and spiritual fulfilment as initial inducements. The cult maintains a number of dedicated Internet sites, which receive up to 1,000 hits a day. The Aum homepage features pictures of the guru along with many of his sayings.

The Web site message concludes unambiguously: 'There is no mistake in what our supreme master says.'[79]

Aum lives. And still looks east at the biggest target in the world. America.

CHAPTER THIRTY-THREE

'Walkers, Floppers & Goners'

'. . . God help us if it's smallpox.'
Renaldo Campana, senior FBI official, 1998

The Western world's most prominent Plague Wars defender is a tall, frenetic New York civil servant who crackles with enough electricity to light Broadway in mid-winter. Jerome (Jerry) Hauer is one of those people who makes things happen, fast, on time, and the way he *wants* it to happen. The static almost arcs around him as he talks on the phone, watches CNN, and barks at his assistants at the same time.

He is very tall, shirt-sleeved, and hands-on everything – as you might expect from the Director of New York's Office of Emergency Management, the man at whose feet the disaster buck stops when there is a serious city crisis, be it a biological or chemical terrorist attack or a natural catastrophe.

New York is the archetypal vulnerable big city. It has 7.5 million inhabitants crammed into a series of concrete jungles; it also happens to be the centre of the Western world's financial system and the enduring symbol of the capitalist way of life. It is a city groaning with people, commerce, narrow streets, inaccessibly tall buildings, and an infrastructure, which, even without an emergency, seems permanently on the verge of collapse.

New York may be vibrant, exciting, and the adrenalin centre of the Western world, but it is, like London, Tokyo, or Paris, a dream target for a biological terrorist. When Jerry Hauer's fizz subsides, he is gloomily aware of what he's up against.

'I'm taking the biological terrorist threat very, very seriously,' he says. 'I have a public health background, and I know what the implications are. I've created a special BW advisory group including microbiologists, infectious disease experts, epidemiologists, and law enforcement officers. I think that with everything we have lined up here, we now lead the world.'[1]

Certainly the world, including London's Metropolitan Police and representatives from numerous other countries, now beats a path to Wall Street and Hauer's twentieth-floor office to sit at his feet and learn about the business from the master. For the past two years, even President Clinton has been taking his advice.

Lesson number one?

'It was always a mistake,' he says, 'for cities to integrate their responses to nuclear/chemical attacks with biological terrorist attacks. You have got to separate the biological side. The disciplines involved are completely different.'

Hauer is paradoxically publicity shy. He dislikes, above all else, to discuss the awful reality of a serious biological warfare attack upon his city. When he does address the subject, his voice lowers to a whisper. 'Yeah, we are vulnerable to disruption,' he agrees. 'There's going to be a lot of panic, there will be civil unrest, people will break into pharmacies to get medicines, there will be problems burying the dead, we've looked at scenarios, and yes, they include, *in extremis*, the possible use of lime pits and crematoria.'

In fact, there would be insurmountable problems in handling the transportation and burial of the large number of corpses. The catastrophic consequences of an all-out, effective biological attack on New York are hard to imagine. If an infectious agent were effectively unleashed, it might kill as many as three million people. There simply are no effective or possible medical countermeasures to handle such an event. It is impossible to stockpile enough vaccine. Nor could it be administered in time.[2] In a viral attack, the mass casualties would have to be buried immediately to prevent the spread of infection. This would not only be a logistical nightmare, but it would violate Judaeo-Christian ethics for decent burial. The only way to handle the overflow of corpses, as Hauer discreetly agrees, would be mass graves filled with lime and other disinfectants.[3]

Martial law? Hauer is uneasy at the thought. He prays the police department, with 40,000 cops who are partially trained for city's biological terrorism, will be able to hold the line, but it is disingenuous to imagine that the National Guard and military will not move in as chaos breaks out.

Hauer is equally reluctant to talk about the biological war games they have run in the city, or on how the city may have to be sealed to imprison terrified people desperate to flee; or how public transport, including airports, will have to be closed down; or how anarchy might take over.

Is an act of biological terrorism in New York inevitable? Hauer's wattage dims, there is an uncharacteristic pause. 'Yes' – a firm response – 'within the next five to ten years.'

He draws by hand a death chart on the back of an envelope: Day One – nothing; Day Two, the deaths begin rising and reach a peak by Day Five. On Day Six, they begin to drop again. 'If we begin treatment early, we can reduce that spike,' he says, tapping the apex of the death curve with his pen, 'but we'll have to move damn fast.'

The worst case scenario? 'Smallpox – we would have to shut down all of New York's eighteen exits, the military would have to come in. It would be catastrophic – truly awful.'

At least Hauer is working on a plan, at least he is a true Plague Wars defender; at least he knows what he's talking about. 'The truth is,' he reflects, 'I need to know *within minutes* not within three days of any suspicious BW death. We're still not there yet.'[4]

Jerry Hauer understands only too well the reality of the terrorist threat to New York (site of the 1993 World Trade Centre bombing by Islamic militants). As the most densely populated area in the US, New York public health officials have reported that the city is 'uniquely vulnerable' to infectious diseases.[5]

Dr Marcelle Layton, New York City's chief of infectious disease control since 1994, summarized the city's situation by saying: 'Most of us ... have grave concerns about whether or not our current public health system has the capacity to respond. Are we prepared? No.'[6]

If the language is restrained, it is because of a logical desire to avoid current panic. But the truth is that even New York, the most wide-awake city in the world to a biological attack, does not have enough beds, vaccines or antibiotics in the huge quantities required. So the response to a BW attack relies on containment, that dreadful Vietnam War word – triage, and long-term 'consequence management' (including quarantine, decontamination, and medical treatment).

Under the direction of Hauer and his boss, Mayor Rudolph Giuliani, New York City is taking the best practical steps it can to handle a biological (or chemical) attack. Hauer is anxious to emphasize the positive side of his BW defence strategies:

1. A crisis management centre has been built near the twin towers of the World Trade Centre. (Prior to 1995, New York's crisis command centre would be set up as needed in an ordinary conference room on the top floor of police headquarters.)[7] With a biological terrorist attack very much in mind, the new facility's ventilation system has the unique feature of 'positive pressure', which means air from the inside flows out, thus keeping any airborne bacteria or viruses from contaminating the city's command, control, and communications centre. The centre has secure and direct access to the news media – for accurate and timely information distribution, a crucial function in a crisis. Plans for handling crisis reports have already been worked out with the senior management of the media outlets.[8]

2. Beginning in September 1997, about 4,000 members from New York's police, fire, and emergency units, and 1,500 doctors and nurses, have undergone military-style training in how to deal with biological attacks. These front-line public defenders are called 'first responders', and they have been issued special protective masks to cover their nose and mouth. The masks, unlike most, are not just slipped on the face with a single elastic band, but need to be custom fitted and contain HEPA ('High Efficiency Particulate Absorbing') filters.

3. Emergency hospitals have been assessed for their preparations and illness reporting procedures. In 1998, New York officials began to monitor patterns of emergency hospitalization so as to be in a position to detect an unusual occurrence. This tracking programme, known as 'Citywide Daily Health', is particularly important in determining a biological attack, because the grim truth is that one will simply not know it has happened until it is too late.

    William Nagle, Hauer's deputy director from 1996–98, has

explained that the 'first recognition' of an unacknowledged bio-logical-terror attack will come 'when the health system becomes taxed'. By then, once the symptoms have shown, there will be little 'window of opportunity' to respond to save lives.[9]

Nagle has described what will occur if an anthrax attack occurs. 'The first wave of people who start showing up at hospitals and doctors' offices will probably be treated for flu,' he said. 'They're going to be sent home, and told to get some rest and drink plenty of fluids. In 24 to 48 hours later, they're going to be back in the hospital. Then it's going to be in their lungs . . . and no amount of treatment is going to do them any good.'[10]

As a result, Hauer's office has already started a comprehensive daily surveillance plan of all NY City hospitals. Each morning at 7 a.m., Hauer receives a statistical report from the prior twenty-four hours of all hospital admissions and EMS runs. From those numbers, his office can compute the normal base-line figures for different times of the year. The data shows there are usually 3,000 EMS runs per day, so if that number suddenly spiked to 5,000, the red lights would flash in Hauer's office. His staff would then launch an immediate investigation seeking patterns and causes, and, if necessary, alert the hospitals to look for a possible biological attack.[11]

Senior FBI officials, who praise Hauer's prescience, still admit that the detection of a BW attack by doctors and nurses remains 'the weakest link' and 'the critical issue' in the armoury of the plague defenders. Most hospitals and physicians are not fully trained yet, warns Renaldo Campana, Chief of the FBI's Weapons of Mass Destruction Countermeasures Unit. He explains that an integrated intelligence system is needed for emergency room physicians to know the difference between anthrax or smallpox and a common virus or cold.[12]

Dr Marcelle Layton, who is responsible for the city's medical planning in the face of a major biological attack, has warned: '. . . Panic and terror could be expected, even among the health care providers themselves.'[13]

4. There is a doomsday scenario. To cope with the overflow of patients from the city's 59 emergency hospitals, Hauer's office has spotted large buildings and outdoor sites near each hospital which can hastily be converted into 'Alternate Care Facilities'. In other words, useful but very basic medical refuge centres. For the pyramids of bodies anticipated after a biological attack, Hauer has

plans to stack the dead into specially refrigerated warehouses – 'Alternate Morgue Facilities'.[14]

5. Biological sensors are in development – but efficient ones, that are affordable, are still several years away. When they are eventually deployed at vital spots around the city, there will inevitably be horrendous problems with false alarms, and the permutations for coping with them are infinite; but, even more seriously, what will Jerry Hauer's New York officials do once an *accurate* alarm goes off?

By then, depending on weather conditions, the wind will probably have carried the bio-threat past the sensor and it will already be too late to prevent the infection from spreading. And that's only the start of the nightmare. How will the responders know the extent of the spread of the contamination or where the deadly spores or germ clouds are heading? Where should emergency medical teams send assistance? How and when will they begin the business of sending out general warnings and what on earth will people be told to do? Those unfortunates under the lethal plume will have already left the scene and dispersed by the time city officials issue the information. Many people won't hear the news immediately anyway. What should people who hear the announcement do if they believe they have been infected? If putative victims make their way to a hospital, will they be further spreading the infection? The questions and dilemmas are endless.[15]

There are other pro-active steps that a city can take. Hauer authorized $1 million to purchase two mobile emergency trailers filled with containment vessels of different sizes that can isolate, analyse, and transport samples of dangerous germs or chemicals. (The vehicles also carry antidotes, medicines, and other useful equipment.) These systems are not perfect, but they are better than nothing.

Meanwhile, medical supplies and vaccines are being stockpiled at the city's hospitals, and the city is negotiating an agreement with drug companies to manufacture and distribute antibiotics quickly in the event of an attack – an emergency 'surge' capacity. The trouble is, it will never be enough, and it is impossible to store the tens (possibly hundreds) of millions of necessary doses in advance. It sounds like a logistical nightmare.

'If there's a biological attack, such as anthrax,' Nagle has said, 'it's going to require tons and tons of medication. . . . We're going to run out of medication very quickly.'[16]

The FBI's Renaldo Campana is more pessimistic. 'New York City and the pharmaceutical companies couldn't produce enough stuff to deal with an incident,' he has said. 'You know why? There just isn't enough there.'[17]

Campana adds: '. . . and God help us if it's smallpox.'

'There is some unhappiness with the pharmaceutical companies,' Hauer says heavily. 'It's a big financial problem for them, we will have to sort it out.'[18]

The good news about medicines is sparse. An inhalation anthrax attack can be effectively treated in the first twenty-four hours, before the onset of symptoms, by commonly available antibiotics. USAMRIID officials estimated in 1993 that about six million doses of Ciprofloxacin (Cipro), the preferred antibiotic, could be made available to New York within that first day window. In 1993, Cipro was manufactured by one pharmaceutical company, Miles, in Westhaven, Connecticut, which can produce an additional one million doses per day. Miles had a contract with the Defense Department to make such amounts in an emergency. Cipro treatment involved a 500-mg oral dose twice a day for thirty days, at about $1 per dose.[19] (If all 7.5 million New Yorkers needed to take two antibiotic pills per day for a month, it would require a total of 450 million doses!)

In the event of an anthrax attack, Hauer would do as the Israelis have done and look toward another antibiotic, Doxycycline, as his first line of defence, rather than the more expensive ciprofloxacin. Doxycycline is available in similar quantities from five drug companies based in New Jersey. Doxycycline requires a 100-mg dose twice a day for thirty days, but is considered only as an emergency substitute for Cipro because it does not provide as much protection and has some deleterious side effects.[20]

And if the anthrax were antibiotic resistant? Hauer shrugs and scowls.

He will not acknowledge any such thing as an insuperable problem. So Hauer, when faced with the worse case scenario, will simply put his head down and push, like a defensive tackle on a goal-line stand – close your eyes and give it everything you've got. The obstacles seem overwhelming: he needs enough medicine for a whole city; he needs to distribute the medicine; he needs a distribution method, and staff to do it; he needs to prevent primitive *sauve qui peut* panic.

So his office has developed two overlapping programmes, one called 'Canvass,' which will take medications to the people; the second, 'Points of Distribution,' which will require residents to make their way to centralized pick-up locations to collect the medicine.[21]

In order to distribute a five-day supply of Cipro (ten tablets) to all the city's 7.5 million residents within 48 hours at central pick-up sites, they will need an entire army of 45,000 personnel to dispense the 75 million tablets. Home delivery to everyone, using the Canvass program, would require another 100,000-to-200,000 distributors citywide. The plan doesn't even look good on paper; the practice of it, no matter how well intentioned, would, of course, be wholly chaotic.

Hauer also has studied the terrorist attacks on the World Trade Centre and Oklahoma City in great detail and knows that many injured victims seek medical assistance on their own – through their doctors and hospitals, many miles away from the crime scene. Given the unique circumstances of a biological attack, namely the inevitable delay between infection and symptoms, there is no doubt that the infection process will continue unwittingly. Once people in a city start coming down with flu-like symptoms (never mind dying), it will be too late to stop the effects of the disease.

'In the case of anthrax,' Hauer has noted, 'which produces flu-like symptoms, if an attack happened in winter, doctors would see an increase in ordinary-looking ailments and dismiss them as nothing out of the ordinary.'[22]

But the worst case scenario, as Jerry Hauer and his team know only too well, will happen in the metropolitan area's extensive underground system – the New York subway. Of all the city's soft spots, nothing is more vulnerable than the underbelly of its massive transit system, which includes 468 subway stations and 346 miles of tunnels and aqueducts.[23]

As far back as June 1966, the army's Special Operations Branch from Fort Detrick secretly carried out the most thorough simulations ever devised to gauge the vulnerability of the New York City subway system to a terrorist attack involving biological agents.[24] This series of tests over four days involved the three major north–south underground lines in mid-Manhattan, including Seventh Avenue and Eighth Avenue trains. A team of army scientists released a harmless anthrax simulant, BG

(*Bacillus subtilis variant Niger*) – both from inside the tunnels and from the street into the subway stations. Sampling devices were pre-positioned throughout the subway system – to the far ends – to measure the spread. In one test method, which carefully mimicked what an intelligent and dedicated terrorist might do, army scientists travelling on a train dropped light bulbs filled with the simulant onto the tracks. As the glass shattered and released the simulant, they measured just how the agent would spread through the dark tunnel.

The tests revealed that similar transportation systems anywhere in the world were wholly vulnerable to a well-executed attack. More seriously still, the trials proved that the entire city could be contaminated with small amounts of highly transmissible biological agents spread through the subway system.[25] The underground tunnels, with their strong wind flows and absence of natural light, are the perfect environment for the survival and distribution of most kinds of bacterial and viral agents.

Even after thirty years, most of the details of those military tests remain classified, because the results were quite appalling. They showed that a very small amount – a mere ten grams – of a dried BW agent (like anthrax or Tularaemia) could infect *several hundred thousand* passengers in a very short time. Some of the agent could be placed inside hand-sized, sealable containers – the army used standard light bulbs. As few as six of these breakable containers could be put on the rails at different points in the subway system. Once they were run over and broken, and the agent was released, passengers breathing normally would inhale more than ten infectious doses after just five minutes on a train or platform. Each time another train passed through the initial impact site, a secondary lethal plume would be spread. Eventually, the entire interconnected underground system would become contaminated.[26] These systems are deliberately not airtight and self-contained – they are constructed to allow ventilation to and from the street. Entrances to tube stations and pavement/street gratings allow the escape of airborne gases and germs. As the bacterial agents make their way from underground to overground, the infection spreads into the city.

'Suppose that somebody throws a little bit of anthrax into the subway,' asks Dr Donald Henderson, a former White House science adviser, rhetorically. 'When do we decide that it's safe to go back into that subway? The answer is, nobody knows.'[27]

A similar 'table top' exercise called Civex '93, held in Washington in

November 1993, postulated the consequences of several terrorist groups releasing anthrax spores inside New York's subway system. This domestic war game, which involved several federal agencies, including the FBI and the army, produced even more horrific conclusions. Within days, there was a mass exodus from New York City – the ultimate nightmare scenario.[28]

In order to try to counter some of these irremediable problems, a small group of scientists is trying to devise innovations to prevent the uncontrollable spread of biological agents through subway tunnels. One suggested method would install particle detectors that would emit an electrostatic-charged mist of hydrogen peroxide if contaminated particles were present. The charged mist would cling to the particles, increase their size, and prevent further spread. Another defensive technique would send ultra-violet light through the tunnels.[29] But huge budgets, and many further technical refinements, will be required to install such devices.

Sceptical BW experts, including Britain's David Kelly, doubt the efficacy of these countermeasures.[30] They believe false alarms will plague the system and the measures will never work on the sheer scale of the decontamination required. At the moment, they argue, the only safe way would be the hard way – to spray every inch of the tunnels and stations manually, with formaldehyde (or newly developed foams); time consuming, very, very expensive, but almost guaranteed.[31]

Hauer also has been poring over the findings from one other BW war game scenario, picking whatever crumbs of comfort he can from a staged disaster inside a typical Manhattan office building. On Wednesday, 15 April 1998, more than fifty scientists, government officials, and state and local emergency preparedness teams met in secret on the outskirts of Washington, D.C. to enact this exercise.

According to the script, some 1,000 people in a fifteen-storey midtown building were exposed to a highly infectious germ, Tularaemia, disseminated through the unfiltered air ducts. The aerosolized bacteria spread quickly throughout the building, which, like most modern office structures, had sealed windows. Within fifteen minutes, virtually the entire building was infected.[32]

Two days later, eighty people were ill with fever, aches, and pneumonia-like symptoms. Some stayed home the next day; others called their doctors. By the weekend, 450 more were unwell; some went to hospital emergency rooms. By Sunday, another 550 went down with the same symptoms and only then did alarm spread through New York's medical community.

As the exercise unfolded, the players realized just how unprepared they were for such an event in New York City, despite the dedicated training of police officers, firemen, emergency medical teams, and other first responders who would be called upon to cope with a germ attack. By the time doctors diagnosed the mysterious illness as Tularaemia and began prescribing the correct antibiotics, the epidemic had already run its course. Even before the defence had begun, the offence had ended in victory. The good news was that a bacterial agent had been selected with a 35 per cent mortality rate, so only a third of the 1,080 people who fell ill actually died.

'The city's detectives were really good; so were the firemen, no kidding,' said a federal official who attended the meeting. 'The mayor's office was extremely impressive, very professional. They were great at controlling crowds and cordoning off areas; they did all the right things. But still we got the maximum amount of lethality from the maximum number of infections from the Tularaemia terrorist attack. The scenario utterly defeated them.'[33]

To assess another worrisome possibility, Hauer studied a different war game. In this one, a small boat, manned by biological terrorists, makes the 20-mile trip from Battery Park (the southern tip of Manhattan) to City Island (the entrance to Long Island Sound) in about three hours at six knots. The weather is good and a light wind (8 mph) is blowing from the southeast. Using this simple scenario, the terrorists launch their attack. They are equipped with a cheap aerosol disperser filled with an anthrax strain containing 10^9 spores/ml and producing aerosol at the rate of about 500 ml/min. They are carrying a total of 90 litres (24 gallons) of the agent.

Hauer read the mathematics of this scenario with increasing gloom. If only half the target population were actually exposed; and if only half of those developed pulmonary anthrax; and if only half the cases result in deaths (these are all conservative assumptions), then the final death toll in the city he must protect would be well over half a million.[34]

*

It was Jerry Hauer's high-voltage approach that directly led to President Clinton's heightened awareness of the threat of biological terrorism. There'd been the Aum affair in Tokyo, the Iraqi wake-up call, hearings led by Senator Sam Nunn, some scary headlines and TV news stories, but somehow the President was still not juiced up about the issue. Hauer then read Richard Preston's gripping novel, *The Cobra Event*, which tells the realistic, though fictional, story of an attempted attack on New York by a lone, technically adept terrorist who carries a lethal, genetically engineered cocktail of smallpox and cold viruses into the Manhattan subway.

Hauer passed the novel to a friend, who passed it to a friend, who passed it to Defense Secretary William Cohen, who passed it to the President of the United States, who, in the words of Cohen, 'Then took this book and biological warfare very seriously indeed. It's fair to say that book did the trick.'[35]

Ironically, everything that Clinton had previously learned about biological terrorism from official sources did not have as much effect on him as the Preston novel. The book found a curious resonance within Clinton, which lead to a profound interest and concern about the threat. Indeed, Clinton was so alarmed by what he read that he asked US intelligence experts to assess the book's credibility. (He even urged other senior officials and then-House Speaker Newt Gingrich to read it.)[36]

At about the same time, in March 1998, the White House held its own top-secret war game to play out what would happen if terrorists struck along the Mexican-American border with a genetically engineered virus. They chose a chimera of smallpox and Marburg – in deference to Ken Alibek's warning that Russian scientists were indeed researching such a viral mixture. Forty federal officials from more than a dozen agencies met secretly in a room across the street from the White House to determine what would happen if biological terrorists used such a virus in several southwest states and California.[37] The answers were ugly.

Because this was a chimera virus, and could not be easily identified, thousands of victims fell ill, and began to die within days. The speed and lethality of a combined smallpox/Marburg virus do not bear thinking about. Predictably millions of people panicked, and extensive shortcomings were revealed in pre-planning, logistics, legal authority, and medical care. Federal quarantine laws were too outdated to address the demands;

few jurisdictions had regulations for how to care for those infected patients who *were* isolated. Arguments broke out between state and Federal officials, as no one seemed to be in charge and turf wars became vicious.

As if that was not enough to spoil the entire day, the domestic disaster rapidly escalated into an international crisis as the epidemic threatened to spread into Mexico. The Mexican government even threatened defensive military measures to prevent Americans from fleeing the epidemic by heading south. It is no great surprise that full details of this war game remain very tightly classified.

'The thing that really worried the President,' recalls Hauer, 'was the problem of genetically engineered biological and viral agents, and the sheer bang per buck value of biological terrorism. I talked to him at some length about this and about the problems that will occur with civil unrest, the problems that Federal government would have to face and the huge problems of demands on medical facilities, both human and physical.'[38]

Faced with the enormity of the federal war-game conclusions and the Preston scenario, President Clinton became sufficiently involved in the whole issue of biological terrorism to call a special White House meeting, which Hauer attended, on 10 April 1998. The President invited a group of seven respected bio-medical experts for a briefing to explore new medical and policy ideas that might address and confront the bio-terrorism problems. The location for this unprecedented session was the Truman Room, where Cabinet meetings are held. Those present agree the President demonstrated a deep engagement with the issues, and for ninety minutes the visitors answered his well-focused and pertinent questions about the threat.[39] (To Clinton's credit, he had been awake most of the night before discussing the final peace-making settlement concerning Northern Ireland.)

The Chief Executive was flanked by an impressive array of very senior officials who were responsible for biological terrorism issues. They included his National Security Council staff, Attorney General Janet Reno, Secretary of Defense William Cohen, Secretary of Health Donna Shalala, CIA Director George Tenet, and the Vice Chairman of the Joint Chiefs of Staff, General Joseph Ralston. These heavyweights sat on the President's side of the table. The invited delegation, which sat on the other side of the table, included Jerry Hauer; Dr Frank Young, the

outspoken former head of the federal Office of Emergency Planning; Dr
Lucille Shapiro, a leading genetics professor and chairman of the biology
department at Stanford University; Dr Barbara Rosenberg, the director
of biological arms-control projects at the Federation of American Scientists; Dr Thomas Monath, currently a vice-president of vaccine developer,
OraVax, of Cambridge, Massachusetts, who had earlier served as a top
virologist at USAMRIID at Fort Detrick; and Dr J. Craig Venter,
president of the Institute for Genomic Research, a non-profit biotechnology group in Rockville, Maryland, and a pioneer of genetic engineering who had decoded the smallpox virus and other microbes.

Finally, the most world-renowned member of the visiting group was
the balding, bearded, and bespectacled seventy-two-year-old Dr Joshua
Lederberg, president emeritus of Rockefeller University. Lederberg
received the Nobel Prize for medicine in 1958, at the age of thirty-three,
for his discoveries concerning genetics of bacteria. His special interest is
the study of the emerging pathogens – infectious diseases of the future,
such as new strains of flu for which there is currently no defence.[40]

Lederberg has quietly advised the Pentagon and CIA on biological
warfare issues for many years. A cautious man, usually reluctant to
express alarmist views, he had broken free of habit a few months earlier
when, at a college lecture, he had warned: '[Biological] terrorism is
moving away from the theatre and moving to the aggressive killing of
massive amounts of people.' He noted that biological agents have not yet
become a standard weapon in the terrorist arsenal. But he warned of
imminent change, adding with indisputable logic: 'The hijacking of
airplanes never happened until the first one.'[41]

Lederberg has also conceded that it will be impossible to be warned
about a biological terror attack in advance. 'The cat is out of the bag,'
Lederberg has said. 'It's the thought of this kind of work going on *sub
rosa* that is really the black cloud now hanging over us.'[42]

As the meeting ended, Clinton asked for advice on what the White
House should do to detect and deter the consequences of a terrorist
biological attack, with a budget of what it would cost. 'He left no doubt
that he intended to act on it right away,' recalls one of the guests.[43]

On 6 May, the panel delivered its confidential, sixteen-page, follow-
up document to the President. The members urged him to increase
federal funding for medical research, strengthen the public-health
response to bio-terrorism, streamline the federal crisis management

system, adopt new verification measures for enforcing the BWC, and financially help the unemployed BW scientists in Russia who might be tempted to offer their skills to terrorists or 'rogue states'.[44]

Most importantly, the report called for the US to develop the capacity to accelerate production of antidotes, antibiotics, and vaccines to counter the most common BW agents. The group cited five agents which posed the greatest threat – anthrax, smallpox, Plague, Tularaemia, and botulinum toxin. An increased drug and vaccine stockpile, they recommended, should include up to 40 million doses against smallpox. Such a stockpile, the report said, could help 'reduce the death and illness 10 to 100 fold'. The total cost over five years was estimated at $420 million.[45]

Since it would be hugely expensive (literally billions of dollars) and quite impractical for every city and town to maintain an adequate supply of vaccines and medicines, the experts proposed a 'national stockpile' that could be quickly dispatched to a crisis zone. A further problem needed addressing – stockpiles of vaccines don't last for ever. For example, a 1998 audit of the US stockpile of 15.8 million doses of smallpox vaccine found that only 4.9 million were still fit for human use.[46] And even effective vaccines do not invariably provide a guaranteed defence, especially against something new that has been biologically engineered.

To fund the plans suggested at the April meeting, President Clinton asked Congress one month later to add $294 million to federal counter-terrorism spending in 1999, a near 30 per cent increase in the previous $1 billion-a-year financing. The increase was the largest single supplement to the federal budget ever requested specifically to bolster civilian and military defences against biological (and chemical) terrorism.[47]

Hauer left the White House pleased that a new, energized federal approach had been launched against the problem of biological terrorism. However, he, and especially the FBI, continued to worry about profiling the kind of persona who would be the aggressor.

There is a new breed of terrorist today, motivated less by political ideology than ferocious ethnic and religious hatreds or by a conviction of the coming apocalypse for which anybody, or anything, or any city can be held responsible. The Japanese Aum sect was the perfect example, and Hauer and FBI officials have studied and restudied their history. This shift in motivations is significant because terrorists with a political agenda, however extreme, have tended not to use weapons of mass destruction, because it would alienate their political constituencies or political sponsors. But the so-called Apocalyptic Sects have no constituency other than their equally deranged colleagues, therefore, even less sense of 'responsibility'. If the world is coming to an end anyway, what damage is done by taking a city or two out a little earlier? Other groups who might use biological warfare would be secular and would include those who have a passionate hatred of all federal institutions. This is a new and disturbing movement developing in America's heartland and far Western states; it is epitomized by the vicious 1995 bombing in Oklahoma City of a government building in which 168 people were killed.

According to Renaldo Campana, chief of the FBI's Weapons of Mass Destruction Countermeasures Unit, the Bureau sees the biggest terrorist threat as the 'lone unstable individual'.[48] In the past, these oddballs were restricted in the damage they could cause. Nuclear and chemical weapons are simply too large and impractical for one man to employ, but biological weaponry is now down to the size of a can of hairspray. These violent, fanatical loners are the most unpredictable. FBI agents fear that a terrorist with technical proficiencies like the Unabomber, Theodore Kaczynski, will try to send their enemies packages or letter bombs armed with anthrax instead of explosives. The truth is that just one lone person with an aerosol can and a few grams of anthrax has the potential to infect an entire skyscraper. As Hauer knows only too well, the threats and hoaxes have already started – against abortion clinics, government agencies, and even President Clinton. FBI officials also concede it will be very difficult, if not impossible, to detect a skilled biological criminal cum terrorist.

The only good news is that, to date, with the exception of the Japanese Aum group, the number of serious, attempted, BW terrorist attacks is still quite small.[49] But no one believes it will stay like that.

As a pre-emptive defensive measure, military units have now been assigned to help protect New York (and other cities) against a chemical or biological attack by well-organized terrorists. Recently, the Pentagon set up the Chemical/Biological Rapid Response Team (C/B-RRT). This new group, based on the capabilities of the army's long-standing response team, the Technical Escort Unit, will rush to the assistance of local and state officials to detect, neutralize, contain, dismantle, and dispose of biological (or chemical) materials. The team includes elements from the army's TEU, the Army 52nd Ordnance Group, USAMRIID, US Navy Medical Research Lab, and US Naval Research Lab.

The goal of this alphabet-soup of military units is to deploy anywhere in the US within four hours (though eight hours is more realistic for some distant or inaccessible locations). It includes support staff with expertise for ordnance disposal, lab analysis, and medical advice.

Although the appearance of the army rumbling through the narrow thoroughfares of New York may give some comfort, unfortunately this second wave of federal responders would arrive on the scene hours after any incident begins. Too late. The chief of the FBI's countermeasures unit, Renaldo Campana, concedes that the local first responders will likely be on their own for 'up to twelve hours' before 'the FBI and federal family . . . come onto the scene'.[50]

Complementing the C/B-RRT, the Marine Corps has set up the Chemical Biological Incident Response Force (CBIRF), a specially trained 375-person team based in Camp Lejeune, North Carolina. Formed in July 1995, CBIRF uses the most advanced protective gear, high-tech equipment, computer programs, and medical techniques to assist local responders who are operating inside a 'hot zone'. All of CBIRF's personnel are immunized against the main anticipated BW agents and the Force is dedicated to sending a 120-person rapid response team anywhere in the US. But once again, they will arrive *post hoc*.

CBIRF's role at the scene of an attack would first focus on sizing up several crucial tactical factors. What is the agent? – find and analyse. How many people are still at risk? – work out and protect. The Recon team also maps the spread of the bacterial plumes and uses computers and weather data to predict the down-wind hazard.

How many and what kind of casualties exist (in both biological and chemical incidents)? A Medical team locates them, and then performs casualty triage, advanced life-saving support, and patient evacuation. Victims are prioritized into three groups, depending on their medical condition – what the Marines somewhat brutally call 'walkers, floppers and goners'. The victims are tagged and bar-coded, with their personal information entered into a computer – to speed hospital care and ensure their whereabouts can be tracked for worried families. Meanwhile, a Security team isolates and evacuates the site, handles crowd control, and extracts hostages (if necessary). The Decontamination team takes charge of disinfecting victims, personnel, and equipment. A Command team manages the Marine operations and provides satellite communications systems, which can connect by computer and telephone to the Pentagon and top experts across the country for on-going advice.

CBIRF was deployed for the first time at the 1996 Summer Olympics in Atlanta, then in January 1997 at President Clinton's second inauguration in Washington, and then at the June 1997 G-7 summit of world leaders in Denver. Not all of the leaders who attended the meeting may have known it, but military precautions had been taken to protect them from a possible BW attack.[51]

All these precautions are fine, of course, when dealing with a pre-announced terrorist threat, or a chemical attack (where visible effects are immediate), or as an act of sensible prophylaxis. But that's not how the big biological terrorist attack will happen. It will come by stealth, as a complete surprise, and may remain undetected for days in a city like New York. By then, Hauer may need only the military's bulldozers – for digging grave pits.

Even the commander of CBIRF, Lieutenant Colonel Arthur Corbett, has admitted that his special Marine unit has mainly symbolic value. Employing one of the military's best-engineered euphemisms, Corbett has said: 'It's called perception management, we have to show there is a cavalry, and America is not impotent in the face of a biological terrorist threat. But we're no panacea. There has to be a broader effort.'[52]

So could he actually cope with a serious BW attack? 'It would,' admits Corbett, in another tortuous evasion, 'be a stretch.'[53]

If the cavalry can mainly show up to bury the dead, what are the chances for the brave 'first responders'? What is the ability of medical personnel to perform their duties for several hours, hold the fort, and still survive in a lethal hot zone? In studies of simulated biological warfare incidents, between 4 and 10 per cent of the responders were rendered useless because of psychological symptoms (predominantly claustrophobia, anxiety, or panic).[54]

So, after studying the Aum attack, the National Security Council asked the US Public Health Service to devise a national plan to address the medical consequences of a biological, nerve gas, chemical, or accidental event. As a key component of the plan, the Public Health Service, a part of the Department of Health and Human Services, proposed another acronymic nightmare, MMSTs (Metro Medical Strike Teams), for the major cities, like New York, that were at highest risk. The idea was to have a highly trained, fully equipped, state-of-the-art group of about forty experts (with two back-up teams on stand-by) from a variety of medical disciplines – doctors, nurses, paramedics, and emergency responders. During a verified crisis, this expert team would quickly self-deploy from around the metropolitan region, rather like a volunteer fire department responds to a fire alarm. These specialists would arrive at the scene as soon as possible to co-ordinate and supplement the earliest life-saving medical treatments. The teams carry specialized equipment to confront a biological warfare attack: test kits for quick identification of the agents used; protective suits; supplies of antidotes; decontamination systems; and communications equipment.[55]

Starting in 1997, medical strike teams were to be established in twenty-seven major metropolitan areas to direct emergency responses to a biological (or chemical) attack. The first cities included Washington, New York, Chicago, Los Angeles, San Francisco, Boston, Kansas City, and Denver. The goal now is to have strike teams in the country's 100 largest cities within five years.[56]

Back inside Hauer's crowded and chaotic office, as the phones ring and lights flash and he still generates ever more energy, there is a distinct sense that this is where Americans are at their can-do best in confronting future shock, such as the prospect of biological terrorism. Hauer's last frenetic act is to leap to a locked cupboard and produce two biological sensors, now available to his city in large numbers. One is the size and shape of an airline's pat of butter; the other looks like a large, broad fingernail. They are not, it transpires, for individual use, but for environmental sampling; and yes, it's true, they have a twenty-minute time delay and cover only six known biological agents, but it's all better than nothing, and it's a prime example of positive thinking. The confidence alone is infectious.

Postcript

It is difficult to feel confident about any similar tactics in London. The United Kingdom, and London in particular, is as vulnerable to a biological attack by terrorists as is New York, but London doesn't have a Hauer, and whatever the big plan may be it remains largely obscured. In

Britain, MI5, the Security Service, has primary responsibility for monitoring the threat of all types of terrorism. There is none of the openness of New York here, rather the inevitable shroud of secrecy blankets the facts.

In November 1995, Britain's Home Office did hold a major BW war game in Manchester at the Greater Manchester police training school. The then-Home Secretary Michael Howard played an active part in the exercise, which was code-named 'Firestorm' and involved a terrorist attack using anthrax. As the plume was driven by the wind, motorways were closed down, the airport was shut, and the City Council was relocated to a place of safety. Emergency planners soon found themselves overwhelmed by information. Rioting broke out at nearby Strangeways prison. The exercise ended with an argument between police and the local authorities over whether to evacuate 200,000 people from Manchester. There was considerable criticism of police handling of the media (one senior officer appeared on screen, sweating profusely, to advise people not to panic).

Co-ordination was handled by the Home Office through COBRA, the government's emergency response headquarters in Downing Street. Problems quickly spread to France, where the authorities were under pressure to close the channel tunnel. American officials offered to send in a team to help.

The conclusions of Firestorm have remained, wisely perhaps, a secret. It was not regarded as a successful exercise in terms of demonstrating a capable defence against a biological attack by terrorists.[57]

Local authorities throughout the UK have their own emergency planning officers, but BW seems to be integrated with chemical, nuclear, and conventional terrorism – the one thing Jerry Hauer believes should not happen. A mixed group of British officials from the Home Office, police forces, Porton Down, and the security services did visit Tokyo after the Aum attacks, but Britain has no plans for the mass production of vaccines or antibiotics.[58]

The third edition of the official Home Office publication 'Dealing with Disaster' does not refer to biological warfare.

CHAPTER THIRTY-FOUR

The Future

'Genetic engineering for biological agents? There'd be no protection.
These are the weapons of the future and the future is coming closer
and closer.'

William Cohen, US Secretary of Defense, 1998[1]

In the autumn of 1998, the Western press reported that the Israelis were
developing a so-called ethnic bullet, a genetically engineered biological
weapon that would miraculously target only Arabs, and not Jews.[2]

The story was a follow-up to an intriguing account first published in
London by the reputable *Foreign Report* two years earlier. That report
quoted the former head of Sweden's Defence Research Establishment,
General Bo Rybeck, as saying that genetic weapons might be around the
corner.[3]

Rybeck speculated that influenza or diphtheria could be designed to
affect only blacks, that a designer toxin could be aimed at Serbs, or that
people with blue eyes might be given Alzheimer's disease. It was indeed
speculative and provocative stuff, but from an authoritative source.

In October 1998, *Foreign Report* followed through with an intriguing
ethnic bullet story – which was then widely publicized.[4] Quoting from
unconfirmed South African sources, the magazine alleged that the 'ethnic
bullet' had originally been a South African concept to deal with blacks
during the apartheid era.[5] Cooperation between South African and Israeli
scientists was close during that period, and the article suggested that the
Israelis had taken over the project after the South Africans terminated it
in 1993.

One of the Israeli conclusions was that there was a genetic difference between Arabs (particularly Iraqis) and both Ashkenazi (East European) Jews and Sephardim (Jews of Arabic origin). The Israeli scientists had also supposedly identified an illness that could be transmitted through Baghdad's water supply and affect only Iraqi Arabs.

A senior aide to then-Israeli Prime Minister Benjamin Netanyahu rejected the allegations, saying news reports proved there was no limit to human gullibility. Asked by the Associated Press if he was denying the story, the aide added, somewhat elliptically: 'This is the kind of story that does not deserve a denial.'[6]

The real truth behind all the politically motivated speculation is less dramatic, but, in its own way, far more troubling. The world has some twenty years, experts predict, before genetic engineering will effectively make biological warfare invulnerable to biological defence.

Ken Alibek, who helped run the secret Soviet BW programme, has warned that the Russians are trying to create a 'chimera virus', an horrendous 'marriage' of Marburg and Ebola, which would combine the speed of infection of one with the lethality of the other.

Science is now moving ahead so quickly and inexorably that there will be no natural or manufactured defence against a plague war, other than a pre-emptive strike. It's as brutal as that.

There are at least four new horizons for work on bacterial and viral agents, which, most microbiologists believe, will be scientifically attainable before the year 2020.

One accomplishment will be the ability to take benign micro-organisms and splice a foreign gene into them, so that they become genetically altered – allowing the creation of new, exotic, and unpredictable biological and viral agents. Leading from this achievement will be the ability to make lethal bacteria antibiotic resistant – hence untreatable in humans once they have become infected. In addition, some micro-organisms will be genetically engineered in such a way as to make them more stable in an aerosol dispenser – the ultimate BW weapon. And finally, it will be possible to so alter some micro-organisms that they will become immunologically different, so that the human body will not even recognize their presence until it is too late for effective treatment.

All this science fiction will be science fact within two decades.

A little further on in the future, science will be able to manufacture a novel micro-organism which will be ethnically specific when used as a weapon.[7] It is a fact that different races have different genes which, theoretically, can be targeted by hostile bacteria, toxins, or viruses. In South Africa, there were attempts (which failed) to manufacture all three types of these agents, aimed specifically at the black majority.

The successful creation of an ethnic biological weapon will depend on three major factors. Firstly, the completion of the Human Genome Project – the mapping of all human genes – which will be sequenced within the next five years. Secondly, the mapping of the specific differences between races, which is something that can effectively be done now. Lastly, the use of gene therapy to make the biological weapon. This step will involve using a viral or physical vector to insert foreign DNA into the victim's DNA, something that is still twenty or so years off. But the main point is that all three steps can and will be achieved. There is no scientific implausibility about this future, no scientific breakthrough is needed. Just hard work.

No one should underestimate the speed of development that the ancient science of biotechnology is now undergoing. Human beings have been at it since wine was first produced, foods were preserved, and plants were domesticated and selected for their biggest and best crops. By 1953, biotechnology took the step into genetics, when the structure of DNA (deoxyribonucleic acid), the key genetic material of all cells, was first described.

Since then, an explosion has occurred in the field of molecular genetics and modern biotechnology. By 1973, microbiologists were able to remove a gene from the DNA of one type of cell and splice into the DNA of another type of cell. This procedure has come to be known as recombinant DNA technology, the posh expression for genetic engineering.[8]

US Secretary of Defence William Cohen has recently voiced his deep concern about ethnic weapons. He called them agents that could be 'designed to take out just certain types of people, depending on their genetic make-up'. He insisted that the science community is 'very close' to being able to manufacture such weapons.[9]

Dr Vivienne Nathanson, the head of science and ethics at the British Medical Association, shares the concern about these ethnically specific genetic weapons. 'One could imagine in Rwanda,' she says, 'a weapon which targeted one of the two tribal groups, the Tutsi and Hutu. While these weapons do not exist, so far as we know, it is not very far away scientifically. The effects of a genetic weapon also could be delayed so that it only affects the next generation.'

For example, it could be possible to design an agent to create sterility (something the Nationalist apartheid regime in South Africa worked on in the 1980s) or pass on a lethal hereditary defect. 'What makes it really frightening,' she says, 'is that it could be done in ways that are much more insidious and less obvious.'[10]

And humans need not be the only direct victims of the genetically engineered biological weapons of the future. A further possibility, and one already entertained by Iraq, is crop warfare: a country would engineer a strain of plants resistant to a pathogen, such as wheat rust, while, at the same time, it introduces the pathogen into another country and damages their economy.[11]

There are already effective ways in which to protect deployed BW agents. Dr Malcolm Dando, the distinguished biologist and Professor of International Security at the Department of Peace Studies at the University of Bradford, England, talks of microencapsulation, a process whereby BW agents can be coated and protected against a variety of harmful outside factors, particularly their natural enemies light and heat. This process also allows agents to survive longer and to be inhaled more easily, which increases the likelihood of infection and death. Currently, the detection and identification of microencapsulated BW agents is more difficult than for non-encapsulated materials.[12] (The Soviets crossed this scientific threshold years ago and were able to 'spray' their offensive bacterial and viral agents that were resistant to the sun's rays.)

In fact, microencapsulation can already be tailored for the mission. For example, you can apply one coating for added protection from heat, and then another one for the effects of sunlight. A germ would need both coatings if it were packed inside a missile warhead and then had to survive explosive decompression at its target, together with sudden exposure to sunlight.

Even a naturally resistant, spore-forming bacterium like anthrax can be modified by genetic engineering, so that the spore is less hostile to the environment. In this way, it is possible to create a variety of anthrax or other biological agents that is highly virulent, but has a very short life-span. That would be perfect for an attacker who wants his enemy infected as quickly as possible, but also needs to occupy a decontaminated battleground soon afterwards. Gruinard Island was used by Britain for anthrax tests during World War II and remained contaminated for half a century. The new 'smart' anthrax spores would perish very quickly and eliminate that lingering problem.

Professor Steve Jones, Professor of Genetics at University College London, remains sceptical that a genetically engineered biological weapon will see the light of day for another decade. 'It will require an enormous amount of work,' he explains. Dr Dando agrees that there is 'much grinding work, a long slog' before that barrier is crashed.

But neither expert believes it will not happen.

To the contrary, Dr Dando presumes it to be inevitable. 'It will occur,' he says, 'unless we manage to negotiate a strong verification protocol into the existing BWC [Biological Weapons Convention]. If we fail to do that, I have a very real concern about what will happen over the next ten to fifteen years.'[13]

The grim truth is that the world does now face the very real prospect of an outbreak of plague wars either locally or internationally within our lifetime. That prospect is not some ill-focused nightmare from which we will awake sweating, but safe; nor can we seriously delude ourselves into believing that 'something will happen, it always does'.

The BW clock is ticking relentlessly towards midnight.

But are we listening?

CHAPTER THIRTY-FIVE

Geneva

An Ad Hoc Group of the States Parties to the Biological Weapons Convention have spent the last five years in Geneva attempting to draw up a legally binding Protocol to strengthen confidence in compliance with the Convention. This Protocol would introduce the much-missed verification regime and is likely to comprise mandatory declarations of the most relevant activities. It would also include on-site challenge inspections to ensure that such declarations are truthful and complete. Such a Protocol would not end a biological warfare arms race, but it *could* deter it or slow it down. The truth is that without real political commitment a state that wishes to cheat on its biological warfare programmes can do so with impunity. (One need only examine the case of Iraq.) Despite five years of talks, the optimists believe that 1998 saw an increasing tempo in the negotiations, with clear signs of political engagement – suggesting a new will to complete the Protocol. There is now a sixth draft on the table, and the Ad Hoc Group will meet five times for a total of sixteen weeks in 1999. The prayer is for a Protocol to be agreed upon before the millennium; however, there are international timetables – involving such events as presidential elections in Russia and the US – which could see a further delay of up to a decade.

The BWC

The Convention on the Prohibition of the Development, Production and Stockpiling of Bacteriological (Biological) and Toxin Weapons and on their Destruction (the BWC) of 1972 prohibits the development, production, stockpiling or acquisition of microbial or other biological agents, or toxins of types and in quantities that have no justification for prophylactic, protective or other peaceful purposes. Western counter-proliferation agencies generally recognize a core list of 19 bacteria; 43 viruses; 14 toxins; and 4 rickettsiae as potential threats. In addition, those genetically modified micro-organisms which contain nucleic acid sequences associated with pathogenicity are derived from organisms on the core list. The essential definitions and differences between the various groups are as follows:

1. Bacteria

Bacteria are single cell, independent, and living organisms. They vary in shape and size from spherical cells (cocci) – with a diameter of 0.5–1.0 micrometres (1/1000 mm), to long, rod-shaped organisms (bacilli) – which may be from 1–5 micrometres. The rigid cell wall of the bacterial cell will determine the shape. The interior of the cell contains DNA, cytoplasm, and the cell membrane that the bacterium needs to live. Under special circumstances, some bacteria can transform into spores, which are a dormant form of bacteria. Like the seeds of plants, spores can germinate under the right conditions. Bacteria can cause disease in humans either by invading the tissues or by producing toxins, and some can do both.

2. Viruses

Viruses are sub-microscopic infective agents composed of DNA or RNA that require living cells in order to replicate. They are much smaller than bacteria and vary in size from 0.02 to 0.2 micrometres (1/1000 mm). Unlike bacteria, they lack a system for their own metabolism and have to live in cells in order to survive and to multiply. In that sense, they are dependent and not self-contained like bacteria. These host cells can be from humans, animals, plants, or bacteria, but each type of virus requires a specific type of host cell for its support system. Host cells can be created in laboratory situations that deal with specific viruses, but viruses can also be cultivated by allowing them to grow on membranes from fertilized eggs. The virus, however, normally changes the host cell to such an extent that the cell dies.

3. Toxins

Toxins are any toxic (poisonous) substances of natural origin produced by animal, plant, or microbe. They tend not to produce secondary or person-to-person exposures. Some toxins are more toxic when delivered by aerosol. Others can be delivered orally or through blood-to-blood contagion. Some toxins, like botulinum toxins, are less toxic when delivered via aerosol. Some toxins are limited in their potential as BW agents by their low toxicity, while others, like saxitoxin, are highly toxic, but can only be produced in tiny quantities. Several toxins cause major illness, but stop short of causing death – and it is these poisons that are often used as BW incapacitating agents.

4. Rickettsiae

Rickettsiae fall between bacteria and viruses. They are large, complex, intracellular parasites found in vertebrates, including man, which cause a variety of diseases, including typhus and Rocky Mountain Spotted Fever.

Description of BW Agents

Bacteria

Anthrax (*Bacillus anthracis*)

Bacillus anthracis, the bacterium that causes the notorious anthrax, is invariably the biological agent of choice for tactical and strategic attacks. Cattle, sheep, horses, and other hoofed animals host the microscopic, rod-shaped bacteria. Anthrax lends itself superbly to the purposeful dissemination of spores. Transmission is made through scratches or abrasions of the skin, wounds, inhalation, eating insufficiently cooked infected food, or by flies. Inhalation anthrax, the favoured biological agent due to its high mortality and virulence, begins after an incubation period of one-to-six days, dependent upon the dose. The onset of illness is gradual. Fever, malaise, and fatigue come first, sometimes together with a cough and mild chest discomfort. These initial symptoms are followed by a short period of improvement (hours to two to three days), followed by a sudden reversal and the abrupt development of severe respiratory distress – with shortness of breath and the obstruction of the upper airways which can literally turn the patient blue. Death usually follows quickly. Mortality is very nearly 100 per cent. Gastrointestinal anthrax (which would make an inefficient BW agent) results from eating infected meat and has a 50 per cent mortality rate. Anthrax can be treated with antibiotics, but almost all cases of inhalation anthrax are fatal if treatment begins after patients are symptomatic.

PLAGUE WARS

Cholera

Cholera, the scourge of third-world nations through the ages, is caused by the bacterial agent *Vibrio cholerae*, which does not spread easily from human to human. To be effective as a BW agent, major drinking water or food supplies would have to be contaminated. This dispersal is easy to achieve, and, once effected, cholera spreads rapidly, contaminating entire drinking water systems. It is an ideal biological warfare agent for 'disguised' use, as the disease is often indigenous and an outbreak can be explained as an 'act of God'. The onset of the disease is very sudden after an incubation period that lasts 12–72 hours, dependent upon the dose the victim has received. The first symptoms are intestinal cramping and painless diarrhoea, followed by vomiting, malaise, and headache. The patient suffers severe loss of body fluids. In untreated cases, mortality can range as high as 50–80 per cent. The disease can be treated with rehydration therapy and antibiotics.

Plague (*Yersinia pestis*)

Yersinia pestis is the most infamous bacterial agent of history – bubonic plague – which has ravaged mankind for centuries and killed on a vast scale. Plague in man can appear as either bubonic or pneumonic. Fleas which live on rodents pass *Yersinia pestis* onto humans, who then suffer from the bubonic form, which is normally seen in the lymph nodes of the legs, the most commonly 'flea-bitten' part of the human body. It was this form of the disease that wiped out populations during great pandemics in past centuries. Bubonic plague is also an ideal BW agent. The incubation period is two to ten days and the onset is acute. The victim suffers from malaise, high fever, and tenderness in the lymph nodes, liver and spleen. Skin lesions and then pustules may appear, as well as large black patches, which gave the disease its sobriquet – the 'Black Death'. The pneumonic form is an infection of the lungs due to the inhalation of the organisms (normally from the breath of an infected person). After an incubation of two to three days, the onset of the disease is acute. The victim suffers from malaise, high fever, chills, headache, aching muscles, and a cough that produces bloody sputum. Pneumonia then progresses rapidly, and the patient's respiratory functions begin to collapse. Death results from respiratory failure and circulatory collapse. In man, the mortality rate of untreated bubonic plague is approximately 50 per cent, whereas in pneumonic plague the mortality rate is nearly 100 per cent if untreated. Plague can be treated with antibiotics, although mortality rates remain high, particularly with pneumonic plague. Pneumonic plague makes the most efficient BW weapon and it can be disseminated in aerosol form.

Tularaemia

Tularaemia is caused by the highly infective bacterium *Francisella tularensis*. First identified in 1911 in Tulare County, California, it is a disease that commonly affects wild rabbits, squirrels, and mice. Humans acquire the disease under natural conditions by entry through abrasions in the skin or mucous membranes of blood or tissue fluids from infected animals, or bites from infected deerflies, mosquitoes, or ticks. Less commonly, inhalation of contaminated dusts or ingestion of contaminated foods or water may produce clinical disease. The bacteria is a highly potent BW agent as it resists freezing (and temperatures below freezing) and can also remain viable for weeks in water, soil, carcasses, and hides. It is easily aerosolized, and, used in this way, inhalation causes typhoidal Tularaemia, which often results in the victim also contracting pneumonia. After an incubation period of two to ten days, symptoms appear suddenly and powerfully. A Tularaemia victim contracts either ulceroglandular disease, which involves localized skin or mucous membrane ulceration, swollen glands, fever, chills, headache, and malaise – or the more virulent typhoidal Tularaemia, which is likely to occur after a BW attack. Without effective treatments, ulceroglandular Tularaemia has a mortality rate of 4 per cent, while typhoidal Tularaemia kills 35 per cent. Antibiotics can be used to treat the disease.

Viruses

Crimean-Congo haemorrhagic fever

Crimean-Congo haemorrhagic fever virus (Nairovirus) is one of many agents that cause viral haemorrhagic fevers (VHF). It is extremely infectious and sufficiently stable to be effectively delivered by aerosol. The disease can mimic a surgical emergency, such as a bleeding gastric ulcer. In its natural form, it is carried by ticks and normally infects cattle and goats. In humans, symptoms begin to appear between four and twenty-one days after infection, causing an acute febrile illness characterized by extreme fatigue, generalized signs of increased vascular permeability, and abnormalities of circulatory regulation. It is highly lethal.

Other significant VHFs which can infect humans, and have been studied as potential BW agents, include Lassa fever and Rift Valley fever from Africa; and Argentine HF (Junin) and Bolivian HF (Machupo) from South America.

Ebola and Marburg

Ebola, and its close cousin Marburg, are severe haemorrhagic fevers (Filovirus) which originated in sub-Saharan Africa. Ebola was discovered in 1976 and is named after a river in Zaire, near the site of the first epidemic. Marburg was discovered in 1967 when African green monkeys, used in medical experiments, carried the disease to a vaccine factory in Marburg, Germany. Ebola is a virus which attacks every single organ and tissue in the human body (except skeletal muscle and bone), and eventually turns most of the body into a digested slime of virus particles. After an incubation of some ten days, the first symptoms appear as fever, vomiting, and body aches. As the virus storms through the body making copies of itself, small blood clots appear in the bloodstream, the blood thickens and slows, and the clots begin to stick to the walls of blood vessels. Eventually, the skin develops red spots called petechiae, which are haemorrhages under the skin. Subsequently, spontaneous tears appear in the skin and blood pours from the wounds; huge bruises will appear and join up, the skin goes soft and pulpy, and can tear off. Soon every orifice in the body begins to bleed. The skin of the tongue can slough off causing indescribable pain. The heart bleeds into itself, the eyeballs fill with blood. And it gets considerably worse before death. Currently, there is no vaccine and there is no cure (although American scientists are attempting to develop a vaccine using advanced genetic engineering techniques). It is a robust virus highly amenable to dissemination through the air.

Q Fever (*Coxiella burnetii*)

Coxiella burnetii is a rickettsia-like organism that causes Q fever, an intense disease (often found in cattle, sheep, and goats) that is not normally fatal to humans, but temporarily incapacitates the victim. After inhalation of the *C. burnetii*, the organisms multiply in the lungs. Following an incubation period of ten to twenty days, the patient develops influenza-like symptoms: fever, severe headache, respiratory distress, and, in some cases, pneumonia. Fatigue, weight loss, and aching muscles are also common. Recovery is usually completed within two weeks, although the disease can be fatal if it is not treated with antibiotics. A vaccine does exist for those who are particularly at risk. *C. burnetii*, the causative agent, is an ideal incapacitating weapon, but a poor killer. It is resistant to heat and is highly infectious by the aerosol route. A single inhaled organism can produce clinical illness. In tests it was shown that 50 kg of *C. burnetii* dumped by an airplane along a 2-km line upwind of a population centre of 500,000 people in a developing country would kill just 150 people, but incapacitate 125,000.

Smallpox

Smallpox (caused by the Variola virus) is the most notorious of the pox viruses, which belong to the family *Poxviridae*. Until relatively recently smallpox was the scourge of mankind, killing as many as 30 to 40 per cent of populations during epidemics. It has only recently been conquered; the last occurrence of endemic smallpox was in Somalia in 1977, and the last human cases were laboratory-acquired infections in 1978. After an incubation period of some twelve days, the earliest symptoms of the virus are lethargy, fever, shaking chills, vomiting, headache, and backache – and 15 per cent of victims develop delirium. Two to three days later, a rash appears over the face, hands, and forearms, which spreads across the entire body, turning into large pustules. These lesions become very painful and the body's immune system begins to collapse, succumbing to the infection, which can, at the end, cover the entire skin surface of the body. Smallpox is a robust virus, very easily transmitted; it survives in the air for a long time and, crucially, will also survive explosive blast dissemination, making it an ideal offensive biological warfare weapon.

Venezuelan Equine Encephalitis

Venezuelan Equine Encephalitis (VEE) virus is an alphavirus that is endemic in the northern part of South America and Central America –

primarily in horses and mules. Natural infections are acquired from mosquito bites, although the feature that distinguishes VEE from many other insect-borne viruses is that it is also transmissible by aerosol. In laboratories, it can easily be developed into a condensed form that is a highly effective incapacitating agent against humans. As a military weapon, VEE would not be chosen for its capacity to kill; rather, a BW spray attack of VEE could render entire military units ineffective by incapacitating nearly everyone. After an incubation period of one to five days, the victim suffers from generalized malaise, a fever that violently comes and goes, shaking chills, severe headache, photophobia, and aching muscles in the legs and lower back. Nausea, vomiting, cough, sore throat, and diarrhoea may follow. This acute phase lasts 24–72 hours and is followed by a prolonged period of malaise and lethargy, with full health regained only after one to two weeks. There is no therapy for the condition. The fatality rate is less than 1 per cent.

Yellow Fever Virus

Yellow fever virus is a member of the *Flaviviridae*, one of the groups of viruses that cause viral haemorrhagic fevers (VHF), and is found throughout tropical Africa and South America – transmitted most often by female *Aedes aegptii* mosquitoes. VHFs lead to fever, aching muscles, extremely low blood pressure, a reddening of the eyes, flushing and small spots of blood beneath the surface of the skin. Full blown VHF typically leads to generalized bleeding from the mucous membranes and is often accompanied by damage to the nerve system, bone-marrow, and lungs. Yellow fever virus, which takes effect after a three-to-six-day incubation period, also damages the liver from jaundice and haemorrhages – and victims often vomit blood, which may have turned black. The best vector for yellow fever distribution in a BW attack would be mosquitoes which were specially bred to carry the virus – though delivery is difficult to manage and the results are unreliable. Yellow fever is normally not lethal, though it can result in death rates of up to 10 per cent.

Toxins

Botulinum Toxin

Botulinum toxin (there are seven different types) is the ultimate killer. It belongs to the family of Clostridial neurotoxins – the most toxic substances known to man. Humans have no natural protection against these non-contagious toxins, which have been extensively researched to establish how effective they might be in biological warfare. In its natural form, the toxin most often appears through spores in the anaerobic conditions frequently encountered in the improper cooking, canning, or preservation of foods. When delivered through this vector, the symptoms appear several hours (up to one to two days) after the contaminated food is eaten. The earliest symptoms are difficult to dissociate from food poisoning and might result in a number of effects, including blurred vision, drooping eyelids, the inability to swallow or talk, and apparent muscle weakness. This leads to breathing difficulties. Death results from muscular failure, paralysis, and ventilation failure. Effective treatments are virtually non-existent. In order to solve the problem of the spore's vulnerability to oxygen, military microbiologists have taken the *Clostridium botulinum* organism, grown it in a liquid medium, and produced botulinum toxin from it (which is no longer anaerobic). This toxin can then be converted into a powder, aerosolized, and used against a target – although it has much less potency in this form.

Ricin

Ricin is a potent toxin derived from the beans of the castor plant, and, therefore, potentially widely available. Castor beans are ubiquitous worldwide and the toxin is fairly easily produced from them. When inhaled as a small particle aerosol, this toxin can cause illness within eight hours, and death may be caused by respiratory failure within 36–72 hours. If, however, ricin is ingested, the victim will suffer severe gastro-intestinal symptoms followed by vascular collapse and death.

Treatment of victims is extremely difficult, because ricin acts rapidly and irreversibly, therefore antibiotics cannot be used effectively, as they can with other, slower acting toxins. Ricin is ideal for individual assassinations. It was the biological agent used in the famous assassination of

Bulgarian dissident Georgi Markov in London in 1978, when he was stabbed in the thigh by an umbrella with a tiny ricin pellet hidden inside the engineered tip. Ricin poisoning leads to local pain and a feeling of weakness within five hours. There is a high temperature within a day, followed by profuse vomiting. These symptoms are then followed by fever, swollen lymph nodes in the groin area, then low blood pressure, vascular collapse, the vomiting of blood, and then death. Ricin is more than twice as deadly as VX nerve agent.

Staphylococcus aureus Toxins

Staphylococcus aureus produces a number of toxins, the most important of which is Staphylococcal enterotoxin B, or SEB. The non-contagious SEB is a very common cause of food poisoning in humans. The toxin, however, can also be delivered in aerosol form and be inhaled, which leads to a different, more severe range of clinical symptoms, from systemic damage to septic shock. The use of this toxin in troop staging posts or ports would be invaluable for causing incapacitation for up to two weeks (a very low dose would affect 50 per cent of those exposed). Very high exposure levels can be lethal, but only in less than 2 per cent of the cases. Most victims will feel the onset of symptoms within three to twelve hours and suffer from fever, headache, chills, aching muscles, and a cough. More severe cases will develop shortness of breath and chest pain. Nausea, vomiting, diarrhoea, and major fluid loss occurs in some cases. There is no vaccine for SEB.

Notes

Chapter 2: 1999

1. Associated Press, 22 January 1999; Reuters, 22 January 1999, citing Clinton speech on the future of terrorism at the National Academy of Sciences
2. Agence France Presse, 19 April 1999
3. Sue Pleming, Reuters, 23 January 1999
4. Ashton Carter, John Deutch, and Philip Zelikow, 'Catastrophic Terrorism: Tackling the New Danger', *Foreign Affairs* (Council on Foreign Relations), November/December 1998
5. Statement by Clarence Edwards, Director of the FPS, quoted by Stephen Fehr, *Washington Post*, 2 July 1998
6. Andrew Quinn, Reuters, 16 November 1998
7. John Broder, *New York Times*, 23 January 1999
8. Judith Miller and William Broad, *New York Times*, 22 January 1999
9. David Ljunggren, Reuters, 23 October 1998
10. Associated Press, 16 February 1999
11. James Bennett, *New York Times*, 23 May 1998; Thomas Lippman, *Washington Post*, 23 May 1998; Reuters, 8 June 1998
12. Address by Richard Clarke at Conference on Biological Terrorism, Johns Hopkins University Center for Civilian Bio-Defense Studies, Arlington, Virginia, 16 February 1999
13. Jim Landers, *Dallas Morning News*, 9 February 1999
14. Vernon Loeb, *Washington Post*, 23 January 1999; James Gerstenzang, *Los Angeles Times*, 22 January 1999; *Dallas Morning News* [2, 13]
15. *New York Times* [2, 8]
16. *New York Times* [2, 8]
17. *Washington Post* [2, 14]

Chapter 3: Unit 731

1. Sumiko Oshima, *Japan Times*, 19 February 1998
2. Major sources for this chapter include:

   a. Sheldon H. Harris, *Factories of Death: Japanese Biological Warfare, 1932–45, and the American Cover-Up*, London: Routledge, 1994. The authors wish to acknowledge Professor Harris and his important and impressively researched book, which has been widely accepted as an authoritative work on Gen. Ishii's programme.

   b. Peter Williams and David Wallace, *Unit 731: The Japanese Army's Secret of Secrets*, London: Hodder and Stoughton, 1989

   c. Tsuneishi Kei-ichi, *The Germ Warfare Unit That Disappeared: Kwantung Army's 731st Unit*, Tokyo: Kai-mei-sha Publishers, 1981

   d. Report by Norbert H. Fell, Chief, Pilot Plant and Engineering Division, Camp Detrick, Maryland, 'Brief Summary of New Information about Japanese BW Activities', US Army, 20 June 1947. See also report by Edwin V. Hill, MD, Chief, Basic Science, Camp Detrick, Maryland, to Gen. Alden C. Waitt, 'Summary Report on BW Investigations', US Army, 12 December 1947.

   e. V.V. Tomilin and R.V. Berezhnai, 'Exposure of Criminal Activity of the Japanese Military Authorities Regarding Preparation for Bacteriological Warfare', *Military-Medical Journal*, (Moscow), no.8, 1985
3. Williams and Wallace [3, 2b], p. 7 and passim
4. Williams and Wallace [3, 2b], p. 7
5. Harris [3, 2a], p. 18
6. Harris [3, 2a], p. 21, citing Tsuneishi Kei-ichi [3, 2c], pp. 50–51
7. Williams and Wallace [3, 2b], p. 13; Harris [3, 2a], p. 10
8. Harris [3, 2a], pp. 13, 19
9. The Foreign Affairs Association of Japan, *Japan Year Book, 1935*, Tokyo: Kenkyusha Press, 1935, pp. 1202–3
10. Harris [3, 2a], pp. 23–6
11. Harris [3, 2a], pp. 27–8, citing Segment 36 in 'The Night of Shock: The Last Will and Testament of a General: The Diary of General Endo Saburo', *Mainichi Shimbun*, Tokyo, 21 December 1982
12. Harris [3, 2a], p. 70, citing testimony from Major General Kawashima Kyoshi at Khabarovsk, Japanese War Crimes Trial, 1949, p. 62
13. Harris [3, 2a], p. 28, citing Mr Han Xiao, Deputy Director of the Unit 731 Memorial Museum in Ping Fan, 'Bacterial Factory in Beiyinhe, Zhong Ma City', *Harbin Historical Chronicle*, vol. 1, 1984, pp. 80–83
14. Harris [3, 2a], p. 54; *Los Angeles Times*, 5 June 1994

15. Harris [3, 2a], pp. 33–5
16. Harris [3, 2a], p. 44, citing Tsuneishi [3, 2c], p. 71
17. Tomilin and Berezhnai [3, 2e]
18. Tomilin and Berezhnai [3, 2e]. See also Harris [3, 2a], p. 55.
19. Harris [3, 2a], p. 59
20. Harris [3, 2a], pp. 62–3
21. Tracy Dahlby, 'Japan's Germ Warriors', *Washington Post*, 26 May 1983
22. Harris [3,2a], p. 63
23. Nicholas D. Kristof, 'Unlocking a Deadly Secret', *New York Times*, 17 March 1995. The former medical assistant, now a farmer, insisted on anonymity.
24. *New York Times* [3, 23]
25. *New York Times* [3, 23]
26. Testimony given by Yoshio Tamura while facing war crimes charges in Beijing, 10 October, 1954
27. Harris [3, 2a], pp. 67–9
28. Harris [3, 2a], pp. 74–5, citing Tsuneishi [3, 2c], p. 40
29. Harris [3, 2a], p. 77, citing Han Xiao, 'Compilation of Camp 731 Fascist Savage Acts', *Unforgettable History*, China: Harbin, 1985
30. Hiroshi Matsumoto interview, August 1997 (BBC *Panorama* research interview by Fuyuko Nishisato). See also Harris [3, 2a], pp. 101–112.
31. Matsumoto [3, 30]
32. Patrick E. Tyler, 'Germ war, a current world threat, is a remembered nightmare in China', *New York Times*, 4 February 1997
33. *New York Times* [3, 32]
34. *New York Times* [3, 32]
35. *New York Times* [3, 32]
36. *New York Times* [3, 32]
37. *Japan Times* [3, 1]
38. *Washington Post* [3, 21]
39. William Patrick, 'History of Biological Warfare', *Proliferation*, ed. Kathleen Bailey, Lawrence Livermore Library, 1994, p. 11
40. US Army, Interview of Lt. Col. Naito Ryoichi by Lt. Col. Murray Sanders, 6 October 1945, Ft. Detrick Archives. See also Harris [3, 2a], p. 60.
41. *Washington Post* [3, 21]; *New York Times* [3, 23]
42. *New York Times* [3, 23]
43. Ishio Kobata interview, April 1998 (by Fuyuko Nishisato)
44. Shoichi Matsumoto interview, April 1998 (by Fuyuko Nishisato)
45. Harris [3, 2a], p. 177, citing Tsuneishi Kei-ichi and Asano Tomizo, *The Bacteriological Warfare Unit and the Suicide of Two Physicians*, Tokyo: Schincho-Sha Publishing Co., 1982, p. 56
46. Harris [3, 2a], pp. 177–8, citing *Japan Times*, 5 September 1982

47. Harris [3, 2a], p. 178, citing anonymous letter, 'Contribution concerning Surgeon Lt. Gen. Shiro Ishii', Record Group 331, Box 1772, Case no. 330, The National Archives, 3 September 1946

48. Harris [3, 2a], p. 179, citing *Pacific Stars and Stripes*, 6 January 1946

49. Peter Kalisher, 'SCAP Locates and Questions Gen. Ishii', *Pacific Stars and Stripes*, 27 February 1946

50. Harris [3, 2a], pp. 136–7, 179–82, citing the two transcripts of the first US interrogation of Ishii: Document 004, Stenographic Transcript of Interrogation of Lt. Gen. Shiro Ishii in Tokyo, by Lt. Col. Arvo T. Thompson, on 5 February 1946 and 6 February 1946, Dugway Proving Grounds Library

51. Harris [3, 2a], pp. 190–91, citing 'Activities of the United States in the Field of Biological Warfare', a Report to the Secretary of War by George W. Merck, Special Consultant on Biological Warfare, p. 7, Record Group 165, Entry 488, Box 182, National Archives

52. Harris [3, 2a], p. 191, citing Merck Report, p. 9

53. Harris [3, 2a], p. 191, citing Merck Report, pp. 9–10

54. Harris[3, 2a], p. 197

55. Harris [3, 2a], p. 198, citing Fell Report, 24 June 1947. Dr Norbert H. Fell, from Camp Detrick, interviewed Ishii on behalf of the US Army for three days in May 1947.

56. Harris [3, 2a], p. 198, citing Fell Report, 24 June 1947

57. Harris [3, 2a], p. 201

58. An eight-page version of Dr Fell's report turned up in a 20 June 1947 'Brief Summary'. This document, in the Ft. Detrick archives, contains information left out of the earlier version. The eight-page version is from Fell to the Tech. Dir., Camp Detrick, 'Brief Summary of New Information about Japanese BW Activities'. See also, Harris [3, 2a], p. 201.

59. Williams and Wallace [3, 2b], p. 298

60. Norman M. Covert (Chief, Public Affairs, Ft. Detrick, Maryland), 'Response to Inquiries on Japanese BW Program', Department of the Army, Memorandum, 5 May 1982, p. 3. Three former officials from Camp Detrick confirmed to the authors that the Japanese research was not useful to the US programme after World War II. Dr Riley Housewright interview, February 1998; Thomas Dashiell interview, February 1998; William Patrick interview, February 1998.

61. James Dao, *New York Times*, 27 June 1998; Associated Press, 26 June 1998

62. *Japan Times* [3, 1]

Chapter 4: Arms Race

1. Sheldon H. Harris, *Factories of Death: Japanese Biological Warfare, 1932–45, and the American Cover-Up*, London: Routledge, 1994, citing Stimson to President Roosevelt, FDR Library, 29 April 1942, p. 154
2. Barry Schweid, Associated Press, 14 April 1998, from Secretary Albright's speech at Howard University
3. Major sources for this chapter are:
   a. William Patrick interviews, February 1998 and June 1998; Dr Riley Housewright interview, February 1998. Dr Riley Housewright, a Texan with a Ph.D. in bacteriology from the University of Chicago, was the first chief of safety at Camp Detrick during the war. He served there from 1943 to 1970, during the last 15 years as Ft. Detrick's overall science director.
   b. Thomas Dashiell (a former senior official at Ft. Detrick, 1952–71), 'US Declaration to the United Nations', 20-page report, ACDA, August 1996. This little-noticed document was submitted by ACDA to the UN in 1996, with no fanfare. It was written by Mr Dashiell (now deceased), who was one of the top US experts on all aspects of the US offensive BW programme.
   c. Rexmond C. Cochrane (Historical Section, Office of Chief, Chemical Corps), 'History of the Chemical Warfare Service in World War II, 1940–1945', *Biological Warfare Research in the United States*, Vol. II, November 1947, declassified September 18, 1975
   d. Department of the Army, 'US Army Activity in the US Biological Warfare Programs', Vols. I and II, 24 February 1977
   e. Norman Covert, *Cutting Edge: A History of Fort Detrick, Maryland*, Ft. Detrick: Public Affairs Office, Third Edition, 1997. Covert was the chief of public affairs at Ft. Detrick 1977–97.
   f. William Patrick, 'Biological Warfare: An Overview', *Proliferation*, ed. Kathleen Bailey, Lawrence Livermore Library, 1994, pp. 1–7 and William Patrick, 'A History of Biological and Toxin Warfare', *Proliferation*, ed. Kathleen Bailey, Lawrence Livermore Library, 1994, pp. 9–20
   g. Testimony of Dr Ira Baldwin, Committee on Biological Warfare, The Pentagon, 15 May 1951. Dr Baldwin was the first science director at Camp Detrick.
4. *The Observer*, 15 December 1996; Gary Thatcher, *Christian Science Monitor*, 13 December 1988; Robert Harris and Jeremy Paxman, *A Higher Form of Killing*, New York: Hill and Wang, 1982, pp. 68–74, 96
5. Dashiell, [4, 3b]; Cochrane [4, 3c]; Covert [4, 3e], p. 17; Barton J. Bernstein, 'Churchill's Secret Biological Weapon', *Bulletin of the Atomic Scientists*,

January/February 1987, pp. 46f.; Seymour Hersh, *Chemical and Biological Warfare*, Indianapolis: Bobbs-Merrill, 1968, p. 12

6. Barton Bernstein, 'The Birth of the US Biological-Warfare Program', *Scientific American*, June 1987, pp. 116f.

7. Dashiell [4, 3b]; Patrick [4, 3f], pp. 1–7

8. Dr Ira Baldwin speech, Ft. Detrick Silver Anniversary Luncheon, 2 May, 1967.

9. Housewright [4, 3a]; Patrick [4, 3f], pp. 1–7; Hersh [4, 5], pp. 68–9, 87

10. Housewright [4, 3a]; Patrick [4, 3f], pp. 1–7; Hersh [4, 5], pp. 68–9, 87

11. Dashiell [4, 3b]; Cochrane [4, 3c]; Department of the Army [4, 3d], Vol. I, Section 1, p. 2

12. Cochrane [4, 3c]; Covert [4, 3e], pp. 9, 17

13. Dashiell [4; 2b]; Cochrane [4, 3c]; Department of the Army [4, 3d], Vol. I, Section 1, p. 2

14. Cochrane [4, 3c]; Harris, p. 157; Frederick Sidell, Ernest Takafuji, and David Franz, *Textbook of Military Medicine*, US Government Printing Office, August 1997, p. 427. In 1943, there were 3,800 military personnel in the entire BW programme at all sites – mostly army and navy personnel.

15. Department of the Army [4, 3d], Vol. II, p. E:1

16. Patrick [4, 3f], pp. 1–7

17. Bernstein [4, 5]

18. Bernstein [4, 5]

19. Dashiell [4, 3b]; Sidell, Takafuji, and Franz [4, 14], pp. 43–4; Bernstein [4, 5]; Harris and Paxman [4, 4], p. 104; Associated Press, 15 January, 1987. A post-war examination of German labs and secret documents by US Army intelligence officers found the Nazis had no large-scale offensive BW weapons. The head of the Manhattan Project, Maj. Leslie Groves, sent a team of officers to Germany to investigate German progress on nuclear weapons and CBW. The team, code-named 'Alsos' (Greek for 'grove'), checked 70 German facilities, labs, institutes, companies, universities, and concentration camps; they also captured all of the German intelligence files on BW. They found no evidence of an active Nazi offensive BW programme. Hitler had ordered that only defensive aspects of bio-warfare could be studied. The Germans sent one million doses of Plague vaccine to the front in Stalingrad in case the Soviets used Plague as a weapon – but the vaccine was never used. In 1943, the Waffen SS had set up a lab in Posen, Poland, with the intention of conducting offensive experiments on humans (similar to those conducted by Gen. Ishii), but the lab was abandoned before it was made operational (Cochrane [4, 3c], pp. 136–41).

20. Cochrane [4, 3c], p. 142

21. Dashiell [4, 3b]. The army also continued a small World War II anti-animal

programme, which included rinderpest, hog cholera and Newcastle virus; and an anti-crop programme, which included several fungus spores, like wheat stem rust, rye stem rust, and rice blast.

22. *Frederick Post* (AP), 22 January 1960; *Chicago Tribune*, 23 August 1955

23. Dashiell [4, 3b]

24. Dashiell [4, 3b]; US Congress, Office of Technology Assessment, *Technologies Underlying Weapons of Mass Destruction: Background Paper*, US Government Printing Office, 1993, p. 88; Sidell, Takafuji, and Franz [4, 14], p. 429; Department of the Army, 8 March 1977, Information for Members of Congress, 'US Army Activities in the US Biological Warfare Program' p. 8; Department of the Army [4, 3d], Vol. I, Section 3, p. 1, Section 3, p. 2, Section 4, p. 1; Patrick [4, 3f], pp. 9–20. See also Harris and Paxman [4, 4], p. 160; Hersh [4, 5], pp. 133–7.

25. Dashiell [4, 3b]. Five British BW tests at sea were disclosed to Parliament in January 1994:

1. 'Operation Harness', a series of 22 experiments at Parham Sound off the coast of Antigua, from August 1948 through February 1949.

2. 'Operation Cauldron', tests of Brucellosis and Plague, in Scottish waters, off Stornaway in Isle of Lewis, from May–December 1952. Clouds of BW agents were released above animals (guinea pigs, mice, rabbits, and monkeys) tethered to rafts set adrift at sea by the Royal Navy transport ship, HMS Ben Lomond.

3. 'Operation Hesperus', tests of Brucellosis and Tularaemia in Scottish waters, from May to August 1953.

4. 'Operation Ozone', long-range tests of Brucellosis, Tularaemia, and VEE in the Caribbean, 18 miles off Nassau, Bahamas (a British colony) from February through May 1954.

5. 'Operation Negation', in the Caribbean, off the Bahamas, from November 1954–March 1955.

(Harris and Paxman [4, 4], pp. 157–8; *The Observer* [4, 4]; *Sunday Telegraph* (London), 2 February 1997)

26. Dashiell [4, 3b]; US Chemical Corps, 'Summary of Major Events and Problems', Fiscal Year 1959, January 1960. See also Robin Clarke, *The Silent Weapons*, New York: David McKay Co., 1968, p. 118; Harris and Paxman [4, 4], pp. 166–7; Malcolm Dando, *Biological Warfare in the 21st Century*, London: Brassey's (UK) Ltd, 1994, pp. 51–2.

27. This experiment was documented in Special Report, No. 117, 'Study of the Vulnerability of the Pentagon to Sabotage with BW Agents Via the Air-Conditioning System', 12 October 1949

28. Dashiell [4, 3b]; Sidell, Takafuji, and Franz [4, 14], p. 429

29. Dashiell [4, 3b]; Department of the Army [4, 3d], Vol. I, Section 2, p. 4

30. Department of the Army [4, 3d], Vol. II, Table 1, pp.E:1:1, F:1 to F:5 and Vol. I, Section 3, p. 2; Harris and Paxman [4, 4], p. 156; Sidell, Takafuji, and Franz [4, 14], p. 429; *Frederick Journal*, 19 December 1984; *San Francisco Chronicle*, 22 December 1976; *San Francisco Chronicle*, 23 December 1976; Drew Featherston, *Newsday*, 21 November 1976

31. Department of the Army [4, 3d], Vol. II, pp. F:1 to F:5 and Vol. I, Section 3, p. 2; Harris and Paxman [4, 4], p. 156; Sidell, Takafuji, and Franz [4, 14], p. 429

32. The one 1950 death, Edward J. Nevin, was linked to the SM test. The army later discontinued use of SM. Medical authorities today believe SM causes a variety of gastrointestinal disorders and infections (*San Francisco Chronicle*, 22 December 1976; *San Francisco Chronicle*, 23 December 1976; Drew Featherston, *Newsday*, 21 November 1976).

33. Department of the Army [4, 3d], Vol. II, Table 33, pp.E3:1–E3:2

34. Dashiell [4, 3b]; Associated Press, 15 May 1997; Heather Knight, *Los Angeles Times*, 15 May 1997

35. In 1997, a National Research Council science panel, under a request from Congress, studied the Large Area Coverage test documentation and health records. The 15-member panel concluded that no illness or adverse effects could be traced to the use of the army's simulant, zinc cadmium sulphide, since people were exposed to such small amounts of the compound (Warren Leary, *New York Times*, 15 May 1997; Associated Press [4, 34]; *Los Angeles Times* [4, 34]).

36. A problem remained: how to maintain the virulence of the agents if they were released by a plane over Spot A, at 20,000 feet, and then drifted down a day later to Spot B, several hundred miles away. By then, the heat, humidity, and wind speed in the atmosphere would kill many of the tiny organisms and render them harmless (Robin Clarke [4, 26], pp. 124–7).

37. Sidell, Takafuji, and Franz [4, 14], p. 59; Patrick [4, 3a], June 1998

38. Patrick [4, 3a], June 1998; Sidell, Takafuji, and Franz [4, 14], p. 59; Robin Clarke [4, 26], pp. 47–8; Harris and Paxman [4, 4], p. 171

39. Patrick [4, 3a], June 1998

40. Sidell, Takafuji, and Franz [4, 14], p. 60; Patrick [4, 3f], pp. 9–20

41. Dashiell [4, 3b]; Patrick [4, 3f], pp. 9–20

42. Patrick [4, 3a], June 1998

43. Dashiell [4, 3b]

44. Patrick [4, 3f], pp. 1–7

45. Dashiell [4, 3b]; Patrick [4, 3a], June 1998

Chapter 5: The Soviet Programme

1. Report of the Russian Federation, 'Declaration of Past Activity in Regard to Offensive and Defensive Programmes of Biological Research and Development', United Nations Form F, DDA/4-92/BWIII, 1992
2. Ken Alibek with Stephen Handelman, *BIOHAZARD: The Chilling True Story of the Largest Covert Biological Weapons Program in the World*, New York: Random House, 1999, p. 33; confidential interview, April 1999
3. Confidential interview, October 1998. See also Arkadiy Pasternak and Oleg Rubnikovich, 'The Secret of Pokrovskiy Monastery', *Nezavisimaya Gazeta*, 17 November 1992, p. 6; Robert Harris and Jeremy Paxman, *A Higher Form of Killing*, New York: Hill and Wang, 1982, pp. 141–2; Anthony Rimmington, 'From Military to Industrial Complex? The Conversion of Biological Weapons' Facilities in the Russian Federation', *Contemporary Security Policy*, Vol. 17, no. 1, April 1996, Frank Cass: London, pp. 99–100, note 7.

    GRU defector Col. Oleg Penkovskiy informed the CIA in 1960 that the Soviets had a BW storage centre on a 'small island' near the city of Kalinin, where they kept 'large containers with bacilli of plagues and other contagious diseases.' This reference to Kalinin, which is near Lake Seliger, was presumably the same site as Gorodomyla Island (Oleg Penkovskiy, *The Penkovskiy Papers*, Garden City, New York: Doubleday & Co., 1965, pp. 246–7).
4. Confidential interview, October 1998; US Congress Joint Economic Committee, testimony of Dr Kenneth Alibek, prepared statement, 20 May 1998
5. Igor Domoradski, *Znanie-Sila* ('Knowledge Itself Is Power': a Russian journal), November and December, 1996
6. Alibek, with Handelman [5, 2], p. 34
7. Alibek, with Handelman [5, 2], p. 35
8. Ken Alibek lecture, Chemical and Biological Arms Control Institute, Washington, DC, 19 May 1998 (author notes); Alibek, with Handelman [5, 2], p. 36; confidential interview, April 1999. See also Viktor Shalygin, 'Kirov: Secret Scientific Research Institute Does Not Fear Even Meteorites', *Moscow Spaseniye*, 30 August 1992, p. 5; Rimmington [5, 3], pp. 80–112.
9. Alibek lecture [5, 8]; Viktor Litovkin, 'We Have No Bacteriological Weapons', *Moscow Izvestiya*, 12 June 1992, translated in FBIS-SOV-92-116, 16 June 1992; Rimmington [5, 3], p. 85
10. Ken Alibek interview, January 1998; US Congress Joint Economic Committee [5, 4]; Alibek, with Handelman [5, 2], pp. 30–31
11. Confidential interview, November 1998; confidential interview, April 1999; Alibek, with Handelman [5, 2], p. 37

12. Alibek [5, 10]; confidential interview, November 1998; US Congress Joint Economic Committee [5, 4]

13. Report of the Russian Federation [5, 1]

14. Harris and Paxman [5, 3], pp. 140–41; Seymour Hersh, *Chemical and Biological Warfare*, Indianapolis: Bobbs-Merrill, 1968, pp. 12–17; V.V. Tomilin and R.V. Berezhnai, 'Exposure of Criminal Activity of the Japanese Military Authorities Regarding Preparation for Bacteriological Warfare', *Military-Medical Journal*, (Moscow), no. 8, 1985

15. Report of the Russian Federation [5, 1]; Vladimir Umnov, 'The Bomb for the Poor', *Moscow News*, 4–10 February 1994; *The Arms Control Reporter*, Chronology 1986, 23 August 1985, p.B:15; Rimmington [5, 3], p. 86

16. Alibek, with Handelman [5, 2], pp. 36–7; confidential interview, April 1999

17. Confidential interview (a former Soviet military microbiologist who worked on the island during the 1980s), July 1997 (by Nick Sturdee); Irina Begmetova interview (the first Kazakh journalist to be allowed onto the island in 1992), July 1997 (by Nick Sturdee); Mukhtar Shakhanov interview (the head of a Kazakh environmental group, Aral Avia Kazakhstan), July 1997 (by Nick Sturdee). See also Sergey Kozlov, 'Scientists Quit A Secret Laboratory', *Nezavisimaya Gazeta*, 23 June 1992; Report of the Russian Federation [5, 1]; Rimmington [5, 3], p. 86.

18. Dr Nikolai Fedotov interview (a former Soviet military microbiologist), July 1997 (by Nick Sturdee); Soviet military microbiologist [5, 17]; V. Umnov, 'After 20 Years of Silence the Soviet Microbes are Talking', *Moscow Komsomolskaya Pravda*, 30 April 1992, translated in JPRS-TND-92-104, 4 May 1992

19. Soviet military microbiologist [5, 17]

20. Alibek, with Handelman [5, 2], pp. 15–18

21. Gen. Anatoli Vorobyov interview, July 1997 (by Nick Sturdee). (Gen. Vorobyov is the former first deputy director of Biopreparat.)

22. Soviet military microbiologist [5, 17]

23. Ken Alibek interview, June 1998; British official, confidential interview, April 1998

24. Alibek [5, 23]; British official [5, 23]

25. Alibek [5, 23]; British official [5, 23]

26. Confidential interview, November 1998; Alibek, with Handelman [5, 2], pp. 30–31; confidential interview, April 1999

27. Soviet military microbiologist [5, 17]; Fedotov [5, 18]

Chapter 6: CIA

1. Confidential interview, February 1998
2. Confidential interview, November 1998
3. Joseph Douglas and Neil Livingstone, *America the Vulnerable: The Threat of Chemical/Biological Warfare*, Lexington, Mass: Lexington Books, 1987, p. 110, citing Walter Hirsch, 'Soviet Chemical Warfare and Biological Warfare Preparations and Capabilities, 1935–45', translated by Zaven Nalbandian, Intelligence Branch, Office of the Chief Chemical Corps, US Army, 1951, declassified 6 June 1974, by Foreign Science and Technology Center
4. CIA, 'Soviet Gross Capabilities For Attack on the US and Key Overseas Installations and Forces in 1965 [Classification: Top Secret]', Special National Intelligence Estimate 11-10-55, 2 August 1955; CIA, 'Soviet Gross Capabilities For Attack on the US and Key Overseas Installations and Forces Through Mid-1959 [Classification: Top Secret]', National Intelligence Estimate 11-56, 6 March 1956; CIA, 'Soviet Gross Capabilities For Attack on the Continental US in Mid-1960 [Classification: Top Secret]', Special National Intelligence Estimate 11-6-57; CIA, 'Soviet Capabilities and Intentions With Respect to the Clandestine Introduction of Weapons of Mass Destruction into the US [Classification: Top Secret]' National Intelligence Estimate 11-7-60, May 17, 1960. (These documents, released in 1997, were obtained by the authors from the National Archives.)
5. CIA [6, 4], NIE 11-56, 6 March 1956; CIA [6, 4], SNIE 11-6-57
6. CIA [6, 4], NIE 11-56, 6 March 1956; CIA [6, 4], SNIE 11-6-57; CIA [6, 4], NIE, 11-7-60, 17 May 1960
7. CIA [6, 4], NIE 11-7-60, 17 May 1960
8. Dino Brugioni interview, February 1998; Gregory W. Pedlow and Donald E. Welzenbach, *The CIA and the U-2 Programme, 1954–74*, CIA, Center for the Study of Intelligence, 1998, p. 104
9. Brugioni [6, 8]. The U-2 target list was prepared by a special advisory group first called the Ad-hoc Requirements Committee. A Scientific Intelligence Committee – with members from CIA, FBI, Atomic Energy Commission, Pentagon, and each armed service – met regularly and maintained a close watch over CBW intelligence gained from the flights.
10. Confidential interview, February 1998
11. Dino Brugioni, *Eyeball to Eyeball: The Inside Story of the Cuban Missile Crisis*, New York: Random House, 1990, p. 43. The other Soviet targets on Powers' flight included the Tyura Tam Missile Test Center, several nuclear plants in the Urals, an ICBM base at Yurya, a missile test centre at Plesetsk, and naval bases at Murmansk. He was supposed to land in Bodo, Norway.

12. Brugioni [6, 8]

13. CIA/NPIC, Photographic Interpretation Report, 'KH-4 Mission 1042-1, 17–22 June 1967 [Classification: Top Secret]'

14. CIA, 'Soviet Capabilities and Intentions with Respect to Biological Weapons [Classification: Secret]', National Intelligence Estimate 11-6-64, 26 August 1964. (This document, released in 1997, was obtained by the authors from the National Archives.)

15. CIA [6, 14], NIE 11-6-64, 26 August 1964

16. CIA [6, 14], NIE 11-6-64, 26 August 1964

17. CIA [6, 14], NIE 11-6-64, 26 August 1964

18. CIA [6, 14], NIE 11-6-64, 26 August 1964

19. The only instances when such weapons were likely to be used, the CIA guessed, would be during a 'clandestine attack' or if Warsaw Pact forces were retreating in the face of an Allied assault (CIA, 'Soviet Chemical and Biological Warfare Capabilities [Classification: Secret]', National Intelligence Estimate 11-11-69, 13 February 1969. This document, released in 1997, was obtained by the authors from the National Archives).

   The CIA now believed the USSR had the 'technical capability' to produce and stockpile 'militarily significant quantities' of biological agents. But the CIA conceded it still did not know if the USSR had actually developed any such weapons. The report noted: 'We have ... insufficient evidence on which to base an estimate of the types and quantities of BW agents which might be available to the Soviets for offensive use' (CIA, NIE 11-11-69, 13 February 1969).

20. Confidential interview, February 1998

21. Confidential interview, October 1998

Chapter 7: The Treaty

1. Office of the White House Press Secretary, 'US Policy on Chemical Warfare Program and Bacteriological/Biological Research Program' and 'Statement by the President', White House Press Release, 25 November 1969

2. [7, 1], 'Statement by the President'

3. That same day, Henry Kissinger signed National Security Decision Memorandum 35, which noted that the US would still continue to research 'offensive aspects' of biological agents if it was 'necessary to determine what defensive measures are required' (National Security Decision Memorandum 35, November 25, 1969).

4. The British proposal, from the British Minister of State for Disarmament, Fred Mulley, was submitted on 16 July 1968 to the Eighteen-Nation Disarma-

ment Conference in Geneva (US State Department, 'Chemical Weapons Arms Control: Chronology of Key Events, 1899–1989', unclassified memo, 1989).

5. Richard Nixon, *RN: The Memoirs of Richard Nixon*, New York: Grosset & Dunlap, 1978, pp. 369–70

6. Seymour Hersh, *The Price of Power: Kissinger in the Nixon White House*, New York: Summit Books, 1983, p. 35; Walter Isaacson, *Kissinger: A Biography*, New York: Simon & Schuster, 1992, p. 204; Roger Morris, *Uncertain Greatness*, New York: Harper & Row, 1977, pp. 96–103; Marvin Kalb and Bernard Kalb, *Kissinger*, Boston: Little, Brown and Company, 1974, pp. 106–7

7. Hersh [7, 6], p. 71; Nixon [7, 5], p. 339; Mark Perry, *Four Stars*, Boston: Houghton Mifflin Company, 1989, p. 244

8. Melvin Laird interview, April 1998

9. James Leonard interview, March 1998

10. Laird [7, 8]

11. The Chairman of the JCS from 1964–70 was Gen. Earle G. Wheeler, US Army.

12. Laird [7, 8]

13. Leonard [7, 9]

14. Leonard [7, 9]

15. Leonard [7, 9]

16. Laird and Kissinger respected each other, but were bitter rivals. They disagreed on many key policy matters confronting the Nixon Administration, including how to pursue the Vietnam War. Both Kissinger and Nixon mistrusted Laird, and believed he was leaking damaging information to the press, as a way of influencing policy his way. Nixon eventually ordered wiretaps on the phones of Laird and a top aide to gauge their loyalty. These so-called 'national security' wiretaps never uncovered any unethical behaviour (Hersh [7, 6], pp. 71, 90, 576–7; Kalb and Kalb [7, 6], p. 89).

17. Hersh [7, 6], p. 35

18. Thomas Dashiell, 'US Declaration to the United Nations', ACDA, August 1996

19. Nixon [7, 5], p. 339

20. Department of the Army, 'US Army Activity in the US Biological Warfare Programs', Vol.1, 24 February 1977, p. 7:3

21. Michael Getler, *Washington Post*, 19 December 1970; Charles Cordry, *Baltimore Sun*, 19 December 1970

22. Office of the White House Press Secretary, White House Press Release, 14 February 1970; National Security Decision Memorandum 44, 'US Policy on Toxins', 20 February 1970; Robert Harris and Jeremy Paxman, *A Higher*

Form of Killing, New York: Hill and Wang, 1982, p. 211; Dashiell [7, 18]; Leonard [7, 9]

23. Department of the Army, 'US Army Activity in the US Biological Warfare Programs', Vol. 1, 24 February 1977, p. 7:4; Dashiell [7, 18]; *Washington Post* [7, 21]; *Arkansas Gazette*, 19 December 1970; *Baltimore Sun* [7, 21]

24. Leonard [7, 9]

25. Leonard [7, 9]

26. Leonard [7, 9]; Alan Neidle interview, April 1998. (Neidle was Leonard's deputy at ACDA.) The US reasoning for not specifying verification measures went as follows:

    1. The US would not do anything differently – about the unilateral US BW ban – if the Soviets kept making biological weapons. The US was not turning back.

    2. A treaty might inhibit the Soviets' BW development activities, because abiding by a treaty might become a matter of conscience to their scientists.

    3. A treaty might prevent other nations from developing bio-weapons. Those other countries would not be as hard to read, or as opaque, as the USSR. A treaty would become the focus of their national decision to make such weapons. Rogue states (like North Korea) would still be a problem, but they probably could not be stopped anyway if they decided to cheat.

27. Leonard [7, 9]

28. Leonard [7,9]

29. Alan Neidle, a State Department lawyer since 1957 and veteran negotiator of international treaties, headed ACDA's working group in Washington, while Leonard handled the negotiations in Geneva. Neidle played an active role in urging the US and UK teams to stick to their position. He argued against joining CW and BW, as the Soviets wanted, largely because he felt a BW treaty was attainable and because it was generally believed that a CW treaty would need more extensive on-site verification to be effective. If the US and UK gave up, he noted, they would get nothing in return (Neidle [7, 26]).

30. Leonard [7, 9]

31. Leonard [7, 9]

32. Leonard [7, 9]

33. Leonard [7, 9]

34. Leonard [7, 9]

35. ACDA, *Arms Control and Disarmament Agreements: 1996 Edition*,'Convention on the Prohibition of the Development, Production, and Stockpiling of Bacteriological (Biological) and Toxin Weapons and their Destruction', pp. 98–100

36. ACDA [7, 35]; Leonard [7, 9]. See also US House of Representatives, 'Biological Warfare Testing', Hearing of Joint Subcommittees of Foreign

Affairs, Interior, and Armed Services, testimony of James F. Leonard, 3 May 1998, pp. 70–74.

37. ACDA [7, 35]; Leonard [7, 9]
38. Leonard [7, 9]
39. ACDA [7, 35]
40. ACDA [7, 35]. Sweden remained a major holdout. Swedish officials objected to the imprecise arrangements that were made in case a violation was proven. The treaty stated that if a violation was alleged, the dispute would be taken to the Security Council for a decision. The Swedes responded that the veto power on the Security Council – by any of the members – meant that this system wouldn't work, because an accused country could ask an ally for a veto as a favour. The US asked if the Swedes had a better idea of how to do it. No one did. So the US and the rest of the world went ahead as planned.
41. Simultaneous signing ceremonies were held at three sites: Washington, London and Moscow. Three sites were needed because of the complex and conflicting diplomatic relations that the various signers maintained with the US, UK and USSR; not every country was welcome at each site.

    Numerous countries signed the treaty later, mostly in 1972, but extending until February 1975, when Sweden finally signed. As of 1996, 109 nations had signed the treaty and 91 had ratified it (ACDA [7, 35], pp. 101–104).
42. The US added one stipulation to the Protocols – that it reserved the right to respond in kind against any nation that used chemical weapons first (US State Department [7, 4]).
43. Leonard [7, 9]
44. Nixon made no mention of his momentous November 1969 announcement in his 1,090-page memoir. He recalled in his book only that his most pressing foreign policy issue was the Vietnam War; and his major arms control concern was SALT (Nixon [7, 5], p. 347).
45. William Safire, 'On Language', *New York Times Magazine,* 19 April 1998

Chapter 8: Cheating

1. Melvin Laird interview, April 1998
2. Laird [8, 1]
3. William Beecher, *Boston Globe,* 28 September 1975; Associated Press, 15 June 1976. See also Robert Harris and Jeremy Paxman, *A Higher Form of Killing,* New York: Hill and Wang, 1982, p. 219
4. Arkady Shevchenko, *Breaking With Moscow,* New York: Alfred A. Knopf, 1985, pp. 172–4, 179, 202. See also Anthony Marro, *New York Times,* 18 April

1978; 'A Defector's Story', *Time*, 11 February 1985; David Stout, *New York Times*, 11 March 1998 (Shevchenko obituary); Bart Barnes, *Washington Post*, 12 March 1998 (Shevchenko obituary).

5. Shevchenko [8, 4], pp. 179, 202
6. Shevchenko [8, 4], p. 173
7. Shevchenko [8, 4], pp. 173–4, 179, 202
8. Co-author Tom Mangold interviewed Shevchenko for BBC *Panorama* after his defection. At that time, Shevchenko's revelations went unquestioned by intelligence analysts on both sides of the Atlantic.
9. V. Umov, 'The Danger of a Biological War Remains', *Moscow Komsomolskaya Pravda*, 19 September 1992, translated in JPRS-TAC-92-030, 8 October 1992; Sergey Leskov, 'Plague and the Bomb', *Moscow Izvestiya*, 26 June 1993, translated in JPRS-TND-93-023, 19 July 1993

Chapter 9: Incident at Sverdlovsk

1. On a Russian television documentary in 1993, A. Volkov, the senior technician/engineer on the shift during the accident, confirmed that all of the equipment in the plant 'was designed to insert anthrax spores into munitions'. He said everyone worked inside the lab wearing gas masks and full rubber protection suits. He explained the cause of the accident: 'The filters were faulty. A dust cloud escaped into the atmosphere. It appears that the wind was blowing toward the ceramics plant and the whole zone was contaminated' (Aleksandr Pashkov, *Izvestiya* correspondent, 'The Generals and Anthrax', Russian Television Network (Moscow), 16 September 1993).

A similar version was first published in the Soviet press in 1991. Gen. Andrei Y. Mironyuk, the acting head of counterintelligence for the Urals Military District, told *Izvestiya* that the accident was caused by a lab employee who failed to turn on 'the safety filters and other protective mechanisms' in the anthrax production plant (Aleksandr Pashkov, 'I Know Where the Anthrax in Sverdlovsk Came From', *Izvestiya*, 23 November 1991).

2. Russian Television Network [9, 1]; Peter Gumbel, 'The Anthrax Mystery', *Wall Street Journal*, 21 October 1991
3. Ken Alibek interview, February 1998
4. No one knows the exact amount of anthrax that was released. Matthew Meselson's team estimated one kilogram was released. The US Defense Department estimated about 'ten pounds' (3.5 kilograms) in 1988 (Matthew Meselson, Jeanne Guillemin, Martin Hugh-Jones, Alexander Langmuir, Ilona Popova, Alexi Shelokov, and Olga Yampolskayal, 'The Sverdlovsk Anthrax Outbreak of 1979', *Science*, Vol. 266, 18 November 1994, pp. 1202–1208; US

Senate, Committee on Government Affairs, Permanent Subcommittee on Investigations, 'Global Spread of Chemical and Biological Weapons', testimony of Dr Barry Erlick, US Army BW Analyst, February 1989, p. 38).

5. Nikolai Shigapov interview, March 1998 (by Nick Sturdee). (He was union head of the ceramics factory in 1979.) Alevtinova Nekrassova, interview, March 1998 (by Nick Sturdee). (Her father, Vassilii Ivanov, then 49, lived close to Compound 19 and suffered an apparent heart attack while walking to work at the nearby meat factory. He was taken to a hospital and died soon afterwards – his body puffed up, covered in blotches. The cause of death was listed as 'poisoning by unknown substance'.) Elizaveta Prokhorova interview, March 1998 (by Nick Sturdee). (Her brother, Valerii Prokhorov, then 32, worked at Compound 32 and fell ill in late April. After three days of extremely high fever, he was taken to a hospital and died the next day with stains on his skin.)

See also Richard Burt, 'New Reports on Soviet Anthrax Convince US of Germ War Tie', *New York Times*, 29 March 1980; Barry May, 'What Really Happened at Sverdlovsk?', Reuters, 30 May 1980; Peter Gumbel, 'Anthrax: The Survivors Speak', *Wall Street Journal*, 23 October 1991; *Science* [9, 4]; Lidiya Usacheva, 'Code 022 – Death', *Poisk* ['Search'] (Moscow), 14–20 December 1990; Lt. Col. David Twining, 'Sverdlovsk Anthrax Outbreak', *Air Force Magazine*, March 1981, pp. 124–8.

6. Mararita Ivanova Ilenk interview, March 1998 (by Nick Sturdee). (She was the head doctor at Hospital 24 in 1979.) See also *Poisk* [9, 5]; V. Chelikov, 'Plague in the Backyard: Has the USSR Stopped Developing Bacteriological Weapons?', *Komsomolskaya Pravda*, 20 November 1991; S. Parfenov, 'Consequences of Alleged 1979 Sverdlovsk Anthrax Outbreak Explored', *Znamya Yunosti* ['Banner of Youth'] (Minsk), 24–25 October 1990, two parts, reprinted from the magazine *Rodina*, No. 5, 1990; N. Zenova, 'Military Secret: Reasons for the Tragedy in Svedlovsk Must be Investigated', *Literaturnaya Gazeta* ['The Literary Gazette'], 22 August 1990, no. 34, Part I and 'Accident At Sverdlosk', no. 39, 2 October 1991, Part II; *Science* [9, 4]; Philip Hilts, *New York Times*, 15 March 1993.

7. The pathologist was Dr Faina Abramova (*Znamya Yunosti* [9, 6]).

8. *Poisk* [9, 5]; *Znamya Yunosti* [9, 6]; *Science* [9, 4]

9. Ilenk [9, 6]. See also *Poisk* [9, 5]; *Znamya Yunosti* [9, 6]; *Science* [9, 4].

10. *Financial Times*, 20 March 1980; Associated Press, 20 March 1980

11. *Znamya Yunosti* [9, 6]

12. Peter Pringle, *Independent*, 29 November 1991; A. Pashkov, 'The End of the Urals Anthrax Legend', *Izvestiya*, 11 December 1991

13. Ilenk [9, 6]; *Poisk* [9, 5]; Thomas Kent, 'Soviets Made No Mention of Biological Warfare Tests in Anthrax Warnings', Associated Press, 9 June

1980; Boris Yarkov, 'The Disease Was in the Epaulets,' *Kuranty* (Moscow), 1 November 1990; *Wall Street Journal* [9, 5]; *Independent* [9, 12]

14. *New York Times* [9, 5]; *Science* [9, 4]

15. Ken Alibek interview, January 1998; confidential interview, March 1998; *Znamya Yunosti* [9, 6]

16. Mararita Ivanova Ilenk, the head doctor at Hospital 24, estimated in 1998 that about 600 people died from the accident. She said that 'over 100 people died' at her facility alone; and, she said, the same amount died at Hospitals 20 and 40. In addition, she said that the rest, about 300, were military casualties (Ilenk [9, 6]).

Ken Alibek, former Deputy Director of Biopreparat, said in 1998 that the death toll was in the hundreds. One Sverdlovsk hospital director told *ABC News* in 1998 she documented 259 victims, but the KGB confiscated all her records (Tim Weiner, *New York Times*, 25 February 1998; ABC News, *PrimeTime*, 'Germ Warfare: Weapons Of Terror', 25 February 1998).

The Soviets did not include any military deaths in their numbers. The CIA and DIA knew in 1980 – from eavesdropping on the Soviet military – that a number of military people had died. The DIA's first estimates (in June 1980) guessed that the range of deaths was from 40 to 1,000. The CIA believed in 1980 that the casualties were more likely 200–300 Soviet civilians. But, publicly, the US never fixed on a precise total number after 1980 (George Wilson, *Washington Post*, 29 June 1980; Walter Taylor, 'US Believes Soviet Anthrax Killed 200–300', *Washington Star*, 19 March 1980; confidential interview, March 1998).

17. Ilenk [9, 6]

18. Fred Hoffman, 'US Officials Say Soviet Biological Warfare Plant Exploded', Associated Press, 3 April 1980

19. *Wall Street Journal* [9, 5]; *Komsomolskaya Pravda* [9, 6]; *Znamya Yunosti* [9, 6]

20. Confidential interview, November 1998

21. Dr Zhores Medvedev, 'The Great Russian Germ War Fiasco', *New Scientist*, 31 July 1980

22. David Floyd, 'The Great Russian Germ War Disaster', *NOW*, 26 October 1979, pp. 54–5. See also Leslie Gelb, 'Keeping An Eye on Russia', *New York Times Magazine*, 29 November 1981; Robert Harris and Jeremy Paxman, *A Higher Form of Killing*, New York: Hill and Wang, 1982, pp. 220–21; *New Scientist* [9, 21].

23. *New Scientist* [9, 21]; *New York Times Magazine* [9, 22]; Harris and Paxman [9, 22], p. 220

24. *Bild Zeitung*, 13 February 1980, ACDA translation, 'Bacteriological Explosion Near Kashino Reported', 14 March 1980; Jim Anderson, UPI, 18 March 1990.

See also Harris and Paxman [9, 22], pp. 220–21, citing Robert Moss, *Daily Telegraph*, 11 February 1980.

25. John K. Cooley, *Christian Science Monitor*, 30 June 1980

26. US House of Representatives, Permanent Select Committee on Intelligence, Report, 'Soviet Biological Warfare Activities', 30 June 1980; *Washington Post* [9, 16]; UPI, 21 March 1980

27. Confidential interview, March 1998; Dino Brugioni interview, February 1998

28. *New York Times Magazine* [9, 22]

29. Reuters [9, 5]; *New York Times Magazine* [9, 22]

30. US House of Representatives [9, 26]; *New York Times Magazine* [9, 22]; DIA report, 'Soviet Biological Warfare Threat', 1986; Associated Press [9, 18]

31. Reuters [9, 5]. Popovsky also testified before the House Intelligence Committee in June 1980.

32. Robert Cullen, 'Some US Officials Doubt Soviets' Anthrax Explanation', Associated Press, 21 March 1980, citing *Maariv* (Tel Aviv), 20 March 1980

33. Confidential interview, March 1998

34. *Washington Star* [9, 16]; *Washington Post* [9, 16]; UPI [9, 26]

35. *Washington Post* [9, 16]; *Associated Press* [9, 18]; Col. David Huxsoll interview, May 1998

36. *New York Times Magazine* [9, 22]; *Air Force Magazine*, [9, 5]

37. R. Jeffrey Smith, 'Despite Soviet Account of Anthrax Outbreak, Questions Remain', *Washington Post*, 14 April 1988

38. Jim Anderson, UPI, 18 March 1990; Jim Anderson, UPI, 19 March 1990; *New York Times*, 19 March 1980; *New York Times Magazine* [9, 22]; Harris and Paxman [9, 22], p. 221

39. UPI [9, 38], 19 March 1990; Reuters, 21 March 1980

40. On 20 March, the Soviet news service Tass accused NATO of illegally making and storing biological weapons. Tass also accused the CIA of planting the *Bild* story to justify a secret US programme to make these bioweapons (*Air Force Magazine* [9, 5]).

41. *New York Times Magazine* [9, 22]

42. UPI, 20 March 1980; *New York Times*, 21 March 1980; DIA report [9, 30]; *New York Times Magazine* [9, 22]; Harris and Paxman [9, 22], p. 221; I.S. Bezdenezhnykh and V.N. Nikiforov, 'An Epidemiological Analysis of the Incidences of Anthrax in Sverdlovsk', *The Journal of Microbiology, Immunology, and Epidemiology* (Moscow), no. 5, May 1980 (US State Department translation)

43. US State Department, transcript of daily press conference, 21 March 1980; Reuters [9, 39]

44. Bezdenezhnykh and Nikiforov [9, 42]

45. *Washington Post* [9, 16]; Reuters, 14 May 1980

46. US House of Representatives, Permanent Select Committee on Intelligence, Subcommittee on Oversight, Hearing, 'The Sverdlovsk Incident: Soviet Compliance with the Biological Weapons Convention', 29 May 1980; US House of Representatives [9, 26]; Rep. Les Aspin, 'Aspin Says Soviets Covering Up On Anthrax', Press Release, 30 June 1980; Rep. Les Aspin, 'Aspin Says Administration Plays Politics With Anthrax Issue', Press Release, 9 July 1980

47. Aspin [9, 46], 30 June 1980; *Christian Science Monitor* [9, 25]; US House of Representatives [9, 26]

48. Aspin [9, 46], 30 June 1980

49. Moscow Radio, 9 July 1980 and Tass, 12 June 1980; M. Mishin, *Literaturnaya Gazeta*, 6 August 1980, translated in FBIS-SU, 12 August 1980

50. Jeanne McDermott, *The Killing Winds*, New York: Arbor House, 1987, p. 41; *New Scientist*, 'Shameful War of Words on Yellow Rain', 5 June 1986, p. 25
    See also Raymond Zilinskas, 'Anthrax in Sverdlovsk: Epidemic on BW?', *Bulletin of the Atomic Scientists*, June/July 1983, pp. 24–7; Vivian Wyatt, 'Anthrax: Recipe for a Blunt Weapon', *New Scientist*, 4 September 1980, pp. 721–2.

51. Matthew Meselson, 'The Biological Weapons Convention and the Sverdlovsk Anthrax Outbreak of 1979', *Journal of the Federation of American Scientists*, Public Interest Report, Vol. 41, No. 7, September 1988; *Wall Street Journal* [9, 2]

52. Col. David Huxsoll interview, May 1998; R. Jeffrey Smith, 'Soviets Offer Account of '79 Anthrax Outbreak,' *Washington Post*, 9 October 1986; David Dickson, 'Soviets Discuss Sverdlovsk', *Science*, 10 October 1986, p. 144.

53. Confidential interview, November 1998; Milton Leitenberg, 'A Return To Sverdlovsk', *Arms Control* (London), Vol. 12, No. 2, September 1991, p. 166; R. Jeffrey Smith, 'Soviets Deny 1979 Outbreak Involved Germ Lab', *Washington Post*, 13 April 1988

54. *Washington Post* [9, 53]; *Washington Post* [9, 37]; Eliot Marshall, 'Sverdlovsk: Anthrax Capital?', *Science*, 22 April 1988, Vol. 240, pp. 383–5; Meselson [9, 51]

55. R. Weiss, *Science News*, Vol. 133, April 1988; Meselson [9, 51]

56. Marshall [9, 54]

57. Marshall [9, 54]

58. Meselson [9, 51]. See also US Senate Committee on Government Affairs [9, 4], testimony of Matthew Meselson, May 1989.

59. The first major, independent Soviet press investigation that concluded the Sverdlovsk accident involved the BW plant was conducted by Natalya Zenova, Urals correspondent for Moscow's *Literaturnaya Gazeta* (Zenova [9, 6]).

The other important articles, in order, included: *Znamya Yunosti*, [9, 6]; *Kuranty* [9, 13]; Usacheva [9, 5]; Aleksandr Pashkov, 'How We Have Been "Inoculated" with Anthrax', *Izvestiya*, 11 November 1991; *Izvestiya* [9, 1], 23 November 1991; *Izvestiya* [9, 12]; Chelikov [9, 6].

60. *Wall Street Journal* [9, 2]; Peter Gumbel, 'Death in the Air', *Wall Street Journal*, 22 October 1991; *Wall Street Journal* [9, 5]

61. The whole epidemic, the Soviet officials had argued convincingly, had been traced to a single, 29-ton lot of bone meal sold a month before the outbreak from a plant in Aramil, a village about ten miles south of Sverdlovsk. But the director of Aramil's animal feed supplier explained to Gumbel that the village had no sterilization equipment, never produced any bone meal supplements, never saw any contaminated feed, and never saw any cases of anthrax (*Wall Street Journal* [9, 2]).

    The finding that the Aramil processing plant did not exist (and thus no contaminated bone meal was produced) was first reported by Soviet journalist Natalya Zenova in 1991 (Zenova [9, 6]).

62. Meselson later claimed that the reference to Aramil had been caused by a mistake in either note taking or the translation of the 1988 session with the three Soviet scientists. However, Meselson's own secret report, which he circulated in the US after his trip to Moscow in 1986, stated clearly that the Aramil plant was the cause of the accident. He repeated this statement in his 1988 report of the Soviet team's visit to the US (Milton Leitenberg, 'Anthrax in Sverdlovsk: New Pieces of the Puzzle', *Arms Control Today*, Vol. 22, Number 3, April 1992, p. 13, note 3; Matthew Meselson, 'Discussions in Moscow Regarding Sverdlovsk Anthrax Outbreak', 25 September 1986, seven-page letter; Meselson [9, 51]; *Wall Street Journal* [9, 2]; Marshall [9, 54]).

63. *Wall Street Journal* [9, 2]; Meselson [9, 51]. See also Marshall [9, 54].

64. *Izvestiya* [9, 1], 23 November 1991. See also *Independent* [9, 12]; Steve Connor, 'How the Russians Poisoned Their Own', *Independent*, 29 March 1993. Gen. Mironyuk did not know what the Soviet Army was doing inside this secret facility, but he confirmed that the decontamination efforts had included both Compound 19 and 32, and that military personnel had died inside both compounds. If the cause was contaminated meat, none of this would have occurred. Mironyuk also revealed, somewhat damningly, that the KGB had confiscated and destroyed all medical records and then concocted the elaborate cover story that was fed to the West (*Izvestiya* [9, 1], 23 November 1991).

65. *Izvestiya* [9, 12]

66. D. Muratov, Yu Sorokin and V. Fronin, *Komsomolskaya Pravda*, 27 May 1992; R. Jeffrey Smith, *Washington Post*, 16 June 1992. (In May 1992, Yeltsin

told a Soviet interviewer: 'the KGB admitted that our military developments were the cause of the release of anthrax spores.')

67. Yeltsin insisted he had no idea what the military was doing at Compound 19 before 1979. He said he only knew that it was a 'closed research centre'. After the epidemic started, he said he personally asked the Ministry of Defence to find out what had happened. He requested that they remove the research lab because it was 'endangering the lives of hundreds of thousands of citizens of Sverdlovsk'. He said the military did not inform him about the 'results of their work' (*Kuranty* (Moscow) [9, 13]).

68. Marshall [9, 4]; *New York Times* [9, 6]; Philip Hilts, *New York Times*, 18 November 1994. The medical evidence showed that the victims suffered anthrax poisoning in their lymph nodes and not in the gastrointestinal tracts.

69. *Wall Street Journal* [9, 60], 22 October 1991; *Literaturnaya Gazeta* [9, 6]; *Znamya Yunosti* [9, 6]. The key medical evidence showed that 42 victims at one hospital had each inhaled an estimated 10,000 or more microscopic particles of anthrax spores. These unusually small sized particles, in such exceptionally high concentration, did not appear in nature and could only have come from a biological weapons facility (*Independent* [9, 64]; *Literaturnaya Gazeta* [9, 6]; Russian Television Network [9, 1]).

A respected member of Meselson's team, Dr David H. Walker, a pathologist from the University of Texas, Galveston, reported after the trip that 42 victims had died of inhalation anthrax – based on examination of slides and preserved organs saved by doctors in Sverdlovsk (David H. Walker, Olga Yampolska, and Lev M. Grinberg, 'Death at Sverdlovsk: What We Have Learned?', *American Journal of Pathology*, June 1994, Vol. 144, No. 6; Michael Heylin, *Chemical and Engineering News*, 22 March 1993).

70. Robert Lee Hotz, 'Anthrax Deaths Tied To Soviet Lab', *Los Angeles Times*, 18 November 1994

71. *New York Times* [9, 68], 18 November 1994

72. Meselson [9, 4]; Matthew Meselson, *ASA Newsletter*, 8 April 1993, cited in *The Arms Control Reporter*, 1993, p. B:112; Nicholas Wade, 'Armed With Integrity', *New York Times Magazine*, 18 December 1994; Peter Pringle, 'Anthrax Answer Was Blowing In the Wind', *Independent*, 18 November 1994

Chapter 10: The Juniper Channel

1. Confidential interview, April 1998; confidential interview, March 1998

2. Confidential interview, April 1998

3. Confidential interview, April 1998; confidential interview, March 1998

4. Confidential interview, April 1998; confidential interview, May 1998
5. Confidential interview, March 1998
6. US Senate, Committee of Government Affairs, 'Global Spread of Chemical and Biological Weapons', testimony of Assistant Secretary of State H. Allen Holmes, 1989, p. 184
7. Robert Gates interview, May 1998
8. Defense Intelligence Agency, 'Soviet Biological Warfare Threat', 1986, DST-1610F-057-86; US Department of Defense, *Soviet Military Power*, April 1984, cited in Milton Leitenberg, 'The Conversion of Biological Warfare Research and Development Facilities to Peaceful Uses', in *Control of Dual-Threat Agents*, ed. Ehrhard Geissler and John P. Woodall, Oxford University Press: Oxford, 1994, p. 91; Jack Anderson and Dale Van Atta, 'Poison And Plague: Russia's Secret Terror Weapons', *Readers Digest*, September 1984, pp. 54–8; *The Arms Control Reporter*, 1986, p. B:15; *Christian Science Monitor*, 'Poison in The Wind', 13 December 1988, p. 35; Bill Gertz, 'Biological Weapons Made in Soviet Union, Report Says', *Washington Times*, 19 January 1989.

   Both Sverdlovsk and the Vozrozhdeniye Island test site were cited publicly by the Defense Intelligence Agency in their 1986 report on the Soviet BW programme (DIA [10, 8]).

   Limited parts of the CIA's information were publicly confirmed by the Soviets themselves in 1987, after the US and USSR agreed to an exchange of information at the 1986 BWC review conference in Geneva. The Soviets claimed they had five military laboratories conducting lawful, defensive bio-research. Three of them were on the CIA's list of alleged violators: Sverdlovsk, Zagorsk, and Aralsk (near Vozrozhdeniye Island). Two were not mentioned by CIA: Leningrad and Kirov. The Soviets also listed fourteen legitimate civilian labs, including the one at Kol'tsovo (Information presented by the USSR, Exchange of Data on Research Centers and Laboratories, UN Department of Disarmament, 13 October 1987, cited in *Biologicals*, Vol. 21, Number 3, September 1993; Milton Leitenberg, 'Commentary: The Biological Weapons Program of the Former Soviet Union', pp. 187–91; *Christian Science Monitor* [10, 8]).
9. Jack Anderson and Dale Van Atta, *Washington Post*, 7 May 1986, cited in *The Arms Control Reporter*, 1986, pp. B:21–2
10. Confidential interview, May 1998
11. This account is based on interviews with three senior officials who have read 'Juniper' reports. Confidential interview, March 1998; confidential interview, April 1998; confidential interview, May 1998. 'Juniper' lasted until 1994, making it one of the longest-running secret channels of that era. By then, the second year of the Clinton Administration, the access list had grown to about 150 officials.

12. David Hoffman, 'President Plans To Intensify Arms-Control Diplomacy', *Washington Post*, 3 September 1989

13. Confidential interview, May 1998

14. Gates [10, 7]

15. Robert Gates, *From the Shadows*, New York: Simon & Schuster, 1996, p. 423

16. Gates [10, 15], pp. 431–2

17. Gates [10, 15], pp. 468–71

18. Gates [10, 15], pp. 482–4

19. Don Oberdorfer, *The Turn: From Cold War to a New Era*, New York: Poseidon Press, Simon & Schuster, 1991, pp. 370–72; Gates [10, 15], pp. 475–80; confidential interview, May, 1998

20. ACDA Annual Report, 1994, p. 105

21. Confidential interview, May 1998

22. Confidential interview, May 1998

Chapter 11: The Defector

1. Dr Chris Davis interview, 'Plague Wars', BBC *Panorama*, 20 July 1998 (taping session), transcript, pp. 3, 9; confidential interview, March 1998; confidential interview, November 1998. (Dr Davis, chief of the Biological Warfare Desk of the Defence Intelligence Staff, was one of Pasechnik's principal British debriefers.)

   See also Mark Urban, BBC *Newsnight*, 21 January 1993, BBC transcript, pp. 1–23; Mark Urban, 'The Cold War's Deadliest Secret', *The Spectator*, 23 January 1993, pp. 9–10; James Adams, *The New Spies*, London: Century Hutchinson, 1994; James Adams, 'The Red Death', *Sunday Times* (London), 27 March 1994; Bill Gertz, *Washington Times*, 4 July 1992.

   On 21 January 1993, Dr Vladimir Pasechnik made his first public appearance during a BBC *Newsnight* interview with BBC reporter Mark Urban (who published an accompanying article in *The Spectator*). On the programme, British Foreign Minister Douglas Hurd supported Pasechnik as a credible source who reinforced other intelligence the West possessed.

2. Confidential interview, November 1998; Davis [11, 1], p. 9

3. Confidential interview, November 1998

4. Confidential interview, October 1998

5. Confidential interview, November 1998; Davis [11, 1], pp. 3, 9; Dr David Kelly interview, 'Plague Wars', BBC *Panorama*, 20 July 1998 (taping session), transcript, p. 2; Gary Crocker interview, March 1998; Ken Alibek, with Stephen Handelman, *BIOHAZARD*, New York: Random House, 1999, p. 43.

See also Urban, BBC [11, 1]; Urban, *The Spectator* [11, 1]; Adams, *The New Spies* [11, 1]; Adams, *Sunday Times* [11, 1].

6. Confidential interview, November 1998

7. In 1972, Yury Ovchinnikov, a highly respected Soviet molecular biologist and vice president of the Academy of Sciences, urged the sceptical Ministry of Defence to establish the USSR's first genetics programme to develop biological weapons – because he noticed, from reading Western scientific journals, that the USSR was way behind the US in this field. Up to that point, no Soviet military laboratories or researchers were devoted to genetic engineering. Ovchinnikov privately convinced President Leonid Brezhnev and his advisers that this new programme was important to national security, and, in 1973, Brezhnev gave his approval by secret decree (which also established Biopreparat). The programme, code-named 'Ferment', was empowered to make new, genetically altered bacteria and viral agents which were resistant to antibiotics and vaccines. Ovchinnikov, who remained a strong supporter of Biopreparat, died in 1987 (Alibek, with Handelman [11, 5], pp. 40–41).

8. Urban, BBC [11, 1], p. 7; Urban, *The Spectator* [11, 1]; Davis [11, 1], pp. 6, 32–3, 39

9. Davis [11, 1], pp. 6, 32–3, 39; Urban, BBC [11, 1], p. 8

10. Adams, *Sunday Times* [11, 1]

11. Confidential interview, November 1998

12. Urban, BBC [11, 1], p. 9

13. Davis [11, 1], p. 3. The West's knowledge of the Soviet's strategic weapons and plans, originally from Pasechnik, was greatly enhanced in 1992 when Ken Alibek arrived in the West. Alibek, a military doctor who served at Biopreparat headquarters, possessed more detailed and current information about military doctrine. This section on Soviet military doctrine and delivery systems is based on information from Ken Alibek (Ken Alibek interview, February 1998).

14. There were two possible scenarios during which the USSR planned to use ICBMs carrying BW warheads. The decision to launch would be based on the circumstances and the type of war that broke out:

    1. If 'total war' started, but both sides decided to use only conventional weapons, and not nuclear missiles, and then the opponent used BW first against the USSR, the Soviets would counter with BW. The USSR would not use nuclear missiles first in that circumstance, because they understood that this step meant Mutual Assured Destruction (MAD).

    2. If a total war started and all possible weapons of mass destruction were used, including nuclear missiles, then BW would be used as part of the overall arsenal.

15. Alibek [11, 13]; Davis [11, 1], p. 4; Alibek, with Handelman [11, 5], p. 7

16. No 'special orders' were ever sent out by the Kremlin or Ministry of Defence. No historical circumstances after 1972 even approached the issuance of mobilization instructions (Alibek [11, 13]).

17. Alibek, with Handelman [11, 5], pp. 5–6, 8. Biopreparat researchers calculated that 220 lbs of dry anthrax, delivered under optimum conditions, could fatally infect up to three million people. At that death rate, one SS-18, which could carry a total of 880 lbs of anthrax in its ten warheads, would kill everyone in New York or London.

18. Ken Alibek interview, April 1999; confidential interview, April 1999; Alibek, with Handelman [11, 5], pp. 140–41

19. Dr Chris Davis, one of Pasechnik's debriefers, says that keeping these 'tiny micro-organisms' alive in missile warheads, through the atmosphere, and back to earth, so that they were still 'alive and kicking and will get into the body and multiply and injure and kill' was an 'enormous achievement' for the Soviet scientists – though not one to applaud (Davis [11, 1], p. 7).

20. Urban, BBC [11, 1], p. 11

21. Confidential interview, November 1998

22. Adams, *Sunday Times* [11, 1]

23. Adams, *Sunday Times* [11, 1]; Alibek, with Handelman [11, 5], p. 139

24. Confidential interview, November 1998

25. Adams, *Sunday Times* [11, 1]; Alibek [11, 13]. As of 1993, Pasechnik was reportedly working contentedly for a British company in his preferred field, civilian bio-research (Adams, *Sunday Times* [11, 1]).

26. Alibek [11, 13]

27. Confidential interviews, November 1998; Alibek, with Handelman [11, 5], pp. 12, 22–3

28. Confidential interviews, November 1998. See also Alibek, with Handelman [11, 5], p. 12.

29. Alibek, with Handelman [11, 5], pp. 12, 22–3

30. Alibek, with Handelman [11, 5], pp. 9–11

31. Confidential interviews, November 1998

32. Confidential interviews, November 1998

33. Confidential interview, November 1998

34. Confidential interview, November 1998; confidential interview, April 1998; confidential interview, March 1998; Davis [11, 1], p. 9

35. Confidential interview, November 1998; confidential interview, April 1998; confidential interview, March 1998

36. Confidential interview, April 1998; confidential interview, March 1998

37. James Baker, with Thomas DeFrank, *The Politics of Diplomacy*, New York: G.P. Putnam's and Sons, 1995, p. 660n.

38. The UNGROUP advisers in 1990 included: Douglas MacEachin, from CIA; Ronald Lehman, director of ACDA; Reggie Bartholomew and Jim Timbie from the State Department; Steven Hadley from the Defense Department; Howard Graves from the Joint Chiefs of Staff; Vic Alessi from the Energy Department; and the NSC's senior arms control expert, Arnie Kantor, who served as chairman (Baker, with DeFrank [11, 37], p. 660n; confidential interview, March 1998).
39. Confidential interview, April 1998; confidential interview, March 1998
40. Confidential interview, April 1998; confidential interview, March 1998
41. Confidential interview, March 1998
42. Confidential interview, May 1998; confidential interview, March 1998
43. Confidential interview, April 1998; confidential interview, May 1998
44. Confidential interview, November 1998
45. Confidential interview, November 1998
46. Gary Crocker interview, March 1998

Chapter 12: Protests

1. Ambassador Jack F. Matlock, Jr. interview, April 1998; Robert Gates interview, May 1998; Dr Chris Davis interview, 'Plague Wars', BBC *Panorama*, 20 July 1998 (taping session), transcript, p. 9; confidential interview, October 1998; confidential interview, November 1998
2. Matlock [12, 1]
3. James Baker, with Thomas DeFrank, *The Politics of Diplomacy*, New York: G.P. Putnam's and Sons, 1995, pp. 248, 252
4. Baker with DeFrank [12, 3], pp. 247–9. For a description of Trinity St Serguis and Zagorsk, see Jack Anderson and Dale Van Atta, 'Sanitation Institute A Soviet Front', *Washington Post*, 3 August 1989.
5. Confidential interviews, March 1998
6. PBS *Frontline*, 'Plague War', James Baker interview, 13 October 1998; confidential interview, March 1998
7. Baker, PBS [12, 6]; confidential interview, March 1998
8. Baker, with DeFrank [12, 3], p. 247
9. Baker, with DeFrank [12, 3], p. 252
10. Ken Alibek interview, May 1998. According to Ken Alibek, Gorbachev was sent a memo on Pasechnik's defection in 1988, but the military downplayed the significance of the loss. They misled the Kremlin by insisting the Leningrad director's flight to Britain was not a big security concern.
11. Confidential interview, March 1998; confidential interview, October 1998; confidential interview, November 1998

12. On 18 May, at formal talks in Moscow between British Defence Minister Tom King and Soviet Minister of Defence, Dmitry Yazov, the hard-line Soviet Marshall dismissively told King that it was inconceivable that the Soviet Union would develop or possess biological weapons. In denying everything, Yazov claimed that this issue had nothing to do with the Ministry of Defence. Any biological research by the military, he said, was intended only to collect intelligence about potential epidemics and to prevent animal diseases – like anthrax, cholera, and Plague – from breaching Soviet borders. Yazov added, for good measure, that the West's misinformation was coming from an 'insane scientist' (Pasechnik) who was a liar with personal problems (confidential interview, October 1998; confidential interview, November 1998).

     Marshall Yazov, a strong critic of Shevardnadze for cutting defence spending and power, was one of the Committee of Eight who led the attempted coup against Gorbachev in August 1991. (See Carolyn McGiffert Ekedahl and Melvin Goodman, *The Wars of Eduard Shevardnadze*, University Park, PA: The Pennsylvania State University Press, 1997, pp. 92–4, 254–5).

13. Confidential interview, May 1998

14. Sir Percy Cradock interview, December 1998. Ken Alibek maintains that four Kremlin officials were fully briefed about the BW programme – Gorbachev, Defence Minister Dmitry Yazov, KGB chief Vladimir Krychkov, and Lev Zaikov (the Politburo member in charge of military industries). According to Alibek, Gorbachev signed a secret Five-Year Plan for Biopreparat in 1986 which approved $1 billion in new funding and called for an expanded building programme, including a new virus production plant at Yoshkar-Ola, Mordovia; a new military virus and bacteria production plant at Strizhi, Russia; and a new smallpox reactor at Vektor (Ken Alibek, with Stephen Handelman, *BIOHAZARD*, New York: Random House, 1999, pp. 117–18, 150; Ken Alibek interview, February 1998).

15. Cradock [12, 14]. Ken Alibek has written that senior Soviet Foreign Ministry officials, including Shevardnadze, were deliberately kept uninformed about all activities at the secret BW facilities of Biopreparat and the Army's 15th Directorate. At high-level meetings, Generals Kalinin and Yevstigneev told senior diplomats only that their organizations made vaccines and performed defensive functions at these sites. Alibek has written that Shevardnadze was furious with the generals in 1990 because he was learning about the illegal BW program for the first time from 'foreigners' (the US/UK diplomats and démarches) (Alibek, with Handelman [12, 14], pp. 146, 149).

16. Today, Shevardnadze, the President of Georgia, is still despised by many senior Russian military leaders, who blame him personally for destroying the USSR. Many Georgians believe that Russian generals have plotted to over-

throw or kill Shevardnadze to teach him a lesson and to bring other former Soviet states to heel (Stephen Kinzer, *New York Times*, 3 May 1998).

17. Gary Crocker interview, March 1998
18. Matlock [12, 1]
19. Ken Alibek confirms that the test chambers at Stepnogorsk, for instance, were closed in May 1990, after Gorbachev's order was issued (Alibek [12, 10]).
20. Alibek [12, 14]; confidential interview, November 1998. In early 1990, Ken Alibek, then deputy director of Biopreparat, wrote a memo for Gorbachev that explained how he could close the Soviet offensive BW programme. Gen. Yuriy Kalinin, the director of Biopreparat, did not support the idea, but he did not try to block Alibek from sending the memo to the Kremlin. However, once the memo was submitted, Kalinin's allies in the Kremlin added one paragraph to the four-paragraph addendum before Gorbachev saw it. Kalinin's addition stated that if Russia closed the BW programme's research and development operations, it would still retain all of the production facilities as 'mobilization capacities' in case a 'special period' was declared prior to war.

   Kalinin's new clause was a clever way to outmanoeuvre the intent of the memo. It meant that the offensive BW programme would continue unchanged, with everything now explained by the necessity of having these capabilities in case of war. Gorbachev signed the memo – with this addendum – on 5 May 1990. From this episode, and other earlier ones, Alibek argues that Gorbachev knew the full extent of the Soviet BW programme (Alibek [12, 14]).
21. Confidential interview, April 1998
22. David Hoffman, *Washington Post*, 4 June 1990; Baker, with DeFrank [12, 3], p. 252; Don Oberdorfer, *The Turn*, New York: Poseidon Press, Simon & Schuster, 1991, pp. 410–30
23. Confidential interview, October 1998; confidential interview, November 1998. See also Mark Urban, BBC *Newsnight*, 21 January 1993, BBC transcript, p. 9; James Adams, 'The Red Death', *Sunday Times* (London), 27 March 1994; John Barry, 'Planning A Plague?', *Newsweek*, 1 February 1993.
24. Urban, BBC [12, 23], p. 9
25. Confidential interview, April 1998; Oberdorfer [12, 22], pp. 412–18, 422
26. Jack Matlock, *Autopsy of an Empire: The American Ambassador's Account of the Collapse of the Soviet Union*, New York: Random House, 1995, p. 367; Oberdorfer [12, 22], p. 412
27. Confidential interview, October 1998; confidential interview, November 1998. See also Urban, BBC [12, 22], transcript, p. 1; *Vecherniy Peterburg* (St Petersburg), 25 January 1993; Bill Gertz, *Washington Times*, 4 July 1992.

28. Urban, BBC [12, 22], transcript, p. 4

29. Confidential interview, October 1998

30. Gates [12, 1]

31. Confidential interview, October 1998; confidential interview, April 1998; confidential interview, March 1998; confidential interview, May 1998; Gates [12, 1]; Crocker [12, 17]

32. Confidential interview, April 1998; confidential interview, March 1998; confidential interview, May 1998; Gates [12, 1]; Crocker [12, 17]

33. Gates [12, 1]

34. Gates [12, 1]

35. Confidential interview, May 1998; confidential interview, November 1998

36. Confidential interview, May 1998

37. Confidential interview, April 1998; confidential interview, May 1998; Gates [12, 1]

38. For background on Baker's trip to Irkutsk, see Baker, with DeFrank [12, 3], p. 3; Matlock [12, 26], pp. 409–10; Michael Beschloss and Strobe Talbott, *At the Highest Levels*, Boston: Little, Brown & Company, 1993, p. 243; Margaret Garrard Warner, 'The Moscow Connection', *Newsweek*, 17 September 1990.

39. Confidential interview, October 1998; confidential interview, November 1998; confidential interview, April 1998.

40. Confidential interview, October 1998; confidential interview, November 1998

41. 'Baker raised it with Shevardnadze in a limousine,' Robert Gates confirmed. 'Baker handed him a paper in the limo. President Bush knew exactly what was going on – that this scenario would be played out' (Gates [12, 1]).

42. Confidential interview, April 1998; confidential interview, March 1998; Gates [12, 1]

43. Confidential interview, October 1998; confidential interview, November 1998

44. Confidential interview, October 1998; confidential interview, November 1998

45. Confidential interview, October 1998; confidential interview, November 1998

46. Ambassador John Hawes interview, May 1998

47. Confidential interview, April 1998; confidential interview, March 1998

48. Confidential interview, October 1998; confidential interview, November 1998

Chapter 13: Inspection

1. James Baker, with Thomas DeFrank, *The Politics of Diplomacy*, New York: G.P. Putnam's and Sons, 1995, p. 474; confidential interview, May 1998

2. Carolyn McGiffert Ekedahl and Melvin Goodman, *The Wars of Eduard Shevardnadze*, University Park, PA: The Pennsylvania State University Press, 1997, pp. 43–8, 237–54

3. Ken Alibek interview, May 1998; confidential interview, November 1998

4. Alibek [13, 3]. Alibek conferred regularly with Gen. Kalinin about these issues, and attended numerous Biopreparat strategy sessions. He also spoke to one of Shevardnadze's deputies who was in charge of the interagency commission which handled the inspection planning process.

5. Since October, Ambassador John Hawes, a veteran State Department official, had been co-leader of the US team, in charge of the diplomacy, but he did not accompany the group to the USSR, due to another assignment.

6. Confidential interview, November 1998. Officially, the Soviets only used three levels of bio-containment, up to what they called their BL-3; however, Western experts contend that the Soviets used this three-tiered system as a means of hiding the fact they had BL-4 equivalent labs that could work on the most dangerous pathogens, like smallpox and Ebola.

7. Confidential interview, April 1998; confidential interview, September 1998

8. Dr Frank Malinoski interview, February 1998; Dr Chris Davis interview, 'Plague Wars', BBC *Panorama*, 20 July 1998, taping session, transcript, p. 20

9. Malinoski [13, 8]

10. Alibek [13, 3]

11. Confidential interview, April 1998

12. Alibek [13, 3]; Davis, BBC [13, 8], p. 11; Ken Alibek, with Stephen Handelman, *BIOHAZARD*, New York: Random House, 1999, p. 197

13. Dr David Kelly interview, 'Plague Wars', BBC *Panorama*, 20 July 1998, taping session, transcript, p. 23

14. Kelly, BBC [13, 13], p. 23

15. Confidential interview, October 1998

16. Malinoski [13, 8]; Kelly, BBC [13, 13], p. 1; confidential interview, October 1998

17. Malinoski [13, 8]; Davis, BBC [13, 8] p. 13; confidential interview, October 1998. For background on Obolensk, see also John Barry, 'Planning A Plague?', *Newsweek*, 1 February 1993; Anthony Rimmington, 'From Military to Industrial Complex? The Conversion of Biological Weapons' Facilities in the Russian Federation', in *Contemporary Security Policy*, Vol. 17, no. 1, London: Frank Cass, April 1996, p. 86; Vitaliy Kaysyn, 'Visiting the Caged Beast', *Pravda* (Moscow), 4 February 1992, translated in JPRS-TAC-92-008, 9 March 1992.

18. Davis, BBC [13, 8], p. 13; Ken Alibek interview, 'Plague Wars', BBC *Panorama*, 20 July 1998, broadcast transcript, p. 8; confidential interview, October 1998

19. Confidential interview, April 1998; Davis, BBC [13, 8]; Kelly, BBC [13, 13], p. 1; Malinoski [13, 8]. See also *Newsweek* [13, 17].

20. Alibek [13, 3]; Davis, BBC [13, 8], p. 11; Kelly, BBC [13, 13], p. 1

21. Alibek [13, 3]; Davis, BBC [13, 8], p. 11; Kelly, BBC [13, 13], p. 1

22. Alibek [13, 3]

23. Davis, BBC [13, 8], p. 12; Kelly, BBC [13, 13], p. 2; Malinoski [13, 8]; Alibek [13, 3]; confidential interview, April 1998

24. Davis, BBC [13, 8], p. 12; Alibek [13, 3]

25. Davis, BBC [13, 8], pp. 12–13

26. Davis, BBC [13, 8], pp. 12–13

27. Davis, BBC [13, 8], pp. 12–13. According to Ken Alibek, the Soviet escort panicked in the heat of the moment and did not give Dr Davis the rehearsed explanation of the unusual marks inside the chamber. Instead of implausibly blaming 'hammering' for causing the marks on the door, the preferred answer should have been that the marks were made by explosives used in testing aerosols during lawful 'bio-defence' research. This plausible response would have made it more difficult for the West to accuse the Soviets of a violation (Alibek, with Handelman [13, 12], p. 200).

28. Kelly, BBC [13 13], p. 1

29. Ken Alibek has confirmed that the Soviets lied to Kelly and Davis (Alibek, BBC [13, 18], p. 9).

30. Davis, BBC [13, 8], p. 13

31. Confidential interview, April 1998

32. Dr Chris Davis interview, September 1998

33. Confidential interview, April 1998; Malinoski [13, 8]; Alibek [13, 3]

34. Malinoski [13, 8]

35. Malinoski [13, 8]; Alibek, with Handelman [13, 12], p. 153

36. Before the inspectors could enter the BL-4 laboratory, the Soviets wanted the US/UK team members to give them blood samples. They insisted there were strict rules prohibiting people from entering the laboratories without the proper vaccines. The Soviets claimed they needed the blood to make sure the visitors were adequately protected from certain pathogens. The Soviets already knew what vaccinations the visitors had taken, because they had submitted their shot cards. The blood would confirm the written information.

The Americans suspected another reason was behind the blood request: the Soviet military wanted to see what antibody profiles were in the visitors' blood, so they would know what types of vaccines the US and UK were using. From this information, the Soviets would have state-of-the-art knowledge of Western antibody defences.

The Soviets also wanted the blood samples to make sure that the visitors who entered the laboratory did not make false claims later about contracting diseases during the tour.

Frank Malinoski, Chris Davis, David Kelly, and several others gave blood samples at Obolensk (Malinoski [13, 8]).

37. Malinoski [13, 8]
38. Malinoski [13, 8]
39. Malinoski [13, 8]
40. Confidential interview, October 1998
41. Confidential interview, October 1998
42. Malinoski [13, 8]
43. Malinoski [13, 8]; confidential interview, September 1998; confidential interview, October 1998
44. Malinoski [13, 8]; confidential interview, September 1998; confidential interview, October 1998
45. Confidential interview, April 1998; Malinoski [13, 8]
46. Confidential interview, April 1998; confidential interview, September 1998; Davis, BBC [13, 8], p. 15
47. Dr Lev Sandakhchiev interview, May 1998
48. Sandakhchiev [13, 47]; Malinoski [13, 8]; Ken Alibek interview, February 1998; Davis, BBC [13, 8], p. 15; Alibek, with Handelman [13, 12], pp. 118–19
49. Dr Frank Malinoski [13, 8]
50. Confidential interview, October 1998
51. Davis, BBC [13, 8], p. 34
52. Malinoski [13, 8]; confidential interview, September 1998; confidential interview, October 1998
53. Malinoski [13, 8]; Kelly, BBC [13, 13], p. 4
54. Malinoski [13, 8]; David Kelly interview, January 1998; Davis, BBC [13, 8], p. 37
55. Malinoski [13, 8]
56. Alibek [13, 48]; confidential interview, October 1998. Ken Alibek knew about this computer-modelling project as early as 1976, because he supplied Dr Sandakhchiev with data generated at the Biopreparat facilities where he served.
57. Alibek [13, 48]; confidential interview, October 1998
58. Alibek [13, 48]; confidential interview, October 1998
59. Malinoski [13, 8]; Alibek [13, 8]; Kelly, BBC [13, 13], p. 3; confidential interview, October 1998. See also Rimmington [13, 17], p. 108.
60. Alibek [13, 3]; Alibek, BBC [13, 18], p. 10. See also ABC News, *Prime Time Live*, 25 February 1998.
61. Alibek, BBC [13, 18]; Ken Alibek interview, 'Plague War,' PBS *Frontline*, 13 October 1998
62. Alibek [13, 3]; Alibek, BBC [13, 18], p. 10
63. US Congress Joint Economic Committee, testimony of Dr Kenneth Alibek, 20 May 1998
64. Confidential interview, April 1998; confidential interview, September 1998

65. Malinoski [13, 8]; Davis, BBC [13, 8], p. 16; confidential interview, September 1998; confidential interview, October 1998

66. Confidential interview, September 1998

67. Confidential interview, April 1998

68. Malinoski [13, 8]; confidential interview, September 1998; confidential interview, October 1998

69. The US/UK team briefly considered sending two men into the restricted Vektor laboratory and risking the quarantine. But they decided it was not a good idea to leave a twosome behind under the circumstances – alone and in isolation – so they passed (Confidential interview, September 1998).

70. Malinoski [13, 8]; Davis, BBC [13, 8], p. 36; confidential interview, September 1998. See also Malcolm Dando, *Biological Warfare in the 21st Century*, London: Brassey's (UK) Ltd, 1994, pp. 153–5.

71. The Russian scientist was Nikolai Ustinov, who became infected on 13 April 1988 in a laboratory accident. (See Chapter 18.)

72. Kelly, BBC [13, 13], p. 5; Davis, BBC [13, 8], p. 15; Malinoski [13, 8]; confidential interview, September 1998; confidential interview, April 1998

73. Malinoski [13, 8]

74. In the early 1980s, the World Health Organization (WHO) approved the plan to keep just two repositories for smallpox – one at CDC in Atlanta and the other at the Ivanofski Institute for Viral Preparations in Moscow. The Soviets claimed that their smallpox sample was transferred from Moscow to Vektor because it was more secure at the more modern facility in Kol'tsovo. But the switch was done secretly, without telling the WHO, and in circumvention of WHO guidelines.

According to Ken Alibek, the real reason that the Soviet smallpox samples were moved to Vektor was that Dr Lev Sandakhchiev wanted the samples in his laboratory for advanced 'offensive' BW research. After the 1991 US/UK discovery of the sample at Vektor, Sandakhchiev cleverly arranged for an after-the-fact transfer authorization from the WHO – which was apparently deceived about his true intent and the circumstances (Alibek [13, 48]; Alibek [13, 61]; Kelly, BBC [13, 13], p. 5).

Chris Davis says: 'The real reason [for the transfer from Moscow to Vektor] is that a production requirement was put on Vektor to make more sophisticated smallpox.' Davis confirmed this work was meant to produce an offensive weapon. 'I don't think there's any doubt at all,' he says (Davis, BBC [13, 8], pp. 15–17).

75. The Soviet smallpox samples were moved to Kol'tsovo for one other reason – because the Soviets feared Pasechnik had told the West about the military's ongoing smallpox research. The Soviets needed a rational explanation to

rebut Pasechnik's information. Their excuse was that Vektor was mapping the smallpox DNA (confidential interview, November 1998).

76. Malinoski [13, 8]. Ken Alibek worries that only a 'small accident' with smallpox at Vektor might cause a 'serious epidemic'. In spite of the danger, he adds: 'Vektor scientists have continued working on industrial techniques to manufacture biological weapons with smallpox. They are using hundreds of litres of highly concentrated smallpox. They just don't care about the consequences. No one cared' (Alibek [13, 48]).

77. Kelly, BBC [13, 13], pp. 4, 25

78. Kelly, BBC [13, 13], pp. 4–5

79. Davis, BBC [13, 8], p. 16

80. Malinoski [13, 8]

81. Kelly, BBC [13, 13], p. 5

82. Malinoski [13, 8]; Davis, BBC [13, 8], pp. 16–17

83. Davis, BBC [13, 8], p. 17; Kelly, BBC [13, 13], p. 3. See also V. Umov, 'The Danger of a Biological War Remains', *Komsomolskaya Pravda*, 19 September 1992, translated in JPRS-TAC-92-030, 8 October 1992.

84. Kelly, BBC [13, 13], p. 3

85. When the authors went to visit Dr Sandakhchiev in 1998, he gave broadly the same answers to the same questions.

86. Malinoski [13, 8]

87. Kelly, BBC [13, 13], p. 3; confidential interview, October 1998

88. Alibek [13, 48]; confidential interview, September 1998; confidential interview, October 1998

89. Alibek [13, 48]; confidential interview, September 1998; confidential interview, October 1998

90. Alibek [13, 48]; confidential interview, September 1998; confidential interview, October 1998

91. Alibek [13, 48]; confidential interview, September 1998; confidential interview, October 1998

92. Confidential interview, October 1998; confidential interview, April 1998; confidential interview, March 1998; Malinoski [13, 8]; Kelly, BBC [13, 13], p. 8

93. Confidential interview, April 1998; confidential interview, October 1998

94. Confidential interview, October 1998

95. Davis, BBC [13, 8], p. 34

96. Confidential interview, September 1998

97. Confidential interview, April 1998

98. Alibek [13, 3]

99. Alibek [13, 3]

Chapter 14: Gorbachev

1. Confidential interview, October 1998; confidential interview, November 1998. In mid-March 1991, first Secretary of State Baker and then Prime Minister Major held separate meetings with Gorbachev, during which they stressed that the inspectors' recent visit had heightened, rather than allayed, the West's fears about the continuing Soviet offensive programme.

On 25 March, the new Soviet Foreign Minister, Alexander Bessmyrtnykh, was given copies of two US/UK papers containing detailed complaints about the on-going Soviet BW programme (based on the inspectors' January visit). The first US/UK paper noted eight points that indicated the Soviet offensive BW programme was not dismantled:

1. The existence of new explosive test chambers.
2. Extensive production capacity – beyond any justification.
3. Extensive bio-containment facilities and labs – far beyond defensive needs.
4. Unusual quarantine requirements – which point to secretive and dangerous work.
5. Extensive research on pathogens that were not health threats to the USSR.
6. Extensive new construction at the sites – indicating an expanding programme.
7. Biopreparat received 40 per cent of its funding from the Ministry of Defence, which was all classified; and most senior Biopreparat officials were military officers.
8. Only military officials were able or allowed to answer many of the visitors' questions.

The second paper, on the future steps that the USSR could take to give the West confidence that it was in compliance with the BWC, cited ten points:

1. Dismantle all explosive test chambers.
2. Stop all work on smallpox, except at a WHO approved lab in Moscow.
3. Stop all open-air testing of dangerous pathogens.
4. Destroy all hardened bunkers at BW facilities.
5. Destroy all BW production buildings.
6. Destroy either 'Corpus One' at Obolensk or 'Building 6A' at Kol'tsovo.
7. Reduce the production capacity to defensive standards at one BW facility.
8. Reduce bio-containment at any one site.
9. Reduce research at one site on pathogens that are not a public health risk.

10. Cut back significantly on the military's role in classified research on dangerous pathogens.

2. Additional US/UK-Soviet diplomatic contacts after March 1991 included the following: on 31 May in Lisbon, Baker informed Bessmyrtnykh that the previous Soviet response/rebuttal was unconvincing. On 20 June in Berlin, Baker handed Bessmyrtnykh a letter from President Bush to Gorbachev which reiterated the West's serious concerns. On 11 July, Gorbachev wrote to Bush, repeating that the Soviet Union had no offensive BW programme. On 17–18 July in London, at the G7 summit, Bush and Major again raised the issue of non-compliance with Gorbachev in separate, private discussions. No progress was made, save that Bush and Major agreed to Gorbachev's proposal to hold trilateral talks about the nature of treaty violations in late August in Moscow.

3. Confidential interview, March 1998; confidential interview, October 1998; confidential interview, November 1998

4. Confidential interview, November 1998

5. Confidential interview, October 1998; confidential interview, November 1998. See also John Barry, 'Planning A Plague?', *Newsweek*, 1 February 1993.

6. Confidential interview, March 1998; confidential interview, April 1998. Robert Gates, then the new CIA Director; Gary Crocker, then from the State Department; Michael Moodie, then from ACDA; and Billy Richardson, then Deputy Assistant Secretary of Defense, also confirmed to the authors that the document was prepared by the UNGROUP and given to Yeltsin.

7. Confidential interview, March 1998; confidential interview, April 1998; confidential interview, October 1998; confidential interview, November 1998

8. Confidential interview, November 1998; confidential interview, October 1998

9. Confidential interview, October 1998; confidential interview, November 1998

10. Confidential interview, November 1998

Chapter 15: The Soviet Visit

1. Col. Jim Bushong interview, May 1998
2. Bushong [15, 1]
3. Lisa Bronson interview, June 1998
4. Bushong [15, 1]
5. Bushong [15, 1]
6. Bushong [15, 1]
7. Bushong [15, 1]. The Defense Department even devised a mundane 'cover

story' in case the secrecy was blown. The press would be told only that it was a cooperative visit sponsored by the US Defense Department and Soviet Ministry of Defence for US and Soviet scientists.

8. Ambassador John Hawes interview, May 1998

9. Robert Gates, *From the Shadows*, New York: Simon and Schuster, 1996, p. 525

10. Bushong [15, 1]

11. Bushong [15, 1]; Bronson [15, 3]; Col. Charles Bailey interview, May 1998; Col. David Franz interview, May 1998; Ken Alibek interview, May 1998

12. Bushong [15, 1]; Bronson [15, 3]; Bailey [15, 11]; Franz [15, 11]; Alibek [15, 11]. As of February 1993, Vasileyev was head of the Russian Ministry of Defence's Biological Defence Directorate. A Russian TV interview he did that month typified his views. He said that the Soviet Union and Russia had only produced 'experimental samples' of bio-agents that were tested in 'laboratory and field conditions'. He added: '. . . no biological weapons were produced or stockpiled in our country. We had no biological weapons' (Ostankino Television, 17 February 1993, in FBIS-SU, 1 March 1993, cited in *The Arms Control Reporter*, 1993, p. B:110).

13. Bushong [15, 1]; Alibek [15, 11]

14. Bushong [15, 1]; Alibek [15, 11]. Col. Louis Jackson and Col. Bill Miller were also brought in on temporary assignments to assist Bronson.

15. Bushong [15, 1]; Alibek [15, 11]; confidential interview, September 1998

16. Bushong [15, 1]; Hawes [15, 8]

17. Bushong [15, 1]

18. Bushong [15, 1]

19. Bushong [15, 1]

20. Bailey [15, 11]

21. Franz [15, 11]

22. Franz [15, 11]

23. Bushong [15, 1]

24. Bailey [15, 11]

25. Bailey [15, 11]

26. Bailey [15, 11]. Col. Vasileyev showed Ken Alibek the map at USAMRIID HQ and said he wanted to examine the strange building with the round top – based on the Soviet overhead photos.

27. Bronson [15, 3]

28. Bailey [15, 11]

29. Franz [15, 11]; Bushong [15, 1]

30. Franz [15, 11]

31. Bushong [15, 1]; confidential interview, April 1998

32. One of the authors visited the Pine Bluff Arsenal. The former BW facilities

were found to be in a partially decayed and patently disused and unusable condition. The facility was quite clearly not the most fiendishly clever Potemkin deception – as the Soviets would later allege.

33. Bushong [15, 1]; confidential interview, April 1998

34. Two years later, the Russian government released a highly edited video to the United Nations which accused the US of violating the BWC. This presentation, which showed innocent scenes from US facilities in the worst possible light, included Vasiliyev's taping of the Section 5B 'mosquito room' (confidential interview, April 1998; Gary Crocker interview, March 1998).

35. Alibek [15, 11]

36. Bronson [15, 3]. Alibekov was still largely an unknown quantity to the US, since he had revealed little about himself and was a military officer – believed to be firmly in line with Ministry of Defence policies. Alibekov was not considered a target of recruitment (confidential interview, April 1998).

37. Bushong [15, 1]

38. Bronson [15, 3]

39. Bushong [15, 1]

40. Bushong [15, 1]; Bronson [15, 3]

41. Gates [15, 9], p. 525

42. Bushong [15, 1]; Bronson [15, 3]

43. Bushong [15, 1]

44. Alibek [15, 11]

45. Alibek [15, 11]. Ken Alibek confirmed to Bailey that this accusation about the Eight-Ball was contained in the Soviet report, which was not made public.

46. Alibek [15, 11]

47. Alibek [15, 11]

48. Alibek [15, 11]

Chapter 16: Yeltsin

1. Confidential interview, October 1998; confidential interview, November 1998

2. Confidential interviews, October 1998; confidential interview, November 1998

3. Confidential interviews, October 1998

4. Dr Chris Davis interview for 'Plague Wars', BBC *Panorama*, 20 July 1998 (taping session), pp. 26, 42. British official Chris Davis confirms that Yeltsin alluded to sites and people in the Soviet BW programme during his discussion with Hurd, indicating Yeltsin clearly had received briefings on the matter. 'I think he [Yeltsin] felt that he had been deceived by the outgoing regime – by President Gorbachev,' Davis recalls, 'and that in fact

he had discovered that the biological weapons programme was continuing inside the former Soviet Union ... This was quite an admission.'

5. James Baker interview, PBS *Frontline*, 'Plague War', 13 October 1998; James Baker, with Thomas DeFrank, *The Politics of Diplomacy*, G.P. Putnam's and Sons, 1995, pp. 622–3

6. *The Arms Control Reporter*, 1992, p. B:88; Ann Devroy and R. Jeffrey Smith, *Washington Post*, 2 February 1992; Bill Gertz, *Washington Times*, 3 March 1992; Milton Leitenberg, 'The Conversion of Biological Warfare Research and Development Facilities to Peaceful Uses', in *Control of Dual-Threat Agents*, ed. Ehrhard Geissler and John P. Woodall, Oxford University Press: Oxford, 1994, pp. 77f.

7. Confidential interviews, October 1998; confidential interview, November 1998

8. Confidential interview, March 1998; confidential interview, April 1998; confidential interview, March, 1998; confidential interview, October 1998; confidential interview, November 1998. See also *Washington Post* [16, 6]; *Washington Times* [16, 6]; *The Arms Control Reporter* [16, 6]; Leitenberg [16, 6]; M. Zakharov, 'A Visit with the President', *Izvestiya*, 22 April 1992, translated in JPRS-TND-92-104, 4 May 1992; Rowland Evans and Robert Novak, *Washington Post*, 24 June 1992.

9. Yeltsin offered his version of his summit conversation with Bush to an *Izvestiya* correspondent several months later. He confirmed that he warned the President that the Russian military was trying to hide the ongoing BW programme from him.

   'I said I could not give him firm assurances of cooperation. Certainly, this is not acceptable among politicians, but I said this: "We are still deceiving you, Mr Bush. We promised to eliminate bacteriological weapons. But some of our experts did everything possible to prevent me from learning the truth. It was not easy but I outfoxed them. I caught them red-handed ..."' (*Izvestiya* [16, 8]; *Washington Post* [16, 8]).

   How had Yeltsin 'outfoxed' them? Yeltsin said he 'found two test sites' where BW experts were experimenting with anthrax on 'wild animals'. Yeltsin's account did not explain what happened to the rest of the Soviet BW facilities that the West had identified.

10. Confidential interviews, March 1998; confidential interview, April 1998

11. Confidential interview, March 1998. See also D. Muratov, Y. Sorokin, and V. Fronin, *Komsomolskaya Pravda*, 27 May 1992, translated in FBIS-SU, 28 May 1992, cited in *The Arms Control Reporter* [16, 6], p. B:94.

12. Confidential interviews, March 1998

13. Baker and De Frank [16, 5], pp. 623–5

14. *Washington Post* [16, 6]; *The Arms Control Reporter* [16, 6]; *Washington Times*

[16, 6]. Yeltsin's spokesman was his senior military adviser, General Dmitri Volkogonov. Yeltsin's statement that the programme was dismantled has never been accepted by top British and American government experts. Dr David Kelly said in 1998: 'As yet, we have not been able to verify that President Yeltsin's statement is correct' (Dr David Kelly interview for *Panorama* [16, 4], p. 9).

15. Confidential interview, October 1998; confidential interview, November 1998
16. *Rossiyskaya Gazeta* (Moscow), 28 February 1992
17. Confidential interview, October 1998
18. Confidential interview, October 1998
19. Gary Crocker interview, March 1998; confidential interview, March 1998. See also *The Arms Control Reporter* [16, 6], p. B:89, citing Associated Press, 22 March 1992; R. Jeffrey Smith, *Washington Post*, 31 August 1992; Michael Gordon, *New York Times*, 1 September 1992.
20. Confidential interview, November 1998
21. Confidential interview, October 1998; confidential interview, November 1998
22. Confidential interview, October 1998
23. General Anatoliy Kuntsevich interview, October 1997 (by Nick Sturdee). See also John Barry, *Newsweek*, 1 February 1993; Associated Press, 17 April 1992; *Rossiyskaya Gazeta* [16, 15]; *Krasnaya Zvezda* (Moscow), 30 March 1994, p. 3, interview with General Yevstigneev; Daniel Leshem, *Jerusalem Post*, reprinted in *Washington Jewish Week*, 8 May 1997.
24. Confidential interview, March 1998; confidential interview, May 1998
25. Confidential interviews, October 1998
26. Confidential interview, October 1998; confidential interview, November 1998
27. Confidential interview, October 1998; confidential interview, November 1998
28. *New York Times* [16, 19]
29. Confidential interview, October 1998
30. Confidential interviews, October 1998; confidential interview, November 1998
31. Confidential interview, March 1998; Report of the Russian Federation, 1992, DDA/4-92/BWIII, United Nations Form F, 'Declaration of Past Activity in Regard to Offensive and Defensive Programmes of Biological Research and Development'; *Washington Post* [16, 8], [16, 19]; *Washington Times* [16, 6]
32. Confidential interview, March 1998; Report of the Russian Federation [16, 31]; *Washington Post* [16, 8], [16, 19]; *Washington Times* [16, 6]
33. Confidential interview, March 1998; Report of the Russian Federation [16, 31]; *Washington Post* [16, 8], [16, 19]; *Washington Times* [16, 6]
34. Confidential interview, March 1998; Report of the Russian Federation [16, 31]; *Washington Post* [16, 8], [16, 19]; *Washington Times* [16, 6]
35. Confidential interview, October 1998; confidential interview, May 1998; confidential interview, March 1998

36. Confidential interview, October 1998; Davis [16, 4], p. 24; confidential interview, May 1998; *Washington Post* [16, 19]

37. Confidential interview, October 1998

38. A sampling of the questions that Ambassador Hamner asked General Kuntsevich included:
    • Was Russia still researching and producing Plague for offensive purposes (Temple Fortune's allegation)? No, Kuntsevich replied, the Russians had more than 100 facilities that researched Plague – and they were all defensive.
    • Why was the Sverdlovsk accident omitted from the declaration and what was the real cause? Nothing needed to be said, Kuntsevich responded, because the Russian government had already provided full disclosure about the outbreak.
    • What progress had the Russians made in destroying their BW weapons stockpile? There was no stockpile, Kuntsevich said, so the destruction question was not a problem. (Confidential interview, October 1998)

39. Confidential interview, October 1998

40. Confidential interview, October, 1998

41. Michael Dobbs and Don Oberdorfer, *Washington Post*, 18 June 1992; Andrew Rosenthal, *New York Times*, 18 June 1992; Michael Wines, *New York Times*, 17 June 1992; *Congressional Quarterly Weekly Report*, 20 June 1992, pp. 1825–7; confidential interview, October 1998

42. *Washington Post* [16, 41]; Rosenthal, *New York Times* [16, 41]; Wines, *New York Times*, [16, 41]; *Congressional Weekly Report* [16, 41]

43. Bill Gertz, *Washington Times*, 24 July 1992; *Washington Post* [16, 41]; confidential interview, October 1998

44. Confidential interview, October 1998

45. *Washington Times* [16, 43]

46. *Washington Times* [16, 43]; *Washington Post* [16, 41]

47. Confidential interview, October 1998

48. Confidential interview, October 1998

49. Confidential interviews, October 1998; confidential interview, November 1998; confidential interview, March 1998

50. Confidential interviews, October 1998. James Baker was no longer involved in the process. On 13 August, Baker resigned as Secretary of State – to become President Bush's Chief of Staff and the director of his floundering re-election campaign. Baker was replaced by his deputy, Lawrence Eagleburger (Rosenthal, *New York Times*, 14 August 1992; Devroy, *Washington Post*, 14 August 1992).

51. Confidential interviews, October 1998; *Washington Post* [16, 19]; *New York Times* [16, 19]; BBC *Newsnight*, 21 January 1993, transcript, pp. 18–19

52. *Newsnight* [16, 51], p. 1; Mark Urban, *The Spectator*, 23 January 1993. The

Hurd/Eagleburger démarche read, in part: 'We are very concerned that some aspects of the offensive biological warfare programme which President Yeltsin acknowledged as having existed and which he then banned in April, are in fact being continued, covertly and without his knowledge. This issue could undermine the confidence in the US and UK's bilateral relationships with Russia.'

The letter then cited specific concerns that the Russians were still developing 'industrial production of a strain of Plague resistant to cold and heat and to sixteen antibiotics – for offensive purposes.'

53. Confidential interview, October 1998

54. Confidential interview, October 1998

55. Confidential interview, October 1998

56. Confidential interview, October 1998; *Washington Post* [16, 19]; *New York Times* [16, 19]

57. Confidential interview, October 1998; *Washington Post* [16, 19]

58. *Washington Post* [16, 19]

59. The official US government position is that Russia never satisfactorily amended the UN declaration. The 1996 annual report of ACDA states: 'The Russian Federation's 1993, 1994, and 1995 BWC data declarations contained no new information and its 1992 declaration was incomplete and misleading in certain areas' ('Adherence to and Compliance with Arms Control Agreements', ACDA Report, 1996, pp. 66–7).

Chapter 17: Trilateral Agreement

1. Ambassador Reed Hamner interview, May 1998; confidential interview, March 1998; confidential interview, June 1998. The account of the US trip to Moscow is based on interviews with three US officials who participated, the concurrent notes of one senior US official, and interviews with three knowledgeable British officials. See also R. Jeffrey Smith, *Washington Post*, 31 August 1992.

2. Hamner [17, 1]

3. Hamner [17, 1]

4. Confidential interview, May 1998

5. Confidential interview, October 1998

6. Hamner [17, 1]; confidential interview, March 1998. The US team also included Ambassador Reed Hamner, Deputy Director of ACDA; four UNGROUP representatives: Steven Hadley from Defense, Jim Timbie from State, Douglas MacEachin from CIA, and Lt. Gen. G. MacCaffree from the Joint Chiefs of Staff; and Lisa Bronson from the Pentagon.

7. The British team also included Paul Hatt, head of the Disarmament and Arms Control Unit of the Ministry of Defence, and Peter Verreker, a senior diplomat from the non-proliferation Department of the Foreign Office (confidential interview, October 1998; confidential interview, September 1998).

8. Confidential interview, October 1998

9. Hamner [17, 1]

10. Hamner [17, 1]; confidential interview, March 1998. The Russians began the talks with a neat opening gambit. They invited the visitors immediately to inspect their St Petersburg facility and the Lakhta site (at which 'Temple Fortune', the second Russian defector to MI6, had warned there was work planned on a new kind of Plague bacterium). The Russians offered to board a train north that very afternoon to allay US/British concerns about Plague, as expressed in the August démarche. Quite properly, the Americans and British didn't walk into that one. Diplomats are not qualified to conduct, and therefore should not undertake, complex scientific investigations (especially if attempts have been made to sanitize the establishment under inspection). The two sides agreed that another team would return at a later date for that visit – after an agreement was hammered out.

    (See also Joint US/UK/Russian Statement on Biological Weapons, US Department of State, 14 September 1992; Michael Gordon, *New York Times*, 15 September 1992; John-Thor Dahlburg, *LA Times*, 15 September 1992.)

11. Hamner [17, 1]; confidential interview, October 1998

12. Hamner [17, 1]; confidential interview, October 1998

13. Confidential interview, November 1998

14. Confidential interview, November 1998. A week later, General Kuntsevich charged publicly that Pasechnik had 'invented a lot in order to bump up his price' and 'to show how important he was' (*Rossiyskiye Vesti* (Moscow), 22 September 1992, translated in FBIS-SU, 24 September 1992, cited in *The Arms Control Reporter*, 1992, p. B:101).

15. *Rossiyskiye Vesti* [17, 14]

16. *Rossiyskiye Vesti* [17, 14]. See also *LA Times* [17, 10]; *Nezavisimaya Gazeta* (Moscow), 15 September 1992, FBIS-SU, 16 September 1992, cited in *The Arms Control Reporter* [17, 14]; Nikolai Krupenik, ITAR-TASS, 11 November 1992, translated in FBIS-SU, 23 November 1992 and Sergei Leskov, *Izvestiya*, 25 November 1992, translated in FBIS-SU 25 November 1992, cited in *The Arms Control Reporter* [17, 14], p. B:104.

17. Confidential interview, October 1998

18. Hamner [17, 1]; confidential interview, October 1998

19. Hamner [17, 1]; confidential interview, October 1998. See also *Izvestiya* (Moscow), 17 April 1992, interview with General V.I. Yevstigneev, translated

in JPRS-TAC-92-016, 18 May 1992; *The Arms Control Reporter* [17, 14], p. B:90.

20. Confidential interview, October 1998; Hamner [17, 1]
21. Confidential interview, October 1998; Hamner [17, 1]
22. The Trilateral Agreement contained three sections.

   Section One delineated Russian reductions in staff and budget and called for a formal investigation of the St Petersburg lab – with US/UK monitors present.

   Section Two listed four steps the Russians would take: 1) allowing non-military visits to Russian sites, followed by similar visits to US and UK commercial facilities; 2) provide the US/UK with information about the steps they were taking to dismantle their BW facilities; 3) give the UN more detailed official information about their past offensive BW programme; and 4) allow independent scientists to review their future BW compliance.

   Section Three established 'working groups' to address numerous concerns: 1) to plan and adjudicate the future reciprocal visits to Russian, American and British sites; 2) to enhance verification of the BWC; 3) to develop confidence building measures; 4) to determine if any party still retained illegal BW equipment; 5) to plan conversion measures based on cooperation; 6) to establish procedures for public reporting of legitimate biological research activities; and 7) to exchange scientists for bio-defence research.

   (Joint US/UK/Russian Statement on Biological Weapons [17, 10]; Edward J. Lacey, 'Tackling The Biological Weapons Threat: The Next Proliferation Challenge', *The Washington Quarterly*, autumn 1994, pp. 53–64; Martin Sieff, *Washington Times*, 15 September 1992.)

23. *The Washington Quarterly* [17, 22]
24. Joint US/UK/Russian Statement on Biological Weapons [17, 10]
25. Joint US/UK/Russian Statement on Biological Weapons [17, 10]
26. Joint US/UK/Russian Statement on Biological Weapons [17, 10]; US State Department Background Briefing, official transcript, 'Russian Biological Warfare Programs', 14 September 1992. See also *Washington Times* [17, 22]; *New York Times* [17, 10]; *LA Times* [17, 10]; ITAR-TASS, 14 September 1992, translated in JPRS-TND-92-033, 16 September 1992; Umit Enginsoy, *Defence News*, 21 September 1992; Vitaliy Kasyn, *Pravda*, 6 October 1992, translated in JPRS-TAC-92-031, 29 October 1992; *The Washington Quarterly* [17, 22].
27. R. Jeffrey Smith, *Washington Post*, 15 September 1992; *Washington Times* [17, 22]; *New York Times* [17, 10]; *LA Times* [17, 10]
28. *LA Times* [17, 10]
29. US State Department [17, 26]; confidential interview, October 1998. See also *Washington Post* [17, 27]; Michael Gordon, *New York Times*, 1 December 1993; *LA Times* [17, 10].

30. US State Department [17, 26]; confidential interview, October 1998. See also *Washington Post* [17, 27]; *New York Times* [17, 29]; *LA Times* [17, 10].
31. US State Department [17, 26]; confidential interview, October 1998. See also *Washington Post* [17, 27]; *New York Times* [17, 29]; *LA Times* [17, 10].
32. Confidential interview, October 1998
33. Dr Chris Davis interview, October 1998

Chapter 18: Alibekov

1. Confidential interview, June 1998
2. Ken Alibek interview, April 1999. See also Ken Alibek, with Stephen Handelman, *BIOHAZARD: The Chilling True Story of the Largest Covert Biological Weapons Program in the World*, New York: Random House, 1999, pp. 251–3.

   In early 1992, Alibekov befriended a Russian businesswoman who lived in New York and often travelled back and forth to Moscow. He didn't know her well, but she was his only link to the US, so he was forced to rely on her. He asked her to phone Lisa Bronson, to see if she could help arrange for his family to emigrate to the US. Her initial contact, before July, was very encouraging; she reported back that the Americans were 'very interested' and that he would be 'welcome in the US'.

   When Alibekov visited New York in September on business (without his family), he met privately with the businesswoman at his hotel. Bronson had given the woman names of officials in Washington that Alibekov was supposed to contact. Alibekov refused an obligatory American offer to defect on the spot, since he would not leave Russia without his family. The woman then passed along to him instructions of how he would get himself and his family out of Russia – including the names of officials in several countries (including Russia and Kazakhstan) who would help. For security reasons, Alibekov has declined to discuss any of this sensitive information about who else assisted him.
3. Ken Alibek interview, January 1998. This chapter is primarily based on five interviews with Alibek from January 1998 through June 1998; a two-hour, videotaped interview of Alibek for BBC *Panorama* in February 1998 for the programme 'Plague Wars: Apocalypse Delayed' which aired 20 July 1998; and a follow-up PBS-BBC interview in September 1998 for PBS *Frontline*, 'Plague War', which aired 13 October 1998.
4. Alibek interview, May 1998; US Congress Joint Economic Committee, testimony of Dr Kenneth Alibek, prepared statement, 20 May 1998
5. ABC News, *Prime Time Live*, 'Germ Warfare: Weapons of Terror', 25 February 1998

6. Alibek, with Handelman [18, 2], p. 87

7. Alibek, with Handelman [18, 2], pp. 18–19; confidential interview, April 1999

8. Alibek, BBC *Panorama* [18, 3]

9. Alibek interview, May 1998

10. Alibek interview, February 1998. See also Alibek, PBS *Frontline* [18, 3]; Alibek, 'Russia's Deadly Expertise', *New York Times*, 27 March 1998; Tim Weiner, *New York Times*, 25 February 1998

11. Alibek interview, February 1998; confidential interview, November 1998. None of the resistant bacteria had been fully weaponized by 1992, when Alibek left Russia.

12. Alibek interview, February 1998; Alibek, with Handelman [18, 2], pp. 19, 111–21

13. Alibek, with Handelman [18, 2], pp. 112–14

14. Alibek, with Handelman [18, 2], pp. 117–21; confidential interview, April 1999

15. Alibek interviews, February 1998; Alibek, BBC *Panorama*, [18, 3], transcript, p. 20. See also US Congress Joint Economic Committee [18, 4]; *New York Times* [18, 10]; Richard Preston, 'The Bioweaponeers,' *The New Yorker*, 9 March 1998, pp. 52f.; ABC *Prime Time Live* [18, 5].

16. Alibek interviews, February 1998. See also, Alibek, with Handelman [18, 2], pp. 258–62

17. Dr Lev Sandakhchiev interview, May 1998; confidential interview, April 1999. See also Weiner, *New York Times* [18, 10].

18. Alibek, with Handelman [18, 2], p. 43

19. Alibek interview, February 1998; Alibek, BBC *Panorama* [18, 3]; confidential interview, November 1998

20. Alibek interview, February 1998; Alibek, BBC *Panorama* [18, 3]; confidential interview, November 1998

21. Alibek interview, February 1998. See also Alibek, BBC *Panorama* [18, 3]; ABC *Prime Time Live* [18, 5].

22. Alibek interview, February 1998. See also Alibek, BBC *Panorama* [18, 3]; ABC *Prime Time Live* [18, 5].

23. Alibek interview, February 1998. See also Alibek, BBC *Panorama* [18, 3]; ABC *Prime Time Live* [18, 5].

24. Alibek interview, May 1998. See also Weiner, *New York Times* [18, 10].

25. Alibek interview, January 1998

26. Alibek, with Handelman [18, 2], pp. 23–8. In 1981, Alibekov's main assignment at Omutninsk was to turn around Biopreparat's failing Tularaemia weapons programme for Gen. Kalinin. No one in the world before then had ever produced a vaccine-resistant Tularaemia weapon; if Alibekov could do this, it would prove the usefulness of Biopreparat to the Ministry of Defence and the Kremlin (and would boost Kalinin's prestige).

The Tularaemia bomblet that Alibekov produced by 1982 was the first new weapon that Biopreparat ever tested at Vozrozhdeniye Island; all prior tests there had been run by the Ministry of Defence. About 500 monkeys had to be immunized beforehand in order to determine if the new Tularaemia packed inside twenty, carefully prepared bomblets could defeat the vaccine. After the tests worked (nearly all the immunized monkeys died), a very pleased Gen. Kalinin phoned Alibekov to congratulate him. After more tests were successful a year later, the weapon was officially added to the Soviet military arsenal. This achievement made Biopreparat a significant player in the Soviet weapons establishment for the first time, established Kalinin as a much stronger figure, and greatly enhanced Alibekov's reputation within Biopreparat.

27. Alibek interview, May 1998; British official, confidential interview, April 1998; US Department of Defense, Cooperative Threat Reduction, 5 February 1998, Report on the 'Demilitarization of the BioMedPreparat Facility at Stepnogorsk'

28. In 1990, after Gorbachev ordered the halting of BW production, Alibek spent a half-year overseeing the complete disinfection of Building 221 (Alibek interview, May 1998).

29. Alibek, with Handelman [18, 2], p. 90

30. Alibek interview, February 1998. See also Alibek, with Handelman [18, 2], p. 78. Vladimir Sizov later served as one of Alibek's deputies, a department chief, in Moscow in the 1980s.

31. Alibek, with Handelman [18, 2], p. 105

32. Alibek interview, January 1998; US Congress Joint Economic Committee [18, 4]. Alibek was told in 1989 – during a conversation with a Colonel from the Army's 15th Directorate, that the Soviet military had spread glanders in Afghanistan between 1982 and 1984. Alibek was unable to confirm this allegation, since there was no paperwork about it at Biopreparat. He suspects the glanders was dropped from Soviet planes against mujahedin fighters to disable their valuable horses, which were relied on to carry munitions around the rugged terrain. Knowledgeable Western analysts support his conclusion (Alibek interview, February 1998; Alibek, BBC *Panorama* [18, 3]; Alibek, with Handelman [18, 2], pp. 268–9; confidential interview, April 1999).

33. Alibek interview, January 1998

34. Alibek interview, February 1998; Alibek , PBS *Frontline* [18, 3]; British official, confidential interview, April 1998

35. Yevgenia Ustinov interview, May 1998; Alibek interview, May 1998; Alibek, BBC *Panorama* [18, 3]. This account first appeared in the *Mail On Sunday* Review (London), Tom Mangold and Jeff Goldberg, 'Plague Wars', 12 July 1998.

Alibekov was fully informed about the Ustinov case. The day of the accident, Dr Lev Sandakhchiev, director of Vektor, sent a coded message – a cryptogram – to Alibekov in Moscow with a full description of the accident and the measures that were being taken to handle Ustinov. Throughout the two-week death vigil, senior officials in Moscow, from Gen. Kalinin upwards to the Kremlin, were very worried that news of the accident would leak to the West (creating another Sverdlovsk-like publicity disaster). Alibekov continued to receive a detailed cryptogram each day describing Ustinov's worsening condition. Alibekov briefed Kalinin daily, and the General, in turn, informed other, more senior officials (Alibek interview, February 1998; Alibek, with Handelman [18, 2], pp. 123–31).

36. When Ustinov's accident was reported to Moscow, Alibekov ordered an army team from Zagorsk to fly to Kol'tsovo with some of their tiny supply of antiserum for Marburg. He hoped the treatment might help Ustinov, even though it would arrive two days after the infection began. The desperate effort proved to be futile. Alibekov later concluded that Biopreparat officials had been careless in starting the Marburg work at Vektor without having the antiserum on hand.

A subsequent Ministry of Health investigation of the accident found that Ustinov had been at fault for not following proper safety procedures. He had violated standard precautions by holding the guinea pig in his hands – he was supposed to strap the animal onto a wooden board – and by not wearing the full protective suit and thick mitts normally used in such high risk work (Alibek, with Handelman [18, 2], pp. 126–31).

37. Alibekov confirmed that Variant U was successfully weaponized in late 1989. He went to Stepnogorsk twice to supervise the dangerous tests of Marburg bomblets. All twelve test monkeys infected by the virus died within three weeks. By early 1990, Variant U was ready for Ministry of Defence approval (Alibek interview, February 1998; Alibek, with Handelman [18,2], pp. 132–3).

38. Alibek interview, January 1998; confidential interview, October 1998; confidential interview, November 1998

39. Alibek interview, May 1998; Alibek, BBC *Panorama* [18, 3]

40. Alibek interview, May 1998; Alibek, BBC *Panorama* [18, 3], transcript, p. 7

41. Alibek interviews, February 1998 and May 1998

42. Alibek interviews, February 1998 and May 1998

43. Alibek interviews, February 1998 and May 1998

44. Alibek interviews, February 1998 and May 1998

45. Alibek interview, February 1998

46. Alibek interview, February 1998

47. Alibek interview, February 1998; Alibek, BBC *Panorama* [18, 3]

48. Alibek interview, February 1998; Alibek, with Handelman [18, 2], pp. 245–6
49. Alibek interview, February 1998
50. Alibek interview, February 1998. See also Alibek, with Handelman [18, 2], pp. 253–6.
51. Today, Alibek's official legal status in Russia is unknown. He does not know if he is classified as a defector or if he would be arrested and prosecuted if he returned. He does not expect he will ever go back to find out. However, he has been told privately that he would receive harsh treatment. When he recently met a high-ranking Russian official – who was on an official visit to the US – the former colleague told him: 'General Kalinin told me that if you ever came back to Russia, you would be "liquidated"' (Alibek interview, February 1998).
52. Alibek interview, February 1998

Chapter 19: A Walk Through Pokrov

1. President Bush's final statement on Russian biological warfare compliance, made through his Arms Control and Disarmament Agency, spoke for itself: 'The United States,' the report noted, 'has determined that the Russian offensive biological warfare programme, inherited from the Soviet Union, violated the BWC through at least March 1992.' (That meant *after* Yeltsin took over, and up to the point Temple Fortune left Russia.) 'The Soviet offensive BW programme was massive,' the report continued, 'and included production, weaponization, and stockpiling. The status of the program since then [March 1992] remains unclear.' The report complained specifically that 'old hands' (i.e. the Ministry of Defence) continued to lead the Russian BW programme. It also warned that 'the modernization of biological agent capability' – a euphemism for super-Plague and genetic engineering – 'remains a concern' in Russia (White House, Office of the Press Secretary, 19 January 1993, President's Annual Compliance Report to Congress).
2. Confidential interviews, March 1998; confidential interview, June 1998
3. Confidential interview, June 1998; confidential interview, October 1998
4. Confidential interview, November 1998
5. Col. David Franz interview, May 1998; confidential interview, June 1998; confidential interview, September 1998; confidential interview, October 1998. Col. David Franz, Deputy Director of USAMRIID, was an important new participant on the US/UK team. Franz was new to the Soviet/Russian visits, but he had experience leading UN inspections to Iraq earlier that year.

6. Confidential interview, October 1998

7. Ken Alibek interview for BBC *Panorama*, 'Plague Wars,' 20 February 1998 (taping session)

8. Dr David Kelly interview for *Panorama* [19, 7], transcript, pp. 6–7, 19. Kelly says there is 'no evidence' that the virus production at Pokrov 'has stopped' as of 1998.

9. Kelly [19, 8], transcript, pp. 6, 19

10. Franz [19, 5]; confidential interview, October 1998

11. Franz [19, 5]; confidential interview, November 1998

12. Franz [19, 5]

13. Franz [19, 5]; confidential interview, June 1998; confidential interview, September 1998

14. Franz [19, 5]; confidential interview, June 1998; confidential interview, May 1998; confidential interview, October 1998

15. Confidential interview, April 1998

16. Dr David Kelly interview, October 1998

Chapter 20: The Pfizer Fiasco

1. Confidential interview, June 1998. See also *The Arms Control Report*, 1994, pp. B:123–4.

2. Confidential interview, June 1998

3. See also Edward J. Lacey, 'Tackling the Biological Weapons Threat: The Next Proliferation Challenge', *The Washington Quarterly*, Autumn 1994, pp. 53–64; 'Biological Weapons Convention: Chronology 1994', *The Arms Control Reporter*, 14 February 1994, p. B:115.

4. Lacey [20, 3]; *The Arms Control Reporter* [20, 3]

5. Lacey [20, 3]

6. Jonathan Tucker, 'Verification Provisions of the CWC and Their Relevance to the BWC', in 'Biological Weapons Proliferation: Reasons for Concern Course of Action', Henry L. Stimson Centre Report, #24, January 1998, p. 96, citing Terence Taylor and L. Celeste Johnson, 'The Biotechnology Industry of the United States: A Census of Facilities', Centre for International Security and Arms Control, Stanford University, July 1995; 'US Pharmaceutical and Biotechnology Industries White Paper on Strengthening Biological Weapons Convention', 1996, p. 4

7. 'US Pharmaceutical and Biotechnology Industries White Paper' [20, 6], pp. 6, 13; Tucker [20, 6], p. 96

8. Confidential interview, October 1998

9. Confidential interview, October 1998

10. Confidential interview, June 1998; Michael Moodie interview, May 1998
11. *The Arms Control Report* [20, 1], p. B:124
12. As of 1996, Pfizer had 46,500 employees worldwide and total sales revenues of $11.3 billion. Pfizer marketed a wide range of cardiovascular, anti-fungal and antibiotic products (Pfizer Web Site, 1998).
13. *The Arms Control Report* [20, 1], p. B:123–24
14. Confidential interview, June 1998. See also *The Arms Control Report* [20, 1], pp. B:123–4.
15. Confidential interview, June 1998; Col. David Franz interview, May 1998
16. Dr Roger Breeze interview, May 1998. (Dr Breeze was director of the Plum Island facility in 1993.) See also *The Arms Control Reporter* [20, 1], p. B:124; John McDonald, 'Plum Island's Shadowy Past', *Newsday,* 21 November 1993; John McDonald, *Newsday,* 3 March 1994; John McQuiston, *New York Times,* 2 March 1994.
17. *Newsday* [20, 16], 3 March 1994
18. Nikolay Burbyga, 'US/UK Bioweapons Production Intentions Viewed', *Izvestiya,* 5 April 1994; Moscow Radio World Service, 'Radio on "Unfounded" Charges on Biological Weapons', 12 April 1994, translated in JPRS-TND-94-010, 5 May 1994
19. *Izvestiya* [20, 18]; Moscow Radio World Service [20, 18]
20. *Izvestiya* [20, 18]; Moscow Radio World Service [20, 18]
21. *Izvestiya* [20, 18]; Moscow Radio World Service [20, 18]
22. Dr Gillian Woollett, PhRMA, interview, May 1998; Dr Alan Goldhammer, Biotechnology Industry Organization, interview, May 1998. See also Gillian R. Woollett, 'Industry's Role Concerns, and Interests in the Negotiations of a BWC Compliance Protocol', in 'Biological Weapons Proliferation', Henry Stimson Centre Report, #24, January 1998, pp. 39–52; 'US Pharmaceutical and Biotechnology Industries White Paper' [20, 6]; 'Reducing the Threat of Biological Weapons – A PhRMA Perspective' (report by PhRMA), November 1996.
23. Woollett [20, 22]
24. Confidential interview, October 1998; *Izvestiya* [20, 18]
25. Woollett [20, 22]; PhRMA Executive Committee Statement, 'PhRMA Position on a Compliance Protocol to the BWC', 9 January 1997. The pharmaceutical industry does not believe that random 'visits' to commercial sites serve any useful function. 'Routine visits serve no purpose and should not be part of any final verification regime,' an industry White Paper states ('US Pharmaceutical and Biotechnology Industries White Paper' [20, 6]).

First, the industry says there is no basis for these fishing expeditions. Second, the selected site, if it wanted to, could clean out (through sterilization) all traces of incriminating evidence within a few hours before the visit.

The only worthwhile inspections, they say, are short-notice 'challenge inspections' based on 'substantial' specified suspicions that offensive BW activities are occurring at a site (like UNSCOM's work in Iraq). In these instances, the inspectors can use intrusive regulations to uncover specific, alleged violations (Woollett [20, 22]; Goldhammer [20, 22]; see also 'Reducing the Threat of Biological Weapons – A PhRMA Perspective' [20, 22]; Woollett, Henry Stimson Centre Report, [20, 22]).

Chapter 21: Postscript: Russia

1. Ian Brodie, *Daily Telegraph* (London), 8 April 1994; *Washington Post*, 8 April 1994; ITAR-TASS, 7 April 1994, translated in FBIS-SOV, 7 April 1994, cited in *The Arms Control Reporter*, 1995, p. B:126
2. *New York Times* (AP), 24 October 1995; *Newsweek*, 23 February 1998. In November 1995, the State Department formally imposed sanctions on Kuntsevich for violating several sections of US arms control acts (Department of State, Public Notice 2295, 'Imposition of Chemical and Biological Weapons Proliferation Sanctions on a Foreign Person', *Federal Register*, vol. 60, no. 234, 6 December 1995).
3. Confidential interview, April 1998; confidential interview, October 1998. See also *The Arms Control Reporter* [21, 1], p. B:129.
4. Confidential interview, April 1998; confidential interview, October 1998
5. R. Jeffrey Smith, *Washington Post*, 17 May 1995
6. See also Raymond Zilinskas, 'The Other Biological Weapons Worry', *New York Times*, 28 November 1997.
7. Confidential interview, October 1998
8. National Academy of Sciences, 'Controlling Dangerous Pathogens: A Blueprint for US-Russian Cooperation', 27 October 1997, p. 4
9. June Preston, Reuters, 10 March 1988
10. Confidential interview, November 1998
11. Sir Percy Cradock interview for BBC TV, 1998. Notes prepared by him for reference.
12. William Broad, *New York Times*, 14 February 1998; Laurie Garrett, *Newsday*, 19 February 1998
13. John Diamond, Associated Press, 14 September 1998; *Defense Week*, 14 September 1998 (citing written submissions to the Senate Intelligence Committee)
14. Associated Press [21, 13]; *Defense Week* [21, 13]
15. Confidential interview, November 1998
16. Judith Miller with William J. Broad, *New York Times*, 8 December 1998
17. National Academy of Sciences [21, 8]

18. *New York Times* [21,16]
19. Confidential interview, April 1998
20. Confidential interview, April 1998
21. Repeated requests to film at Vektor Laboratories in 1998 were approved by Dr Sandakhchiev but then denied by General Kalinin, who invited the BBC *Panorama* team to 'ask again next year'.
22. Confidential interview, November 1998
23. Joint Statement by Presidents Clinton and Yeltsin on a Protocol to the Convention on the Prohibition of Biological Weapons, 2 September 1998

Chapter 22: Rhodesia, 1978

1. Ethan Schwartz, *Washington Post,* 14 October 1989
2. ANC bases were located in Tanzania only until the early 1970s, after which its HQ moved to Zambia. After 1975, the ANC's main military forces were in Angola.
3. Henrik Ellert, *The Rhodesian Front War: Counter-Insurgency and Guerrilla War in Rhodesia 1962-1980,* Zimbabwe: Mambo Press, 1989, p. 122
4. Stephen Ellis, *Journal of Southern African Studies,* vol. 24, #2, June 1998
5. Atalia Ngwenya interview, March 1998
6. Meryl Nass interview, August 1996. See also Meryl Nass, MD, 'Anthrax Epizootic in Zimbabwe, 1978–1980: Due to Deliberate Spread?' *The PSR Quarterly,* vol. 2, no. 4, December 1992.
7. J.C.A. Davies, 'A Major Epidemic of Anthrax in Zimbabwe', *The Central African Journal of Medicine,* vol. 28, no. 12, December 1982
8. Defense Intelligence Agency, ref: DoD 5200-1-R, August 1990. This report was declassified under the Freedom of Information Act on 1 February 1994.
9. Defense Intelligence Agency [22, 8]
10. G.B. Carter, *Porton Down: 75 Years of Chemical and Biological Research,* London: HMSO, 1992, pp. 52–4
11. Exchange of letters between Dr Timothy Stamps and Dr Mark Bradley, Ministry of Health and Child Welfare, Harare, March/April 1997
12. Dr Timothy Stamps interview, March 1997
13. Col. Lionel Dyck interview, March 1997
14. Dyck [22, 13]
15. The authors are indebted to David Martin, the distinguished *Observer* correspondent in Rhodesia/Zimbabwe, for his help in this matter.
16. Confidential communication held by David Martin
17. Jeremy Brickhill, 'Zimbabwe's Poisoned Legacy: Secret War in Southern Africa', *Covert Action,* no. 43, Winter 1992/93

18. Ellert [22, 3], pp. 146–7
19. Ellert [22, 3], pp. 146–7
20. Ellert [22, 3], pp. 146–7

Chapter 23: Nothing Personal

1. Peter Stiff, *See You in November*, South Africa: Galago, 1985
2. Jeremy Brickhill, *Covert Action*, no. 43, Winter 1992/93
3. 'Taffy' interview, June 1998
4. Connie Braam interview, February 1998
5. Braam [23, 4]
6. Braam [23, 4]
7. Frank Chikane interview, March 1998
8. Chikane [23, 7]
9. Chikane [23, 7]
10. Schalk Van Rensburg testimony, Truth and Reconciliation Commission hearings, 9 June 1998 (author notes of the hearing)
11. South Africa signed the BWC on 10 April 1972 and ratified it on 5 November 1975.

Chapter 24: Wouter Basson

1. Letter from Office of the Attorney-General of South Africa to the Truth and Reconciliation Commission, 3 June 1998
2. The authors are indebted to Stephen Ellis of the Africa Centre in Leiden, Holland for his paper: 'The Historical Significance of South Africa's Third Force', *Journal of South African Studies*, vol. 24, no. 2, June 1998.
3. General Niels Knobel interviews, April–May 1998
4. Ellis [24, 2]
5. TRC Hearings, 18 June 1998, transcript, p. 1219
6. TRC Hearings [24, 5], p. 1151
7. Jan Lourens interview, June 1998
8. The Seventh Medical Battalion had three wings: one for 'Parabats' parachutists; one for Special Forces; and one for Intelligence Group. There was also a group that supported police security.
9. TRC, Document #14
10. General Niels Knobel interview, May 1998
11. A detailed investigation by Britain's MI5, the Security Service, has failed to substantiate the allegation that he visited Porton Down. Basson told the

authors, however, that he frequently used false names and false passports during these visits.

12. Jim Shortt interviews, September 1997 and March 1998

13. 'Bizarre Experiments at SADF Research Firms', *South Africa Mail and Guardian*, 15 December 1994

14. Confidential interview, November 1998; Schalk van Rensburg interview, June 1998

15. Beatrice Wiltshire, letter to *Sunday Tribune* (South Africa), 'SADF's Roode-plaat Laboratory Used to Blowtorch Baboons for the Benefit of Mankind', 26 June 1996

16. Confidential interview, November 1998

17. Confidential Western intelligence briefings, March 1998 and June 1998

18. William E. Burrows and Robert Windrem, *Critical Mass*, New York: Simon & Schuster, 1994, pp. 185–6

19. Daan Goosen interview, June 1998

Chapter 25: 'Gert'

1. Jacques Pauw, *Into the Heart of Darkness*, Johannesburg: Jonathan Ball, 1997, pp. 17–18

2. General Magnus Malan, submission to the Truth and Reconciliation Commission, May 1997

3. Pauw [25, 1], p. 188. Testimony of Brigadier Jack Cronje, former head of Northern Transvaal Security Branch, and self-confessed killer of forty activists.

4. Pauw [25, 1], p. 188

5. Malan [25, 2]

6. Confidential interview, November 1998

7. Confidential interview, November 1998

8. Pauw [25, 1], pp. 221–30

9. Confidential interview, November 1998

10. It was reported in December 1998 that Executive Outcomes had wound up its business affairs.

11. Nico Palm interview, March 1998

12. 'Gert' interview, March 1998

13. Francois Misser, 'Ebola: The Military Connection', *New African*, March 1996

Chapter 26: Truth and Reconciliation

1. Truth and Reconciliation Commission hearings, evidence of Daan Goosen, 11 June 1998 (author notes of the hearing)
2. Confidential interview, June 1998
3. TRC hearings, testimony of Dr Schalk van Rensburg, 9 June 1998 (author notes of the hearing)
4. TRC Document #52
5. TRC hearings, testimony of Dr Mike Odendaal, 8 June 1998 (author notes of the hearing)
6. US scientists seized on *Brucella* as a biological weapon as early as 1942; two years later, they had successfully weaponized it into bomblets and tested it using animal targets. It was eventually dropped from their offensive arsenal in 1967, two years before the US abandoned offensive biological warfare altogether.
7. Frederick Sidell, Ernest Takafuji, and David Franz, *Textbook of Military Medicine: Medical Aspects of Chemical and Biological Warfare*, US Government Printing Office, 1997, pp. 516–18
8. Confidential interviews, March 1998; Daan Goosen interview, June 1998
9. TRC hearings, testimony of Dr Jan Lourens, 8 June 1998 (author notes of the hearing)
10. Confidential interview, November 1998
11. Klaas de Jonge interview, February 1997
12. Daphne White interview, April 1998
13. Confidential briefings, January 1998
14. Torie Pretorius spoke to Daphne White for several hours at her Maidstone house on 23 October 1998.
15. TRC hearings, remarks by Counsel for the TRC, June 1998 (author notes of the hearing)
16. Lourens [26, 9]

Chapter 27: Revelations

1. The authors have been unable to find an original copy of the Steyn Report. There is talk that he never produced one, just a series of notes and conclusions. What *was* widely disseminated became known as the 'Steyn Portfolio' (twenty-one pages). Its authenticity, and pedigree, remain unchallenged; its conclusions remain a source of impotent rage among hardliners in the SADF.

2. The authors are grateful to Stephen Ellis for his interpretations of the Steyn Portfolio.

3. F.W. de Klerk interview, March 1998

4. De Klerk [27, 3]

5. For additional background on Basson's Libyan connection, see James Adams, 'South Africa: Libya Said Seeking Secret Biological Weapons', *Sunday Times* (London), 26 February 1995; Erik Leklem and Laurie Boulden, 'Exorcising Project B: Pretoria probes its shady chemical past', *Jane's Intelligence Review*, August 1997.

6. Raymond Bonner, *New York Times*, 2 December 1997; Joshua Sinai, *Washington Post*, 29 January 1998

7. Western intelligence sources today do not believe that Libya has successfully developed a BW programme. This is partly due to an extreme shortage of home-grown expertise. For background on Libya's BW programme, see also US Arms Control and Disarmament Agency, 'Adherence and Compliance with Arms Control Agreements, 1998', p. 7; US Office of the Secretary of Defense, 'Proliferation: Threat and Response', November 1997, p. 37; Robert Waller, 'The Deterrence Series, Case Study 2, Libya', Chemical and Biological Arms Control Institute, 1998.

8. There is now no doubt that Basson was originally invited to Libya to help them with chemical warfare facilities at Rabta. There was nothing illegal per se about these visits (confidential interview, November 1998).

9. Confidential interview, November 1998; confidential interview, April 1998. See also Adams [27, 5].

10. De Klerk [27, 3]

11. Confidential interview, June 1998

12. Confidential interview, May 1998

13. Confidential interview, December 1997

14. Confidential interview, April 1998

15. Confidential interviews with British and American intelligence sources, April 1998 and May 1998

16. Confidential interview, November 1998

17. Confidential interview, April 1998

18. Confidential interviews with Western intelligence sources, June 1998 and November 1998

19. Dr Wouter Basson interview, June 1998

20. Confidential interview with Western intelligence sources, June 1998

21. Confidential interview, November 1998

22. *Cape Argus Independent*, 28 February 1997

Chapter 28: Arrest

1. Dr Wouter Basson interview, June 1998
2. Juergen Jacomet interview, May 1998
3. Jacomet [28, 2]
4. Detective Superintendent Giel Ehlers interview, June 1998 (by BBC *Panorama* producer Peter Molloy)
5. Confidential interview, November 1997 and March 1998
6. Confidential interviews, March 1998
7. Report of the Truth and Reconciliation Commission, published 28 October 1998 (summary by the South African Press Agency, 29 October 1998)
8. Torie Pretorious interview, November 1998
9. Letter from the Office of the Attorney General of the Republic of South Africa to the TRC, Reference PDS940188, 3 June 1998; Emsie Ferriera, Agence France Press, 24 March 1999; Alister Bull, Reuters, 24 March 1999

Chapter 29: Iraq

1. This chapter is based, in part, on the following sources:
a. Major interviews:
David Kelly, October 1998 and January 1999; Richard Spertzel, October 1998; Scott Ritter, January 1999; Richard Butler, October 1998 and January 1999; Rolf Ekeus, January 1999; William Patrick, June 1998; Charles Bailey, May 1998
b. Major official sources:
UNSCOM Report to Security Council, 214-S/1995/864, 11 October 1995; UNSCOM Report to Security Council, S/1996/848, 11 October 1996; US Department of Defense, JPO-BIODEFENSE, 'UNSCOM Known/Suspect Iraqi BW Agents and Delivery Systems', 15 November 1997; US Government Report, unsigned (prepared by US intelligence agencies), 'Iraqi Weapons of Mass Destruction Programs', officially released by the Department of Defense, 13 February 1998 (seventeen pages); Richard Spertzel, 'UNSCOM and Iraq's WMD programs', The Washington Institute, 23 January 1998 (lecture); US Senate Committee on Government Affairs, Permanent Subcommittee on Investigations, 'Global Proliferation of Weapons of Mass Destruction', 13 March 1996, Testimony of Ambassador Rolf Ekeus, pp. 90f.
c. Major press sources:
William J. Broad and Judith Miller, 'How Iraq's Biological Weapons Program Came to Light', *New York Times*, 26 February 1998; R. Jeffrey Smith,

'Iraq's Drive for a Biological Arsenal', *Washington Post*, 21 November 1997; John Barry and Gregory Vistica, 'The Hunt For His Secret Weapons', *Newsweek*, 1 December 1997; John Barry, 'Unearthing The Truth', *Newsweek*, 2 March 1998; James Bone, 'Chemical Agents', *The Times Magazine* (London), 13 December 1997; CNN/*Time, Impact*, 'The Inspectors' Story', one-hour special TV report, 1 March 1998

2. Rick Atkinson, *Crusade*, New York and Boston: Houghton Mifflin Company, 1993, pp. 85–90; Michael Gordon and General Bernard Trainor, *The Generals' War*, Boston: Little, Brown and Company, 1995, pp. 135–7, 182–3. See also Norman Schwarzkopf, with Peter Petrie, *It Doesn't Take A Hero*, New York: Bantam Books, 1992, pp. 390, 415; Colin Powell with Joseph Persico, *My American Journey*, New York: Random House, 1995, pp. 503–4

3. C.J. Peters and Mark Olshaker, *Virus Hunter*, New York: Anchor Books, 1997, p. 292

4. Patrick [29, 1a]

5. Peters and Olshaker [29, 3], p. 284; Atkinson, [29, 2], p. 89

6. Atkinson [29, 2], p. 90

7. Bailey [29, 1a]

8. Kelly [29, 1a], January 1999

9. Institute of Medicine, National Academy of Sciences, 'Health Consequences of the Persian Gulf War: Initial Findings and Recommendations', January 1995, pp. 54–5; US Senate Banking Housing and Urban Affairs Committee, Report of Senator Donald Reigle, Jr., 'US Chemical and Biological Warfare-Related Dual Use Exports and Their Possible Impact on the Health Consequences of the Persian Gulf War', 25 May 1994, p. 135

10. BBC TV *Panorama* interviews at US Army Chemical School, Bio-Defense Branch, Fort McClellan, Alabama, May 1998 (by Tom Mangold)

11. Smith [29, 1c]; US Department of Defense, [29, 1b: JPO-BIODEFENSE]

12. US Department of Defense, Office of the Secretary of Defense Report, 'Proliferation Threat and Response', November 1997, p. 32

13. Smith [29, 1c]

14. ACDA, 1996 report, 'Adherence to and Compliance with Arms Control Agreements', p. 67; US Senate Armed Services Committee, 27 March 1996, testimony of Gordon Oehler; UNSCOM, [29, 1b], 214-S/1995/864; UNSCOM press release, IK/43, 5 August 1991; Anthony Goodman, Reuters, 14 January 1998, citing UNSCOM, [29, 1b], 214-S/1995/864

15. ACDA [29, 14]; UNSCOM [29, 1b], 214-S/1995/864

16. UK Ministry of Defence, Communication to Members of Parliament, 13 November 1998

17. Confidential interview, November 1998

18. Confidential interview, November 1998

19. Confidential interview, November 1998
20. Kevin Merida and John Mintz, *Washington Post*, 10 February 1994; *Washington Post* [29, 1c]; *New York Times* [29, 1c]
21. *Washington Post* [29, 1c]; *The Times Magazine* (London) [29, 1c]
22. *Washington Post* [29, 20]; UNSCOM [29, 1b], 214-S/1995/864; ACDA [29, 14], p. 67
23. *Aerospace Daily*, 24 December 1998. UNSCOM had no evidence to confirm that these tanks on the L-29 planes actually contained anthrax (Kelly [29, 1a], January 1999).
24. Spertzel [29, 1b]; *Washington Post* [29, 1c]; UNSCOM [29, 1b], 214-S/1995/864
25. R. Jeffrey Smith, *Washington Post*, 26 August 1995; US Senate Committee [29, 1b], p. 92; James Baker, with Thomas DeFrank, *The Politics of Diplomacy*, New York: G.P. Putnam's and Sons, 1995, pp. 358–9
26. David Kelly advises that the figure of 157 bombs is based on the diary of an officer employed in the destruction of the bombs. Iraq's own figures have been inconsistent; UNSCOM itself has no precise figure of how many weapons were filled (Kelly [29, 1a], January 1999).
27. Secretary-General of the United Nations, Note by the Secretary-General, United Nations Security Council, 11 October 1995, S/1995/864
28. General Wafiq al-Samarra'i interview, January 1998. For background on Wafiq al-Samarra'i's defection see Jonathan Calvert, Mark Skipworth, Hala Jabar, and John Swain, 'The Anthrax Connection', *Sunday Times* (London), 'Insight', 19 February 1995; Reuters, 7 February 1998, citing *Der Spiegel* interview with al-Samarra'i.
29. For background on Hussein Kamel's defection see 'Inside Saddam's Brutal Regime', interview with Hussein Kamel al-Majid, *Time*, 18 September 1995; *Newsweek* [29, 1c: Barry and Vistica]; *Newsweek*, 9 October 1995; *Newsweek* [29, 1c: Barry]; *New York Times*, [29, 1c]; Douglas Waller, *Time*, 4 September 1995; Christopher Dickey, *Newsweek*, 4 September 1995.
30. Kelly [29, 1a] October 1998
31. Kelly [29, 1a] January 1999; *Washington Post*, [29, 1c]; *New York Times*, [29, 1c]
32. US Department of Defense [29, 12], pp. 32–3
33. Confidential interview, November 1998
34. *Time*, 17 November 1997
35. Confidential interview, December 1998

Chapter 30: The Inspectors

1. This chapter is based primarily on interviews with current and former senior UNSCOM officials and inspectors conducted from October 1998–February 1999, including: Richard Butler; Gabriele Kraatz-Wadsack; Nikita Smidovich; David Kelly; Hamish Killip; Terry Taylor; Scott Ritter; Richard Spertzel; Rod Barton; and Rolf Ekeus. The authors wish to thank Richard Spertzel, the senior officer on UNSCOM's BW team from 1995–8, for his generous cooperation and important insights.

2. This document nearly became a *casus belli* in November 1998 when a new crisis with Iraq developed.

3. Richard Butler interview, November 1998

4. Gabriele Kraatz-Wadsack interview, October 1998

5. Richard Spertzel interview, October 1998

6. Nikita Smidovich interview, October 1998

7. Hamish Killip interview, November 1998

8. Most of the growth medium was exported by British companies in the late 1980s; UNSCOM believes these sales were made under the assumption that Iraq was running extensive civilian medical and research programmes. The British exporters have refused, however, to discuss the matter with the authors.

9. David Kelly interview, October 1998

10. Rod Barton interview, November 1998

11. Camel pox causes illness like any other pox virus. It raises pustules on the body, becomes debilitating, and is highly lethal to camels. It could possibly affect humans too, and there is speculation that the Iraqis may be attempting some simple genetic engineering to make it as virulent as smallpox. But UNSCOM has no proof of this suspicion. Camel pox is also related to monkey pox, which is slowly emerging as a threat in Africa.

12. David Kelly says UNSCOM can account for only one Venturi valve. The rest are unaccounted for. There has never been a dedicated UNSCOM inspection to find them or to establish how many were fitted to experimental, or actual, drop tanks (Kelly [30, 9]). Former senior UNSCOM inspector Richard Spertzel believes that these precious valves remain hidden in Iraq (Spertzel [30, 5]).

13. Spertzel [30, 5]

14. Confidential interview, October 1998

15. Peter J. Boyer, 'Scott Ritter's Private War', *The New Yorker*, 9 November 1998

16. Ritter was not the first to make the Israeli connection. This contact was pioneered by another inspector, Annick Paul-Henriot (now deceased), and

led directly to UNSCOM's huge break that uncovered the Iraqi purchase of growth medium from Britain.

17. David Makovsky, 'Hide and Seek with the Palace Guard', *Ha'aretz*, 29 September 1998

18. Barton Gellman, 'Arms Inspectors Shake the Tree', *Washington Post*, 12 October 1998

19. The full and complex story of this dramatic period is well described in articles by Barton Gellman in the *Washington Post*, 11–12 October 1998.

20. The US government, including the FBI, launched investigations into the possibility that Ritter was working for the Israelis.

21. Scott Ritter interviews, February 1999

22. Butler [30, 3]

23. Confidential interviews, November 1998

24. As the November 1998 crisis came to a head, Secretary General Kofi Annan, notably, was not seen to be as helpful to Iraq as he had been in February.

25. Letter from Ambassador Richard Butler to UN Secretary General Kofi Annan, 15 December 1998

26. 'UN Arms Inspector Faces the Bombing Backlash', *The Times* (London), 21 December 1998

27. *The Times* [30, 26]

28. 'Secrets, Spies and Videotapes – The Unscom Story', BBC *Panorama*, 1 March 1999, revealed the full details.

Chapter 31: Rogue State

1. Associated Press, 2 February 1999 (Tenet's testimony to the US Senate Armed Services Committee)

2. See also Marguerite Holloway, 'Profile: Joseph Needham', *Scientific American*, May 1992, p. 56

3. 'China, North Korea Fabricated US Germ Warfare Charges', *Kyodo News Service* (AP), 8 January 1998; Mike Feinsilber, 'Proof Soviets Lied About US Warfare', Associated Press, 16 November 1998; Bruce Auster, 'Unmasking an old Lie,' *US News and World Report*, November 16, 1998.

   The Soviet documents were first disclosed in January 1998 by the Japanese daily newspaper, *Sankei Shimbun* (see Yasuro Naito, *Sankei Shimbun*, 8 January 1998). Cold War historians Milton Leitenberg and Kathryn Weathersby also retrieved and verified the documents later in 1998. See Milton Leitenberg, 'New Russian Evidence on the Korean War Biological Warfare Allegations', *Cold War International History Project Bulletin 11*, Woodrow Wilson International Center for Scholars, Winter

1998, pp. 185–99; and Kathryn Weathersby, 'Deceiving The Deceivers: Moscow, Beijing, Pyongyang, and the Allegations of Bacteriological Weapons', *Cold War International History Project Bulletin 11*, Winter 1998, pp. 176–84.

For an earlier attempt to discredit the North Korean/Chinese accusations, see Mary Rolicka, 'New Studies Disputing Allegations of Bacteriological Warfare During the Korean War', *Military Medicine*, Vol. 160, March 1995.

4. Associated Press, 16 November 1998

5. Major published sources for this chapter include:

   a. Bruce Bennett, 'Implications of Proliferation of New Weapons on Regional Security', a Rand Study, November 1996. See also Barbara Opall, 'Study: Chemical, Biological Weapons Could Boost N. Korea', *Army Times*, 18 November 1996; G.E. Willis, 'Analysts: N. Korea Could Have Pearl Harbor Character', *Army Times*, 5 May 1997.

   b. Joseph S. Bermudez, Jr., *The Deterrence Series, Case Study 5: North Korea*, Chemical and Biological Arms Control Institute, 1998

   c. Theresa Hitchens, 'Wargame Finds US Falls Short in Bio War', *Defense News*, 28 August 1995; Theresa Hitchens, 'US Needs To Clarify Response to Biological War Threat', *Defense News*, 11 September 1995; 'Officials Address Realm Of Germ Attack Against US By Lesser Powers', *Army Times*, 11 September 1995

6. Memo by South Korean government, 'Biological Weapons of North Korea', 1992; Joseph Bermudez, *Jane's Intelligence Review*, 1 May 1993; Bermudez [31, 5b], p. 12

7. Bermudez [31, 5b], p. 12

8. Secretary of Defense, 'Proliferation: Threat and Response,' Office of the Secretary of Defense, April 1996; South Korean Government report, 'Biological Weapons of North Korea', 1992; Bermudez [31, 6]; Bermudez [31, 5b]

9. Bermudez [31, 6]

10. The account of Global 95 is derived from interviews with three former senior US officials who were knowledgeable about the proceedings (confidential interview, March 1998; confidential interview, February 1998; confidential interview, May 1998). See also Hitchens [31, 5c], 28 August, 1995.

11. The full Global 95 scenario included a special simulation of a domestic terrorist attack by Iraqi agents using biological weapons on Norfolk, Virginia (the US Navy's major East Coast home port) and Washington, DC. The results of those simulations have remained highly classified to this day (Hitchens [31, 5c], 28 August 1995).

12. South Korea has discovered four tunnels under the DMZ. Allied intelligence estimates that as many as twenty tunnels could still be undetected and ready

for use by infiltrating special operations troops (*Army Times* [31, 5a], 5 May 1997).

13. Confidential interview, March 1998

14. Confidential interview, March 1998. BIDS is the acronym for the army's Biological Integrated Detection System.

15. Confidential interview, May 1998. Disheartened by the results of Global 95, in 1997 the Pentagon decided to follow up with another, even bigger 'table top' exercise on North Korea, code-named 'Coral Breeze'. The point of this second secret war game was to test what had been learned from Global 95. The exercise, this time, was held at a US base in South Korea and included the full participation of representatives from the host country. The scenario, which included North Korean missile launches with biological and chemical warheads, went into much greater detail than Global 95 about how the combined US and South Korean forces would respond to the attack from the North.

   Coral Breeze has led to certain defensive measures being taken and a modification of the 'Peninsula Intelligence Estimate', the classified guidelines produced by the US Combined Forces Command in Korea, to increase attention to CBW scenarios. The existing American war plan, for example, called for rapid reinforcement of the front lines with South Korean troops stationed at rear areas. The Coral Breeze exercise, however, revealed serious questions about whether the reserves would be sufficiently well equipped, with such basics as masks and protective suits, to respond effectively. Steps have since been initiated to increase CBW training and equipment for South Korean forces.

16. Confidential interview, March 1998

17. Confidential interview, March 1998. See also Bermudez [31, 5b], pp. 19–22. The North Koreans have not yet put BW warheads on ICBMs, like the Soviets did. However, US intelligence believes that they are capable of launching such warheads on SCUD and No-dong missiles (which can reach Japan). See Bermudez [31, 5b], pp. 20–21; Bennett [31, 5a]; *Army Times*, 18 January 1996.

18. The preparations for such a two-front war is now an essential component of Pentagon planning and strategy. Then Secretary of Defense William J. Perry told an interviewer in 1997: 'My own opinion is that two major regional conflicts is an existential fact. It's not anything you decide on or don't decide on' (*Army Times*, 6 January 1997).

19. Hitchens [31, 5c], 28 August 1995

20. Confidential interview, May 1998

21. Confidential interview, March 1998

22. Confidential interview, February 1998

23. Confidential interview, February 1998

24. Confidential interview, February 1998

25. Dr Billy Richardson interview, March 1998. Richardson served as Deputy Assistant Secretary of Defense for Chemical and Biological Warfare from 1989–93, during the Bush Administration. See also Bermudez [31,6], 1 May 1993.

26. Confidential interview, March 1998

27. See also Bermudez [31, 6], 1 May 1993

28. Lee Sun Ok interview, August 1998. See also Robert Burns, 'Defector Tells of Prison Horror', Associated Press, 26 February 1998; Lee Sun Ok, ten-page prepared statement, press conference, Washington, DC, 26 February 1998; Suzanne Sholte, 'Behind North Korea's Dark Curtain', *Washington Times*, 3 April 1998; 'Survivors of North Korean Political Prisoner Camps', research paper on Lee Sun Ok, nine pages, Defense Forum Foundation, February 1998.

29. *Washington Times* [31, 28]

30. Lee Sun Ok, press conference [31, 28]. She also was subjected to water torture, during which she would be fastened to a wooden bed and forced to drink water from a kettle hanging down from the ceiling. The spout of the kettle was shaped so that no water could leak out when it was inserted in her mouth, and any attempt to breathe would result in the intake of more water. When she fainted, a board was placed on her stomach and guards would stamp on it until she vomited up the water that she had drunk.

31. Defense Forum Foundation [31, 28]. In recent years there have been several high-ranking officials who have defected from North Korea. Most notable amongst them is Hwang Jang Yop, a professional man who was one of the eleven secretaries of the ruling Workers Party. Previously, Mr Hwang was the tutor to Kim Il Sung's son, Kim Jong Il, now the nation's ruler (*New York Times*, 13 February 1997).

Amongst other things, Mr Hwang claimed that North Korea has an arsenal of 'high-grade' chemical and biological weapons (*Washington Times*, 5 June 1997). While this accusation may be true, such high-ranking officials should be treated with a degree of scepticism, as they may have been thoroughly briefed by South Korean officials for propaganda purposes. One former senior CIA official warns that one must 'be careful' of anything relating to such high-ranking officials. 'If the South Koreans get hold of them first,' he says, 'then you can't be sure if what they tell you is true' (confidential interview, February 1998).

Hwang Jang Yop provided the US with very little new information about the North's BW programme.

32. Lee Sun Ok interview [31, 28]

33. Lee Sun Ok interview [31, 28]
34. Defense Forum Foundation [31, 28]
35. 'US General Cites North Korea Threat', Associated Press, 14 May 1997
36. Bermudez [31, 5b] pp. 17–19

Chapter 32: Apocalypse Delayed

1. 'Germ Warfare', *60 Minutes*, CBS News, 18 February 1996
2. Major sources for this chapter include:
   a. 'Global Proliferation of Weapons of Mass Destruction', US Senate Committee on Governmental Affairs, Permanent Subcommittee on Investigations, Hearings, Part I, 31 October 1995
   b. John Sopko, 'A Case Study On The Aum Shinrikyo', Staff Report, US Senate, Permanent Subcommittee on Investigations, 31 October 1995, pp. 47f.
   c. Australian Federal Police, 'The Australian Investigation of the Aum Shinrikyo Sect', prepared for the United States Permanent Subcommittee on Investigations, US Senate, Permanent Subcommittee on Investigations, 31 October 1995, pp. 610f.
   d. Australian Federal Police, Overview of Aum Shinrikyo Investigation in Australia, Strategic Intelligence Division, 27 June 1995
   e. Ron Purver, Strategic Analyst, 'Chemical And Biological Terrorism: The Threat According to the Open Literature', Canadian Security Intelligence Service, June 1995
   f. David E. Kaplan and Andrew Marshall, *The Cult at the End of the World*, New York, Crown Publishers Inc., 1996
   g. D. W. Brackett, *Holy Terror: Armageddon in Tokyo*, New York: Weatherhill, 1996
   h. Sheryl WuDunn, Judith Miller, and William Broad, 'How Japan Germ Terror Alerted the World', *New York Times*, 26 May 1998; Judith Miller, 'Some in Japan Fear Authors of Subway Attack are Regaining Ground', *New York Times*, 11 October 1998
3. Sopko [32, 2b], p. 47
4. US Department of Defense, 'Proliferation: Threat and Response', November 1997, p. 50
5. Testimony of John Sopko [32, 2a], p. 16
6. Sopko [32, 2b] p. 49; Kaplan and Marshall [32, 2f], p. 8
7. Kaplan and Marshall [32, 2f], p. 9; Brackett [32, 2g], p. 61
8. Brackett [32, 2g], pp. 61–2
9. Kaplan and Marshall [32, 2f], p. 11
10. Kaplan and Marshall [32, 2f], pp. 12–13

11. Kaplan and Marshall [32, 2f], pp. 14–17
12. Kaplan and Marshall [32, 2f], p. 16
13. Kaplan and Marshall [32, 2f], p. 17
14. Sopko [32, 2b], pp. 56–7
15. Kaplan and Marshall [32, 2f], pp. 28–34
16. Kaplan and Marshall [32, 2f], pp. 31–3
17. Confidential interview, March 1998
18. Kaplan and Marshall [32, 2f], p. 52
19. Confidential interview, March 1998; confidential interview, June 1998; John Sopko, 'Aum Shinrikyo's Activities with Biological Agents', US Senate memo, 3 May 1996; *New York Times* [32, 2h], 26 May 1998; *The Daily Yomiuri*, 5 May 1995; Purver [32, 2e], p. 165
20. Confidential interview, March 1998
21. Purver [32, 2e], p. 165
22. Confidential interview, March 1998
23. Confidential interview, February 1998
24. Kaplan and Marshall [32, 2f], pp. 52–3
25. *New York Times* [32, 2h], 26 May 1998. It is quite simple to obtain substances like botulinum in Japan. As in many industrial nations, Japan does not have a regulatory system to register or inspect legitimate medical and scientific laboratories that handle pathogens like anthrax and botulinum. Professional trade journals routinely carry advertisements to sell these organisms through the mail, in a freeze-dried state, ready for laboratory use (Kaplan and Marshall [32, 2f], p. 56).
26. *The Daily Yomiuri*, 25 May 1995; Kaplan and Marshall [32, 2f], p. 53
27. Kaplan and Marshall [32, 2f], p. 57
28. *New York Times* [32, 2h], 26 May 1998; Yuri Kagayama, Associated Press, 26 May 1998
29. *New York Times* [32, 2h], 26 May 1998
30. *New York Times* [32, 2h], 26 May 1998
31. Sopko [32, 2b], pp. 69–72.
32. Sopko [32, 2b], pp. 71–2; Alan Edelman testimony [32, 2a], p. 27. See also Brackett [32, 2g], p. 91.
33. Edelman testimony [32, 2a], pp. 27–8
34. Kyodo News Service (AP), 23 April 1997
35. Sopko [32, 2b], pp. 59, 71–2; Sopko testimony [32, 2a], pp. 202–1. See also Brackett [32, 2g], p. 92; Kaplan and Marshall [32, 2f], pp. 106–12.
36. Sopko [32, 2b], p. 63; John Sopko, US Senate memo, 30 October 1995; Kaplan and Marshall [32, 2f], p. 97
37. Purver [32, 2e], p. 165
38. Edelman testimony [32, 2a], p. 33; Sopko [32, 2b], p. 78

39. Edelman testimony [32, 2a], p. 33; 1995, Sopko [32, 2b], p. 77
40. Kaplan and Marshall [32, 2f], p. 93
41. Kaplan and Marshall [32, 2f], p. 93
43. Kaplan and Marshall [32, 2f], pp. 94–5
44. Kaplan and Marshall (32, 2f], p. 96; *New York Times* [32, 2h], 26 May 1998
45. Kaplan and Marshall [32, 2f], p. 96
46. *New York Times* [32, 2h], 26 May 1998; confidential interview, February 1998
47. *New York Times* [32, 2h], 26 May 1998
48. Australian Investigation of the Aum Shinrikyo Sect [32, 2c]; Overview of Aum Shinrikyo Investigation [32, 2d]; Sopko [32, 2b], pp. 73–6; Edelman testimony [32, 2a], pp. 30–31. See also Kaplan and Marshall [32, 2f], pp. 126–8.
49. Overview of Aum Shinrikyo Investigation [32, 2c]; Kaplan and Marshall [32, 2f], pp. 126–7
50. The Australian Investigation of the Aum Shinrikyo Sect [32, 2c]. Overview of Aum Shinrikyo Investigation in Australia [32, 2d]. See also Kaplan and Marshall [32, 2f], pp. 128–9.
51. Overview of Aum Shinrikyo Investigation [32, 2c]
52. Edelman testimony [32, 2a], p. 31
53. Sopko [31, 2b], p. 76; Edelman testimony [32, 2a], p. 32; Kaplan and Marshall [32, 2f], pp. 265–6
54. Confidential interview, February 1998
55. Confidential interview, June 1998
56. *New York Times* [32, 2h], 26 May 1998
57. *New York Times* [32, 2h], 26 May 1998
58. Testimony of Gordon Oehler, [32, 2a], p. 212; testimony of Gordon Oehler, Director, CIA Non-Proliferation Center, Senate Armed Services Committee, 27 March 1996; Edelman testimony [32, 2a], pp. 27–8; John Sopko, memo, 'Aum Shinrikyo', US Senate, PSI, 24 July 1995; Purver [32, 2e], p. 164; *Jane's Defence Weekly,* May 1995
59. 'Guru Planned Global Germ War by Balloon', Agence France Press, 16 October 1996
60. Lynda Richardson, *New York Times,* 4 June 1996
61. *The Daily Yomiuri* [32, 19]; Sopko memo [32, 36]; Purver [32, 2e], p. 164
62. Kaplan and Marshall [32, 2f], pp. 234–5
63. Sopko [32, 2b], p. 63; Kaplan and Marshall [32, 2f], p. 235
64. Sopko [32, 2b], p. 63
65. Kaplan and Marshall [32, 2f], p. 236
66. Kaplan and Marshall [32, 2f], p. 257
67. Kaplan and Marshall [32, 2f], pp. 280–81
68. Kaplan and Marshall [32, 2f], p. 281
69. US Senate [32, 2a], p. 151

70. US Senate [32, 2a], p. 275
71. US Senate [32, 2a], pp. 275–6
72. Sopko memo [32, 19]
73. Knut Royce, 'Gas Masks Ordered in US Never Made it to Japanese Cult', *Newsday*, 27 September 1995
74. Kyodo News Service, 26 August 1997
75. Reuters, 27 December 1998; Kyodo News Service, 20 December 1997
76. Reuters, 2 March 1998
77. Reuters [32, 75]
78. *New York Times* [32, 2h], 11 October 1998; Reuters [32, 75]. As of late 1998, Aum had 500 hardcore, 'ordained' followers who run 18 branches in Japan, with an estimated total of 2,000–5,000 members.
79. Associated Press, 3 February 1998

Chapter 33: 'Walkers, Floppers & Goners'

1. Jerome Hauer interview, November 1998
2. William Patrick interview, June 1998
3. Patrick [33,2]; Hauer [33, 1]
4. Hauer [33, 1]
5. 'A Special Report: Emerging Infectious Disease Threats: Why New York City is Especially Vulnerable', New York City Department of Health, City Health Information, 14 (4), September–December 1995
6. Laurie Garrett, *Newsday*, 7 April 1998
7. Confidential interview, December 1997
8. William Nagle, 'Seminar on Emerging Threats on Biological Terrorism: Recent Developments', Proceedings Report, presentation for Potomac Institute for Policy Studies, Arlington, Virginia, 16 June 1998
9. Nagle [33, 8]
10. Nagle [33, 8]
11. Nagle [33, 8]
12. Renaldo Campana, 'Seminar on Emerging Threats on Biological Terrorism: Recent Developments', Proceedings Report, presentation for Potomac Institute for Policy Studies, 16 June 1998
13. Garrett [33, 6]
14. US Senate Health, Education, Labor, and Pensions Committee, prepared testimony of Jerome M. Hauer, 25 March 1999
15. Maj. Gen. George Friel interview, January 1998. (Friel was then commander of the US Army's Chemical and Biological Defense Command, Aberdeen Proving Ground, Maryland.)

16. Nagle [33, 8]

17. Campana [33, 12]

18. Hauer [33, 1]

19. Hauer [33, 1]; 'Senior Policy Forum, Civex 93: Player's Guide', FEMA, 30 November–1 December 1993, a 27-page booklet, p. A:2

20. Hauer [33, 1]; 'Civex 93: Player's Guide' [33, 19]

21. Hauer [33, 14]

22. Bradley Graham, *Washington Post*, 14 December 1997

23. Mark Jacobson, 'Battered City Syndrome', *New York*, 16 March 1998

24. In 1964–5, additional vulnerability tests with BG were carried out at National Airport and the Greyhound Terminal in Washington, DC. Special Army officers from Ft. Detrick, posing as passengers, used five aerosol blowers hidden inside fake suitcases to spray the simulant BG (*Bacillus subtilis variant Niger*) through the airline terminal. In August 1965, they staged a simulated attack on the Pennsylvania Turnpike (Ken Ringle, *Washington Post*, 5 December 1984; *New York Times* (UPI), 4 December 1984, citing released army documents; *Frederick Post*, 9 March 1977).

25. Patrick [33, 2]; Robert Harris and Jeremy Paxman, *A Higher Form of Killing*, New York: Hill and Wang, 1982, p. 159, citing *Washington Post*, 23 April 1980; William Patrick, 'History of Biological Warfare', *Proliferation*, ed. Kathleen Bailey, Lawrence Livermore Library, 1994, p. 17; Norman Covert, *Cutting Edge*, Ft. Detrick: Public Affairs Office, 1997, p. 60; Department of the Army, 24 February 1977, Vol. 1, p. 6:3. The official report was entitled: 'A Study of the Vulnerability of Subway Passengers in New York City to Covert Action with Biological Agents', Department of the Army, Ft. Detrick, January 1968.

26. Frederick Sidell, William Patrick, and Thomas Dashiell, *Jane's Chem-Bio Handbook*, Jane's Information Group, 1998, p. 253

27. Laurie Garrett, 'Germ Terror: Is the US Ready?', *Newsday*, 6 April 1998

28. 'Civex 93: Player's Guide' [33, 19]; Patrick [33, 2]; Dr Charles Bailey interview, May 1998

29. Dr Randy Curry, 'Electro Technologies to Counter Biological Terrorism', Proceedings Report: 'Countering Biological Terrorism,' Potomac Institute for Policy Studies, August, 1997

30. David Kelly interview, January 1999

31. Chemists from the US government's Sandia National Laboratories in New Mexico have recently invented a new extra-bubbly and long-lasting foam to fight a variety of BW agents (including anthrax) and nerve gases that are released inside confined spaces, like buildings and tunnels. Delivered by high-powered sprayers, the foam combines readily available ingredients, including wetting substances from hair-conditioning creams and oxidizing compounds used in toothpaste. As tested so far, the foam would destroy the

BW agents within one hour, but, unlike other caustic detoxifying sprays, it will not harm materials inside the building or leave any dangerous residue. (Malcolm Browne, *New York Times*, 16 March 1999).

32. Judith Miller and William J. Broad, 'NYC Plans Defence Against Biochemical Attack', *New York Times*, 18 June 1998

33. Miller and Broad [33, 32]

34. B. J. Berkowitz et al., 'Superviolence: The Civil Threat of Mass Destruction Weapons', ADCON (Advanced Concepts Research) Corporation, Santa Barbara, CA, Report A72-034-10, 29 September 1972

35. William Cohen interview, June 1998

36. Judith Miller and William Broad, *New York Times*, 7 August 1998

37. Judith Miller and William Broad, *New York Times*, 26 April 1998

38. Hauer interview [33, 1]

39. Confidential interview, May 1998. See also Associated Press, 10 April 1998; *New York Times* [33, 36].

40. James Pritchard, *The Stanford University Daily*, 13 January 1998; Hillary Johnson, 'Killer Flu', *Rolling Stone*, 22 January 1998

41. *The Stanford University Daily* [33, 40]

42. *Newsday* [33, 27]

43. Confidential interview, May 1998

44. Confidential interview, May 1998

45. *New York Times* [33, 34]; *New York Times* [33, 36]; Bradley Graham, *Washington Post*, 21 May 1998; Douglas Kiker, Associated Press, 22 May 1998

46. *New York Times* [33, 36]

47. White House Fact Sheet, Office of the Press Secretary, 'Preparedness for a Biological Weapons Attack', 22 May 1998; Judith Miller, 'Clinton Seeks More Money to Counter Germ Warfare', *New York Times*, 9 June 1998; Robert Suro, *Washington Post*, 25 June 1998; Reuters, 8 June 1998

48. Campana [33, 12]

49. No individual or group in the US or UK has yet to actually attempt an aerosol BW attack. Only one BW attack has occurred in the US where anyone was injured. From August to September 1984, members of the Rajneeshee religious cult in Oregon tried to influence a local election by spreading salmonella through the salad bars of ten popular local restaurants. More than 750 people became ill, but there were no fatalities.

Around the world, a number of groups, cults, and individuals have acquired BW agents and contemplated using them. In April 1997, the previously unknown 'Counter Holocaust Lobbyists of Zion', sent a petri dish with the misspelled label 'anthrachs' to the Washington headquarters of Bnai B'rith. The dish was filled with strawberry gelatin. In February 1997, James Dalton Bell, an MIT graduate, wrote an Internet essay about killing government officials after he allegedly investigated toxins. Bell had a previous arrest for possessing ingredients for manufacturing meth-amphetamine. In May 1992, the anti-tax group 'Minnesota Patriots Council' plotted to kill federal officials using ricin. (They planned to smear ricin mixed with a solvent on door handles and steering wheels of vehicles of the US Marshall and IRS agents – they called the resulting illness the 'bureaucratic flu'. Four men were found guilty and sentenced to up to four years in prison.) In the mid-1980s, the Tamil secessionist group in Sri Lanka threatened to infect humans and crops with pathogens. In October 1981, in 'Operation Dark Harvest', environmentalists spread dirt around a Conservative Party gathering; the dirt had been collected from a Scottish island that had been used as a testing area for germ warfare during World War II. In November 1980, a French cell of the revolutionary group, Red Army Faction, allegedly tried to manufacture botulinum toxin. In June 1976, an unknown person called 'B.A. Fox' threatened to mail tickets infected with pathogens. In January 1974, the Symbionese Liberation Army allegedly investigated biological warfare. In January 1972, a group called RISE tried to put typhoid in the Chicago water supply. In November 1970, the Weathermen planned to poison a city's water supply with germ weapons. They intended to steal the germs from Ft. Detrick, Maryland, allegedly by blackmailing a gay officer into helping them.

For the most complete history of bio-terrorism incidents, see W. Seth Carus, 'Bioterrorism, Biocrimes, and Bioassassination: Case Studies', Center for Counterproliferation Research, National Defense University, 8 January 1998.

50. Campana [33, 12]
51. Capt. John Pedersen (CBIRF) interview, January 1998; CBIRF 1997 Mission and Structure briefing materials, 1998; Robert Burns, 'Marine Unit Trained on Terrorists', Associated Press, 30 April 1997
52. *Washington Post* [33, 22]
53. *Washington Post* [33,22]
54. Matthew S. Slater, MD and Donald D. Trunkey, MD, 'Terrorism in America: An Evolving Threat', *Archives of Surgery*, October 1997
55. Capt. Mike Moultrie interview, January 1998. Moultrie, Captain of the emergency management unit in the Arlington, Virginia Fire Department, is a founder and leader of the Washington area MMST.
56. Huntly Collins, *Philadelphia Inquirer*, 16 June 1997; Lisa A. Towle, *National Fire and Rescue*, Spring 1997
57. Confidential interviews, April 1998 (by Gerard Davies)
58. Briefing at the UK Home Office, April 1998

Chapter 34: The Future

1. William Cohen interview, May 1998
2. 'Israel Develops New Weapons', Associated Press, 15 November 1998
3. *Foreign Report*, 'Genetic Weapons', 14 March 1996
4. *Foreign Report*, 'Genetic Warfare', 29 October 1998
5. The authors are satisfied that these theories were indeed researched by Dr Wouter Basson and his aides at Roodeplaat Laboratories in Pretoria, as part of the notorious Project Coast.
6. Associated Press [34, 2]
7. Dr Malcom Dando interview, December 1998
8. 'Soviet Biological Warfare Threat', Defense Intelligence Agency, 1986, pp. 9–10
9. *Jane's Defence Weekly*, 'Interview' (with William Cohen), 13 August 1997
10. *The Electronic Telegraph* (London), 30 September 1996
11. *The Washington Quarterly*, The Center for Strategic and International Studies and the Massachusetts Institute of Technology, Spring 1986, p. 5
12. Dr Malcolm Dando interview, November 1998
13. Dando [34, 12]

Select Bibliography

Adams, James, *The New Spies: Exploring the Frontiers of Espionage*, London: Century Hutchinson, 1994

Alibek, Ken, with Handelman, Stephen, *Biohazard: The Chilling True Story of the Largest Covert Biological Weapons Program in the World*, New York: Random House, 1999

Atkinson, Rick, *Crusade: The Untold Story of the Persian Gulf War*, New York and Boston: Houghton Mifflin Company, 1993

Bailey, Kathleen (ed.), *Proliferation*, Lawrence Livermore Library, 1994

Baker, James A., with DeFrank, Thomas M., *The Politics of Diplomacy: Revolution, War, and Peace, 1989–92*, New York: G. P. Putnam's Sons, 1995

Bennett, Bruce, *Implications of Proliferation of New Weapons on Regional Security*, Rand Study, November 1996

Bermudez Jr., Joseph S., *The Deterrence Series, Case Study 5: North Korea*, Chemical and Biological Arms Control Institute, 1998

Beschloss, Michael and Talbott, Strobe, *At the Highest Levels: The Inside Story of the End of the Cold War*, Boston: Little, Brown & Company, 1993

Brackett, D.W., *Holy Terror: Armageddon in Tokyo*, New York: Weatherhill, 1996

Brugioni, Dino A., *Eyeball To Eyeball: The Inside Story of the Cuban Missile Crisis*, New York: Random House, 1990

Burrows, William E., and Windrem, Robert, *Critical Mass: the Dangerous Race for Superweapons in a Fragmenting World*, New York: Simon & Schuster, 1994

Carter, G. B., *Porton Down: 75 Years of Chemical and Biological Research*, London: HMSO, 1992

Carus, W. Seth, *The Poor Man's Atomic Bomb?: Biological Weapons in the Middle East*, Washington, D.C.: Washington Institute for Near East Policy, 1991

—'Bioterrorism, Biocrimes, and BioAssassination: Case Studies,' January 8, 1998, Center for Counterproliferation Research, National Defense University

Clarke, Robin, *The Silent Weapons*, New York: David McKay Co., 1968

Cole, Leonard A., *Clouds of Secrecy: The Army's Germ Warfare Tests Over Populated Areas*, Totowa, N.J.: Rowman & Littlefield, 1989

—*The Eleventh Plague: The Politics of Biological and Chemical Warfare*, New York: W.H. Freeman, 1997

Covert, Norman, *Cutting Edge: A History of Fort Detrick, Maryland*, Fort Detrick: Public Affairs Office, 1997

Dando, Malcolm, *Biological Warfare in the 21st Century: Biotechnology and the Proliferation of Biological Weapons*, London: Brassey's (UK) Ltd, 1994

Douglass, Joseph D., and Livingstone, Neil C., *America the Vulnerable: The Threat of Chemical and Biological Warfare*, Lexington, Mass.: Lexington Books, 1987

Ekedahl, Carolyn McGiffert, and Goodman, Melvin A., *The Wars of Eduard Shevardnadze*, University Park, PA: The Pennsylvania State University Press, 1997

Ellert, Henrik, *The Rhodesian Front War: Counter-Insurgency and Guerrilla War in Rhodesia 1962–1980*, Zimbabwe: Mambo Press, 1989

Garrett, Laurie, *The Coming Plague: Newly Emerging Diseases in a World Out of Balance*, New York: Farrar, Strauss, and Giroux, 1994

Gates, Robert M., *From the Shadows: The Ultimate Insider's Story of Five Presidents and How They Won the Cold War*, New York: Simon & Schuster, 1996

Geissler, Erhard (ed.), *Biological and Toxin Weapons Today*, Oxford and New York: Oxford University Press, 1986

Gordon, Michael R., and Trainor, General Bernard E., *The Generals' War: The Inside Story of the Conflict in the Gulf*, Boston: Little, Brown & Company, 1995

Harris, Robert, and Paxman, Jeremy, *A Higher Form of Killing: The Secret Story of Chemical and Biological Warfare*, New York: Hill and Wang, 1982

Harris, Sheldon H., *Factories of Death: Japanese Biological Warfare, 1932–45, and the American Cover-Up*, London and New York: Routledge, 1994

Hersh, Seymour M., *Chemical and Biological Warfare; America's Hidden Arsenal*, Indianapolis: Bobbs–Merrill, 1968

Hersh, Seymour, *The Price of Power: Kissinger in the Nixon White House*, New York: Summit Books, 1983

Isaacson, Walter, *Kissinger: A Biography*, New York: Simon & Schuster, 1992

Jane's Information Group, *Countering Chemical and Biological Weapons: Government Programs, Industry Opportunities*, Washington, D.C., November 19, 1997

Kaplan, David E., and Marshall, Andrew, *The Cult at the End of the World: The Terrifying Story of the Aum Doomsday Cult, from the Subways of Tokyo to the Nuclear Arsenals of Russia*, New York: Crown Publishers Inc., 1996

Leitenberg, Milton, Chapter 8 in *Control of Dual-Threat Agents: The Vaccines for Peace Programme*, E. Geissler and J.P. Woodall (eds), SIPRI and Oxford University Press, 1994, pp. 77–105

—'Biological Weapons Arms Control,' Project on Rethinking Arms Control, Paper 16, May 1996, Center for International and Security Studies at Maryland

Matlock, Jack M., *Autopsy of an Empire: The American Ambassador's Account of the Collapse of the Soviet Union*, New York: Random House, 1995

McDermott, Jeanne, *The Killing Winds: The Menace of Biological Warfare*, New York: Arbor House, 1987

Nixon, Richard, *RN: The Memoirs of Richard Nixon*, New York: Grosset & Dunlap, 1978

Oberdorfer, Don, *The Turn: From Cold War to a New Era*, New York: Poseidon Press, Simon & Schuster, 1991

Pedlow, Gregory W., and Welzenbach, Donald E., *The CIA and the U-2 Programme, 1954–74*, CIA, Center for the Study of Intelligence, 1998

Penkovskiy, Oleg, *The Penkovskiy Papers*, Garden City, New York: Doubleday & Co., 1965

Perry, Mark, *Four Stars: The Inside Story of the Forty-Year Battle Between the Joint Chiefs of Staff and America's Civilian Leaders*, Boston: Houghton Mifflin Company, 1989

Peters, C. J., and Olshaker, Mark, *Virus Hunter: Thirty Years of Battling Hot Viruses Around the World*, New York: Anchor Books, 1997

Piller, Charles, and Yamamoto, Keith R., *Gene Wars: Military Control Over the New Genetic Technologies*, New York: Beech Tree Books, William Morrow, 1988

Potomac Institute for Policy Studies, 'Conference on Countering Biological Terrorism: Proceedings Report, PIPS 97–2', Arlington, VA; August 12–13, 1997

Potomac Institute for Policy Studies, 'Seminar On Emerging Threats of Biological Terrorism: Proceedings Report', PIPS 98–3, Arlington, VA; June 16, 1998

Powell, Colin, with Persico, Joseph E., *My American Journey*, New York: Random House, 1995

Preston, Richard, *The Cobra Event*, New York: Random House, 1997

—*The Hot Zone*, New York: Random House, 1994

Ritter, Scott, *Endgame: Solving The Iraq Problem – Once And For All*, New York: Simon & Schuster, 1999

Schevchenko, Arkady N., *Breaking With Moscow*, New York: Alfred A. Knopf, 1985

Schwarzkopf, General Norman H., with Petre, Peter, *The Autobiography: It Doesn't Take A Hero*, New York: Bantam Books, 1992

Sidell, Frederick R., Takafuji, Ernest T., and Franz, David R. (eds), *Medical Aspects of Chemical and Biological Warfare* (Textbook of Military Medicine. Part 1, Warfare, Weaponry, and the Casualty, V. 3.), US Government Printing Office, August 1997

Sidell, Frederick, Patrick, William, and Dashiell, Thomas, *Jane's Chem-Bio Handbook*, Jane's Information Group, 1998

Stiff, Peter, *See You in November*, South Africa: Galago, 1985

Tsuneishi, Kei-ichi, *The Germ Warfare Unit That Disappeared: Kwantung Army's 731st Unit*, Tokyo: Kai-mei-sha Publishers, 1981

Tsuneishi, Kei-ichi, and Asano, Tomizo, *The Bacteriological Warfare Unit and the Suicide of Two Physicians*, Tokyo: Shincho-Sha Publishing Co., 1982

US Arms Control and Disarmament Agency, *Arms Control and Disarmament Agreements, Texts and Histories of the Negotiations*, Washington: US Government Printing Office, 1996

US Army, USAMRDC, *Biological Defense Research Program*, April 1989

US Central Intelligence Agency, *The Biological & Chemical Warfare Threat*, Langley, VA, 1997

US Congress, House of Representatives, Permanent Select Committee on Intelligence, Report: 'Soviet Biological Warfare Activities,' June 30, 1980

US Congress, Office of Technology Assessment, *Proliferation of Weapons of Mass Destruction, Assessing the Risks*, Washington: US Government Printing Office, 1993

US Congress, Office of Technology Assessment, *Technologies Underlying Weapons of Mass Destruction: Background Paper*, Washington: US Government Printing Office, 1993

US Congress, Senate Committee on Governmental Affairs, Permanent Subcommittee on Investigations, *Global Proliferation of Weapons of Mass Destruction*, Hearings, Part I, October 31, 1995, Washington: US Government Printing Office, 1996

US Congress, Senate Committee on Human Resources, Subcommittee on Health and Scientific Research, *Biological Testing Involving Human Subjects by the Department of Defense, 1977*, Hearings, March 8 and May 23, 1977, Washington: US Government Printing Office, 1977

US Congress, Senate Committee on Governmental Affairs, Permanent Subcommittee on Investigations, *Global Spread of Chemical and Biological Weapons*, Hearings, February 1989, Washington: US Government Printing Office, 1990

US Defense Intelligence Agency, *Soviet Biological Warfare Threat*, Washington, D.C.: The Agency, 1986

US Secretary of Defense, *Proliferation: Threat and Response*, Office of the Secretary of Defense, April 1996 and November 1997

Williams, Peter and Wallace, David, *Unit 731: The Japanese Army's Secret of Secrets*, London: Hodder and Stoughton, 1989

Wright, Susan (ed.), *Preventing a Biological Arms Race*, Cambridge, Mass.: MIT Press, 1990

Zilinskas, Raymond A. (ed.), *The Microbiologist and Biological Defense Research: Ethics, Politics, and International Security*, New York, N.Y.: New York Academy of Sciences, 1992

Index

Index

Index

Index

Acknowledgements

This book owes its existence to the vision and persuasive powers of William Armstrong of Macmillan, and to the encouragement of Clare Alexander, whose unequivocal support turned gestation into birth.

We owe a special debt to David Irvine, whose work on several chapters was invaluable.

We are much indebted to our research team: in London, Gerard Davies and Julia Hannis; in Moscow, Nick Sturdee; in Pretoria, Evelyn Groenink and Dewet Potgieter; in South Korea, Andrew Wood. Our thanks also to Peter Molloy, who produced the BBC documentaries *Plague Wars*, and who joined in.

Peter Horrocks, editor of the BBC's *Panorama*, was generous with time off and gave the book his encouragement.

In addition, we wish to thank a small team who were always at our side when we needed them and whose specialized knowledge held focus on the research: Dr David Kelly, CMG; Dr Chris Davis, OBE; and Colonel Terry Taylor, OBE – three formidable arms control inspectors. The Right Honourable Sir Percy Cradock, G.C.M.G., strategically placed during his years at the JIC and as Lady Margaret Thatcher's foreign policy adviser, was essential to this text for his judgements and overview.

Thanks also to Professor Malcom Dando and Graham Pearson for some careful hand holding.

This project would never have developed in the way it did without the help and guidance of other primary sources in London, Washington, Pretoria, and Western Europe who cannot be identified by name. They know who they are and that we owe them more than we can say.

We are very grateful to a number of people (and their organizations) in the US who generously gave of their time and shared their files with us, including: Ken Alibek and Jennifer Guernsey; Dr Charles Bailey; Bruce Bennett, Rand Corporation; Joseph Bermudez; Norman Covert, USAMRIID; Gary Crocker; James Genovese, CBDCOM; Dr Riley Housewright; Milton Leitenberg, University of Maryland; Peter Benwell-Lejeune; Erik Leklem, Arms Control Association; Michael Moodie and Javid Ali, Chemical and Biological Arms Control Institute; Dr Meryl Nass; Alan Neidle; William Patrick; Dr Billy Richardson; John Sopko; Dr Jonathan Tucker, Monterey Institute of International Studies; Gillian Woollett, PhRMA; and Dr Raymond Zilinskas, University of Maryland.

Also, we thank our literary agent Bill Hamilton of A.M. Heath in London, whose enthusiasm and commitment were crucial.

Our most special thanks are owed to Catherine Whitaker, who is blessed with the three qualities that make a great literary editor, accessibility, judgement, and a large, wide, dry shoulder. The efficient copy-editing of Ann Cooke also proved to be invaluable.

Our deep appreciation goes to our families for their understanding, patience, and unwavering support. To George and Teddy, Robbi and David Goldberg, you always responded beyond the call – thanks.

Finally to Sarah, Abigail and Jessica – thanks for being around on the dark days.